Jewish Legends
of the Second Commonwealth

The Jewish Publication Society of America

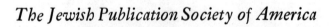

PHILADELPHIA   5743/1983

Judah Nadich

Jewish Legends of the Second Commonwealth

Copyright © 1983 by The Jewish Publication Society of America
First Edition   All rights reserved
Manufactured in the United States of America
Designed by Adrianne Onderdonk Dudden

Library of Congress Cataloging in Publication Data
Main entry under title:

Jewish legends of the second commonwealth.

Translations from rabbinic and Hellenistic literature.
Bibliography: p.
Includes index.
1. Legends, Jewish.   2. Aggada—Translations into English.
3. Jews—History—586 B.C.—70 A.D.—Miscellanea. I. Nadich, Judah,
1912–

BM530.J48   296.1'9   82-7195
ISBN 0-8276-0212-X   AACR2

כי עוד נמשכת השלשלת

For two generations:
our children and grandchildren
who are our hope for the future—
Leah Nessa and Aryeh Meir
Shira Adina and James L. Levin
Nahma Meira Nadich

Natan Menachem, Adin Yehoshua, and Vered Simha Meir
Alexander Nadich and Gideon Ribalow Levin

IN MEMORIAM

Isaac, Lena, and Nettie Nadich
Yael Hana Meir
Gertrude Nadich Liss
Menachem, Rose, and Harold U. Ribalow

Contents

Introduction

1

It is the aim of this book to set forth Jewish legends of the Second Commonwealth, that period in Jewish history between the return of the Jews from exile in Babylonia during the last third of the sixth century B.C.E. to the destruction of the Second Temple by the Romans in 70 C.E.

The word *legends* as used here requires some comment. *Webster's New World Dictionary* defines legend as "any unauthentic narrative handed down by tradition and having a basis in fact; a tradition; fictitious or nonhistorical narrative; fiction, fable, myth." The contents of this book will often be true to such definitions but frequently will be even more inclusive. What we mean by *legends* is the equivalent of that classic body of Jewish lore known as Aggadah.

In the rabbinic sense of the word Aggadah is coupled with its opposite Halakhah ("law"); it is thus that part of the rabbinic literature, Talmud and Midrash, which is not Halakhah. Such Aggadah is the primary source of our material. It may include stories and anecdotes, fables and myths, sometimes told about biblical personalities, sometimes told independently. It also embodies ethical and moral instruction; a historical description, as of the sacrificial system in the Temple; and biographical data about historic personalities, kings, high priests, soldiers, and sages. It also comprehends astronomy and astrology, mathematics and science, homiletics and the interpretation of biblical texts, medicine and poetry, proverbs and aphorisms, and theology and mysticism. Leopold Zunz wrote that "everything the imagination can conceive is found in the Aggadah, with one exception: idle laughter and frivolity."

There are universal aspects in the Aggadah, that is, legends similar to those that may be found in the folklore of other peoples. But even in such cases there is often a difference in format, in emphasis, or in conclusion, reflecting a different ethical and moral matrix. Stories are often much older than the time of the story-teller. They may have been in the possession of the people in earlier times, retold by one generation after the other, until receiving their final form by a particular teacher or preacher. Preachers used such stories for instructional purposes, for oratorical emphasis, to illustrate a biblical phrase or verse, or to bring home in popular style a moral lesson. The legends thus served their didactic purpose and at the same time assured the stories a long life.

The Aggadah, it can be seen, is a rich mine whose precious ores are of various elements. It is a source not only for historic data but for Jewish attitudes to historic persons, peoples, and events. Louis Ginzberg called Jewish legends "the people's verdict upon history." The Aggadah, of course, casts light upon the political, economic, and social conditions of the times. Since the legendary material so often can be said to have been produced by the people and to have appealed to the people, from the Aggadah we can learn much about the people, their hopes and their disappointments, their calamities and their comforts, their anxieties and their ideals, their concerns and their judgments. The same aggadic treasure trove can supply us with the theology of the ancient rabbis, their thoughts and beliefs about God, His powers and self-limitation, His relations with humankind and the world, the problems of good and evil, reward and punishment, the Messiah and the world to come, the role of Israel and the nations, and the Shekhinah and heavenly beings. It was taught, "Do you wish to know the One who by His command brought the world into being? Study Aggadah!" (Sifrei, Ekev, 49). Hence, some of the aggadic material is told allegorically. A story may make sense and, indeed, be appealing purely as a tale, but often it is to be understood metaphorically.

The Aggadah is the source for learning the practical wisdom of the rabbis, the standards of right conduct they counseled, the values to be cherished, the goals to be sought for in life, and the purposes to be enshrined. There may be among the rabbis differences in stress and accent but, as in their teachings in Pirkei Avot (Ethics of the Fathers), there is a great measure of agreement concerning the principles of human conduct. Between Halakhah, Jewish law itself, and Aggadah there is a reciprocal relationship, as the Hebrew poet Hayyim Nahman Bialik observed: "The Halakhah is the exemplification and crystallization of the Aggadah, while the Aggadah is the crucible of the Halakhah."

The Halakhah and the Aggadah are not discretely separated

in the Talmud. They intermingle without organization or structure. Almost a third of the contents of the Babylonian Talmud is aggadic, a smaller proportion in the Palestinian Talmud. The period of the Talmud is usually described as the first five centuries of the common era. But parts of the Talmud are much older. For example, the conflict of laws in different parts of the Bible required solution, for Jews lived in accordance with its commandments. Thus, the Bible prohibits labor on the Sabbath yet calls for the circumcision of a male child on the eighth day, which may occur on the Sabbath. So, too, marriage with a sister-in-law is prohibited yet the Scriptures establish levirate marriage with a sister-in-law. Exegetical study of the Bible during pre-Maccabean centuries must have resulted in the resolution of such conflicts. Similarly, aggadic material may be traced to pretalmudic times, to the time of the scribes. Biblical exegesis, midrash, included nonhalakhic matter as well as legal. Louis Ginzberg points to such early exegetical material in the Septuagint, Philo, Josephus, and the Targumim. These sources contain legends narrated in the Talmud as well. For example, the Septuagint translates *ve-khol ẓeva'am* (Gen. 2:1) as "and all their order." The Talmud (Rosh Ha-Shanah 11b) offers a similar explanation. Philo explains that the human being was created last because God prepared everything else first, as a feast is prepared for a guest. The Talmud (Sanhedrin 38b) says that this may be compared to a king who prepares a feast for his guest. Josephus tells that the wife of Potiphar feigned illness so as not to attend a feast on the day she thought to be opportune to meet Joseph, a story found in the talmudic tractate of Sotah 36b.

Aggadic midrashim were set down much earlier than halakhic literature because there was no objection to writing them. Rav, in the third century, is reported to have read *sifrei de-aggadata*, books of Aggadah. Collections of aggadic material date from the second to the fourteenth centuries and, together with the aggadic portions in the Talmud, constitute the major source of Jewish legends. The stream has never run dry, however, and new stories came into being during the Middle Ages and beyond in the kabbalistic and Hasidic literatures.

Midrashic literature consisting almost entirely of Aggadah was first compiled and, most likely even written down, during the tannaitic period of the first two centuries. The fourth century saw the first edited aggadic work. The oldest midrashic collections are Genesis Rabbah and the Pesikta, exegetical and homiletical works, respectively. Although tannaitic in origin, they were probably compiled during the fifth and early sixth centuries. Other midrashic works of tannaitic origin include the Mekhilta on Exodus and the Sifrei on Numbers—ascribed to the school of Rabbi Ishmael—and the Sifra on Leviticus and the Sifrei on Deuteronomy—ascribed to the school of Rabbi Akiba. These tannaitic midrashim, largely halakhic in character, began their development with collections compiled during the second century but did not receive their final form until later centuries. Other tannaitic works include Seder Olam, biblical chronology based on biblical exegesis, Megillat Ta'anit, a listing of special days in the calendar marking historic events, and the Thirteen Middot of Rabbi Eliezer.

The midrashim on the Five Megillot (Scrolls) came afterward: Lamentations Rabbah, Songs Rabbah, Ruth Rabbah, Ecclesiastes Rabbah, and Esther Rabbah. The Scrolls were, and still are, read during synagogue services on festivals, and, in one instance, on a fast day and therefore were the subjects of much exegetical and homiletical interpretation. Later aggadic works include the midrashim on the other books of the Pentateuch: Leviticus Rabbah, compiled soon after Genesis Rabbah, followed in later centuries by Exodus Rabbah, Deuteronomy Rabbah, and Numbers Rabbah. Apart from this cycle of large midrashim on the Five Books of Moses, there is another midrashic cycle of early origin known as Midrash Tanḥuma or, as it was called formerly, Midrash Yelamdenu. It covers the entire Pentateuch and is of homiletic nature. The Pesikta, referred to earlier, frequently called Pesikta de-Rav Kahana, is a collection of homilies on the portions of the Pentateuch for special Sabbaths and festivals, on certain prophetic portions, and on the theme of repentance. It is one of the earliest midrashic works. Pesikta Rabbati is much later; the date 845 is mentioned in the book itself. It too contains homilies on the pentateuchal portions and prophetic lessons, the special Sabbaths, and holidays.

There are midrashic collections attached to other biblical books: Psalms, Proverbs, and Samuel, all probably the products of the tenth and eleventh centuries.

Aggadic material of an ethical nature may be found in Pirkei Avot (the Sayings, or Ethics, of the Fathers), a collection of ethical maxims included in the Mishnah and edited about 200 c.e. Later works in the same category are Avot de-Rabbi Natan, a much larger expansion of the earlier book; Pirkei de-Rabbi Eliezer, probably an eighth-century work blending ethical instruction with narrative embellished with stories; and Seder Eliyahu, or Tanna de-ve-Eliyahu, an ethical religious work composed toward the end of the tenth century.

Subsequent writers collected aggadic material from earlier sources, some of them lost, and published such popular works as the Yalkut Shimoni of the thirteenth century, in which the material is arranged according to the order of the twenty-four books of the Bible. Modern collections, containing short midrashim and midrashic fragments, include those prepared by Adolph Jellinek, S. A. Wertheimer, Salomon Buber, and J. D. Eisenstein. A systematic collection of aggadic source material is to be found in *Sefer ha-Aggadah*, edited by Hayyim Nahman Bialik and Y. H. Ravnitzky. The classical work in English, of course, on the Jewish legends associated with the biblical period, is Louis Ginzberg's seven-volume *The Legends of the Jews*.

The legends in this book have been culled from the various rabbinic sources, talmudic and midrashic, noted above. These have been combined to produce a continuous narrative in a connected form, rather than isolated tales and exegetical comments scattered across rabbinic literature. Two useful tools for talmudic Aggadah, used in the preparation of this book, were *Yefei Mar'eh*, a collection of aggadic material in the Palestinian Talmud, by Shmuel Yafeh Ashkenazi, and *Ein Ya'akov*, a collection of such material in the Babylonian Talmud, by Jacob Ibn Habib. However, these works are not complete and reference, therefore, is made to the talmudic text itself.

The translations are usually those of the Soncino English renderings of the Talmud and Midrash Rabbah, the English translations of Pesikta de-Rav Kahana by William G. Braude and Israel J. Kapstein, of Pesikta Rabbati and Midrash on Psalms by William G. Braude, and of Mekhilta de-Rabbi Ishmael by Jacob Z. Lauterbach. I have permitted myself the liberty of changing words or phrases and, at times, retranslating entire passages. My intention in translating was to stay as close as possible to the original except for changes required for clarification or stylistic necessity. The translation of biblical verses almost always follows the new Jewish Publication Society translation of the Scriptures. Where a story is found in more than one version—at times the same tale will be told in two different tractates of the Talmud or in the Talmud and again in the Midrash—I have usually attempted to blend the varying elements into one tale, explaining the sources in the notes. Where the differences are minor and few, I have set forth the fuller version and given the variations in the notes. The same person or event may be treated in two or more parts of the book. For example, tales about Rabban Johanan ben Zakkai are to be found both in the section "The First Generation of Tannaim," and in the section "The Last Years of the Second Commonwealth." Recourse will have to be made to the index by the reader wishing to find all the information in this book on a particular individual or event. In most cases the material is organized sequentially and is grouped by persons, places, institutions, and historic events.

II

For the purpose of setting the legends in historical context it may be useful to offer a brief résumé of that period of history into which the legends fit.

Four great empires of antiquity—Babylonia, Persia, Greece, and Rome—reached the zenith of their power during this period, and the Jews, among many others, were their subjects. The period actually begins with the decline and fall of the Babylonian empire and its conquest by Cyrus the Great of Persia by 539 B.C.E. Soon after his incorporation of Jerusalem into his territories, he issued an edict permitting the Jews who had been exiled by the Babylonians under Nebuchadnezzar to return to their own land of Judea. Only a minority, less than fifty thousand, chose to return to restore their people's homeland and to build a Second Temple. The country to which they came back was no land of milk and honey. Economic conditions were difficult and the work of rebuilding a Temple was obstructed by the non-Jews who in the meantime had settled in Judea. Some twenty years elapsed before the Temple, a modest structure, was completed in 515 B.C.E. The return of the first group of exiles is associated with the leadership of Zerubbabel. The spirits of the returned Jews were uplifted by the prophets Haggai and Zechariah.

The years immediately following the construction of the Second Temple are covered by a veil of darkness. In Babylonia, the Jewish community grew stronger. Fraternal ties were close between the two communities. When the Jews of Babylonia learned of the hardships suffered by their fellow Jews in Judea—their economic privation, the hostility of such neighbors as the Ammonites, the Edomites, and the Samaritans, the weakening of religious practice and of moral fiber decried by the prophet Malachi—they were dismayed. They determined to send off another group of Jews, some eighteen hundred, led by Ezra, a strong religious leader, who would succeed in reforming the spiritual life of the Jews of Judea. Nehemiah, who had occupied high office in the Persian court, came to Jerusalem in 444 B.C.E. with permission to rebuild the city walls for security against the hostile neighbors. Moreover, he had been appointed governor of Judea as well. He gave the young Jewish community of the Second Commonwealth political form and organization. After a shaky start, the small community of Jews had gained a foothold once again on its ancestral soil and continued the cultivation and growth of its people's values and traditions. Thus it continued until Alexander the Great and his armies set foot upon the soil of Judea, ushering in a new era. (The legends of part 1, "The Persian Period," are set against the backdrop of these historic events and personalities.)

Alexander, dramatic character that he was and, in addition, kindly disposed to the Jews of Judea, became a favorite subject for Jewish legend. In 334 B.C.E. he crossed into Asia and by the time of his death in 323 had conquered all of the Middle East. In 332 he had overrun Judea, but he did not level the harsh measures against Jerusalem that he imposed upon other cities and countries. His troops were accompanied wherever they marched by an invisible but real companion—the culture of Greece. True, it was not Greek culture at its apogee. When Greece met the people of Judea, it had already given to humankind the finest fruits of its flowering. Yet Greek language and culture were still sufficiently attractive, even in decline, to draw into their web the peoples of the Middle East, whose history, religions, and cultures were much older. Ancient cultures merged into the new dazzling Hellenistic civilization. All but one. Judea stood out alone—but not completely so, for during the Jewish exile in Babylonia before the rise of Cyrus, there had existed among the exiles a strong tension between identity and assimilation. Babylonia was powerful, its culture attractive, and economic conditions were more than satisfactory. Before Ezra's arrival in Judea the same tension between identity and assimilation held the Jews of the small returning community in its grip. It was difficult to hold fast, and intermarriage was common. Now the refulgent splendor of Greek art and literature had come to Asia. Jews, too, could not help but be influenced. Built in Palestine alone were some thirty Greek cities, with their theaters, gymnasia, temples, and agoras. If Hellenistic culture was not the same as that of the great Greek philosophers and tragedians, it still possessed an enticing glitter. Many Jews opted for assimilation, wholly or partially, rather than for Jewish identity. Even among the rest, Greek influences had their impact.

After Alexander's death his empire was divided among three of his generals. Judea, situated at the crossroads between Asia and Africa, was batted like a shuttlecock between two opponents—the Seleucid empire of Syria and that of the Ptolemies of Egypt. In 198 B.C.E., after a century and a quarter of fighting over Judea by the two successor empires—during which time the Jewish land was included first in the one empire and then in the other—Judea finally came under Syrian governance. During the periodic rule of Judea by the Ptolemaic kings of Egypt, many Jewish captives were carried off to Egypt to serve as soldiers or slaves. Under Ptolemy II the slaves regained their freedom. The size of the Jewish community in Alexandria grew, and the Jews spoke Greek rather than Hebrew or Aramaic, which was displacing Hebrew in Judea. But the Jews remained loyal to their faith and traditions and wished to have their Scriptures made available to them in Greek. The Greek translation of the Bible, the Septuagint, may have been done at their initiative or, if the legend telling of its miraculous creation has a kernel of truth in it, it may have been instigated by their king or with his sanction in order that it might be added to the books of the great library of Alexandria. (Part 2, "The Greek Period," should be read against this particular background.)

In Judea, now firmly anchored in the Seleucid empire of Syria, the rift grew wider between the lovers of Hellenistic culture and those Jews who remained staunchly loyal to Judaism. Once Judea came under Seleucid rule the government gave full support to a campaign of Hellenization. The Jewish upper classes who were involved with the Hellenized Syrians in managing political affairs favored the foreign culture, while the masses remained steadfast in their traditional ways. It was against the latter that Antiochus IV Epiphanes of Syria aimed a new oppressive effort, introducing compulsory pagan practices in Jerusalem itself as well as in the other cities and villages. The resentment and rancor of the people swelled into a short-lived revolt against Syrian rule and the high priesthood, whose occupants—Jason and his successor Menelaus— had bribed their way into office. The spark that had kindled the outburst was the news of Antiochus's death in his campaign against the Egyptians. The rumor proved false, and the enraged king killed thousands of Jews, profaned the Temple, and forbade Jewish religious practices.

Open rebellion began in the village of Modi'in when the king's representatives arrived to enforce pagan worship. The priest, Mattathias, and his five sons trained their followers in the nearby mountains to fight guerrilla warfare which, under the leadership of Mattathias's son Judah, called Maccabee (the Hammer), repeatedly inflicted casualties upon the foe. After three years of fierce fighting, Jerusalem was liberated, and the Temple was returned to divine worship on the twenty-fifth day of Kislev in 165 B.C.E., marked thereafter as Hanukkah. Identity had triumphed over assimilation.

But it was not until twenty-three years later that full independence and peace came to Judea under Simon, the last surviving Hasmonean brother. He dispatched a delegation to Rome to renew the treaty of friendship between Judea and the new ascending world power, an understanding originally concluded by Judah the Maccabee. The Roman Senate in 139 B.C.E. recognized the independence of the Jewish state. A convocation of Jewish priests, elders, and laity named Simon prince and high priest, to be succeeded by his descendants after him.

Simon was followed by his son John Hyrcanus in 135 B.C.E., but while the Hasmoneans continued to rule they no longer enjoyed the favor of the people. The house of liberators became a dynasty of petty despots and minor imperialists as the descendants of the Maccabees sought greater power. John Hyrcanus waged wars to gain territory in Samaria, Idumea, and Transjordan, forcibly converting the Idumeans to Judaism. He designated himself as both head of the Jewish state and high priest. The secular character of the state, united in the person of the ruler, with the leadership of the Temple, displeased those who advocated the purity of Jewish traditional teaching and who represented the majority of the people. They separated themselves from participation in the affairs of state and came to be called Pharisees, the separatists. Their opponents, allying themselves with the government, led by priests belonging to the family of Ẓadok, were called Sadducees (Zadokites)—at least, so one theory as to the origin of the name goes. The Pharisees opposed the royal house and its imperialistic policies; the Sadducees supported them. The Pharisees saw religion and its study, practice, and growth through reinterpretation, as the best means for preserving the Jewish people; the Sadducees thought that political power would better serve that end.

Aristobulus, who succeeded his father John Hyrcanus in 104 B.C.E., emulated his father's example, for he gained his throne through the murder of his mother and elder brother. He conquered and Judaized the northern part of the country, all of Galilee and part of Lebanon. He died of an illness after a one-year reign and was succeeded by his brother Alexander Yannai, who ruled for twenty-seven years. Like his father and grandfather, he was known for his cruelty and striving after aggrandizement. He was constantly engaged in warfare, even using mercenaries and negotiating agreements with Cleopatra to further their mutual political aims. He alienated the people and their pharisaic leaders completely; on one festival of Sukkot, when he committed in the Temple what the Pharisees taught was an incorrect practice, the people pelted him with their *etrogim* (citrons). The Pharisees had urged him to surrender the office of high priest, but he had refused. After this act of lese majesty committed by the people, the enraged Alexander Yannai had thousands killed. The people rebelled against him, calling upon Syria for assistance against their own king. The civil war lasted six years, and upon his return to power, the king mercilessly slaughtered large numbers of his opponents, many of them fleeing into exile, including leaders of the Pharisees.

After Alexander Yannai's death in 76 B.C.E., his widow Salome Alexandra came to the throne, and for the nine years of her reign the people enjoyed a rare peace, the only such calm period during the eighty years of Hasmonean rule. The wars ceased, the exiles returned, and the queen, influenced by her brother Simon ben Shetaḥ, favored the Pharisees. She invited Judah ben Tabbai and other pharisaic teachers to set up a system of elementary education. Pharisees replaced Sadducees in the Sanhedrin, which was legislature and supreme court together. The Pharisees could count on the support of the majority of the population, but the wealthier classes—the aristocracy, the priests, and the military—supported the Sadducees.

Salome Alexandra was the last independent ruler of Judea. After her death in 67 B.C.E., her two sons Hyrcanus and Aristobulus fought a civil war for the throne. The first stage of the fighting ended with Hyrcanus the loser, but Antipater, the Idumean whose father had been appointed governor of his country by Alexander Yannai, prevailed upon Hyrcanus to renew the war. They were aided by the Nabatean Aretas, and Aristobulus, defeated in battle, retreated to Jerusalem and the Temple. Ḥoni, a pious man, known for his successful prayers for rain, was asked by the besiegers to pray for the success of their cause. Instead he prayed for the welfare of both sides and for his pains was stoned to death.

At this time Roman power was growing in the eastern Mediterranean. The Roman general Pompey had been sent to Asia and had already scored several decisive military victories when his attention was drawn to the state of affairs in Jerusalem. Both sides asked for Pompey's help, while the people wanted neither claimant for the throne. A deputation of Pharisees asked Pompey that there be a return to the theocratic state governed by a high priest with the advice of a popular council. Pompey at first favored Aristobulus, but afterward the latter turned against the Romans and secured himself with his troops in the Temple fortifications. After a three-month siege, the Romans broke through and massacred thousands. Jerusalem and the entire country were made subject to Rome. Hyrcanus was appointed high priest by the Romans but with his royal prerogatives sharply reduced. Rome looked kindly upon the Idumeans and Antipater had the actual power in the land. His two sons, one of whom was Herod, were made governors over local areas. (This is the historical background for part 3, as well as for sections of parts 5, 6, and 7.)

The Second Temple served not only as the religious center for the Jews of Judea but as a means for unifying Jews scattered throughout the lands of the Diaspora. The annual Temple tax was voluntarily paid by Jews wherever they lived, and funds for the Temple in Jerusalem flowed from as far away as Spain and the Asian hinterland. It was the dream of Jews living at a distance to join their people in Judea in making a pilgrimage to the Temple on one of the holy days. Herod rebuilt the Temple, sparing no expense, and it became known far and wide for its magnificent beauty, and work on it continued long after Herod's death, until close to the time of its destruction. Tens of thousands of pilgrims crowded the streets of Jerusalem and the Temple area during each of the festivals. The Temple services were dramatic and moving, incorporating the religious fervor of the people and symbolizing their desire for closeness to God. The services on Yom Kippur were awe-inspiring, and those on Sukkot, occasions of great rejoicing.

One of the halls of the Temple, the Hall of Hewn Stones, was the meeting place of the Sanhedrin, which had served as the supreme legislative and judicial body since the early days of the Second Commonwealth. Its seventy-one members were headed by the high priest. With the beginning of Roman power in Judea, the Sanhedrin was shorn of all political power, and its influence was restricted to religious and civil affairs. The office of the high priest declined in importance and lost the respect of the people when, first, the oppressive Hasmonean kings considered themselves the high priests, and later, when the office was filled by the appointees of either Herod and his descendants or of a Roman procurator. They replaced high priests at will, depending upon the size of the bribe. In later years the Sanhedrin was presided over by the nasi, assisted by the av bet din, both offices filled by the leading sages of the generation.

Another religious institution was growing in effectiveness during the days of the Second Temple—the synagogue. It had its roots in Babylonia when the exiled Jews would meet on the Sabbath to hear the words of the prophets and the holy writings. After the return to Judea and despite the construction of the Second Temple, the meetinghouse continued as a place where the people of the neighborhood gathered to hear the Torah and prophets read. Here public meetings were held and cases tried before local judges. In the people's gathering place, or "synagogue," from the Greek word *synagoge*, or in an adjoining hall, the scribes taught and interpreted the Torah. The Great Assembly, an institution that continued into the third century B.C.E. and met from time to time to interpret the existing laws or to enact new ordinances, was succeeded by the scribes, teachers, scholars, and sages. Simon the Just was the bridge between the two eras. It was to the sages that the people looked for religious leadership and for strengthening Jewish identity. The Temple had served as the bond uniting the Jews for centuries, but even before its destruction by the Romans in 70 C.E., the academy and the synagogue were beginning to take its place. (The above may serve as background for parts 5 through 8.)

Herod, half Jew and half Idumean, was appointed king of Judea by decree of the Roman Senate, and in 39 B.C.E. he returned from Rome to Judea to take over his kingdom. Hyrcanus, who had been restored to the throne by Pompey, had fallen victim to the Parthian invasion of the country. The Parthians had set Antigonus, son of Aristobulus and nephew of Hyrcanus, on the shaky throne. The Romans saw in Herod a strong and loyal vassal who could hold Judea for them against the Parthians. The Roman legions

drove out the Parthians, but Jewish support for Antigonus and opposition to Herod kept the fighting going. Eventually Jewish resistance was crushed; Jerusalem was besieged and taken; Antigonus,
the last of the Hasmonean rulers, was executed; and Herod was
firmly placed in power. It has been estimated that over a hundred
thousand Jews fell in the thirty years from the start of the civil war
between the sons of Salome Alexandra and Herod's accession to
the throne.

Herod's reign was marked by extraordinary achievements in
construction and commerce but by abysmal failure in his personal
affairs and his relations with the people. He built new cities, recon-
structing Samaria as Sebaste, and Straton's Tower as Caesarea, naming both for his patron Caesar Augustus. Caesarea was to become
the Roman capital of the land. He constructed palaces, stadia, gymnasia, theaters, and, in the pagan cities, temples to the pagan gods.
The improved harbor at Caesarea helped to increase foreign trade.
Herod encouraged commerce and adopted measures to combat
poverty and famine, but his taxes were a heavy burden on the people. He rebuilt the Second Temple so that its beauty became legendary. He built fortresses—two of them were called Herodium—
for security against foreign attacks, but as his reign continued he
needed them for protection against his own people. For Herod was
hated as few rulers have been. His false pretense at Hellenistic culture was seen for what it was. His origins were not forgotten. But
worst of all was his cruelty. He executed his wife, the princess
Mariamne of the Hasmonean house, his two sons by her and another son born of his first wife, his mother-in-law, his brother-in-
law, and the aged high priest Hyrcanus. The premature news of
his own death ignited a popular uprising that he quelled by ordering forty-two of its leaders burned alive. He died unmourned in
4 B.C.E. After his death his achievements were forgotten, and the
rabbis who spun legends about the glories of the Temple he had
adorned and embellished despised his memory. The two most eminent sages during his time were Hillel and Shammai.

Herod's will arranged for the continuation of royal power by
his sons, but Rome, having the final say, confirmed Herod's son
Archelaus not as king but as ethnarch or prince over Judea, Samaria, and Idumea. Another son, Antipas, was appointed tetrarch
of Galilee and part of Transjordan, while a third son, Philip, was
assigned the tetrarchy of another small province in northern Transjordan. Archelaus possessed only the cruelty of his father and none

of his abilities. His reign began with the massacre of several thousand Jews gathered on the Temple steps at Passover. The Jews had opposed his appointment, having appealed to Rome to rule directly without any Herodian intermediary. Revolt followed upon revolt, each put down with bloody severity until Augustus acceded to the joint request of both the Jews and the Samaritans and banished Archelaus to distant Gaul, his ten-year reign ending in 6 C.E.

Thereafter Rome ruled Judea through its own procurators—who exercised supreme judicial power as well—except for several years when Agrippa, Herod's grandson, ruled as king by imperial appointment. It was not so much the unhappiness of the Jews with Archelaus that motivated Rome to establish direct rule but the combination of the strategic importance of Judea and the seemingly constant turbulence of its inhabitants. The Roman procurators ruled with a heavy hand, determined to establish peace and quiet among the rebellious Jews. They lacked understanding of Jewish religious beliefs and practices and frequently violated them, trampling with impunity upon the most sacred Jewish traditions. Not only did they lack sympathy for Jewish sensitivities, but they regarded Jews as barbarians and fools because they did not adopt Roman civilization in all its aspects. In addition, the procurators were corrupt and aimed at enriching themselves during their foreign service. Six procurators followed one another in rapid succession as governors of Judea and Samaria between 6 and 41 C.E., when Agrippa was made king over Judea. The longest rule was that of Pontius Pilate who governed from 26–36 C.E. Determined to Romanize the Jews, he ruled with force, and Judea and Galilee seethed with rebellion.

Years of civil wars, Herodian tyranny, and the Roman procurators' greed and severity, joined to continuing economic deprivation and heavy taxation, caused great unrest among the people. Jewish theology taught that when life would become unbearable apocalyptic events would herald an end to human history and usher in a messianic era. The people lived with such expectations. Some were seized by religious ecstasy and preached an early end to Roman rule and the beginning of God's kingdom on earth. When their followers multiplied, the preachers were arrested by the Romans and punished as rebels and troublemakers. Sects arose whose members isolated themselves from society, living in the desert and following rules of simplicity and purity. But more and more Jews were becoming convinced that the solution lay in an open revolt against Rome.

For a brief while, during the reign of Agrippa, it seemed the course of history might be changed. Agrippa, companion of the emperor Caligula, was appointed king of Galilee and northern Transjordan in 38 C.E. Three years later, the emperor Claudius expanded Agrippa's kingdom to include Judea and Samaria. The new king showed sensitivity to Jewish religious life and participated in its practice. Like any ordinary Jew, he brought the firstfruits to the Temple and each day an offering was made at his expense. The Pharisees and the people at large showed him their affection and, in contrast to their attitude toward his grandfather Herod, hailed him as one of their own. He began the building of a north wall to protect Jerusalem from attack at its weakest side, but the emperor ordered the work stopped. Unfortunately, sudden death overtook Agrippa in 44 C.E., and the emperor was dissuaded from appointing Agrippa's son as his successor, instead assigning him to a small area in Lebanon, although later his kingdom was enlarged.

Once again Roman procurators ruled, and they were even more harsh than their predecessors. The best of them had no sympathy for Jewish beliefs and practices, the worst drove Jews to rebellion through their harsh oppression and corrupt greed. Would-be prophets appeared, rebels were crucified, and disturbances increased. The Zealots, who were advocates of open rebellion, multiplied, and assassins, Sicarii, struck down pro-Roman sympathizers with their daggers. Disorder was rife throughout the land. The last two procurators were the worst, looting private and public funds and plundering entire communities. When Florus, the last procurator (64–66 C.E.), dared to take money from the Temple treasury, the people mocked him by carrying baskets and asking for coins of charity to aid the poor Florus. The enraged procurator set his Roman soldiers upon the people. Looting and killing by the soldiers were followed by the outbreak of open rebellion by the Jews. There was no unanimity of opinion on the part of the Jews. A peace party, which included representative pharisaic leaders, opposed the revolt, but the war party gained the upper hand, particularly after a spectacular military defeat of the Roman twelfth legion and auxiliary troops.

Determined to crush the rebellion, the emperor Nero sent one of his ablest generals, Vespasian, to command the Roman troops.

Vespasian's son Titus led a segment of the soldiers, who numbered some sixty thousand. The Jewish garrison in the north under Josephus were the first to feel the brunt of the Roman force and after his defeat, Josephus surrendered to Vespasian. (Josephus's famous books are an important source, subjective as they are, for this period of history and constitute a source for tales included in this collection.) By the end of 67 C.E. all of the north had been taken by the Romans.

The Zealots gained complete control of Jerusalem as a result of the military disasters in the north, and those sympathetic to peace with Rome were imprisoned or killed. Simon ben Gamaliel and other leaders of the Pharisees tried to use their influence against the internal strife and terrorism. Meanwhile, Vespasian conquered almost all of Transjordan, Idumea, and the Judean plain. He was engaged in preparations for the siege of Jerusalem when, at Caesarea in June 68 C.E., he received the news of Nero's death. He waited for the establishment of a new emperor's reign, but the murder of the next emperor, Galba, in January 69 C.E. further delayed him. But in June of the same year, he renewed his campaign, capturing Hebron, and all of the land was in Roman hands except Jerusalem and three fortresses south of it. Before the end of the following month, Vespasian was proclaimed emperor by the legions stationed in the East, and the command of the war against the Jews was left to his son Titus.

In Jerusalem three men had risen to military leadership— Johanan of Gush Ḥalav, Simon Bar Giora, and Eleazar ben Simon —each commanding a different sector of the city and contending with one another, even burning the supplies of their rivals. Only when Titus's troops began battering Agrippa's unfinished wall in the spring of 70 C.E. did Johanan and Simon come to terms with each other, Eleazar having been deprived of power. The first wall fell in May. The defenders fought valiantly without regard for their lives, and famine and plague raged in the beleaguered city. On the seventeenth day of Tammuz the daily morning and evening sacrifices offered in the Temple were discontinued, and Titus, overcoming Jewish resistance yard by yard, prepared for an assault upon the Temple area. Repeatedly repulsed, the Romans finally set fire to the Temple gates on the ninth day of Av in order to make their way into the area. But the flames spread rapidly within, and soon the entire Temple was engulfed in flames. Another month yet passed before the remaining Jewish resistance in Jerusalem was overcome, and three years more were required to subdue the three fortresses of Machaerus, Herodium, and Masada. In Masada the Jewish patriots slew each other to deprive Rome of the final victory.

Jewish independence had finally come to an end, although true freedom had not been the lot of the Jews for a long time. The Temple, the center of Jewish religious life and the bond uniting Jews the world over, was reduced to ashes. Titus's triumphal procession in Rome celebrated his great victory and the conquest of the Jews. But the work of the sages in developing Jewish law and scholarship, in making the study of Torah and the life of Torah a new central force in Jewish existence, assured Jewish survival and creative continuity. While the Roman battering rams were still smashing away at the walls of Jerusalem, Rabban Johanan ben Zakkai was establishing an academy of learning in the village of Jabneh. Its efforts and those of its successors resulted in the enhancement of Jewish values, the furtherance of Jewish ideals, and the raising of Jewish standards. These would hold the Jewish people together in a closely knit unity throughout the ages.

III

I express appreciation to the many who have helped make this work possible. First and foremost, there are the men who introduced me to the world of Talmud and rabbinic literature. At the beginning, in my native city of Baltimore, Mr. Abraham Steinbach was my first Talmud teacher. Later, at the Rabbi Isaac Elchanan Theological Seminary, it was my privilege to study with Rabbi Ephraim Steinberg, Rabbi Moshe Aaron Poleyeff, Rabbi Samuel Olshefsky, and Rabbi Moshe Soloveitchik, all of blessed memory. My talmudic studies continued at the Jewish Theological Seminary of America, where I had the singular privilege of being exposed to the erudition and wisdom of Professor Louis Ginzberg of blessed memory. In later years it was my good fortune to study under Professor Saul Lieberman, the renowned Talmudist—*yibadel le-ḥaim tovim ve-'arukhim*. Whatever knowledge I have been able to acquire in the study of rabbinic literature is due to my teachers. Needless to say, any errors I acknowledge as my own.

I am grateful to the library of the Jewish Theological Seminary of America, to its head, Dr. Menahem Schmelzer, and to Dr.

Herman Dicker for the courtesies rendered me. My secretary, Mrs. Norma Daub, has typed much of the manuscript with diligence and devotion, and I thank her.

A word of special thanks is due to my congregational family, the Park Avenue Synagogue in New York City, whose loyalty and friendship I cherish most profoundly. They have understood the need for a rabbi to retreat at times from a very busy congregational calendar and find renewal and strength in our Torah. For their understanding I shall be ever grateful.

As always, I am indebted to my wife, Martha Hadassah, who shares all that I do and all that I am.

New York City
17 Elul 5742/September 5, 1982

Judah Nadich

Part I

The Persian Period

1

Returning from
the Babylonian Exile

The Jews who returned from their exile in Babylonia brought with them traditions originating among them in that land. For example, they taught that when God wrote the Torah, He delayed the recording of the incident of the Golden Calf until after the description of the construction of the Tabernacle—this to show His compassion and love for Israel despite their sins.[1] They brought back also the homiletic interpretation that wherever the words *vayehi bimei* ("and it came to pass in the days of") occur in the Scriptures, they signify a tale of misfortune.[2] They also brought back with them the names of the months of the year used by the Babylonians,[3] and these are the names used in the Hebrew language to this day.

They left behind them in Babylonia their inclination to idolatry. That country was then the center of the pagan world.[4] Their numbers were few when they returned; hence, to them the rabbis applied the verse, *We have a little sister* (Songs 8:8), *little*, because their numbers were small.[5] Their spirit was shaken. In Babylonia they trembled and the trembling accompanied them still as they made their way back to Judea. But another opinion has it that the return to the Holy Land healed them of their trembling.[6]

2

Cyrus

Cyrus, liberator of the Jews from Babylonian captivity, was God's instrument brought to the throne of Persia as part of the divine plan. Darius the Mede and Cyrus of Persia were both door-keepers of the chamber of King Belshazzar of Babylonia. They plotted against Belshazzar, and Darius suggested that should they succeed, Cyrus should reign first. But Cyrus quoted from the prophecies of Daniel as proof that Media was to precede Persia upon the fall of Belshazzar.

When the king learned that conspiracies were being planned against him, he alerted his military commanders. But God told him his military preparations would be futile, for no mortal can avert His decree, and God Himself would punish Belshazzar. After the monarch heard the interpretation by Daniel of the strange writing on the wall, warning of his imminent downfall, he instructed his doorkeepers to admit no one to his chamber. Even should such a person claim that he was the king himself, no credence should be given to his utterance, and his head should be severed from his shoulders forthwith. It happened that very night that the king had to relieve himself and left his chamber without the doorkeepers noticing him. Upon his return he demanded admission. To their inquiring as to his identity he insisted that he was the king.

"Ah, the king warned us of such a possibility," they said. Whereupon they seized a branch of a nearby candlestick and broke his head with it.[7]

The Jewish people wondered why God had chosen Cyrus to be its liberator rather than some righteous Jew. The community of Israel asked the Holy One, blessed be He, "Sovereign of the Universe, rather than to have performed all the miracles through Cyrus, would it not have been better to have performed them by the hand of Daniel or some other righteous man?"

God replied simply, "I am decreeing for the best."[8]

When Cyrus came to the throne he found in Daniel a loyal confidant and trusted friend. But he could not understand why so wise a man did not worship the great god Bel whose idol consumed so much flour, oil, and sheep each day. Daniel, in reply, asked that the usual amount of food be left in the idol's temple and that the doors be then locked and sealed. Daniel cleverly scattered ashes all over the temple floor.

By morning the food had disappeared, but Daniel showed the king that the ashes on the floor revealed the footprints of the priests, their wives, and children, who had come in during the night by a secret entrance under the table and taken away the provisions.

The king was convinced, and he ordered the priests killed and the temple destroyed.[9]

The people became angry at Daniel, and their temper mounted because he had denied the divinity of the serpent worshiped by the king, and he had killed it by feeding it lumps of fat, hair, and pitch. The mob demanded Daniel's death. The king reluctantly acceded to their pressure and ordered Daniel locked in the lions' den. The lions were given nothing to eat, but they did not molest Daniel. He himself was fed miraculously by the prophet Habakkuk, who had been snatched up in Judea by an angel, as the prophet was carrying food to some reapers. The prophet instead gave the food to Daniel, and the angel again caught up Habakkuk by his hair and flew him back to Judea. On the seventh day the king came to the den to mourn Daniel but instead found him alive. He freed Daniel and offered praise to his God. Daniel's enemies, in their fright, fled into the den and were devoured immediately by the lions.[10]

Cyrus was a descendant of Japheth, son of Noah. Noah's blessing to his son, *May God enlarge Japheth* (Gen. 9:27), is an allusion to Cyrus, whose empire was vast and who in his magnanimity ordered the Temple to be rebuilt.[11] At the destruction of the Temple by the Babylonians, Cyrus had wept, and as a reward for this sense of sympathy his people were given dominion over the world.[12]

The winter of the Babylonian exile was past and the springtime of redemption was heralded by the voice of "the good explorer" in the land, the voice of Cyrus granting permission for the Jews to return to Judea to build the house of the Lord.[13] The winter of that exile was seventy years in duration, although the actual time that elapsed from the time of the Temple's destruction until Cyrus's defeat of the Babylonians was only fifty-two years. The eighteen years' difference is accounted for as constituting that period of time at the beginning of the seventy years during which there was a constant dinning into the ears of Nebuchadnezzar by a heavenly voice, saying, "You shameless servant, go up and lay waste the house of your Master, since the sons of your Master do not obey Him."[14]

Cyrus commendably extolled God for having given him all the kingdoms of the earth, but in his self-adulation he tended to exaggerate.[15] Yet he was a pious and good king, so that he was worthy of being numbered among the Jewish kings. Except for Nebuchadnezzar, he was the only non-Jewish king to sit on Solomon's throne. The wicked Nebuchadnezzar used force majeure, but Cyrus was deemed worthy of the privilege.[16] Unfortunately, his conduct was not consistent throughout his life. In the beginning, he was a worthy king, and therefore his years on the throne were counted in accordance with the practice of Jewish royalty, starting the year with the month of Nisan. But afterwards he changed, when he ordered the Second Temple to be built with timber as well as stone so that if the Jews would rebel against him he could more easily set it afire. While Solomon's Temple was also constructed partially of wood, that wood was in the upper part of the building, on the inside of the wall, and was covered with cement. Cyrus saw to it that in the Second Temple the wood should be in the lower part of the building, on the outer side of the wall, and bare—all to make the structure more flammable.[17]

God Himself became disappointed in the king whom He had chosen to be the instrument for the liberation of His people. God said to the Messiah, who is destined to liberate all Israel, "I must complain against Cyrus. I wanted him to rebuild the Temple and to take all the exiles back to the Holy Land. All he did was to issue a proclamation permitting those who wished to return to do so."[18]

In the beginning Cyrus was wise and his words were therefore gracious: *Anyone of you of all His people—may his God be with him and let him go up to Jerusalem* (Ezra 1:3). But later in his life, Cyrus became foolish. He retracted his words and reversed his policy.[19]

Cyrus went forth to tour his capital and saw it deserted. He asked for an explanation, "Where are the artisans, those who work in gold and silver?" He was told, "But was it not you who decreed that the Jews have permission to build their Temple? It was they who were the craftsmen in silver and gold and they have returned to their country to build their sanctuary."

At once he ordered that those Jews who had already crossed the Euphrates could continue on their way, but whoever had not as yet crossed should halt. The Jewish people were cast into great despair. They called upon Cyrus to revoke this decree but he was deaf to their plea.[20] It was at that time that Daniel and his associates went up to Palestine. They said, "It is better that we should eat the food of the land of Israel and bless God for it."[21]

Had all the Israelites in a united phalanx shown their determination to leave Babylonia for the land of Israel and solidly as a wall crossed the Euphrates to Judea, the Temple would not later have been destroyed a second time.[22]

As a matter of fact, it may be said that Cyrus was not so wise even at the beginning. For he described the Lord as *the God that is in Jerusalem* (Ezra 1:3), limiting God's dominion to that city alone. Eventually, he spoke words of grievous madness when he retracted and annulled his decrees, ordering that no more Jews leave Babylonia for Judea.[23]

For his original decree, permitting the exiled Jews to return to their ancestral land and to erect the Second Temple, Cyrus was rewarded materially by God. Nebuchadnezzar had amassed vast riches and was so niggardly that his wealth remained intact. As he felt his end approaching, he rebelled against the thought of leaving his great fortune to his successor, Evil-merodach. He therefore loaded all his money on specially constructed brass barges that he then ordered sunk in trenches dug alongside the Euphrates River. The water was then channeled over the trenches and concealed the treasure completely. On the day Cyrus decreed that the Temple might be rebuilt, God revealed to him the hiding place of the treasure.[24]

3

Persia

Persia was so named from the word *prusot* ("segments"), because the Persian Empire grew in size, segment by segment—one section in the time of King Tarda, one in the days of Adrakhion, and the last will be added in the time to come. This last will be the fulfillment of Micah's prophecy, *And that shall afford safety should Assyria invade our land* (Micah 5:4).[25] And in the future Rome will be conquered by Persia.[26]

Sometimes the country is called Persia and sometimes Media. Frequently, it is called by both names together, Persia and Media, or Media and Persia, the precedence depending on which of the two lands was the birthplace of the reigning king.[27] It was called Media from the word meaning "to bow," for Media bows to the will of God. The kings of Media were men of character, and God had no complaint against them except for their having been idolaters. Even on that score they were not altogether to blame, as the practice of idolatry had been transmitted to them by their ancestors.[28]

Ten portions of physical beauty were distributed throughout the world; nine were given to Media and one to the rest of the world.[29] So too are there ten portions of bravery in the world, nine in Persia and one in the rest of the world.[30] On the other hand, there are ten portions of vermin in the world, nine among the Persians and one in the rest of the world.[31] For Persians are hairy like bears, eat and drink like bears, are fleshy like bears and, like bears, they enjoy no peace.[32]

The Persians are descendants of Japheth, son of Noah, by Japheth's son, Tiras.[33] The prophet Haggai accurately predicted the overthrow of their kingdom, the prophecy being fulfilled thirty-four years after the restoration of the Temple.[34]

The Persians' rule over the Jews resulted from an ill-fated temporary replacement of Gabriel, the protecting angel of the Jews, by Dobiel, the guardian angel of the Persians. This had occurred because God had punished Gabriel for his delay in carrying out God's orders against Jerusalem. Gabriel had received the command to fill both his hands with coals of fire from between the cherubim and to dash them against the city in order to destroy Jerusalem. For three years Gabriel held the coals in his hands, hoping that Israel would repent and make his tragic mission unnecessary. As a result of his tardiness in executing God's judgment, Gabriel was deposed from his high celestial office, and his place was taken by Dobiel for twenty-one days. Dobiel made the most of his new power and arranged for the subjection of twenty-one kingdoms to Persia, including the kingdom of Judah. Still not satisfied, he asked that the Persians have the right to levy special taxes against Jewish scholars. He received a written promise to that effect, but just as the heavenly seal was to be placed upon it, a voice was heard exclaiming, "O Master of the Universe, if all the scholars were placed in one scale of the balance and Daniel in the other, would he not outweigh them all?" It was Gabriel's voice coming from beyond the curtain, for he had been expelled from God's presence. Only the family of celestial beings are permitted on God's side of the curtain.

When God heard the voice, He asked, "Who is this, pleading for My children?" When told it was Gabriel, He rescinded his decree and permitted Gabriel to return to His presence. When he came back to God's side of the curtain, Gabriel noticed the writ in Dobiel's hands and tried to seize it. But Dobiel quickly swallowed it, and thus it became blurred. That is why the Persian levy of taxes against Jewish scholars in later centuries was not universally carried out. On another occasion, when the guardian angel of Greece received temporary dominion over the Jews, all of Gabriel's efforts to mitigate the evil effects were unsuccessful.[35]

═══ **4** ═══

The Four Empires

The defeat of Babylonia and the benevolence of Cyrus were both part of God's plan, and it was He who rescued His people. God would have done more had the Jews not been guilty of sin. He would have liberated them by a great miracle as He had done for their ancestors in Egypt, but their transgressions made that impossible. So He worked through natural rather than through supernatural means.[36] The Four Empires, Babylonia, Persia, Greece, and Rome,[37] whose pagan religions were inferior to the worship of the One God, nevertheless ruled over the Jews, each in its turn. None could deliver the Jews out of their hands but the Holy One, blessed be He.[38] It was God who led the Jewish people through *the great and terrible wilderness with its serpents, fiery serpents, and scorpions* (Deut. 8:15). *Serpents* refers to Babylonia, *fiery serpents* to Persia, and *scorpions* to Greece.[39]

The patriarchs and the prophets were informed about the future subjugation of their people by the Four Empires. The Holy One, blessed be He, when Abraham was on the point of sacrificing Isaac his son, showed Abraham a ram caught in the thicket by its horns, tearing itself free from one thicket only to become entangled in another. God said to him: "In similar fashion will your descendants be seized by one nation after another—conquered and liberated only to be conquered again. First Babylonia, then Persia, afterward Greece, later Rome. But their ultimate redemption will be signaled by the messianic blast of the ram's horn."[40]

Just as Jewish history began with Abraham's military engagement with four kings, so in later days would four powers harass the Jewish people. Abraham warred against Chedorlaomer, Tidal, Amraphel, and Arioch. Later his descendants would be involved with Babylonia, Persia, Greece, and Rome. Shinar, land of King Amraphel, is an allusion to Babylonia. Elam, land of Chedorlaomer, refers to Media, or Persia. Ellasar, country of Arioch, alludes to Greece. Goiim (which means *nations*), the land of Tidal, is an allusion to wicked Rome, which levies troops from all the nations of the world.[41]

Abraham foresaw the Four Empires engaged in their subsequent activities. After he had performed the ritual of sealing the covenant with God through the sacrifice and division of the heifer, goat, and ram and the offering of the turtledove and pigeon, *a trance fell upon Abram, and a deep dark dread descended upon him* (Gen. 15:12). *Dread* refers to the Babylonian exile; *dark* to Persia and the evil days there in the time of Haman. The word *deep* alludes to Greece, famed for its military leadership, and the word *fell* to Rome whose fall would cause the earth to quake.[42] The animals and birds involved in the sacrifice are themselves also symbolic. The three-year-old heifer is an allusion to Babylonia and its three kings who played a part in Jewish history—Nebuchadnezzar, Evilmerodach, and Belshazzar. The three-year-old goat refers to Persia and its three kings, Cyrus, Darius, and Ahasuerus; the three-year-old ram to Greece, which extended its dominion in three directions—westward, northward, and southward. The turtledove and pigeon represent Rome, a seeming turtledove but of predatory character.[43]

When God had thus shown Abraham the four captivities, He said to him, "As long as your descendants will study the Torah and offer sacrifices, they will be saved from these captivities. But a time will come when they will cease offering sacrifices. Choose, therefore, which your children will then suffer, Gehenna or captivity?" Abraham chose captivity, some say because God so advised him.[44] Abraham was assured, however, that just as his descendants would be enslaved by the Egyptians, who would be punished in their turn, so too would the Four Empires be successively subjugated.[45]

Jacob's dream of the ladder stretching from heaven to earth with angels ascending and descending was also a vision of the future relations between the Four Empires and Jacob's descendants. For the angels were the divine protectors of the nations of the world. The protector of Babylonia ascended seventy rungs of the ladder, the protector of Persia fifty-two, the protector of Greece one hundred eighty, while the protector of Rome climbed so high that he vanished from Jacob's sight. Jacob was seized by fear, thinking that this signified that Rome's power would be everlasting. But God reassured him that even if Rome's protector were to ascend to the heights of the throne of God Himself, he would be cast down.[46] Jacob himself was invited by God to climb the ladder after he had witnessed the ascent and descent of the four protectors. He was concerned lest he too be made later to descend, which would be an ill omen for his progeny, so he demurred. God urged him again, promising that there would be no descent for him. But Jacob sinfully would not believe the divine word and refused to climb the ladder. Whereupon, God told him, "Had your faith been strong so that you would have mounted the ladder, nevermore would you have come down. But because you were of little faith, your descendants are now destined to be subject to Four Empires in this world, paying them duties, imposts, fines, and taxes."

Jacob, distraught, asked if their subjection would last forever. The comforting message came that one day the Jewish exile would end. Jacob's descendants would through suffering be cleansed of their wrongdoings, the cause of their exile, and would return to their own land from all the distant countries, from Babylon, Persia, Greece, and Rome, even from Gaul and Spain and the territories adjoining them.[47]

When Jacob resumed his journey and came to the land of the Easterners, he saw a well, which alludes to Zion. He also beheld three flocks of sheep lying beside the well. They allude to the first three powers destined to hold sway over Zion—Babylonia, Persia, and Greece.[48]

Under divine inspiration Jacob and, later, Moses compared the Twelve Tribes to certain animals. Judah was likened to a lion because Judah's descendants, Daniel, Hananiah, Mishael, and Azariah would successfully fight against Babylonia, which is compared to a lion. He compared Benjamin to a wolf, as Mordecai, of the tribe of Benjamin, would one day triumph over Persia, also compared to a wolf. Moses pitted the tribe of Levi against the Greek Empire, for the Hasmoneans were of the tribe of Levi. Joseph was prophetically assigned to oppose Rome, for Rome will be defeated by the Warrior-Messiah descended from Joseph, and, in addition, there is a tradition that Rome will fall only through the hands of the descendants of Rachel.[49]

Moses saw an allusion to the Four Empires in the ritually unclean animals prohibited as food for the children of Israel. The camel refers to Babylonia, the rock badger to Persia, the hare to Greece, and the swine to Rome.[50]

No mention is made of iron in the construction of either the tabernacle or the Temple because Rome was compared to iron. Moses does take from the children of Israel their contributions of gold, silver, and brass for the building of the tabernacle. In Daniel's vision, these three metals were the symbols of Babylonia, Persia, and Greece, respectively. So in the time to come, God will accept gifts from all the kingdoms save from Rome. For, although Babylonia destroyed a Temple even as did Rome, she did not raze it utterly to the ground as Rome did, destroying even its foundations.[51]

The symptoms of leprosy, as described to Moses and Aaron (Lev. 13:2), also hinted at the characters of the Four Empires. A *swelling* is an allusion to Babylonia, a *rash* to Persia, a *discoloration* to Greece, and the *scaly infection* to Rome.[52] The verses dealing with the removal of leprous persons from the camp of the children of Israel may also be taken as allusions to the successive exilic periods of the Jewish people, caused in turn by Babylonia, Persia, and Rome. Greece is not referred to here in order to link Babylonia and Rome more closely together, for both destroyed the Temple and exiled Israel.[53]

When Moses warned his people of the consequences of the violation of the divine law, he hinted at the unhappy subjection of Israel to foreign masters. *In the morning you shall say, "If only it were evening"* (Deut. 28:67). *In the morning*, that is, when Israel's captivity in Babylonia would be at its beginning, the Jews will yearn for the *evening*, for its end. When Babylonia's power would be at its peak, the harassed Israelites will hope for its decline. So too, in turn, with Persia, Greece, and Rome. Similarly, when Babylonia's strength would be at its greatest, the Jews will long for the rise of Persia's might so that it triumphs over Babylonia. But when Persian force would be uppermost, the hope will then be for the ascendancy of Greece. And when the latter's victories would give her dominance, the Jews will seek relief in the future triumph of Rome. But all in vain. Their situation will continue to go from bad to worse.[54]

The four beasts seen by Daniel in his vision (Dan. 7) were symbolic of the Four Empires. The *lion with eagle's wings* referred to Babylonia, the *bear* to Persia, the *leopard* to Greece, the fourth beast, *fearsome, dreadful, and very powerful*, to Rome. Daniel saw the first three during a vision one night and the last on another night, for the fourth animal was equal to, or even more powerful than, the other three—that is, Rome's power was as great as or even greater than the might of the preceding three empires combined.[55] Egypt, the first country to enslave the Jews, was compared to a fox, for just as the fox is smaller than the four aforementioned beasts, so Egypt was smaller than any of the Four Empires.[56]

Indeed, all the prophets foresaw the oppression of the Jewish people by the Four Empires, for the allusion to them is already found in the first book of the Bible. The four rivers stemming from the river that came out of Eden (Gen. 2:10–14) call them to mind by association. Pishon refers to Babylonia, Gihon to Persia, Tigris to Greece, and Euphrates to Rome.[57]

A prophecy of Jeremiah may also be interpreted in like manner. *It is turned to darkness,* for lack of words of Torah and prophecy, *and becomes a deep gloom* (Jer. 13:16) in Babylonia, then in Persia, later in Greece and, finally, in Rome.[58] And when the prophet says a *lion of the forest strikes them down, the wolf of the desert ravages them, a leopard lies in wait by their towns; whoever leaves them will be torn in pieces* (Jer. 5:6)—*lion* refers to Babylonia, the *wolf* is Persia, the *leopard* is Greece, and *torn in pieces* an allusion to Rome.[59]

And when the prophet Amos (5:19) describes a man running *from a lion,* he means Babylonia. *Attacked by a bear* refers to Persia. The *indoors* into which the man escapes from the lion and bear alludes to Greece during whose era in history the House of God was still standing. The *snake* biting him thereafter is a designation for Rome.[60]

The four horns seen in a vision by Zechariah (2:1)—horns in the Bible are frequently symbols of power—represent the Four Empires.[61] So too with the four chariots drawn by different-colored horses seen by the prophet in another vision. The bay horses denote the kingdom of Babylonia, which shed much blood in Israel. The black horses symbolize the Kingdom of Persia, which darkened the face of Israel during Haman's time. The white horses represent the Kingdom of Greece, which blanched the face of Israel with blasphemies and reproaches. The spotted or dappled horses indicate the Roman Empire, which issued multiple decrees, each different from the other, against the Jewish people.[62]

Passages in the Hagiographa may be similarly understood. In the Song of Songs (5:2) the phrase *Let me in my own* refers to Israel in the Babylonian captivity; *my darling* to Persia; *my dove* to Greece; *my faultless* to Rome. *Dove* refers to Greece, for during the Greek period Israel used to offer pigeons and doves on the Temple altar.[63] The *little foxes* connote the Four Empires *that ruin the vineyards* (Israel) (Songs 2:15), as it is written, *For the vineyard of the Lord of Hosts is the House of Israel* (Isa. 5:7).[64]

The words of the verse in Psalms (18:7), *In my distress I called on the Lord*, refer to the Babylonian period; *cried out to my God*, to the Persian; *in His temple He heard my voice*, to the Greek; *my cry to Him reached His ears*, to the hoped for redemption from Rome.[65]

Job's description of his uneasiness (Job 3:26) may be similarly interpreted: *I had no repose* on account of Persia; *no quiet, no rest* on account of Greece; and *trouble came* with Rome.[66]

When Ecclesiastes (5:15) compares the similarity of end to beginning, the reference is to the conclusion of history and its early chapters. Early scriptural history (Gen. 14:1) mentions the four kingdoms of Shinar, Ellasar, Elam, and Goiim. History will close with four kingdoms: Babylonia, Persia, Greece, and Rome.[67]

Each of the Four Empires came against Israel not singly but in pairs: Babylonia with Chaldea, Persia with Media, Greece with Macedonia, and Rome with the descendants of Ishmael. They alternated in the severity of their treatment of the Jews. Babylonia was severe, Persia more lenient, Greece severe, and the Ishmaelites more lenient.[68]

But in all four exilic periods of its history, the Jewish people remained faithful to God and adamantly refused to deny Him. He resolved to go with them into each of these exiles, even as He had been with them in Egypt, in order that their reputation might be untarnished during their stay in the various foreign lands.[69]

In the end God will not permit the oppressors to go unpunished. It was He who delivered Israel into the hands of the alien empires because of Israel's sins. In due time He will redeem Israel and judge the nations, just as He had delivered Israel from Egypt and Babylonia. This is the reason why the word *who* is written six times in one verse (Prov. 23:29), alluding to the six times when Israel was exiled among the nations, all of whom were punished or will be punished on its account. The six nations are Egypt, Assyria, Babylonia, Persia, Greece, and Rome.[70]

Meanwhile, however, Israel suffered greatly, one harassment succeeding another without a breathing spell. The community of Israel stood before the Holy One, blessed be He, and voiced its complaint: "Sovereign of the Universe, you used to give us at least some measure of light between one night and another"—that is, between the night of Egypt and the night of Babylonia, between the night of Babylonia and the night of Persia, between the night of Persia and the night of Greece, between the night of Greece and the night of Rome—"but now that I sleep neglectful of the Torah and its precepts, one night follows immediately upon another."[71]

Just as God rescued the Jews from Babylonia, Persia, and Greece, so will He eventually keep His covenant with them by ushering in the messianic era. Such is the promise revealed in the verse, *Yet, even then, when they are in the land of their enemies, I will not reject them or spurn them so as to destroy them, annulling My covenant with them: for I the Lord am their God* (Lev. 26: 44). The statement *I will not reject them* refers to the Babylonian period; the word *spurn* to the Persian; *destroy* to the Greek; *annulling My covenant with them* to the Roman; *for I the Lord am their God* to the messianic era.[72]

The four cups of wine drunk each Passover at the Seder table were instituted by the sages, according to one opinion, as an allusion to the Four Empires who subjugated the Jewish people. Another opinion has it that the reference is to the four cups of fury that God, in the end of days, will make the nations of the world drink. Corresponding to these, He will give Israel four cups of salvation to drink.[73]

Like a woman conceiving and giving birth in travail again and again, so Israel suffers troubles repeatedly. But from all of them will she be delivered. Hence all the songs sung by Israel are designated by the feminine form of the word *shirah*. Babylonia and Persia, Greece and Rome have subjected Israel, but in the messianic age there will be no more trouble. At that time Israel will recite a song in the masculine form, *shir*, as the psalmist suggests, *Sing to the Lord a new song (shir)* (Ps. 96:1).[74]

When the Messiah will come, God will judge all nations and reward them in accordance with the extent to which they have devoted themselves to the study of Torah. The first to come before God will be Rome. God will ask Rome, "With what have you occupied yourselves?" Rome will answer, "We have established many marketplaces, built many bathhouses, gathered much silver and gold, and all this we did only for the sake of the Jews, that they might have leisure for occupying themselves with the study of Torah." God will reply: "Fools! All that you did you did for yourselves. You established marketplaces in order to settle harlots in them. You built bathhouses in order to revel in them. You gathered gold and silver but these precious metals really belong to Me. But you did not study Torah and you will receive no reward." Crushed in spirit, the Romans will depart. After the Romans, the Persians will appear. God will ask them, "With what have you occupied yourselves?" The Persians will answer, "We have built many bridges, conquered many cities, waged many wars, and all this we did only for the sake of the Jews, that they might have leisure for occupying themselves with the study of Torah." God will reply: "Fools! All that you did you did for the sake of yourselves. You built bridges to collect tolls. You conquered cities so as to impose forced labor upon their inhabitants. Your wars were not your own doing but Mine, so that My people might be liberated from Babylonian exile. But you did not study Torah and you will receive no reward." The Persians, like the Romans, will depart abashed.[75]

= 5 =
Haggai, Zechariah, and Malachi

The three prophets, Haggai, Zechariah, and Malachi, were among those Jews who returned from the Babylonian exile. Each made his contribution toward the rebuilding of the Temple.[76] Haggai showed the people the plan for the new altar, to be larger than the original one in the First Temple. Zechariah told them where the altar was to be placed. He knew the location because, in a vision, he had seen the angel Michael sacrifice there. Malachi informed them that they might bring their offerings to be sacrificed upon the altar even before the Second Temple would be completed. Moreover, one of these prophets instructed the Jews to give up the old form of the Hebrew alphabet, and he rewrote the Torah in the "Assyrian" characters in use to the present time.[77] It was these three prophets, it is said, who introduced the terminal forms of the five elongated letters.[78] Zechariah's father, Iddo, was also a prophet.[79] Malachi was the same person called at other times Ezra, and again, Mordecai.

When Zechariah called upon the people to repent and give up the evil ways of their fathers, saying, *Where are your fathers now?*, the people retorted, "And the prophets who did not sin, where are they?" But the prophet replied, *And did the prophets live forever?* (Zech. 1:5). Thereupon the people acknowledged the justice of God and testified to the fulfillment of His words.[80]

The three prophets were with Daniel when he saw the vision of the man clothed in linen whose loins were girded with fine gold (Dan. 10:7). But they saw nothing. In one respect they ranked higher than Daniel because they were prophets and he was not. On the other hand, he ranked higher than they because he saw the heavenly vision and they did not. Yet they were suddenly seized with fright because their guardian angels saw the vision and communicated the sensation to them.[81]

The Targum, the Aramaic translation of the prophets, was composed by Jonathan ben Uzziel under the influence of these three prophets.[82] Haggai's authority was invoked for the acceptance of Kardites and Tardumites as proselytes to Judaism.[83] The Talmud quotes him as the author of several legal decisions.[84] He and Zechariah wrote several of the psalms.[85]

The three stood in an intermediate position between the prophets who had preceded them and from whom they had received the tradition and the Men of the Great Assembly, which they helped found, who followed them and to whom they transmitted the tradition.[86] They themselves were the very last of the prophets.[87] With their death, the prophetic spirit departed from the Jewish people, although holy inspiration remained with them.[88]

There were seven great leaders of the Jews during the period following the return from Babylonia: Joshua the high priest, Zerubbabel, Ezra, Nehemiah, Haggai, Zechariah, and Malachi.[89]

These seven were primarily responsible for the rebirth of the Jewish commonwealth and the rebuilding of the Temple.

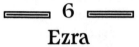

6

Ezra

Ezra or, as he was sometimes called in the Bible, Malachi,[90] did not return from Babylonia to Judea with the first group of Jews. He delayed his journey because he wished to complete his studies with his teacher, Baruch ben Neriah, who had been the disciple of the prophet Jeremiah. Baruch himself could not make the trip because he was a heavy man and very old and was unable to travel even when carried in a palanquin. But it was fortunate that Ezra did not return with the first party. For had he gone then, there might have been strife as to the selection of the first high priest to serve in the Second Commonwealth. Satan the Accuser would have had the opportunity to stir up mischief by saying, "It is better for Ezra to serve as high priest rather than Joshua ben Jehozadak." But the latter merited the office more than Ezra. Ezra was indeed a righteous man, but his lineage was unlike that of Joshua who was a high priest and son of a high priest.[91]

Had all the Jews remaining in Babylonia returned with Ezra, they would have possessed incorruptible strength.[92] Unfortunately, only a fraction of the Jews accompanied him. Ezra's group was called a heavenly treasure stored up for the Jewish people, like those who were with Moses, Joshua, David, and Hezekiah in earlier times and like the associates of Hillel, Rabban Johanan ben Zakkai, and Rabbi Meir in later days.[93] Among those who had been the first to return were the heads of the clans of Judah because it was the tribe of royalty, of Benjamin because the Temple was in its territory, of the priests because they were required to minister in the Temple, and of the Levites because of their Temple duties.[94] However, not too many Levites accompanied Ezra. Therefore, they were punished by the loss of the traditional tithes that had been assigned to the priests during the period of the Second Temple.[95] Strangely enough, God had wished to abolish the practice of the tithe altogether at this time, but the Jews themselves decreed its continuation. They recorded their decision in a document and deposited it in the Temple. The next day they found the document mysteriously stamped with God's seal, *Emet* ("Truth"). This is one of the three things that an earthly court decreed that were later ratified by God.[96]

When the Second Temple was nearing completion, the priests prepared to offer the first sacrifices. But they could not find the sacred flame with which to kindle the perpetual fire on the altar. Ezra prayed to God, together with Nehemiah, Mordecai, Joshua, and Zerubbabel: "Master of all worlds, You have stirred the spirit of the kings of the earth and have given them the desire to build Your Temple, to send forth the poor of Your people and Your priests to offer Your sacrifices and peace offerings as our ancestors have done. We have come to this holy place and prepared Your altar and have presented sacrifices and set wood for the burnt offering. We had thought that fire would at once descend from before You, O Lord, and would consume our sacrifice. We looked for it but it did not descend.

"Now, O Lord our God, how can we kindle on the altar a strange fire not commanded by You? That would be a sin against You."

After they had prayed, one of the oldest priests arose and said, "Now I remember the place where the holy fire was hidden by Jeremiah, prophet of the Lord." Upon the request of the heads of the community the old man walked to a place outside the camp, followed by the elders of Israel. He showed them a pit closed by a large whitewashed stone. Rolling away the stone, they saw water in the pit, thick as oil.

Ezra was informed of the matter and, hastening to the pit, he commanded the priests to take a handful of the water in their palms and carry it to the Temple of the Lord. They threw the water upon the altar, the offering, and the wood. At once a great flame burst forth and set ablaze the wood and the sacrifice. The flame continued growing in intensity until it enveloped all the sacred vessels and purified them. The frightened priests fled. But after it had purified the Temple and its vessels, the flame grew smaller until only a small fire flickered upon the altar. From that day on the priests regularly placed wood upon it and kept the fire burning continuously upon the altar. It was not extinguished until the children of Israel were exiled a second time from their land.[97]

Ezra was greatly concerned about the maintenance of the purity of the Jewish people. He investigated his own lineage while still in Babylonia. His research into his own genealogy resulted in his writing the Book of Chronicles in the Bible and the book called by his own name. The Book of Ezra was finished, however, by Nehemiah.[98] Before his departure from Babylonia for Judea, Ezra established the lineal purity of the families remaining behind and took with him those of mixed or questionable ancestry.[99] However, he excluded the Gibeonites, though proselytes, from membership in the Jewish people.[100]

A second significant contribution made by Ezra to the fashioning of the Second Commonwealth was his role in the revival of the study of Torah. The Torah was largely forgotten among the Jews in Judea until Ezra came from Babylonia and rekindled interest in it.[101] As a matter of fact, he was worthy enough for the Torah to have been given through him to Israel had it not been that Moses preceded him.[102] But though the Torah was not transmitted originally through him, he was responsible for the change in its script. For at the outset, the Torah was given to the Jewish people in the primitive Hebrew characters and in the Hebrew language. In Ezra's day, it may be said, it was given to them again, this time in the "Assyrian" type letters and in the Aramaic language. Eventually, the Jewish people themselves settled upon the "Assyrian" script and the Hebrew language for the Torah. It is called "Assyrian," either because it was brought by Jews from Assyria, or because the script is praiseworthy in character.[103]

Ezra did other things to stimulate study and knowledge of Torah. He was primarily responsible for the division of the Torah into portions to be read publicly at synagogue services each Sabbath.[104] He further established the practice of public reading of the Torah at services on Sabbath afternoons and on Monday and Thursday mornings.[105] He arranged too for the opening of more schools for children, even though there apparently was a sufficient number. His reasoning was that the competition among the schools could only bring benefit to the students.[106] He was author of parts of the Scriptures—not only of most of the book called by his name, but also of Chronicles and a number of the Psalms.[107] Some say he was also responsible for the diacritical points to be found above certain letters in the text of the Torah, for the letters thus marked constitute words difficult to defend in the sacred text. Ezra reasoned that if Elijah came to remonstrate against the inclusion of those letters, Ezra could reply that he had placed points over the letters as a sign that these letters were to be disregarded. If Elijah gave his approval to their inclusion, Ezra could then erase the marks.[108]

He himself possessed a masterful knowledge of the Torah. Yet it was said that even if a scribe knows the Torah as well as Ezra, he must not write a Torah scroll by memory but copy it from another.[109] Were it not for the fact that Nehemiah was his contemporary, it would have been said of Ezra, as it was said only of Moses before him and of Rabbi Judah ha-Nasi after him, that Ezra was unique in his time as possessing both knowledge of Torah and supreme leadership.[110]

He was responsible for some ten different practices thereafter followed by the people: reading from the Torah at Sabbath afternoon services and also at services on Monday and Thursday mornings, court sessions on these latter two days, that laundry work be done on Thursdays, eating of garlic on Friday as a sex stimulant, baking of Sabbath loaves on Friday morning rather than in the afternoon, wearing by women of a garment called *sinar*, combing the hair before entering the ritual bath, bathing for the ritually unclean to cover the case of the man who wishes to pray or study Torah, and permitting peddlers to sell cosmetics to women in towns.[111]

When asked why the Torah should be read twice on Saturday, morning and afternoon, Ezra explained that it was to benefit the peddlers who all week long were out working in the rural areas and so had no opportunity to hear words of Torah except on the Sabbath. As for his suggestion that bread be baked early on Friday, his reason was that the poor come during the morning to beg for bread for the Sabbath. Let it then be baked early in the day so that none of the needy be turned away. Those who would follow this advice would receive God's blessing.[112]

Ezra and the other leaders of the Jewish people were greatly concerned about the people's lack of good character. So soon after the destruction of the First Temple and the Babylonian exile, caused by sin, the people were again sinning. They were once more guilty of jealousy, envy, slander, and other evil things. Ezra and his associates prayed, therefore, that the inclination toward evil placed by God in every mortal be eradicated. For, although the evil inclination had been created so that man might conquer it and be rewarded, it would be preferable, they felt, that there be neither the evil inclination nor the reward. In answer to their prayers a note fell from the heavens. Upon it was written one word, "Truth." It was a sign that their prayers had been successful.

They fasted three days and nights, and the evil inclination was then handed over to them for their disposal. It came charging out of the precincts of the Holy of Holies like a fiery lion. The prophet Zechariah identified it, crying, "This is the Wickedness!" As the leaders of the people approached to seize it, one of its hairs was pulled out. Its loud bitter scream was heard at a distance four hundred parasah away from Jerusalem. The frightened people asked the prophet for his advice. He counseled placing it in a lead cauldron with a lead cover on top. After they had done so, the prophet warned them not to slay it lest all the world perish.

The evil inclination was in their power three days. The hens stopped laying eggs, and not an egg could be found in all the land, not even to feed the sick. The captors of the evil inclination now did not know what to do—to kill it would mean disaster, for hens and cows would no longer reproduce, to ask God to deprive it of half its power would be unthinkable, for God does nothing partially. They concluded that it would be best to blind it and send it forth free. This they did. Its strength was weakened so that it could not cause men to sin as greatly as before, nor could it entice them to unspeakable abominations as in earlier times.[113]

Ezra himself was able to rule his evil inclination and master it. The entire generation of such a man depends on him.[114] God Himself praised Ezra for his good character, pointing out that the existence of the Temple was no guarantee of righteousness. For when the First Temple still stood, there were such wicked men as Ahaz, Manasseh, and Amon; while—to the contrary—with the Temple in ruins there were Daniel, Mordecai, and Ezra.[115]

Ezra felt for his people's woes, and once he complained to God about His treatment of the Jewish people. They wallowed in misfortune while the heathen peoples prospered. The angel Uriel then appeared to explain that all evil must run its course. But Ezra was still dissatisfied, and so seven visions were granted him, all interpreted by the angel. They cast light both upon the entire past of history and its future. With the last vision, there came a voice from a thorn bush, as to Moses, warning him not to reveal the secret things he had seen. He was told too that his death was imminent. He asked God to let the divine spirit rest upon him before he died, so that he might record all that had happened since Creation as set down in the Torah, in order to guide men upon the path leading to God.

God told him to take five experienced scribes to a secluded place and to dictate to them for forty days. With Sarga, Dabriah, Seleucia, Ethan, and Aziel, he went into isolation, far from men and cities. After one day he heard a voice asking him to open his mouth and to drink what would be given him. A chalice was presented to him filled with a liquid that flowed like water, but in color resembled fire. His mouth opened to drink and then was not closed again for forty days. For Ezra dictated unremittingly for that entire period to the five scribes in the newly adopted Hebrew characters, which the scribes did not understand. At the end of the forty days, God commanded Ezra to publish the twenty-four books of Holy Scripture for all to read, the worthy and unworthy alike. The remaining seventy books that he had dictated during the forty days were to be reserved for study by the wise alone. On account of his literary creativity, Ezra is called "the scribe of the science of the Supreme Being unto all eternity."[116]

Some say Ezra died in Jerusalem.[117] The date of his death was the second day of Tevet, the date of Nehemiah's death as well. Therefore, the day was later observed as a fast day.[118] However, others say that he died outside the Holy Land, at Khuzistan in Persia on a journey to the king of that land.[119] Perhaps this was the realization of the curse pronounced upon him by the Jews of Yemen, who were angered when Ezra cursed them first for their refusal to return to Judea. His malediction upon them was that they and their descendants would forever live in poverty. In turn they cursed him that he would end his days outside the Holy Land.[120]

Just before Ezra's death, the city of Babylon was completely destroyed by the Persians and all the prophecies of the prophets against it were fulfilled. There is still a spot on the site where it once stood that no animal can pass over unless some of the earth of the place is first strewn upon it.[121]

In later times the highest appellation that could be bestowed upon a man distinguished for both holiness and scholarship was "worthy disciple of Ezra."[122]

7

Zerubbabel and Nehemiah

Zerubbabel was of royal descent. God had retracted the oath He had sworn through His prophet, Jeremiah, that King Jehoiachin would have no descendants to rule after him. For the punishment of exile atones for all wrongdoings. Therefore, in Babylonia Jehoiachin fathered Zerubbabel. The sincere repentance of Jehoiachin succeeded in reversing the decree of childlessness.[123] He was known as Assir, because his mother was pregnant with him when she was in prison. He was also known as Shealtiel because his father was born impotent, but God altered his state and made it possible for him to plant his seed. Another explanation for Shealtiel is that God revoked His earlier vow that Jehoiachin would be childless. He was given the name of Zerubbabel because he was born in Babylonia. He was also called Nehemiah.[124]

Zerubbabel was a member of the royal bodyguard serving Darius, the king of Babylonia, and later Cyrus appointed him head of the Jews of the land.[125] He is included among the "famous men whose praises were sung in later generations."[126] Once when Darius was asleep, Zerubbabel and the other two bodyguards engaged in a contest of wits. Each was to write down what he considered the most powerful thing in the world. The king awoke to find three notes under his pillow awaiting his immediate decision. The first note said wine was the strongest of all things, for it can overcome the mightiest man. The second note judiciously hailed the monarch as the most powerful of all on earth. The third, the one written by Zerubbabel, called woman stronger than any man, for woman can cause man to succumb to her, but strongest of all is truth. Each writer defended his selection. The first explained that wine is so potent that it causes a man to forget even grief. The second sang the praises of the king. Zerubbabel described the power of woman who can humble kings. "Truth, however, is supreme over all," he continued. "The earth demands it; the heavens sing its praises. All creation trembles before it, and there is no blemish in it. To it belong dominion, power, and glory. Blessed be the God of truth!"

The entire assembly present in the royal court shouted its approval. The king was so taken by the wisdom of Zerubbabel that he asked how he might reward him. Zerubbabel replied that he wanted nothing for himself but that he would plead for his people. He asked for permission for the Jews to restore Jerusalem and rebuild the Temple and for the return of the sacred vessels that had been carried off to Babylonia. The king at once gave his consent and, in addition, gave letters of safe-conduct to Zerubbabel, special privileges to the Jews who would accompany him to Judea, and his own royal gifts for the future Temple.[127] As a matter of fact, the idea of returning the sacred vessels had been the king's own. Before he had ascended the throne he had made a vow to God that should he become king, he would send all the sacred vessels to Jerusalem. Zerubbabel's request served to remind him of this vow.[128] Before Darius's death he transmitted his desires concerning the Jews to his successor, Cyrus. He, in turn, carried out these wishes in the first year of his reign, decreeing that the Jews might return to Judea and rebuild the Temple. Cyrus undertook this action both because of his own pious nature and because he was anxious to fulfill the last request of his predecessor.[129]

God gave to Zerubbabel a knowledge of future events. This was arranged especially through the medium of the archangel Metatron, who not only revealed to him when the Messiah would appear but even arranged a meeting between the two. Zerubbabel would have a special role to play in messianic times. He would have the honor of reciting the special kaddish prayer upon conclusion of the lecture to be delivered by God on the subject of the new Torah that He would reveal through the Messiah. All men, including non-Jews and even the wicked in hell, upon hearing the kaddish would answer, "Amen." As a result, God would have compassion upon all His creatures, not even excluding the sinners. He would have the angels Michael and Gabriel open the gates of hell to set free all its inmates. Moreover, Zerubbabel would enjoy, at that time, the privilege of joining with Elijah in clarifying all the obscure passages in the Written Law and Oral Law. At the call of Zerubbabel the angels Michael and Gabriel would launch the final war of annihilation against the world of paganism. In the company of Elijah and the Messiah, Zerubbabel would ascend the

Mount of Olives, where the Messiah would signal Elijah to blow the trumpet.[130]

Nehemiah was a name for Zerubbabel, but Nehemiah was also called the Tirshatha because the authorities absolved him from having to observe the decree of Daniel and his three companions against using wine touched by heathens and allowed him to drink it with the king, whom he served as cup-bearer.[131] Yet, it was Nehemiah and his associates who were responsible for the rigid law that no utensil or vessel is to be handled on the Sabbath. However, this was because the people had become lax in their observance of the Sabbath. When their faithfulness to the sacred day was renewed, this excessive restriction was annulled.[132]

When the Jews returned to Judea and wished to relight the flame on the Temple altar, Nehemiah played an important part in discovering the secret place where the celestial fire had been hidden.[133] However, he lacked certain human qualities. He was a braggart and, in addition, he spoke ill of those who had been in the royal service before him. He even maligned Daniel. Therefore, the Book of Ezra in the Bible, although composed by Nehemiah, was not called by his name.[134]

Notes

I. THE PERSIAN PERIOD

1. Returning From the Babylonian Exile

1. Songs Rabbah 1:12.
2. Leviticus Rabbah 11:7; Numbers Rabbah 10:5; Yalkut Esther, Pesikta Rabbati 5.
3. Yerushalmi Rosh Ha-Shanah 1:2; see Zech. 1:7, 7:1.
4. Rashi on Zech. 5:11; Yerushalmi Berakhot 4:17a calls Babylonia the dregs of the world.
5. Songs Rabbah 8:9.
6. Ibid., commenting on Deut. 28:65.

2. Cyrus

7. Songs Rabbah 3:4, commenting on Dan. 5:5, Ps. 75:7 f., and Dan.

5:30. For the identification of Cyrus with Darius, see *Aggadat Esther,* ed. Salomon Buber (Cracow, 1897), p. 8.

8. Songs Rabbah 5:3.

9. This is the story of Bel in the Apocrypha, most likely a story written by a Jew of Alexandria early in the first century B.C.E. in order to warn Jews in Egypt against succumbing to the local idolatrous religion by exposing its shams. See also *Bereshit Rabbati* of R. Moses Hadarshan, quoted from a manuscript in Epstein, *Magazin für die Wissenschaft der Judentum* 15 (1888):78–79; Raymondo Martini, *Pugio fidei* (Farnborough, 1967), p. 956; Louis Ginzberg, *The Legends of the Jews* (7 vols., Philadelphia, 1909–46), 6:432, n. 6.

10. This is the story of the Dragon in the Apocrypha. Theodotion alone gives the king's name as Cyrus. The Septuagint describes this story as having been taken from the prophecy of Habakkuk son of Jesus, or Joshua, of the tribe of Levi. This apocryphal work says that Daniel was of priestly descent, but the rabbis say he was descended from the royal house. The name Dragon is taken from the Greek and Latin words for serpent, *drakon* and *draco.* This story, like the preceding one about Bel, was most likely written before the middle of the first century B.C.E. to ridicule the idolatrous religions of the Egyptians. The stories were added to the Book of Daniel by its Greek translator and then rewritten by Theodotion about the middle of the second century C.E., when he translated Daniel from Aramaic and Hebrew into Greek.

11. Genesis Rabbah 36:8, and Yoma 10a, where Japheth's son, Tiras, is identified as the ancestor of the Persians.

12. Seder Eliyahu Rabbah, ed. M. Friedmann (Vienna, 1900) chap. 20, p. 114; Esther Rabbah 1:2, 13; Pirke de-Rabbi Eliezer, ed. S. Luria (New York, 1946), p. 11; Midrash Aseret Melakhim, ed. J. D. Eisenstein (in *Ozar midrashim,* New York, 1915), p. 44; 1 and 2 Targum on Esther 1:2.

13. Songs Rabbah 2:13; a play of words on *tor,* "turtle," in Songs 2:12. Read as *tayyar,* "explorer," and taken to refer to Cyrus and his proclamation, Ezra 1:2 ff.

14. Songs Rabbah 2:13. An interpretation of *For now the winter is past, the rains are over and gone* (Songs 2:11). *Winter* is the seventy-year period; *the rain* refers to the fifty-two years in actual captivity.

15. Megillah 11a; 2 Chron. 36:23 ff.; and Leviticus Rabbah 13:5; see also Ezra 1:2 ff.

16. See supra n. 13.

17. Rosh Ha-Shanah 3b, 4a.

18. Megillah 12a based on Isa. 45:1.

19. Ecclesiastes Rabbah 10:12–13 on Eccles. 10:12. The rabbis here identify Cyrus with Artaxerxes who ordered the rebuilding of the Temple halted, Ezra 4:17 ff. See also Midrash Aseret Melakhim, p. 44.

20. Songs Rabbah 5:5–6.

21. Songs Rabbah 5:5, "bless God"—in the recital of grace after meals.

22. Songs Rabbah 8:9 and Yoma 9b. Ezra 2:64 states that only 42,360 Jews left Babylonia, a fraction of the total number.

23. Ecclesiastes Rabbah 10:13 on Eccles. 10:13 and Ezra 4:17 ff.

24. Esther Rabbah 2:1, explaining that King Ahasuerus inherited his wealth from Cyrus and basing the legend upon the verses Isa. 45:1, 3.

The ambivalence of the feeling of the rabbis toward Cyrus may be explained, Ginzberg says, by whether they were Palestinian or Babylonian. The Palestinian rabbis were more favorable to the Persian king because they suffered under the Roman yoke and they sympathized with the Persians, also conquered by Rome, whom they regarded as more friendly. On the other hand, the Babylonian rabbis were conscious of Jewish persecution by the priests of Mazda who were powerful in the Sassanid Empire and they considered the Romans the lesser evil. They, therefore, regarded Cyrus, the founder of the Persian Empire, with less warmth. See Ginzberg, *Legends*, 6:433, n. 7.

3. Persia

25. Esther Rabbah 1:18. *Prusot* may possibly also be understood as "at intervals" in time, the thought being that the empire was not continuous, especially since this midrash says that the Persian Empire will again exist in the future. The king, Tarda, is otherwise unknown. One conjecture equates him with Mithridates. Adrakhion was a king of Parthia. The verse quoted from Micah 5:4 refers to Assyria but the rabbis confused the name with Persia, which was in the same general direction from Palestine.

26. Yoma 10a, based either on an interpretation of Jer. 49:20 or on a fortiori argument.

27. Esther Rabbah 1:18; also cf. Megillah 12a.

28. Esther Rabbah 1:18.

29. Esther Rabbah 1:17; cf. Kiddushin 49b.

30. Kiddushin 49a.

31. Esther Rabbah 1:17; cf. Kiddushin 49b.

32. Megillah 11a, based on an interpretation of Dan. 7:5; cf. also Kiddushin 72a; Avodah Zarah 2b; Yalkut Isaiah 316.

33. Yoma 10a.

34. See Rashi on Haggai 2:22.

35. Ezek. 10:2. The rabbis identify Gabriel as "the man clothed in linen" (see Yoma 79a). Notice that Dobiel, the name of Persia's guardian angel, is composed of *dov*, "bear," and *el*, "God," alluding to Dan. 7:5. In rabbinic literature the bear is the symbol of Persia.

4. The Four Empires

36. Sanhedrin 98b, commenting on Exod. 15:16; see also Sotah 36a.

37. Destined to rule the world, according to the interpretation of Dan. 7.

38. Lamentations Rabbah 5:8, commenting on the phrase, *slaves are ruling over us* (Lam. 5:8). Greece in rabbinic literature refers not so much to the Greek world empire of Alexander the Great as to the successor Hellenistic kingdoms of the Seleucids and the Ptolemies, more often the former; see also Songs Rabbah 5:5.

39. Leviticus Rabbah 13:5; see also Genesis Rabbah 44:17.

40. Leviticus Rabbah 29:10, explaining the word *aḥer* in Gen. 22:13, which may mean "another" or "after" and is, moreover, superfluous. The first explanation offered by the Midrash is that the de-

scendants of Abraham are destined to be caught by iniquities and entangled in troubles, ultimately to be redeemed by the Messiah whose coming will be heralded by the blowing of the ram's horn, mentioned in this connection in Zech. 9:14.

41. Genesis Rabbah 42:2, 4 on Gen. 14:9.

42. Genesis Rabbah 44:17. Another rabbinic opinion interprets *dread* as referring to Edom or Rome, *darkness* to Greece, *deep* to Media or Persia, and *fell* to Babylonia; see also Leviticus Rabbah 13:5 and Exodus Rabbah 51:7.

43. Genesis Rabbah 44:15 on Gen. 15:9.

44. Exodus Rabbah 51:7.

45. Genesis Rabbah 44:19 on Gen. 15:14.

46. Leviticus Rabbah 29:2, interpreting *But you have no fear, my servant Jacob* (Jer. 30:10).

47. Ibid.

48. Genesis Rabbah 70:8 on Gen. 29:2.

49. Genesis Rabbah 99:2.

50. Leviticus Rabbah 13:5 on Lev. 11:4–7. The rabbis offer varying interpretations likening these animals to the Four Empires. Some associate the hare with Persia, the rock badger with Greece.

51. Exodus Rabbah 35:5 on Exod. 25:3, Dan. 2:32 ff., and Ps. 137:7.

52. Leviticus Rabbah 15:9 on Lev. 13:2. The Midrash explains the associations of the symptoms with the Four Empires.

53. Numbers Rabbah 7:10.

54. Esther Rabbah, Proem 2. In the first two comments on the verse, *morning* is interpreted as the beginning and *evening* as the end. In the third comment, *morning* is interpreted as the peak of one era and *evening* as the beginning of the next historical era.

55. Leviticus Rabbah 13:5. See also Esther Rabbah, Proem 5, where the second beast is taken by one rabbi to be a wolf, which he regards as the designation for Persia. And in Exodus Rabbah 23:5 the lion is the symbol for both Babylonia and Persia, the leopard for Rome.

56. Exodus Rabbah 22:1, referring to Songs 2:15; see also Songs Rabbah 2:15.

57. Leviticus Rabbah 13:5 on Gen. 2:10 ff.; see also Genesis Rabbah 16:4.

58. Lamentations Rabbah, Proem 25.

59. Esther Rabbah, Proem 5.

60. Esther Rabbah, Proem 5.

61. Targum on Zech. 2:1 renders "the Four Kingdoms," and Kimḥi enumerates them as Babylonia, Persia, Greece, and Rome.

62. See Rashi on Zech. 6:1 and the rabbinic interpretation of the different colors of the horses in Zech. 6:2–3.

63. Esther Rabbah, Proem 5.

64. Songs Rabbah 2:15.

65. Esther Rabbah, Proem 5. The link between "Temple" and "Greece" is the same as in the previous interpretation of Songs 5:2. Most of the citations refer to Greece of the Seleucid dynasty.

66. Exodus Rabbah, 26:1.

67. Ecclesiastes Rabbah 5:15; see also Genesis Rabbah 42:2.

68. Lamentations Rabbah 1:42, on the interpretation of the word *niskad.* Radal (Rabbi David Luria) would emend the text for greater

historical accuracy as follows: the Chaldeans were severe, but Babylonia lenient; Persia severe but Media lenient; Greece severe but Macedonia lenient; Rome severe but Ishmael lenient.

69. Exodus Rabbah 15:6, interpreting Songs 6:10.

70. Numbers Rabbah 10:2 on Prov. 23:29.

71. Songs Rabbah 3:1.

72. Esther Rabbah, Proem 4. Cf. Megillah 11a, where the phrases of Lev. 26:44 are interpreted to refer to the days of Antiochus, Vespasian, Haman, the Romans, and the wars of Gog and Magog, respectively. In this midrashic passage a second interpretation is also offered, with a slightly different order: Vespasian, Turquinus, Haman, the Romans, and the era of Gog and Magog.

73. Genesis Rabbah 88:5.

74. Exodus Rabbah 23:11.

75. Avodah Zarah 2a,b, quoted in the name of Rabbi Simlai, friend of Rabbi Judah II, middle of third century C.E. Other nations in the story then advance their own pleas, all to no avail. None is mentioned by name other than Rome and Persia because, according to this talmudic tale, only these two empires will last until messianic times.

5. Haggai, Zechariah, and Malachi

76. Zevaḥim 62a.

77. Tosefta Sanhedrin 4:7–8; Sanhedrin 21b–22a; Yerushalmi Megillah 1:21b–21c; see Ginzberg, Legends, 6:443, n. 44, and infra, n. 105, and text to which it refers.

78. Shabbat 104a; Megillah 2b; Yerushalmi Megillah 1:9; Tanḥuma Koraḥ 12; Genesis Rabbah 1:11; Numbers Rabbah 18:21; Pirke de-Rabbi Eliezer, chap. 48.

79. Leviticus Rabbah 6:6. This is the opinion of R. Johanan, whose argument is that wherever both the prophet's name and his father's name are mentioned in the Bible, it is an indication that both were prophets. This is the case with Zechariah, but not with Haggai, in Ezra 5:1. (In Zech. 1:1 the father is Berekhiah and the grandfather Iddo.) His colleagues overruled him, however, suggesting that it is to be assumed in all cases that a prophet is the son of a prophet. The Masoretic accentuation of Zech. 1:1 upon the title of prophet belongs to Iddo. Iddo is mentioned among the leading prophets who returned from exile under Zerubbabel and Joshua in 536 B.C.E. (Neh. 10:4, 16).

80. Megillah 15a.

81. Megillah 3a; see also Sanhedrin 93b, 94a.

82. Megillah 3a.

83. Yevamot 16a.

84. Yevamot 16a.

85. See the Septuagint, where the heading to Ps. 138 reads "A Psalm of David, Haggai, and Zechariah." Similarly with Pss. 146–49. The Vulgate and the Peshitta add similar superscriptions to additional psalms.

86. Avot de-Rabbi Natan 1:3.

87. Bava Batra 14b.

88. Yoma 9b; see also Sotah 48b; Sanhedrin 11a; and Songs Rabbah 8:9. The meaning of bat kol has been the subject of much scholarly

discussion, and it is here translated as "holy inspiration."

89. Kimḥi on Zech. 3:9, quoting the explanation of his father of "the seven facets" mentioned in the verse.

6. Ezra

90. Megillah 15a; see also Targum on Malachi 1:1 and Jerome's introduction to his commentary on Malachi.

91. Songs Rabbah 5:5.

92. Yoma 9a on Songs 8:9.

93. Leviticus Rabbah 2:11 based on Songs 7:14.

94. Songs Rabbah 5:5.

95. Yevamot 86b based on Ezek. 8:15.

96. Genesis Rabbah, beginning of Sidrah Vayeḥi, second section, as printed at the end of the Vilna edition in new version of Jacob's Blessing (printed originally in *Mishpetei Shavu'ot* by Rabbenu Hai Gaon, Venice, 1601); based on Ps. 57:3 in a statement by Rabbi Joshua ben Levi. The other two things decreed by mortals and later approved by God occurred in the days of Joshua and of Mordecai.

97. Josippon, chap. 3, related to the legend found in 2 Macc. 1:19–2:12, but not based on it, according to Ginzberg; see infra. n. 133, and text to which it refers.

98. Malachi 2:10; Bava Batra 15a.

99. Kiddushin 69b–71a,b.

100. Numbers Rabbah 8:4; Yerushalmi Kiddushin 4:65c; Midrash Shemuel ed. S. Buber (Cracow, 1893), p. 134.

101. Sotah 20b; Sifrei, Vezot ha-berakhah, Soferim, chap. 16.

102. Sanhedrin 21b.

103. Sanhedrin 21b–22a. The second fanciful theory is based on a play of words, *ashurit*, the name of the script, and *me'usheret*; see supra, n. 77, and sentence to which it refers.

104. Megillah 31b.

105. Bava Kamma 82a–b; Ketubbot 5a; Bava Batra 22a.

106. Bava Batra 21b.

107. Bava Batra 15a and, for the source concerning authorship of Psalms, Songs Rabbah 4:4; cf. Bava Batra 14b; Ecclesiastes Rabbah 7:19. The statement is made that Ezra was one of ten men who composed the Book of Psalms.

108. Numbers Rabbah 3:13. As a precursor to the Messiah, Elijah would resolve all difficult problems in Jewish learning.

109. Genesis Rabbah 36:8.

110. Gittin 59a. Ezra shared leadership with Nehemiah and, therefore, just missed meriting this description.

111. Bava Kamma 82a–b; Ketubbot 5a; Bava Batra 22a. The ten ordinances of Ezra are given somewhat differently in Yerushalmi Megillah 4:75. See the critical study by Solomon Zeitlin "Takkanot Ezra," *Jewish Quarterly Review*, n.s. 8(1917–18):761, and by Moses Löb Bloch, *Sha'are torat ha-takkanot* (3 vols., Vienna, 1879–1906), 1:107–38. It was believed that garlic was a sex stimulant and, therefore, the counsel to eat it on Friday. The rabbis held that Friday night was a fitting time for conjugal relations, in opposition to the Samaritans and other sectarians who forbade sexual intercourse on the Sabbath because

of the sacredness of the Sabbath (see Mishnah Ketubbot 5:6; Ketubbot 62b; Mishnah Nedarim 3:10). The word *sinar* is taken by Louis Ginzberg to be derived from the Aramaic transliteration of the Greek word for belt. It was a garment worn by women over the lower part of the body. Jastrow translates it as a sort of petticoat or breech-cloth. Modern Hebrew uses it for apron.

112. Ibid.

113. Yoma 69b.

114. Songs Rabbah 4:4 ff. The thought is found some four times in these midrashic passages.

115. Songs Rabbah 4:4.

116. Ezra 4:3–14; see Ginzberg, *Legends,* 6:445, n. 50.

117. Josephus, *Antiquities,* 11.5.5.

118. Megillat Ta'anit (addition) 24.

119. *Travels of R. Benjamin of Tudela* (London, 1784), p. 73.

120. See Ginzberg, *Legends,* 6:431, n. 5 for this legend told by Yemenite Jews.

121. Berakhot 67b; see Rashi ad locum.

122. See Songs Rabbah 8:9 and Sanhedrin 11a, where Hillel is so called.

7. Zerubbabel and Nehemiah

123. Jer. 22:30; Numbers Rabbah 20:20.

124. See 1 Chron. 3:17 (Jeconiah=Jehoiachin) and Sanhedrin 38a. The explanations of the several names are based on similar sounding Hebrew words: Assir from *asor,* "to bind," and *bet ha-'asurim,* "prison"; Shealtiel from *shatol,* "to plant," and *el,* "God"; the second interpretation, *sha'ol,* "to ask," and *el,* "God"; Zerubbabel from *zaro'a,* "to plant seed," and *bavel,* "Babylonia."

125. Josippon 3:5b; also Ezra 3 and Josephus, *Antiquities,* 11.3.3–9.

126. Ben Sira 49:11 ff.

127. 1 Esd. 3–4; Josephus, *Antiquities,* 11.3.3–9; Josippon 3:10a–11a. Cf. also Bava Batra 10a, where wine is also called one of the ten most powerful things in the world. The story seems to have been influenced by the Greek exaltation of Truth, as compared to the more customary Hebraic praise of Wisdom.

128. Josephus, *Antiquities,* 11.3.1.

129. See the commentary of Abarbanel on Isa. 45. According to Josippon it was Darius who was chiefly responsible for the return of the Jews from Babylonia although it took place during the reign of Cyrus.

130. See Alfa Beta de-Rabbi Akiba in *Bet ha-midrash,* ed. A. Jellinek (6 vols., Jerusalem, 1938), 3:27–28; *Halakhot gedolot,* ed. A. Hildesheimer (Jerusalem, 1971), 223; Pirkei Mashiah in *Bet ha-midrash,* ed. A. Jellinek, 3:75; Kalir's elegy, "Bayamim Ha-heim," found at the end of the *kinot* of the Roman rite.

131. See Neh. 8:9, *ha-tirshata,* from *hatar,* "to absolve," and *shatah,* "drink"; Avodah Zarah 36b; Yerushalmi Kiddushin 4:65b; Midrash Aseret Melakhim, ed. Chaim Meir Horowitz in *Bibliotheca Haggadica* (2 vols., Frankfurt-am-Main, 1881), 1:44.

132. See Shabbat 123b; and cf. Josephus, *Wars of the Jews,* 2.8.9.

133. 2 Macc. 1:19–2:12; cf. Josippon 3:11d–12a. See supra, n. 97 and the story to which it is appended.

134. Sanhedrin 93b. The Books of Ezra and Nehemiah are spoken of by the rabbis as the Book of Ezra; for example, see Bava Batra 15a.

Part II

━━ ━━ ━━ ━━ ━━ ━━

The Greek Period

1

Alexander the Great

When Alexander first invaded the land of Israel, his intention was to harm the Jews, but instead he became their friend and protector. The Samaritans, whose religious center was Mount Gerizim, plotted against the Jews. They petitioned Alexander to destroy the Temple, claiming that the Jews had rebelled against him. He listened to their presentation sympathetically. When this news came to the high priest, Simon the Just, he donned the garments of his office and asked the priests and the leading citizens of Jerusalem to accompany him to the emperor. Carrying torches, they marched all night long, half on one side of Simon, half on the other. When dawn broke, they were seen in the distance by Alexander. He asked the Samaritans who were with him the identity of these people. "These are Jews, who have rebelled against you," they replied.

By the time the sun had risen high in the skies, the two facing columns met each other at the town of Antipatris. The moment that Alexander laid eyes upon Simon the Just he descended from his chariot and bowed low before him. The men of his entourage exclaimed in amazement, "So great a king as you bowing before that Jew!" He explained, "Before each military victory I would see in a vision the glistening image of this man." He then asked the Jews why they had come. They replied, "Is it possible that the Temple in which we pray for you and your empire should be destroyed by your decree because conspirators have deceived you?" He asked, "Who are these people?" They replied, "These very Samaritans standing near you." "They are yours to do with as you please," the king then said.

Immediately the villains were dragged across briar and bramble to their own sanctuary at Mount Gerizim. Their temple was then destroyed and its site ploughed over and seeded with horsebeans, just as the Samaritans had plotted to do to the Temple in

Jerusalem. The day when all this occurred, the twenty-fifth day of Tevet, was made a festival; thereafter, when a funeral took place on that day, no eulogy was delivered, as is the practice on joyous days. The day was given the name of Mount Gerizim Day.[1]

When Alexander had first expressed the wish to visit the Temple at Jerusalem, the Samaritans had at that time told him that the Jews would not permit him, a heathen, to enter their Holy of Holies. They thus hoped to arouse Alexander's anger against the Jews, knowing that no one was permitted to enter the Holy of Holies but the high priest and he only on the Day of Atonement. A certain Jewish hunchback by the name of Gebiha ben Kosem, the doorkeeper, learned of this and went to Alexander's camp with a gift for the king, a pair of felt shoes set with two precious stones worth twenty thousand silver zuzim. When the king approached the Temple Mount, Gebiha said to him, "Your majesty, remove your shoes and put on these felt shoes so that you may not slip on the smooth pavement." (Of course, the real reason was that one may not enter the Temple Mount in ordinary shoes.) When they came to the Holy of Holies, Gebiha said to him, "Thus far may we go, but no farther," indicating that Jews too were not permitted to go beyond that point.

The emperor was displeased and threatened Gebiha, "When we come out, I shall strike your hump so hard, it will straighten out!" But Gebiha put him off with a jest. "If you could do that, you would become famous as a great surgeon and receive rich fees!"[2]

Gebiha served his people brilliantly on another occasion before Alexander when the welfare of the Jews was endangered. The Ishmaelites, Canaanites, and Egyptians came before the monarch, each to plead a case against the Jews. "Who will argue in our defense?" it was asked among the Jews. "I shall go and argue against them," said Gebiha ben Kosem. "Be careful not to allow them to win their case and prove that the land is theirs," he was cautioned. "I shall go and argue against them," he replied. "If I defeat them, it will be well; if not, you can say, 'Who is this hunchback to take up our cause?'" Alexander, acting as judge, asked the first plaintiff to state his case. The Ishmaelites declared, "We base our claim on their own laws in which it is written, *He must accept the first-born, the son of the unloved one, and allot to him a double portion of all he possesses* (Deut. 21:17). And Ishmael was Abraham's first-born!" Gebiha then responded, "Your majesty! Cannot a man do as he likes with his sons?" "Yes," replied the monarch. "Then," argued Gebiha, "it is written, *Abraham willed all that he owned to Isaac* (Gen. 25:5)."

But the judge, while agreeing that a gift given by a father during his lifetime does not come within the bounds of a legacy, asked, "Where is the announcement of gifts to the other sons?" For a father cannot give all to one son and disinherit the others, even in his lifetime. If he does, his action is null, and the ordinary laws of inheritance become operative.

Gebiha answered, "*But to Abraham's sons by concubines Abraham gave gifts* (Gen. 25:5)." Thereupon, the Ishmaelites, having been put to shame, departed. Then the Canaanites pleaded, "We base our suit against them on their own Torah. In it this country is referred to so often as 'the land of Canaan.' If so, let them return our country to us." Gebiha argued, "Your majesty! Cannot a man do as he likes with his slave?" "Yes," replied Alexander. "Then," continued Gebiha, "it is written, *Cursed be Canaan; the lowest of slaves shall he be to his brothers* (Gen. 9:25). Therefore, they are now our slaves." The Canaanites fled in shame.

The Egyptians then advanced their claim, "We base our case against them on their own Torah. Six hundred thousand Hebrews left us laden with silver and gold utensils, as it is written, *Thus they stripped the Egyptians* (Exod. 12:36). Let them return all our silver and gold!"

Gebiha argued, "Your majesty! Six hundred thousand men served them two hundred and ten years. Among them were silversmiths and goldsmiths. Let them pay for their labor at the rate of a dinar a day." The mathematicians then calculated what was owing the Hebrew slaves for their labor. Before they reached the sum owing for the first hundred years, the Egyptians were found to be forfeit for the amount due. They too then departed in shame.[3]

Alexander's kindness to the Jews was acknowledged by them in unique fashion. Josippon says the name Alexander was given to every boy born to the priests of Judea during the year following Alexander the Great's arrival in Jerusalem.[4] Others say it was a stratagem on the part of Simon the Just. For Alexander, perceiving the reverence in which the Temple was held by the Jews, requested of Simon that an image of himself be placed near the altar. Simon, however, explained, "Our God has prohibited all images in His Temple. But let not the king think therefore that his honor is not precious to us. We shall do something in your honor that will be an everlasting remembrance. Every son born this year to the priests, the descendants of Levi, shall be named Alexander in your honor, so that the name of Alexander will be carried forward through all future generations."[5]

Alexander put ten questions to the elders of the south.[6] He asked, "Which is farther, from heaven to earth or from east to west?" They replied, "From east to west. The proof is that when the sun is in the east all can look at it, and when it is in the west all can look at it, but when it is in the middle of the sky, no one can look at it."[7] He said to them, "Were the heavens created first or the earth?" They replied, "The heavens, as it is said, *In the beginning God created the heaven and the earth* (Gen. 1:1)."[8] He asked, "Was light created first or darkness?"

They answered, "This question cannot be solved." Why did they not reply that darkness was created first, since it is written, *The earth being unformed and void, with darkness* . . . and after that, *God said, "Let there be light"; and there was light* (Gen. 1:2–3)? They thought to themselves, perhaps he will go on to ask what is above and what is below, what is before and what is after.[9] If that is the case, they should not have answered his question about the creation of the heavens either. At first they thought that he just happened to ask that question, but when they saw that he was pursuing the same subject, they thought it better to answer him no further along this line of questioning.

He asked them, "Who is wise?" They replied, "He who understands what is to come to pass." He asked, "Who is called a mighty man?" They answered, "He who subdues his passions." He asked, "Who is the wealthy man?" They replied, "He who rejoices in his portion."[10] He said to them, "What shall a man do to live?" They replied, "Let him mortify himself."[11] He asked, "What shall a man do to kill himself?" They replied, "Let him concentrate on keeping himself alive."[12] He asked, "What should a man do to make himself acceptable to others?" They answered, "Let him shun the king and the governing authorities."[13]

He said to them, "I have an answer better than yours. Let a person cultivate friendship with ruler and government so as to be able to influence them to do good for men."[14]

He asked, "Where is it preferable to dwell, on sea or dry land?" They replied, "On dry land, for those who set out to sea are not free from anxiety until they reach dry land again." He asked them, "Which among you is the wisest?" They answered, "We are all equal as can be seen from the fact that all our previous answers were given unanimously." He asked, "Why then do you oppose me?"[15] They replied, "Satan is powerful."[16] He said to them, "Behold I can slay you by royal decree." They answered, "Indeed power is in the king's hands, but it does not become the king to be false."[17] He immediately had them clothed in purple raiment and gold chains placed on their necks.[18]

Alexander said to the elders of the south, "I wish to go to the land of Africa." They said, "You will find it impossible because the way there is blocked by mountains and clouded by darkness both by day and by night." He exclaimed, "That is not enough to stop me. And was it for such a statement from you that I asked? I asked you to tell me how to go." They replied, "Get Libyan donkeys that know their way in the dark and take coils of rope, and as you go through the mountain passes uncoil the rope at the side of the road. Thus you will be able to guide yourself by the rope on your way back and return safely."[19]

He followed their advice, and he came to a place in which only women lived. He wanted to launch a war against them but they said to him, "If you win and kill us, people will say, 'He was victorious only against women!' and if you lose and we kill you, they will laugh, 'The king who was slain by women!' "

He was convinced and said to them, "Bring me bread." They brought him bread of gold on a golden table. Whereupon he asked them, "Do people here eat bread of gold?" To which they replied, "If you wanted ordinary bread, had you no bread in your own country that you found it necessary to travel here?" When he left the place he wrote on the gate of the city, "I, Alexander of Macedon, was a fool until I came to the city of women in Africa and learned wisdom from them."[20]

Continuing on his journey, he came to a spring alongside which he sat down to eat. He dipped his salted fish into the water, and at once they gave off a sweet smell. "Ah!" he said, "the water of this spring must come from Paradise (the Garden of Eden)." Some say he took some of the water and washed his face with it. He traced the source of the water until it led him to the gate of Paradise. He cried out, "Open the gate for me!" The answer came back, *"This is the gateway to the Lord—the victorious shall enter through it* (Ps. 118:20)." He replied, "I too am a king and deemed of some consequence. If you will not admit me, at least give me something."

A skull was given him. He went and weighed all the gold and silver he had with him as against the skull, but he could not weigh it down. He then asked the rabbis, "How can this be explained?" They said, "It is because of the eyeball of mortal man that can never be satisfied." "Prove it," he challenged them. They took a little dust and covered the eyeball, and immediately it was weighed down. So is it written: *Sheol and Abaddon cannot be satisfied. Nor can the eyes of man be satisfied* (Prov. 27:20).[21]

Alexander of Macedon, when he wished to ascend into the air, used to rise higher and higher until he saw the world look like a ball and the sea like a dish. On account of this he is depicted with an orb in his hand. And why not with a dish as well? Because he has no dominion over the sea. But the Holy One, blessed be He, has dominion both on sea and on land; He can deliver on sea and rescue on land.[22]

It was Alexander's desire to ascend to the heavens and to descend to the depths in order to know what was in both places. In addition he wished to know what was in the uttermost limits of the earth. So the Holy One, blessed be He, to frustrate him, split his kingdom in all directions.[23]

When Alexander sought to know what was in the heavens, he made a yoke, harnessed two eagles in it, and suspended meat above it as do those who fowl with hawks. Seeing the meat, the eagles would fly higher and higher until they saw the world before them like a ring in his hand.[24]

In pursuit of his desire to explore the depths, Alexander kept lowering ropes into the ocean for three and a half years, until he heard a heavenly voice that warned him that the king would come to an end before his rope would give out. He then made chests of glass into which he placed men and lowered the chests into the Mediterranean—all this in order to learn how the waters praise the Holy one, blessed be He. When the men were brought up, they said, "We have heard the waters of the Great Sea praise the Holy One in this manner: *The Lord, majestic on high* (Ps. 93:4)."[25]

Alexander of Macedon went to visit King Kazia.[26] The latter showed him much gold and silver. Whereupon Alexander said to him, "I do not need your gold and silver. I have come only to see your ways; how you dispense justice." While they were engaged in conversation, two men came before the king for judgment. One said that he had bought a field and in cleaning it had found a treasure of dinars in a dunghill. The purchaser said, "I bought the dunghill but did not buy the treasure." The seller said, "I sold the dunghill and all it contained."

The king called to one of them, "Have you a son?" "Yes," was the reply. He asked the other, "Have you a daughter?" "Yes," he answered. Whereupon the king said, "Let them be married to each other and the treasure will belong to both."

Alexander began to laugh and Kazia asked him, "Why are you laughing? Have I not judged well? Had this case come before you, how would you have judged?" He replied, "We would have killed them both and the treasure would have gone to the king."

Kazia said to him, "How much you must love gold!" He ordered a meal prepared for him of meat and chickens fashioned of gold. Alexander asked, "Can I eat gold?" King Kazia, thinking to himself, "A curse upon the man's soul!" said, "If you do not eat gold, then why do you love gold so much?"

Kazia then asked, "Does the sun shine in your country?" "Yes," Alexander replied. "Does rain fall in your country?" "Yes," was the answer. "Do you have small cattle in your country?" "Yes," Alexander said. King Kazia, thinking to himself, "A curse upon the man's soul!" said to him, "You live only because of the merit of the small cattle, as it is written, *Man and beast You deliver, O Lord* (Ps. 36:7)."

Alexander paid honor to the bones of the prophet Jeremiah. The Jews in Egypt had stoned the prophet to death because of his continuing censure of their misdeeds after they had compelled the prophet to accompany them to Egypt when the First Temple had been destroyed. The Egyptians had the prophet buried because they were grateful for his prayers on their behalf. Alexander reburied the remains in the city of Alexandria.[27]

He brought the wondrous throne of Solomon to Egypt. Originally this extraordinary throne, possessing occult powers, had been captured by Nebuchadnezzar when he had destroyed the Temple and razed Jerusalem. Nebuchadnezzar brought the throne to Babylonia, and it became the possession of the heads of the succeeding empires. Alexander carried it down to Egypt.[28]

The Greek conqueror is alluded to in the Scriptures. The words *Radiant as the sun* (Songs 6:10) refer to the Greek kingdom.

Alexander the son of Helios was his name and the sun is called a hero, as it is said: *Like a hero, eager to run his course* (Ps. 19:6).[29]

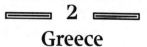

2

Greece

The Greeks are descendants of Japheth, son of Noah, their direct ancestor being Javan, son of Japheth. The people of Thrace came from another son of Japheth, Tiras.[30]

The might of Greece extended over vast dominions. Some say she was served by one hundred and seventy-one governors and one hundred and twenty-seven commanders; another opinion has it that the number was one hundred and twenty governors and the same number of commanders; and still another, one hundred and twenty generals. The majority opinion of the rabbis was that the number was sixty in each category, for Greece is compared to a scorpion and a scorpion lays sixty eggs at a time or, others say, it casts sixty young at a time.[31]

When the Jews were exiled by the power of Greece, God Himself accompanied them.[32] However, a contradictory opinion affirms that the forces of Antiochus did not exile the Jews from their land. But the Greeks defiled the Sanctuary with their idolatrous practices.[33]

The Jewish people, deploring its wretchedness, complained before the Almighty: "Lord of the Universe, I sit here pondering on the number of years that elapsed before You redeemed us from Egypt and, similarly, on the number of years that went by before You redeemed us from Babylonia. I now ponder on how many have been the years of servitude under Greece." Therefore, does the psalmist say, *My thoughts turn to days of old, to years long past* (Ps. 77:6).[34]

When the Seleucid dynasty ruled Judea, lawlessness and immorality were common. The Jews, under Hellenistic influence, fell away from the high standards of the Torah so that the Jewish courts had to adopt severe measures, even more stringent than the

Torah itself provides. Thus it happened that a man was stoned for riding a horse on the Sabbath. Another was whipped for behaving indecently in public.[35] As many as a leopard's spots were the decrees of the Seleucid Greeks against Israel, fulfilling Jeremiah's prophecy: *A leopard lies in wait by their towns* (Jer. 5:6).

═══ **3** ═══

The Greek Language
and the Septuagint

The Bible may be translated into Greek; and a scroll of the Torah and sacred books may be written in Greek, but not phylacteries and mezuzahs. For such is the interpretation of Noah's blessing of his sons: *May God enlarge Japheth and let him dwell in the tents of Shem* (Gen. 9:27)—that is, the words of Shem (or his descendants, the Jews) may be rendered in the languages of Japheth (the ancestor, by his son Javan, of the Greeks).[36] By a play on words, deriving the name of Japheth from the Hebrew word meaning "beauty," the rabbis said, "Let the most beautiful possession of Japheth, the Greek language, dwell in the tents of Shem" (among the Jews).[37]

Four languages are of special value to society: Greek for song, Persian for lamentation, Hebrew for conversation, and Latin for military purposes. A certain villager is responsible for the birth of Latin, fashioning it out of Greek so that the former is, in reality, no more than an offshoot of the latter.[38]

But it was the Greek language that Jews could study, not other areas of Greek culture. And even the permission to study the language was limited, in one opinion, to the translation of the Torah. This was allowed because of an important event that took place during the reign of Ptolemy, the king of Egypt. It happened that this king brought seventy-two elders from Jerusalem and placed them in seventy-two separate rooms, without revealing his purpose to them beforehand. He then visited each elder in his room and asked each one to write a Greek translation of the Five Books of Moses. The Holy One, blessed be He, so inspired the elders that they wrote seventy-two copies of a Greek translation, identical to each other in every respect.

For example, instead of translating the opening words of the Bible according to the sequence in the Hebrew original (Gen. 1:1), they all wrote, "God created the beginning." So too did they all adopt the following new translations: "I will make man in an image and a likeness," instead of *in My image, after My likeness* (Gen. 1:26); "And God finished on the sixth day and rested on the seventh day," instead of *on the seventh day God finished the work* (Gen. 2:2); "He created him," not *them* (Gen. 5:2); "Let Me go down and confound their speech there," instead of *us* (Gen. 11:7); "And Sarah laughed among her relatives," instead of *to herself* (Gen. 18:12); "For in their anger they slew an ox and in their self-will they houghed a fattened ox," instead of *men* (Gen. 49:6), in the first clause; "And Moses took his wife and sons, mounted them on a human carrier," instead of *an ass* (Exod. 4:20); "The time the Israelites remained in Egypt and in other lands was four hundred and thirty years" (Exod 12:40, inserting the phrase, "and in other lands"); "He delegated the respectable men among the Israelites," instead of *the young men* (Exod. 24:5); "I have not taken one precious thing from them," instead of *one ass* (Num. 16:15); "These the Lord your God allotted to light to the other peoples" (Deut. 4:19, inserting "to light"); "Something I never commanded to worship" (Deut. 17:3, inserting "to worship"); "the slender-footed," instead of *the hare* (Lev. 11:6), because Ptolemy's wife was named Hare in its Greek equivalent, and the elders were concerned lest Ptolemy think the Jews were mocking him by inserting his wife's name in the Torah in an unflattering reference.[39]

In addition there were eighteen other changes from the Hebrew text that the Jewish elders introduced; among these "male with his apertures created He them," instead of *male and female* (Gen. 1:27). This change was made in order to explain the plural *them* and also, since God created the human in His image, to avoid the implication that God is both male and female.[40] The reason for their revising *Let us, then, go down and confound their speech there* (Gen. 11:7), to "Let Me, then, go down," was to remove the thought of plurality in God.[41] By slightly emending one word in the Hebrew text, they changed *And Sarah laughed to herself* (Gen. 18:12) to "before her relatives," so that Ptolemy might understand that God was angry with Sarah because she had laughed at the divine promise publicly, while Abraham kept his doubts to himself.[42]

Knowledge of the Greek language is helpful in lending further clarification to a number of biblical verses. So, for example, the name of the oak tree, *alon bakhut*, under which Deborah, the nurse of Rebecca, was buried was explained by one rabbi as follows: *alon* is from the Greek meaning "another," hence *alon bakhut* means "another weeping," indicating that while Jacob was grieving for Deborah, news reached him of the death of his own mother.[43]

In Greek the word for swords is *mekirin*. This sheds light upon the verse describing Simeon and Levi, *Their weapons are tools of lawlessness (mekheiroteihem)* (Gen. 49:5); therefore, not *their weapons* but "their swords."[44]

Similarly, Greek is helpful in resolving an apparent contradiction between two verses relating to the slaying of Shechem and Hamor and their townsmen by Simeon and Levi. One verse reads: *and slew all the males* (Gen. 34:25); the other, *For when angry they slay men* (Gen. 49:6). But the explanation lies in the fact that all the men were as one before God, as it says, *See (hen), the nations are but a drop in a bucket* (Isa. 40:15). The word, *hen*, comes from the Greek, meaning "one."[45] The same word, *hen*, is found again the verse in the Book of Job: *See (hen), God is beyond reach in His power* (Job 36:22). Since *hen* may be derived from the Greek, meaning "one," the verse may be understood to mean, "One is our God who strengthens (the righteous) with His power—that they should perform His will."[46] Again, the word *hen* appears in Isaiah, *Why (hen), you are less than nothing* (Isa. 40:17). Since *hen* in Greek means "one," the verse may be interpreted to mean: "The Holy One, blessed be He, said to Israel, 'You are a one and only nation to Me out of the nations of the world.' "[47]

In the Book of Lamentations (4:15) the verse reads, "*Away! Unclean!*" *people shouted at them,* "*Away! Away!*" (*suru, suru*). The Greek expression is *seron, seron* meaning "Sweep! Sweep!"[48]

Whoever has not seen the basilica synagogue in Alexandria has not seen Jewish glory. The huge basilica had a double colonnade and sometimes it held twice the number of people that went forth from Egypt. There were in it seventy-one gold cathedras, corresponding to the seventy-one members of the Great Sanhedrin, each containing no less than seventy-one talents of gold, and a wooden platform upon which stood the attendant of the synagogue with a scarf in his hand. When the time came to answer "Amen" (to a benediction recited by the officiant) he waved his scarf and all the congregation responded ("Amen"). They did not occupy seats at random, but goldsmiths sat together, silversmiths together, blacksmiths together, metalworkers together, and weavers together, so that when a poor man entered the place he could recognize the members of his craft and apply to them for work, so obtaining a livelihood for himself and for the members of his family.[49]

Notes

II. THE GREEK PERIOD

1. Alexander the Great

Alexander the Great is a popular subject for legends in the cultures of both West and East, their origin going back to the Hellenistic literature of Alexandria. Jewish literature is no exception. Legends about Alexander are found in ancient rabbinic literature, i.e., the Babylonian and Palestinian Talmuds, Megillat Ta'anit, the Mekhilta, Midrash Rabbah on the Pentateuch and the Five Scrolls, Midrash Tanḥuma, Pesikta de-Rav Kahana, Pirkei de-Rabbi Eliezer, Midrash Tehillim, Midrash Yonah, Midrash Aseret Melakhim, Targum Sheni, Midrash Aggadah, and Yalkut Shimoni.

At the very outset there is the Hellenistic Jewish work, known as the Pseudo-Callisthenes, which, according to Israel J. Kazis, is "the basic source for most of all the legendary accounts of the life of Alexander." The reader with special interest in the legends relating to Alexander may profitably examine Dr. Kazis's excellent work, *The Book of the Gests of Alexander of Macedon*, published by the Mediaeval Academy of America in 1962, a work to which I am greatly indebted.

Josephus is another source for such legendary material about Alexander in both the *Antiquities* and *Against Apion*. For the references to Alexander in Josephus, see Adolf Büchler, "La Relation de Josèphe concernant Alexandre le Grand" in *Revue des Études Juives* 36 (1898): 1–26; I. Spak, *Der Bericht des Josephus über Alexander den Grossen* (Königsberg, 1911); Ralph Marcus, "Appendix C," in Josephus, Classical Library (London, 1937), 6:512–32.

Jewish sources in medieval literature include Josippon, five other Hebrew versions of the Alexander Romance, including the one published by Kazis, and two other Hebrew works, *Muserei ha-pilosofim* (by Hunayn ibn Ishaq al-Ibadi, translated into Hebrew by Judah al-Ḥarizi, Frankfurt am Main, 1896) and *Sod ha-sodot* (Hebrew version of *Secretum secretorum,* ascribed to Aristotle, translated by M. Gaster, London, 1908). The legends given in the text are drawn from the ancient rabbinic sources, but the notes will indicate parallels in other sources.

1. This story of the meeting of Alexander the Great and the high priest is found in the Talmud, Yoma 69a. The tale is also found in Megillat Ta'anit, chap. 9, with slight variations; for example, there the date is the twenty-first of Kislev. In Leviticus Rabbah 13:5 the midrash in two separate passages refers to this legend, one of which adds that Alexander, upon first seeing Simon, exclaimed, "Blessed be the Lord, God of Simon the Just!"

The story is inaccurate historically. Simon the Just lived after Alexander's time. The first high priest by that name is dated 310–291 or 300–270 B.C.E.; the second, 219–199 B.C.E. The Samaritan temple on Mount Gerizim was destroyed not in the days of Alexander but two hundred years later in the time of John Hyrcanus I. The town of Antipatris, the supposed locale of the meeting of Alexander and the high priest, was not known by that name until Herod gave the name to the town built by him in honor of his father, Antipater. (Although most likely there was a town on the same site before, an important crossroads linking the west-east road and the north-south road. In Israel today the Yemenite village of Rosh ha-Ayin is situated on that site or near to it.)

The story is told in greater detail in Josephus, *Antiquities,* 11.8.3–5. The high priest here, however, is not Simon the Just, but Jaddua; the meeting place is not Antipatris, but Sapha or Mount Scopus outside Jerusalem. The villains are Sanballat, a Cuthite like the Samaritans, appointed satrap over Samaria by Darius, emperor of Persia, and his son-in-law, Manasseh, brother of Jaddua, the high priest. The temple on Mount Gerizim was built for Manasseh by Sanballat, who had received permission first from Darius, later from Alexander. Alexander's ire had been aroused against the Jews because they had refused to honor his request for provisions for his troops in their siege of Tyre. But later he prostrated himself before Jaddua, saying that he had seen him before in a dream at Dios in Macedonia when the king had been deliberating whether or not to invade Asia. The figure in the dream had counseled invasion, promising victory against Persia. Alexander even offered sacrifices in the Temple at Jerusalem after the meeting with the high priest and was happy to identify himself as the one prophesied in the Book of Daniel who was destined to overthrow Persia. He granted the Jews their requests to observe their own laws and to be exempt from tribute during the seventh year, the sabbatical year, as well as an extension of the same privilege to observe their own laws for the Jews of Babylon and Media. Many Jews joined his army. The Samaritans were denied the privileges granted the Jews.

The version in Josephus is equally unhistorical. Sanballat lived during the era of Nehemiah, long before Alexander. Josephus evidently combined two tales with a resultant contradiction between details in both. The Book of Daniel is dated 150 years after Alexander.

The version in Pseudo-Callisthenes stresses Alexander's admiration of the Jewish God. Here no high priest is mentioned. Alexander is awed by the saintly appearance of the priests and affirms that their God will be his God. The tribute brought by the Jews he consecrates to Temple use, together with his own personal contribution. See C. Müller, "Pseudo-Callisthenes" in *Arriani Anabasis et Indica* (Paris, 1846), pp. 82–85; F. P. Magoun, *The Gests of King Alexander of Macedon* (Cambridge, Mass., 1929), pp. 15–62; J. Zacher, *Pseudocallisthenes* (Halle, 1867). The episode of Alexander's visit to Jerusalem as found in Pseudo-Callisthenes (though it is found only in Codex C) is regarded by both Donath and Pfister as an interpolation in the text, the apologetic work of an Alexandrian Jewish author. This author was also responsible for a similar interpolation that tells how Alexander founded the city of Alexandria and there proclaimed the one true God. See L. Donath, *Die Alexandersage in Talmud und Midrasch* (Fulda, 1873), pp. 13 ff.; F. Pfister, "Eine jüdische Grundungsgeschichte Alexandrias" in *Sitzungsberichte der Heidelberger Akademie der Wissenschaften philosophisch-historische Klasse* (1914, abh. 11), 17–19, 22–23, 30–32. See also A. Ausfeld, *Der griechische Alexanderroman* (Leipzig, 1907), p. 17, where he claims that the author of Codex C was Jewish.

Louis Finkelstein regarded the talmudic version as an obvious emendation born out of the affection in which Simon was held by the ancient rabbis. He also denies that it could have been Jaddua who welcomed Alexander. See his *Mavo le-masekhtot Avot ve-Avot de-rabbi Natan* (New York, 1950), p. xlvii.

Victor Tcherikover saw kernels of truth in the narratives, while denying the historicity of a visit by Alexander to Jerusalem. From Greek sources it would appear that the Samaritans rebelled against Alexander and that the revolt was put down quickly and with severity. The Jews, on the other hand, must have sent a delegation to the new conqueror as he made his way through their land. The two most likely subjects on the agenda for such a meeting were the continuing controversy with the Samaritans and a confirmation of the domestic autonomy of the Jews, which was usually granted by their overlords.

2. Genesis Rabbah 61:7. *Gebiha means* "hunchback." The story is found with slight variations in Megillat Ta'anit, scholium to chap. 3. There the name is Gebiha son of Pesisa. But both Kosem and Pesisa come from roots having the same meaning, "to cut." The parallel source adds one important item, found nowhere else in rabbinic literature or Josephus, that while Gebiha and Alexander stood at the entrance to the Holy of Holies, a serpent darted out and bit the king. Donath, in *Die Alexandersage*, suggested that this is a confusion of Alexander for Ptolemy Philopator who, according to 3 Maccabees, was suddenly smitten with deafness and convulsions when he dared to enter the Holy of Holies. The story told in Genesis Rabbah is found also in Yalkut Shimoni, Ḥayei Sarah 25.

3. Genesis Rabbah 61:7 on Gen. 25:7. The story is found with variations in Sanhedrin 91a and in Megillat Ta'anit, scholium to chap. 3, where the name is Gebihah son of Pesisa (see supra n. 2). The talmudic version has the three peoples coming at different times, rather than together. Gebiha's words to his fellow Jews are slightly different as are the proof-texts cited by the Canaanites and Ishmaelites. The story in Sanhedrin calls the first plaintiffs "Africans," instead of Canaanites; the order there is Africans, Egyptians, Ishmaelites, and the descendants of Keturah. A talmudic tradition has it that when the Canaanites heard that the Israelites were about to enter Canaan, they migrated to Africa.

In both parallel sources Alexander gives the plaintiffs in each case three days to answer Gebiha's argument, but all in vain. The Oxford manuscript of Megillat Ta'anit edited by A. Neubauer, *Medieval Jewish Chronicles and Chronological Notes*, vol. 2 (Oxford, 1895), contains a few variant readings. The argument of Gebiha against the Egyptians has its parallel in Hellenistic Jewish literature, in Philo's *Life of Moses* 1.25.140–42. Philo says that the Jews had a moral and legal right to the Egyptian booty: morally, in return for the deprivation of freedom; legally, as payment for their service; and, in accordance with prevailing military law, as victors. See also Israel Lévi, "La Dispute entre les Égyptiens et les Juifs devant Alexandre," *Revue des Études Juives* 63 (1912):211–15, and idem, "Alexandre et les Juifs," in *Gedenkenbuch zur Erinnerung an David Kaufmann* (Breslau, 1900), 346–54. Tertullian also used the same argument, *Adversus Marcionem* 2.20. In Yalkut Shimoni, Ḥayei Sarah 25, both versions of the story are related, the first and fuller tale that of the midrash, the second and abbreviated form that of the Talmud.

4. This statement is found only in Josippon, Venice ed. (1544), p. 17d; Berdichev ed. (1896–1913), p. 63.

5. Seder Hadorot 448.

6. Tamid 32a.

7. Therefore, they reasoned the sun must be nearer, i.e., heaven is closer to earth than east is to west.

8. The Talmud (Ḥagigah 12a) records a controversy on the subject between the school of Shammai, which argued the heavens were created first, and the school of Hillel, which held the earth was created first. Donath, *Die Alexandersage*, pp. 26 ff., attributes the answer of the elders here to a follower of the Shammaite school.

9. Such speculation was forbidden; see Ḥagigah 11b.

10. See Avot 4:1 and 2:13.

11. Literally, "let him kill himself." The commentary on Tamid by Rabbi Shemaiah, a pupil of Rashi, explains "let him make himself exceedingly modest."

12. Literally, "let him make himself live," explained by Rashi as "let him exalt himself," i.e., let a person be full of pride and engage in luxurious living and in self-indulgence.

13. Rashi explains that when a person is close to the governmental authorities, he arouses jealousy, suspicion, and hatred on the part of others. Donath, *Die Alexandersage*, pp. 26 ff., understands this as a reflection of the rabbinic hatred of Roman tyranny.

14. Ibid. This answer reflects the views of those Jews who favored a policy of peace with Rome.

15. Rashi understands this to mean: Why do you cling to your faith and not accept mine? Do you not know that we are the majority and you are subject to us? S. Rapoport, *Sefer erekh millin* (Warsaw, 1914), pp. 125–27, argues that "the elders of the south" in this legend were the Indian gymnosophists. He says that Alexander's question here supports his theory since there is no record of Jews opposing Alexander. The Indian gymnosophists did persuade "the free nations to oppose him" and Sabbas to revolt. Plutarch, *Lives*, transl. Dryden, revised Clough (Modern Library, New York, n.d.), pp. 844, 846–47, says that Alexander had several of the Indian philosophers hanged. However, it should be noted that the Jews did oppose Alexander; according to

Josephus's version of the legend of Alexander's meeting with the high priest (see supra, n. 1), they had refused his request for provisions for his troops during their siege of Tyre. Rapoport continues his theory by saying that the answers given here about the wise man, the strong man, and the wealthy man were originated by the Indian philosophers, and Ben Zoma in Avot 4:1 borrowed from them. His different answer, "He who learns from all men," to the first question, "Who is wise?" is an indication that it is permissible to quote non-Jews. Donath, op. cit., pp. 26 ff., affirms that Ben Zoma was the original author, and his aphorisms and Rabbi Simon's answer, Avot 2:13, given here as the answer to the question "Who is the wise man?" were later attributed to "the elders of the south" so as to invest them with greater authority. Lévi, "La légende d'Alexandre dans le Talmud et le Midrasch," *Revue des Études Juives* 7 (1883):78–93 (hereafter cited as Lévi, "Alexandre dans le Midrasch") agrees that the answers here were taken from Avot. The redactor of the legend quoted from memory and hence used R. Simon's answer instead of Ben Zoma's.

16. Rashi explains, "Your argument that you are the majority is of no worth, for Satan leads men astray daily."

17. Lévi ("Alexandre dans le Midrasch") points to Plutarch as the source of this legend and especially the threat to execute the sages. Rashi comments that the elders here remind Alexander that he had promised to do no harm and it would be a poor reflection on so great a king to be deceitful, for so is it written in Prov. 16.

18. Kazis, *Gests of Alexander*, p. 14, says that most scholars identify "the elders of the south" with the gymnosophists of India. "It has been suggested that this legend is of Hellenistic origin and that it reflects the notion, found in Greek literature, that the Jews are a philosophical people and are descended from Indian philosophers. The idea was, according to this view, employed in Hellenistic Jewish literature in order to prove the antiquity of the Jews as well as their pre-eminence in the field of philosophy." See Rapoport, *Sefer erekh millin*, pp. 125–27; Donath, *Die Alexandersage*, pp. 26 ff.; Lévi, "Alexandre dans le Midrasch," p. 78 ff.; and idem, "La légende d'Alexandre dans le Talmud," *Revue des Études Juives* 2 (1881):293–300 (hereafter cited as Lévi, "Alexandre dans le Talmud"); A. Wünsche, "Die Alexandersage nach jüdischen Quellen," in *Die Grenzenboten* 33 (1879):272–74; L. Wallach, "Alexander the Great and the Indian Gymnosophists in Hebrew Tradition," in *Proceedings of the American Academy for Jewish Research* 11 (1941):47–83. However, Azariah dei Rossi was of the opinion that "the elders of the south" were Jewish, *Me'or einayim* (Vilna, 1863), 10:69a.

This legend, found in the Talmud (Tamid 32a), has its parallel in Plutarch's *Lives* (loc. cit., p. 847), but both the questions and the answers are different. In Plutarch the account is of a dialogue between Alexander and ten Indian philosophers, called gymnosophists, whom the king had taken prisoner because they had persuaded Sabbas to revolt and had caused the Macedonians much trouble. Wallach (*Alexander the Great*, pp. 48–52) asserts that the talmudic version is based on an older Greek source than that underlying Plutarch's tale. Lévi ("Alexandre dans le Talmud," p. 293; "Alexandre dans le Midrasch," p. 78) thinks that the talmudic narrative comes from an older Palestinian Aramaic version that was closer to the account in Plutarch. Wünsche

("Alexandersage," p. 274) declares it difficult to decide which version represents the original tale. Kazis (*Gests of Alexander*, p. 15) says that "while the talmudic version has its origin in Hellenistic sources, the account as found in the Talmud bears a definite rabbinic stamp and represents the product of much interpolation and elaboration. The passages in Aramaic represent the older layer while the Hebrew ones represent the later elements." Still another account of the dialogue is found in Pseudo-Callisthenes, 3.6. This too differs from the talmudic version.

19. Tamid 32a. The mountains of darkness are mentioned again in the legends about Alexander's visit to the king of Kazia. See later and infra, n. 26.

20. Tamid 32a–b. This legend is found in other rabbinic sources with slight variations: Leviticus Rabbah 27:1; Midrash Tanhuma (ed. S. Buber, Vilna, 1885); Vayikra, Emor 9; Pesikta de-Rav Kahana (ed. S. Buber, Vilna, 1925), Piska 9:24. In all these the place is called Carthage. Buber points out that in other manuscripts of the Tanhuma there is a variant reading of *Kartigra* instead of *Kartigna* as we have it here. (The Latin, of course, is *Carthago*.) Another variant is *Kartinda*. Buber cites the theory that the word is compounded from the Aramaic, *karta*, "city," and the Greek, *gyne*, "woman." Most authorities today believe that the name of Carthage was compounded of two Aramaic words— *karta*, "city," and *hadasht*, an old Aramaic word meaning "new," i.e., Carthage, the "new city" in Africa of the original settlers from the Middle East. Buber relates the fact that this city is mentioned in both the Babylonian and Palestinian Talmuds and in the midrashim: Berakhot 29a; Yerushalmi Shabbat 7:2; Kilayim 1:9; Shevi'it 6:1; Genesis Rabbah 44. It is his opinion that the city is the well-known Carthage of antiquity, not far from the present city of Tunis. Kazis says there is a partial parallel to this story in Pseudo-Callisthenes, 3.25–26, and the legend may also be found in *Hibbur ma'asiyot* (Verona, 1647), p. 7a, where the trial held before King Kazia (see infra, n. 26) is here held before the women. Lévi ("Alexandre dans le Midrasch," p. 83) says that while this legend is found in various versions in other literatures, the part dealing with the gold bread is Jewish in origin.

21. This legend is found in the Babylonian Talmud, Tamid 32b. Kazis points out that parallel elements are found in Pseudo-Callisthenes, 2.39–41, where, however, the journey is to the spring of eternal life. Variations of this legend of the journey to the spring of life are found in the Persian, Arabic, and Turkish versions of the Alexander Romance. See Wünsche, "Alexandersage," pp. 275–80, and F. Spiegel, *Die Alexandersage bei Orientalen* (Leipzig, 1851), pp. 29, 63. An elaborated account of the journey to Paradise is found in the twelfth-century Latin work, *Alexandri Magni iter Ad Paradisum* (see Magoun, *Gests of King Alexander*, p. 29, n. 6, and G. Cary, *The Medieval Alexander* [Cambridge, 1956], pp. 19–21).

Donath's opinion (*Die Alexandersage*, pp. 36 ff.) is that the versions of the legend in the Talmud and in Pseudo-Callisthenes come from a common Jewish source; Wünsche's ("Alexandersage," pp. 276– 80), that the origin is Persian; Lévi's ("Alexandre dans le Midrasch," pp. 82–84 and "Alexandre dans le Talmud," pp. 298–300), that the account in Pseudo-Callisthenes is older, and the medieval Latin work is a translation of a more detailed Jewish source older than the version in the

Talmud. Wallach ("Alexander the Great," pp. 56–63, 81–82) believes that these several Alexander legends in Tamid are reflections of Hellenistic-Jewish apologetic literature where popular stories and themes in general Hellenistic literature were cast into a Jewish form to show the antiquity of the Jewish people and to place them in a favorable light vis-à-vis the Greeks and Egyptians.

22. Numbers Rabbah 13:14; also Yerushalmi Bava Meẓia (ed. Krotoschin, 1866), 3.1, 42c.

23. Yalkut Shimoni, 1 Kings 18, sec. 211, p. 758; also Pirke de-Rabbi Eliezer 11.28b–29a.

24. Midrash Aseret Melakhim in *Oẓar midrashim*, ed. J. D. Eisenstein (New York, 1915), 2:463. See the emendations of two words in the text made by Kazis, *Gests of Alexander*, p. 185, nn. 68–69. Lévi ("Alexandre dans le Midrasch," p. 93) believes that the versions of this legend in rabbinic literature as given here are based on the version in Pseudo-Callisthenes, 2.41. Kazis (*Gests of Alexander*, p. 19) says it is possible that all derive ultimately from a common source.

25. Midrash Tehillim, ed. S. Buber (Vilna, 1891), Psalm 93, sec. 6. See also *Midrash on Psalms*, ed. William C. Braude (2 vols. New Haven, 1959), 2:127–28. Found also in Yalkut Shimoni on Psalm 93, sec. 848, p. 946. In both sources the text reads "Hadrian." Kazis, following Lévi, suggests that this represents a scribal error and that the emperor referred to is Alexander. He bases his argument on the fact that Alexander's desire to descend to the depths is mentioned, together with his desire to ascend to the heavens, in two rabbinic sources, Pirke de-Rabbi Eliezer 11, and Yalkut Shimoni, 1 Kings 18, sec. 211. In addition, this legend is associated with Alexander in Pseudo-Callisthenes, 2.38. Lévi's opinion is that the rabbinic version is based on this last. In the Greek narrative, Alexander's purpose in plumbing the ocean's depths is to find pearls; typically, in the Jewish version, he is concerned with learning how the waters praise God, in accordance with Ps. 93:4, *Above the thunder of the mighty waters, more majestic than the breakers of the sea.* Kazis suggests that both versions may stem from one common source. See Israel Lévi, "Alexander the Great" in the *Jewish Encyclopedia*, 1:343; idem, "Alexandre dans le Midrasch," p. 93; Kazis, *Gests of Alexander*, pp. 19–20.

In the rope story the text in Midrash Tehillim reads "Adriatic Sea." But since the second story specifies the Mediterranean and since also the other source, Yalkut Shimoni, reads "the ocean," usually denoting the Mediterranean, for the rope story as well, both Buber and Braude feel that in both stories it is the Mediterranean that is meant. Braude further points out that the maximum depth of the Adriatic is about 800 fathoms or 4,800 feet, and the king would not have needed three and a half years to measure it. See Braude 2:499, n. 9.

26. Three versions of this legend are found in rabbinic literature with only minor variations among them. The story told here is found in the Talmud Yerushalmi, Bava Meẓia, 2.5, 8c. A second version occurs in Genesis Rabbah 33:1; Leviticus Rabbah 27:1, Pesikta de-Rav Kahana 9:24; Midrash Tanḥuma, Emor 9. The differences in the latter version are the following: (1) the place is specified as "Beyond the Mountains of Darkness" and "another land whose name is Africa"; (2) upon his arrival Alexander is presented with golden apples, golden pomegranates, and golden bread. He asks, "What is the meaning of this? Is gold eaten

in your country?" He is given the answer, "Is it not so in your country, else why have you come here?" To which he responds, "It is not your possessions that I have come to see but your administration of the law." (3) Leviticus Rabbah calls the locale of the treasure "a carob tree" instead of "a dunghill" but in the Aramaic the two words are almost identical, ḥruva and ḥurva, respectively, and the correct word is undoubtedly "dunghill." Leviticus Rabbah explains why each litigant wants the other to have the treasure—each fears being accused of theft. (4) The preparation of the meal of gold is told only in the version in the Talmud Yerushalmi.

The third version, found in Yalkut Shimoni, Psalm 36, sec. 727, includes both the offering of the golden items of food to Alexander upon his arrival and the golden meal later and is evidently (since the Yalkut is a comparatively late compilation) a combination of elements contained in the two earlier versions.

The location of Kazia's kingdom is placed in Africa by several of the sources: Pesikta de-Rav Kahana, Leviticus Rabbah, and Midrash Tanḥuma. Rabbinic interpreters of the Midrash derive his name from the Hebrew word kez, meaning "end," and deduce that his kingdom was, therefore, at the uttermost limits of Africa as then known. Wallach, believing that the legend is reminiscent of Alexander's meeting with the Indian gymnosophists, suggests that Kazia is the name of either an Indian ruler or place (see Wallach, "Alexander the Great," p. 75). This conjecture was made much earlier by an eighteenth-century scholar, the author of the Penei Moshe, a commentary on the Talmud Yerushalmi (see his comment on Bava Mezia, 2.5.8c).

As to the origin of this legend, Wallach holds to his view that this legend, like the four found in Tamid—the conversation with the elders of the south, the journey to the region of darkness, the arrival at the gate of Paradise, and the meeting with the women rulers—are all Greek in origin, fashioned anew in Hellenistic Jewish literature of an apologetic vein in order to show Jewish superiority (see Wallach, op. cit., p. 65). However, Lévi ("Alexandre dans le Midrasch," p. 84) thinks the legend may be of Jewish origin.

The legend has no parallel in Pseudo-Callisthenes. But its moral, Alexander's greed for gold and its absurdity, is found in another story there: the Brahman philosophy is expounded by Dirdimus, king of the Brahmans, who ridicules Alexander's greed for gold. Kazis also points out that it is met again in another form in Plutarch's Morals (ed. W. H. Goodwin, Boston, 1870), 1:382–83. Of course, it is mentioned earlier in the talmudic version of the legend of Alexander and the African kingdom of women; see supra, n. 20.

27. Midrash Aggadah (ed. S. Buber, Vienna, 1894), 2.157 on Num. 30:15. This legend is alluded to in Pseudo-Callisthenes, 1.32. An interesting parallel is found in Pseudo-Epiphanius, Vitae Prophetarum, which tells that Alexander brought serpents from Greece to Alexandria and placed them in the Nile to destroy the serpents and crocodiles there. Unsuccessful in this project, Alexander then removed Jeremiah's bones from his grave and placed them in a circle around the city. The malevolent reptiles vanished (see the Vitae Prophetarum in E. Nestle, Marginalien und Materialen [Tubingen, 1893], pp. 16 ff.). In Midrash Aggadah, Jeremiah's prayer for the Egyptians that aroused their gratitude was for them to be protected against the evil denizens of the Nile.

The story of the bones of Jeremiah is found also in the *Historia Scholastica* of Peter Comestor and in other medieval writings (see G. Cary, *The Medieval Alexander*, p. 132).

28. This legend is found only in Targum Sheni, chap. 1, sec. 2. The source misplaces Alexander in the line of succession, placing him immediately after Nebuchadnezzar, with Shishak of Egypt, Antiochus Epiphanes, and Cyrus (*sic*) following.

29. Exodus Rabbah 15:6. The word for "sun" in Greek is *helios*.

[Before concluding these notes on the Alexander legends in rabbinic literature, it should be mentioned that the Talmud states (Sukkah 51b): "Alexander of Macedon killed the Jews of Alexandria. They were punished because they had transgressed the commandment (Exod. 14:13), *For the Egyptians whom you see today you will never see again*. Yet they returned and resided in Egypt. When Alexander came he found them reading the verse (Deut. 28:49), *The Lord will bring a nation against you from afar, from the end of the earth*. He said, 'My voyage should have taken ten days but the winds blew and brought me here in five. It must have been for this purpose.' So he fell upon them and killed them." However, the Alexander referred to here must have been Tiberius Julius Alexander, a renegade from Judaism, who as governor of Alexandria during the sixth decade of the common era had the Roman garrison attack the Jews when riots broke out between the latter and the non-Jewish inhabitants of Alexandria. According to Josephus (*Wars of the Jews*, 2.18.7–8), fifty thousand Jews were slain and the Delta, the Jewish quarter, was devastated. The words "of Macedon" following the name of Alexander in the talmudic text may have been added by a later scribe, or there may have been confusion in the mind of the narrator of the legend, the third-century scholar, Abaye (see Azariah dei Rossi, *Meor einayim*, part 3, chap. 12, p. 170).

The Book of Josippon, a popular history of the Jews dealing principally with the era of the Second Commonwealth, contains many legends dealing with Alexander, most from nonrabbinic sources. Scholars vary in their estimates of the book's date of composition, placing it from the fourth to the tenth centuries, but all agree that many interpolations have been introduced into it, including the Alexander legends. These deal with all the various phases of Alexander's brief but extraordinary life from birth to death (see Kazis, *Gests of Alexander*, pp. 28–31).]

2. Greece

30. In rabbinic literature "Greece" can mean either the empire of Alexander, or the later Hellenistic empire of the Seleucid kings of Syria, and more often the latter. Genesis Rabbah 37:1 on Gen. 10:2; see also Yoma 10a, and Yerushalmi Megillah 1:9.

31. Genesis Rabbah 44:17 on Gen. 15:12 and Leviticus Rabbah 12:5. The comparison of Greece to a scorpion is derived from Deut. 8:15 where *serpents, fiery serpents, and scorpions* are symbolically applied to Babylonia, Persia, and Greece, respectively.

32. Lamentations Rabbah 1:19 on Zech. 9:13–14 and Jer. 31:21.

33. Numbers Rabbah 7:10.

34. Exodus Rabbah 45:2.

35. Yevamot 90b.

3. The Greek Language and the Septuagint

36. Genesis Rabbah 36:8; see also Deuteronomy Rabbah 1:1.

37. Mishnah Megillah 1:8.

38. Esther Rabbah 4:12. Another opinion is that the second language mentioned is not Persian but Syrian.

39. Megillah 9a–9b. The king was probably Ptolemy II Philadelphus, at whose order the Septuagint translation is said to have been produced. See also Genesis Rabbah 1:11, 38:10, 48:17, 98:5 (where, on the Greek translation's change from slew *a man* to *an ox*, in Gen. 49:6, the theory has been advanced that it was done because of the then current libel that the Jews captured a Greek every year for a sacrifice, which might conceivably have been supported by the present Hebrew reading!). See also Exodus Rabbah 5:5, Mekhilta Bo', chap. 14; see Sotah 49a and Mishnah Sotah 9:14 concerning the prohibition against studying Greek philosophy and science; also Kiddushin 83a. The house of Rabban Gamaliel II, of Jabneh, was permitted to study Greek culture because of its association with the government.

40. Genesis Rabbah 1:11.

41. Genesis Rabbah 38:10.

42. The change from *be-kirbah* to *bi-kerovehah* did not change the letters of the original word, only its vocalization. See Genesis Rabbah 48:17 and Rashi's comments on Megillah 9a.

43. Genesis Rabbah 81:5 on Gen. 35:8. The rabbi quoted is Rabbi Samuel ben Nahman.

44. Genesis Rabbah 99:7. It is Rabbi Johanan who is responsible for this comparison with the Greek, in which the word is *maxairan* ("sword").

45. Genesis Rabbah 99:7.

46. Exodus Rabbah 12:1 on Exod. 9:13.

47. Exodus Rabbah 27:7. The rabbi who uses the Greek in both this passage and the previous one is Rabbi Berekhiah. He equates *me-'ayin*, "nothing," in the verse with "the nations of the world," basing it on the verse, *All the nations are as naught in His sight* (Isa. 40:17).

48. Leviticus Rabbah 16:1. Rabbi Meir is the author of this comment on the Greek words *seron* from *saira*, "sweep."

49. Sukkah 51b; Tosefta Sukkah 4. From the beginning of Alexandria in the days of Alexander the Great, the Jews constituted a significant segment of the city's population and had their own places of worship and other rights and privileges. Because of the tremendous size of the basilica, the voice of the officiant could not be heard by the worshipers; hence the waving of the scarf as a signal to the people to answer the officiant's prayer with "Amen." Philo describes a beautiful synagogue in Alexandria but whether it was the same as depicted here is not certain.

Part III

The Hasmonean Period

The Greek Persecution
and the Maccabean Revolt[1]

When Onias was high priest, there was peace in the holy city and God's laws were observed. He was a man who could not tolerate wickedness. All the kings of neighboring countries paid honor to Jerusalem and sent precious gifts to the Temple. Seleucus, the Greek king of Syria, sent offerings for sacrifices. But a certain Simon of the tribe of Benjamin, the superintendent of the Temple, hated the high priest who had prevented him from doing evil in the city. Fearing personally to attack the high priest he told Appolonius, governor of Aram and Tyre, that the Temple was full of rich treasure of silver and gold that the king ought to seize. Appolonius informed the king, who sent his treasurer, Heliodorus, to Jerusalem to confiscate the treasure.

The high priest informed him that the entire tale was false. The funds in the Temple were of a comparatively small amount and were to be used for widows and orphans. In addition, Hyrcanus ben Tobias, had deposited some of his personal wealth on trust. The envoy replied that, nevertheless, he would have to obey the royal command and bring whatever treasure was in the Temple to the king.

The city was shocked at this proposed desecration of the Sanctuary. The priests prostrated themselves in prayer before the altar. The people left their homes and gathered together to cry aloud to the Lord that His house should not so be defiled and put to shame. The women donned sackcloth and ashes.

Heliodorus and his men entered the Temple and proceeded to the treasure room. Suddenly, the Lord's presence was felt, and all the men shook with fear. They saw a terrifying rider in gold mail sitting upon a horse with a beautiful caparison. The horse lifted its front hooves and struck out at Heliodorus. At the same time, two young men of fine appearance stood beside him and beat him continually. He fell to the ground in a faint, and his men carried him out. Seeing this, the people praised the Lord, and the Temple resounded with rejoicing, for the Lord had performed a great wonder before their very eyes.

The friends of Heliodorus came to the high priest asking that he pray for the official's life. The priest agreed for he was concerned lest the king think the Jews had attacked his legate. So he offered a sacrifice and prayed. Suddenly, the same two mysterious young men appeared before Heliodorus and said, "Give honor to the priest and bless him, for the Lord spares your life for his sake. And now rise, and declare our God's glory among the peoples." They then vanished.

Heliodorus offered a sacrifice to the Lord and made a vow unto Him for having restored his life. He thanked Onias, and with his military escort he returned to the king. There he told of all the great wonders of the Lord that his own eyes had seen. And when the king asked, "Whom shall I now send to seize the treasure in Jerusalem?" Heliodorus replied, "If you have an enemy or one who plots against your throne, send him! For if he will return at all, he will be a beaten and scourged man. For this God who dwells in the heavens is awesome in that place. His eyes are upon it always to protect it, and he who lifts a hand against it is marked for death."[2]

Therefore, when the Syrians planned to desecrate the Temple in Jerusalem, they thought it would be safer for them if a Jew were to defile it first. They persuaded a Jewish renegade, Joseph of Shitta, to enter first, bribing him with the promise that he could keep whatever he brought out from the sanctuary. He came out carrying the golden candelabrum. But they denied it to him saying that a commoner ought not use a golden candelabrum. They asked him to enter the sanctuary again for some other prize for himself. Now, having repented of his error, he refused. He was offered a release of taxes for three years, but he still refused. "Is it not enough that I have angered my God once," he exclaimed, "that I should anger him again?" They placed him in a carpenter's vise and began sawing him asunder. All the while he cried out, "Woe, woe, that I angered my Creator!"[3]

A similar fate later befell Jakum of Zerorot, a nephew of the sage Jose ben Joezer of Zeredah. During the time of the religious persecution Jakum (or Alcimus as he is sometimes called), whom the Greeks had appointed high priest, rode by just as Jose, bearing the beam for the gallows, was going forth to be hanged. Taunting his learned uncle, a pious priest,[4] Jakum said, "Look at the horse that my master gives me to ride, and look at the horse (the beam for the gallows) that your Master gives you to ride!"

Jose replied, "If so much is given to such as you who provoke Him, how much more will be given to those who obey His will!" "Has any man been more obedient to God's will than you?" Jakum jeered. Jose replied, "If so much is done to those who are obedient to His will, how much more shall be done to those who provoke Him!" These words pierced Jakum instantly like the poison of a snake. He went away and, in remorse, imposed upon himself the four legal death penalties: stoning, burning, death by the sword, and strangulation. How did he execute them all upon himself? He took a pointed beam and drove it into the ground. To this stake he tied a rope. Around the beam he heaped sticks of wood and surrounded them with a wall of stones, the base of which had been set upon the wood as well. Amidst the pile of wooden sticks, he placed a sword, pointing upward. He lit a fire with the kindling wood under the stones; then he hanged himself from the beam, strangling himself. The flames spread and soon leaped up, causing the rope to break, and he fell upon the sword in the fire. The wooden base beneath the stones was consumed by the flames, and the wall of stones tumbled upon his body in the fire. The soul of Jakum departed, and because of his repentance it was instantly received in heaven.

In the meanwhile Jose ben Joezer was being put to death. When his soul was expiring, he saw the bier of Jakum flying through the air. He exclaimed, "Look how he precedes me by a brief moment into Paradise!"[5]

The Syrians issued various decrees against Judaism. The Jews were ordered to inscribe upon the bars across their doors the words "I have no share in the God of Israel." The people at once removed all such bars from their homes. The same words were to be carved on the horns of every ox. Whereupon, the people sold their oxen.[6]

When the Syrians entered the Temple, Miriam, of the priestly family of Bilgah, who had married a Syrian captain and had forsaken her faith, beat the altar with her sandal, exclaiming in her anger, "O ravenous wolf, how long will you consume the wealth of the Jewish people, but when trouble comes, you do not protect them!" When the sages heard of her blasphemy, they abolished all the future priestly privileges of the Bilgah clan.[7]

There was a wise and scholarly old man, handsome in appearance, by the name of Eleazar. The oppressors forced his mouth open to feed him swine's flesh. He spat it out before them, for he had decided to submit himself to torture and to suffer death, maintaining his integrity, rather than live at the cost of his convictions. The men in charge of this abominable procedure had known Eleazar for some time and felt sorry for him. Taking him aside, they whispered to him, "We shall feed you kosher meat and all who see you eating it will think it the flesh of the idolatrous sacrifice commanded by the king." They proposed this plan in order to spare his life, for they had compassion upon him.

But in keeping with his gray hairs and the path he had trod since childhood in observance of the Lord's commandments, Eleazar replied: "Send this old man straightway to the netherworld! For it is not fitting for an old man like me to live a lie! Why should the young say, 'Ninety-year-old Eleazar became an idolater too!' And why should I mislead my people and shame my old age in order to prolong my life by a few days more? What good does it do to escape from death? Can I escape from God either in life or in death? Therefore, I am now prepared to go to my death with a peaceful heart as befits an old man like me. And I shall be an example for all my people to offer their lives willingly and with peaceful hearts for the Torah of the Lord and His commandments."

When he had finished, they began to torture him. Their former pity now turned into bitter hatred, for they said, "He is a stiff-necked man." As they smote him murderously, he groaned, "O Lord, God! Before You are all hidden things revealed. You know that I could have saved myself from such mortal agony, but I willingly chose to bear it for Your great name's sake." His spirit expired and he died. And in his dying he became a lesson and example to both young and old to love the Lord and to revere Him.[8]

A woman and her seven sons were seized and brought before the ruler. The oldest son was commanded to do obeisance to an idol. He refused, saying, "It is written in the Torah, *I the Lord am your God* (Exod. 20:2)."

He was led forth at once to be executed. The second son

was then ordered to worship the idol. He answered, "It is written, *You shall have no other gods beside Me* (Deut. 5:7)."

He was killed forthwith. The third son received the same command and his response was, "It is written in the Torah, *You must not worship any other god* (Exod. 34:14)." After his execution the next son was brought forth. He too rejected the order given him, saying, "It is written in the Torah, *Whoever sacrifices to a god other than the Lord alone shall be proscribed* (Exod. 22:19)." He was slain.

The fifth son was summoned and his reply was, "It is written in the Torah, *Hear, O Israel! the Lord is our God, the Lord alone* (Deut. 6:4)." After his death, the sixth son was given the same order as his brothers. His retort was, "It is written in the Torah, *Know therefore this day and keep in mind that the Lord alone is God in heaven above and on earth below; there is no other* (Deut. 4:39)." He too was executed.

The youngest was then brought before the ruler and told to worship the idol. He answered, "God forbid! For it is written in the Torah, *You have affirmed this day that the Lord is your God . . . and the Lord has affirmed this day that you are . . . His treasured people* (Deut. 26:17–18). We have already sworn to the Holy One, blessed be He, that we shall never exchange our God for another, and He has sworn that He will never exchange our people for any other."

The ruler then said to him, "Your older brothers have all seen something of life and have had their pleasures. But you are so young. You have gotten as yet no joy from living. I urge you, bow down to the idol!"

The boy replied: "It is written, *The Lord will reign for ever and ever* (Exod. 15:18) and *The Lord is king for ever and ever; the nations will perish from His land* (Ps. 10:16). You will be nothing as will your kingdom, but the Holy One, blessed be He, lives and shall exist always!"

The king, anxious to save the situation, said to the boy, "Look, your brothers are all slain. I shall throw my signet ring in front of the idol. All you need do is to bend down and pick it up. People will then say that you finally submitted to the authority of the king."

"Alas for you, O king," the lad replied, "if you are so zealous for your honor, how much more so ought we be for God's honor!"

As he was being led away to the place of execution, his mother asked for permission to give him a farewell kiss. When her request was granted, she pleaded that she be killed first. But the king refused, saying, "Is it not written in your Torah that *no animal . . . shall be slaughtered on the same day with its young* (Lev. 22:28)?"

"O wicked man!" she exclaimed, "have you then fulfilled all the commandments of the Torah save this one alone?"

At once the ruler commanded that the boy be killed. The mother fell upon the lad, embracing him and kissing him and sobbed, "Go, my son, and tell Abraham: My mother says to you, you set up one altar to sacrifice one son and that was but to test you. But I have erected seven altars and I have sacrificed seven sons!"

They slew her son before her eyes. She then ascended to the roof and jumped to her death. As she lay dying, a heavenly voice was heard proclaiming, *As a happy mother of children* (Ps. 113:9).[9]

All were afraid of the Greek kingdom of Syria for it was like the scorching rays of the sun in summer that none can withstand. But Mattathias the priest and his sons stood firm in their faith in God with the result that the Greek legions fled from before them and were all slain. Hence God said unto them, *Beat your ploughshares into swords, and your pruning hooks into spears. Let even the weakling say, "I am strong"* (Joel 4:10).[10]

The appearance of Mattathias and his Hasmonean sons in the days of Antiochus was in fulfillment of God's promise, *I will not reject them or spurn them so as to destroy them, annulling My covenant with them: for I the Lord am their God* (Lev. 26:44). The words, *I will not reject them*, refer to the days of the Chaldeans when God brought to the Jews Daniel, Hananiah, Mishael, and Azariah; *or spurn them*, to the days of Haman, when God gave them Mordecai and Esther; *so as to destroy them*, to the time of Antiochus, when God set before them Simon the Just and Mattathias, son of Johanan the Hasmonean high priest, and his sons; *annulling My covenant with them* refers to the Roman period, when God placed before them the dynasty of Rabbi Judah ha-Nasi and the scholars of the various generations; *for I the Lord am their God*, refers to the time to come, when no heathen people or tongue will have dominion over them.[11]

The coming of Judah the Maccabee was predicted by the

prophet Zechariah with the words, *Rejoice greatly, Fair Zion;
raise a shout, Fair Jerusalem! Lo, your king is coming to you. He
is victorious, triumphant* (Zech. 9:9).[12]

The victories of the Maccabees against the Greeks were also
forecast by the same prophet (Zech. 9:13–14):

*For I have drawn Judah taut,
And applied [My hand] to Ephraim as to a bow,
And I will arouse your sons, O Zion,
Against your sons, O Javan,
And make you like a warrior's sword.
And the Lord will manifest Himself to them.
And His arrows shall flash like lightning;
My Lord God shall sound the ram's horn
And advance in a stormy tempest.[13]*

God raised up for the Jewish people Simon the Just, Mattathias, son of Johanan the Hasmonean, and his sons so that Israel
might not be destroyed by the Greeks.[14] It was appropriate that
the Greek power should have been humbled by the Hasmoneans,
who were of the tribe of Levi. For just as Levi was the third
tribe so were the Greeks the third world empire. As the word
"Levi" is constituted of three letters (*l-v-i*), so too the word
"Greece" (*y-v-n*). The priests of the tribe of Levi blew trumpets
in the Temple, and the Greeks blew trumpets in time of war.
The priests wore mitres and the Greeks helmets; the priests, the
uniform of ecclesiastical garments, and the Greeks, the military
uniform. The soldiers of the priests were few in number, while
the Greeks were many. But the many fell into the hands of the
few.[15]

When the Greeks had entered the Sanctuary they defiled all
the sanctified oil. After their defeat by the Hasmoneans, the
victors searched the Temple and found only one unopened cruse
of oil still bearing the seal of the high priest. Normally, it would
have been enough for but one day. Miraculously, it lasted for
eight days. In later years these eight days of the year were fixed
as festive days for praise and thanksgiving. This then is the explanation for Hanukkah.[16]

There is another explanation for the practice of lighting
candles during Hanukkah. When the victorious Hasmoneans entered the Temple, they searched for the golden menorah, but

Antiochus had taken it away. But they came upon eight iron spits. These they set up with candles in them and lit them.

Still another explanation has it that the Maccabees sent for oil to Teko'a, famed for having always supplied the best oil for the Temple. Normally, the journey there and back took sixteen days. This time, miraculously, it took only eight.[17]

When the wicked Antiochus heard that his army had been put to flight by Judah the Maccabee and his men, he became very angry. He decided that he himself would crush the rebellion and destroy the Jews, making Jerusalem a cemetery for them all. He mounted his war chariot and ordered the army to ride day and night. But God's anger overtook him. He was smitten with an incurable disease that racked his bowels. But he was still full of arrogance and insolence, continuing to rage against the Jews. He commanded his chariots to go even faster. Because of the high speed he fell from his chariot and was badly hurt, suffering injuries to all parts of his body. Thus the man who, in his pride, had thought he could command the ocean's waves, weigh the mountains in a balance, and reach to the very stars of heaven was now cast down to the ground, showing to all the power of God.

Antiochus, tormented by pain, was carried by his men in a litter. His disease caused his body to rot away, creating a loathesome stench. Only then did his pride leave him, and he acknowledged that mortal man must never liken himself to God but subject himself to Him. He vowed that he would give Jerusalem its liberty and make the Jews the equals, in rights and privileges, to the citizens of Athens. The Temple that he had already plundered, he would enrich with lavish gifts, restoring all the holy vessels. Even more, he pledged that he himself would become a Jew and would go through all the inhabited world to declare the power of God. But his vows were of no avail. His pains did not cease. God's full justice was upon him.

Seeing that his end was near, Antiochus wrote a letter to the Jews, calling them "the good Jews, my citizens" and urging them to be loyal to his son. The murderer and blasphemer suffered most grievously as he had caused others to suffer, and so he died a miserable death in a strange land among the barren mountains of the wilderness.[18]

Antiochus's son and successor sent a large army to conquer Judea. Judah the Maccabee with his few men hastened to meet the foe at Gilead. But his soldiers were soon exhausted by the battle and the overwhelming odds against them. Perceiving this, Judah lifted his eyes toward heaven and prayed, *O Lord, deliver us* (Ps. 118:25).

At once five handsome young men garbed in gold raiment and riding upon fiery steeds appeared before him. Their swords flashed like lightning, and shields of gold protected their chests. While Judah still stared in amazement, three of them made for the enemy hosts and cut men down right and left. The two remaining placed their shields over Judah to protect him.

Judah rejoiced greatly and he cried out to his warriors, "Be strong, my valiant men! Heaven itself fights for us!" Renewing their effort, his soldiers fell upon the enemy with such might that the Greeks fled in all directions.

Afterward, a new army was sent against the Jews, with Lysias as its commanding general. Judah and his band advanced to meet them at Betar, but when they saw that the Greek soldiers were as many as the sands of the seashore, their hearts melted within them. Judah asked his men to fast and pray and they did so. The fast ended with the blast of the shofar. At that moment the heavens opened and the entire area was suffused with light. A figure like an awesome angel of God, clad in gold mail, appeared between heaven and earth, his horse a fiery creature.

"God has not forsaken us!" Judah exclaimed to his men. "See how He has sent His angel to take vengeance against those who would destroy Israel!"

Their spirits strengthened, his soldiers followed him into battle. In a surprise attack they routed the army of Lysias who, in his fear, made a solemn treaty of peace with Judah.[19]

The Greek general Nicanor was dispatched a second time at the head of a large army to crush the Hasmonean rebellion. In his haughtiness Nicanor had already planned the monument he would erect to commemorate his victory over Judah the Maccabee. But Judah trusted in God and lent courage and hope to his men by reminding them of how God had helped them upon earlier occasions. He raised their spirits with words from the Torah and the prophets. So he armed them not only with shields and spears but with faith and spiritual strength.

In addition, he told them a wonderful dream that he had recently had. In his dream he saw the late righteous high priest, Onias, standing with arms raised toward heaven, praying for his people Israel. Suddenly, there appeared a glorious form of another man with gray hair and majestic figure. And Onias said to Judah, "This is the prophet Jeremiah, who prays constantly for his brethren and for Jerusalem." Then Jeremiah stretched forth his right hand and gave Judah a sword of gold. "Take this holy sword, a gift from God," he said, "and go forth to smite the enemy."

The men were greatly encouraged by the account of Judah's dream and determined to launch the attack at once. Meeting their enemies with prayer on their lips, they won a mighty victory.

Nicanor, the Greek general, each day during his siege of Jerusalem would shake his fist at the city and exclaim, "When will it fall that I may tread it under foot?" When the Hasmoneans triumphed, they cut off his thumbs and big toes and hung them on the city gates and his head on the highest tower of the city wall, saying, "Let justice be done to the mouth that spoke with arrogance, the hands that were raised against Jerusalem, and the feet that hastened against Judea." Thereafter, those gates were called "Nicanor's Gates."[20]

During the Greek regime, it was the practice to hang wreaths of lilies upon the gates of the Greek temples, shops, and courtyards, accompanied by songs hailing the gods. They would also place inscriptions upon the foreheads of oxen and donkeys that their owners disassociated themselves from the God of Israel. When the Hasmoneans triumphed, they abolished these practices.[21]

The Greeks had prohibited the use of God's name. When the Hasmoneans were victorious, they decreed that God's name could again be used, even in commercial documents. For example, a contract would begin, "In such and such a year of the high priesthood of John, priest of the most high God." However, the sages objected because, they pointed out, a man would pay his debt, claim his document, and then throw the canceled contract bearing God's name into the garbage. So they forbade the use of the divine name for such purposes.[22]

When Antiochus V Eupator sent the largest attacking army under Lysias to annihilate Judea, it was with the counsel of the traitor Menelaus, then at the Syrian king's court. He who had served as high priest now volunteered to go with the enemy hosts for he boasted that he knew the land well, including the secret caves where the Hasmoneans would hide. The young king himself accompanied the great army, which included war elephants as part of the force.

But the elders of Israel cried out, *They* [*call*] *on chariots,* *they* [*call*] *on horses, but we call on the name of the Lord our* *God* (Ps. 20:8).

Judah the Maccabee saw in the enemy camp a young man with a golden shield, riding upon a mighty elephant, and he surmised that this must be the king. He called for a volunteer. Eleazar his brother stepped forward with a shout, "Salvation is of the Lord!" He ran quickly into the camp of the foe, smiting with his sword right and left, and the soldiers fell like ears of corn before the harvester. Reaching the elephant, he stood beneath it and thrust his sword upward into its belly. The elephant fell upon Eleazar, killing him. The story of his valor quickly spread among the soldiers of Judah, and heartened by the example of his heroism, they rushed to attack the enemy and overwhelmed them. The king returned to his tent and there found a messenger with the news that others in his homeland were plotting to take his crown. He sued for peace with Judah, who replied, "Peace is precious in the sight of the Lord and to all who live by the law of the Lord."

The renegade Menelaus, fearing the worst, fled into one of the towers of Jerusalem to hide. The king commanded his men, "Find Menelaus who persuaded me to go up against Judea, bind him and bring him to me."

The men saw him running among the towers and pursued him. Menelaus hid on a roof of a high tower, but when he heard the approaching footsteps of the soldiers, he leaped from the roof, falling into a pit of ashes. He sank into it and was suffocated. All who heard of it said that he had received his just deserts for he had sinned against the Lord and His people, Israel, and he had enticed the kings of Syria to do harm to Israel and to profane the altar whose ashes were sacred. Therefore, he was suffocated among ashes and died the death of a wicked man.[23]

When peace had been established and the priests had returned to the Temple service, the sages of Israel remembered how Miriam, daughter of Bilgah the priest, had committed sacrilege when she had beaten the altar with her sandal and had blasphemed against God.[24] They now prevented the priestly watch to which her family belonged from participating in the service at the altar. But the priests of this watch protested. "Why do you thus punish us?" they asked.

"Because of the transgression of Miriam, daughter of Bilgah, head of your watch," the sages answered. "If one woman sins, shall all the priests of the watch suffer?" they replied. "Had Miriam not heard contemptuous remarks in her father's home about the sacrifices in the Lord's House, she would not have smitten the altar with her shoe nor uttered her blasphemous words!" retorted the sages. "Suppose Miriam, her father, and her mother have sinned, why should we be penalized?" the priests persisted. The wise men then said, "Does not an ancient proverb say, 'Woe to the wicked and woe to his neighbor; well to the righteous and well to his neighbor'?"[25]

═══ 2 ═══

The Hasmonean Rulers

The Hasmoneans at the outset were righteous and fulfilled the commands of the Torah.[26] The army of John Hyrcanus rested on the Sabbath and festivals,[27] and when he conquered the Idumeans, he permitted them to remain in their land upon condition that they would accept Judaism, including the rite of circumcision.[28]

John Hyrcanus, king and high priest, heard a heavenly voice as he officiated in the Temple. The voice spoke from out of the Holy of Holies, saying, "The sons of the high priest who went forth to battle against Antiochus have been victorious."[29] Thus had it happened previously with Simon the Just who also had heard a voice issuing forth from the Holy of Holies, speaking similarly in the Aramaic tongue, saying, "The enemy's plan to destroy the Temple has been brought to naught and Gaskalgas has been slain and his decrees, therefore, are no longer in force."[30] Hyrcanus was a righteous ruler at first. It was only later in his reign that he changed. For eighty years he served faithfully as high priest, and only toward the end did he become a Sadducee.[31]

John Hyrcanus was succeeded by his son Aristobulus, who only reigned for a short while. He was succeeded by his brother Alexander Yannai who, according to the Jewish law of levirate marriage, married his dead brother's widow, Salome Alexandra. During Hyrcanus's reign, the area of the kingdom had expanded to the size of that of Solomon, and Alexander Yannai conquered even more territory.

There was a city belonging to the king that would produce each week six hundred thousand basinfuls of salted fish for the fellers of the fig trees in the area. The king had a single tree from which would be collected every month forty measures of young pigeons of three different broods.[32]

King Yannai possessed sixty myriads of cities. The population of each was equal to that of the number who were liberated from Egypt except three cities whose populations were double that number. These three cities were Kfar Bish ("village of evil"), Kfar Shiḥlayim ("village of watercress"), and Kfar Dikhraya ("village of male children"). The first was called by its uncomplimentary name because there was no hospice for strangers within it. The second got its name because its inhabitants earned their livelihood through that plant. The name of the third, according to one opinion, derived from the fact that its women gave birth first to boys, afterward to girls, and then had no more children.[33]

Two thousand towns belonging to King Yannai were destroyed because their people swore true oaths. How is this possible? A man would say to his friend, "On my oath, I shall go and eat such and such a food at such and such a place, and I shall drink such and such a drink at such and such a place." They would go and do as they had sworn and would then die the death of the wicked. All because they had sworn to trifles, using God's name lightly. If this is the fate of one who swears to a truth, although trivial, how much more so of one who swears to a falsehood![34]

Once when a slave of King Yannai committed murder, Simon ben Shetaḥ said to the sages, "He must be tried for his crime." The information was sent to the king who ordered his slave to appear before the court of the sages. But they sent back word that he himself must also appear at the trial, in keeping with the biblical teaching that when a creature belonging to a person does injury, the owner is also required to be present in court.[35] The king came and was seated.

"Stand! King Yannai," said Simon ben Shetaḥ, "so that the witnesses may testify against you. Know that you rise not for our honor but for the honor of Him at whose command the world came into being, even as the Torah requires."[36] The king answered, "It will not be as you alone say, but as all your colleagues will say." Simon then turned to his right, but the other sages cast their eyes downward, fearing to speak. He turned to the left but again, the same reaction. Indignant, he burst out, "In your minds are considerations other than those of justice. May He who probes man's mind mete out justice to you!" At once the angel Gabriel appeared and smote them to the ground and they died.[37]

Once it happened that King Yannai went to Koḥalit in the desert, conquering sixty cities. Upon his return he was jubilant and invited all the sages of Israel to join him in celebration. He said to them, "When our ancestors were engaged in the construction of the Second Temple, in their poverty they ate salt plants. Let us too eat them in memory of our ancestors, recollecting our humble beginnings and in thanksgiving to God." Salt plants were then served, but upon tables of gold, and they ate.

There was present a certain base, evil-hearted scoundrel by the name of Eleazar ben Poirah. He said to the king, "O King Yannai, these Pharisees are secretly against you." "How can I tell?" inquired the king. "Put on the high priest's gold frontlet," was the reply.

He did so. An old man, Judah ben Gedida by name, spoke up to the king. "The crown of royalty should suffice you! Leave the crown of the high priest for the descendants of Aaron!" For it was bruited about that his mother, years before, had been a captive of the enemy in Modait—and a son of a woman taken captive may not serve as priest. The matter was investigated, and the rumor was not proven. The king's great anger set up a wall between him and the sages—for they had not denounced their colleague.

Eleazar ben Poirah then advised the king, "O King Yannai, are you then a commoner that you should thus be put to shame? Are you not both king and high priest?"

"What should I do?" asked the king.

"If you listen to my advice, tread them all under foot!"

"But what will become of the Torah?" asked Yannai.

"You need not be concerned. Let the Torah stay wrapped in its corner, and he who may wish to study it will come and study."

The king was persuaded by this heinous man, and all the sages of Israel were slain. The world was void of learning until later, when Simon ben Shetaḥ, brother of Queen Salome Alexandra, who had gone into hiding, restored the study of Torah to its pristine glory.[38]

King Yannai and his queen were eating together and since he had killed all the sages, he had no one to recite the grace after the meal. Turning to his wife, he asked, "Where can we get someone to recite the grace for us?"

She said, "Swear that if I bring you such a man you will not harm him." He swore. She then summoned her brother Simon ben Shetaḥ.

The king placed him between the queen and himself and said to the scholar, "See how much honor I pay you!"

The rabbi replied, "It is not you who is the cause of my honor, but the Torah, as it is written, *Hug her to you and she will exalt you; she will bring you honor if you embrace her* (Prov. 4:8)."

The king said to his wife, "Do you not see how these Pharisees are unwilling to accept royal authority!"

Nevertheless, he gave Simon a cup of wine for the recital of grace. But Simon asked ironically, "How shall I offer the grace? Shall I say, 'Blessed be He from whose food Yannai and his friends have eaten?'" For he himself had been given nothing. Whereupon he drank the contents of the cup and was then given another with which he recited the grace.[39]

Once it happened that three hundred Nazirites came to Jerusalem each to offer the three sacrifices at the Temple required upon the termination of the period of their vows. But they could not afford to purchase the necessary animals. Simon ben Shetaḥ was consulted. For one hundred and fifty, he found a way out of their difficulty. He discovered flaws in their vows that were legal grounds for absolution. But for the remaining one hundred and fifty he could find no such grounds. He went to King Yannai and told him, "There are three hundred Nazirites who wish to offer nine hundred sacrifices but have not the means. If you give half from your resources, I shall give half from mine."

Yannai agreed and the one hundred and fifty brought their offerings. Afterward it was reported to the king that Simon had contributed nothing. The king was enraged and Simon, hearing of it, fled.

Some time later, certain dignitaries from Persia were seated at the king's table. While dining they observed, "Your majesty, we recall that there used to be here a wise old man who would expound to us the wisdom of the Torah."

The king turned to the queen, who was Simon's sister, and said, "Send for him." She replied, "Give me your word that no harm will befall him, and he will come." He did so and Simon came. He seated himself between the king and the queen. The king asked him, "Why did you flee?"

He replied, "I heard that his majesty, the king, was angry with me and I was afraid that you might kill me, so I fled, in keeping with the verse, *Hide but a little moment, until the indignation passes* (Isa. 26:20)."

The king then inquired, "Why did you deceive me?" Simon exclaimed, "Heaven forbid! I did not deceive you. You paid with your resources—money. I paid with my resources—learning. So is it written, *For to be in the shelter of wisdom is to be also in the shelter of money* (Eccles. 7:12)."

"If so, why did you not tell me this beforehand?" asked Yannai. "Had I told you," answered Simon, "you would not have given." "And why have you seated yourself between the queen and myself?" asked the king. "Because it is written in the book of Ben Sira, '*Hug her* [*wisdom*] *to you and she will exalt you* (Prov. 4:8) and cause you to sit among princes.' "[40]

The king commanded his servants, "Pour a cup of wine for him that he may recite the grace." Whereupon Simon recited, "Blessed be He for the food eaten by Yannai and his friends." Angrily the king exclaimed, "You still persist in your stubborn ways! Never have I heard grace recited in this fashion, mentioning my name in the blessing!" "What then should I have said," replied Simon, "the usual words, 'Let us bless Him of whose bounty *we* have eaten'? I have not eaten!" The king ordered food for Simon and he ate. Then he offered grace in the usual manner.[41]

King Yannai one day said to his wife, "Fear neither the Pharisees nor the Sadducees. Beware only of the hypocrites who pretend to be real Pharisees, but in reality their deeds are like those of Zimri, while they ask the reward of Phinehas."[42]

Once during the festival of Sukkot, when the ceremony of water libation was to take place in the Temple, Yannai, acting as high priest, poured the water on the ground at his feet instead of against the altar, as was the tradition. The people pelted him with their citrons and reviled him as the son of a mother who had been once a captive, which disqualified him from serving as a priest. The infuriated king ordered his mercenary troops to attack the worshipers and six thousand people were slain.[43]

When King Yannai was lying on his deathbed, he ordered that seventy elders be seized and flung into prison. To the warden of the prison he sent word, "As soon as you hear of my death, kill them all. Then the Jews will mourn so for their teachers that they will not be able to rejoice at my death."

But good Queen Salome Alexandra frustrated the plan. When the king died, and before the news had spread, she removed the king's ring from his finger and sent it to the warden with the message that it was the king's order that the sages be released. Only afterward did she announce the fact that the king had died. The day of his death was made a day of rejoicing.[44]

After the death of Alexander Yannai and the reign of his widow, Queen Salome Alexandra, their sons Hyrcanus and Aristobulus engaged in a civil war for the throne. It happened that Hyrcanus, the elder son, to whom the throne had been promised, was besieging Jerusalem, where the forces of Aristobulus had seized power. There was in the land a very pious man called Ḥoni Ha-Me'aggel, Ḥoni the Circle Drawer, so named because he would draw a circle about himself and within it would pray. His prayers would be answered. When he prayed for rain during a severe drought, the rains fell in abundance. Since he was thus beloved of God, the followers of Hyrcanus sought him out in his place of concealment and asked him to place a curse upon Aristobulus and his supporters within Jerusalem, both priests and laity. Ḥoni refused but finally was made to yield. He then prayed, "O God, King of all the people, since those who stand now near me are Your people and those besieged are also Your priests, I beseech You not to hearken to the others against these nor to bring to pass that which these ask to be done to the others." So enraged were Hyrcanus's men when they heard this prayer that they at once stoned the man.[45]

The festival of Passover came, and since there were no animals within Jerusalem for the temple sacrifices, the priests asked their fellow Jews besieging the city to send them the animals, offering to pay any price. An exorbitant price was demanded, one thousand drachmas for each animal. Aristobulus and the priests agreed and let down the money by rope over the city walls. Hyrcanus's men took the money but broke their promise and did not deliver the animals. The disappointed priests prayed to God to punish these impious men who had defrauded them and the Temple. The punishment was not long delayed, for God sent a strong windstorm that destroyed all the crops of the land.[46]

During the changing episodes of the continuing civil war an arrangement was made for the besieged forces to lower gold dinars in a basket over the city wall each day in exchange for the animals required for the daily sacrifices. Among those within the city was a treacherous old man, learned in Greek culture. He sent word to the besiegers, "As long as the Temple service continues, those in the city will never fall before you." The next day, when the basket of dinars was lowered, a swine was sent up. Halfway up, its feet struck Jerusalem's wall and the land of Israel was shaken for a distance of four hundred miles.[47]

With the execution of Antigonus, son of Aristobulus, the Hasmonean dynasty came to an end.[48] There remained of the royal house only an unmarried woman who climbed to the roof and exclaimed, "Whoever will claim in the future to be a descendant of the Hasmonean house is but a slave!" Whereupon she leaped from the roof to her death.[49]

Notes

III. THE HASMONEAN PERIOD

1. The Greek Persecution and the Maccabean Revolt

1. Throughout this chapter and the following, "Greek" is used in the sense of the Hellenistic successor empire of the Seleucid kings of Syria.

2. 2 Macc. 3. Onias the high priest is Onias III; Seleucus is Seleucus IV Philopator. A similar tale is found in 3 Macc. telling of an attempt by Ptolemy Philopator to break into the Holy of Holies. The high priest prayed that God would defend the sanctity of His house, and a miracle occurred. God smote the king to the ground, paralyzing him in all his limbs. His retinue carried him away, and he left the city with angry threats. Victor Tcherikover (*Hellenistic Civilization and the Jews* [Philadelphia, 1959], p. 435, n. 98) believes that a comparison between the two stories points to the originality of 2 Macc. He says of the basic tale that it is "a legend of the usual Hellenistic type, and

I do not think it worthwhile to look for a historical germ in the story . . ." (ibid., p. 158). But he accepts as historical fact the dispatch of Heliodorus by Seleucus to confiscate the Temple gold and silver and the return of the envoy without them. Perhaps, he conjectures, an agreement may have been made between Onias and Heliodorus that was acceptable to both. Onias III was the son of Simon the Just. The bitter feeling between him and Simon, the Temple overseer, is explained by the internecine quarreling among the Jews as to whether their support should go to the Egyptian empire of the Ptolemies or the Syrian empire of the Seleucids, both successors to the domains of Alexander the Great. Tcherikover points out that Simon, who was the brother of Menelaus and Lysimachus, could not have been of the tribe of Benjamin as stated in 2 Macc. For how could Menelaus have served as high priest if he were a Benjaminite and not of priestly descent? However, the Latin translation of 2 Macc. reads "of the tribe of Belgea," this being the name of a well-known priestly clan, "Bilgah." (See Neh. 12:5 and the later story in this part about Miriam from the same priestly family.) This must have been the original correct reading. Simon evidently demanded an extension of power from the high priest who was becoming suspect by the supporters of the Seleucids as sympathetic to Ptolemy, as was Hyrcanus. In addition to his post as overseer of the Temple, Simon asked for the position of *agoranomos*, whose functions were administrative or juridical and perhaps even supervisory over markets and police. The exact functions of this post are unknown, but evidently its holder was a leading official vis-à-vis the ruling power, at this time, Seleucid Syria. When Onias refused his demand, Simon resorted to Appolonius, the Syrian governor of the provinces of Coele-Syria and Phoenicia, telling him that great wealth was stored in the Temple treasury. As to why moneys were kept in the Temple storehouses, temples in ancient times served as financial as well as religious centers. This was true in Babylonia, Egypt, Greece, and Rome. Josephus points out that great wealth accumulated in the Temple in Jerusalem (*Antiquities* 14.110). In addition to public funds, money of private individuals was also kept on deposit in the Temple treasury since it was the safest place in the city. Thus, in a sense it served as a forerunner to the modern bank. The Hyrcanus spoken of in the story was not the son of Tobias but his descendant, a member of a wealthy and influential family, which was related also to the family of the high priest (see Tcherikover, *Hellenistic Civilization*, chap. 4).

3. Genesis Rabbah 65:22. This story and the following one are linked in the Midrash with the verse Gen. 27:27, where a play on words reads *begadav*, "his raiment," as *bogdav*, "traitors against Him." Thus the verse is related to the wicked of Israel who ultimately sanctified God's name. *Shitta* is most likely a place-name.

4. See Mishnah Pe'ah 2:7.

5. Genesis Rabbah 65:22 and Midrash Tehillim on Ps. 11:7, with some slight variations between the two versions. Also Yalkut Shimoni, Genesis, 115. See Tcherikover, *Hellenistic Civilization*, pp. 228–31. He points out (p. 487, n. 47) that this legend has so many imaginary features that it cannot serve as a reliable historical source. Jakum or Jehoiakim or Alcimus was a man "who of his own free will had contaminated himself in the period of disturbances," in the words of 2

Macc. 14:3. The date of his appointment as high priest is not sufficiently clear in the sources (see 1 Macc. 7:5; 2 Macc. 14:3; and Josephus, *Antiquities*, 12.9.7), though Tcherikover believes that Josephus's chronology is apparently the correct one. Max Margolis and Alexander Marx, *A History of the Jewish People* (Philadelphia, 1945), p. 143 ff., state that Alcimus replaced the executed Menelaus as high priest in 163 B.C.E. See also Solomon Zeitlin, *The Rise and Fall of the Judaean State* (3 vols., Philadelphia, 1962–78), 1:112–20, who points out that Alcimus died of a paralytic stroke in the summer of 160 B.C.E.

Jakum is identified by historians as the high priest Alcimus, leader of the Hellenists among the Jews. It is possible that Ẓerorot is a corruption of Ẓeredah, the native city of Jose ben Joezer, his uncle. (Wolf Jawitz, *Toldot Yisrael* [14 vols. in 7, Tel Aviv, 1932–40], 4:108, n. 2.) See Abraham Geiger, *Das Judenthum und seine Geschichte* (Breslau, 1910), p. 64; G. F. Moore, *Judaism in the First Centuries of the Christian Era* (3 vols., Cambridge, Mass., 1950–54), 1:45; and Louis Finkelstein, *Ha-Perushim ve-Anshei Keneset ha-Gedolah* (New York, 1950), p. 57, who theorize that Jose was among the sixty pious Jews or company of scribes slain by Bacchides at the instigation of Alcimus the high priest. Geiger bases his theory upon the midrashic text that tells that Alcimus was present when his uncle Jose was led to his execution. Alcimus, reminded by his uncle of the retribution awaiting him, was then gripped by remorse and committed suicide. Sidney B. Hoenig, *The Great Sanhedrin* (New York, 1953), p. 29, rejects the entire theory.

A later version of the story is found in Midrash David, pp. 3–4. This version is more elaborate, telling that Jakum was an apostate who became a high ranking officer of the government with a hundred attendants carrying rods of gold. On a rainy day, when Jakum was riding in the street, one of his attendants pushed his uncle out of the way and into the mud. The nephew, seeing his uncle's plight, begged him to forsake Judaism and his poverty. No mention of the name Jakum is made in the story; the character is simply called "the apostate." Jose answered that if God gives such honor in this world to the wicked like his nephew, how much more honor would He bestow upon the righteous in the world to come. And if such poverty and suffering are the lot of the righteous in this world, how much greater would be the suffering of the wicked in Hell in the world to come. The words affected the apostate so that he at once returned home and divided his property in equal thirds—for his family, for the sages and the poor, and for his attendants. He then killed himself in the same elaborate fashion detailed in the earlier version. When God saw how he had repented and taken upon himself the four legal methods of execution, a voice from Heaven declared that he would be granted life in the world to come. This later version does not mention Jose's execution.

6. Leviticus Rabbah 13:5 commenting on Jer. 5:6, and Midrash le-Ḥanukkah.

7. Sukkah 23a, 56b, and Talmud Yerushalmi.

8. 2 Macc. 6:18–31.

9. 2 Macc. 7:1 et seq., and 4 Macc.; Gittin 57b; Lamentations Rabbah 1:16; Yalkut Shimoni on Lam. 2, Seder Eliyahu, chap. 28. The story, as found in Gittin, is quoted in the name of Rabbi Judah who tells it as an illustration of the verse, *It is for Your sake that we are slain all day long, that we are regarded as sheep to be slaughtered* (Ps. 44:23). A comprehensive article on the various versions of this

story in Jewish literature was written by Gerson D. Cohen in *Sefer Ha-yovel*, essays in honor of the seventieth birthday of Mordecai M. Kaplan, published by the Jewish Theological Seminary of America, New York, 1953, pp. 109–22.

The fullest versions of the story are found in Lamentations Rabbah and Seder Eliyahu. The version found in Midrash ha-Gadol, *parashah* Ki Tavo on Deut. 28:50, is an abbreviated rescension of the version in Lamentations Rabbah. Two shorter forms of the story are found in the Talmud, Gittin 57b, in Midrash Lamentations Zuta 21 (ed. S. Buber, Vilna, 1899, p. 69), and in Yalkut Lamentations 10:7–9, the talmudic version most likely serving as the basis for the others, the additions coming perhaps from the Lamentations Rabbah version. Still another version is found in Pesikta Rabbati, chap. 43, which differs from the other versions in a number of details. It served as the source for the story in Midrash Aseret ha-Dibrot (see Jellinek, *Bet ha-midrash* 1:70).

In all the versions in rabbinic literature, except for that in the Babylonian Talmud, the mother's name is given as Miriam, daughter of Tanhum or Menahem and the time as the period of the Hadrianic persecutions in the second century of the common era. But Cohen explains the transference of the date and the difference of the name by relating the later embellishments of the story to actual Roman legal practices, the historical conditions of the times, and similarities in early Christian martyrology.

Josippon 19 (in the longer rescension) gives the name of the heroine as Hannah and restores the date to the Maccabean period. It was this source that particularly influenced later medieval literature and the folk mind so that Hannah and her sons became a popular symbol for martyrdom (see Cohen, op. cit., p. 118). Cohen explains how Josippon came to call the heroine, nameless in the earliest version in the Book of Maccabees, by the name of Hannah (ibid., pp. 118–21). The story of Hannah and her seven sons, so popular among the people, was woven into the liturgy in *piyuttim* for the Sabbath of Hanukkah and Tisha B'Av (ibid., pp. 121–22). The popular folk volume, *Zena u-r'ena*, telling the story of its vast reading audience over the centuries, helped make the story of Hannah and her sons one of the most popular of all Jewish legends.

10. Exodus Rabbah 15:6 in a comment based on Ps. 19:7.

11. Megillah 11a. This passage is quoted in the Talmud as a variant baraita. Samuel, a third-century amora, interprets the several phrases of the verse as referring to the following: the days of Antiochus, the times of Vespasian, the days of Haman, the Roman period, and the future time of Gog and Magog.

12. So Ibn Ezra on Zech. 9:9; however, Rashi says that the verse can refer only to the Messiah.

13. See Rashi, Ibn Ezra, and other medieval Jewish commentators on Zech. 9:13–14. *Javan* is the Hebrew name for Greece. Jerome says that in his time the Jews interpreted this text as a reference "to the times of the Maccabees, who conquered the Macedonians, and after a space of three years and six months, cleansed the Temple defiled by idolatry."

14. Megillah 11a.

15. Genesis Rabbah 99:2. The Hasmoneans were *kohanim*, priests descended from Aaron who was of the tribe of Levi, the third son of Jacob. Hence the tribe of Levi was the third in the order of the tribes

of Israel. The rabbis spoke of four world empires: Babylonia, Persia, Greece, and Rome. Hence Greece—in this instance, the Syrian kingdom of the Seleucids is meant—was the third in order of the empires.

16. Shabbat 21b; Megillat Ta'anit 9.

17. Pesikta Rabbati 2; Menaḥot 28b for the story of the spits and Teshuvot Hage'onim for the story of the oil of Teko'a.

18. 2 Macc. 9; 1 Macc. 6; Josippon 9; see Josephus, *Antiquities*, 12.9.1.

19. Josippon 21, 22.

20. Ta'anit 18b; 1 Macc. 7; 2 Macc. 15. Nicanor was sent in the year 162–161 B.C.E. by Demetrius at the head of a strong army against Judah the Maccabee. See 1 Macc. 7:29; 2 Macc. 14:23 ff.; Josephus, *Antiquities*, 12.10.5. Previously, in the spring of 166 B.C.E. Nicanor had served as a general in the army of Lysias, sent by Antiochus IV to quell the Hasmonean revolt. Judah the Maccabee surprised Nicanor's army at Bet Ḥoran, about twelve miles from Jerusalem. He defeated it decisively, and Nicanor was slain. The date of the victory, I Adar 13, in the year 161 B.C.E. was declared a festive day to be celebrated annually as "Nicanor's Day."

21. Megillat Ta'anit 2:3; Megillah 6b.

22. Megillat Ta'anit 7; Rosh Ha-Shanah 5b.

23. Josippon 24; see also 1 Macc. 6:43–46; 2 Macc. 13:3–8; Josephus, *Antiquities*, 12.9.7. The two latter sources place Menelaus's death at the hands of the Syrians at Berea in Syria, his execution counseled by Lysias, although 2 Macc. says the suggestion was put in the king's mind by "The King of kings." The latter source also tells of death by suffocation among ashes, a cruel Persian practice (see Tcherikover, *Hellenistic Civilization*, p. 487, n. 44, citing Hugh Bévenot, *Die beiden Makkabaerbuecher*, Bonn, 1931).

Menelaus, brother of the Temple treasurer, Simon, a leader of the Seleucid party in Jerusalem, was appointed high priest to replace Jason and died in 163 B.C.E.

24. See the story about Miriam earlier in this chapter.

25. Sukkah 46b. The priests who ministered in the Temple were divided into twenty-four watches or groups, each serving its tenure in sequence during the course of the year.

2. The Hasmonean Rulers

26. Targum on Songs 6:7.

27. Josephus, *Antiquities*, 13.8.4.

28. Josephus, *Antiquities*, 13.9.1.

29. Sotah 33a and Songs Rabbah 8:9. See also Josephus, *Antiquities*, 13.10.3. The opinion of Margolis and Marx, *History of the Jewish People*, p. 152, is that this legend refers to the decisive victory won by Aristobulus and Antigonus, sons of John Hyrcanus, against the Samaritans. Despite the intervention of Antiochus IX Cyzicenus (113–95 B.C.E.) of Syria on the side of Samaria, the enemy was beaten and the Samaritan temple on Mount Gerizim was razed to the ground. The second source, Songs Rabbah, locates the battle at Antioch, a confusion with the name of the reigning king, Antiochus IX.

30. Sotah 33a and Songs Rabbah 8:9.

31. Berakhot 29a. Abaye, in the talmudic discussion, confuses John Hyrcanus with Alexander Yannai. Rava distinguishes between the two, father and son, and indicates that while Alexander Yannai sympathized with the Sadducees from the outset, Hyrcanus did so only toward the close of his reign. John Hyrcanus, son of Simon the Hasmonean, displayed attachment for the law. See Sotah 47a–b; also Sidney B. Hoenig, *The Great Sanhedrin*, p. 37, and Solomon Zeitlin, *Who Crucified Jesus?* (New York, 1942), and idem, "The Am Haarez," *Jewish Quarterly Review* 23 (1932):45–61, for the activities of John Hyrcanus in this regard.

The talmudic view is that John Hyrcanus appointed the first *zugot*, the "pairs" of scholars listed in Avot, chap. 1, the leading sages in the five generations preceding the tannaim. According to tradition, the first named of each pair was president (nasi) and the other, senior judge of the court (av bet din). See Sotah 9:10 and 48a and Yerushalmi Sotah 24a. But Hoenig, op. cit., p. 37, says this refers to the two overseers of the tithe collections who executed the king's decrees concerning *demai*, "dubious produce."

Margolis and Marx, *History of the Jewish People*, p. 153, say that the more traditional Jews objected to the assumption by John Hyrcanus of both the functions of king and high priest. In addition, the character of the Hasmonean dynasty was becoming more and more secular. Since these pietists were in the minority in the Council of State, they withdrew from participation in the government. Hence they became known as Pharisees or Separatists. Those allied with the government, being largely priests belonging to the Zadok clan, were called Sadducees. The rift thus started during the reign of John Hyrcanus widened under his successors.

Josephus, *Antiquities*, 13.10.5, says that "they that were the worst disposed to him [John Hyrcanus] were the Pharisees." But he indicates that earlier "Hyrcanus was a disciple of theirs and greatly beloved by them." According to Josephus the bitterness broke out after a certain Eleazar had charged that the king's mother had been a captive during the reign of Antiochus Epiphanes and that, therefore, John should lay down the high priesthood. The king was greatly provoked by this false story, and grew embittered at all the Pharisees because they said that Eleazar should be given a light sentence. Thereafter, influenced by his friend, Jonathan, a Sadducee, the king severed his associations with the Pharisees and nullified their decrees. This account is similar to the talmudic explanation of the rift between Alexander Yannai and the Pharisees.

32. Berakhot 44a. These tales and those following are obvious hyperboles to express the great extent of Yannai's kingdom and its prosperity. The second tale here and the one following are quoted in the Talmud in the name of the same amora, Ravin, as stories related by him when he came to Babylonia.

33. Gittin 57a; Yerushalmi Ta'anit 4:69a; Lamentations Rabbah 1–2:2. Notice the number of 600,000 for the total of the cities and the same number for the population of each city. The three larger cities have, supposedly, twice that number. Kfar Bish may be Capharabis in upper Idumea (see Lamentations Rabbah 1–2:2). Kfar Shiḥlayim may be a town, Shiḥlaya, in the mountains of Ephraim. The version in the Yerushalmi explains that this town was given its name because its dwellers raised their children with great care, as carefully as watercress

must be cultivated. The version in Lamentations Rabbah says it is because the inhabitants raised their children on dishes of watercress.

34. Numbers Rabbah 22:1.

35. Exod. 21:29. The clause, *And warning has been given to its owners*, is interpreted in the Talmud (Sanhedrin 19a) to mean that the owner must appear in court together with his goring ox.

36. Deut. 19:17–18. *The two parties to the dispute shall appear before the Lord, before the priests or magistrates in authority at the time and the magistrates shall make a thorough investigation.*

37. Sanhedrin 19a–b, and Midrash Tanḥuma, Judges 6:26. The Talmud tells the story to explain why the rabbis ruled that kings of Israel must neither judge nor be judged. However, the rule does not apply to kings of the Davidic dynasty. The Tanḥuma version varies slightly. Hoenig, *The Great Sanhedrin*, p. 186, says that historically the reference here is believed to apply to Herod's trial (see Josephus, *Antiquities*, 14.9.3).

38. Kiddushin 66a. See supra, n. 5, and the narration of a similar tale by Josephus, *Antiquities*, 13.10.5. There, however, the king is John Hyrcanus, father of Alexander Yannai, and the villain is Jonathan, a Sadducee and the king's friend. See also Berakhot 48a.

39. Berakhot 48a.

40. It is only the last part of this quotation that comes from Ben Sira (or Ecclesiasticus) 11:1; the first part is from Prov. 4:8. For the offerings required of the Nazirite see Num. 6:14.

41. This tale, similar in certain respects to the previous one, is found in Genesis Rabbah 91:3; Ecclesiastes Rabbah 7:12; Berakhot 48a; Yerushalmi Berakhot, chap. 7, and Nazir, chap. 5.

42. Sotah 22b; Yerushalmi Sotah, chap. 3:4; for the story of Zimri and Phinehas see Num. 25:1–15.

43. Josephus, *Antiquities*, 13.13.5; see also Mishnah Sukkah 4:9, and Tosefta Sukkah 3:16. The general assumption is that these rabbinic sources, which do not name the offender, refer to Yannai. Zeitlin disagrees, *The Rise and Fall of the Judean State*, 1:498, n. 32, and idem, *Ha-Zedukim ve-ha-Perushim* (Jerusalem, 1936), p. 26, n. 92.

44. Megillat Ta'anit 11. See Josephus, *Antiquities*, 13.15.5, which tells a different story of Alexander Yannai's death; cf. Josephus, *Wars*, 1.4.6. It is of interest to note that some scholars identify Alexander Yannai with "the Wicked Priest" of the Dead Sea Scrolls.

45. Josephus, *Antiquities*, 14.2.1.

46. Josephus, *Antiquities*, 2.2.14.

47. Sotah 49b; Menaḥot 64b; Bava Kamma 82b; Yerushalmi Berakhot 16b–17a. The first two sources place the armies as in our story. The third source says the opposite, that the besiegers were the followers of Aristobulus while Hyrcanus and his men were within the city. Dio Cassius reports a violent earthquake in the Middle East in the year 65 B.C.E., and Justin tells that 170,000 lives were lost, with many cities destroyed in the Syrian earthquake. See Zeitlin, *The Rise and Fall of the Judean State*, 1:347–48 and 501, nn. 17–20.

48. Josephus, *Antiquities*, 14.16.4.

49. Kiddushin 70b. "A slave," because, as Rashi explains, Herod killed off all the Hasmonean house and then misappropriated the name of the dynasty. Since he himself had once been a slave, those descended from him merited not the Hasmonean title but that of Herod's original status, "slave."

Part IV

The Apocrypha

1

The Story of Tobit[1]

Tobit was a man of Galilee of the tribe of Naphtali, but unlike the others who worshiped the golden calf erected by Jeroboam, Tobit was a faithful Jew who would go regularly to the Temple in Jerusalem. He scrupulously observed the law of the tithes and the firstfruits. His wife's name was Hannah, and his son's name, like his own, Tobias.[2] He taught his son to revere the Lord and to refrain from doing evil.[3]

When the Jews of the northern kingdom of the Ten Tribes were exiled to Nineveh in Assyria, Tobit and his family were with them, but he did not eat forbidden foods as did the rest. Moreover, he observed all the laws of God and the prescribed statutes. He walked always in the way of truth and justice and did that which was right in the eyes of God. He was particularly a fortress of strength to the poor, coming to their aid at all times.

The Lord, therefore, blessed him, and he enjoyed the favor of King Shalmaneser, ruler of Assyria, whose purchasing agent he became. He went about among all his exiled brothers, comforting them and lifting up their spirits. He gave alms to the needy, bread to the hungry, clothing to the naked, and whenever he saw the abandoned corpse of a Jew, he himself would bury it.[4] In his traveling, he once came to the city of Ragae[5] in Media, and finding there a poor Jew in need of help, he loaned him ten talents of silver and took a receipt for the sum.

When Shalmaneser died and was succeeded by his son Sennacherib, the fortunes of Tobit changed. The new king hated the Jews, and when he returned from his debacle in Judah, in his anger he had many of the Jews executed. Tobit buried the bodies, against the king's orders. When the king learned of it, he ordered Tobit killed and his possessions confiscated. Tobit hid with his kinsmen, but he himself lost everything. Soon, however, the king was assassinated and the new ruler, Esarhaddon, appointed Aḥikar,

Tobit's nephew, as his vizier, and Tobit's home was restored to him.

Despite the fact that the royal edict prohibiting the burial of executed Jews remained in force, Tobit resumed his pious practice of performing this righteous deed, but only after nightfall when none might see. Once, when so engaged, a bird's droppings fell into his eyes; a white film formed, and he became blind, so that he was compelled to rely upon his wife's labor for support. She taunted him, asking of what avail was all his piety. In his distress he prayed to God, acknowledging divine justice but asking that death relieve him from his torment.

Meanwhile, in the distant city of Ecbatana in Media a similar prayer was being offered by a woman in great grief. Sarah, daughter of Raguel, had been married seven times, but each time the demon Asmodeus[6] had slain the husband in the bridal chamber. Her maids mocked her and she too prayed for death. The Lord heard the prayers of Tobit and Sarah, and the angel Raphael[7] was sent to bring healing to both.

Tobit remembered that he had once loaned a sum of money to a Jew in Ragae in Media, and, being now in need, he sent his son to collect it. But first he gave him a series of ethical and moral admonitions because the younger man was now going out on his own into the world. He directed him to find a guide and traveling companion for the journey, and Tobias engaged the angel Raphael, now disguised as a man named Azariah, and the two set off together.

At the end of the first day's journey they reached the river Tigris[8] at whose banks they lodged for the night. When Tobias went to wash in its waters a great fish leaped forth and frightened him. Raphael instructed him to seize the fish by its fins and drag it out upon the dry land, then slit it open and extract its heart, liver, and gall. These Tobias salted and wrapped well, and he took them with him when they continued the journey. He asked the angel Raphael, whom he knew as the man Azariah, of what good were these fish organs. Raphael explained that the smoke rising from the heart and liver placed on a fire could drive away evil spirits, while the gall was useful for healing blindness.[9]

Arriving in Ecbatana, they visited Sarah's father Raguel, a kinsman of Tobit. Her sad story had been told Tobias by his guide who had impressed upon him his religious obligation to marry Sarah since Tobias was her only marriageable kinsman.[10] The young man feared the fate of Sarah's previous husbands, but Azariah reassured him that the fish's heart and liver would be efficacious against evil spirits. Tobias was warmly greeted by Raguel, who consented to give his daughter in marriage to her kinsman.

That night in the marriage chamber, Tobias remembered the words of his guide, and he placed the fish's heart and liver upon the hot coals of the hearth. The smoke drove away the evil spirit who was then banished by Raphael to Upper Egypt. The young couple rose from their bed to pray and then peacefully slept through the night.[11] The grave already prepared by Raguel for his latest son-in-law was happily not needed for Tobias, and the marriage feasting continued for fourteen days. In the midst of it, Tobias sent Azariah to Ragae to collect the money due his father, and Azariah did so. Upon the completion of the feasting, Raguel insisted upon dividing his property with his son-in-law, and his half remaining would go to Tobias after the death of Raguel and his wife. Thus personally enriched and in possession of the considerable sum belonging to his father, Tobias, together with Sarah and Azariah, set out on the homeward journey. Tobias's parents had worried about him because of his long absence, and his mother had chided his father for having sent him on so perilous a journey. But Tobit assured his querulous wife that their son would return.

Approaching Nineveh, Azariah instructed Tobias to go ahead with him, taking the fish's gall. Tobias's mother ran out to greet them, and blind Tobit, too, stumbled forward. Tobias anointed his father's eyes with the gall, and when the eyes smarted, Tobit rubbed them. The white layer upon them fell away, and Tobit could see again. He wept and offered thanks to God. Tobias told his parents of all that had befallen him, and they went to the city gates to welcome Sarah. A second wedding feast was held for seven days.

Tobit reminded his son to reward his extraordinary guide handsomely, and Tobias offered Azariah half of all he had brought back with him. But Azariah then took father and son aside and revealed to them that he was the angel Raphael, one of the seven holy angels, and that he had been sent by God to answer the prayers of both Tobit and Sarah. He exhorted them to do good, to give charity, to pray, to fast, and to praise God; then he vanished. Tobit offered a prayer of rejoicing and thanksgiving in which he predicted a glorious future for Jerusalem.[12]

He lived to a very old age to see his children's children. He warned Tobias to move the entire family to Media, for Jonah's prophecy about Nineveh's destruction would one day be fulfilled. The Jews, he predicted, would return from their exile to build a second Temple in Jerusalem, not quite like the first. But when that next age would end, all the Jews would come back from their various places of exile and build up the Temple and Jerusalem gloriously, as the prophets had spoken. Then all the nations would bury their idols and worship God.

After the death of his parents, Tobias departed with his wife and children to Ecbatana. There he came into possession of the full estate of his father-in-law. Before he himself died, a very old man, he heard the news of the destruction of Nineveh and the news pleased him greatly.

━━ **2** ━━

The Story of Judith[13]

Nebuchadnezzar, the king of Assyria, sent a powerful army, under the command of his general Holofernes, to war against Judea. For the Jews had earlier spurned his request for help against his enemy Arphaxad, who reigned over the Medes in Ecbatana.[14] Holofernes marched his mighty forces across many lands, conquering, looting, and destroying as he went, until he came to Bethulia[15] in Judea. The Jews, who had only recently returned from captivity, were afraid for the Temple and Jerusalem, as well as for themselves. Therefore, Joachim, the high priest,[16] charged the defenders of Bethulia to stand fast, for the conquest of their town would lay bare the passages through the hill country toward Jerusalem. Then all the people of Israel fasted and prayed, crying aloud to their God to save them.

When Holofernes learned that the Jews were preparing to

resist him, he became very angry and summoned the princes of the neighboring countries to Judea to explain to him the nature of this people. The leader of his Ammonite allies, Achior, related to him the history of the Jews and pointed out that only when they disobeyed their God could the Jews be overcome. As long as they are faithful, no one can subdue them. The words of Achior[17] infuriated the other chieftains present at the war council, and they would have slain him. But Holofernes intervened and, expressing his contempt for the God of Israel, he ordered Achior bound and cast at the foot of the hill below Bethulia.

The Jews of the town took him in, and, after listening to his story, they praised him greatly. But then the Assyrians seized the springs outside the town from which the people obtained their water and laid siege to the town. The Jews suffered greatly from thirst, and they demanded that their elders surrender the city. This they agreed to do if God sent no deliverance within five days.

There lived in Bethulia a pious and virtuous widow, Judith, a woman of great beauty. She rebuked the elders for their readiness to yield and for presuming to put God to the test. They could not understand the workings of a man's heart. How could they search out God and know His mind or comprehend His purpose? Yet, she assured them, on that very night she and her servant would go forth from the city, and within five days the Lord would bring deliverance by her hand.

After having prayed for strength, she dressed herself in her finest garments and jewels and gave food and wine[18] to her maid to carry. They left the city and made their way to the Assyrian camp and to the tent of Holofernes. When halted by guards she explained that she knew an effective way to overcome the defenders of Bethulia; the plan itself she set before Holofernes. The Jewish leaders, she reported, had inquired of the authorities in Jerusalem whether, in their hunger and thirst, they might eat food normally forbidden them—the firstfruits and the tithes usually designated for use in the Temple. When permission would be forthcoming, she would inform Holofernes, and he would then be able to destroy them that very day. For only when the Jews disobey their God can they fall before their enemies. God had sent her as His instrument to Holofernes. She and her maid would remain in his camp, and each night, with his consent, she would go forth into the valley below the city to pray alone to her

God.[19] He would tell her when the Jews would have broken His laws, and she would then inform the general.

Holofernes was greatly taken by her beauty and agreed to the plan. At his command she was permitted to go freely from the camp at night into the valley. She ate only of her own food and, each night, she would go to the valley, bathe in the waters of the fountain there, and offer her prayers.

On the fourth day Holofernes made a feast and instructed Bagros,[20] his eunuch, to persuade Judith to join him. Judith agreed and dressed in her finest clothes. At the feast, she ate and drank only what her maid had prepared. When the banquet was over and all had withdrawn except for Judith and Holofernes, he fell into a drunken sleep. From the moment he had first seen her he had planned to deceive her, but now the wine had proved to be his undoing.[21] She offered a brief prayer for the success of her mission, then quickly drew his sword and cut off his head.[22] Together with her maid, she left the camp as was their usual practice each night, the head of Holofernes in her provision bag. Judith went straight away to Bethulia and displayed the general's head to the people. Achior identified the head and, overwhelmed by this display of God's protection of Israel, at once asked to be converted to Judaism.

At the advice of Judith the head was hung on the city wall the next morning, and the Jewish soldiers charged forth to the attack. The Assyrians, having discovered the loss of their leader, were thrown into a panic. They fled in all directions with the Jews in pursuit, leaving behind great spoil.[23]

The high priest and the elders of Jerusalem came to Bethulia to hail Judith. She sang a song of thanksgiving, in which she was joined by all the people. For three months, feasting continued in Jerusalem before the Sanctuary where the people offered their sacrifices and gifts. Judith dedicated to the Lord the possessions of Holofernes that had been given her. She lived to old age in great honor, and none attacked the children of Israel during her lifetime or for a long time afterward.

The Story of Susanna [24]

Susanna was the beautiful wife of Joachim, a leading Jew of Babylon. Besides being beautiful she was a pious woman, having been taught the law of Moses by her parents. Her husband was a wealthy man with a large house and garden to which the leaders of the Jewish community often came. Two of these elders became greatly enamored of her but were ashamed to confess their lust for her to each other. Yet they daily kept a diligent watch to see her. One day after gazing upon her, they parted, supposedly each to go to his home to dine. But then each stealthily made his way back, and encountering one another, they openly acknowledged their passion for her. They then plotted to find her alone in the garden, and this came to pass one warm day when Susanna went into the garden to bathe. She sent her two maids into the house to bring her bath oil and washing balls, and she told them to shut the garden doors. The elders, who had hidden, now came out and threatened to swear that they had found her in the arms of a lover, if she would not submit to them. She repulsed them and cried for help. The elders shouted too, and when the servants of the house came running, they insisted that they had surprised her with a youthful lover, and that they had attempted to seize him but he had gotten away.[25]

When she was brought to trial the next day before the assembly of the people, the elders testified against her. She was found guilty of adultery and condemned to death, for the elders constituted the two witnesses required by Jewish law for the true establishment of a fact.[26]

She prayed to God and the Lord heard her voice. As she was being led to the execution, a young man by the name of Daniel[27] came forth from the crowd to halt the proceedings. He was not convinced of her guilt, he declared, and could not share the responsibility of the people in condemning her to death.[28] He asked them to return to the place of the trial and there he examined the two witnesses separately, asking each elder under which tree in the garden the tryst of Susanna and her supposed lover had taken place. The first said under a mastic tree, to which Daniel sternly proclaimed that God's angel would masticate him.[29] The second elder said under an oak tree and Daniel replied that the angel of God would cut him in two. The people perceived the contradiction in the testimony of the two elders. The two lying witnesses had convicted themselves by their own words.[30] According to the law of Moses they were sentenced to that which they had maliciously intended to do to their victim. They were both executed while Susanna was set free.[31]

Notes

IV. THE APOCRYPHA

1. The Story of Tobit

1. The story of Tobit is recounted in the Book of Tobit, a work of the Apocrypha. Scholars differ as to the date, the place, and the original language of this book. Tobit's reference, in his last prayer, to a seemingly inferior building of the then existing Temple would seem to place the date of the composition of the book well before the time of Herod who refurbished the Second Temple. It was most likely written about 200 B.C.E. in Egypt and certainly before the Maccabean uprising. Some scholars argue that the original language was Hebrew, for the style of the book and its prayers and speeches would fit that language more naturally. If that is so, its purpose would have been to remind the Jews living in Egypt in Hellenistic times of the ideal Jew portrayed in the character of Tobit, of his devotion to God's law even in exile, of his complete trust in God, and his faith even amidst affliction. Other scholars maintain that the book was written in Greek, not only for Hellenized Jews but also to exalt the Jewish ideal in the eyes of the gentiles and win them over to Judaism.

2. The name of the son is identical with that of his father—*Tuviah*, in Hebrew—but to avoid confusing the two, the name Tobias has been here retained for the son, as is usually found in English translations.

3. Tobit is the ideal Jew, revering God and doing good to his fellowman. He is observant of both the ritual and the ethical injunctions. Living in exile, he is devoted to the land of Israel. He is kind and com-

passionate not for the sake of reward but because this way of life inherited from his ancestors he hopes to bequeath to his children. When smitten with blindness, even as a result of his performing a good deed at the risk of his life, he does not complain, but sees in it a test of his faith in and love for God. He reminds us of Job, but the explanation offered here of the suffering of the righteous is that it constitutes a divine test of man. Tobit withstands the test. He attempts to transmit his faith to his wife and, especially, to his son, whom he also instructs in ethical and moral behavior.

4. The burial of the dead is an important *mizvah* in Judaism. It is "the last kindness," the "kindness of truth," since the dead cannot reciprocate by giving any reward to the living. It is among those righteous deeds for which no limit is prescribed (Mishnah Pe'ah 1:1).

5. Ragae or Rhages was an ancient city on whose site Teheran now stands.

6. Asmodeus is frequently described as the king of the evil spirits. Although the name is possibly derived from the Hebrew word *shamod*, "to destroy" (so Asmodeus would be "the destroyer"), more likely the origin comes from the Persian *Aëshma Daëva*, meaning "evil spirit." Despite the fact that the author of the story of Tobit stresses the ideal Jew and the purity and strength of his faith, there are mixtures of Persian and Egyptian influences in the story. One pagan tale of antiquity, the Egyptian work *The Tractate of Khons*, describes how Khons, the Theban deity, cast out a demon from a princess. Part of its action, like the Book of Tobit, is placed in Ecbatana; the use of the organs of the fish for healing resembles some practices of Egyptian medicine, and the story of Aḥikar, well known in Egypt, also influenced the author of Tobit.

The Persian influence can be seen especially in the appearance of angels and demons, a new development in Judaism, but common in Persian religion. In the complete story a dog follows Tobias on his travels, recalling the dog that accompanied the Persian Sraosha on his journey. The dog was sacred in Zoroastrianism but generally despised by Jews.

There are other pagan tales that describe how virtuous men perform the good deed of burying the uncared for dead. However, in such stories the dead return to this earth to reward their kind benefactors. This is not true here, where Tobit is given his recompense by God. However, because of the mingling of Greek and Jewish ideas, Goodspeed suggests that Tobit was written in Egypt where under the Ptolemies Greek and Jewish currents of thought mingled freely. (See Edgar Goodspeed, *The Story of the Apocrypha* [Chicago, 1939], p. 13.)

7. As noted in n. 6, the appearance of angels is a new phenomenon in Judaism and reflects Persian influence, probably in the Magian stage of the Persian religious development. Tobit, in turn, influenced the New Testament, foreshadowing the very specific demonology and celestial hierarchy of the Gospels and Revelation (see Goodspeed, op. cit., pp. 18–19). Raphael, like Gabriel and Michael, is among the seven holy angels (Rev. 12:15). Joseph of Arimathea is like Tobit in his scrupulous observance of the *mizvah* of burial of the dead (cf. Matt. 27: 57–59; Mark 15:43–46; Luke 23:50–53; John 19:38–40). The story of Sarah and her seven husbands has its parallel in the Sadducees' story of the woman who had seven husbands and no children (Matt. 22:23–28).

The picture of the New Jerusalem in the twenty-first chapter of Revelation is reminiscent of Tobit's dream of the future glory of Jerusalem with its jeweled walls and gold battlements.

8. The author of Tobit errs in the geography of southwestern Asia, which would not be unnatural for an Egyptian Jew. He writes as though the Tigris were east of Nineveh on the way to Ecbatana (Tob. 6:1), as the Greeks supposed. In reality Nineveh was located on the east bank of the river.

9. The use here made of the organs of the fish was similar to actual practices of Egyptian doctors.

10. This is reminiscent of the practice of levirate marriage; see also the biblical stories of Tamar (Gen. 38) and Ruth (3:9–12, 4:5–10).

11. In the Vulgate version of Tobit and, therefore, in the earliest English Bibles, Tobias and Sarah are depicted as having devoted the first three nights after their marriage to prayer and postponing the consummation of their marriage until the fourth night. This, therefore, became the religious ideal of pious Christians in the Middle Ages. It was followed by Louis IX (Saint Louis) of France and his queen upon their marriage in 1234. In the earliest Book of Common Prayer (1549), the ideal pair is not Abraham and Sarah, but Tobias and Sarah: "And as Thou didst send Thy angel Raphael to Thobie and Sarah, the daughter of Raguel, to their great comfort, so vouchsafe to send Thy blessing to these Thy servants."

12. See supra, n. 7.

2. The Story of Judith

13. See the Book of Judith in the Apocrypha. The story is reminiscent of that of Jael and Sisera (Judg. 4). Scholars generally agree that Judith was written during the second century B.C.E., perhaps at the time of the Maccabean struggle or soon afterward. A clue to the latest possible date is found in the mention of Ashdod (Jth. 2:28), which was desolated by Jonathan about 147 B.C.E., and it seems to have been still inhabited at the time of the writing of Judith. Philo says that the book was written by Jeshua, son of Jozadak the high priest, near the beginning of the Second Commonwealth. It was probably written in Hebrew and soon translated into Greek, perhaps by Alexandrian Jews. The Hebrew original was lost, and the current Hebrew versions are translations from the Greek and Latin.

The story of Judith as found in the minor midrashim differs in many details from the apocryphal text (see J. D. Eisenstein, Ozar midrashim [New York, 1915], 1:203–9; Jellinek, Bet ha-midrash, 2:12–22, whose version is that found in Nathan Haazati, Ḥemdat yamim, vol. 2 [Livorno, 1763]). The latter version is not a literal translation of the apocryphal book but a free retelling of the story with an enlargement of the various prayers offered by Judith and the Jews of the city. An abbreviated version of the story by Rabbi Nissim ben Jacob was printed in Amsterdam without Judith's name ever being mentioned. Another version with the king's name as Achior was printed in Venice (1650) and in Mantua (1725) in Sippur ha-ma'asim. The longer version of the story was translated into Hebrew by Rabbi Akiba Levi of Halberstadt in 1679. A German translation by Meir ben Asher

Katz of Königsberg was printed together with *Megillat Antiochus* in Berlin in 1766. A brief version of the story of Judith, *Ma'aseh Yehudit*, is found in Jellinek, *Bet ha-midrash*, 1:130–31, where it is the king of the Greeks who is the villain. In this version the story of Judith is linked with the Maccabees and the story of Hanukkah, and this was the popular belief during the Middle Ages. In the *yozer* prayers for the first Sabbath of Hanukkah, "Aliforni" is a Greek king besieging Zion. Judith cuts off his head, and it is this that is the miracle of Hanukkah and the reason for the recital of *Hallel* and the kindling of the candles.

14. The story of Judith, although not historical, includes historical names. Nebuchadnezzar historically, of course, was the king of Babylonia who destroyed the First Temple. Holofernes was a general in the army of Artaxerxes Ochus, 359–338 B.C.E. This Persian king, who ruled just prior to Alexander's conquests, sent his army against Syria and Egypt, which had rebelled against him, under the command of Holofernes. It is possible that the Jews too had participated in the rebellion. The name of Arphaxad appears in Gen. 10:22 as one of the sons of Shem and a grandson of Noah.

15. This is most likely a fictitious name. In other versions of the story the locale is Jerusalem itself (see Jellinek, op. cit.). Such a town, either in the Valley of Jezreel or near to the approaches to Jerusalem and the Judean hills, may have figured in the campaign of Artaxerxes Ochus. Goodspeed, *The Story of the Apocrypha*, p. 45, says it may mean Shechem.

16. In the version printed in Jellinek, *Bet ha-midrash*, 2:12–22, (and elsewhere), the head of the Jews is Uzziah ben Micah, the prince ruling over Israel.

17. In *Midrash le-Ḥanukkah* the role of Achior is taken by the king's astrologer and counselor.

18. In Jellinek's version, Judith's provisions consist mainly of cheese and milk. The original author of the tale wished to show the importance of observing Jewish law faithfully at all times and places, and all through the story runs the constant concern for observing the law in matters of food, fasts, ablutions, tithes, and firstfruits.

19. In Jellinek's version, Judith asks permission to leave the camp at night and at dawn.

20. The name of a participant in the Egyptian campaign of Artaxerxes Ochus of Persia in 351 B.C.E., in which the Jews were involved.

21. In some of the versions Holofernes is gentlemanly and asks Judith to be his wife.

22. Judith with the head of Holofernes was a favorite subject of Renaissance artists, as was Tobias walking with his guide, and Susanna surprised by the elders.

23. This is perhaps reminiscent of the Hasmonean victory over Nicanor (2 Macc. 15:35–36).

3. The Story of Susanna

24. The word, "Susanna," in Hebrew, *Shoshanah*, means "lily" (see Hos. 14:6). It may have been chosen for the name of the heroine because of its association with purity. It is not found in the Jewish

Bible as a proper name, but in the New Testament it appears in Luke 8:3 as the name of one of the women who took care of Jesus.

25. In the Roman legend concerning Tarquin and Lucrece, the latter is put to a similar test. The story also recalls that of the adulterous woman in John 8:1–11, although the details are different.

26. See Num. 35:30; Deut. 17:6.

27. The name Daniel in Hebrew means "God is my judge" and, therefore, its bearer might have been thought to be possessed of special gifts enabling him to ferret out conspiracies to pervert justice. Because of the name of the young hero this story, evidently written in Hebrew early in the first century before the common era, was combined with the Greek translation of the Book of Daniel after first being rewritten and expanded. It is one of the three additions to Daniel made by the Greek translators, the others being the Song of the Three Holy Children and Bel and the Dragon, both contained in the Apocrypha. Daniel, written in Hebrew and Aramaic at about the time of the Maccabean revolt, 165 B.C.E., was embellished with these three short additions when it was translated into Greek about a century later. The Septuagint placed Susanna and Bel and the Dragon at the end of the Book of Daniel. But another translator, Theodotion, early in the second century of the common era, thought Daniel's youthful victory on behalf of justice ought properly to serve as the earliest chapter in his story and, therefore, set it at the beginning of the Book of Daniel. The early Church preferred this latter version and the order found in the Septuagint was almost completely forgotten: only a single Greek manuscript of it survives. The Book of Susanna, as the first part of the Greek text of the Book of Daniel, was part of the Greek Bible of the early Church. Among the Church Fathers, Irenaeus and Tertullian quoted it; Hippolytus allegorized it; Origen's friend, Julius Africanus, challenged it; and Origen defended it. (Julius Africanus, in a letter written about 240 C.E., argued that the story could not be accepted as part of the text of Daniel since the Greek plays on words in the names of the trees in the story's climax mark it of Greek, not of Hebrew or Aramaic origin, and the style of the Greek was too good to be a translation. Origen defended the Hebrew origin of the story of Susanna but admitted that he could get no Hebrew parallels for any such plays on words from Jews he had questioned.) Jerome, in the Vulgate, placed the story of Susanna at the end of Daniel. The Church of England has a liturgical reading from Susanna in November. The Roman Catholic Church has such a reading during Lent, and among the prayers of the Church is found, "Lord, free the soul of thy servant as thou didst free Susanna from a false charge." The first English Bibles called it a "Story," the King James Version the "History of Susanna."

28. See Lev. 24:14.

29. In the Greek version there is a play on words in associating each of the two trees with the punishment by the angel.

30. A Jewish tradition identifies the two lying, lascivious elders with the two false prophets Ahab and Zedekiah (Jer. 29:21–23), whom Jeremiah described as having performed vile deeds for which they were executed by the king of Babylon.

31. See Deut. 19:19. Goodspeed, *Story of the Apocrypha*, pp. 65–66, 69, supports the theory that the story of Susanna was written during the early years of the first century before the common era in order to

urge acceptance of the law concerning the offering of false testimony. The Pharisees, the party of the people, suffered from the hatred of the Hasmonean king, Alexander Yannai, who had thousands of them killed. Their leader was Simon beh Shetah. The Sadducees, the party of the aristocracy and close to the king, arranged through false witnesses to have the son of Simon beh Shetah, leader of the Pharisees, condemned to death. Before he could be executed, however, the witnesses confessed that they had testified falsely. Under the law, since the execution had not taken place, they could not be punished. The Pharisees pressed for a reinterpretation of the law so that perjurers could be punished whether or not their intended victim had actually been executed through their false testimony. It was to stimulate this interpretation of the law, Goodspeed says, that the tale of Susanna was written. When the Pharisees came to power after the death of Alexander Yannai in 76 B.C.E., they reorganized the Sanhedrin and required a more rigorous examination of accusatory witnesses. Goodspeed concludes that a gifted Pharisee of Jerusalem wrote Susanna in Hebrew, and not long after in Egypt it was translated and expanded in Greek and added on to the Greek translation of Daniel. It finally became (in Theodotion's Greek translation of the second century of the common era) the introduction to Daniel. Perhaps the original brief Hebrew text, long since lost, did not contain the Greek puns on the names of the trees nor call the young hero Daniel.

Part V

The Second Temple

1

The Building of the Second Temple

Three times was the Temple destined to be built within the territory of the tribe of Benjamin: once in the days of Solomon, again in the days of the exiles who returned from Babylonia, and the third time in the future days of the Messiah.[1] But it was from the tribe of Judah that Solomon came, who built the First Temple, and Zerubbabel, who built the Second Temple; and from that tribe will come the Messiah who will rebuild the Temple.[2] In a vision God showed Adam the events of the distant future, that Nebuchadnezzar would destroy the Temple but that Darius would authorize its rebuilding.[3]

The study of Torah, however, is more important than the building of the Temple, as can be seen from the fact that as long as Ezra's teacher, Baruch ben Neriah, lived, Ezra did not leave Babylonia for Jerusalem.[4] Among the families who left Babylonian exile to return to Jerusalem were those of Bakbuk, Hakufa, and Harhur, an illustration of unpleasant names associated with pleasant deeds. The family names connote "doubt," "smiting," and "anger" respectively, yet these were among the families who were privileged to go up to Jerusalem to rebuild the Temple.[5]

King Ahasuerus, or Artaxerxes, at first wished to issue a decree permitting the rebuilding of the Temple, but his queen, Vashti, persuaded him not to do so. She argued, "Would you build what my ancestors have destroyed?" and therefore she met her unhappy fate.[6] Because he hindered the construction of the Temple, Ahasuerus ruled over only half the world.[7] When the king was told in a letter by Rehum, his chancellor, and Shimshai the scribe, the son of Haman, that the Jews were the kind of people who would not pay taxes such as the land tax or poll tax or do forced labor, he ordered a halt on the construction of the Temple.[8] Scripture equated him, therefore, with Nebuchadnezzar, who destroyed the Temple, whereas he hindered its rebuilding.[9]

But his son, Darius, ordered that the Temple's construction go forward. When Darius renewed the permission to build the Temple, originally given by Cyrus, his counselors came before him and asked, "Your father decreed it should not be built. Will you order to the contrary, seeing that the laws of the Medes and Persians are unalterable?"

He said to them, "Bring the scrolls from the archives." They did so at once and pointed to the earlier royal decree, which read, "Make you now a decree to cause these men to cease."

But he queried, "Does that say that it would be for all time? Does the text not also say, 'Until another decree shall be issued by me'? Perhaps if my father were alive today he would have issued a new decree permitting the resumption of the building of the Temple."[10]

In the rebuilding of the Temple Haggai the prophet showed the people the plan of the altar and Zechariah marked its exact location. The third prophet of the time, Malachi, taught the people that sacrifices might be offered on the holy place even before the completion of the Temple.[11] While they were excavating for the Temple the workmen found the skull of Aronah the Jebusite, the original owner of the site in the days of David. The priests, unlearned and inexperienced, could not decide if the place was thereby ritually defiled or not, and the prophet Haggai, therefore, rebuked them.[12] When the first altar was dedicated in the wilderness in the days of Moses, sixty rams, sixty goats, and sixty lambs were sacrificed. These numbers symbolize the Second Temple, whose dimensions were sixty cubits high by sixty cubits wide.[13] So great was the poverty among the Jews who built the Second Temple that their fare consisted of saltplants of the desert.[14]

Herod later rebuilt the Temple in glorious fashion, which happened because of his sense of guilt and the advice given him by the rabbi, Baba ben Buta, to help him ease it. Herod the Idumean had been a slave in the royal house of the Hasmoneans and had set his eyes upon a maiden of the royal family.[15] One day he heard a mysterious voice that said that the day was propitious for any slave who would rebel. Whereupon he slew all the Hasmoneans except for the young girl. When she understood that he was planning to marry her, she ascended to the roof and cried out, "Should anyone in the future claim that he is descended from the Hasmoneans, he lies! He is descended only from a former slave. For no one is left of the Hasmoneans but myself and now I shall put an end to my life!" She then leaped from the roof and was killed. Herod took her corpse and preserved it for seven years in a honey compound, seeking to create the impression that she was not dead but married to him, thus validating his seizure of the throne.

But Herod was concerned lest the rabbis stir up popular opposition to him, for they were familiar with the scriptural injunction, *Be sure to set as king over yourself one of your own people; you must not set a foreigner over you, one who is not your kinsman* (Deut. 17:15). He, therefore, killed all the rabbis except for Baba ben Buta whom he spared so as to have him available as a counselor. But he had him blinded.

One day Herod came to visit him and, disguising his voice, said, "Look what that shameful slave, Herod, has done! He has killed all the rabbis and the men of authority." The rabbi replied, "What can I do about it?" "Curse him!" was the answer. "No, for it is written, *Don't revile a king even among your intimates* (Eccles. 10:20)." To which Herod retorted, "But in reality he is not a king."

"Even if he were only a rich man, I could not do it either," said the rabbi, "for the same verse goes on to say, *Don't revile a rich man even in your bedchamber.*"

"But," argued Herod, "Is it not written, *You shall not . . . put a curse upon a chieftain among your people* (Exod. 22:27) and that must mean only when the ruler is of your people, who acts as do your people, and that does not, therefore, apply to Herod."

"I am afraid of him," the rabbi finally admitted. "There would always be someone who would report me to him."

"But there is no one here, only you and I."

"The verse I quoted before continues, *For a bird of the air may carry the utterance* (Eccles. 10:20)."

"I am Herod!" the king at last declared, "and had I known how circumspect the rabbis are, I would not have killed them all. Now, advise me, what can I do to make up for it?"

Whereupon the rabbi asserted, "You have extinguished the light of the world. Go, therefore, and busy yourself in rekindling the light of the world.—Who are the light of the world? The rabbis, as it is written, *For the commandment is a lamp, the*

teaching is a light (Prov. 6:23). Rekindle the light of the world
—rebuild the Temple, as it is written, *And all the nations shall
gaze on it with joy* (Isa: 2:2)."[16]

Others say that the rabbi said to him, "You put out the eye
of the world— i.e., the rabbis, as the verse says, *it being hid
from their eyes* (Num. 15:24)[17]—therefore, go and busy yourself with the eye of the world—i.e., the Temple, as it is written,
My Sanctuary . . . the delight of your eyes (Ezek. 24:21)."

"But I fear the Roman government," replied Herod. The
rabbi advised him, "Send an envoy to Rome to ask permission.
It will take him a year to journey there. Another year will he
have to tarry before he will complete the negotiations. A third
year will be required for the return trip. Start the work now
and within three years you will have completed the reconstruction."

Herod did so. After three years the envoy returned with
the reply from Rome: "If you have not demolished any of the
old structure, do not do it. If you have, but have not put up the
new edifice, stop where you are. But if you have already completed the project, let it alone. Such is the practice of bad servants;
after the thing is done, they ask permission. But if you strut
with your sword because of this stratagem, remember that your
record is with us, stating that you are really neither king nor son
of king, but Herod the slave who has made himself a freedman."[18]

Herod built the Temple with blue, yellow, and white marble,
the sections not in a straight line, but alternately projecting and
receding. He wanted to cover it with gold overlay but was
advised by the rabbis not to do so because it looked better as it
was, having the appearance of a surging sea. It was said that he
who had never seen the Temple of Herod had never truly seen
a beautiful structure.[19]

In the scriptural verse *one goat for a sin offering* (Num.
7:64) one can see an allusion to the edifice that Herod erected,
for it was built by a sinful king as an atonement for having slain
the sages of Israel.[20] But the work received heavenly approval,
for during Herod's reconstruction of the Temple, the rains would
fall during the night only. In the morning a wind would blow
and scatter the clouds, and the sun would shine and dry up the
earth. The laborers could rise each morning sure to go on with
their work.[21]

2

Differences between the First and Second Temples

The prophet Haggai predicted that the glory of the Second Temple would outshine that of the First, and the prophecy was fulfilled because of the longer duration of the Second Temple and its greater beauty as embellished by Herod.[22] But there were five items present in the First Temple that were missing from the Second: the Ark, the Urim and Tummim, the heavenly fire, the Divine Presence, and the Holy Spirit. Some sources say that the oil of anointment was also missing.[23]

When the First Temple was destroyed by the Babylonians, the candlestick was mysteriously stored away through divine intervention. It was one of five things so concealed and, therefore, absent from the Second Temple: the Ark, the candlestick, the fire which had originally descended from heaven and had always remained on the altar, the Holy Spirit, and the cherubim. When the Holy One, blessed be He, in His mercy will again build His Temple and His Holy Place, He will restore them to their position in order to gladden Jerusalem.[24] The Divine Presence rested permanently in the First Temple for the Ark was there, but in the Second Temple the Divine Presence only tarried. After the disappearance of the Ark the Foundation Stone took its place.[25]

The altar in the Second Temple was larger than the one in Solomon's Temple. The fire on the altar during the time of the First Temple took on the form of a lion; during the Second Temple, that of a dog.[26]

Some sages say that when the First Temple was destroyed, the Ark was taken away to Babylonia, but others are of the opinion that it disappeared in its very place in the Temple; while still others maintain it was mysteriously concealed in the wood storage. Once a priest serving in the Second Temple noticed that one of the paving stones of the compartment where wood was stored seemed to be irregular. With an axe still in his hands, he went to tell his fellow priests of it, but before he could finish his story, he dropped dead. On another occasion two priests whose physical blemishes rendered them unfit for serving at the altar were engaged in selecting wood that was not moldy, when the axe of one of them accidentally fell at that mysterious spot, and at once a flame leaped forth and consumed him. Thus it was known that the Ark of the Covenant must have its place of concealment in the Temple's woodshed. In later years the sages would bow in its direction, respecting that sacred tradition transmitted by their ancestors.[27]

In the Second Temple all the building was overlaid with gold except the backs of the doors, but in Solomon's Temple even they were covered with gold.[28] The handles of all the vessels used on the Day of Atonement were of gold, paid for by King Monobaz. His mother, Queen Helene, contributed a golden candlestick that was placed over the Temple entrance. When the sun rose, sparkling rays were reflected from it, and the people of Jerusalem knew that it was time to recite the morning Shema. She also presented the Temple with a tablet of gold upon which were inscribed the biblical verses concerning the suspected wife.[29] The table in the Temple was made of gold and when the sun rose at dawn, its rays sparkled off the table's surface. That was an indication to those nearby within the sanctuary that the hour had arrived for the recital of the Shema of the morning. One opinion has it that it was a sign for the people in Jerusalem that it was the correct hour for the reading of the Shema.[30]

The two lots used on the Day of Atonement for the ritual of the selection of one goat for sacrifice and another for destruction in the wilderness were made of gold. This was done by Joshua ben Gamla when he was chosen as high priest, and he was remembered for it thereafter with praise.[31]

Twelve stopcocks were made for the laver by Ben Katin. Earlier it had but two. He also made a device for the laver so that its water would not be rendered unfit by standing overnight. The noise of this device could be heard as far away as Jericho.[32]

The Gates of Nicanor in the Temple reminded onlookers to praise his name too. It is told that Nicanor went to Alexandria to get these gates. During the voyage back there was a mighty gale, and one of the gates was flung overboard to lighten the load, but the sea continued to rage. When they seized hold of the other gate to cast it too into the sea, he clung to it and said, "Throw me in with it!" They did so and at once the sea became calm. He and the gate were rescued, but he was unhappy at the loss of the first gate. When the ship arrived at the harbor of Acre, the missing gate came up from the water under the sides of the ship. Others say that a sea monster swallowed it and spat it out on the dry land. Therefore, all the gates of the Sanctuary were changed for golden ones except for the Nicanor Gates because of the miracles that had happened with them. But some say it was because the bronze of which they were made had a golden hue, one sage explaining that it was Corinthian bronze that shone like gold.[33]

Proper reverence for the Temple included the prohibitions against one's entering it with a staff or money bag or shoes or with dust upon his feet. The Temple grounds were not to be used as a shortcut, and it was forbidden to expectorate upon them. All this was true not only during the time of the Second Temple but even after its destruction, i.e., the same respect must be shown for the ground upon which the Temple once stood.[34]

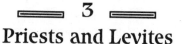

3
Priests and Levites

The priests who had served idols during the days of the First Temple were disqualified by the Holy One, blessed be He, from service in the Second Temple.[35] The high priests who served in the First Temple ministered uprightly, and therefore only eighteen high priests held office, beginning with Aaron. In the Second Temple, however, because they would bribe their way into office or, as some say, because they used witchcraft to do away with their predecessors to gain office, many more held the post of high priest. The opinions as to the total vary from eighty to eighty-five. Simon the Just held office for forty years, but after his death the old practice of purchasing the office was again followed so that the lives of his successors were shortened.

The total of eighteen priests during the four hundred and ten years of the First Temple can be compared to the more than three hundred priests who ministered during the four hundred and twenty years of the Second Temple. If you deduct the forty years service of Simon the Just, the eighty years of Johanan the high priest, the ten years of Ishmael ben Phiabi, and, as some say, the eleven years of Rabbi Eleazar ben Harsom, it can be seen that none of the rest completed even one year of service. This was because they rose to the office not through merit but through bribery. For example, Martha, the daughter of Boethus, brought a measure full of dinars to King Alexander Yannai to persuade him to nominate her husband Joshua ben Gamla, for the high priesthood.[36]

Once a certain man coveted the office of high priest and sent his son with two silver measures full of silver pieces together with two silver leveling instruments. But a rival sent his son with two golden measures full of gold pieces with two gold leveling instruments. People said, "The fool has upset the candlestick," by which they meant that the second man had outbid the first.

To the high priests who ministered in the First Temple can be applied the words, *The fear of the Lord prolongs life*. But to the priests of the Second Temple, the second half of the verse is applicable, *while the years of the wicked will be shortened* (Prov. 10:27).[37]

The high priest should properly be distinguished from the rank and file of priests in five ways: in countenance, strength, wealth, wisdom, and appearance. It happened once that a poor priest, Phinehas the stonecutter, was elevated to the high priesthood. His fellow priests found him cutting stones at a quarry. They would not permit him to continue but, in his presence, filled the quarry hole with gold dinars to enrich him.[38]

The high priest ministered in eight garments and the ordinary priest in four—tunic, breeches, headdress, and girdle. In addition the high priest wore the breastplate, ephod, robe, and the frontlet. The tunic symbolized atonement for bloodshed, the breeches for sexual offenses, the headdress for arrogance, the girdle for theft and double-dealing. The breastplate was the symbol of atonement for perversion of justice, the ephod for idolatry, the robe for slander, the frontlet for impudence and blasphemy. And the death of the high priest provided atonement for him who killed another accidentally.[39] The eight items of apparel worn by the high priest are an allusion to the rite of circumcision, which takes place eight days after birth. The same word, *covenant,* is used in connection with both circumcision and the high priesthood.[40]

The high priest did not enter the Holy of Holies attired in the golden apparel so Satan had no opportunity of accusing the Jewish people by saying, "In the past they made for themselves a god of a golden calf, now they seek to officiate in the holiest place in garments of gold!" Gold is a reminder of the great sin of old, and, as the proverb has it, "the accuser cannot act as defender." But there also are other explanations. One is that the golden items were not worn so often in order to save Israel expenses. Another that it was a provision against haughtiness, as the Scriptures say, *Do not exalt yourself in the king's presence* (Prov. 25:6).[41]

There are two people who take precedence over a high priest: a sage and a king, in that order; for if a sage dies, none can replace him, while if a king dies, all Israelites are eligible for the crown. But a high priest takes precedence over a prophet, and one anointed with the anointing oil outranks one consecrated only by the additional vestments. A prophet takes precedence over a priest anointed for war, while the latter outranks a deputy high priest, who takes precedence over a chief of the watch. This latter takes precedence over the chief of a priests' division, who outranks an *amarkal,* who in turn takes precedence over a temple treasurer, who outranks an ordinary priest. Thereafter, the order of precedence is priest, Levite, Israelite, bastard, *natin,* proselyte, freed slave. But when does this order of precedence apply? Only when they are equal in all other respects. But if the bastard be a scholar, he takes precedence over a high priest who is an ignoramus. Some of the rabbis thought that this entire matter of precedence concerned only the ransoming of a captive, the saving of life, and clothing, not, however, the order of seating at the academy of learning. In regard to this last there was a difference of opinion since the possession of wisdom is more important than even the privilege of regular admission into the innermost precincts of the Sanctuary.[42] When the high priest entered the Holy of Holies, he had to his credit bundles upon bundles of merits to aid him in his pleas before God. He entered with the merits of Torah, the rite of circumcision, the observance of the

Sabbath, Jerusalem, Judah, the heave offering, the tithes, and the sacrifices.[43]

Once a certain high priest entered the Holy of Holies on Yom Kippur and prayed for so long a time that the other priests became alarmed, thinking that he might have suddenly died within the holy place. They decided to enter the Holy of Holies, against the established practice, to see what had happened to him. As they were about to enter, he came out. They asked him, "Why did you prolong your prayers so?"

He replied, "Is it of such little worth to you that I offered prayer for you and for the Temple, that it might not be destroyed?"

They said, "Do not make it your custom to pray at length for we have learned the tradition that a high priest should not do so lest he frighten the people."[44]

The sacred name of God, the Tetragrammaton, may not be transmitted to every man, nor to one who is not in his prime but only to one who has lived most of his years. It may be transmitted only when the persons are standing and only in an undefiled place and on or near a body of water where no people would be present to overhear it. At first it was transmitted to all the priests, but when the sinners among them multiplied, it was transmitted only to the priests who lived by high moral standards. They would deliberately muffle its pronunciation amidst the chanting of the priests, so that the others should not hear it clearly during the benediction.

Rabbi Tarfon once reported that with his uncle Samson he ascended the platform where the priests intoned the benediction and he inclined his ears toward the high priest to catch the exact name, but it was muffled amidst the chanting of the priests. But once he did hear it and he fell upon his face in awe. The people who were near the high priest and heard the ineffable name fell upon their faces. Those who were further away, seeing this sight, would exclaim, "Praised be His sovereign glory for ever and ever." But none among the people who had knowledge of the name ever left the place retaining it for, miraculously, it would be erased from his memory.[45]

The high priest would offer a brief prayer privately in the outer chamber not within the hearing of others. This was done in order that the people not become fearful. He would pray, "May it be Your will, O Lord our God, that this coming year have plentiful heat and rain." Some interpreted the prayer to mean that if there were to be great heat, then let there also be sufficient rain and dew, and let not the prayers of travelers who ask for the cessation of rain be accepted. Others said that the high priest prayed additionally, "May sovereignty never depart from the house of Judah; further, may Your people Israel not have to depend for livelihood upon charity either from Jews or non-Jews."[46]

As Joshua was told, *Remove your sandals from your feet* (Josh. 5:15), so wherever the Shekhinah, the Heavenly Presence, appears, one must not go about with shoes. Therefore, the priests ministered in the Temple barefooted.[47]

The first prophets instituted twenty-four watches from various parts of the country. Each had its shift of priests, Levites, and ordinary Israelites. When the turn of the shift came, the priests and Levites went to Jerusalem to serve in the Temple together with the Israelites of that watch who lived nearby. The other Israelites in the shift who lived far from Jerusalem would gather in their respective towns to read the story of the Creation. The reading schedule would be as follows: Sunday, Genesis 1:1–5; Monday, 1:6–8; Tuesday, 1:9–13; Wednesday, 1:14–19; Thursday, 1:20–23; Friday, 1:24–31. The longer section of the day was read by two persons and the shorter, by one, during *shaharit* and *musaf* services. But for the afternoon prayers they would assemble and say the appropriate selection by heart, as the Shema is recited. On Friday afternoon they would not assemble, however, because of the honor due the Sabbath.[48] Were it not for the prayers and Torah readings of the men of the respective watches, heaven and earth would cease to exist. Since the Temple's destruction, the sacrifices and the words of the men of the watch have been replaced by the reading of the order of the sacrifices in the daily prayer service.[49]

The Israelites who had accompanied the priests and Levites of their watch to the Temple would pray that the sacrifices offered by their brethren be favorably accepted. The other Israelites of the watch who had not gone up to Jerusalem would gather in their local synagogues and fast for four days. Monday's fast was for those who sailed the seas; Tuesday's for the travelers crossing the deserts; Wednesday's for children, so that they might not catch the croup. Thursday's fast was for pregnant women and nursing mothers, so that the former might not suffer a miscarriage and the latter might be able to nurse. They did not fast on Friday because it was the eve of the Sabbath nor on the Sabbath because of the honor due the day. They did not fast on Sunday because it would be dangerous for their health to go from a day of rest and festivity to a day of fasting and fatigue. Others explained that it was out of fear of the non-Jews who might say, "Because we celebrate Sunday, the Jews fast on that day!" However, the sages pointed out that in the time of the Temple there was no fear of the non-Jews.[50]

Priests were judged for physical or family defects by the Great Sanhedrin that sat in the Court of Hewn Stones in the Temple. If disqualified by the court, the priest donned black clothing and departed. If not, he dressed in white and joined his fellow priests in service. A festive day would be made of the occasion as they would proclaim, "Blessed be the Omnipresent that a disqualifying defect has not been found in this descendant of Aaron and blessed be He who has chosen Aaron and his descendants to minister before Him in the Temple of the Holy of Holies!"[51] An ignorant priest is not to be one's associate for he will ultimately feed his friend with the heave offering forbidden to nonpriests.[52]

Once there were three priests who were discussing the amounts of their priestly shares. One said, "Mine was as large as a bean." The second reported, "Mine was as large as an olive." The third said, "Mine was as large as a lizard's tail." Because of his indecorous expression the third priest was investigated and a blemish of descent was discovered, which disqualified him. Others say that his very use of improper language rendered him unfit for the priesthood.[53]

Throughout the forty years that Simon the Just served as high priest, the lot "For the Lord," drawn during the Yom Kippur ritual of the two goats, would always come up in the right hand. Thereafter, it would at times come up in the right, at times in the left. During his term of office the crimson-colored strap, tied between the horns of the bullock, would always become white, indicating forgiveness of Israel's sins. Afterward, there were times when it turned white and times when it did not. During his tenure the westernmost light on the menorah continued burning after the others had gone out, despite the fact that no more oil had been placed in it and it had been kindled first, an omen that the Heavenly Presence rested over Israel. After his time that light at times would burn, at times go out. Similarly, in his day the wood kept burning on the altar, though it had been kindled in the morning, so that the priests did not have to add any wood to the original two logs. Afterward, there were times when the fire burned strongly and times when the flame went low so that the priests would have to bring wood throughout the day. During his term of service the omer, the two breads, and the bread of display were so blessed that every priest who received a piece even if no larger than an olive ate it and was sated, even leaving something over. Afterward, such was not the case, so that when every priest received a piece no larger than a bean, the well-mannered priests would not appear eager for it, but the gluttons would grasp it and devour it at once. Once when one of these gluttons grabbed not only his own portion but that of his fellow priest, they called him "Grasper" until his dying day.[54]

On Yom Kippur of the last year of his life Simon the Just predicted that his death would occur in that same year. He was asked how he knew it, and his reply was, "On every Yom Kippur in the past an old man dressed all in white would join me, entering the Holy of Holies with me and leaving it with me. Today I was joined by an old man dressed all in black, who entered with me but did not leave with me." After the festival of Sukkot he was sick for seven days and then died. That year his fellow priests omitted the mention of the ineffable name in pronouncing the blessing.[55]

One Yom Kippur the high priest, Simon ben Kimḥit, left the Temple service to converse with the visiting king of the Arabians when, accidentally, a streak of saliva spurted out from the king's mouth upon the garments of the high priest. The sages declared the high priest unclean, disqualifying him from carrying out the duties of his office on the most sacred day of the year. His brother, Judah, at once took his place and served as high priest. That day their mother saw two of her sons act as high priests.

The sages say that Kimḥit had seven sons and all of them served in the office of high priest. The sages once called upon her and asked, "What good deeds have you performed to have merited such high honor?" She replied, "May Heaven so help me! In all my life the rafters of my house have never looked down upon the uncovered hair of my head." They exclaimed, "All kinds of flour are flour, but the flour of Kimḥit is the finest!" They applied to her the verse, *All the glory of the royal princess is best seen within her palace* (Ps. 45:14).[56]

Four cries were heard to issue forth at various times from the Temple court itself. The first was, "Depart from this place, sons of Eli, who have defiled the Sanctuary of the Lord!" The second cry was, "Leave here, Issachar, man of the village of Barkai, who honors himself but desecrates Heaven's sacred offerings!" For what was his practice? He used to wrap his hands in silk and then perform his priestly service. The third cry was, "Lift up your heads, O ye gates, and let Ishmael ben Phiabi, disciple of Phinehas, enter and serve as high priest!" The fourth cry was, "Lift up your heads, O ye gates, and let Johanan ben Narbai, disciple of Pinkai, enter and let him fill his stomach with Heaven's sacred offerings!"[57]

It was said of Johanan ben Narbai that he would eat at a meal three hundred cakes, drink three hundred bottles of wine, and, for dessert, consume forty measures of pigeons. It was said of him further that never during his lifetime was any part of the priestly portion of the sacrifices left over.[58]

The end of Issachar of the village of Barkai happened in this fashion. Once the king and queen were discussing the relative merits of kid and lamb. The king said kid meat was better, the queen, lamb. Whom could they call to settle the matter? Surely, the high priest would know, for he was involved with various kinds of sacrifices daily. He arrived and, waving his hand arrogantly, declared, "If kids were better, they would be used for the daily sacrifices instead of lambs." The king asserted, "Because he showed no respect for the throne, in waving his hand so arrogantly, let his right hand be cut off!" The high priest bribed the executioner, who then cut off his left hand. But the king heard of it and ordered the right severed. Thus Issachar lost both hands.[59]

In Jericho there were trunks of sycamore trees that the priests forcibly appropriated for their own use. The owners then consecrated them for Temple use, so that no individual could afterward make use of them. Of these priests and such like them Abba Saul ben Batnit said (quoting Abba Joseph ben Ḥanin), "Woe is me because of the house of Boethus and their lances! Woe is me because of the house of Ḥanin and their whispering! Woe is me because of the house of Katros and their pens! Woe is me because of the house of Ishmael ben Phiabi and their fists!" For they were all high priests, their sons the Temple treasurers, their sons-in-law the Temple officers, and their servants would beat the people with rods.[60]

A certain high priest was leaving the Temple upon the conclusion of the Yom Kippur services and crowds of people accompanied him. When they saw the sages Shemaiah and Avtalyon, the people left the high priest for the sages. Later Shemaiah and Avtalyon came to take their leave of the high priest. He said to them sneeringly, "May the descendants of the heathen depart in peace!" They retorted, "The descendants of the heathen may go in peace because they do the peace-loving deeds of Aaron; but the descendants of Aaron may not have peace because they do not do the deeds of Aaron!"[61]

Certain priestly families, because of their actions, were afterward mentioned unfavorably. The house of Garmu was expert in baking the bread of display but would not teach the knack to others.[62] The sages sent for skilled bakers to Alexandria in Egypt. They could bake as well as the priests of the house of Garmu, but they did not know how to take the loaves down from the oven as well as they. The Alexandrians heated the oven from the outside and baked from the outside, while the priests of the house of Garmu heated the oven from within and baked from within. The bread of the former became moldy, but the bread of the latter never did. The sages recalled the priests of the house of Garmu but they refused to come. Their salary was doubled and they returned. Instead of twelve minas per day, they got twenty-four; another source has it that they got forty-eight instead of twenty-four. The sages asked them why they refused to teach others their skill. Their answer was, "In our father's house it is known that the Temple is to be destroyed, and perhaps some unworthy person, having been taught this skill, will then use it in the service of idolatry." But the house of Garmu was praised for the fact that fine bread was never to be found in their children's hand, so that people should not say that they were making personal use of the bread of display.[63]

The house of Abtinas was expert in preparing the incense but would not teach the knowledge to others. The sages sent for specialists to Alexandria in Egypt. They knew how to mix the ingredients as well as the priests of the house of Abtinas, but they could not make the smoke ascend as well as they. The smoke of the incense compounded by the house of Abtinas went straight up like a stick, while the smoke of the Alexandrians was diffused in every direction. The sages, therefore—since only the best should be in the Temple—recalled the priests of the house of Abtinas, but they refused to come. Their salary was doubled and they returned. One opinion is that their salary went from twelve minas to twenty-four; another, from twenty-four to forty-eight. The sages asked them why they refused to instruct others. Their reply was, "In our father's house it is known that the Temple is to be destroyed, and perhaps some unworthy person, having been taught this skill, will then use it in the service of idolatry." But the house of Abtinas was praised for the fact that never did a bride of their house go forth perfumed, and when they married a woman from elsewhere, they forbade her to be perfumed, so that people would not say that they were making personal use of the ingredients of the incense.[64]

One day, many years later, after the Temple had been destroyed, Rabbi Ishmael ben Loga and a boy descended from the house of Abtinas were gathering herbs in the fields, and he saw the boy crying and laughing. "Why do you cry?" he asked him.

He replied, "Because I recall the past glory of my ancestors that is no more."

"Then why do you laugh?"

"Because the Holy One, blessed be He, will restore it to us with the rebuilding of the destroyed Temple."

"What caused you to recall all this?"

"Because I see the plant called 'smoke-raiser' before me."

"Show it to me!"

"We have a tradition in our family not to show it to anyone."[65]

Rabbi Johanan ben Nuri told the story that once he met an old man who had a scroll containing a formula for making incense. He asked him his ancestry and the old man said that he was descended from the house of Abtinas. He asked what was in the old man's hand and was told it was a scroll listing the ingredients for the incense. "Give it to me," he asked. The old man replied, "As long as my father's house was active, they would pass it on from one generation to the next and show it to no one. But now that the Temple is destroyed, here it is. Be careful about it, for it is the scroll of the proper ingredients for the incense."[66]

When Hygros ben Levi tuned his voice to a trill, he would put his thumb into his mouth and place his finger on the division line between the two parts of his mustache. At the sound his brethren the priests would stagger backward with a sudden movement.[67]

Ben Kamẓar was able to hold four pens between his fingers, and if there was a word of four letters, he could write them all at the same time. He was the only priest possessing a special skill who refused to teach it to others without being able to offer any excuse for his refusal.[68]

═══ 4 ═══
In and about the Temple

The land of Israel is the navel of the earth, placed at its center. Jerusalem is situated at the center of Israel and the Temple at Jerusalem's center. The Sanctuary is the center of the Temple, the Ark at its center, and the Foundation Stone was placed in front of the Sanctuary. The Foundation Stone was associated with the earth's foundation.[69] At the time of the Second Temple, when the Ark had disappeared, the Foundation Stone stood in its place. This Stone had been there since the days of the early prophets and of Samuel and David.[70] The Sanctuary, wide in front and narrow at the back, resembled a lion.[71]

The heavenly Holy of Holies is directly opposite the Holy of Holies on earth. The spring that came forth from the Holy of Holies in its beginning resembled the antennae of grasshoppers. As it reached the entrance to the Sanctuary it became like the thread of the spinner's warp. As it reached the door of the main hall it became like the thread of the woof. Upon reaching the entrance of the Temple court it became as large as the mouth of a small flask. Thereafter it grew larger and wider until it reached the entrance to the House of David where it became like a swiftly flowing brook in which the ritually unclean would wash to purify themselves.[72]

There was a round place in the middle of the altar for collecting the ashes, and at times there were in it as much as three hundred kurs of ashes. A vine made of gold was hung from beams at the entrance to the Sanctuary and people would attach to it their offerings of a golden berry or grape cluster. Once so much had been suspended from it that three hundred priests were summoned to clear it. The thickness of the Temple curtain was a handbreadth. It was woven of seventy-two cords, each cord made of twenty-four strands. Its length was forty cubits, its width twenty. It had been woven of eight hundred and twenty thousand threads, and two such curtains were made each year. It took three hundred priests to immerse it in water to clean it.[73]

There was a smooth-surfaced narrow reed pipe in the Temple that dated back to the days of Moses. The king had it overlaid with gold, and afterward it lost the sweetness of its tones. When its gold overlay was removed, it played as sweetly as before.[74] There was also a brass cymbal in the Temple going back to Moses' time. Its music was melodious but then it was damaged. The wise men summoned artisans from Alexandria to fix it but its musical sound was impaired. When the mending material was removed the sound was as melodious as before.[75] The family of Ben Arẓa had charge of the cymbal.[76]

So too was there in the Temple a bronze mortar dating back to Moses' time, used for mixing spices. It was damaged and the sages sent to Alexandria for artisans to mend it. It did not work thereafter as well as it had before. But when the mending matter was removed, it was once again as effective as ever. These three items were the ones that had remained from the First Temple and were later damaged and repaired, but the mending of them was in vain.[77]

There was a musical instrument in the Temple called *magreifah*. It had ten openings, each of which emitted ten different notes. Altogether, therefore, it could play one hundred notes. In size it was a cubit square. It also had a projection extending from it containing ten openings, each of which was capable of producing one hundred notes—in sum, one thousand.[78] The sound of this instrument could be heard as far as Jericho. This was equally true of the reed pipe and the cymbal, the daily blowing of the shofar from the Temple, and the sound of the singing. In Jericho could be heard too the sound of the opening of the great Temple gate, the turning of the huge wheel in the Temple well that had been made by the high priest Ben Katin, and the daily morning announcement by the priest Gebini when he aroused his fellow priests to their service. Some say that even the voice of the high priest pronouncing the ineffable name of God could be heard as far away as Jericho. Even the smell of the incense reached as far as Jericho.[79]

The harp in the Temple had seven strings. The harp of the days of the Messiah will have eight strings. The harp of the world to come will have ten strings.[80]

There were two chambers in the Temple called by the names of Chamber of Secret Gifts and Chamber of Vessels, respectively. Sin-fearing people would place their gifts in the Chamber of Secret Gifts unbeknown to others, and the poor who were descended from the virtuous would be supported from it without anyone's knowledge. Those whose gifts were vessels would throw their contributions into the Chamber of Vessels. Every thirty days the treasurers would open it. Any vessel that could be used in the Temple was kept. All others were sold and the proceeds were used for the repair of the Temple.[81]

There were three courts of judgment, one at the entrance to the Temple Mount, the second at the entrance to the Temple Court, and the third in the Chamber of Hewn Stones.[82]

Just as there were three camps in the wilderness—the camp of the Divine Presence, the camp of the Levites, and the camp of the Israelites—so too were there three camps in Jerusalem. From the gates of Jerusalem to the gate of the Temple Mount was the Israelite camp; from the gate of the Temple Mount to the Gate of Nicanor was the camp of the Levites; from the Gate of Nicanor inward was the camp of the Divine Presence. This last corresponded to the space within the Tabernacle hangings in the wilderness.[83]

In the roof beams of the Sanctuary's porch there were fastened golden chains by means of which the novitiates in the priesthood would climb to see the crowns on the ledge (originally for Joshua and Zerubbabel), as it is written, *The crowns shall remain in the Temple of the Lord as a memorial* (Zech. 6:14).[84] From the windows in the Temple light would stream out for the world. They were transparent and opaque, narrowing toward the inside and broadening toward the outside, so as to let the light out to the world. This is unlike the manner of a king who builds a palace for himself with windows narrow on the outside and broadening inward so that light will enter the interior. With the Temple windows the opposite was true so it would send forth a great light.[85]

The scholars who taught the priests the laws concerning ritual slaughter, reception and sprinkling of the blood, and taking a handful of the frankincense from the meal offering received their payment from the Temple funds. So too did the experts who examined the sacrificial animals for blemishes, the sages who checked the Torah scroll in the Temple Court, the two judges who tried robbery cases in Jerusalem, and the women who wove the veil for the Ark.[86] The judge, Karna, would collect a silver coin from each litigant.[87] As a woman ties up her hair behind, and this is an ornament for her, so did the Great Sanhedrin sit behind the Temple and it was an ornament for the Temple.[88]

=== 5 ===

Services and Practices in the Temple

The people of Israel used to offer two regular sacrifices every day, one in the morning and one before evening. The morning sacrifice was offered for sins committed during the night, the evening one for those perpetrated during the day. So it was that no man spent a night in Jerusalem with sin on his conscience. Thus was the verse fulfilled, *where righteousness dwelt* (Isa. 1:21).[89]

The altar seized the sacrifices as a wolf its prey, the one lamb in the morning, the other at dusk.[90] God said to Israel, "Ten animals have I permitted you for food, three of them domestic, seven wild. The three domestic animals are the ox, the sheep, and the goat. The seven wild animals are the ram, the deer, the roebuck, the ibex, the antelope, the buffalo, and the mountain goat. I have not put you to the bother of climbing mountains or wearying yourselves in forests to bring an offering before Me. You need bring only those that are in your immediate possession, that feed at your trough."[91] The ox is pursued by the lion, the sheep by the wolf, the goat by the leopard. The Holy One, blessed be He, said, "Bring before Me as an offering not from among the pursuers but from among the pursued."[92]

Once a poor man brought a meal offering to the Temple all the way from Apamea. When he saw that the priest took a handful for the altar and ate the rest, he said, "Woe unto me! All the trouble I have gone to was for the benefit of this man." The people present pacified him, saying, "Even though this priest has gone to no more bother than to take two steps between the hall and the altar, he has, nevertheless, earned the right to enjoy the greater part of your offering. How much more so, then, will you, who have taken all this trouble receive for your merit the good that is treasured up. Moreover, it is written concerning the priests' share, *And the remainder of the meal offering shall be for Aaron and his sons* (Lev. 2:3)."[93]

King Agrippa desired to bring a thousand burnt offerings in one day. He sent word to the high priest, "Let no man but me be permitted to bring an offering this day." When a poor man with two doves in his hand came and said to the high priest, "Offer up these doves for me," the high priest replied, "The king charged me that no man but he be allowed to bring an offering this day." But the poor man pleaded, "My lord high priest, each day I capture four doves; two I eat and two I offer up. If you do not offer these up for me, you endanger my livelihood." The high priest rose and offered up the doves.

In a dream it was disclosed to Agrippa, "A poor man's offering preceded yours!" Agrippa sent word to the high priest, "Did I not say to you, 'Let no man except me be allowed to bring an offering this day?'" The high priest replied, "A poor man came with two doves in his hand and said to me, 'Offer up these for me.' I said to him, 'Thus and thus has the king charged me,' and he said to me, 'Each day I capture four doves; two I offer up and two I eat. If you do not offer up for me, you endanger my livelihood.' Should I not have offered them up?" Agrippa replied to the high priest, "You have done well. For it is written, *For He did not scorn, He did not spurn the plea of the lowly* (Ps. 22:25)."[94]

Once it happened that an ox being led to the altar would not move along. A poor man came along with a bunch of endives and held it out to the ox who ate it and allowed itself to be led after it. In a dream it was revealed to the owner of the ox, "The poor man's sacrifice of his herbs preceded your offering of the ox!"[95]

When a poor woman once brought a handful of fine flour for a meal offering and the priest ridiculed her, saying, "See what she offers! What is there in this to offer up? What is there in this to rise as incense?" Then in a dream it was disclosed to the priest, "Do not despise her! It is regarded as if she had offered up her very life."[96]

Why does the Bible use different language with the bringing of a meal offering, describing the bringers as *nefesh*, "a soul" or "a life"? It is because the Holy One, blessed be He, said, "Who brings a meal offering? A poor man. When he does, I deem it as though he had offered his very soul, his very life!" The Holy One, blessed be He, said, "The handful of the poor man's offering is more precious to Me than the fistfuls of the high priest's frankincense."

Therefore, the meal offering alone has five different kinds of preparation. It is like an earthly king who knows how poor is his beloved friend who has invited him for a meal. He says to his poor friend, "Make for me these five kinds of preparations from the same food source so that I may enjoy myself."[97]

In the Temple the threefold priestly benediction was recited as one blessing without the interruption of Amen. The priests would pronounce the ineffable name of God in the benediction. As they uttered the benediction they would raise their hands above their heads, all except the high priest who would not raise his hands higher than the gold frontlet on his forehead. Outside the Temple the benediction was recited as three blessings with an Amen response after each section. The ineffable name was not pronounced; substitutes were used, and the priests would raise their hands to a level with their shoulders.[98] One of the rabbis said that he who gazed upon the priests in the Temple while they pronounced the threefold benediction uttering the ineffable name causes his eyesight to grow dim. So too with one who stares at a rainbow or at the nasi.[99]

The Jews, as they made their way to the Temple on their regular pilgrimages, were under divine protection. To them may be applied the verse, *How lovely are your feet in sandals* (Songs 7:2).[100] If, during a pilgrim's absence from his home, he had left his cow pasturing in a field, no wild animal would harm it. If his chicken had been left pecking at the dungheap, no weasel would hurt it. Once a pilgrim left for Jerusalem and forgot to lock the doors of his home. Upon his return he found a snake entwined around the fastening ring of his entrance gate. Another pilgrim left his home and forgot to bring in his chickens. When he came back from the Temple he discovered ripped-up cats in front of his chicken yard. Still another pilgrim had forgotten a pile of wheat in the field. Upon his return he found lions surrounding the wheat.

There were two wealthy brothers who lived in Ashkelon. Their neighbors were wicked non-Jews who could not wait until the two brothers would go off to the Temple for the festival. For they said, "When will these Jews go up to Jerusalem to pray and we shall then be able to break into their homes to plunder all they possess?" The time came and the two brothers went up to Jerusalem. The Holy One, blessed be He, arranged for two angels to take on the appearance of the two brothers, and they would go in and out of the house during the absence of the true owners. When the two brothers returned, they brought gifts for their neighbors, sharing with them whatever they had purchased in Jerusalem. "Where have you been?" asked their neighbors. "Jerusalem," they replied. "When did you go?" "On such and such a day." "And when did you return?" "On such and such a day." "Whom did you leave in your homes during your absence?" "We left no one." Whereupon the neighbors exclaimed, "Blessed be the God of the Jews who has not forsaken them and who will never forsake them!"[101]

The pilgrimage to the Temple in Jerusalem for the three festivals was to be undertaken for its own sake. That is why the choice fruits that grow around the Sea of Galilee do not grow in Jerusalem. Similarly, that is why the hot springs are not found in Jerusalem but in Tiberias. So that pilgrims should not say, "Had we gone up to Jerusalem only to eat the choice fruits, it would have been enough!" Or, "Had we gone up to Jerusalem only to bathe in the healing waters of the hot springs, it would have been enough!" For the pilgrimage to the Temple in Jerusalem was to be done for its own intrinsic worth as the fulfillment of a *mizvah* and not for the sake of personal pleasure.[102]

Once the ruling powers prohibited the bringing of the firstfruits to the Temple in Jerusalem. To make certain the decree would be obeyed they stationed guards on the roads as Jeroboam ben Nebat had once done to prevent the pilgrims from going up to Jerusalem. What did the pious sin-fearing people of that generation do? They brought their baskets of firstfruits, covering them with a layer of dried-out figs. Carrying their baskets and with a pestle on their shoulders, they approached the guards. The latter asked, "Where are you going?" The pilgrims replied, "To make flat pressed cakes of these dried figs with the pestle on our shoulders and the mortar that is a short distance ahead." When they had passed the guards, they wreathed their baskets with garlands and brought them to Jerusalem.

Another time the authorities forbade the bringing of firewood for the Temple altar. Guards were stationed on the roads as in the days of Jeroboam ben Nebat when he had sought to keep the Jews from their pilgrimages to Jerusalem. What did the pious and sin-fearing folk of that generation do? They took pieces of wood and made ladders of them. Carrying the ladders on their shoulders, they walked along until they came to the guards. The latter asked, "Where are you going?" The reply was, "To take down the pigeons from the dovecote a short distance ahead, by means of these ladders on our shoulders." Once they had safely passed the guards they broke up the ladders and carried the pieces of wood to Jerusalem. To them and to those like them was the verse applied, *The name of the righteous is invoked in blessing* (Prov. 10:7).[103]

The officer of the Temple Mount used to go round to every watch with burning torches carried before him, and if any member of the priestly watch did not rise at his approach and say to him, "Peace be with you, supervisor of the Temple Mount," it was a sign that he was asleep. The officer would strike him with his stick, and he was also permitted to burn his clothes. The other priests, hearing the tumult, would ask, "What is that noise in the Azarah? It is the cry of a member of the tribe of Levi who is being beaten and whose clothes are being burned because he was asleep at his post." Rabbi Eliezer ben Jacob said, "Once my mother's brother was found asleep and his clothes were burned."[104]

In the beginning whichever priest wished to remove the ashes from the altar did so, and if there were a number of them, they would run and mount the ramp leading to the altar, and he who came first within four cubits obtained the privilege. It once happened that two were even as they ran to mount the ramp and one pushed the other so that he fell and broke his leg. Once it happened that two priests were exactly even as they ran to mount the ramp and when one came first within four cubits of the altar, the other took his knife and plunged it into his heart. Rabbi Ẓadok stood on the steps of the hall and cried out, "Brothers of the House of Israel, hear ye! Behold it is written, *If, in the land that the Lord your God is giving you to possess, someone slain is found lying in the open ... your elders and magistrates shall go out ...* (Deut. 21: 1–2). On whose behalf shall we offer the heifer whose neck is to be broken, on behalf of the city or on behalf of the Temple Courts?" All the people burst out weeping. The father of the young priest came and found him in the throes of death. He said, "May he be an atonement for you. My son is not yet dead and the priestly knife has not become unclean."[105] When the court saw that this practice involved danger, they changed it in favor of a new method of selection. The cleansing of the altar was henceforth to be done by a kind of lottery.[106]

The sacrifice of the paschal lamb was made by three different groups. The first group would enter until the Temple Court was full, at that point its doors would be closed. The shofar was sounded: *teki'ah, teru'ah, teki'ah.* The priests stood in rows with silver and gold basins in their hands. Those with silver basins stood in separate rows from those with gold basins. The basins had no rounded rest at the bottom lest they be set down and the blood in them congeal. An Israelite would sacrifice his paschal lamb; then a priest would catch the blood in his basin and pass it on to the next priest; then this priest to the next, and so on. The priest closest to the altar would dash the blood against its base. Each priest would pass on a full basin and receive an empty one in turn.

The first group was succeeded by the second and it by the third. The latter two did the same thing as the first. During the slaughtering of the animals the Hallel was recited. If it was finished before all the animals had been slaughtered, it was recited a second and a third time, although it never happened that the third recital would go to the very end of the Hallel.

There were iron hooks fixed on the walls and pillars on which the slaughtered animals were hung and flayed. If all the hooks were taken, there were thin smooth rods which a man would place on his shoulders and those of another man. Upon the rod the animal would be hung and its skin stripped. It would then be cleaved open and the parts to be offered on the altar removed. These were placed on a tray and burned on the altar. When the first group left it would congregate on the Temple Mount, the second at the Hel, the third remaining in its place. When it would grow dark they would then all leave and roast their paschal lambs.[107]

Despite the large crowds in the Temple at Passover time, only once, during one Passover in the days of Hillel, was an old man accidentally crushed to death in the Temple Court. That particular Passover was later called the Passover of the Crushers.[108]

Once King Agrippa, anxious to know the number of people in Israel, instructed the high priest to keep a watchful eye on the number of paschal lambs. The latter took a kidney from each lamb, counted them, and found that there were twice sixty myriad kidneys, double the number of those who came out of Egypt. This did not include those who were ritually impure and those traveling. Since there were at least ten people who ate each paschal lamb, the total census represented six hundred myriads. That Passover was thereafter known as the Crowded Passover.[109]

A certain pagan, not telling anyone that he was not an Israelite, used to go up to Jerusalem each year and partake of the paschal lamb. Once he came before Rabbi Judah ben Batyra and said to him tauntingly, "It is written, *No foreigner shall eat of it* (Exod. 12:43) and *But no uncircumcised person may eat of it* (Exod. 12:48); nevertheless, I have eaten of the very best of it." Rabbi Judah ben Batyra asked him, "Have they given you a piece of the fat-tail?" The pagan replied, "No." The rabbi then told him, "The next time you go there ask them to give you a piece of the fat-tail." When he went up to Jerusalem, he said to them, "Give me a piece of the fat-tail." Shocked, they exclaimed, "What are you saying! The fat-tail is always offered upon the altar!" They asked him, "Who advised you to ask for it?" and he answered, "It was Rabbi Judah ben Batyra." "What can this mean?" they asked. They investigated him and, discovering that he was a pagan, executed him. They then sent a message to Rabbi Judah ben Batyra, "Peace be unto you, Rabbi Judah ben Batyra! You live in Nisibis, yet your net is cast in Jerusalem."[110]

The following was the procedure for the offering of the omer, the first barley, during the festival of Passover. On Passover eve the agents of the court went out to the fields and bound up the sheaves while they still stood implanted in the earth so that they would be easier to cut. The villagers of the surrounding area would gather so that the cutting might be done with great éclat. As soon as it would grow dark, the reaper would ask them, "Has the sun set?" They would answer, "Yes." Three times he would ask the same question and three times they would give the same answer. "With this sickle?" he would then ask. "Yes," they would reply. "In this receptacle?" he would ask next. "Yes," they would say.

On the Sabbath he would ask additionally, "On this Sabbath?" And they would answer in the affirmative. "Shall I now cut?" They would say, "Cut!" Each question was asked thrice and similarly answered. Why so much? Because of the Boethuseans who said there is no cutting of the omer at the expiration of the first day of the festival. They then would cut it, place it in the boxes, and bring it to the Temple Court. They parched it over the fire by placing it in a perforated iron tube so that the fire could get to all of it. Then they spread it out in the Temple Court where the wind blew over it. Later they would put it in a grist mill, and pound it and sift it in thirteen sieves so that they got in the end a tenth of an ephah from three seahs. Then they offered it. When the omer had been offered, they would go out and find the markets of Jerusalem full of new flour and parched grain ready for sale.[111]

Once it happened that it was time for offering the omer and the authorities did not know where there was newly grown grain to offer. They issued a public announcement, and a deaf-mute came and with one hand pointed to a roof (*gag*) and with the other to a hut (*zerif*). One of the wise men asked, "Is there a place called Zerifin-Gagot or Gagot-Zerifin?" They investigated, found such a place, and brought the new grain from there.

Once when the time came for the baking of the two loaves and no raw materials were available, a public announcement was issued and a deaf-mute came and put one hand on his eye (*ayin*) and the other on a bolt (*sokher*). One of the wise men asked, "Is there a place called Ein Sokher or Sokher Ayin?" They investigated, found such a place, and brought the necessary ingredients from there.[112]

How were the firstfruits brought up to Jerusalem? The men of the smaller towns of the *ma'amad* would assemble in the principal town of the region, spend the night in the town square, and not enter the houses. Early in the morning the leader of the caravan would cry out, *Come, let us go up to Zion, to the Lord our God* (Jer. 31:6). The men near Jerusalem brought fresh figs and grapes; those from more distant places brought dried figs and raisins. An ox went before them, its horns overlaid with gold and a wreath of olive leaves on its head. The flute was played before them until they came close to Jerusalem. When they approached Jerusalem they sent messengers ahead and garlanded their firstfruits. Officials of the priests and Levites as well as the Temple treasurers would come out to meet them, the number and rank depending upon the honor due to the particular group of pilgrims. All the craftsmen in Jerusalem used to rise up before them and greet them, "Brothers, men of such and such a place, we bid you welcome!" The flute would continue playing before them until they reached the Temple Mount. When they had reached the Temple Mount, even Agrippa the king would take his basket on his shoulder and enter the Temple precincts as far as the Temple Court. When they reached the Court the Levites would sing, *I extol You, O Lord, for You have lifted me up and not let my enemies rejoice over me* (Ps. 30:2). The pigeons that were hung on the baskets were sacrificed as burnt offerings and that which the people carried in their hands they gave to the priests. While the basket was still on his shoulder a man would recite the entire passage, beginning, *I acknowledge this day before the Lord your God* (Deut. 26:3). Rabbi Judah, however, says he would recite the passage up to *My father was a fugitive Aramean* (Deut. 26:5), and when he reached those words he would take down the basket from his shoulder and grasp it by its rim. The priest would place his hand beneath it and wave it, and then the man would recite from *My father was a fugitive Aramean* until the end of the passage. He would leave the basket at the side of the altar, bow low, and depart. In earlier days all who could recite the prescribed passage did so and those who did not know it repeated the words after the priest. But when the latter, because of their embarrassment, refrained from bringing their firstfruits, it was ordained that both those who knew the passage and those who did not should repeat the words after the priest. The rich brought their firstfruits in baskets overlaid with silver and gold and the poor brought them in wicker baskets of peeled willow branches. Both the baskets and the firstfruits were given to the priests.[113]

How did the priest wave the sheaf of the firstfruits? He moved it forward and backward, upward and downward; forward and backward to symbolize that the act was in honor of Him to whom all the world belongs; upward and downward to symbolize that the act was in honor of Him to whom belong the regions on high and the regions below. Simon ben Joshua interpreted it otherwise. He said the movements forward and backward were a form of petition to ward off the effects of harmful winds and the movements upward and downward were to counteract the effects of harmful dews. At the season of the firstfruits the pilgrims coming to Jerusalem were like a cataract that stops neither by day nor night.[114]

On Yom Kippur, the holiest of days, the Temple services were elaborate. Seven days before the Day of Atonement the high priest was taken from his own house and secluded in the counselors' chamber. Another priest was made ready to serve as an alternate in case anything occur that would render the high priest ineligible. Elders of the court would be assigned to read before him the prescribed rituals of the day, and they would say to him, "My lord high priest, read it yourself as well. Perhaps you have forgotten or have never studied it." On the day preceding Yom Kippur in the morning they would make him stand at the East Gate and have pass before him oxen, rams, and sheep so that he might quickly distinguish among them and be more familiar with the service. Throughout the seven days they did not withhold food and drink from him, but toward nightfall on the day before Yom Kippur they would not let him eat too much for heavy eating causes sleep. The elders of the court would hand him over to the elders of the priesthood, who would bring him up to the upper chamber of the house of Abtinas. They had him take an oath, and then they would take their leave and depart. The oath they administered was as follows: "My lord high priest, we are the agents of the court and you are our agent and the agent of the court. We ask you to swear by Him who made His name to dwell in this house that you will change nothing of what we have told you." He would turn aside and weep, and they too would turn aside and weep. If he was a sage he would expound the Scriptures; if not, the scholars would expound before him. If he was versed in the reading of the Scriptures, he would read; if not, they would read before him. And from what texts? From Job, Ezra, and Chronicles. Zechariah ben Kabutal adds, "Many times I read before him from the Book of Daniel." If he became drowsy the young priests would snap their middle fingers into their palms and say, "My lord high priest, drive away this sleep by taking a walk on the cold marble floor." They would divert him until the time drew near for the offering of the sacrifice.

The official in charge would say to them, "Go see if the time has come for the slaughtering." If the time had come, the one perceiving it would cry out, "Daybreak!" Mattiah ben Samuel says, "He that perceived it would be asked, 'Is the entire eastern sky alit as far as Hebron?'" And he would reply, "Yes." Why was all this procedure required? Because once the light of the moon was so bright that they thought it was the dawn and they slaughtered the daily offering and then had to take it away to the place of burning.

Then they would lead the high priest down to the place of immersion. He would immerse himself five times and sanctify his hands and his feet by washing them ten times that day. They would spread a linen sheet between him and the people. He would strip off his clothes, go down and immerse himself, and come up and dry himself. They then brought him garments of gold; he would put them on and sanctify his hands and feet. They then brought him the daily sacrifice. He would make the incision and another priest would complete the slaughtering for him. He would receive the blood, toss it at the altar base, and go inside to burn the morning incense and trim the lamps. If the high priest were old or weak they would heat water and mix it with the cold water of the ritual bath to take off its chill.

They then would bring him to the Parvah Chamber within the sacred precincts. They would spread a linen sheet between him and the people. He would sanctify his hands and feet and take off his clothing. He would immerse himself, come up, and dry himself. Then he would put on white garments and sanctify his hands and feet. In the morning he was clothed in Pelusium linen worth eighteen minas, in the afternoon in Indian linen worth twelve minas. These were furnished by the people, but if the high priest wanted more expensive garments, he would have to pay for them himself.

He would come to his bullock, which was standing between the hall and the altar, its head to the south and its face to the west. He would set both hands upon it and make his confession: "O God, forgive, I beseech You, the iniquities, transgressions, and sins that I have committed, transgressed, and sinned before You, I and my house, as it is written in the Torah of Moses, Your servant, *For on this day atonement shall be made for you to cleanse you of all your sins; you shall be clean before the Lord* (Lev. 16:30)." And they answered, "Praised be His sovereign glory forever and ever!" He would come to the east of the Court to the north of the altar with his deputy on his right and the chief of his father's house on his left. There were two male goats there together with a casket in which there were two lots. They were made of box-wood, but Ben Gamla made them of gold and he was remembered for good. He would shake the casket and take out the two lots. On one was written "For the Lord" and on the other "For Azazel." If the lot bearing the name of God came up in his right hand the deputy high priest would say to him, "My lord high priest, raise your right hand," but if it came up in his left hand the chief of his father's house would say to him, "My lord high priest, raise your left hand." He would put them on the two male goats and exclaim, "A sin offering to the Lord!" And they would answer after him, "Praised be His sovereign glory forever and ever!"

He would tie a thread of crimson wool on the head of the goat to be sent forth into the wilderness and turn it toward the way by which it was to be sent out. He also would tie a thread around the throat of the one to be slaughtered as a sin offering. Then he would go back to his bullock, place his two hands upon it, and make confession: "O God, I have committed iniquities, I have transgressed and sinned before You, I and my household and the children of Aaron, Your holy people. O God, forgive, I beseech You, the iniquities, transgressions, and sins that I have committed, transgressed, and sinned before You, I, my household and the children of Aaron, Your holy people, as it is written in the Torah of Moses, Your servant, *For on this day atonement shall be made for you to cleanse you of all your sins; you shall be clean before the Lord* (Lev. 16:30)." And they would answer after him, "Praised be His sovereign glory forever and ever!"

He then would slaughter the bullock, catch its blood in a basin, and give it to a priest who would stir it on the fourth terrace of the Sanctuary so that it not congeal. He would take the fire pan, go up to the top of the altar, clear the coals on both sides, and then scoop out glowing cinders from below. Then he would come down and set the fire pan on the fourth terrace in the court. On all other days he would scoop with a fire pan of silver and empty the cinders into one of gold. On this day he scooped with the gold fire pan, in which he also brought down the cinders. On all other days it was of greenish gold, today of red gold.

They would bring out to him the ladle and the fire pan, and he would put two handfuls of incense into the ladle. The amount depended on the size of the man's hand; if it was large or small, so was the measure. Then he would take the fire pan in his right hand and the ladle in his left and walk through the Sanctuary until he came to the space between the two curtains—a cubit's space—

separating the Sanctuary from the Holy of Holies. The outer curtain was looped up on the south side and the inner one on the north side, and he would walk between them until he reached the north side. Then he would turn around to the south and walk with the curtain on his left until he reached the Ark. When he reached the Ark he would put the fire pan between the two bars and heap up the incense on the coals. Soon the entire place became filled with smoke. Afterward, he would come out the way he had gone in and in the outer place offer a brief prayer. The prayer was brief in order not to frighten the Jews. (After the Ark had been taken away, a stone from the time of the early prophets remained on the spot, which was called *Shetiyah*. It was three finger-breadths above the ground, and upon it the high priest would set the fire pan.)

He would take the blood from whoever was stirring it and enter the place he had entered before and stand upon the spot he had previously stood upon and sprinkle the blood, once upward and seven times downward, not as one intending to do so but as though he were wielding a whip. And he used to count, "one, one and one, one and two, one and three, one and four, one and five, one and six, one and seven." He would then come out and put the basin on the golden stand in the Sanctuary.

They would bring the male goat to him, and he would slaughter it and catch its blood in a basin. He would reenter the same place, stand on the same spot, and sprinkle the blood once upward and seven times downward, again like a man using a whip, counting as before. He would then come out and place it on a second golden stand in the Sanctuary.

He then would come to the scapegoat to be sent off into the wilderness and, as he laid his two hands upon it, he would make confession: "O God, Your people, the House of Israel, have committed iniquity, transgressed, and sinned before You. O God, forgive, I beseech You, the iniquities, transgressions, and sins which Your people, the House of Israel, have committed, transgressed and sinned before You, as it is written in the Torah of Moses, Your servant, *For on this day atonement shall be made for you to cleanse you of all your sins; you shall be clean before the Lord* (Lev. 16: 30.)" When the priests and the people standing in the Court heard the ineffable name of God come forth from the mouth of the high priest, they knelt, bowed, and fell on their faces and exclaimed, "Praised be His sovereign glory forever and ever!"

The scapegoat was handed over to the one who was to lead it away. All were eligible to do it, but the custom was established that an Israelite should not. However, it once happened that Arsela of Sepphoris led it away and he was an Israelite. A causeway was made for it because the Babylonian Jews who were gathered at the Temple used to pull its hair as it was led past them, crying out to it, "Bear our sins and be gone! Bear our sins and be gone!" Some of the distinguished people of Jerusalem would accompany the leader of the goat to the first booth. There were ten booths from Jerusalem to the ravine, ninety ris away. At each booth they would say to the man leading the goat, "Here is food and water," and they would go with him to the next booth, but never from the next to the last booth to the last booth, and none would go with him to the ravine but they would stand at a distance and see what he did.

What did he do? He would divide the thread of crimson wool, tying half to the rock and half between its horns. He would push it from behind, and before it had fallen half way down, it would break into pieces. Then he would return and sit down at the last booth until dark.

The high priest then would come to the bullock and male goat to be burned, and he would burn the sacrificial portions on the altar. The people would tell the high priest, "The male goat has reached the wilderness." How did they know this? They would set up sentinels along the route and from them towels were waved so that the signal was communicated back. Rabbi Ishmael said there was another sign. A thread of crimson wool was tied to the Sanctuary door, and when the male goat reached the wilderness the thread would turn white, as it is written, *Be your sins like crimson, they can turn snow-white* (Isa. 1:18).

Then the high priest would read from the Scriptures, and if he wished to read while still in his linen garments, he could do so. Otherwise he could read in his own white garment. The sexton of the synagogue would take a scroll of the Torah and give it to the chief officer of the synagogue. He in turn would give it to the deputy high priest who gave it to the high priest who received it standing and so read the portions beginning, *After the death of the two sons of Aaron* . . . (Lev. 16) and *Mark the tenth day* . . . (Lev. 23:26–32). Then he would roll up the scroll of the Torah and hold it to himself and say, "More than I have read before you is written here." By heart he recited from Numbers, beginning, *On the tenth day* . . . (Num. 29:7–11). He then pronounced eight benedictions: for the Torah, for the Temple Service, for the Thanksgiving, for the Forgiveness of Sin, for the Temple, for the Israelites, for the Priests, and a general prayer for the rest.

They would bring him the vestments of gold, and he would put them on. He would sanctify his hands and feet by washing and go out and offer his ram and the ram of the people. He then would sanctify his hands and feet, strip off his clothing, and immerse himself. After he came up, he would dry himself and put on the white garments they brought him. He again would sanctify his hands and feet and go in to bring out the ladle and fire pan. Again he would sanctify his hands and feet, take off his garments, and immerse and dry himself. He would put on the golden vestments they brought him and sanctify his hands and feet. He then would go in to burn the afternoon incense and trim the lamps, and again he would sanctify his hands and feet and take off his vestments. Finally they brought him his own clothing to put on, and they would accompany him to his house, where he would make a feast for his friends to celebrate his having come out safely from the Sanctuary.[115]

What was the form of the high priest's prayer on Yom Kippur when he would leave the Sanctuary? He would pray: "May it be Your will that the coming year shall be marked by ample rain and if the rain be excessive, may there be sufficient warmth to counteract it. May it be blessed with dew; a year of favor, a year of blessing, a year of plenty, a year of trade, wherein Your people Israel shall not be dependent upon each other nor shall any dominate another. Neither turn You to the prayer of the wayfarers." The rabbis of Caesarea said, "It was concerning our brethren in Caesarea that the high priest prayed that they might not assume too much authority." The rabbis of the south said, "Concerning our brethren who are in the Sharon the high priest prayed that their homes not become their tombs."

The high priest was able to tell at the beginning of the year, on Yom Kippur, what its outcome would be. How was that possible? When he would see the smoke of the altar rise toward the south he knew that the south would have plenty. If it rose toward the west he knew that the west would be prosperous. If it rose toward the east he knew that the east would enjoy abundance, and so with the north. If the smoke went straight up toward the middle of the sky he knew that it would be a year of plenty for all the world.[116]

There were no greater days of joy among the Jews than Yom Kippur and the fifteenth day of Av. On those days the maidens of Israel would go forth in white robes borrowed for the occasion (in order not to embarrass the poor who had none of their own). The white robes had first to be immersed in a ritual bath to purify them. Dressed in these robes the maidens of Israel would go forth to dance in the vineyards. The young men would also go, and to them the maidens would sing, "Young man, lift up your eyes and see whom you will choose. Pay no attention to beauty but rather to the quality of the family."[117]

One Yom Kippur there was a Sadducean high priest who, following Sadducee teaching, arranged and lit the incense outside and then brought it already smoking into the Holy of Holies. As he left he was very glad. His father met him and said, "My son, although we are Sadducees, your deed has made me fearful because I fear the Pharisees." The high priest answered, "All my life, I was saddened by the verse, *For I appear in the cloud over the cover* (Lev. 16:2). I would say, when shall I have the opportunity to fulfill it as we Sadducees interpret it? Now that the opportunity has come, should I not have made the most of it?" Only a few days later he died. His body was thrown on the dungheap and worms came forth from his nose. Others say that he was smitten as he came out of the Holy of Holies. The high priest, following the usual practice in coming out of the Holy of Holies, was walking backward so as not to turn his back on the Holy of Holies. Reaching the threshold, his back emerged behind the curtain. An angel came and, outside the curtain, struck him on the back between the shoulders. He fell forward into the Holy of Holies, his face to the ground. The noise was heard outside in the Temple Court and the priests came in and found him lying there, the trace of a calf's foot upon his shoulder, as it is written, *The legs of each were [fused into] a single rigid leg, and the feet of each were like a single calf's hoof* (Ezek. 1:7). They picked him up and threw him out.[118]

In earlier days when the first day of Sukkot fell on a Sabbath, the men would bring their palm branches on the eve of the Sabbath to the Temple Mount, and the officials would take them and place them in order on top of the portico. The older people put theirs in a special chamber. They were all taught to say, "Whoever gets possession of my *lulav*, let it be his as my gift." On the next day they would arrive early and the officials would throw down the *lulavim* and the people would snatch them. In so doing they would sometimes injure each other. When the Court saw that the situation was dangerous they decreed that each person should use the *lulav* in his home.[119]

How was the *mizvah* of the willow branch fulfilled? There was a place below Jerusalem called Moza, where they would go and cut young willow branches and bring them back to set them up at the sides of the altar so that their tops were bent over the altar. They then would blow the shofar, first a sustained blast, then a quavering one, then a sustained one. Each day for the first six days of the festival they would circle the altar once in procession, saying, *O Lord, deliver us! O Lord, let us prosper!* (Ps. 118: 25). Rabbi Judah says that what they said was "*Ani ve-ho!* Save us, we pray! *Ani ve-ho!* Save us, we pray!" On the seventh day they circled the altar in procession seven times. When they left what did they say? "All this beauty for You, O altar! All this beauty for You, O altar!" Rabbi Eleazar says they said, "To the Lord and to You, O altar! To the Lord and to You, O altar!"

On the Sabbath the practices were exactly the same except that they gathered the willow branches on Sabbath eve and placed them in gilded troughs containing water so that they might not wither. Rabbi Johanan ben Beroka says that they would bring palm branches and beat them on the ground at the sides of the altar and that day was called the Day of the Beating of the Branches. The children would then cast away their *lulavim* and eat their citrons.[120]

On whose behalf were the seventy bullocks offered during the seven days of the Sukkot festival? On behalf of the seventy nations of the world. And on whose behalf was the one bullock sacrificed on the Eighth Day of Solemn Assembly? On behalf of the one, unique people, Israel. It is like an earthly king who says to his servant, "Prepare a small meal for me so that you may bring me some joy." "Woe to the nations of the world," said Rabbi Johanan, for they have suffered a grievous loss and they are not even aware of what they have lost. As long as the Temple stood, its altar atoned for their sins. Now what atones for them?"[121]

How was the water libation performed during the seven days of the Sukkot festival? They would fill a golden pitcher holding three logs with water from the brook of Siloam. When they reached the Water Gate with it they blew three notes on the shofar, a sustained blast, a quavering one, and again a sustained blast. The priest whose turn of duty it was went up the altar ramp and turned to his left where there were two silver bowls. At the bottom each was perforated with a hole like a nostril. The bowl to the west, for water, had a narrower hole, that to the east, for wine, a wider one, so that both bowls emptied themselves at the same time. To the priest who performed the libations they would say, "Raise your hand high!" For once a Sadducean high priest poured the libation over his feet and the people pelted him with their citrons. On that same day the horn of the altar was damaged, and it was temporarily repaired by plugging the hole with a lump of salt so that the altar might not be seen in a damaged state.[122]

On the Sabbath they would perform the ritual the same way except that on the eve of the Sabbath they would fill with water from the brook of Siloam a golden jar that had not been hallowed and placed it in a special chamber. If it was upset or uncovered, they would refill it from the laver, for wine or water uncovered is invalid for the altar.[123]

At the close of the first day of the festival of Sukkot the priests and Levites would go down to the Court of the Women where temporary changes had been made in preparation for the large crowds expected. They would have golden candelabra there with four golden bowls on top of each. At each candelabrum four ladders were placed. Four young priests stood by and in their hands were pitchers of oil holding one hundred and twenty logs, which they poured into all the bowls. They made wicks from the worn out breeches and girdles of the priests and with them lit the candelabra. The light at this ceremony of the water libation was so great that there was not a courtyard in Jerusalem that did not reflect it. Men of piety and good deeds used to dance with burning torches in their hands, singing songs and praises. Levites would play on harps, lyres, cymbals, and all other kinds of musical instruments. On the fifteen steps leading down from the Court of the Israelites to the Court of the Women, which correspond to the fifteen Songs of Ascents in the Psalms, the Levites stood with their instruments and played music.

Two priests stood at the upper gate, which leads down from the Court of the Israelites to the Court of the Women, with two trumpets in their hands. At cockcrow they blew a sustained blast, a quavering one, and again a sustained one. When they reached the tenth step they blew again in the same manner. When they reached the Court of the Women they blew the same three notes once more, and they continued like this until they reached the gate that leads out to the east. Upon reaching it, they turned their faces to the west, toward the Temple, and exclaimed, "When our fathers were in this place they stood with their backs toward the Temple of the Lord and their faces toward the east and they bowed down eastward toward the sun, but as for us, our eyes are turned toward the Lord." Rabbi Judah says that they used to repeat the words, "We are the Lord's and our eyes are turned toward the Lord." When they departed from each other, what did they say to each other? They would say, *May the Lord bless you from Zion; may you share the prosperity of Jerusalem all the days of your life, and live to see your children's children. May all be well with Israel* (Ps. 128:5–6).[124]

He who never witnessed the rejoicing at these ceremonies of the libation of the water has never really seen rejoicing in his life.[125] They related of Hillel the Elder that when he would rejoice at these ceremonies, he would say, "If I am here, all are here and if I be not here, who is here? To the place I love there my feet take me." So does the Holy One, blessed be He, say, "If you will come to My house, I shall come to your house, as it is said, *In every place where I cause My name to be mentioned I will come to you and bless you* (Exod. 20:21)."[126] Of Rabban Simon ben Gamaliel it was said that when he would rejoice at these ceremonies of the water libation he would take eight flaming torches in his hands, throw them upward and catch them, without one ever touching another. When he would fall prostrate he would press both thumbs against the floor stretching out low, then kiss the floor and lift himself up straight, a feat no other person could do.[127]

There were among the visitors at the libation ceremonies those who said, "Blessed was our youth that does not now embarrass our old age." These were the pious and the men of good deeds. Others said, "Blessed is our old age that has atoned for our youth." These were the repentant. Both used to say, "Blessed is he who has not sinned and let him who has sinned return and he will be forgiven."[128] Rabbi Joshua ben Ḥananiah said, "When we participated in the rejoicing at the libation ceremonies our eyes saw no sleep. How so? The first hour was devoted to the daily morning sacrifice, then to the morning prayers, next to the additional festival sacrifice, then to the additional festival prayers, afterward to the study hall, then to eating and drinking, then to the afternoon prayers, next to the daily evening sacrifice, afterward we rejoiced at the libation ceremonies until morning."[129]

How was the ceremony performed in which the king read from the Torah? Every eighth year, the year following each sabbatical year, on the night following the first day of Sukkot, a wooden platform was prepared for the king in the Temple Court. On this he sat, as it is written, *Every seventh year, the year set for remission* . . . (Deut. 31:10). The sexton of the congregation would take a scroll of the Torah and give it to the head of the congregation. He would hand it over to the deputy high priest who would give it to the high priest. He then handed it over to the king. The king would receive it standing, then sit to read from it. King Agrippa would receive it standing and would also stand while reading from it and for this the sages praised him. When he would reach the verse, *You must not set a foreigner over you, one who is not your kinsman* (Deut. 17:15), tears flowed from his eyes. The rabbis called to him, "Be not concerned, Agrippa, you are our brother, you are our brother, you are our brother!"

The Torah reading was from the beginning of Deuteronomy to *Hear, O Israel* . . . (Deut. 6:4–9); then, *If, then, you obey the commandments* . . . (Deut. 11:13 ff.); followed by, *You shall set aside every year a tenth part* (Deut. 14:22); then, *when you have set aside in full the tenth part* (Deut. 26:12 ff.); and finally, the section dealing with the king (Deut. 17:14–20), the Blessings (Deut. 27:15–26), and the Maledictions (Deut. 28:26–28)—until the end of the section. With the same blessings with which the high priest blessed them the king blessed them except that he pronounced the blessing for the festivals instead of that for the forgiveness of sin.[130]

After the seven days of Sukkot have been concluded, *on the eighth day you shall hold a solemn gathering* (Num. 29:35). This is what is meant by the verse, *They answer my love with accusation and I must stand judgment* (Ps. 109:4). For during the seven days of Sukkot Israel offers seventy bullocks as sacrifices on behalf of the seventy nations of the world. Therefore, they should love us. But not only do they not love us; they hate us! Therefore, the Holy One, blessed be He, said to the Jewish people, "During the seven days of Sukkot you have offered sacrifices before Me on behalf of the peoples of the world, but now offer a sacrifice for yourself." Therefore, *on the eighth day you shall hold a solemn gathering* (Num. 29:35).

On the eighth day *you shall present a burnt offering . . . one bull, one ram* (Num. 29:36). This may be compared to a king who made a feast lasting seven days to which were invited all the people of the country. When the seven days of feasting were over the king said to his beloved friend, "Our duties to the people of the country are ended. Now let the two of us celebrate with whatever you can find, a litra of meat or fish or vegetables." So did the Holy One, blessed be He, say to Israel, "All the sacrifices that you have offered during the seven days of the Sukkot festival were on behalf of the peoples of the world, but *on the eighth day you shall hold a solemn gathering!* Make do with whatever you can find, *one bull, one ram.*[131]

On Purim even the priests who engaged in the Temple service, the Levites who stood on the platform for the chanting of the Psalms, and the lay Israelites at their station were to halt their activities and come to listen to the reading of the Book of Esther. Even the study of Torah is to be halted for this reason. Not that it is to be inferred, however, that the study of Torah is more important than the Temple service. The sacrifices on behalf of the people take precedence over study of the Torah; the latter over sacrifices offered on behalf of individuals.[132]

═══ 6 ═══

Extraordinary Events in the Temple

Rabbi Ishmael ben Elisha said, "Once when I entered the Holy of Holies to burn the incense I saw the crowned God, the Lord of Hosts, seated on a lofty and exalted throne. He said to me, 'Ishmael, My son, bless Me.' I said to Him, 'May it be Your will that Your mercy overcome Your anger and Your compassion overrule Your judgmental attributes. May Your conduct toward Your children be governed by mercy and may You judge them with more compassion than justice requires." He nodded His head in assent.[133]

When the Jews would come up to Jerusalem for the festivals they would stand in the Temple closely pressed together, so great was the crowd, yet they were able to prostrate themselves with wide space between them. This was one of the ten miracles wrought in the Temple. The others were: no woman ever miscarried from the odor of the holy flesh; the holy flesh never became putrid; no fly was ever seen in the slaughterhouse; no pollution ever befell the high priest on Yom Kippur; no rain ever quenched the fire of the woodpile on the altar; neither did the wind ever overcome the column of smoke rising from it; no disqualifying defect was ever found in the omer, in the two loaves, or in the bread of display; never did a serpent or a scorpion injure anyone in Jerusalem; nor did any man ever say to another that there is insufficient space in Jerusalem for me to stay overnight. There were other miracles as well. The fragments of earthenware in which the flesh of sin offerings was boiled and which had to be broken were swallowed up in the very place where they were broken. The crop, the feathers, and the ashes removed from the inner altar and the candlestick were swallowed up in the very place where they were taken off. When the bread of display was removed it was as fresh as when it was put on the table.[134]

On the night following the last day of the Sukkot festival all the people looked upon the smoke rising from the pile of wood on the altar. If it inclined toward the north, the poor rejoiced and the wealthy were downcast because that meant the rains of the coming year would be abundant, their fruits would spoil more quickly, and so they would have to be sold fast and inexpensively. If the smoke turned southward, the poor were unhappy and the wealthy rejoiced, for there would be little rain that year and the fruit would be preserved. If it turned toward the east, all rejoiced because it meant average rainfall, and plenty of fruit with no danger of rotting so that moderate prices could be charged. If westward, all were downcast because the seeds would dry up resulting in famine. Does not this entire passage seem to contradict the statement in the previous passage that the winds never overcame the column of smoke rising from the altar? The explanation is that while the wind was bent in a straight line in different directions, it never broke and scattered. That was the miracle of it.[135]

From Jerusalem to Jericho the distance was ten parasangs. The sound of the turning hinges of the Temple doors were heard the length of eight Sabbath limits. The goats in Jericho used to sneeze because of the aroma of the incense. The women in Jericho did not need to perfume themselves because of the scent of the incense. A bride in Jerusalem did not have to perfume herself because of the aroma of the incense. Rabbi Jose ben Diglai said, "My father had goats on the mountains of Mikwar and they used to sneeze because of the smell of the incense." Rabbi Ḥiyya bar Avin quoted Rabbi Joshua ben Korḥa as saying, "An old man told me, 'Once I was walking toward Shiloh and I could smell the odor of the incense.' "[136]

From Jericho the people could hear the noise of the opening of the great gate, the sound of the shovel-shaped musical instrument, the noise of the wooden device made by Ben Katin for the laver, the voice of Gebini the public crier, the sound of the flute, the noise of the cymbal, the sound of the singing, the sound of the shofar. Some say, even the voice of the high priest could be heard pronouncing the divine name on Yom Kippur.[137]

Notes

V. THE SECOND TEMPLE

1. The Building of the Second Temple

1. Numbers Rabbah 14:8.
2. Genesis Rabbah, Shitah Ḥadashah for Jacob's Blessing, chap. 2.
3. Exodus Rabbah 40:3.
4. Megillah 17b; Songs Rabbah 5:5; see also Ginzberg, *Legends* 6:441, n. 35.
5. Genesis Rabbah 71:3; the names of these families are found in Ezra 2:51.
6. Esther Rabbah 5:2; Ahasuerus is identified in this and the following rabbinic passages with Artaxerxes.
7. Exodus Rabbah 9:7; see Ezra 4:6, 4:21; and cf. Esther Rabbah 1:5; Songs Rabbah 5:7.
8. Esther Rabbah, Proem 5, 8; see Ezra 4:8.
9. Esther Rabbah 1:1, utilizing as a supporting text Prov. 18:9.
10. Esther Rabbah 1:1. The text in the Midrash reads Cyrus, but it should be Darius, according to Ezra 6:1–15, who ordered the resumption of the Temple's construction. This Darius was identified by the rabbis as the son of Ahasuerus (see also Ezra 4:21). Because of Darius's argument in the legend, the rabbis explain that Artaxerxes (or Ahasuerus, as identified by the rabbis) was also credited with the rebuilding of the Temple (see Ezra 6:14).

11. Zevaḥim 62a; see Ginzberg, *Legends,* 6:440, n. 31.

12. Yerushalmi Sotah 5, 20b; Pesaḥim 9, 36c; Nedarim 6, 39d–40a; Sanhedrin 1, 18d; see Ginzberg, *Legends* 6:440, n. 32.

13. Numbers Rabbah 14:18; see Num. 7:88; Ezra 6:3.

14. Kiddushin 66a.

15. Mariamne, daughter of Alexander, son of Aristobulus II. Josephus says she was put to death by Herod several years after their marriage.

16. The verb in the verse means to stream or flow or gaze with joy, but it can also mean to shine, especially in Aramaic.

17. The verse speaks of the error that may be done unwittingly by the congregation in generations to come. Here the interpretation would be that the error is "hid from their eyes," the word *their* referring to the rabbis.

18. M. Jastrow, *A Dictionary of the Targumim, the Talmud Babli and Yerushalmi, and the Midrashic Literature* (New York, 1926), p. 1379, takes this to mean "and, therefore, your country is declared a colony," an anachronistic allusion to the change of the status of Judea to a Roman province upon the banishment of Archelaus.

19. The previous passages concerning Herod are from Bava Batra 3b, 4a; see also Sukkah 50b.

20. Numbers Rabbah 14:8.

21. Ta'anit 23a and Leviticus Rabbah 35:10.

2. Differences between the First and Second Temples

22. Bava Batra 3a–b on Hag. 2:9.

23. Yoma 21b, based on the fact that in Hag. 1:8 the word *ve-'ekavda* is written without the last letter. The rabbis saw in the omission of the letter *heh,* which has the numerical value of five, an allusion to the five missing articles. The inclusion of the oil of anointment among the missing items is found in Songs Rabbah 8:9.

24. Numbers Rabbah 15:10. The rabbis see in the five expressions of joy in Isa. 35:1–2 an allusion to the restoration of the five missing items.

25. Leviticus Rabbah 20:5 and Yoma 53b.

26. Zevaḥim 62a; see Ginzberg, *Legends,* 6:440, n. 31; Yoma 21b.

27. Yoma 54a; Shekalim, chap. 6.

28. Numbers Rabbah 12:4 and Songs Rabbah 3:10. This tradition conflicts with the one stated previously, that the rabbis advised Herod not to cover the Temple with gold overlay, because the differently colored marble was attractive as it was. But perhaps this second tradition refers to the Temple interior, and one must allow for hyperbole.

29. Mishnah Yoma 3:10 and Tosefta Yoma 2:4. King Monobaz II was the son of Monobaz I and Queen Helene of Adiabene, a district of northern Iraq that became an independent kingdom in the first century B.C.E. Queen Helene became a convert to Judaism about 30 C.E. with her sons, Monobaz II and Izates, who supported the Jews during the war against the Romans (66–70 C.E.). The verses concerning the suspected wife are found in Num. 5:12–31. The priest was to write the oath of the ordeal of jealousy upon a parchment and immerse it in water that he then gave the suspected wife to drink. The presentation

of the golden tablet by Queen Helene made unnecessary the use of a Torah scroll from which to copy the verses, for the oath was now transcribed by the priest from the tablet. See Gittin 60a, and Josephus, *Antiquities*, 20.4.1. ff.

30. Yoma 37b.

31. Mishnah Yoma 3:9.

32. Yoma 3:10; Tamid 1:4, 3:8. For the biblical description of the laver see Exod. 30:18–21. Whatever is contained in a sacred vessel becomes holy itself (Zevaḥim 9:7), and any holy thing that remains overnight becomes invalid for use (see Menaḥot 7:4).

33. Yoma 38a; Tosefta Yoma 2:4; Middot 1:4, 2:3, 2:6; Shekalim 6:3; Sotah 1:5; Nega'im 14:8. The Nicanor Gates were those of the great eastern entry into the Temple Court. Corinthian bronze was refined, hence lighter in weight and brighter in color.

34. Yevamot 6a–b.

3. Priests and Levites

35. Numbers Rabbah 12:7, based on Ezek. 44:15 and preceding verses.

36. Yoma 8b, 18a. The measure brought by Martha was a tarkaba, a dry measure containing two kabs. The name of the king in this talmudic passage, Yannai, is frequently used in the Talmud as a general patronymic for Hasmonean and Herodian rulers. Here it is used for Agrippa II; see Josephus, *Antiquities*, 20.9.4.

37. Leviticus Rabbah 21:9, based on Lev. 16:3; Pesikta Rabbati 47:4. The leveling instruments mentioned in the story were used to level off measures of corn, wheat, etc. For the origin of the proverb about the fool and the candlestick see Shabbat 116b.

38. Yerushalmi Yoma, chap. 1; Tanḥuma Hakadum, Emor.

39. Songs Rabbah 4:4; Yoma 71b.

40. Leviticus Rabbah 21:10; see also Exod. 28:4 ff., Gen. 17:12, Mal. 2:5.

41. Leviticus Rabbah 2:10; see also Exod. 28:6 ff.

42. Numbers Rabbah 6:1 on Num. 4:22. This lengthy exposition of precedence is prompted by the numbering of Gershon, the firstborn, after Kohat. See also Horayot, chaps. 3 and 13a and Yerushalmi ad locum; Tosefta, chap. 3, end; Tanna de-ve Eliyahu Zuta, chap. 16. The proof-texts of these orders of precedence are as follows: for wisdom's highest rank, Prov. 3:15; for precedence of a king over a high priest, 1 Kings 1:33; of high priest over prophet, 1 Kings 1:34 and Zech. 3:8 (together with Deut. 13:2). According to the talmudic passage in Keritot 5b, the original oil of anointing was hidden away by Josiah and afterward high priests were consecrated through their additional vestments. The statement here would, therefore, refer to a high priest consecrated before the oil was concealed and another afterward, the first having become infirm, so that both are high priests simultaneously. The chief of the watch was the leader of a group of both priests and Levites serving in rotation, while a priests' division was a subdivision of it. An *amarkal*, as used in this text, was, according to Jastrow, the Temple controller or one of the seven Temple trustees superintending the cashiers. A *natin* was a descendant of the Gibeonites

(see Josh. 9:27). David forbade intermarriage with them (Yevamot 78b). Jews may not intermarry with a *natin* (Mishnah Yevamot 8:3; see also Tosefta Kiddushin 5:4). The last-mentioned difference of opinion is based on a play of words on Prov. 3:15, *Wisdom is more precious than rubies*, where the Hebrew words for "rubies," *peninim*, and "the innermost precincts of the Sanctuary," *li-fnei ve-lifnim*, are compared with each other. The same play on these words is found in Sotah 4a.

43. Leviticus Rabbah 21:6. The various merits are deduced from proof-texts containing the word *this*, as in the verse, *With this shall Aaron enter the Shrine* (Lev. 16:3). Other texts are: Deut. 4:44; Gen. 17:10; Isa. 66:2; Ezek. 5:5; Deut. 33:7; Songs 7:8 (the love poem is interpreted by the rabbis as an allegory of the love between God and Israel); Exod. 25:3; Mal. 3:10; and Lev. 16:3. The high priest alone entered the Holy of Holies and only on Yom Kippur.

44. Yoma 53b.

45. Ecclesiastes Rabbah 3:11; Numbers Rabbah 11:8; Yerushalmi Yoma 40d. The transmission of the secret things of prophecy is to be done under similar conditions as the transmission of God's ineffable name (see Mekhilta, beginning of Bo').

46. Ta'anit 24b.

47. Exodus Rabbah 2:6; see also Genesis Rabbah 97:3.

48. Mishnah Ta'anit 4:2. By "the first prophets" are meant Samuel and David, cf. supra, 27a; see 1 Chron. 23–24. The verses prescribed here were read from a Torah scroll only for the morning services but evidently not for the afternoon services.

49. Ta'anit 27b.

50. Ta'anit 27b; Soferim 17; see R. T. Herford, *Christianity in Talmud and Midrash* (London, 1903; Clifton, N.J., 1966), pp. 171–73.

51. Middot, chap. 5.

52. Nedarim 20a.

53. Pesahim 3b.

54. Yoma 39a–b; see also Kiddushin 53a. Concerning the crimson-colored strap, see Isa. 1:18 and Rashi ad locum. For the miracle of the westernmost light, see Shabbat 22b and Menahot 86b; for the logs for the altar fire, see Yoma 26b; for the two breads, Lev. 23:17.

55. Yoma 39b; see also Menahot 109b. God's ineffable name could be pronounced only when there was an indication that the Heavenly Presence rested on the Temple (see Tosafot, Sotah 38a). With the death of Simon the Just and the disappearance of the many signs of the Heavenly Presence that marked his term of office, the priests hesitated to utter the ineffable name.

56. Numbers Rabbah 2:26; Leviticus Rabbah 20:11; Yoma 47a; Yerushalmi Yoma, chap. 1; Yerushalmi Horayot, chap. 3. The version in Yoma gives the second brother's name as Yeshevav, and there the sages' reply to Kimhit's explanation is, "Many women do so (cover their hair even indoors) and they are not so rewarded." True modesty consisted in the covering of the woman's head in public, but Kimhit went even further and did so even indoors. The sages' question to her was an attempt to discover why such divine favor had been shown her. Her answer in the version in Leviticus Rabbah also adds that the rafters had not looked down upon the seam of her undergarment. Because the accident with the saliva occurred on Yom Kippur,

another high priest had to be appointed immediately to carry out the many functions of the high priest on that day, all of which had to be executed by a high priest in a state of ritual purity. The sages' exclamation is a play on the words *Kimḥit* and *kemaḥ*, "flour." The verse from Ps. 45:14 means that just as the princess's glory is within the palace, so too a woman's glory is in the modest seclusion of the home.

57. Pesaḥim 57a. Rashi explains that Johanan was so favored because he trained many young priests and fed them in his home.

58. Pesaḥim 57a.

59. Pesaḥim 57a–b.

60. Pesaḥim 57a; Tosefta Menaḥot 13:21. The latter text speaks only of the house of Boethus and the house of Ishmael ben Phiabi. The sons-in-law were appointed to the office of *amarkal*, controller. There were seven such Temple trustees who supervised the cashiers. Josephus notes that under the Roman procurators (6–66 C.E.) "the government became an aristocracy and the high priests were entrusted with a dominion over the nation." Rashi, on Mal. 1:10, quotes a midrashic source that tells that for the simplest of services in the Temple, such as the closing of a door or the kindling of a light, a fee was demanded by corrupt priests.

61. Yoma 71b; Shemaiah and Avtalyon were the famous teachers of Hillel and Shammai (see Avot 1:10–12). They were descendants of non-Jews; according to one tradition, descendants of Sennacherib (see Gittin 57b). The high priest referred to their ancestry because of his anger and jealousy at the preference by the people of these sages to him. The sages, in their answer, indicated that his arrogance was a cause of strife, the opposite of the love of peace characteristic of Aaron, the first high priest, and which should have been pursued by him also.

62. Mishnah Yoma 3:11. The twelve loaves of bread of display, placed on the golden table in the Temple from Sabbath to Sabbath (see Exod. 25:30 and Lev. 24:5–9) were thin and fragile. Baked of approximately four quarts of flour, they were about one-half inch thick, twenty-eight inches long, twelve inches wide. They were made with special shapes at the corners, and the trick was to remove these loaves from the oven without breaking them. They were baked on Friday or Wednesday, to be eaten on the Sabbath of the following week, and great baking skill was required to keep them fresh and edible. The priests of the house of Garmu are here taken to task for not passing on to others this skill that they had. They, and the priests of the house of Abtinas, explained, in extenuation, that they did not want others to learn their special skills lest they be used in the services of heathens, but the sages rejected this explanation. The priests of the house of Abtinas knew which special herbs to use for the incense so that its smoke went straight up. The special skill of Ben Kamẓar was that he knew how to hold four pens in one hand and so, simultaneously, write a four-letter name.

63. Yoma 38a; Songs Rabbah 3:6. The latter source differs in the baking procedure. The salary mentioned is quite excessive and is probably an exaggeration.

64. Yoma 38a; Tanḥuma Vayishlaḥ 8; Yerushalmi Shekalim, chap. 5; Yoma, chap. 3; and Songs Rabbah 3:6. The latter source describes the ascent of the smoke differently. The priests of the house of Abtinas

here and of the house of Garmu in the previous passage are praised by the sages in the end, although their refusal to teach their skill is condemned, because they did more than was required by the law. The former would not let their women use perfume at all (and their children as well, according to the midrashic source). The latter would not let their families have fine bread, which they did for appearance' sake, for one must avoid even the appearance of acting wrongly even though one knows he is acting correctly. The Talmud here quotes Num. 32:22; the Midrash also quotes Prov. 3:4. The incense compound of the house of Abtinas is also mentioned in Songs Rabbah 1:14.

65. See supra, n. 64; this is either Ishmael ben Loga or Simon ben Loga (as in the Midrash). The Midrash adds that the boy died soon afterward, an act of Providence, lest he be tempted to reveal the secret. The plant "smoke-raiser" was supposed to be the special ingredient that caused the incense smoke to rise straight up and was known only to the priests of the house of Abtinas who guarded it as a family secret.

66. See supra, n. 64.

67. Yoma 38b; Songs Rabbah 3:5; Yerushalmi Yoma, chap. 3; Shekalim, chap. 5. The priests recoiled at the sound either because of the sudden volume of his music or because they were startled at its beauty. He is also referred to as Hugdes. The midrashic source explains that he succeeded in producing the sounds of all kinds of musical instruments so that his fellow priests would involuntarily turn their heads to look at him.

68. See supra, n. 67. Songs Rabbah 3:6 says it was the house of Kamẓar at fault here, not an individual named Ben Kamẓar, their reading being Bet Kamẓar instead of Ben. It also adds that, because of the inability to offer any explanation for their refusal to teach their skill, they had no descendants. A four-letter word could be the Tetragrammaton (see Rashi on Mishnah Yoma 3:11).

4. In and about the Temple

69. Midrash Tanḥuma Hakadum, Kedoshim.

70. Yoma 5:2.

71. Middot 4:7.

72. Songs Rabbah 4:4; the proof-text for the facing positions is a play on words in Exod. 15:17. The source for the spring is Yoma 77b and 78a. The main court is the *ulam*. The House of David or Zion was the fortress in the wall of the city. The ritually unclean could include men and women suffering from gonorrhea, menstruating women, and women after childbirth (see Zech. 13:1).

73. Ḥullin 90b; Middot 3:8, which adds the word *leaf* to berry and cluster. In all these three instances the rabbis in the Talmud assert that hyperbole was used. Three hundred kurs may equal about 2,830 bushels. The Talmud points to exaggeration as a linguistic style that may be found also in the Pentateuch and the Prophets. Rashi ad locum gives two explanations for the talmudic expression, "And of (or by) eight hundred and twenty thousand was it made." He prefers "threads," but he indicates a variant explanation, that the curtain was made by

820,000 maidens. The priests dipped the curtain in water when it became ritually impure.

74. Arakhin 10b; Tosefta; see also Arakhin 2:3. The king referred to was probably Herod.

75. See supra, n. 74, and also Yerushalmi Sukkah 5:55c–d.

76. Shekalim 5:1, Yerushalmi Shekalim 48d; Tamid 8:3.

77. Arakhin 10b.

78. Arakhin 10b, 11a; Yerushalmi Sukkah 55d. Some think the *magrefah* to have been a kind of organ. Rabbi Naḥman bar Isaac in the talmudic source declares the description of this instrument to be an exaggeration.

79. Tamid 3:8; for Gebini, see Shekalim 5:1 and Yoma 20b.

80. Arakhin 13b; Pesikta Rabbati, beginning of chap. 21 (ed. M. Friedmann [Vienna, 1880], 98b and 99a). The talmudic passage contains the following biblical sources for the seven- eight- and ten-stringed harps, respectively: Pss. 16:11, 12:11, 92:4. However, Josephus (*Antiquities* 7.12.3) says that the Temple harp had ten strings.

81. Shekalim 5:6. Pious persons should avoid publicity for their deeds of philanthropy.

82. Genesis Rabbah 70:8; Sanhedrin 86b.

83. Numbers Rabbah 7:8.

84. Middot 3:8. The crowns were placed as ornaments in the windows of the upper chambers of the porch. According to Asheri the young priests would climb up to see if the crowns were in good order, not merely for pleasure.

85. Leviticus Rabbah 31:7; Midrash Tanḥuma, Ba-ha'alotekha, sec. 2; Menaḥot, chap. 8.

86. Numbers Rabbah 11:3; Songs Rabbah 3:7. The Torah scroll was the authorized one from which other copies were made.

87. Ketubbot 105a. This coin was equal to a common sela or half a zuz.

88. Songs Rabbah 4:1. The seat of the Sanhedrin in the Chamber of Hewn Stones was not in the sacred precinct of the Temple and, therefore, it is called "behind the Temple."

5. Services and Practices in the Temple

89. Songs Rabbah 1:9.

90. Genesis Rabbah 99:3; Num. 28:4. The allusion here is to the description by Jacob of Benjamin as *a ravenous wolf; in the morning he consumes the foe, and in the evening he divides the spoil* (Gen. 49:27). The Temple was in Benjamin's territory although the greater part of Jerusalem was in the portion of Judah.

91. Tanḥuma Hakadum, Emor.

92. Ibid.

93. Leviticus Rabbah 3:6; Midrash Tehillim, Ps. 22:31. Apamea was an important town in ancient Syria. The reference to the good treasured up for the righteous may be an allusion to Ps. 31:20. In the version given in Midrash Tehillim the place of origin of the poor man is "Gaul or Spain or from such distant country."

94. Midrash Tehillim, Ps. 22:31.

95. Leviticus Rabbah 3:5; Midrash Tehillim, Ps. 22:31. The former

version has a passage concerning a needle expelled by the ox when he sneezed upon eating the greens. Buber thinks it a later addition.

96. Leviticus Rabbah 3:5; Midrash Tehillim, Ps. 22:31.

97. Menaḥot 104a and Ecclesiastes Rabbah 4:1. The five kinds of preparation are fine flour, fried on the pan, stewed in sauce, baked as ḥallot, and as wafers.

98. Numbers Rabbah 9:4, 8; Sotah 39b. The priestly benediction is divided into three sections, as found in Num. 6:24–26. The Midrash here states that the Amen response was not made in the Temple, using Neh. 9:5 as its source. Instead of responding Amen, the form of praise was "Blessed be the name of His glorious kingdom forever and ever." The gold plate on the forehead of the high priest is described in Exod. 39:30. That the priestly benediction is to be pronounced outside the Temple is derived from Exod. 20:21.

99. Ḥagigah 16a. The nasi was the chief of the Great Sanhedrin in Jerusalem, and later, of its successor in other sites in Palestine.

100. Sukkah 49a.

101. Pesaḥim 8b; Yerushalmi Pe'ah; Songs Rabbah. Apart from the elaboration upon Songs 7:2, the proof-text is Exod. 34:24.

102. Pesaḥim 8b.

103. Ta'anit 28a; Tosefta Ta'anit 4:7, which explains that these stratagems were for the purpose of bypassing the (Greek) Syrians. See also Mishnah Ta'anit 4:5. See infra n. 117 concerning the fifteenth of Av (cf. Bikkurim 3:3).

104. Middot 1:2; Tamid 27b, 28a. The priests were divided into twenty-four watches, which assumed their functions in the Temple in turn. Each watch consisted of four to nine families or clans. Every week another watch did service in the Sanctuary, being relieved on the Sabbath. During the week the service was distributed among the families. The Azarah was the Temple courtyard.

105. Yoma 23a. The hall (ulam) led to the interior of the Temple. The verses of Deuteronomy refer to the finding of an unknown slain person and the sacrifice of a heifer by the breaking of its neck to be offered by the elders of the city closest to the site of the slain man. Had the young priest been dead, the knife would have at once become ritually unclean. The Talmud explains that this incident preceded the one related earlier of the breaking of the leg. However, it was thought that this attack with a knife was an accident and the old system was continued. But when it was seen that even without such a tragic accident danger was incurred, the new method of counting was enacted (see n. 106).

106. Yoma 2:1, 22a. Any priest of the family whose turn came on a particular day could, originally, remove the ashes from the altar, if he so desired. Since this task had to be done during the night, near dawn, it was thought originally that there would be few volunteers. The ramp of the altar was at its south end and was thirty-two cubits long. The method of the lottery was to place the volunteers in a circle, remove the miter from one, and after having named a number, would start counting from that man by the fingers raised forth by each. The priest with whom the number was reached received the privilege of cleaning the altar.

107. Pesaḥim 64a. Three groups were necessary because of the large number of people who could not be contained within the Temple

courtyard at one time. The Hallel consists of psalms of praise and thanksgiving, Pss. 113–18. The Hel was an area within the fortification of the Temple (see Middot 1:5; Sanhedrin 88b).

108. Pesaḥim 64b.

109. Ibid. The taking of a census by the actual counting of individuals was contrary to Jewish tradition (see Exod. 30:11–16). Some of the later rabbis offered another explanation—that King Agrippa's purpose was to learn the exact strength of Israel for military reasons. Concerned lest he arouse the suspicions of the Roman authorities, he used this roundabout way of taking a census. A myriad is ten thousand. Those who were ritually impure at Passover time were forbidden to take part in the service of the paschal lamb. Those who were traveling at Passover time and were too distant to reach the Temple for the festival were given the opportunity a month later at the second Passover to offer their paschal lamb, as were those formerly impure ritually who were now ritually pure. See Num. 9:9–15.

110. Pesaḥim 3b. Rabbi Judah ben Batyra was of the second generation of tannaim, but as this incident shows, he must have lived before the destruction of the Temple (see *Jewish Encyclopedia*, 2:598). He headed a famous academy at Nisibis in Babylonia, which is expressly recommended together with other famous schools (see Sanhedrin 32b).

111. Menaḥot, chap. 6; Leviticus Rabbah 28:2; also see Menaḥot 6:6–7. The barley was reground and resifted until the quantity of the three seahs was reduced to three-tenths of a seah or one tenth of an ephah, three seahs equaling one ephah. A tenth of an ephah is about a quart. The passage in Leviticus Rabbah adds that the threshing was done with reeds and plant stalks instead of flails to prevent the grain from being crushed.

The Sadducees, dormant for a while after Herod executed some of their leaders, took the name Boethuseans after the family of high priests and became active again under this new guise. (The high priest Simon ben Boethus was Herod's father-in-law.) The Boethusean doctrines were those of the Sadducees. They believed in the absolute power of the high priest as the sole authority on Jewish law and its interpretation. They repudiated the Oral Law and denied providence, resurrection, immortality of the soul, and reward and punishment. In tannaitic literature the terms Boethusean and Sadducee are used interchangeably (see Solomon Zeitlin, *The Rise and Fall of the Judaean State*, 2:100–101, 318, 399, n. 1, and apps. II and III; see also Josephus, *The War against the Jews*, 2.8.14). The Sadducees interpreted the verse concerning the offering of the omer *on the day after the Sabbath* (Lev. 23:11) literally and held that it must always take place on the Sunday of Passover week. The Pharisees understood the "Sabbath" in this verse to be synonymous with "holy day" or "the day of cessation from work," and the context shows that Passover is meant. Therefore, they decreed that the omer was to be offered during the day of Nisan 16. The Septuagint and Josephus support the pharisaic view, which became the established Jewish practice. The Septuagint renders, "on the morrow of the first day." Josephus says, "The offerings of the sheaf took place on the 16th, the first busy work-day of the harvest in relation to which the preceding day might well be called a Sabbath or rest day. . . ."

The reference in the account to the full markets in Jerusalem is a comment on the fact that until the omer was offered, the new flour and grain of the recent harvest could not be sold.

112. Menaḥot 64b; Yerushalmi Shekalim 5:48d. For the two loaves see Lev. 23:17.

113. Bikkurim 3:2–8. The entire country was divided into twenty-four *ma'amadot* (see Ta'anit 4:2). In each there were priests, Levites, and Israelites. When the turn of the priests and Levites came to do service in the Temple, they went to Jerusalem while the Israelites of that *ma'amad* came together in their own towns to read the story of Creation, to fast, and to pray. The ox was intended as a peace offering. For officials among priests and Levites and Temple treasurers, see Shekalim 5:1–2 and Luke 22:52. Professor Louis Ginzberg would explain in class lectures that the passage beginning *My father was a fugitive Aramean* (Deut. 26:5) is found in the Passover Haggadah because in antiquity this was one of the scriptural passages known by heart by the majority of Jews, and since books were rare, it was advisable to use at the Passover seder a familiar passage such as this.

See Kiddushin 33a where a baraita is quoted to the effect that the craftsmen would rise to greet the Israelites bringing their firstfruits to the Temple. The Talmud indicates that they need not interrupt their work to rise for passing scholars, but only for the pilgrims who were strangers and, therefore, should be welcomed. See Bava Kamma 92a, where it is inferred that the rich take back their baskets overlaid with gold or silver and only the baskets of the poor remain with the priests.

114. Leviticus Rabbah 28:5; Lamentations Rabbah 1:17. This passage lists verses recited by the pilgrims that differ from those in the passage from the Mishnah immediately preceding it. The Midrash here related that while on the the road the pilgrims used to exclaim, *Our feet stood inside your gates, O Jerusalem* (Ps. 122:2). Maimonides, however, states that while on the road they exclaimed, *I rejoiced when they said to me: We are going to the House of the Lord* (Ps. 122:1), and when they arrived at the gates of Jerusalem they said, *Our feet stood inside your gates, O Jerusalem.* On the Temple Mount they would say, *Hallelujah. Praise God in His sanctuary* (Ps. 150:1); in the Temple Court, *Let all that breathes praise the Lord* (Ps. 150:6).

115. Yoma, chaps. 1–7. The narrative is more complete in this original source. The counselors' chamber, in Hebrew, *palhedrin*, comes from the Greek, *paredroi*, "assessors, counselors" (see Yoma 8b for an explanation of the name). Abba Saul said (Middot 5:4) it was identical with the wood chamber on the south side of the Temple Court. It has also been identified with the Chamber of Hewn Stones, the locale of the Sanhedrin. See Adolf Büchler, *Das Synhedrion in Jerusalem* (Vienna, 1902), p. 23 ff. The high priest needed a ready substitute in case he became ritually unclean or suffered certain bodily defects during the seven days before Yom Kippur. The elders would read to him the procedures of the day as found in Lev. 16. (For the house of Abtinas, see Tamid 1:1 and Middot 1:1; also supra, n. 64.) In that chamber the family of Abtinas prepared the incense, and there the high priest was taught the careful procedure for taking up the incense without spilling a grain. An oath was administered to him to make certain he would not follow Sadducean practice concerning the incense, i.e., its preparation in the fire pan before entering the Holy of Holies so that he would enter it with the pan smoking (Yoma 19b). He would weep because he was suspected,

and they would weep because they might be suspecting an innocent man.

The biblical books selected for reading were chosen because they would arouse his interest and keep him awake. Sleep was to be prevented because of the risk of pollution. Hebron is mentioned, the Yerushalmi says, for the historic importance of the cave of Machpelah where the patriarchs and matriarchs were buried. (For the place of burning, see Pesahim 8:2, 9:9; the place of immersion, Tamid 1:1; the Parvah Chamber, Middot 5:3—it was in the Temple Court, south of the Court of the Priests.)

The first immersion was on top of the Water Gate on profane ground. The next immersion, however, had to be performed on holy ground as part of the Yom Kippur service. The name *Parvah* is explained in the Talmud (Yoma 35a) as the name of a Persian magus. Rabbenu Ḥananel says that some scholars believe that Parvah had dug a cave under the ground of the Sanctuary so that he might watch the high priest during the Yom Kippur service. The digging was discovered and the cave was found, so the chamber was, thereafter, called by his name. One mina equaled one hundred dinars or zuzim or fifty shekalim.

The trimming of the lamps involved cleaning them, providing them with oil and wick, and, according to Maimonides, also lighting them. The white garments for Yom Kippur were four: the tunic, the breeches, the girdle, and the miter (Lev. 16:4). The golden garments of the high priest were eight: tunic, breeches, miter, girdle, breastplate, ephod, robe, and frontlet (Exod. 28:2 ff.). The luxurious golden garments were exchanged on Yom Kippur for the simple white ones as a symbol of humility and of assurance of God's forgiveness for sins. White, the rabbis say, is symbolic of hopefulness.

The high priest's bullock was brought by himself (Lev. 16:3, 6). The second bullock was an additional offering (Num. 29:8). The hall (ulam) connected the Temple Court with the *heikhal*, which led to the Temple interior. The priest turned the bullock's head toward the *heikhal*, so that its horns, between which the priest pressed his hands, faced the *heikhal*. He stood at the bullock's side, his face toward the Holy of Holies, his back to the altar. In each of the three confessions that follow, the Tetragrammaton was pronounced, the name of God being spoken only by the high priest and only on this occasion. Upon hearing the ineffable name of God the priests and people standing in the Temple Court would prostrate themselves. The chief of the father's house was an officer of the *ma'amad*, the priestly clan. There were twenty-four such *ma'amadot* (1 Chron. 24:1–19), which served in turn in the Temple a week at a time. Each *ma'amad* was divided into "father's houses," each ministering one day of the seven (see Tamid 2:8). For the male goats see Lev. 16:5, 7. Ben Gamla was a wealthy high priest. For Azazel see Lev. 16:10; Azazel was the hardest of the mountains, says the Talmud (Yoma 67b). It seems to be the name of a craggy cliff rather than a demon, as has been suggested. Again the Tetragrammaton was pronounced by the high priest in the selection of the male goat and the crowd in the Court would fall prostrate. The high priest would utter the ineffable name of God ten times during Yom Kippur (Tosefta Yoma 2:2, and Yoma 39b). When the lot bearing it came up in the right hand it was considered a good omen. This is the order of the three confessions:

first the high priest had to confess his own sins, then those of his family and priestly fraternity, and only then could he atone for the sins of all the people. For the fourth terrace or pavement see Middot 3:6; for scooping the cinders see Tamid 1:4. Between the two curtains there was a narrow corridor one cubit wide (see Exod. 25:13 f.). The reference to the time of the early prophets is to the period of David and Solomon. *Shetiyah* means "foundation." From it, the talmudic legend says, the world was founded. The high priest did not offer too long a prayer in the Sanctuary lest the people become afraid that a mishap had occurred. For the sprinkling, the high priest again entered the Holy of Holies, stood between the two staves, and sprinkled upward toward the Ark Cover and downward.

For the causeway for the goat see Shekalim 4:2. According to the Talmud (Yoma 66b; Menaḥot 100a), the Babylonians mentioned here were not actually Babylonian Jewish priests but Alexandrians whom the Palestinian sages called Babylonians as a term of contempt. There are seven and a half ris to the mile; ninety ris would be about twelve miles. "Ravine," according to Maimonides, is incorrect for *ẓok*, the original word, which he says is a place name. Others translate it as peak or precipice. For the red thread turning white, see the discussion in the Talmud (Yoma 67a; Rosh Ha-Shanah 31b).

The high priest came to read in the Court of the Women, the eastern portion of the Temple rectangle. The texts are from Lev. 16, 23:26–32; Num. 29:7–11. Of the eight benedictions the second, third, and fourth would correspond to the seventeenth, eighteenth, and sixth in the Shmoneh Esreh (the Eighteen Benedictions) or the Amidah (the Silent Devotion). The Mishnah contains an additional blessing for Jerusalem. Certain editions, however, do not, and neither does the Yerushalmi. For the final offerings and ceremonies see Lev. 16:3; Num. 29:8; and Exod. 30:8, 27:21.

116. Leviticus Rabbah 20:4. The midrash is based on Job 39:29, the subject of which is homiletically interpreted to be the high priest. Wayfarers who travel a lot always pray for dry weather so that the roads will not be muddy, but were their prayers answered the resultant drought would be disastrous for the nation. Caesarea, once again flourishing in contemporary Israel, was a maritime city founded by Herod in which the Roman influence was strong. The Sharon is the northern part of the coastal plain. The strange prayer for its inhabitants may have been necessary either because its sandy soil caused the periodic collapse of houses built upon it, or because the region was subject to earthquakes or sandstorms that may have buried the dwellers in their homes.

117. Ta'anit 4:8, 30b; Lamentations Rabbah, Proem 33. The passage is quoted in the name of Rabban Simon ben Gamaliel. Note the sensitivity to the poor and the desire to furnish them with equal opportunity for making a match in the requirement that all the garments be borrowed. They had to be immersed in the ritual bath in case they had been previously worn by a woman in a state of ritual uncleanness (see Lev. 15:19 ff.). The cry of the maidens is reminiscent of Prov. 31:30, quoted in the Mishnah in the first source cited above. Other sages in the Talmud (Ta'anit 30b, 31a) offer other explanations for the gaiety on Yom Kippur and the fifteenth day of Av: Yom Kippur, of course, primarily because it is a day of forgiveness and

pardon, and on it the second Tablets of the Ten Commandments were given (Seder Olam 6). The fifteenth of Av was noted for gaiety because it was the day on which permission was first given to the tribes to intermarry (Num. 36:6–7); the day on which the tribe of Benjamin was permitted to reenter the congregation of Israel (Judges 21:1); the day on which the generation of the wilderness ceased to die out; the day on which Hosea ben Elah removed the guards whom Jeroboam ben Nebat had stationed on the roads to prevent Jews from going up to Jerusalem on pilgrimage (see Gittin 88a); the day when permission was granted by the Romans for those Jews killed at Betar during the Bar Kokhba revolt to be buried (see Gittin 57a); and the day on which, each year, no more trees were cut for the altar firewood because thereafter the wood would be too moist and harbor worms, and so the wood would become unfit for the altar.

118. Yoma 19b. For the dispute between the Sadducees and Pharisees concerning when the high priest was to light the incense on Yom Kippur, see Yoma 53a. The controversy centered upon the interpretation of Lev. 16:2. *For I appear in the cloud over the [Shrine] cover.* The Sadducees said this meant that God is to be seen only with the cloud of the incense already upon the Shrine cover. The entire verse, according to them, is to mean, "Let him not come into the holy place except with the cloud [of incense]," for only thus, with the cloud, "am I to be seen over the Shrine cover." Hence the Sadducees insisted that the high priest should enter the Holy of Holies with the fire pan smoking, prepared, and lit outside. The Pharisees, in reply, pointed to Lev. 16:13. *He shall put the incense on the fire before the Lord,* as clearly showing that the incense was to be lit inside. The Pharisees explained the Sadducean text as teaching the need for putting into the incense a certain plant whose effect lay in producing a straight, rising smoke. The verse from Ezekiel is quoted as evidence that an angel had kicked him with his foot. The "four creatures" in Ezekiel 1 here are identified with angels. For this story see Yerushalmi Yoma 1:5, and J. Z. Lauterbach, "A Significant Controversy between the Sadducees and the Pharisees," *Hebrew Union College Annual* 4 (1927): 173–205.

119. Sukkah 4:4. The word *lulav* means "palm branch" but here, as usual in rabbinical literature, it denotes the palm branch tied together with myrtle and willow branches and carried together with the *etrog*, the "citron" (see Lev. 23:40). Sukkah 3:13 prescribes the bringing of the *lulav* the day before the Sabbath when the first day of the festival is on the Sabbath; the next day each comes, discerns his own, and carries it. But this has to do not with the Temple but a synagogue where the number of people involved is smaller and confusion less likely. For "portico," see Shekalim 8:4 and Pesaḥim 1:5. The Talmud (Sukkah 45a) disputes whether "above the portico" is meant or the seats, like benches, cut into the wall. The people were taught to say this sentence because it would be likely that a man might pick up not his own but another's, and in order to fulfill the obligation properly, the *lulav* had to be his own. Through the declaration that each uttered this end was assured.

120. Sukkah 4:5–7. Moẓa is mentioned in Josh. 18:26 and is a village in Israel today. The shofar notes here are *teki'ah, teru'ah, teki'ah* (see Rosh Ha-Shanah 4:9 and Pesaḥim 5:5). The force of Rabbi Judah's statement is that instead of the repetition of the Lord's name in

the verse, the sounds are modified to *ani ve-ho*. Rashi and other commentators explain that the people took away the *lulavim* from the children and ate their citrons. The text is susceptible to both translations.

121. Sukkah 55b. The passage is quoted in the name of Rabbi Eleazar. The verses detailing the Sukkot sacrifices are Num. 29:13–34; for the Eighth Day of Solemn Assembly, Num. 29:36.

122. Sukkah 4:9, 48b, 49a. A log is about one and a half pints. The shofar notes are *teki'ah, teru'ah, teki'ah*. For the ramp, see Middot 3:3. Since wine flows out more slowly than water, the hole in its bowl was wider, Josephus, in *Antiquities* 13.13.5, tells the story of how Alexander Yannai was pelted with citrons, but he inaccurately relates that it happened when Alexander was standing at the altar about to offer a sacrifice. Enraged he killed 6,000 people. He also built a wooden partition wall around the altar within which only the priests could enter, thus preventing the people from coming close in the future.

123. Sukkah 4:10. If the jar had been hallowed the water could not remain overnight, for it itself becomes holy (Zevahim 9:7), and anything holy that remains overnight becomes invalid and unusable (Menahot 7:4). For the laver, see Exod. 30:18 ff.; for the invalidity of uncovered wine and water, see Terumot 8:4.

124. Sukkah 5:2–4, 51a–b, see Tosafot there; Shabbat 21a. The Court of the Israelites was fifteen steps higher than the Court of the Women (see Middot 2:5). The Talmud says that the candelabra were fifty cubits high. It has been suggested that "men of good deeds" may possibly mean "men who worked miracles," but the use of the same expression elsewhere, as later in the passage concerning the utterances of visitors to the libation ceremonies, would seem to indicate its meaning as "men of good works." The fifteen Songs of Ascent are Pss. 120–34 (see Middot 2:5). The upper gate, Danby says (Herbert Danby, ed. and trans., *The Mishnah* [Oxford, 1933], p. 180, n. 3), is the Nicanor Gate, not the one by the same name in Shekalim 6:3 and Middot 2:6. For the posture of the fathers, see Ezek. 8:16.

125. Sukkah 5:1.

126. Sukkah 53a. Hillel's cry was to hasten the crowd to come more quickly for each person, he taught, should regard himself as all-important.

127. Sukkah 53a. Rabban Simon ben Gamaliel I was of the first generation of tannaim (ca. 10–80 C.E.).

128. Sukkah 53a.

129. Ibid.

130. Sotah 7:8. The Torah was to be read to the people periodically for it is the heritage of all the people and not to be kept as the exclusive possession of either priests or political leaders. In the days of Josephus the reading was done by the high priest, earlier by the king. Deut. 31:10 prescribes the periodic reading of the Torah publicly. Agrippa was the son of Aristobulus and grandson of Herod and, therefore, of Edomite descent. He was appointed king in 37 C.E. by Caligula.

131. Tanhuma Hakadum, Phinehas. A litra equals one half a log, equaling the contents of three eggs.

132. Megillah 3a–3b. A number of lay Israelites were appointed to be present at the offering of the daily sacrifices, which they accompanied with prayer (see Ta'anit 26a, and supra, nn. 113 and 115, on *ma'amad*).

6. Extraordinary Events in the Temple

133. Berakhot 7a.

134. Yoma 21a; Avot 5:8; Leviticus Rabbah 10:9, Ecclesiastes Rabbah 1:7, Ḥagigah 26b. The omer was the new barley offered on the second day of Passover (Lev. 23:10 f.). The two loaves were the firstfruits of the wheat harvest offered on Shavuot (Lev. 23:17). The breads of display were changed each Sabbath and the fresh supply baked before the Sabbath. The stale bread would have had to remain a second week, contrary to the law, if anything was wrong with the new loaves (see Lev. 24:5 f.). The people prostrated themselves in the Temple on Yom Kippur as the high priest pronounced the ineffable name of God in making the threefold confession of sins. The Talmud (Pesaḥim 64b) relates that only once on a certain Passover was a man crushed by the crowd. Serpents and scorpions were found in Jerusalem. Josephus gives huge numbers of people who came to Jerusalem to celebrate Passover. He tells (*Wars*, 2.14.3) that on Passover in the year 65 c.e. not less than three million people were present in Jerusalem. For the breaking of the earthenware vessels, see Lev. 6:21; for the miracle of the bread of display, see the proof-text quoted by the Talmud, 1 Sam. 21:7.

135. Yoma 21b; Bava Batra 47a. See Rosh Ha-Shanah 16a, where at the festival of Sukkot the world is judged concerning the rain to fall during the coming year (see Ta'anit 2a). Therefore, the people watched the smoke for the omen.

136. Yoma 39b; Tamid 3:8. A parasang is a Persian mile. Jericho is about fifteen miles from Jerusalem. The Sabbath limit is 2,000 cubits in every direction, the marked-off area around a town or village within which it was permitted to go on the Sabbath. A cubit is the distance from the elbow to the tip of the middle finger. The place Mikwar has variants: Mikmar and Makvar. It must have been reasonably near to Jerusalem. Some place it in Perea, others east of the Jordan, or east of the Dead Sea.

137. Tamid 3:8. The shovel-shaped musical instrument had ten pipes and each pipe had ten holes; it produced very loud music. Ben Katin's device was for lowering the water into a well below (see Tamid 1:4). Gebini used to call the priests in the Temple to rise for the services (Shekalim 5:1). For the cymbal, see Arakhin 2:5.

Part VI

The Great Assembly and the Sanhedrin

The Men of the Great Assembly

The Great Assembly was established by Ezra and consisted of one hundred twenty men, including some thirty prophets, together with priests, elders, and scribes.[1] In addition to Ezra himself there were among them such illustrious figures as Mordecai, Zerubbabel, Nehemiah, Joshua the high priest, Hananiah, Mishael, and Azariah.[2] They received the Torah from the prophets who received it from the elders, to whom it was given by Joshua who had received it from Moses to whom it was given at Sinai.[3] It was transmitted by one to the next as a ball is thrown from hand to hand without falling to the ground.[4] The merit of the Men of the Great Assembly was recorded so it would be remembered by all Israel.[5] They were so righteous that they did not need the sign of the rainbow as a reminder of God's promise not to destroy the earth again by flood.[6]

The Men of the Great Assembly devoted themselves to the fixing of the biblical canon and the exact text of the Scriptures. For example, they interpreted the expression *the highest heavens, and all their host* (Neh. 9:6) to explain that the hosts, i.e., the sun and the moon, are set in the second *raki'a*, which is above the heaven.[7] They also used the name Abram instead of Abraham for the father of the Jewish people but that was because they were there referring to him at the earlier stage in his life before he was chosen by God who later changed his name.[8]

In a number of instances they emended biblical wording to avoid obviously irreverent or sacrilegious expressions.[9] Moreover, they were responsible for the vocalization of the traditional text of the Scriptures and the separation of the words.[10] They were called scribes (*sofrim*) because they would count (*safor*) all the letters in the Torah in order to fix the exact text of the Scriptures for all time. Thus they pointed out that the letter *vav* in the word *gahon* in Lev. 11:42 is exactly the midpoint of the total number of letters in the Pentateuch. The expression *darash darash* (inquired) in Lev.

10:16 is the midpoint of the total amount of words in the Pentateuch. The verse in Lev. 13:33 is the midpoint of the verses in the Pentateuch. The letter *ayin*, of the word *mi-ya'ar* (out of the wood), in Ps. 80:14, is the halfway mark of all the letters in the Book of Psalms. The verse in Ps. 78:38 is the halfway mark of the verses in the book. The Pentateuch contains five thousand eight hundred and eighty-eight verses. The Psalms have eight verses more, Chronicles eight less.[11] The words of the scribes are compared to the words of the Torah. As the latter are true, so are the former.[12] Among the traditions dating back to the Men of the Great Assembly is the one that says that wherever the expression, *va-yehi*, meaning, *and it came to pass*, occurs in the Bible, it introduces an unhappy event.[13]

The Men of the Great Assembly edited the texts of Ezekiel, the twelve minor prophets, Daniel, and Esther.[14] Earlier authorities would have excluded Proverbs, Song of Songs, and Ecclesiastes from the Bible, but the Men of the Great Assembly, having shown their true interpretation, included them in the canon. They observed twenty-four fasts so that those who write scrolls, phylacteries, and mezuzahs should not become wealthy, for if they became wealthy, they would not write.[15]

It is not surprising, therefore, that the Men of the Great Assembly taught, "Be exceedingly careful in judgment, raise up many disciples, and set a fence about the Torah."[16] They concerned themselves not only with Bible and its study, but also with the classification of the Law and the development of the liturgy. They classified the Oral Law into Midrash, Halakhah, and Aggadah.[17] They established prayers and blessings, including kiddush at the beginning of Sabbaths and holy days and havdalah at their conclusion.[18]

The Great Assembly was called by that title because it restored the attribute of greatness to God. Moses had called Him, *The great, the mighty, and the awesome God* (Deut. 10:17). Jeremiah, who had witnessed the destruction of the Temple, said, "Idol-worshipers are prancing about His Temple site. Where, then, is His awesomeness?" So he spoke of the *great and mighty God* (Jer. 32:18), omitting the attribute, "awesome." Daniel said, "Pagans are oppressing His children. Where, then, is His might?" He, therefore, spoke of the *great and awesome God* (Dan. 9:4), omitting "mighty." The Men of the Great Assembly maintained that this precisely was the manifestation of both His awesomeness and His might. His might lay in His ability to control His anger against the wicked and to be patient with them. His awesomeness was evidenced in the fact that Israel is able to survive among the seventy hostile nations of the world. Therefore, in the thrice-daily prayer of the Amidah they restored all of the attributes to God that Moses had applied to Him: the great God, the mighty, and the awesome. Why were they called Men of the Great Assembly? Because they restored greatness to its pristine status.[19] The Amidah, instituted by these sages, contains eighteen blessings corresponding to the eighteen times the divine name is mentioned in the reading of the Shema and also in the twenty-ninth psalm.[20] The Men of the Great Assembly also introduced the feast of Purim and fixed the days for its celebration.[21]

The great men of this Assembly through the sincerity of their prayers once succeeded in having the Evil Inclination delivered into their hands. It happened in this fashion. They prayed to God, saying, "Woe, woe! It is this Evil Inclination that was responsible for the destruction of the Temple, the burning of the Sanctuary, the slaying of the righteous, and the exile of Israel from its land. And still it dances among us! Why have You given it to us? Is it not that we should receive greater reward for mastering it? We want neither its presence nor the reward!" Suddenly from heaven a tablet fell down before them. Upon it was written "Truth." They fasted three days and three nights. The Evil Inclination was then handed over to them. It appeared as a flame in the shape of a young lion coming out of the Holy of Holies. "Here he is, the Evil Inclination of paganism," a prophet cried out to the Jews. In the process of their catching it a hair was torn out of its mane and it voiced a cry heard for a distance of four hundred parsas. They said, "What shall we do to it? If it cries so loudly, Heaven may take pity upon it." The prophet advised them to cast it into a leaden boiler covered with a leaden top, as lead deadens sound. Then they said, "Since this is a favorable time, let us pray to be forever rid of all sensual desire." They prayed and their prayer was answered. The prophet, however, cautioned them, "Take care! If you kill it, all the world will, in time, be destroyed." They bound it up for three days. It happened that a fresh egg was needed for a sick person. They searched throughout Palestine and none could be found, for sexual desire had disappeared from the world. They understood the reason and did not know what to do. "If we slay desire," they said, "the world will ultimately come to an end. If we pray to have dominion over it only at such times when it be necessary, we have a tradition that Heaven does not do things by halves." What did they do? They blinded it in both eyes and let it go. Some good did result in that it does not excite desire toward one's close relatives.[22]

The Men of the Great Assembly decreed that tithes and *terumah* were to be given even though according to biblical law these should have ceased when the Jews were first exiled. They drew up a document taking upon themselves these obligations and spread it out in the courtyard of the Temple. In the morning they found a heavenly seal affixed to it.[23]

The Men of the Great Assembly drew up a list of three kings and four commoners who have no share in the world to come. The commoners are Balaam, Doeg, Ahitophel, and Gehazi. The kings are Jeroboam, Ahab, and Manasseh. They wanted to include Solomon's name among the latter. A figure with the features of King David came and prostrated itself beseechingly before them, but they paid no attention to it. A fire sprang out from within the Holy of Holies and flared up all around them but they paid no attention to it. A heavenly voice was then heard, "*See a man skilled at his work—he shall attend upon kings* (Prov. 22:29). The man who gave priority to My house over his own and, moreover, built My house speedily in seven years while taking thirteen years to build his own—shall such a man stand before mean men? No indeed, *He shall attend upon kings; he shall not attend upon obscure men* (Prov. 22:29)." But they gave no heed to it. So once again the voice was heard, "*Should He requite as you see fit? But you have despised* [*Him*]*! You must decide, not I. Speak what you know* (Job 34:33). *Do not touch My anointed ones* (Ps. 105:15)." They then refrained from including Solomon in their list.[24]

2

The Sanhedrin

The Great Sanhedrin was the splendor of Israel,[25] the heart of the Jewish people, dear to it as the apple of its eye.[26] Even as the limbs and organs of the body move only by the direction of the eyes, so Israel followed the direction given by the Sanhedrin. Just as the embryo in the mother's womb lives only by the navel, so Israel could do nothing without the Sanhedrin.[27] As the skin covers the flesh and so protects it, so did the Sanhedrin protect Israel.[28]

The Sanhedrin of seventy-one members would meet in the Temple's Hall of Hewn Stones. There were also two courts of twenty-three members each, one sitting at the entrance to the Temple Mount, the other at the entrance to the Temple courtyard. Similar courts of twenty-three were set up in all the cities of Israel. When a legal matter arose, it was first brought before the local court. If the members of that court were aware of a precedent that could be used for making a decision, they decided accordingly. If they knew of no precedent, the case was brought before a nearby court. If that court was aware of a precedent, they decided the case accordingly. If they were unaware of a precedent, the case was brought before the court of twenty-three at the entrance to the Temple Mount. Thereafter, it was taken to the Sanhedrin in the Hall of Hewn Stones where the members sat from the time of the morning sacrifice until the time of the evening offering. If the members of the Sanhedrin knew of an appropriate precedent, they quoted it and based their decision upon it. If not, they voted. If the majority voted that the matter was impure, it was impure. And if the majority voted it was pure, it was so decided.

The Sanhedrin would send written communications to all the cities, indicating that whoever is wise, modest, sin-fearing, and well liked by his fellowmen is eligible to be a judge in his own city. Thence he could be promoted to the court at the Temple Mount, from there to the court at the Temple courtyard, and from that court to the Sanhedrin.[29]

As the navel is the center of the body, so the seat of the Sanhedrin, the Hall of Hewn Stones, was at the center of the Temple in Jerusalem, which is the center of the world.[30] The location of the Sanhedrin was alongside of the altar.[31] The Holy One, blessed be He, honored the members of the Sanhedrin with ripe old age.[32] They enjoyed life tenure, but there were those who voluntarily withdrew from office: the Benei Batyra, Menahem, and Judah ben Tabbai.[33]

A Sanhedrin consisting of angels sits on high before God. So too must the earthly Sanhedrin regard itself as sitting before Him.[34] The Sanhedrin shall never cease either in this world or in the world to come.[35] It shall be established forever as the moon.[36]

Amram, the father of Moses, was the head of the Sanhedrin at the time of Moses' birth.[37] During the days of Moses and Aaron the seventy members of the Sanhedrin were strung after them like pearls on a string.[38] The Sanhedrin, like the priesthood, the service of the Levites, and the institution of royalty, all had their origin in that period when the children of Israel traversed the wilderness of Sinai.[39] During the days of the prophet Samuel, because the men of Bet-shemesh gazed upon the Ark with disrespect upon its return from the Philistines, many perished, including the entire membership of the Sanhedrin.[40] King David, together with the Sanhedrin of his time, made the law by interpreting the words of the Torah.[41] For six months he was smitten with leprosy, the Heavenly Presence left him and the members of the Sanhedrin kept away from him.[42] It was on a Sabbath day that fell on the festival of Shavuot that David died and the members of the Sanhedrin presented themselves before Solomon, his successor. There was a difference of opinion between Solomon and the Sanhedrin as to the procedure to follow—whether or not David's body was to be anointed and washed on the Sabbath. Solomon simply spread a curtain over the body. Others explained that he summoned eagles to spread their wings over the body so that the sun should not beat down upon it.[43]

The prophet Elijah was a native of Jerusalem and was one of those who sat in the Sanhedrin.[44] When Joash was made king, the plan was executed by Jehoiada and Jehoshabeat, but it was the Sanhedrin that supported the action by crowning him.[45] In the very place where the Sanhedrin used to meet and decide upon laws for Israel, the princes of wicked Babylonia sat; as the proverb has it, "Where the master hangs up his armor, there the shepherd hangs up his pitcher." The Holy Spirit exclaimed, *Alongside righteousness there is wickedness* (Eccles. 3:16).[46]

In the same sacred place where the Sanhedrin meted out justice, the prophets Zechariah and Uriah were slain by the people because the prophets had rebuked them for their disobedience. When Zechariah was killed, seven transgressions were committed by the people: they murdered a priest, a prophet, and a judge; they shed innocent blood; they defiled the Temple Court; and this was done on the Sabbath, which that year was also the Day of Atonement.[47]

When the people slew Zechariah they were not as considerate of his blood as they would have been of the blood of a hind or ram offered as a sacrifice. The latter's blood would have been covered with dust but Zechariah's blood ran out upon the stones. Therefore, his blood cried out for vengeance. It seethed and bubbled for two hundred and fifty-two years through the reign of eleven kings. Heaps of earth were thrown upon it and yet it was not stilled but continued foaming. The Holy One, blessed be He, said to the blood, "The time has come for you to collect your debt." The conqueror Nebuzaradan came to destroy Jerusalem. When he saw the bubbling blood he asked, "What kind of blood is this that seethes in this fashion?" He was told that it was the blood of bulls, rams, and lambs offered as sacrifices. He had the same animals sacrificed but their blood was still while the other blood kept seething. He then strung up the people and declared, "Tell me the exact nature of this blood or I shall comb your flesh with an iron comb." They answered, "We see that it is God's will to exact punishment for this blood, so we shall reveal the mystery to you. There was a priest-prophet and judge who many years ago predicted all that you are doing. Our ancestors did not believe him. They arose against him and killed him because he had rebuked them."

Nebuzaradan immediately had eighty thousand priests-in-training brought before him and slain at the site of the seething blood. The blood was not stilled. It gushed forth even more strongly until it reached the grave of Zechariah. Nebuzaradan had the members of the Great Sanhedrin and the Minor Sanhedrin slain alongside the bubbling blood but there was no change. The villain then exclaimed to the blood that would not be stilled, "Are you and your blood better than these men's? Do you desire that I destroy all your people on its account!" At that moment the Holy One, blessed be He, was moved to compassion and commented, "If this wicked cruel man, the son of a wicked father, who came up to destroy My house, is so filled with compassion for them, how much more should I be, for is it not written, *The Lord! the Lord! a God compassionate and gracious* (Exod. 34:6) and *The Lord is good to all, and His mercy is upon all His works* (Ps. 145:9)."

The Holy One, blessed be He, directed the blood to cease and it was immediately absorbed into the ground. When Nebuzaradan witnessed this he debated with himself whether to repent, arguing, "If such vengeance is exacted for the taking of one life, how much more will happen to me for having taken so many lives!" He fled, leaving a document for his family concerning the disposition of his property, and became a convert to Judaism.[48]

When Nebuchadnezzar came up from Babylonia to destroy Jerusalem, he camped in Daphne, a suburb of Antioch. The members of the Sanhedrin went there to meet him and they asked, "Has the time come for the destruction of the Temple?" He replied, "No, but your king, Jehoiakim, has rebelled against me. Hand him over to me and I shall withdraw." They returned and reported to Jehoiakim, "Nebuchadnezzar demands your life." He said to them, "Is this the moral thing to do, to save a life by paying for it with another's? To save your own by surrendering mine? Is it not written, *You shall not turn over to his master a slave who seeks refuge with you from his master* (Deut. 23:16)?" They answered him, "Did not your ancestor behave in the same manner with Sheba, the son of Bichri, whose head was flung over the city wall by its inhabitants at Joab's demand so that the city was spared (2 Sam. 20:21)?" He would not be persuaded to go willingly so they seized him and put him in chains. Nebuchadnezzar displayed him in all the cities of Judah, killed him, and stuffed him inside a split-open donkey, fulfilling the prophecy spoken of him by Jeremiah, *He shall have the burial of an ass* (Jer. 22:19). Another version has it that after being exhibited in all the cities of Judah he was slain, his body was cut into small pieces the size of olives, and the pieces were flung to the dogs, for is not the final burial place of a donkey within the innards of dogs?

After executing Jehoiakim, Nebuchadnezzar crowned the late king's son, Jeconiah, as his successor and returned to Babylonia. The populace of his city came out to greet him with songs of praise. They asked him to tell of his exploits. He recounted how Jehoiakim, king of Judah, had rebelled against him; he had executed him and placed his son, Jeconiah, on his throne. They said, "The proverb has it—'A good whelp cannot be sired by a bad dog.'" He immediately took their advice and returned to his headquarters in Antioch. The members of the Great Sanhedrin again came to greet him. Again they asked, "Has the Temple's time for destruction arrived?" He replied, "No, but hand over to me Jeconiah, king of Judah, and I shall depart." Nebuchadnezzar took Jeconiah and bound him in prison.[49]

Mordecai, before coming to Persia, had been a member of the Sanhedrin and, as such, had knowledge of the seventy languages spoken in the world. This enabled him to understand the conversation between Bigthan and Teresh, the chamberlains of King Ahasuerus, in their conspiring at the king's assassination, and to foil their plot. Not all of the members of the Sanhedrin looked with favor upon Mordecai. A small number turned from him.[50]

During the reign of King Alexander Yannai the Sadducees were favored by him and they filled the ranks of the Sanhedrin. Queen Salome Alexandra sat at the king's side and no member of the Pharisees was with them but Simon ben Shetah. The Sanhedrin was asked questions of law and its members did not know enough to bring any proof or precedent from the Torah. Simon ben Shetah said to them, "Only he whose knowledge enables him to bring proofs from the Torah is qualified to sit in the Sanhedrin; otherwise, he is not qualified." Once a case came before them and none knew of any proof from the Torah for a decision but one old man who babbled childishly, arguing against him. He said to Simon, "Give me until tomorrow and I shall marshall my arguments against you." Simon agreed. The old man withdrew and meditated in private. Since he saw that he could not bring any proof-texts from the Torah, he was embarrassed to return and take his seat in the Great Sanhedrin. Simon ben Shetah appointed one of his disciples in his place for he explained, "The Sanhedrin must contain no less than seventy-one." Thus he took advantage of every such opportunity daily until the Sadducees were all replaced by a Sanhedrin more properly according to his opinion. That day when the Sadducee Sanhedrin was replaced by a Sanhedrin representing the common people of Israel was made a festive day.[51]

The members of the Sanhedrin were seated in a semicircle like a threshing floor or half moon, to be able to see each other. The two scribes of the court sat in front of them, one at the right and the other at the left. The kings of Israel and Judah had followed a similar practice when sitting in judgment.[52] In the world to come the Holy One, blessed be He, sits at the head of the academy on high with the righteous seated before Him in a semicircle, as the members of the Sanhedrin are seated on earth.[53] Three rows of sages sat in front of the Sanhedrin, each sage knowing his place, just as the dove, when entering its cote, recognizes at once its nest and its young.[54] The least of these scholars was as well packed with learning as is a pomegranate with seeds—how much more so those who sat in the Sanhedrin itself![55] Just as when a woman ties up her hair behind her head it is an ornament to her, so when the Great Sanhedrin sat behind the Temple it was an ornament to the Temple. Strangely, the members of the Sanhedrin seemed to be crowded together, yet they had plenty of room.[56] The patriarchal prophecy concerning Judah, that *the scepter shall not depart from Judah* (Gen. 49:10), alludes to the Sanhedrin, which punished and kept law and order. For the majority of the Sanhedrin was descended from the tribe of Judah.[57] Others say that the tribe of Issachar produced two hundred presidents of the Sanhedrin. The law they enunciated was accepted by the people as if it were the law of Moses pronounced at Sinai. Moreover, the sages who sat in the rows in front of the Sanhedrin were drawn largely from the tribe of Issachar.[58]

Jethro's descendants were privileged to be members of the Sanhedrin. He merited this great honor because of his stance when Pharaoh, planning to exterminate the Jews, asked his counsel, together with that of Balaam and Job. Balaam who gave assent to the plan was killed; Job, because he was silent, was doomed to much suffering; Jethro showed his opposition by flight and, therefore, his descendants were privileged to sit in the Chamber of Hewn Stones.[59]

Purity of descent need not be traced beyond membership of one's ancestors in the Sanhedrin because that is sufficient proof of unimpaired stock. Qualifications for membership in the Sanhedrin included not only righteous conduct but unblemished lineage.[60] Only those were to be seated in the Sanhedrin who had these qualities: stature, wisdom, handsome appearance, age, familiarity with sorcery, so as to be able to test those charged with it, and knowledge of the seventy languages of the world, so that the Sanhedrin should not have to listen to testimony through an interpreter. Another opinion added the quality of such keen mental agility as to be able to pronounce ritually clean a reptile classified by the Torah as unclean![61] The members of the Sanhedrin were exhorted to lead Israel in the right path and to give the people instruction and understanding.[62] With their legislation they protected the words of the Torah by building a hedge around it.[63] Just as all derive pleasurable benefit from a heap of wheat, so all who listened to the logic of the Sanhedrin during its discussions derived pleasure.[64] From the Hall of Hewn Stones in the Temple, the locale of the Sanhedrin, Torah went forth to all Israel.[65] The Sanhedrin decided upon the laws and instructed the people in every point of the law, explaining every difficulty.[66] The members of the Sanhedrin kept their knowledge of the law as sharp as a sword so that when a case came before them they should not be in doubt of the law. When a case was tried they all argued how they should decide and pronounce the law, with the fear of the punishment of Gehenna in their minds should they decide wrongly.[67] The Lord set the Sanhedrin among the Jewish people to watch over wrongs and to repair the breaches made by the people in the wall of Jewish practice.[68] So when the Torah commands, *Justice, justice shall you pursue* (Deut. 16:20), it calls upon the individual to follow after the sages in the Hall of Hewn Stones.[69] Once three Torah scrolls were found in the Temple court and the sages nullified one as being an incorrect text and confirmed the other two as being correct.[70]

Seven regulations were ordained by the Sanhedrin. One pertained to the burnt offering sent by a heathen from an overseas land. If he also sent money for drink offerings with it, his drink offerings are offered up too. If he did not, they are offered up at the expense of the community. Another decree of the Sanhedrin stated that during the interregnum between the death of a high priest and the appointment of his successor, the meal offering of the high priest continues at the expense of the community. The Sanhedrin also decreed that the priests may use salt and wood belonging to the Sanctuary for the preparation of their food from such sacrificial meat or other consecrated food assigned to them. Their other ordinances stated that the law of sacrilege did not apply to the ashes of the red heifer and that substitute bird offerings should be offered for those that were invalid and at the expense of the community.[71]

The Sanhedrin was the court that determined whether a priest could no longer serve because of some disqualifying defect. If that were so, the priest donned black garments and left. If the verdict found him fit to continue, he put on white garments and went forth to serve with his fellow priests. The occasion would be made a festive day and they would declare, "Blessed be the All-Present that a blemish was not found in a descendant of Aaron and blessed be He who chose Aaron and his descendants to serve the Lord in the House of the Holy of Holies."[72]

There could be a case where the Sanhedrin would have to decide according to the demands of the law, but God's mercies would be stirred none the less. So when an illegitimate son was born of illicit relations between a man and a married woman, the Sanhedrin would remove such a child from the Jewish fold, as the Torah had commanded (Deut. 23:3). But if the parents of this bastard had committed transgression, why blame the child? What sin has he committed? Therefore, the Holy One, blessed be He, says, "They have no comforter; it shall be My task to comfort them. In this world there is dross in them, but in the world to come I have seen them all pure gold."[73]

Additions to Jerusalem or to the Temple courts may not be made except with the consent of the king, a prophet, the Urim and Tummim, and the Sanhedrin of seventy-one judges. When such extensions are approved it is done with the bringing of two thanks offerings and with singing. A festive procession is formed with the court followed by the two thanks offerings and the people afterward.[74]

It once happened that Rabbi Simon of Mizpah sowed his field with two kinds of wheat and he inquired of Rabban Gamaliel whether he was obligated to leave one corner of his field unharvested for the poor or two. They went up to the Chamber of Hewn Stones to ask of the Sanhedrin. Nahum the Scribe said, "I have received a tradition from Rabbi Measha, who received it from his father, who received it from the *zugot*, who received it from the prophets as a law given by Moses from Sinai, that if a man sowed his field with two kinds of wheat and made them up into one threshing floor, he leaves one corner unharvested for the poor, but if two threshing floors, he must leave two.[75] Rabbi

Ẓadok testified that if flowing water was led through a channel made from the foliage of nuts, it remains valid for mixing with the ashes of the red heifer. Such a case happened at Ahaliya, and when the case came before the Sanhedrin in the Chamber of Hewn Stones the sages declared it valid.[76]

There were occasions when the Sanhedrin meted out punishment heavier than that demanded by the Torah in order to build a protective hedge around the Torah. So, for example, it happened during the days of the Greeks that a Jew rode a horse on the Sabbath and the court ordered that he be stoned—not because the law required it but because the times required it.[77]

Although from Sinai the Sanhedrin had full authority to exact the death penalty, any court that executed one person in a seven-year period was described as "a violent court." Rabbi Eleazar ben Azariah said, "Even once within seventy years." Rabbi Tarfon and Rabbi Akiba said, "Had we been members of the Sanhedrin, a death sentence would never have occurred." To which Rabban Simon ben Gamaliel retorted, "Such scholars would only increase the numbers of those who shed blood in Israel."[78]

When a capital case occurred and a criminal was sentenced to death, upon his reaching a point about ten cubits from the place of execution he was told, "Confess!" For all those who confess have a share in the world to come. If he cannot find the words, he is told, "Simply say, 'May my death be an atonement for all my sins.'" He would be given a cup of wine in which a grain of frankincense had been stirred in order to benumb his senses. The wine and frankincense were donated by the worthy women of Jerusalem. The executed criminal was not buried in his family plot. The court arranged for two special cemeteries, one for those executed by the sword or by hanging, the other for those executed by stoning or burning. In the latter case, after the flesh had been consumed, the relatives gathered the bones and buried them in the proper place. The relatives would come afterward to greet the judges and the witnesses to let them know that they bore no grudge, for the judgment had been a just one. They did not observe the laws of mourning publicly for the executed but grieved privately.[79]

Rabbi Akiba asked: How do we know that the members of the Sanhedrin who have sentenced a man to death are not to taste food all that day? For it is written, *You shall not eat anything with its blood* (Lev. 19:26).[80]

Although the Sanhedrin with its four methods of execution for capital crimes is no more, the four methods of punishment continue in effect. The Holy One, blessed be He, condemns a man who deserves to die by these methods to severe penalties that resemble them. A man committing a crime that in the time of the Sanhedrin would have merited strangulation by hanging, drowns in a river or dies by suffocation or is strangled by idolaters. One who deserves death by stoning falls from a roof or is trampled by a beast or is stoned by idolaters. A man meriting beheading by the sword is attacked and killed by robbers. One who deserves the penalty of burning either falls into a furnace or is bitten by a serpent whose poison burns him. Thus you learn that none can escape the judgment of the Holy One, blessed be He, and avoid being punished measure for measure.[81]

God's presence, the Shekhinah, was exiled ten times and wandered to ten places. So too was it with the Sanhedrin. Forty years before the destruction of the Temple it moved from the Hall of Hewn Stones to Ḥaniyot (no longer did it judge cases of capital crimes), from there back to Jerusalem, then to Jabneh, thence to Usha, from Usha again to Jabneh and back to Usha, then to Shafaram, to Bet Shearim, to Sepphoris, and then to Tiberias. Tiberias was the lowest place of all so that the prophecy was fulfilled, *And you shall speak from lower than the ground, your speech shall be humbler than the sod* (Isa. 29:4). From their last locale the next stage will be redemption, as it is prophesied, *Arise, shake off the dust. Sit [on your throne], Jerusalem* (Isa. 52:2).[82] Thus it was that Jacob on his deathbed blessed Zebulun before Issachar even though Issachar was the older son and should have been blessed first. For Jacob prophetically foresaw that the Temple would be destroyed and the Sanhedrin removed from the tribe of Judah and take its place in Zebulun's part of the land. For the Sanhedrin was exiled from Jerusalem and sat in Jabneh, then to Usha, hence to Shafaram, then to Bet Shearim, from there to Sepphoris, which was in the territory of Zebulun. After that it moved on again to Tiberias.[83] But the Shekhinah, God's presence, did not go into exile with the Sanhedrin. Nor did it go into exile when the ten tribes were exiled, nor when the remaining two tribes of Judah and Benjamin were exiled nor with the exile of the Temple watches. God's presence went into exile only when the school-children were exiled.[84] When the Sanhedrin came to an end, song ceased from the places of feasting, as it said, *They drink their wine without song* (Isa. 24:9). When the fear of the Sanhedrin was upon the people, lewd words were never used in songs, but when the Sanhedrin was abolished vulgar people used to do so.[85]

Notes

VI. THE GREAT ASSEMBLY AND THE SANHEDRIN

1. The Men of the Great Assembly

1. Megillah 17b. Another tradition speaks of eighty-five elders, among them some thirty prophets (see Ruth Rabbah 4:5; Yerushalmi Megillah 1, 70d; Megillah 17b; Yerushalmi Berakhot 2, 4d). The prophets spoken of in the sources quoted above are evidently scholar-prophets, as distinguished from the classical prophets of the Bible. Therefore, these traditions are not in conflict with the talmudic tradition that described Malachi as the last prophet. He was the last of the classical literary prophets. Seder Olam Rabbah records a tradition that in the days of Alexander prophecy ceased in Israel, and this may refer to the scholar-prophets of the Great Assembly (see Sotah 48b; Tosefta Sotah 13.2.318; Yoma 9b; Sanhedrin 11a; Avot de-Rabbi Natan, chap. 1, p. 2 [ed. S. Schechter, trans. Goldin, p. 4]; Seder Olam Rabbah, chap. 6, p. 70 [ed. Ratner, Vilna, 1894–97]). Compare, however, Ephraim Urbach, "When Did Prophecy Cease?" *Tarbiz* 17 (5706): 1–11; Yehezkel Kaufmann, *Toledot ha-emunah ha-yisra'elit* (8 vols., Tel Aviv and Jerusalem, 1955–60), 4:379, n. 2.

It is significant that the Targum Yerushalmi often renders *navi*, "prophet," as *safra*, "scribe," as in Isa. 9:14, 1 Sam. 10:5 ff., 19:24. This rendering must date back to a time when the two titles were interchangeable, i.e., the period of the Great Assembly.

The exact nature of this body of Jewish leaders during the Persian period, the Great Assembly, is not known. Scholars differ as to its origins, functions, and achievements. Rabbinic texts setting forth their activities go a long way toward making the Men of the Great Assembly the fathers of pharisaic and talmudic Judaism. Historians, moreover, are divided into four camps. Some reject the rabbinic traditions concerning this institution as a late invention, or else they deny that the Great Assembly was a separate continuing body. See Henry Englander, "The Men of the Great Synagogue," *Hebrew Union College Annual*, Jubilee Volume (1925): 149–69; E. Bickerman, "Viri Magnae Congregationis," *Revue Biblique* 55 (1948):397–402; Joshua Gutman, "Anshei Kneset ha-Gedolah," *Ha-Shiloah* 21 (1909): 313–60; H. E. Ryle, *The Canon of the Old Testament* (London, 1914), pp. 250–83, for a summary of medieval and modern views.

A second group of historians, at the other end of the spectrum, maintains that the Great Assembly was the official governing body of the Jews, under the presidency of the high priest, during the Persian period, Cyrus having granted the Jews complete autonomy for all national affairs. Ezra, its first head, was a priest, and one of its last survivors was Simon the Just who was high priest (Avot 1:2). When Alexander the Great conquered the Middle East the Persian period came to an end and with it Jewish self-rule and the sway of the Great Assembly. See Naḥman Krochmal, *Kitve Rabbi Naḥman Krochmal*, ed. Simon Rawidowicz (2d ed., Waltham, Mass., 1961), pp. 62 ff., 121, 128 ff.; Eliezer Levi, *Pirkei Avot* (Tel Aviv, 1951–52), p. 5, notes; L. Herzfeld, *Geschichte des Volkes Israel* (Leipzig, 1863), 1:380–95; S. Sachs, "Uber die Zeit der Enstehung des Synhedrins," *Zeitschrift d. religiösen Interessen des Judenthums* 2 (1845):301–12; David Hoffmann, "Männer der grossen Versammlung," *Magazin für die Wissenschaft des Judenthums* 10 (1883):45–63; Samuel Krauss, "The Great Synod," *Jewish Quarterly Review*, o.s. 10 (1898):347–77.

Still other historians argue that the Great Assembly was simply a name given to periodic meetings held in time of need by the leaders of the people: for example, the assembly presided over by Ezra; later, that which appointed Simon the Hasmonean head of state and high priest in 142 B.C.E.; the last one, meeting in 66 C.E. to declare war against Rome. See Solomon Zeitlin, "The Origins of the Synagogue," *Proceedings of the American Academy for Jewish Research* 2 (1930–31):69–81; idem, "Shimon ha-ẓaddik ve-Keneset ha-Gedolah," *Ner Ma'aravi* 2 (1925):137–42; L. Loew, *Gesammelte Schriften* (Szegedin, 1889) 1:399–499; Louis Finkelstein, *The Pharisees* (2 vols., Philadelphia, 1938), 2: 576 ff.; idem., "The Maxim of the Anshe Keneset ha-Gedolah," *Journal of Biblical Literature* 59 (1940):455–69; Sidney Hoenig, *The Great Sanhedrin* (New York, 1953), p. 33.

The principal proponent of the fourth view is Louis Finkelstein. His position is that the Great Assembly was a body of nonofficial religious leaders. It was organized by Ezra as *Keneset ha-Ḥasidim*, the Assembly of the Pious, as mentioned in 1 Macc. 7:12 as taking part in the revolt against the decrees of Antiochus IV. Finkelstein cites several tannaitic passages where the term *keneset* is used as a synonym for Pharisees: Mishnah Yoma 7:1; Mishnah Zavim 3:2; Mishnah Bekhorot 5:5, etc. Ezra's followers rejected the authority of the high priest in religious matters, so they established their own *keneset ha-Gedolah*, Great Court or Great Assembly. See Louis Finkelstein, *Ha-Perushim ve-Anshei Keneset ha-Gedolah* (New York, 1950), pp. 31–38, 51 ff.

Hugo Mantel prefers Finkelstein's theory but modifies it on two counts: (1) The Great Assembly did not come into being until at least a century and a half after Ezra when, with the beginning of the Greek period, Ezra's followers and their successors reorganized themselves along individual or family lines in place of the clans of the Persian period; (2) The Great Assembly was not a court but a national unofficial religious association constituted of delegates from local religious associations, the latter being each called a *keneset*, an assembly, the national body, *keneset ha-Gedolah*, the Great Assembly. See Hugo Mantel, "The Nature of the Great Synagogue," *Harvard Theological*

Review 60 (1967):69–91; idem, *Studies in the History of the Sanhedrin* (Cambridge, Mass., 1961), p. 261 f.

2. Thus Mordecai lived over four hundred years; of course, hyperbole! See Ginzberg, *Legends*, 6:447, n. 56.

3. Avot 1:1; Avot de-Rabbi Natan 1:3. In the latter passage the judges are placed in the chain of the bearers of the tradition, between the elders and the prophets. That source also adds the names of Haggai, Zechariah, and Malachi as having received the Torah from the prophets and transmitted it to the Men of the Great Assembly. Maimonides, in his introduction to the *Mishneh Torah*, sets forth the chain of tradition from Moses to the compiler of the Talmud, Rabbi Ashi. Later authorities extended the chain until the last of the Geonim. See Seder Olam 163–65; Seder Olam Zuta 176; and *Sefer ha-Qabbalah*, ed. by Abraham ibn Daud, trans. by Gerson D. Cohen (Philadelphia, 1967).

4. Ecclesiastes Rabbah 12:11.

5. Esther Rabbah 7:11.

6. Genesis Rabbah 35:2. Two generations are omitted from among all the generations requiring the rainbow for reassurance, that of Hezekiah and that of the Great Assembly. Another sage substitutes for the latter the generation of Rabbi Simon bar Yohai.

7. Genesis Rabbah 6:6. The midrash here states that although Gen. 1:17 is explicit in saying that God set the sun and moon in the second heaven, *raki'a*, the Men of the Great Assembly explained it further. The ancient rabbis thought there were seven heavens, the name of the second being *raki'a*, "firmament" (see Ḥagigah 12b).

8. Genesis Rabbah 46:8 on Gen. 17:5, quoting also Neh. 9:7. Here the authorship of the book of Nehemiah is evidently ascribed to the Men of the Great Assembly (see Exodus Rabbah 51:3; Yerushalmi Bava Batra 15a).

9. Exodus Rabbah 41:4, 13:1; Leviticus Rabbah 11:5. A list of these emendations may be found in Tanhuma Beshallah 16; Sifrei Numbers 84; Yalkut Exodus 247.

10. Nedarim 37b.

11. Kiddushin 30a. The word *sofer* means "count."

12. Numbers Rabbah 14:4.

13. Megillah 10b. This text lists a number of such biblical passages in support of this statement: Esther 1:1; Ruth 1:1; Gen. 6:1, 11:2, 14:1; Josh. 5:13, 6:27; 1 Sam. 1:1, 8:1, 18:14; 2 Sam. 7:1. However, other verses beginning with the same expression are cited where no untoward events take place. The conclusion is then reached that the use of the expression is not conclusive. At times it denotes a calamity; at other times it does not. But where the expression reads, *And it came to pass in the days of* . . . , it does signify that a sad event will transpire.

14. Bava Batra 15a. For the textual word, "write," see Ginzberg, *Legends*, 4:277, n. 90.

15. Sanhedrin 35a. (See also Avot de-Rabbi Natan, version 1, chap. 1 [ed. Schechter, 1b]; compare Tanhuma Beshallah, 16.) For the fasts, see Pesahim 50b.

16. Avot 1:1. See the commentaries ad locum of Eliezer Levi (Tel Aviv, 1951–52); Joseph Hertz, *Sayings of the Fathers* (London, 1943, New York, 1945); Judah Goldin, *The Living Talmud—The Wisdom of the Fathers* (New York, 1957).

17. Yerushalmi Shekalim 5:1:48c.

18. Berakhot 33a.

19. Yoma 69b; Berakhot 33b. See also Yerushalmi Berakhot 7:11c; Megillah 3:74c; also Ginzberg, *Legends*, 6:447, n. 56. The Men of the Great Assembly restored both attributes of God dropped by Jeremiah and Daniel to the opening prayer of the silent devotion, recited thrice daily, and to Neh. 9:32, both works attributed to them either by way of authorship or redaction. For the last answer, the source is Yerushalmi Berakhot 7:24b.

20. Leviticus Rabbah 1:8; Megillah 17b; Yerushalmi Berakhot 2:4:4d. The midrashic passage states also that there are eighteen vertebrae in the spinal column. Ginzberg, *Legends*, 4:359, states that the blessings composing the Amidah "date back to remote ancient times. The Patriarchs were their authors and the work of the Great Assembly was to put them together in the order in which we now have them." (See Ginzberg, *Legends*, 4:360–61, for the rabbinic listing of the sources for each of the eighteen blessings.)

21. See Megillah 2a; Yerushalmi Megillah 1:7:70d; Ruth Rabbah 4:5. Compare Ginzberg, *Legends*, 4:448, n. 193.

22. Yoma 69b. Two views are stated in Songs Rabbah 7:8. One says that the desire for idolatry was rooted out in the time of Hananiah, Mishael, and Azariah, all members of the Great Assembly. The other view holds that this occurred during the days of Mordecai and Esther. Ginzberg, *Legends*, 6:449, n. 57, recounts the Babylonian myth that all creatures lost their desire when the goddess Ishtar descended into hell and was absent from earth for a while. Because the Evil Inclination is now blind, as this legend in our text concludes, its power is diminished; but at the end of history it will disappear altogether and human beings will become like angels (see Genesis Rabbah 48:11).

23. Ruth Rabbah 4:5. The midrash states that this was one of three things ordained by a human court that was approved by a heavenly court.

24. Numbers Rabbah 14:1; Songs Rabbah 1:1; Sanhedrin 104b; Yalkut Shimoni, Proverbs 22. Solomon built the Temple before his own palace, but he was criticized by some of the rabbis for his luxurious ways, for his foreign wives, and for the heavy taxes levied upon the people.

2. The Sanhedrin

25. Lamentations Rabbah 1:6. The Great Sanhedrin, in contradistinction to the lesser courts of twenty-three members, was composed of seventy-one members. It functioned as a supreme court but it had legislative powers as well. It was presided over by a president (nasi) and a deputy (av bet din). It met in Jerusalem daily except for Sabbaths and festivals from morning until midafternoon. Some scholars argue that there were two parallel bodies by the same name, one for political, civil, and criminal matters, one for religious affairs only. This is the position of Jacob Z. Lauterbach and Solomon Zeitlin. The Sanhedrin disappeared from Jewish life before the end of the fourth century. During the sixteenth century an attempt was made by Jewish leaders in Palestine to revive it and talk is heard today about the possi-

bility of reviving such a body in modern Israel. The Jewish assembly called together by Napoleon in 1806 was called by the same name.

26. Lamentations Rabbah, Proems 16 and 2:4; Ruth Rabbah 4:8.

27. Songs Rabbah 1:15, 4:1, 5:12, 7:3, 7:5.

28. Lamentations Rabbah 3:4.

29. Sanhedrin 88b, 11a, 1:6; Yerushalmi Sanhedrin 19c; Genesis Rabbah 71:9; Numbers Rabbah 19:26; Middot 5:4; Sukkah 51b. The Hall of Hewn Stones was located on the southern side of the inner court of the Temple, north of the court of the Israelites (see Middot 5:4). It had two entrances, one from the court of the priests, the other in the Water Gate used by the laity (see also Tosefta Sanhedrin 7:1; Tosefta Ḥagigah 2:9; Tosefta Shekalim 3:27. The latter text indicates that the court of twenty-three other than the one sitting at the entrance to the Temple Mount sat in the Ḥel, a place within the fortification of the Temple; see also Numbers Rabbah 6:3).

30. Sanhedrin 37a; Numbers Rabbah 1:4; Pesikta Ki Tissa; Tanḥuma Ki Tissa.

31. Mekhilta (ed. Lauterbach), 2:292, 3:41.

32. Leviticus Rabbah 30:11.

33. Pesaḥim 66a; Ḥagigah 2:2; Makkot 5b.

34. Exodus Rabbah 30:18.

35. Leviticus Rabbah 2:2.

36. Ecclesiastes Rabbah 12:7 based on Ps. 89:38.

37. Exodus Rabbah 1:13. It need not be said that this midrash and the legends following are not based on historic fact.

38. Songs Rabbah 1:10.

39. Songs Rabbah 3:6. This conflicts with the earlier passage about Amram, but neither is based on fact.

40. Numbers Rabbah 5:9 on 1 Sam. 6:19, quoting Tanna de-ve-Eliyahu.

41. Ruth Rabbah 2:2 on 1 Chron. 4:21.

42. Sanhedrin 107a.

43. Ruth Rabbah 3:2. Another association of the Sanhedrin with Solomon is to be found in Numbers Rabbah 9:3.

44. Exodus Rabbah 40:4; see also Genesis Rabbah 71:9.

45. Ecclesiastes Rabbah 4:9; see 2 Chron. 22:11, 23:11.

46. Ecclesiastes Rabbah 3:15; Leviticus Rabbah 4:1; see also Bava Meẓia 84b, and cf. Isa. 1:21.

47. Ecclesiastes Rabbah 3:15–16. For Zechariah see 2 Chron. 24:20–21; for Uriah, Jer. 26:20–23. Of course, this Zechariah lived much earlier than the literary prophet by the same name whose prophecies are found in the Bible. The former, Zechariah ben Jehoiada the priest, was slain just before the death of King Joash. The latter, Zechariah ben Berekhiah, lived in postexilic times.

48. Gittin 76b; Ecclesiastes Rabbah 3:16 and 10:4; and Lamentations Rabbah, Proem 23, with minor variations among them. In the latter source the prophet is described as arrogant in his rebuke of the people, thus being responsible for his own death and for the sin of the people in slaying him. It also adds to the murders by Nebuzaradan the slaying of schoolchildren and places the killing of the members of the Sanhedrin first (see Yerushalmi Mo'ed Katan). Nebuzaradan was a high officer of Nebuchadnezzar (see Sanhedrin 96b; Gittin 57b). The

murder of Zechariah occurred toward the end of the reign of King Joash (2 Chron. 24:20 ff.). Then followed Amaziah who ruled 29 years, Uzziah 52, Jotham 16, Ahaz 16, Hezekiah 29, Manasseh 55, Amon 2, Josiah 31, Jehoiakim 11, and Zedekiah 11—the total being 252. By the Minor Sanhedrin here the text means the court of twenty-three. For the respective functions of these two courts, see Sanhedrin 2a.

49. Leviticus Rabbah 19.

50. Megillah 11b and 13a, based upon Esther 10:3, *and popular with the multitude of his brethren,* but, argues Rabbi Joseph here, "not by *all* his brethren."

51. Megillat Ta'anit, chap. 10; Menahot 65a. Alexander Yannai reigned from 103 to 76 B.C.E. Pro-Sadducee, he was opposed by the Pharisees and the people. In his last days he regretted his antagonism to the Pharisees and advised his wife to make peace with them. Salome Alexandra succeeded her husband and ruled from 76 to 67 B.C.E. She surrounded herself with advisers from among the Pharisees whose leader was Simon ben Shetah, presumably the brother of the queen. Margolis and Marx, *A History of the Jewish People,* pp. 160–61, say, "The high Council of State, combining legislative and supreme judicial functions, was reorganized so as to admit a large number of Pharisees."

52. Sanhedrin 4:3; Hullin 5a; Exodus Rabbah 5:12; Songs Rabbah 7:3; Genesis Rabbah 44:13; Lamentations Rabbah, Proem 23; Genesis Rabbah 98:8; Leviticus Rabbah 30:11.

53. Leviticus Rabbah 11:8; Ecclesiastes Rabbah 1:11.

54. Sanhedrin 4:4; Songs Rabbah 1:14, 4:1; Genesis Rabbah 70:8; Leviticus Rabbah 30:11. From these rows of sages vacancies in the Sanhedrin were filled.

55. Songs Rabbah 4:4.

56. Songs Rabbah 4:1.

57. Genesis Rabbah 98:8, 10; Ruth Rabbah 2:2.

58. Esther Rabbah 4:1; Songs Rabbah 6:4; Genesis Rabbah 97 (NV), 98:12; Numbers Rabbah 13:15, 17; see 1 Chron. 12:33.

59. Sotah 11a; Sanhedrin 106a, 104a; Exodus Rabbah 1:9, 27:3; Genesis Rabbah 97 (NV).

60. Kiddushin 4:5, 76b.

61. Sanhedrin 17a.

62. Exodus Rabbah 28:2, 23:10 interpreting Isa. 2:5 and Songs 1:5, respectively.

63. Ruth Rabbah 2:2; cf. Avot 1:1.

64. Sanhedrin 37a.

65. Sanhedrin 11:2, based on Deut. 17:10. This is an affirmation of the highest jurisdiction and final authority of the Sanhedrin in matters of law, tradition, and practice.

66. Sanhedrin 103a; Songs Rabbah 1:5.

67. Songs Rabbah 3:7.

68. Leviticus Rabbah 33:2, interpreting Amos 7:7; Bava Batra 91b.

69. Sanhedrin 32b.

70. Yerushalmi Ta'anit 68a. Compare Solomon Zeitlin, "The Hebrew Scrolls: Once More and Finally," *Jewish Quarterly Review,* n.s. 41 (1950):1–58, esp. p. 21, and C. Albeck, *Mishnah Mo'ed* (Jerusalem, 1952), p. 508. The Sanhedrin had the function of preserving the exact text of the Torah, which served as the official copy and the text

to be copied for all other scrolls. See Hoenig, *The Great Sanhedrin,* p. 90.

71. Leviticus Rabbah 2:9; Shekalim 7:6–7; see also Menaḥot 73b; Lev. 6:12–16.

72. Middot 5:4.

73. Leviticus Rabbah 32:8.

74. Shevu'ot 2:2. Shevu'ot 15b argues that the thanks offerings preceded the court.

75. Pe'ah 2:6; Hoenig, *The Great Sanhedrin,* p. 92, calls this an instance of an appeal made to the Sanhedrin. *Pe'ah,* literally "corner"—that is, corner of the field which the farmer is required by Lev. 19:9 and 23:22 to leave unharvested for the benefit of the poor. The Torah sets no limit; the sages fixed a minimum (see Pe'ah 1:2). Simon of Miẓpah and Rabban Gamaliel the Elder were of the first generation of tannaim (ca. 10–80 C.E.), as was Naḥum the Scribe. The scribe kept traditions and records of court proceedings. The *zugot* (see Avot 1:4 ff.) are literally "pairs" of leaders—the president (nasi) and his second in command, the "Father of the Court" (av bet din)—from the time of Jose ben Joezer (ca. 160 B.C.E.) to the time of Hillel and Shammai (second half of first century B.C.E.).

76. Eduyyot 7:4; see also Parah 6:4. The "flowing water" to be mixed with the ashes must come directly from the water source to the vessel. If the water on its way from the source comes in contact with anything susceptible to ritual uncleanness, it becomes invalid. Hoenig, *Great Sanhedrin,* p. 92, calls this another instance of an appeal to the Sanhedrin. Ẓadok, a pupil of Johanan ben Zakkai, lived during the second half of the first century C.E.

77. Sanhedrin 46a.

78. Exodus Rabbah 2:4; Makkot 7a. Rabbi Eleazar ben Azariah was born about 70 C.E. and died about 135 C.E. At the age of eighteen (some say sixteen) his erudition caused his appointment as temporary president of the Sanhedrin at Jabneh. Rabbi Akiba, the greatest scholar and most influential man of his time, was born about 50 C.E. and was executed by the Romans about 135 C.E. Rabbi Tarfon (in Greek, Tryphon) was born about 46 C.E. and died about 117 C.E. Simon ben Gamaliel is Simon III, son of Gamaliel II. He succeeded his father as patriarch in 110 C.E. and served as president of the Sanhedrin. He died in 165 C.E. and was succeeded by his distinguished son, Judah ha-Nasi.

79. Sanhedrin 43a–b, 46a–b.

80. Sanhedrin 63a.

81. Numbers Rabbah 14:6; Ketubbot 30a; Sanhedrin 37b.

82. Rosh Ha-Shanah 31a; Yoma 31a–b; Avodah Zarah 8b; Shabbat 15a; Sanhedrin 41a. *Ḥanuyot* may refer to "stores," the literal meaning of the word, or "marketplace" outside Jerusalem, or the place of Ḥanan, the high priest, or perhaps a station (in Hebrew, *taḥanah*). See Hoenig, *The Great Sanhedrin,* p. 109, for a discussion of this text and its usefulness for historical purposes. Many scholars argue that the Great Sanhedrin ended about 30 C.E. and this text is one of their proofs. There are, however, varying opinions. Louis Finkelstein, *Ha-Perushim ve-Anshei Keneset ha-Gedolah,* p. 84, and David Hoffmann, "Bemerkungen zur Geschichte des Synedrions," *Jahrbuch für die literarische gesellschaft* 5 (1907):225–44, say the end of the Sanhedrin resulted

from the domination of the state by Herod. Isaac Halevy, *Dorot ha-rishonim* (Frankfurt, 1906), 3:62, says it ended in 57 B.C.E. with the arrival of Gabinius and his establishment of his own synedria. Emil Schürer, *Geschichte des judischen Volkes in Zeitalter Jesu Christi* (3 vols., Leipzig, 1898–1901), 2:208, n. 72, says it was in 6 C.E. with the establishment of the procuratorship. Hoenig points out that both the Talmud and Josephus furnish evidence that the Great Sanhedrin functioned until the last years of Jerusalem. Thus Sanhedrin 7:2 records the testimony of Rabbi Eleazar ben Zadok who saw an adulterous daughter of a priest burned at the stake a few years before the destruction of the Temple (see also Sanhedrin 52b; Tosefta Sanhedrin 9:429; Yerushalmi Sanhedrin 24b). Similarly, Rabbi Johanan ben Zakkai examined witnesses as to stalks of figs near the scene of a crime (Sanhedrin 5:2, 41a). Hoenig concludes that the exact date of the Sanhedrin's end was 66 C.E. and the text here should properly be read "four years," instead of "forty years before the destruction of the Temple."

83. Genesis Rabbah, Vayehi, 97 (NV).

84. Lamentations Rabbah 1:6 based on Lam. 1:5–6.

85. Sotah 48a; Lamentations Rabbah 4:15. This text is also used by Hoenig, *Great Sanhedrin*, p. 113, to support his view that the last days of the Sanhedrin were times of great trouble just before the Temple's destruction and the fall of Jerusalem; see supra, n. 82.

Part VII

The Early Sages

1

Simon the Just

Simon the Just was one of the last survivors of the Men of the Great Assembly. He used to say, "By three things is the world sustained, by the Torah, by the Temple service, and by deeds of loving kindness.[1] He was great among his brethren and the glory of his people. How glorious was he when he came out of the Sanctuary—like the full moon on the feast days and like the rainbow becoming visible in the cloud![2]

The verse reading *I will not reject them or spurn them so as to destroy them* (Lev. 26:44), refers to the leaders sent by God to the Jewish people in times of trouble. *I will not reject them* refers to Daniel, Hananiah, Mishael, and Azariah in the Persian period; *or spurn them,* to Mordecai and Esther in the days of Haman; *so as to destroy them,* to Simon the Just and Mattathias, son of Johanan the Hasmonean, the high priest, and his sons.[3] Once Simon the Just heard a voice speaking in Aramaic from out of the Holy of Holies, "The army of the enemy is no more and the intention of the hater of Israel to attack the Temple is frustrated for Gaskalgas has been killed and his decrees are annulled."[4]

Who prepared the ashes of purification from the red heifer? Moses prepared the first, Ezra the second, and, Rabbi Meir says, five were prepared after Ezra. But the sages say seven were prepared after Ezra by the following persons: Simon the Just and Johanan the high priest prepared two each, and Eliehoenai ben Hakof, Hanamel the Egyptian, and Ishmael ben Phiabi prepared one each.[5]

Simon the Just said, "I have never eaten of the guilt offering of any nazirite but one. That happened when a would-be nazirite came up to me from the south, asking that I shave off his hair for he had vowed to become a nazirite. I noticed that he had a handsome appearance and beautiful eyes and his locks were arranged in rows of curls. I asked him, 'My son, why should you want to destroy this lovely hair?' He replied, 'I was a shepherd for my father in my home town. I went to draw water from the fountain and beheld my reflection in the water. My evil inclination surged up within me and sought to destroy me. So I said to it, "Wretch! Why do you plume yourself in this microcosm of my body that is not yours, in that which is destined to become dust to be eaten by maggots and worms! I swear to cut off my locks for heaven's sake!"' At once I arose and kissed him upon his head and said to him, 'My son, may there be many such nazirites as you in Israel. Scripture means such as you when it says, *If anyone, man or woman, explicitly utters a nazirite's vow, to set himself apart for the Lord* (Num. 6:2).'"[6]

Simon the Just held office as high priest for forty years, but after him the office was sold to candidates for a price. Therefore, they did not live long and their tenure was brief.[7] During the forty years that Simon the Just served as high priest the lot for the Lord's goat on Yom Kippur always came up in the right hand of the high priest. Afterward it came up at times in the right, at other times in the left. During his term of office the crimson-colored wool on Yom Kippur always turned white, as a sign that God had heard his prayers and forgiven all the people. Afterward it sometimes became white, sometimes remained red. The westernmost light, from which other lights were kindled in the Temple, burned continually even though not too much oil was added. Afterward it would go out periodically. During Simon's term the fire on the altar would burn strongly even though the priests would bring daily only the two pieces required by Scripture. Afterward the fire would languish despite the fact that the priests would add wood all day long. During Simon's tenure God's blessing rested upon the omer, the two loaves of bread and the bread of display. The priest whose portion was no more than the size of an olive would eat and be sated and sometimes even leave some food. Afterward a curse befell the omer, the two loaves of bread, and the bread of display and the priest got a portion the size of an Egyptian bean. The modest priest would not even take it; the gluttonous would grab it.[8]

In the year in which Simon the Just died he predicted to his friends that he would die within that year. They asked him how he knew. He told them, "Every Yom Kippur in past years when I would enter the Holy of Holies a mysterious old man all dressed in white would enter with me and leave with me. This year an old man dressed in black went in with me but did not come out with me." After the festival of Sukkot he fell ill for seven days and died. Thereafter the priests ceased blessing the people with the Tetragrammaton form of God's name but instead used a substitute form.[9] Before Simon died he was asked, "Who is to succeed you?" He replied, "Onias, my son, will serve in my place."[10]

<hr>

2

Antigonus of Sokho

Antigonus of Sokho received the tradition from Simon the Just. He used to say, "Be not like servants who minister to their master for the sake of receiving a reward. Be rather like servants who minister to their master not for the sake of receiving a reward— and may the fear of Heaven be upon you!"[11]

Antigonus had two disciples who used to study his words, Zadok and Boethus. They taught this doctrine to their students who, in turn, taught it to their own students. They examined this teaching and demanded, "Is it right that a laborer should work all day and not receive his reward in the evening?" So they arose and withdrew from the Torah. Two sects sprang from them: the Sadducees named after Zadok and the Boethusians after Boethus. They used silver and gold vessels all their lives, not because they were ostentatious, but the Sadducees said, "It is a tradition among the Pharisees to live austerely in this world; yet in the world to come they will have nothing."[12]

<hr>

3

Jose ben Joezer and Jose ben Johanan

Jose ben Joezer of Zeredah and Jose ben Johanan of Jerusalem received the tradition from Simon the Just and Antigonus. Jose ben Joezer said, "Let your house be a meeting place for the wise and sit in the dust of their feet and drink in their words with thirst."[13] He was called "the most pious man in the priesthood."[14] Jose ben Joezer and his deputy, Jose ben Johanan, decreed that the law of ritual uncleanliness is to be applied to countries outside of Israel as well as to Israel and to glass vessels.[15]

Jose ben Joezer said that one was not to practice the laying of hands on an offering on a festival before it is sacrificed. His deputy, Jose ben Johanan, said one might. They were followed in these opinions by their successors as presidents and deputies of the Sanhedrin.[16]

They called him "Jose the Lenient" because he permitted three things that other authorities did not. He testified that the Ayal locust may be eaten, that the liquid flowing along the floor of the slaughtering place in the Temple is not susceptible to ritual uncleanliness, and that only he who actually touches a corpse becomes ritually unclean.[17]

Jose ben Joezer had a son who did not behave properly. Once Jose had a measure of dinars that he consecrated to the Temple for its use. His son married the daughter of Gadil, the master of the crowns of King Yannai. When his wife gave birth, he bought a fish for her. When she cut it open, she found a pearl inside. She told her husband, "Do not bring it to the royal treasury (for use in a crown) for they will give you too little. Bring it to the Temple treasurers (for use in the ephod). Do not say, 'I give it to the Temple for such and such a price' for the mere declaration of a gift to the Temple is comparable to legal acquisition in ordinary affairs (and you will not be able to ask a higher price or to withdraw). But let the Temple treasurers (who are expert assessors and God-fearing men) evaluate it and they will not assess it for less than its worth." He did so and the treasurers evaluated the pearl as being worth thirteen measures of dinars. They told him, however, "We only have seven measures in the Temple treasury." He said, "Give me the seven and the remaining six I consecrate to the Temple (for its use)." Whereupon it was recorded: Jose ben Joezer consecrated one measure and his son (of whom he had thought that he did not behave properly) consecrated six measures of dinars. But another version has it otherwise: Jose ben Joezer brought one measure of dinars to the Temple; his son took out seven measures. (For he should not have emptied out the Temple treasury. He should have left, at least, one or two measures. By his action he made it clear that if the Temple treasury would have had the thirteen measures, he would have taken them all and consecrated nothing.)[18]

When Jose ben Joezer of Ẓeredah and Jose ben Johanan of Jerusalem died, that kind of personality ended too—the kind that encompassed all possible qualities. All such personalities, combining learning, piety, and kindness to fellowmen, who rose up for Israel from the days of Moses until the death of Jose ben Joezer taught the Torah like our master, Moses. Thereafter, teachers did not teach the Torah like Moses, our master. All such all-inclusive men who rose up for Israel from the days of Moses until the death of Jose ben Joezer of Ẓeredah were free of all taint of sin. Thereafter, it was not so.[19] Jose ben Johanan of Jerusalem said, "Let your house be opened wide and let the poor be members of your household and talk not overly much with women."[20]

══ 4 ══
Joshua ben Peraḥyah
and Nittai the Arbelite

Joshua ben Peraḥyah and Nittai the Arbelite received the tradition from their predecessors. Joshua ben Peraḥyah said, "Provide a teacher for yourself, acquire a friend, and judge every man charitably." Nittai the Arbelite said, "Keep far away from a bad neighbor; do not associate with the wicked and do not surrender belief in retribution."[21]

Let a person always repel another with the left hand while bringing him close with the right. Not like Elisha who thrust Gehazi away with both hands nor like Rabbi Joshua ben Peraḥyah who did so with Jeshu. When King Yannai killed the rabbis, Joshua ben Peraḥyah and Jeshu fled to Alexandria in Egypt. When peace was restored, Simon ben Shetaḥ sent Joshua a message, "From Jerusalem, the holy city, to my sister, Alexandria in Egypt! My husband dwells with you and I am desolate!" Understanding the message, Joshua arose and started on the way back. Stopping off at an inn where great respect was shown him, Joshua said to his disciple, Jeshu, "How lovely is this lady, the keeper of the inn!" Jeshu objected, "But, master, her eyes are unattractive!"

"Wicked man!" exclaimed his teacher. "Did you think I was referring to her physical beauty? I had reference to her manners." Whereupon Rabbi Joshua had four hundred shofars blown and excommunicated Jeshu. Thereafter, Jeshu came to see his master a number of times to beg his forgiveness but Rabbi Joshua would pay no attention to him. Once it happened that Jeshu came while his master was reciting the Shema. Forbidden to interrupt his prayers the master motioned to him that he had finally forgiven him. Misunderstanding the gesture, Jeshu thought that his teacher was again repelling him. He left and became an idolater. Rabbi Joshua urged him to repent. Jeshu replied, "From you have I learned the tradition that he who sins and causes the many to sin may not atone for his actions." It was said that Jeshu enticed and beguiled many and led Israel to sin.[22]

Rabbi Joshua ben Perahyah said, "In the beginning, had anyone suggested that I seek power, I would have flung him upside down before a lion. But now that I have it, if one were to suggest that I let it go, I should empty a kettle of boiling water upon his head!" So was it with King Saul. At first he fled from power, as it is said, *He is hiding among the baggage* (1 Sam. 10:22), and then, after he had reigned as king, he sought to slay David who was a threat to his power.[23]

═══ 5 ═══

Judah ben Tabbai
and Simon ben Shetah

Judah ben Tabbai and Simon ben Shetah received the tradition from Joshua ben Perahyah and Nittai the Arbelite. Judah ben Tabbai said, "When a judge, do not play the role of attorney for either side; when the two parties in a case stand before you, regard them both with suspicion; but once the case has been adjudicated and both parties have accepted the decision, regard them both as having been cleared."[24]

A case in law was decided by Judah ben Tabbai and he ordered a man executed. Simon ben Shetaḥ rebuked him for not having followed the tradition and, therefore, he had shed innocent blood. Judah immediately took it upon himself never again to render a decision except in Simon's presence. It was told that Judah, for the rest of his life, would visit the grave of the executed man, stretch out upon it, and weep. His voice would be heard at a distance and people thought it was the voice of the executed man. But Judah assured them it was his voice and offered as proof that on the day after his own death the voice would be heard no more.[25] Simon ben Shetaḥ said, "Be very searching in the examination of the witnesses and be most careful with your words lest through them the witnesses learn to lie."[26]

After Alexander Yannai, the king, had the sages executed, the world was a wasteland until Simon ben Shetaḥ returned the Torah to its former glory.[27] It is told that in the days of Simon ben Shetaḥ and Queen Salome Alexandra rain fell on Sabbath nights in such measure that wheat grew to the size of kidneys, barley to that of olive berries, and lentils to that of gold denarii. The sages gathered some and put them away for future generations to show them the cost of sin, as it is written, *It is your iniquities that have diverted these things, your sins that have withheld the bounty from you* (Jer. 5:25).[28]

Simon ben Shetaḥ said, "May I see the consolation of Israel as the following is true. I saw a man running after another person into a ruin. I ran after them and when I caught up with them, I saw a sword, blood dripping from the blade, in the hand of the pursuer and the dying man on the ground shaking convulsively in death throes. I said to the pursuer, 'Wicked man, who killed this poor fellow, was it I or was it you? But what can I do since the requiting of your blood for his is not legally within my power, for the Torah has said, *A person shall be put to death only on the testimony of two or more witnesses; he must not be put to death on the testimony of a single witness* (Deut. 17:6). But may He who knows all men's thoughts exact payment from the man who has killed his fellow man!' " Before they left the place a poisonous snake suddenly appeared, bit the man, and he died.[29]

When Simon ben Shetaḥ was appointed head of the Sanhedrin, he was told that there were eighty witches in a cave at Ashkelon.

On a rainy day he gathered eighty tall young men and gave each a new jar with a clean cloak neatly folded within it. The young men placed the jars upside down on their heads. He told them, "When I whistle once put on the cloaks, when I whistle twice, rush into the cave all of you together, each seize a witch and lift her off the ground. For it is the way of witches that they can do no harm if they have no contact with the earth." They accompanied him to the cave's entrance where he shouted to the women inside, "Ho! Ho! Open up for I belong to your company." They asked him, "Amidst these rains how did you come here dry?" He replied, "I walked between the drops." They asked again, "For what purpose have you come?" He answered, "To learn and to teach. Let each of you show me what she can do." Whereupon one mumbled something and a loaf of bread suddenly appeared. Another mumbled and there was meat. Still another uttered an incantation and, mysteriously, cooked dishes appeared. Another spoke a magic formula and wine came. Then they said to him, "You, what can you do?" He replied, "I can whistle twice and I shall thus bring before you eighty young men dressed in dry cloaks. They will be happy with this trick and will make you happy!" He whistled once and they donned their cloaks. He whistled twice and they all rushed in together. They shouted to each other, "Grab your witch!" They lifted the witches off the ground and carried them off to be executed by hanging.

The relatives of the dead witches in their anger vowed to take vengeance. Two of them came before the court and testified that the son of Rabbi Simon ben Shetah had committed a crime, the penalty for which was death. The court tried him on the basis of this testimony and sentenced the young man to be executed. As he was being led forth to be stoned, he cried out, "If I be guilty of this crime, let not my death atone for my sin. And if I be not guilty, then let my death atone for all my transgressions!" The responsibility wore heavily upon the witnesses and when they heard these words, they repented of their deed and exclaimed, "We are false witnesses." At once Simon sought to have his son brought back and the case reconsidered. Whereupon the son said, "If you aspire to have Israel's welfare strengthened through you, make me the threshold for the law to pass over me—let the law take its course though it cost my life!"[30]

Theodosius of Rome would have the Jews of Rome eat roast kid on the eve of Passover (even as the Jews in the land of Israel ate the roast paschal lamb). Simon ben Sheṭah sent a message to him, "If you were not so distinguished a person, I would place you under the ban, for you give the appearance of feeding Jews outside the land of Israel with sacrifices from the Temple altar!"[31]

It is told of Rabbi Simon ben Sheṭah that once he purchased an ass from an Ishmaelite. His disciples came and found a precious stone suspended from its neck. They said to him, "Master, *It is the blessing of the Lord that enriches* (Prov. 10:22)." Rabbi Simon ben Sheṭah replied, "I purchased only an ass, not a precious stone." He went back to the Ishmaelite and returned the gem to him, whereupon the Ishmaelite exclaimed, "Blessed be the Lord, God of Simon ben Sheṭah!"[32] Simon ben Sheṭah ordered that schools be established in the larger cities in which children could be taught Torah, the Written and the Oral law.[33]

===== 6 =====

Shemaiah and Avtalyon

Shemaiah and Avtalyon received the tradition from Judah ben Tabbai and Simon ben Sheṭah. Shemaiah said, "Love work, hate mastery, and keep your distance from the ruling power." Avtalyon said, "Sages, be careful with your words lest you incur the penalty of exile and be exiled to a place of evil waters and your disciples who come after you drink from them and die. So God's name will be profaned."[34]

They, the descendants of the heathen Sennacherib, taught Torah to the multitudes.[35] So great was their scholarship that they were called "the great men of the generation" and the "exegetes."[36] Despite their reputed origin, they influenced the people greatly and were beloved by them. Once it happened that when the high priest was being escorted home by the people at the end of a Day of Atonement, he was suddenly deserted by them. For the crowd, noticing Shemaiah and Avtalyon, turned aside to follow them. The envy of the high priest was aroused and later when Shemaiah and Avtalyon came to take their leave of him, he said meanly, "The descendants of heathen may depart in peace!" They retorted, "The descendants of heathen may indeed depart in peace because they do that which Aaron did—to love peace and pursue it—but the descendants of Aaron do not have peace because they do not do that which Aaron did!"[37]

Shemaiah was a man of courage. When Herod, then prefect of Galilee, on his own responsibility had Hezekiah, the leader of a band of Jewish patriots in that region, executed together with some of his followers, he was summoned to stand trial before the Sanhedrin. Young Herod showed his defiance of the court by appearing in royal purple, sword at his side, accompanied by a bodyguard of armed men, instead of in the customary humble garments of one accused. The members of the Sanhedrin were frightened. Only Shemaiah was brave enough to break the silence to say, "He who is summoned here to stand trial before us on capital charges seems ready to kill us if we condemn him. Yet more than I condemn him, do I condemn you, the judges, and the king, since you appear ready to commit an injustice and to let him go free. Know, therefore, that the day will come when he will execute all of you together with the king!"[38] Later, Avtalyon used his great influence with the people to persuade the men of Jerusalem to open the gates of the city to Herod. Herod was grateful and rewarded him with honors.[39] Admission to Avtalyon's academy of learning was not free to everyone. Those who wished to enter could do so by paying a daily small fee of one and a half tropaika.[40] Shemaiah said that the great faith in God that Abraham possessed was sufficient cause for God to split the waters of the Red Sea for his descendants, the children of Israel. Avtalyon said the cause was the faith of the children of Israel themselves.[41]

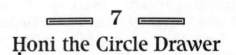

= 7 =
Ḥoni the Circle Drawer

It once happened that the greater part of the month of Adar had already passed and rain had not yet fallen. The disciples of Ḥoni asked him to pray for rain. He instructed them to bring into their homes the clay Passover ovens standing in their courtyards so that they would not distintegrate in the rains he was confident would soon come. He prayed but no rain fell. He drew a circle around him and stood within it, as the prophet Habakkuk had once done. He then prayed, "Master of the universe, Your children have set their faces upon me, as though I were a member of Your household. I swear by Your great name that I shall not move from this place until You have compassion upon Your children." Drops of rain began to fall. Whereupon his disciples said to him, "Master, may we be spared from harm, but we think this small amount of rain has fallen only that you may be released from your vow."

"It was not for a few drops of rain I prayed," said he, "but for enough rain to fill the wells, cisterns, and caves." The rain suddenly came down furiously, until each drop got to be as large as the mouth of a barrel, and the sages estimated that each drop contained the volume of a lug of water. His disciples spoke up again, "Master, may we not be punished, now we are of the opinion that these rains have but come to destroy the world." He prayed once more to God, "Not for such rain did I ask You, but for desirable rain that would be a blessing and a bounty." The rain then fell in the usual way, but it rained so much that the Jews dwelling in lower Jerusalem had to go up to the Temple Mount for safety.

His disciples said to Ḥoni, "Master, just as you prayed for rain to fall, pray now that it cease." He replied, "There is a tradition that one should not pray for an end to an overabundance of good. Nevertheless, bring me a bullock for a thanksgiving sacrifice." They brought him the animal. He placed his two hands upon it and prayed, "Master of the universe, Your people Israel, whom You have brought out of Egypt, can take neither too much misfortune nor too much goodness. When You become angry with them, they cannot stand it. When You shower too much of Your goodness upon them, they cannot stand it either. May it be Your will that the rains cease and the world will profit." Immediately, a wind blew, scattering the clouds, and the sun shone. The people went out and saw that the Temple Mount was covered with truffles and mushrooms.[42]

Simon ben Shetaḥ, evidently displeased by Ḥoni's daring utterances to God, sent word to him, "If you were not Ḥoni, I would pronounce the ban against you. For were these years like those concerning which Elijah said no rain should fall—for the keys to rainfall were in his hands—would not the result of your action have been the desecration of God's name? But what can I do with you, since you offend God but He does your will, like a son who sins against his father, who then fulfills his son's desires. The son asks, 'Father, bathe me in hot water, bathe me in cold, give me nuts, almonds, peaches, pomegranates.' Whatever the son asks, the father gives him. To you may the passage be applied, *Your father and mother will rejoice; she who bore you will exult* (Prov. 23:25)."[43]

The Sanhedrin sitting in the Chamber of Hewn Stones sent a message to Ḥoni the Circle Drawer. "As the Book of Job has it, *You will decree and it will be fulfilled* (Job 22:28), you have decreed below and the Holy One, blessed be He, from above has carried it out. *And light will shine upon your affairs* (Job 22:28)— to the generation in darkness your prayer brought light. *When others sink low, you will say it is pride* (Job 22:29)—the generation cast down you lifted up through your prayer. *For He saves the humble* (Job 28:29)—the generation humble because of its transgressions you saved through your prayer. *He will deliver the guilty* (Job 22:30)—to a guilty generation you brought deliverance through your prayer. *He will be delivered through the cleanness of your hands* (Job 22:30)—why was the generation delivered? Because of the cleanness of your hands."[44] Of Ḥoni it was said that whenever he entered the hall of the Temple the place lit up brightly.[45]

All his life Ḥoni was sorely puzzled by the meaning of the verse in Psalms, *A song of Ascents. When the Lord restores the fortunes of Zion—we see it as in a dream* (Ps. 126:1). He would say, "How is it possible that seventy years of exile should be like a dream? And are there any who sleep seventy years?" One day he was going down a road and saw a man planting a carob tree. He asked him, "Look here, it takes seventy years before a carob tree bears fruit. Are you so sure you will live another seventy years to eat from this tree?"

The man replied, "When I came into the world it had carob trees planted by my ancestors. I too plant for my descendants." Ḥoni sat down near the tree to eat. He grew drowsy and fell asleep. He continued to sleep and a grotto formed around him and concealed him. He slept for seventy years. Upon awaking he saw a man eating from the carob tree. He asked him, "Do you know who planted that tree?" The man answered, "My father's father." Ḥoni, startled, said to himself, "I must have surely slept seventy years." He looked at his ass and saw that several generations of mules had been born to it.

He went home and asked, "Where is the son of Ḥoni the Circle Drawer?" He was told, "His son is no more, but his son's son lives." He then said, "I am Ḥoni!" They refused to believe him. He went to the House of Study and overheard the rabbis say, "This law is as clear to us now as laws were in the days of Ḥoni the Circle Drawer who, when coming to the House of Study, would solve any problem the rabbis had." He exclaimed, "I am he!" They did not believe him nor did they show him proper respect. He was so discouraged that he prayed for death and his spirit expired. Rava said, "This is why people say—either fellowship or death!"[46] Another tradition says that Ḥoni went to sleep at the time of the destruction of the First Temple and did not awake until after the building of the Second Temple.[47]

Still another account reports Ḥoni's death as having occurred in a different manner altogether. After the death of Queen Salome Alexandra, a civil war broke out between the forces of her two sons, Hyrcanus and Aristobulus, each vying for the throne. The troops of Hyrcanus laid siege to the Temple Mount of Jerusalem where were Aristobulus and his followers. Ḥoni, who had hidden himself because of the fighting, was discovered by the soldiers of Hyrcanus. Remembering how his prayers for rain had been answered by God, they brought him to their camp and demanded that he curse Aristobulus and his faction. He demurred and offered various excuses for his refusal, but the men insisted and would not let him go until he spoke. Whereupon he stood up in the midst of them and prayed, "O God, the King of the whole world, since both the besieged as well as the besiegers are Your people, I beg that You will not answer the curses that they may utter against each other." The wicked soldiers, hearing such a prayer, at once stoned him to death.[48]

8

Abba Ḥilkiah

Abba Ḥilkiah was a grandson of Ḥoni the Circle Drawer. When there was need of rain the rabbis would come to him. Once it happened that rain was needed and the rabbis sent two of their younger colleagues to request that he ask heavenly compassion so that rain would fall. They came to his home but did not find him in. They went out to the fields and there they found him hoeing. They greeted him but he did not even turn his face toward them. Toward evening, he started off for home and he brought along some wood, placing the wood and the hoe on one shoulder and his cloak on the other. All the way home he did not wear his shoes except for the fording of a brook. When he came among briars and brambles, he would raise the hem of his garment. As he approached the city he was met by his wife dressed in fine apparel. Upon reaching their home, she entered first, followed by him, then by the two rabbis. He sat down to eat but he did not say to the rabbis, "Come, eat with us." He gave food to his children, one portion to the elder, two to the younger. He then whispered to his wife, "I know that the rabbis came for rain. Let us go up on the roof to pray for divine compassion. It may be the will of the Holy One, blessed be He, to cause rain to fall and then it will not appear as though it came about through us." They went up to the roof, he prayed in one corner and she in another. A rain cloud appeared in the direction of the corner where his wife was standing.

He went back downstairs and, speaking to the rabbis for the first time, asked them, "For what purpose have you come?" They replied, "The rabbis have sent us to ask you to pray for rain." He said to them, "Blessed be the Lord who has made your need of me unnecessary." But they responded, "We know that this rain now falling comes only because of you, but please explain some of your actions that puzzle us. When we greeted you, why did you not turn your face to us?" He answered, "I had been hired as a day laborer and I thought I must not waste even a minute of my employer's time."

"Why did you carry the wood on one shoulder and the cloak on the other, instead of in the customary way, beneath the wood?" He replied, "Because I had borrowed the cloak to wear and not to use as a pad."

"Why did you not wear your shoes all the way home except when it came to fording a brook." "Because all along the way I could see what I was stepping on but in the water I could not."

"And why did you lift your garment where there were prickly shrubs and thorns?" "Because if my leg got scratched it would heal, but if the garment were torn, it could not be mended."

"Why did your wife come out to meet you when you came back to the city?" "So that I should not look at any other woman."

"Why did she enter the house first, then you, then we?" "Because you were unknown to me."

"When you ate why did you not invite us?" "Because there was not enough food and I did not wish to receive your thanks for nothing."

"Why did you give one portion to your elder son and two to the younger?" "Because the elder has been at home today and has probably helped himself while the younger has been at school and is hungrier."

"Why did a rain cloud first appear in the direction of the corner where your wife was praying and then, only later, did a rain cloud appear in the direction of the corner where you were praying?" "Because a woman is at home all day and is thus able to feed the poor who come for help while a man cannot do such direct acts of charity as often. Besides, there were bandits in our area and I prayed that they should die, but she prayed that they should repent. And they repented. Therefore, her prayer was answered before mine."[49]

9

Ḥanin the Hidden

Another grandson of Ḥoni the Circle Drawer was called Ḥanin the Hidden. When the country needed rain the rabbis would send to him the schoolchildren who would take hold of the hem of his garment and cry, "Father, give us rain!" And he would pray to the Holy One, blessed be He, "Master of the Universe, give rain for the sake of these children who do not even know enough to distinguish between a Father who gives rain and a father who does not." Why was he called Ḥanin the Hidden? Because he would, in his modesty, hide himself, so as to keep out of public view.[50]

10

Hillel and Shammai

If a poor man dies and appears before the heavenly court, he will be asked, "Why have you not studied Torah?" If he answers that he could not because of his poverty and the need to earn a livelihood, he will be answered, "Were you poorer than Hillel?"

Hillel used to work each day until he had earned a tarpeik. Half that sum he would give to the gatekeeper at the academy for his admission and half went for the sustenance of his family and himself. One day he could earn nothing and the gatekeeper of the academy refused him admission. He climbed to the roof and swung himself over to the skylight where he was able to hear the teachers, Shemaiah and Avtalyon, expound the words of the living God. Once on a Friday during the wintry month of Tevet snow fell and covered him. When the dawn of the Sabbath day broke, Shemaiah said to Avtalyon, "My brother, by this time each morning the house is light and this morning it is dark. Is it because the day is cloudy?" They looked up toward the skylight and saw the figure of a man upon it. They went up to the roof and found a man covered by a layer of snow three cubits thick. They shook it off him, washed him, anointed him, and placed him before a fire. They said, "For such a man, with so great a desire to learn, even the Sabbath may be violated!"[51]

Hillel chose to be poor. He studied the Torah while his brother, Shevna, was involved in business. Shevna one day proposed to Hillel that the two share their gains. He would divide his financial profit with Hillel while Hillel would share his spiritual merits with him. Hillel declined the offer and remained poor, in obedience to a heavenly voice that proclaimed, *If a man offered all his wealth for love, he would be laughed to scorn* (Songs 8:7).[52]

It once happened that the fourteenth day of Nisan (the day the paschal lamb was sacrificed annually) fell on the Sabbath and the Benei Batyra, the scholarly authorities at the time, forgot what the law should be under such circumstances: should the Passover sacrifice take precedence over the Sabbath or not? They asked the sages if anyone knew the answer. They were told there was a certain man who had come from Babylonia, Hillel the Babylonian by name, who had studied under the two greatest sages of the earlier generation, Shemaiah and Avtalyon, and perhaps he would know. They sent for him and asked him, "Do you know whether the Passover sacrifice supersedes the Sabbath or not?" He replied, "Do we then have only one such case similar to a Passover sacrifice that supersedes the Sabbath? Are there not more than two hundred such instances each year when the Sabbath is superseded by a sacrifice?" They asked him, "What is your scriptural proof?" He answered, "It is said, *at its set time* (Num. 9:3), in connection with the Passover sacrifice, and a similar phrase is used in connection with the daily sacrifice (Num. 28:2). Just as the expression in the case of the daily sacrifice means that it supersedes the Sabbath, so too the use of the wording with the Passover sacrifice must mean the same. Moreover, the argument of a fortiori can be used: if the daily sacrifice, for the neglect of which there is no punishment of *karet*, supersedes the Sabbath, how much more so should the Passover sacrifice, for the neglect of which there is the punishment of *karet*, supersede the Sabbath!"

They immediately appointed him their head and nasi. He sat down and lectured all day long on the laws of Passover. He later rebuked them, "What was responsible for your having made me, who comes from Babylonia, nasi over you? Only your laziness in not having studied under the two greatest sages of the earlier generation, Shemaiah and Avtalyon."

They asked him, "Master, what is the law in such a case where a sacrifice is to be offered on the Sabbath and the man had forgotten to bring the slaughtering knife on Friday? May he bring it on the Sabbath?" He replied, "I have heard what this law is but I have forgotten it. However, leave it to the people. If they are not prophets, they are the descendants of prophets!" On the next day, which was the Sabbath and the fourteenth of Nisan, whoever brought a lamb for the sacrifice had the knife stuck in the lamb's wool. He who brought a kid had the knife stuck between the kid's horns. As soon as Hillel saw this, he remembered that this was the law and said, "This is the tradition I received from Shemaiah and Avtalyon."⁵³

Hillel the Elder expounded seven rules of exegesis in the presence of the Benei Batyra: the inference drawn from a minor premise to a major, the inference drawn from a similarity of words or phrases, a general principle established on the basis of a law contained in one verse or of laws contained in two verses, the rule when a generalization is followed in the text by a specification, and when a specification is followed in the text by a generalization, the inference drawn from an analogous passage elsewhere, and the interpretation of a word or passage from its context.⁵⁴

The descendant of Hillel, Rabbi Judah ha-Nasi, was very modest. He used to say, "I am prepared to do whatever any person tells me except what the Benei Batyra did for my ancestor in that they relinquished their high office and promoted him to it."⁵⁵ Hillel did for his generation what Ezra had done for his. In Ezra's day the Torah had been forgotten in Israel. He came up from Babylonia and reestablished it. Before Hillel, the Torah had again been forgotten. Hillel the Babylonian came up from his country and reestablished it. Therefore, Hillel was rightly called "disciple of Ezra" even though centuries separated them, even as Samuel the Small was later called "disciple of Hillel." Abraham,

Isaac, and Jacob are grouped together, Moses, Joshua, David, and Hezekiah, also Ezra, Hillel, Rabban Johanan ben Zakkai, and Rabbi Meir. Hillel was forty years of age when he came from Babylonia. He studied with the sages for forty years and for forty years he was the spiritual head of his generation. It was said of Hillel that he had not neglected any of the words of the sages but had learned them all. He had studied all manners of speech, even the utterance of mountains, hills, and valleys, the utterance of trees and plants, the utterance of beasts and animals, the speech of demons, popular stories and parables. Why did he study all these things? Because it is stated, *The Lord desires His [servant's] vindication, that he may magnify and glorify [His] teaching* (Isa. 42:21).[56]

Hillel's life ran parallel to that of Moses. Both lived one hundred twenty years. Moses spent forty years in Pharaoh's palace and then left his native land; forty years in Midian in preparation for his career of leadership and then he led his people forty years. Hillel left Babylonia for the land of Israel at forty; forty years he spent in study; forty years he served as the spiritual leader of his people.[57]

There are six pairs whose life cycles were similar each to the other within each pair: Rebecca and Kehat, Levi and Amram, Joseph and Joshua, Samuel and Solomon, Moses and Hillel the Elder, Rabban Johanan ben Zakkai and Rabbi Akiba.[58] A genealogical scroll was found in Jerusalem in which it was written that Hillel was descended from David.[59]

Hillel and Shammai received the tradition from Shemaiah and Avtalyon. Hillel said, "Be of the disciples of Aaron, loving peace and pursuing peace, promoting peace between husband and wife, loving mankind and bringing them near to the Torah." He used to say, "Whoever makes his name great, loses his name; whoever does not increase his knowledge, decreases it; he who does not study deserves death; and he who unworthily exploits the crown of learning will pass away." He also used to say, "If I am not for myself, who will be? And if I am only for myself, what am I? And if not now, when?"[60]

It was said of Hillel the Elder that he would greatly rejoice at the Ceremony of Water-Drawing. He would say, "If you will come to my house, I will go to yours. Wherever my heart desires to go, there my feet lead me." He used to say, "If I am here, all are here; if I am not here, who is here? Turn it and turn it again for everything is in it. With regard to all things, the rule holds—according to the labor, so is the reward."[61]

The story is told of Hillel the Elder that as he was walking along the road he met some men carrying wheat. He asked them, "How much for a seah?" They replied, "Two dinars." Later he met other men carrying wheat and asked them, "How much for a seah?" They answered, "Three dinars." He said to them, "But those who came earlier asked only two dinars." They responded, "You stupid Babylonian, do you not know the rule—according to the labor, so is the reward? And we have brought the wheat from a greater distance, hence our price is higher." He said to them, "You foolish empty-headed persons! I ask you a civil question and you answer me rudely!" Hillel the Elder so influenced them that they were turned to the way of righteousness.[62]

Hillel taught, "Do not separate yourself from the congregation. Do not trust in yourself until the day of your death. Do not judge your fellowman until you have come into his place. Do not say anything which cannot be understood at once, in the hope that ultimately it will be understood. And do not say that when I shall have time, I shall study—perhaps you will never have time."[63] He used to say, "An unlettered person is not sin-fearing, nor is an ignorant person pious. A shy person does not learn nor can the hot-tempered teach, nor is everyone who is greatly involved in business wise. Where there are no men, do try to be a man."[64] Moreover, he once saw a skull floating on the surface of the water. He said to it, "Because you drowned others, you were drowned; and in the end, they who drowned you will themselves be drowned."[65]

He used to say, "The more flesh, the more worms; the more possessions, the more anxiety; the more wives, the more witchcraft; the more female servants, the more immorality; the more manservants, the more theft; the more Torah, the more life; the more schooling, the more wisdom; the more counsel, the more understanding; the more charity, the more peace. He who has acquired a good name has won it for himself. He who has acquired Torah for himself has acquired life in the world to come."[66]

Hillel the Elder said, "When the scholars keep in [the teaching of the Torah], you disseminate it, and when they disseminate it, you keep it in."[67] He used to say, "Why do disciples of the sages [often] die young? It is not because they are immoral nor because they rob, but because they interrupt their study of the Torah to indulge in idle talk. Moreover [when they resume their studies], they do not begin where they left off."[68]

How did Hillel bring his fellowman closer to the Torah? One day Hillel stood in the gate of Jerusalem and met people going out to work. He asked, "How much will you earn today?" One said, "A dinar," another, "Two dinars." He asked them, "What will you do with the money?" They replied, "We shall pay for the necessities of life." Then he said to them, "Come rather with me and gain knowledge of the Torah so that you may gain life in this world and life in the world to come." So did Hillel do all his days and he brought many under the wings of the Heavenly Presence.[69] Hillel explained that the prophet Malachi's phrase, *him who has not served Him* (Mal. 3:18), refers to the man who had studied but who ceased to do so. Only he who studies without cessation is the one *who has served the Lord* (Mal. 3:18).[70]

Hillel was a humble man. He used to say, "My humiliation is my exaltation: my exaltation is my humiliation."[71]

There was a man of a wealthy family who had become poor. Hillel provided him with a horse to ride upon and with a servant to run before him. One day he could not find a servant, so he himself ran before him for three miles.[72]

It once happened that Hillel the Elder had arranged for a certain man to dine with him, when a poor man came and stood at his door and said to Hillel's wife, "I am to marry today and I have no means of livelihood." She took the entire meal that she had prepared and gave it to him. She then kneaded fresh dough, cooked another dinner, and placed it before Hillel and his guest. He said to her, "My dear, why did you not bring it to us sooner?" She told him the entire story. He said to her, "My dear, I really did not judge you in the scale of guilt but in the scale of merit because everything you did was for the glory of Heaven's name!"[73]

The sages taught that a man should always be modest and patient like Hillel and not quick-tempered like Shammai. Once it happened that two men made a wager with each other, betting a total of four hundred zuzim. The wager was that whoever would provoke Hillel to anger would take the money. One of them said, "I shall provoke him to anger." It was the eve of the Sabbath and Hillel was washing his head. The man came to the door of Hillel's house and cried out, "Where is Hillel? Where is Hillel?"

Hillel wrapped himself in his robe and went out to him and asked, "My son, what do you want?" The man replied, "I have a question to ask." "Ask, my son, ask," said Hillel. "Why are the heads of the Babylonians round?" the man asked. Hillel answered, "My son, you have asked a great question. It is because they have no skilled midwives."

The man went away, waited a brief while, and then returned, shouting, "Where is Hillel? Where is Hillel?" Again he dressed, went out to him, and asked, "My son, what do you want?" "I have a question to ask," said he. "Ask, my son, ask," was Hillel's reply. "Why are the Palmyrans bleary-eyed?" was the question. "My son, you have asked a great question," answered Hillel. "It is because they live in a sandy country." The man left, waited a while, and came back again, crying out, "Where is Hillel? Where is Hillel?" Again Hillel wrapped himself in his robe and went out to him, asking, "My son, what do you want?" The man replied, "I have a question to ask." "Ask, my son, ask," said Hillel. "Why do Africans have broad feet?" asked the man. "My son, you have asked a great question," answered Hillel. "It is because they live in marshy places."

The man said, "I have many more questions to ask but I am afraid to ask them lest I make you angry." Hillel wrapped his robe around himself, sat down before the man, and said, "Ask all the questions you may have." The man asked, "Are you Hillel who is called Nasi in Israel?" He said, "Yes." To which the man retorted, "If you are, may there not be many more in Israel like you!" "Why not, my son?" asked Hillel. He answered, "Because I have just lost four hundred zuzim on your account." Hillel replied, "Calm yourself, better that you lose four hundred zuzim on Hillel's account than that Hillel should lose his temper."[74]

Once a pagan came before Shammai and asked him, "How many Torahs do you have?" He replied, "Two, a Written Torah and an Oral Torah." The man said, "The Written Law I am ready to accept but the Oral Law I am not prepared to accept. Convert me to Judaism upon the condition that you teach me—and I accept—the Written Law." Shammai became furious at him and ejected him with a rebuke. The pagan went before Hillel who converted him under the same condition. One day Hillel taught him the first four letters of the alphabet. The next day he deliberately reversed the sequence of the letters so that the *aleph* he now called *daled* and so on. The convert exclaimed, "But yesterday you taught me contrariwise!" "Ah!" commented Hillel, "evidently you put your trust in me to teach you the alphabet correctly. Concerning the correctness of the Oral Law trust me also."[75]

On another occasion a pagan appeared before Shammai and said, "Convert me to Judaism provided that you teach me the entire Torah while I stand on one foot." Shammai pushed him out with a builder's cubit-measure that was in his hand. He went to Hillel who converted him, saying, "What is hateful to you, do not to your neighbor: that is the whole Torah; the rest is commentary; go, study."[76]

Still another pagan once passed by the rear of a synagogue and heard the voice of a scribe saying, *These are the vestments they are to make: a breastpiece, an ephod . . .* (Exod. 28:4). He came to Shammai and asked him, "For whom is all that finery?" He replied, "For the high priest." The pagan thought, "I shall become converted to Judaism so that I may become high priest." He asked Shammai, "Convert me upon the condition that they shall appoint me high priest." Shammai pushed him out with the builder's cubit-measure that was in his hand. He went to Hillel who converted him but then said to him, "Is it possible for a man to be made a king unless he has first become familiar with court procedures? Go study the requisite procedures for the office you seek." The convert went and studied. When he came to the biblical verse, *You shall make Aaron and his sons responsible for observing their priestly duties; and any outsider who encroaches shall be put to death* (Num. 3:10), he asked, "For whom is that verse meant?" Hillel answered, "Even for David, king of Israel" (even he is a "common man" as far as the priesthood is concerned since he is not a descendant of Aaron). "So," reasoned the convert, "if those born Jews who are called the children of God and who, because of His love for them He called, *Israel is My first-born son* (Exod. 4:22), are warned—*and any outsider who encroaches shall be put to death*—how much more so the ordinary convert who comes but with his staff and knapsack!" He then went to Shammai and exclaimed, "Am I then eligible to become a high priest? Is it not written in the Torah, *and any outsider who encroaches shall be put to death?*" He appeared before Hillel and cried out, "O patient Hillel, blessings upon your head because you have brought me under the wings of the Heavenly Presence."

Some time later the three proselytes met in one place. They observed, "The impatience of Shammai could have driven us out of the world. The patience of Hillel brought us under the wings of the Heavenly Presence."[77] The grateful proselyte who had aspired to the high priesthood became the father of two sons. He named them Hillel and Gamaliel. They were known as Hillel's proselytes.[78]

One day Hillel the Elder was returning from a journey. As he approached his neighborhood he heard cries. He said, "I am confident that the cries do not come from my house." This is an illustration of the verse, *He is not afraid of evil tidings, his heart is firm, he trusts in the Lord* (Ps. 112:7).[79]

Shammai taught, "Fix a definite time for your study of Torah. Say little and do much. Greet all men with a cheerful countenance."[80] About Shammai it was said that on every day of the week he would eat in honor of the Sabbath; that is, when he would chance upon a fine animal, he would say, "This shall be for the Sabbath." When he would find a better one, he would eat the first one and save the second for the Sabbath.

But Hillel the Elder had a different practice because all his actions were for the sake of heaven, trusting in God, as it is said, *Blessed is the Lord. Day by day He supports us* (Ps. 68:20). Thus the school of Shammai taught, "Prepare every day for the Sabbath." So too would Shammai the Elder begin to collect firewood for the Sabbath on the preceding Sunday. But the school of Hillel said, "Praised be the Lord day by day."[81]

Ben He He asked Hillel, "What is the meaning of the verse, *And you shall come to see the difference between the righteous and the wicked, between him who has served the Lord and him who has not served Him* (Mal. 3:18)? Are not the terms the same —*the righteous* and *him who has served the Lord*, and *the wicked* and *him who has not served Him?*" Hillel answered, "He who serves God and he who serves Him not may both be righteous men but he who studies his lesson one hundred times cannot be compared to him who studies it one hundred and one times." To which Ben He He retorted, "Because of one additional time a man is described as one who does not serve God!" "Yes," replied Hillel. "Go and learn from the market place. Hire a donkey for ten miles and you pay one zuz. Hire it for eleven miles and you pay two."[82]

One day, after Hillel the Elder had concluded his studies with his disciples, he took his leave of them. They asked him, "Master, where are you going?" He replied, "To perform a religious duty."

They asked, "What may that be?" He answered, "To take a bath." They asked, "Is that a religious duty?" He replied, "Yes, if the statues of kings erected in the theaters and arenas are scoured and washed by the man appointed to look after them and who thereby obtains his livelihood—even more, he is honored for doing well by the great of the kingdom—how much more is it a duty of man to care for his body, since man has been created in the divine image and likeness, as it is written, *For in the image of God was man created* (Gen. 9:6)."[83]

At another time when Hillel the Elder took leave of his disciples upon concluding his studies with them, they asked him, "Master, where are you going?" He replied, "To bestow a kindness upon a guest in my house." They asked, "Have you a guest every day?" He answered, "Is not my poor soul a guest in my body? Today it is here, tomorrow it is gone."[84]

Hillel said, "Do not appear naked among the dressed nor dressed among the naked; do not remain standing among those who sit nor sitting among those who stand; do not laugh among those who weep nor weep among those who laugh. The rule is, Do not deviate from the usage of men."[85]

Hillel the Elder had eighty disciples. Thirty were worthy enough that the Divine Presence should rest upon them as it did upon Moses; thirty were worthy enough that the sun should stand still for their sake as it did for Joshua ben Nun; and twenty were average. The greatest among them was Jonathan ben Uzziel, the least among them, Rabban Johanan ben Zakkai. Yet of the latter it was told that he did not leave unstudied the Bible, Mishnah, oral study, laws, legends, subtle points in the interpretation of biblical laws, special points in rabbinical enactments, both the lenient and the restrictive, the hermeneutical rules of analogy, the calculation of astronomical cycles, arithmetic, the whispering of angels, the whispering of evil spirits, the whispering of palm trees, the fables of laundrymen and the fables about foxes, small things and large things. Large things such as the esoteric mysteries of Ezekiel's vision; small things like the matters that later formed the subjects of the controversies between Abaye and Rava. All this to confirm that which has been written, *I endow those who love me with substance; I will fill their treasuries* (Prov. 8:21). And if the least of the disciples was so learned, how much more so was the greatest among them? It was told concerning Jonathan ben Uzziel that when he sat and was involved in the study of Torah, any bird that flew over his head was immediately consumed in flames.[86]

Once Hillel fell ill and all his disciples came in to visit him. Rabban Johanan ben Zakkai remained in the courtyard. Hillel asked, "Where is he, the youngest among you, he who is destined to be the father of wisdom and the father of generations to come?" They answered, "In the courtyard." Hillel ordered, "Let him come in." When he entered, Hillel applied to him the words of the verse, *I endow those who love me with substance; I will fill their treasuries* (Prov. 8:21).[87]

Rabban Johanan ben Zakkai said of his teacher, Hillel, "If all the heavens were parchments and all the trees were quills and all the seas were ink, it would still be impossible for me to write down even a small part of all that I learned from my teacher. And if I could, all this would only be as much as a fly might pick up when skimming the waters of the sea."[88]

One day a group of wise men were gathered in the upper chamber of a certain Gurya's house in Jericho when a heavenly voice announced, "There is among you one man who deserves that the Divine Presence rest upon him but his generation is not worthy of it." They all fixed their eyes upon Hillel. And when he died they said, "Alas for the pious man, the humble man, the disciple of Ezra!"[89]

It once happened that there was a man whose sons lived reprehensible lives and he, therefore, willed his possessions to Jonathan ben Uzziel. What did Jonathan do when he came into possession of the estate? He sold off one-third for his personal needs, one-third he consecrated for the Sanctuary, and one-third he gave to the dead man's sons. Shammai the Elder came to him with strong rebuke, "You returned one-third to the sons when it was their father's expressed wish to leave them nothing!" Jonathan replied, "If you can find legal grounds for nullifying the third I sold and the second third I consecrated, then you can also nullify what I gave as my gift. If you cannot—because it is my property to sell or to sanctify—then it is also mine to give as a gift." Shammai exclaimed, "A sharp argument and unanswerable!"[90]

Shammai was severe with the members of his family. For although it was legally permissible to wash one hand on Yom Kippur before taking food to feed a young child, Shammai would not permit himself to do so for his young son. Again, although women and children are legally absolved from the *miẓvah* of the sukkah, when Shammai's daughter-in-law gave birth during the Feast of Tabernacles, he broke away some of the roof-plaster and made a sukkah-roofing over the crib for the sake of the child.[91]

Shammai ruled that when one harvests grapes for the wine-press they already fall within the possibility of levitical unclean-ness. Hillel disagreed. He said to Shammai, "Why do you rule this way with grapes and so require them to be harvested in ritually clean vessels but do not rule so with regard to the harvesting of olives?" Shammai replied, "If you provoke me further, I shall so rule even with regard to the harvesting of olives." A sword was stuck into the floor of the academy and it was announced that he who wished to enter could not and he who desired to leave could not so that a quorum for making a decision might be obtained. That day Hillel sat bent in submission before Shammai as though he were his disciple. And that day was as hard for the Jewish people as the day when the Golden Calf was fashioned.[92]

The sages interpreted the verse, *The scepter shall not depart from Judah, nor the ruler's staff from between his feet* (Gen. 49:10), as follows: *The scepter shall not depart from Judah*—that refers to the exilarchs in Babylonia who rule the children of Israel as with a scepter: *nor the ruler's staff from between his feet*—that refers to the descendants of Hillel who teach Torah to the multitudes.[93]

⸺ 11 ⸺
Jonathan ben Uzziel

One of Hillel's great disciples was Jonathan ben Uzziel. He was responsible for the Aramaic translation of the prophets, with the supernatural assistance of Haggai, Zechariah, and Malachi. At the moment he finished the translation a tremor shook the land of Israel for four hundred squares miles and a heavenly voice was heard saying, "Who is the one who has revealed My mysteries to human beings?" Jonathan ben Uzziel stood upon his feet and asserted, "I am the one who has revealed Your mysteries to man but it is surely known to You that I have done it not for my personal fame nor for the glory of my father's house but for the sake of Your glory so that controversies shall not multiply in Israel." He also sought to translate the Writings into Aramaic when a heavenly voice spoke to him and said, "You have done enough! And why? Because in the Writings the secrets concerning the coming of the Messiah are revealed."[94]

Notes

VII. THE EARLY SAGES

1. Simon the Just

1. Avot 1:2; Avot de-Rabbi Natan 4:1. The first high priest to bear the name of Simon the Just, son of Onias, was the one who served 310–291 B.C.E. or 300–270 B.C.E.; the second, his grandson, 219–199 B.C.E. According to the early authorities, Z. Frankel, *Darkhei ha-Mishnah* (Warsaw, 1923), H. Graetz, *History of the Jews* (6 vols., Philadelphia, 1891-98), and I. Halevy, *Dorot ha-rishonim*, the author of this maxim was the former; N. Krochmal, *Ha-aggada u-va'alei ha-aggadah* (Tel Aviv, 1930), and J. Brüll, *Mavo ha-Mishnah* (Frankfurt, 1876–85), say it was the latter. For the former, see Josephus, *Antiquities*, 12.2.5 and 12.4.1, who says Simon was called the Just because of both his piety toward God and his kindness to his fellowmen. Josephus mentions the second Simon—without calling him "the Just"—in *Antiquities* 12.4.10. Concerning the legends associating Simon the Just with Alexander the Great, see part 2. The pretannaitic period of the sages is usually reckoned from 200 B.C.E. to about 10 C.E., but the starting point depends on the identification of Simon the Just.

2. Ben Sira (Ecclesiasticus) 50:1–12.

3. Megillah 11a; Hoenig, *The Great Sanhedrin*, pp. 33–34, rewords this passage to sustain his theory that Simon the Maccabean, brother of Judah the Maccabee, is to be identified with Simon the Just and was head of the Hasmonean court. The Bet Din ha-Gadol, the Great Court, he says, was established during the administration of Simon the Hasmonean. Hoenig reads the passage: "Simon the Just, *the Hasmonean and his sons* and Mattathias the high priest." Simon organized the court, says Hoenig, but, occupied with political concerns, turned over the leadership of the court to Antigonus of Sokho and Jose ben Joezer.

4. Sotah 33a; Yerushalmi Sotah 9:24b; Songs Rabbah 8:9; Megillat

Ta'anit, chap. 11, end. One opinion in the Talmud says that the mysterious voice was that of the angel Gabriel. Jastrow, *A Dictionary of the Targumim, the Talmud Babli and Yerushalmi*, p. 1395, and Jacob Levy, *Wörterbuch über die Talmudim und Midraschim* (4 vols., Berlin and Vienna, 1924), identify Gaskalgas as the Emperor Caligula (37–41 C.E.). If they are correct, then the reading of the text must be wrong. Simon the Just, whether the first or the second, lived much earlier. Hoenig, *The Great Sanhedrin*, p. 33, points to the coupling of Simon the Just with Johanan the high priest in the talmudic passage immediately preceding, which tells how Johanan heard a mysterious voice from out of the Holy of Holies inform him that his sons had just won a battle against the Greeks (see also Josephus, *Antiquities* 13.10.3). Hoenig says that Simon the Just and Johanan the high priest are usually mentioned together in rabbinic sources. Johanan is John Hyrcanus (135–104 B.C.E.), the son of Simon the Hasmonean (142–135 B.C.E.), whom Hoenig seeks to identify as Simon the Just. See supra, n. 3. The two are coupled in other rabbinic passages: Yoma 9a, where it is said that Simon was high priest forty years and Johanan eighty years; Parah 3:5 relates that each of them prepared the ashes of two red heifers.

5. Parah 3:5; Ezra 8:4. Rabbi Meir counts not two each for Simon and Johanan, but one each, for in each case one became invalid. The sages say all were valid.

6. Nedarim 9b; Numbers Rabbah 10:7. The Bible sets forth the regulations concerning the nazirite in Num. 6:1–22. This story is reminiscent of the famous Narcissus anecdote of Ovid, but a comparison of the two will point up the superior moral quality of the Hebraic tale. The Talmud explains that Simon generally was opposed to eating of the sacrifice of a nazirite because usually the nazirite made his vow in a moment of temper or high emotion and later, when his passion would cool, he would regret his vow. Once a man regrets his vow, his sacrifices are profaned and, therefore, forbidden. This nazirite, however, made his vow after due deliberation, in sincerity, and for moral purposes.

7. Leviticus Rabbah 21:9.

8. Yoma 39a. The forty-year term of office mentioned here does not agree with the historical facts relating to either the first or second Simon the Just, 310–291 B.C.E. or 219–199 B.C.E., respectively. The various miracles here have as their purpose the description of Simon's holiness and God's favor toward him and the people on whose behalf he ministered. For the Yom Kippur ritual mentioned here, see Lev. 16:8; for the omer, Lev. 23:10–12; for the two loaves of bread, Lev. 23:17; for the bread of display, Exod. 25:30, 35:13, 39:36.

9. Yoma 39b; Menahot 109b; Leviticus Rabbah 21:12. The Tetragrammaton form of God's name consists of the four letters not pronounced by the observant Jew and for which a substitute form is used. Tosafot, Sotah 38a, says the Tetragrammaton was used no more because the Jews were no longer found worthy to have God reveal His presence to them.

10. Menahot 109b; Yerushalmi Yoma 6:3.

2. Antigonus of Sokho

11. Avot 1:3; Avot de-Rabbi Natan 5:1. Antigonus—note the

Greek name—was a scholar who lived during the first half of the third century B.C.E. Sokho is mentioned in Josh. 15:35, 48 and 1 Sam. 17:1 as a city in Judah. The point of the aphorism here is that one should serve God from pure motives. The law of God is to be kept for its own sake. The moral life is its own reward. On the verse, Ps. 112:1, *Happy is the man who fears the Lord, who is greatly devoted to His commandments,* the rabbis comment (Avodah Zarah 19a), "to His commandments, and not to the reward of the commandments." The fear of God means not dread but awe and reverence. Worship God, Antigonus says, both out of love, without the thought of reward, and out of awe. Do the words, "received the tradition from" mean actual transmission from teacher to disciple? Krochmal says they do; therefore, Simon the Just must have been the second Simon, son of Onias (219–199 B.C.E.). For otherwise how account for the Greek influence in the name of Antigonus and in the spirit of his sayings so soon after Alexander's conquest during whose time or shortly afterward the first Simon son of Onias lived? Z. Frankel, *Darkhei ha-Mishnah,* p. 31, says it was indeed the first Simon (about 300 B.C.E.), but "received the tradition" is not to be taken literally. There could have been a gap of many years between the two men.

12. Avot de-Rabbi Natan 5:2. The Sadducees denied belief in the world to come, for just as a laborer does receive his reward at the end of the working day, so too does a man receive his reward in this life. Besides, Scripture does not specifically mention a world to come or resurrection. On this passage see Finkelstein, *The Pharisees,* p. 80 and p. 633, n. 20; also idem, "Introductory Study to *Pirke Abot,*" *Journal of Biblical Literature* 57 (1938): 13–50, and esp. 35–37. Josephus, *Antiquities,* 18.1.3 says, "The Pharisees live simply and despise delicacies."

3. Jose ben Joezer and Jose ben Johanan

13. Avot 1:4; Avot de-Rabbi Natan, chap. 6. Jose is an abbreviation for Joseph. These two men lived during the first half of the second century B.C.E. Zeredah is mentioned in Josh. 15:35 among the cities of Judah and in 1 Kings 11:26 as the native town in Ephraim of Jeroboam ben Nebat. The Hebrew phrase is that these two "received the tradition from them," meaning either from the two mentioned before, i.e., Simon the Just and Antigonus, or from the unnamed teachers who lived during the period between them and Antigonus. (Another reading is "from him," meaning from Antigonus.) With these two Joses, Mishnah Avot begins a listing of five pairs of sages, called in Hebrew the *zugot* ("pairs"), ending with Hillel and Shammai, a period from approximately 170 B.C.E. to 10 C.E., the end of Hillel's term. The name *zugot* is found in the Mishnah, Pe'ah 2:6. The first named in each pair held the office of nasi, president of the court or Sanhedrin; the second, that of Av Bet Din, literally "Father of the Court," or vice-president or deputy. Some say the order of the third pair is reversed, that Simon ben Shetah was president and Judah ben Tabbai, deputy. (See Hagigah 2:2; and Tosefta Hagigah 2:8, pp. 234–35.) Jose ben Joezer is said to have been the uncle of Alcimus or Jakum (1 Macc. 7:5). I. Halevy, *Dorot ha-rishonim* 1:201 explains that the injunction to let scholars meet in homes was due to the forced closing of the schools by the

Hellenized Syrians at the time. Jose ben Joezer was himself a martyr (Genesis Rabbah 65). To sit in the dust at the feet of the wise may be better understood when it is remembered that it was usual for teachers to sit on benches while their disciples sat on the ground before them (see Bava Meẓia 84b). Louis Finkelstein, *Mavo le-masekhtot*, p. 8, believes that Jose ben Joezer and his deputy, Jose ben Johanan, were the founders of the pharisaic sect.

14. Ḥagigah 2:7; Isaac Weiss, *Dor dor ve-doreshav* (5 vols., New York, 1924), 1:106, thinks he was an Essene.

15. Shabbat 14b. The reason was that the exact location of graves and burial places was unknown in such lands. As for the glass vessels, Professor Louis Ginzberg explained in his class that this was in the nature of a protection for local industry. The pottery made in Israel was susceptible to ritual uncleanliness. The imported glass vessels to which the law of ritual impurity originally did not apply, since they were made of sand, were being purchased in quantity by the Jews and driving the locally made pottery from the market. Hence the application of the law of ritual impurity to glassware as well.

16. Ḥagigah 2:2. The controversy centered about the permissibility on a festival to lay the hands on an animal to be sacrificed since this is done with a man's whole weight, so that, in a legal sense, he is using the animal in making it carry his burden, thus profaning the Sabbath and festival law. The successors mentioned in this text are the following pairs: Joshua ben Peraḥyah and Nittai the Arbelite; Judah ben Tabbai and Simon ben Shetaḥ (some say the order is reversed); Shemaiah and Avtalyon; Hillel and Menaḥem (who did not differ), but Menaḥem left (the Gemara, Ḥagigah 16b, says he left either to enter the king's service or he became irreligious; a modern opinion says he left to join the Essenes), and Shammai took his place. The first person in each pair was president of the Sanhedrin, the second, the deputy.

17. Eduyyot 8:4. The Ayal locust got its name evidently because of its fancied similarity in appearance to a ram, in Hebrew *ayal*. The liquid on the slaughtering place floor would be a mixture of blood and water. Only he who definitely touches a corpse becomes ritually unclean, but if there be any doubt about it, he does not become unclean. Another explanation is that only he who actually touches the corpse becomes ritually unclean but not those whom he touches; it is not transferable.

18. Bava Batra 133b. A dinar was equal to one-half a shekel or one zuz or twelve pondions or six maahs or five aspers or two tropaics or one-fourth of a sela or one twenty-fifth of a golden denarius or zahub or one-hundredth of a mina. As to the purchasing power of these units of money in mishnaic times, see Ketubbot 5:8 for a woman's annual dressing allowance; Me'ilah 6:4 for the price of a mantle and shirt; Ma'aserot 2:5 for the price of fruit; Eruvin 8:2 for bread and flour; Bava Meẓia 5:1 for wheat; Menaḥot 13:8 for lambs, rams, and young bullocks; Bava Batra 5:1 for a yoke of oxen; Bava Kamma 10:4 for an ass; Bava Meẓia 5:2 for the rent of a courtyard. The Yannai cited here could not be Alexander Yannai who reigned 103–76 B.C.E. The name was used to denote any tyrannical ruler who hated the sages. See Wolf Jawitz, *Toldot Yisreal*, 4:108, n. 1; A. Hyman, *Toledot Tannaim va-Amoraim* (3 vols., London, 1910), 2:731, thinks the king was John Hyrcanus; see also Frankel, *Darkhei ha-Mishnah*, p. 34. Con-

cerning the counsel of the wife, words alone do not usually constitute legal transfer or acquisition of property. The only exception is consecration of property to the Temple.

19. Temurah 15b, 16a; Sotah 9:9. There is a play on words in the Hebrew text: *eshkolot* meaning originally "clusters," as of grapes, translated here as an integrated personality or as the text has it, *ish shehakol bo*, literally, "a man in whom there is everything."

20. Avot 1:5. Jose ben Johanan goes beyond Jose ben Joezer. One's home should be opened not only for the wise, but hospitality should be practiced toward guests and the poor. Excessive trivial and wasteful talk should be avoided and too much idle talk with women can also be the first step toward immoral acts. Rashi and Maimonides explain that poor men rather than slaves should be employed. During this period in Jewish history the Sadducees enjoyed the favor of the government but the masses supported the Pharisees. Hence an additional reason for this pharisaic teaching of kindness to the poor. For an expansion of these teachings of Jose ben Johanan, see Avot de-Rabbi Natan, chap. 7.

4. Joshua ben Peraḥyah and Nittai the Arbelite

21. Avot 1:6; Avot de-Rabbi Natan, chaps. 8–9. Joshua was president of the Sanhedrin; Nittai, his deputy, or vice-president (see Ḥagigah 2:2). Arbel was north of Tiberias (see Hos. 10:14; 1 Macc. 9:2). Nittai's teaching may be aimed at the Sadducees.

The Talmud warns that he who judges the righteous with mistrust and suspicion should be whipped (Shabbat 97a). But "he who judges another charitably will himself so be judged" (Shabbat 127b; see also Shevu'ot 30a). Keep your distance from the wicked for "woe to the wicked, woe to his neighbor" (Nega'im 12:6). Do not associate with the wicked even for the study of Torah (Avot de-Rabbi Natan 9:4).

Little is known of Joshua or Nittai. Travers Herford says that Joshua was involved in the persecution of the Pharisees by John Hyrcanus "and it is quite conceivable that his maxims originated in some phase of the controversy now no longer to be traced" (*Pirke Abot*, p. 27). Nittai is perhaps a shortened form of Natanyah. The name Mattai replaces Nittai in Yerushalmi Ḥagigah 2:76d.

Joshua ben Peraḥyah decreed that wheat coming from Alexandria is ritually impure because of the irrigation methods used (Tosefta Makhshirin, chap. 3). Hillel remembered that as a young lad he had seen Joshua authorize the high priest, wearing the garments of his office, to offer the sacrifice of the red heifer (Yalkut Shimoni, Ḥukkat 761).

22. Sotah 47a; Sanhedrin 107b; Yerushalmi Ḥagigah 2:77d; Berakhot 29a; where the king is not Yannai but John Hyrcanus. (See H. L. Strack, *Introduction to the Talmud and Midrash* [Philadelphia, 1931], p. 108.) The folk proverb quoted at the beginning stresses the importance of balancing discipline with love. Some would identify this Jeshu with Jesus although in fact Rabbi Joshua ben Peraḥyah lived a full century earlier. Joshua fled to Alexandria because of Sadducean hostility. However, Yerushalmi Ḥagigah 2:2:77d says it was not Joshua but Judah ben Tabbai; Frankel, *Darkhei ha-Mishnah*, pp. 35–36, supports

that version; Weiss, *Dor* 1:135, supports the version of the Babylonian Talmud; Halevy, *Dorot* 1:465, says the two versions refer to two different events.

23. Menaḥot 109b. Joshua became president of the Sanhedrin. In the Jerusalem Talmud, Pesaḥim, 6:1, this story is told about Rabbi Joshua ben Korḥa.

5. Judah ben Tabbai and Simon ben Shetaḥ

24. Avot 1:8; Avot de-Rabbi Natan 10:1. The tradition is not clear as to which of the two was the head of the Sanhedrin and which the deputy. The order of the two names in Mishnah Avot here indicates that Judah was head and Simon deputy. But Yerushalmi Ḥagigah 2:2:77d says that in later times there was a difference of opinion about this fact. See also Tosefta Ḥagigah 2:8, pp. 234–35. A baraita, Ḥagigah 16b, gives an example where Judah decided a case to show his opposition to the Sadducees. Simon felt the decision was incorrect because it was not in accordance with the tradition. Judah at once agreed that he would, in the future, decide cases only in the presence of Simon. Frankel, *Darkhei ha-Mishnah*, p. 37, states that in the beginning Judah was nasi but after he rendered an improper decision in the case of a false witness (see Makkot 5b), he resigned in favor of his deputy, Simon. See Yerushalmi Ḥagigah 2:2:77d and Yerushalmi Sanhedrin 6:9:23c, which say: he who says Judah was nasi has as support the tale that the people of Jerusalem wished to appoint Judah ben Tabbai nasi but he had fled to Alexandria, and the people then wrote him requesting his return. He who says Simon was nasi has the incident of his ordering the execution of eighty women at Ashkelon as a proof. See Mantel, *Studies*, pp. 8–9, and p. 9, n. 51. These two sages lived during the reigns of John Hyrcanus, Aristobulus, Alexander Yannai, and Salome Alexandra. When Alexander Yannai (103–76 B.C.E.) persecuted the Pharisees, Judah ben Tabbai fled to Alexandria (see Yerushalmi Sanhedrin 6:9, 23c), evidently the same occasion as that told in Sanhedrin 107b where the tale concerns Joshua ben Peraḥyah (see also Sotah 47a; Yerushalmi Sanhedrin 6:9, 23c; and Ḥagigah 2:41d). The party of the Sadducees represented the wealthier, aristocratic, and priestly classes during the two centuries before the Temple's destruction. They denied resurrection and the immortality of the soul and adhered to the literal understanding of the biblical text. The Pharisees were essentially a democratic party representing the broad masses of the people who favored the interpretation of the Scriptures and the consequent development of the Oral Law. (See Louis Finkelstein, *The Pharisees*, and R. Travers Herford, *Pharisaism: Its Aims and Its Method* [London, 1912].) After the death of Alexander Yannai, who favored the Sadducees, and the accession of Queen Salome Alexandra (76–67 B.C.E.), presumably the sister of Simon ben Shetaḥ (see Berakhot 48a), the Sanhedrin was reorganized so as to include a large number of Pharisees (Kiddushin 66a), and Judah ben Tabbai returned from exile in Egypt. Evidently his teaching and that of Simon were especially applicable as guiding principles for the reorganized judicial system to ensure the impartiality of the judges and the attainment of justice. Mantel, *Studies*, p. 18, says that Judah resisted expulsion from office (which office is

unknown, perhaps as head of the Sanhedrin), and he refers to Avot de-Rabbi Natan, version 1, 10:43, and version 2, 10:43.

25. Hagigah 16b; Makkot 5b.

26. Avot 1:9, Avot de-Rabbi Natan 10:4. See n. 24 above. Tales concerning Simon ben Shetaḥ and the Hasmonean king, Alexander Yannai may be found in part 3, section 2, "The Hasmonean Rulers." Simon ben Shetaḥ was, it is said (Berakhot 48a), the brother of Queen Salome Alexandra (76–67 B.C.E.) and enjoyed great influence during her reign. He led in the restoration of pharisaic influence in the royal court and Sanhedrin, after the Sadducean dominance during the reign of the previous ruler, Alexander Yannai (Kiddushin 66a and Megillat Ta'anit 10). He was concerned here about miscarriages of justice either through insufficient examination of the witnesses by the judges or through injudicious words by the judges that might suggest to witnesses methods of distorting testimony. It has been suggested that a personal tragedy motivated this utterance of Simon's. His own son was executed upon the basis of false testimony, uncovered too late (Yerushalmi Sanhedrin 4:23b, 6:9, 23c). He was responsible for the creation of a system of elementary education among Jews in cities.

27. Kiddushin 66a. See part 3, section 2, "The Hasmonean Rulers." Yannai came under the influence of the Sadducees and did violence to many Pharisee sages; others fled. Upon Yannai's death and the accession to the throne by his widow, Queen Salome Alexandra, reputedly Simon's sister, the pharisaic influence was restored and the exiled sages called back. Hoenig, *The Great Sanhedrin*, p. 58, denies the story that all the Sadducees were expelled from the Sanhedrin, whereas Finkelstein accepts it. Hoenig argues that the only evidence for it is the story recorded in the scholion on Megillat Ta'anit 10, but the scholion is posttalmudic, and the Talmud does not mention it. On the contrary, Sanhedrin 52b quotes Rabbi Joseph as saying, "It was a court of Sadducees." Simon only acted to obtain a majority of Pharisees. Therefore, Josephus, *Antiquities* 18.1.4, states that the courts in the first century B.C.E., were generally pharisaic (see also Tosefta Middot 5:3 [648]; Niddah 33a; Yoma 19b).

28. Leviticus Rabbah 35:10, Ta'anit 23a. The tale is linked to Lev. 26:4. A gold denarius was worth twenty-four silver dinars.

29. Sanhedrin 37b. Rabbi Simon was only one witness, not two, as the Torah requires. Moreover, he did not see the act of killing. There was only circumstantial evidence here that led him to conjecture what must have happened. See the mishnah and baraita on the subject of *me'umad*, preceding this story in Sanhedrin.

30. Yerushalmi Sanhedrin 6:23b; Sanhedrin 6:4 and Rashi ad locum; Rashi, Sanhedrin 44b; Sifrei on Deuteronomy 221, p. 114b (ed. Finkelstein, p. 253). Further, for refuted witnesses, see Makkot 5b and 1:6 as to the controversy on the subject between the Pharisees and Sadducees. See supra, n. 24, for the differences of opinion as to whether Judah ben Tabbai or Simon ben Shetaḥ was nasi, head of the Sanhedrin. This story supports those who say it was Simon. One opinion holds that they exchanged positions, Judah yielding to Simon who had been his deputy and he becoming Simon's deputy. H. L. Strack, *Introduction to the Talmud and Mishnah*, p. 8, says, "The statement . . . that the latter [Simon] caused eighty women to be hanged in Ashkelon is erroneous, since the city had been an independent municipality from

104 B.C.E. on." E. Schürer, *Geschichte des judischen Volkes in Zeitalter Jesu Christi*, 1:285, n. 17; 2:121, doubting the traditions about Simon, similarly points out that Simon could not have condemned anyone outside of Judea and in his day Ashkelon was not under Jewish rule. But, Hoenig, *Great Sanhedrin*, pp. 86–87, states that other authorities say that Ashkelon did belong to the Jews and evidence for this can be found in 1. Macc. 10:86, 11:60, 12:33; Josephus, *Antiquities*, 13.5.5; and Tosefta Shevi'it 4:11 (66). So Z. Taubes in *Ha-nasi be-Sanhedrin ha-Gedolah* (Vienna, 1925), p. 37, disagrees with Schürer, saying there were times when Ashkelon did belong to the Jews. Hoenig suggests that even though Ashkelon was not under Jewish civil administration but a Hellenistic city under Roman jurisdiction, nevertheless the Sanhedrin had religious authority over its Jewish residents. Therefore, the decision of its local Jewish court had to be approved by Simon as head of the Sanhedrin in Judea. The execution of Simon's son was probably the reason for Simon's statement in Avot 1:9, quoted earlier, concerning the careful cross-examination of witnesses.

31. Berakhot 19a.

32. Deuteronomy Rabbah 3:3.

33. Yerushalmi Ketubbot 8:32c. Thus Simon may be said to be the founder of the elementary school system. Before his time the instruction of children was the obligation of their fathers.

6. Shemaiah and Avtalyon

34. Mishnah Avot 1:11; Avot de-Rabbi Natan 11:1–5. Shemaiah and Avtalyon were leaders of the Pharisees during the middle of the first century B.C.E., the former, president of the Sanhedrin before and during the reign of Herod, the latter, its vice-president. Both were pupils of Judah ben Tabbai; Avtalyon studied also with Simon ben Shetah. They probably lived in exile in Egypt for a while with their teacher, Judah ben Tabbai, when Alexander Yannai persecuted the Pharisees. This experience as well as Herod's harshness probably motivated their advice to their followers to shun politics and to seek anonymity as far as the ruling powers were concerned. Their advice may have been even more pointed. After the death of Salome Alexandra, during whose reign the Pharisees were influential, her sons Hyrcanus II and Aristobulus fought for the throne and the warning here is that scholars, Pharisees, should stay clear from taking sides. Alexandria was a place where many Greek heretical doctrines circulated and, therefore, its evil waters of heresy could pollute young disciples and cause them to forsake God. Maimonides indicates that Shemaiah warns against three dangers to a man's faith: the disdain of work leading to dishonesty, the lust for mastery leading to all the evils of power, and closeness with the ruling power leading to the enlargement of ambition. The names of Shemaiah and Avtalyon are always linked together as president and vice-president of the Sanhedrin respectively (see Eduyyot 1:3, 5:6; Berakhot 19a; Beizah 23b, 25a; Pesahim 66a, 70b; Yoma 35b, 71b; Yevamot 67a; and here, Mishnah Avot 1:10. Also Tosefta Hagigah 2:8 where Shemaiah supported the theory of *semikhah* and reliance upon contemporary authorities to introduce innovations in the law, as did Hillel after him).

35. Gittin 57b; Sanhedrin 96b; Yoma 71b; Numbers Rabbah 9:28; Yerushalmi Mo'ed Katan 3:81b. See Weiss, *Dor* 1:1. However, H. Graetz, *History of the Jews*, 2:72, rejects this statement and maintains that Shemaiah and Avtalyon were Alexandrian Jews. Akavyah ben Mahalalel spoke slightingly of their origins and was placed under the ban. When he died while in that status, the court stoned his coffin by symbolically placing a stone on it (see Numbers Rabbah 9:28; Eduyyot 5:6; Yerushalmi Mo'ed Katan 3:1).

36. Pesaḥim 66a, 70b. Evidently they were either the originators of the method of *derush*, biblical interpretation according to certain hermeneutical rules, or else they developed the technique more fully than their predecessors. Hence their title here, *darshanim*. It is significant that their pupil Hillel was the first to set forth hermeneutical rules for the interpretation and development of the law. Their method seems to have stirred opposition among the Pharisees (Pesaḥim 70b).

37. Yoma 71b. This high priest was also the king—Antigonus, last of the Hasmonean kings.

38. Josephus, *Antiquities*, 14.9.4. A similar story is found in Sanhedrin 19a, but the names are changed to Simon ben Shetaḥ and King Alexander Yannai, and the dramatic ending comes about through supernatural means as the angel Gabriel appears to smite the cowardly judges. Josephus calls Shemaiah by the name Sameas, and describes him as a regular member of the court instead of its president. Hoenig, *Great Sanhedrin*, p. 41, explains that the trial took place in 47 B.C.E. and only later was Shemaiah appointed head of the court. After Caesar's victory over Ptolemy XIV he showed his gratitude for Hyrcanus's support by naming him hereditary head of the Jewish state. But real power lay in the hands of his astute minister, Antipater, who appointed his sons as prefects. Herod in Galilee and Phasael in Jerusalem. In Galilee a patriotic movement agitated for complete Jewish independence of Rome. Herod, then but twenty-five, seized its leader Hezekiah and a number of his followers and had them executed, contrary to the procedures of Jewish law and its safeguards against capital punishment. After Herod had been summoned before the Sanhedrin with Hyrcanus's consent, the latter received an order from Sextus Caesar, the governor of Syria, to have Herod set free. Hyrcanus then adjourned the session of the court.

39. Josephus, *Antiquities*, 15.1.1. Avtalyon's purpose was perhaps to avoid the slaughter of the population for he saw the futility of challenging Herod's power. Herod had by then been named by the Roman governor of Syria prefect of all of southern Syria, which included Judea, and he returned to Jerusalem with an army to take revenge for the indignity he had been subjected to earlier in the trial before the Sanhedrin, but he was dissuaded from this act by his father, Antipater. But Herod did kill many of the Sanhedrin (see Bava Batra 3b). Louis Ginzberg puts the siege of Jerusalem by Herod referred to by Josephus in the year 37 B.C.E. (*Jewish Encyclopedia*, 1:136). The siege lasted five months. The pharisaic leaders who opposed Antigonus, the last of the Hasmonean rulers, for combining in himself both the high priesthood and the throne, counseled surrender to Herod. Josephus's name for Avtalyon is Pollion. Ginzberg says the name presumably was Ptollion, thus explaining the prefixed *a* in the Hebrew form and omission of the *t* in Josephus. The name recurs in Josephus, *Antiquities*,

15.10.4, but there Ginzberg says Josephus confused Shammai with Shemaiah and, therefore, linked the name of Pollion with it instead of Hillel, since the event referred to in that passage took place in 20 or 19 B.C.E., some time after Avtalyon's death. See also *Pirke Abot*, p. 31.

40. Yoma 35b. The reason, says Ginzberg (*Jewish Encyclopedia*, 1:136), was to prevent overcrowding. Weiss, *Dor* 1:149, says the reason was to limit the number of students of the pharisaic masters so as not to arouse the antagonism of the government. A tropaika was equal to half a dinar.

41. Mekhilta Beshallaḥ, chap. 3; see Gen. 15:6 and Exod. 4:31.

7. Ḥoni the Circle Drawer

42. Ta'anit 23a; Mishnah Ta'anit 3:8 has a slightly different version. Ḥoni Ha-me'aggel ("the circle drawer") lived in the first century B.C.E. Tradition considers him to be a descendant of Moses (Midrash Tanḥuma, Va-eira; see article "Onias," by J. Z. Lauterbach, *Jewish Encyclopedia*, 9:404). He was a scholar of high repute with many disciples, renowned also for his piety. His teaching was marked by clarity and he was readily able to answer all questions and objections put to him (Ta'anit 23a). The mention of Habakkuk in the story is a reference to Hab. 2:1. A lug equals 506 cubic centimeters.

43. Ta'anit 23a; Mishnah Ta'anit 3:8; Berakhot 19a. Simon acted for the Sanhedrin as can be seen from the next tale in the text, Ta'anit 23a. Similar examples of excommunication are to be seen in connection with Akavyah ben Mehalalel, who refused to retract his personal views (Eduyyot 5:5), and with Eleazar ben Enoch (Berakhot 19a).

44. Ta'anit 23a.

45. Yerushalmi Ta'anit, loc. cit.

46. Ta'anit 23a. Rava or Raba (Rabbi Abba) was a renowned scholar, a Babylonian amora of the fourth generation, born about 280 C.E. at Maḥoza, and died there in 352. In addition to the halakhic lectures to his disciples he would give public lectures, usually aggadic in character. These frequently would include popular proverbs and maxims, such as the one cited by him here. This tale might be called the Jewish Rip Van Winkle story. Near Rosh Pinah in present-day Israel there is a village called Kefar Farram. Close to it is a spot reputed to be the tomb of Ḥoni the Circle Drawer. In times of drought some Jews go there to pray for rain (see Zev Vilnay, *Legends of Palestine* [Philadelphia, 1932], p. 410).

47. Yerushalmi Ta'anit 9:1c. Jacob Z. Lauterbach, *Jewish Encyclopedia*, 9:404–5, says that this tradition in the Jerusalem Talmud may refer to Ḥoni's grandfather who was also named Ḥoni, and he cites J. Brüll, *Einleitung in die Mischna* (Frankfurt, 1876), 1:24–25.

48. Josephus, *Antiquities*, 14.2.1. The story is not mentioned in the Talmud. Salome Alexandra reigned from 76 B.C.E., when her husband Alexander Yannai died, to 67 B.C.E. The civil war followed.

8. Abba Ḥilkiah

49. Ta'anit 23a–b. Abba Ḥilkiah was the son of Ḥoni's son. The

reaction of Abba Ḥilkiah and his wife to the bandits may be compared to that of Meir and his wife to the wicked men of their time. See Berakhot 10a.

9. Ḥanin the Hidden

50. Ta'anit 23b. Ḥanin was the son of Ḥoni's daughter.

10. Hillel and Shammai

51. Yoma 35b; see also Pesaḥim 70b. The work Hillel did was manual labor, some say woodcutting. The tarpeik was a coin equal to 4 dinars or 768 prutot or 4 zuzim or 1 sela or 2 rabbinical shekels. A cubit in rabbinical times was 22.1 inches or 56.1 cm. Hillel and Shammai, who lived during King Herod's time, constitute the fifth and last pair of the *zugot*. Each founded a school whose legal opinions figure prominently in the Talmud. According to Sifrei on Deuteronomy 357, Hillel is called "The Elder" to distinguish him from a descendant of the same name, Hillel II, 320–365 C.E. (Others say the title was honorific to indicate his leading position among his contemporaries and in the Sanhedrin.) Hillel was forty at the time he came to Palestine from Babylonia, the land of his origin. The year was probably about 40 B.C.E. He was the leading scholar of the Jewish people from ca. 30 B.C.E. to 10 C.E. The controversies between the schools of Hillel and Shammai concern all areas of Jewish learning: Halakhah, Aggadah, and Midrash. In the memory of posterity Hillel was seen as the gentle, modest, humanitarian sage who made the contents of all Jewish learning his own (see Soferim 16:9). His authority was sufficient to establish as accepted law the decrees handed down in his name. The best known of these was the *prozbul*, which ensured the repayment of loans (Shevu'ot 10:3) despite the law concerning the sabbatical year (Deut. 15:1 ff.; see Gittin 4:3). The purpose was to protect the creditor against loss and to make certain that those requiring loans would find them available. Economic conditions had changed from earlier agricultural times and Hillel's period was one of petty capitalism. A similar legal tendency is found in Hillel's enactment concerning the sale of houses (Lev. 25:30; see Arakhin 9:4).

52. Sotah 21a. "Love" (Songs 8:7) is here understood to mean the love of Torah and its study, which cannot be purchased, no matter how great the sum. It must be acquired only through personal effort.

53. Pesaḥim 66a; see also Yerushalmi Pesaḥim 6:1, 33a; Tosefta Pesaḥim 4:1–2. Hillel's reference to the more than two hundred sacrifices that supersede the Sabbath is to the daily morning and evening sacrifices that are offered also on all the Sabbaths and holy days. The word *karet* means punishment not at the hands of man but divine punishment through premature death (see Num. 9:13). Hillel was responsible for the "seven rules" of hermeneutics for the oral interpretation of the Written Law. Here he uses two: *gezerah shavah* and *kal ve-ḥomer*. On these seven rest the thirteen of Rabbi Ishmael (see Sifra, beginning). They were of the greatest importance for the systematic development of the exposition of the Scriptures (see also Tosefta

Sanhedrin 7, near the end; Sifra, introduction, end; Avot de-Rabbi Natan 37). Hoenig, *Great Sanhedrin*, p. 38, points out that, contrary to Schürer who says that Rabbi Judah ha-Nasi was the first to have that title, this text says that Hillel was the first (cf. Tosefta Pesaḥim 4 (162); Bava Meẓia 85a; Yerushalmi Pesaḥim 6:1, 33a). His descendants after him, among whom was Rabbi Judah ha-Nasi, were called by that title. Hillel is called "Nasi in Israel" in the story told about his humility (Shabbat 31a). His descendants who lived before the destruction of the Temple were each also nasi. This is seen in the passage, "Hillel and Simon (I), Gamaliel (I) and Simon (II) led as nasi before the destruction of The (Second) Temple" (Shabbat 14b, 15a). The title "nasi" meant the permanent president of the High Court or Sanhedrin. During the period of Rabbi Judah ha-Nasi about the beginning of the third century, it was a state title with political significance (see also Hoenig, op. cit., p. 59.

Graetz lists the nesi'im as follows: Hillel, 30 B.C.E.–10 C.E.; Simon I, 10–30 C.E.; Gamaliel I, the Elder, 30–50 C.E.; Simon II, 50–70 C.E.; Gamaliel II of Jabneh, 80–117 C.E., continuing to Rabbi Judah ha-Nasi, editor of the Mishnah, about 200 C.E.

However, some scholars deny that our story in the text means that the position of Hillel was that understood by the later tradition as nasi. For examples of this point of view, see Louis Ginzberg's letter, cited in Mantel, *Studies in the History of the Sanhedrin*, p. 46, n. 266; also C. Albeck, *Ha-Sanhedrin u-nesi'ah* (Tel Aviv, 1942–43), p. 167; J. Klausner, *Historiyah Yisra'elit* (4 vols., Odessa and Tel Aviv, 1909–25), 4:126–27; A. Kaminka, *Kitvei bikoret historit* (New York, 1944), p. 33. Büchler, *Synhedrion*, pp. 145–47, defends the historical accuracy of the story. Louis Finkelstein, *Ha-Perushim*, p. 9, suggests a compromise: that Hillel was appointed nasi over the Benei Batyra, who were a committee in charge of the proper observance of the Sabbath in the Temple and Jerusalem as a whole. So too Solomon Zeitlin, "Historical Books on Judea," *Jewish Quarterly Review*, n.s. 29 (1938-39):287–300; idem., "The Crucifixion of Jesus Re-examined," *Jewish Quarterly Review*, n.s. 31 (1940–41):327–69; 32 (1941–42):175–89, 279–301; and Moses L. Lilienblum, *Kol kitvei* (4 vols., Crakow, 1910), 1:215; Mantel, op. cit., pp. 18–21, accepts the accuracy of the story as referring to Hillel as nasi, president of the Sanhedrin, but not in the sense the title meant in later centuries, political head of the nation. He believes that the Benei Batyra were probably a hereditary committee in the Temple that now submitted to the authority of the Sanhedrin, headed by Hillel (cf. Finkelstein, *The Pharisees*, 2:643). However, some scholars hold that the Benei Batyra collectively held the office of nasi (see G. Alon, *Meḥkarim be-toldot Yisrael* [2 vols., Tel Aviv, 1957–58], 1:219–52; C. Tchernowitz, *Toldot ha-halakhah* [4 vols., New York, 1934–50], 4:213). Others reject this theory (Frankel, *Darkhei ha-Mishnah*, p. 43; see also Ben-Zion Katz, *Perushim, Ẓedukim* [Tel Aviv, 1947], pp. 224–28).

54. Avot de-Rabbi Natan 37:10, 32 a–b; Tosefta Sanhedrin, near end, Sifrei, introduction, near end.

55. Genesis Rabbah 33:3.

56. Sukkah 20b; Soferim 16:9. Hillel is here pictured as the scholar who mastered all the content of Jewish learning. Ezra the Scribe, at the beginning of the Second Commonwealth, and Hillel, four centuries

later, began their activity after periods of Jewish decline. Nahum Glatzer, *Hillel the Elder* (New York, 1956), pp. 29–33, suggests that Hillel, after leaving the academy of Shemaiah and Avtalyon, withdrew to the wilderness, as did many others at the time, to dedicate himself to a life of Torah study and the hasidic way. There he went through a period of contact with groups of men or sects, perhaps the Essenes and the Covenant communities, who lived this kind of Judaism outside the official centers. However, Glatzer adds that he ventures this suggestion "with all the reservation necessary as long as there is no factual evidence to support it." He points, in passing, to the obvious parallel between Hillel's forty years of preparation for his leadership and the forty years that Moses spent in the wilderness before he was ready to lead his people (see Sifrei on Deut. 34:7). For Hillel's description as disciple of Ezra, see Sanhedrin 11a; Songs Rabbah 8:9. For the groupings, see Leviticus Rabbah 2:11.

57. Sifrei on Deut. 34:7. See the previous note for Glatzer's suggestion. Hillel's activity for forty years may be historical and since, according to a reliable tradition, Shabbat 15a, it began one hundred years before the destruction of the Temple, it must have extended from 30 B.C.E. to 10 C.E.

58. Midrash Tannaim on Deut. 2:26.

59. Genesis Rabbah 98:8; Yerushalmi Ta'anit 68a; Kilayim, chap. 9. See Israel Lévi, "L'Origine Davidique de Hillel," *Revue des Études Juives* 31 (1895):202–11; 33 (1896):143–44.

60. Avot 1:12–14; Avot de-Rabbi Natan 12:1–2. Hillel and Shammai were the fifth and last couple of the *zugot*, the "pairs." The first named of each pair was nasi, president, the second, head of the court or deputy (Ḥagigah 2:2). It would seem that at first Hillel's mate in the pair was Menaḥem, but because of a lack of difference between them, Menaḥem was replaced by Shammai (Ḥagigah 2:2). One tradition has Menaḥem becoming an Essene and, therefore, he had to be replaced; another, that he entered the service of King Herod. Hoenig, *Great Sanhedrin*, p. 246, understands the passage in Ḥagigah 2:2 to refer to the abolition of the office of "head of the court" or deputy because there was no difference of opinion between Hillel, the nasi or president, and Menaḥem, his deputy. The two posts had been traditionally filled by two representatives of differing positions of interpretation of the tradition. But Shammai insisted on "the two-party system" and so the office was reinstalled with Shammai as its occupant. It was finally abolished in the next generation when Hillel's son, Simon I, became nasi. Glatzer, *Hillel the Elder*, p. 28, believes that Menaḥem had been influenced by the Essenes even before he joined them and that he was the same Menaḥem the Essene mentioned by Josephus in the story of Herod (see Yerushalmi Ḥagigah 77d, and Louis Ginzberg, *On Jewish Law and Lore* [Philadelphia, 1955], p. 101). Shammai represented the conservative tendency; Hillel the progressive.

In rabbinic legend (Avot de-Rabbi Natan 12:3), Aaron was the great peacemaker. When two men had quarreled, Aaron would seek each one out to convince him that the other regretted his harsh words; thus the erstwhile enemies became reconciled. His kindness to men would cause a man about to do wrong to ask himself, "How shall I be able to face Aaron?" and in this way he restrained men from committing sin (see Mal. 2:6). The middle statement of Hillel (Avot 1:13), is in Aramaic, as is his later utterance in Avot 2:7. It was the language of Babylonia, his native land, and he used it too in the land of Israel. The reference to a name made great is to overreaching ambition. An alternate interpretation points to the danger from the Romans to the Jew who becomes prominent. He who does not study commits spiritual self-destruction for "it is your life and the length of your days." Another rendition is "he who (possessing knowledge) refuses to teach deserves death," for such an action was considered unpardonable. The text then speaks of "the crown," which we have interpreted, following most commentators, as the crown of learning. Another interpretation of the "crown" derives the Aramaic word for crown, *taga*, from the Latin, *toga*, and the meaning would then be that one who takes to the toga—the Roman way of life—passes from his people and its way. Still another interpretation explains the "crown" as the Tetragrammaton, the use of the divine ineffable name, resulting in divine punishment (see Avot de-Rabbi Natan 12:13, 23b). The virtues of peace, study, humility, and self-reliance blended with altruism, as stressed in these utterances, describe Hillel himself.

61. Sukkah 53a; Yerushalmi Sukkah 5:4; Avot de-Rabbi Natan 12:9–10, 23a–b. The last two teachings are quoted in Avot 5:25–26 in the names of Ben Bag Bag and Ben He He respectively, who were reputed to have been Hillel's disciples. The second night of the festival of Sukkot used to be celebrated on the Temple Mount by a unique service associated with the libation of water and marked by great exuberance and enthusiasm. Men danced with burning torches in their hands singing songs and praises of God (see Sukkah 5:4, 53a; Yerushalmi Sukkah 55b; Avot de-Rabbi Natan 2:27). "Coming to my house" is interpreted in Avot de-Rabbi Natan 23a as God being the speaker and the reference is to the house of prayer and study, coming to which will result in God's blessing. "Where my heart desires to go" refers to the Temple. "If I am here . . ." is to be understood as the words of God. Otherwise it would be difficult to understand them. Their seeming conceit conflicts with what we know of Hillel's humility. Therefore, it is suggested that the "I" refers not to Hillel but to God, the divine "I." If that "I" be present at such great festivities as the Ceremony of Water-Drawing and at other times, then all are present. If He is absent, who is present? Another interpretation would have the people of Israel as the speaker. If it be present, all are. "Turn it . . ." refers to the Torah; it is a complete guide to life. "According to the labor, so is the reward" seems to have been a popular proverb, applied here to the study of Torah.

62. Avot de-Rabbi Natan 12:11, 23b. A seah equals 12.148 liters. A silver dinar is worth 6 maot or 192 prutot.

63. Avot de-Rabbi Natan 2:4. The first teaching may be a plea against excessive individualism and for greater identification with the community or it may be a criticism of the sectarians. Hillel's own colleague, Menaḥem, may have withdrawn from leadership to become an Essene. Especially in times of crisis and travail it is reprehensible for a man to forsake his group (see Ta'anit 11a). Also praying with a congregation is more praiseworthy than praying alone (see commentary ad locum of Simon ben Ẓemaḥ Duran [1361–1444]). Not to trust oneself until the day of one's death may be a warning against excessive self-confidence. Even the most pious can relapse into sin or heresy

(i.e., forsaking the majority community for a sect). John Hyrcanus served as high priest for eighty years and then became a Sadducee, says the Talmud (Berakhot 29a). Moreover, a man should be empathetic in judging another, to imagine himself in the position and circumstances of the other before passing judgment. Face the same temptation and overcome it before condemning one who did not (cf. Matt. 7:1). Nor should a teacher teach that which is not clear in the conviction that eventually it will be understood. Teaching should be intelligible and lucid. Or else, do not teach that which should remain secret or esoteric doctrine with the excuse that ultimately it will be known anyhow. The time to study is always the present; as Hillel says elsewhere (Avot 1:14), "If not now, when?"

64. Avot 2:5. A series of teachings that indicate that the presence of certain defects will militate against the attainment of certain qualities. The uncultured person, lacking both knowledge of Torah and character, cannot, normally, be sin-fearing. Since knowledge of the Torah is essential for piety, the ignorant man must fail to achieve that goal. The shy person will not ask the questions essential to the learning process, while the impatient teacher will lose his temper when his students ask questions for clarification of the subject matter. Hillel himself worked for a living (Yoma 35b), so neither he nor the rabbis deprecate labor. They praise it, but excessive pursuit of wealth through business will interfere with learning. The last dictum stands on its own. Where a responsibility demands one to carry it out and no one else steps forward, you do so. Midrash Shemuel ad locum explains, "In a place where no man sees or knows you, do not say I will sin because no one sees or knows me. Even when alone, strive to be a man, true and God-fearing." This last teaching is found in the Aramaic version in Berakhot 63a.

65. Avot 2:6; Avot de-Rabbi Natan 12:12, 23b; Sukkot 53a. The idea here is that of divine retribution working measure for measure (cf. Ps. 7:16–17; Job 34:11, Isa. 3:11; Sanhedrin 100a). He who lives by violence will perish through violence. During Herod's reign violence grew apace.

66. Avot 2:7; see also Avot de-Rabbi Natan 28:9, 28a–b. Hillel condemns all excess—gluttony, greater wealth than one needs, polygamy (in order to win the husband's affection his wives will engage in witchcraft), numerous maidservants and manservants (who steal from their master and from others, and since they are his property, he is legally responsible). On the other hand he praises Torah as leading to more meaningful life on this earth and to life in the world to come (see Prov. 3:1–2, 8:35, 9:11; Deut. 30:20). He commends learning in general, counsel (see Prov. 12:15), charity or, more literally, righteousness (see Isa. 32:17). One can neither inherit a good reputation, transfer it to another, or be deprived of it (see Prov. 22:1, Eccles. 7:1). In summary, Hillel contrasts the life of the man of affairs with the life of the lover of learning.

67. Berakhot 63a; Yerushalmi Berakhot 143a; Tosefta Berakhot 7. This cryptic utterance seems to counsel the scholar as to when he must make the effort to teach many and spread learning and when he must withdraw and devote himself to the gathering in and compiling of learning. Glatzer, in *Hillel the Elder,* p. 30, explains it, "If you see a generation to which the Torah is dear, you spread (its knowledge);

but if you see a generation to which the Torah is not dear, you gather it and keep it to yourself." Another interpretation is, "Learn, where there are teachers; teach, where there are learners." Glatzer conjectures that Hillel is referring to his own withdrawal to live with the sectarians after he had left the academy of Shemaiah and Avtalyon and before his return to Jerusalem.

68. Avot de-Rabbi Natan 26:3, 27b.

69. Ibid., chap. 26.

70. Ḥagigah 9b.

71. Leviticus Rabbah 1:5. Cf. Matt. 23:12 for an almost identical restatement; see also Shabbat 88b, Midrash Tehillim on 86:1. The sense here is that he who humbles himself will be exalted, while he who exalts himself will be humbled.

72. Ketubbot 67b. This tale is referred to in Sifrei on Deut. 15:9. The sages felt that charity should be extended to a person in accordance with his former standard of living. Hillel's readiness to humble himself is also illustrated.

73. Derekh Erez Rabbah 6:2; Kallah Rabbati 9:1. See the earlier story about the wife of Abba Ḥilkiah (Ta'anit 23b).

74. Shabbat 30b–31a. For a variant version see Avot de-Rabbi Natan 15:1, where the order of the questions is different and the answers are given more fully: the Africans have broad feet "because they live in marshy places and constantly walk in the water"; i.e., they walk barefoot, and since their feet are not confined by shoe or sandal they become broader. The reference to the heads of the Babylonians may also have been calculated to irritate Hillel who was a native Babylonian. In the version of the story in Shabbat the man asks, "Are you Hillel who is called Nasi of Israel?" In the version in Avot de-Rabbi Natan the question is, "Is this the manner in which Nesi'im (plural) reply?" The difference is of importance in dating the first nasi (see Mantel, *Studies*, p. 2, and Schechter's edition of Avot de-Rabbi Natan, p. 61, n. 7). A baraita in Shabbat 15a states that Hillel, Simon, Gamaliel, and Simon II held the office of nasi during the last hundred years of the Temple.

Palmyra (Hebrew, Tadmor) was an ancient oasis city in the Syrian desert on the road from Phoenicia to the Euphrates and a large commercial center. The Greeks called it Thedmor, the Romans, Palmyra. It was said to have been founded by Solomon but Cecil Roth (*Standard Jewish Encyclopedia* [Garden City, N.Y., 1959]), p. 1782, says that this rests on a misreading of 2 Chron. 8:4. Palmyrans served in the Roman armies against the Jews, 66–70 C.E., and expressions of hostility to that city are found in the Talmud: Yevamot 16a–b, 17a and Rashi ad locum; Yerushalmi Ta'anit 4:8, 8:46b. Yet, converts from Palmyra were received (Yerushalmi Kiddushin 4:65c). Benjamin of Tudela found two thousand Jews there in the twelfth century. Jews from Palmyra are buried in the necropolis of Bet Shearim, Israel.

75. Shabbat 31a; Avot de-Rabbi Natan 15:3, 24a–b. The latter version differs somewhat from the former in that it would make the questioner not a pagan but a Jew who denies the authenticity of the oral tradition. Hillel makes him understand that oral communication is a part of the learning process and learning ultimately is based on premises resting on faith (see Glatzer, *Hillel the Elder*, p. 75). For a somewhat similar story concerning a proselyte and the letters of the

alphabet but involving the later talmudic masters, Rav and Samuel, see Ecclesiastes Rabbah 7:8.

The Written Law is the Scriptures. The Oral Law is the interpretation of the Scriptures and the evolving legal and nonlegal mass of tradition based upon it, taught by master to disciple from one generation to the next. Eventually the Oral Law was also written down, edited, and codified into the Mishnah about 200 C.E. The process continued, however, with the Mishnah as the base. The developing post-mishnaic Oral Law was edited into the Gemara about 500 C.E. The Mishnah and Gemara together form the Talmud, frequently called the Babylonian Talmud. The Palestinian Talmud, in its completed form—if ever it was completed—dates from the time of the extinction of the Patriarchate in Israel. The patriarch Hillel II (320–365 C.E.) was the last outstanding figure in the long line of the illustrious family founded by his namesake Hillel the Elder.

76. Shabbat 31a. Compare Hillel's reply with Lev. 19:18. Jesus quotes the Golden Rule in the positive formulation (see Matt. 7:12; also Matt. 22:39; Mark 21:31; and Luke 10:27). Early Christian writings other than the Gospels prefer the negative version because of its strong practical appeal (Glatzer, *Hillel the Elder*, p. 95, n. 1). Isocrates in the West and Confucius in the East also state the formulation in the negative.

77. Shabbat 31a. The proselyte was cured of his ambition and realized that he was not discriminated against because he was not born a Jew. But in his studies he discovered other worthwhile reasons for being a Jew. A variant version occurs in Avot de-Rabbi Natan 15:3, 24b. For further sources on the ancient Jewish attitude to converts, on the whole a favorable one, see Philo, *De Poenitentia* 1; *De Monarchia* 1:7; Mekhilta on Exod. 22:20; Leviticus Rabbah 1:2 quoting Hos. 14:8; Midrash Tanḥuma on Gen. 14:1, and on Exod. 37:1; Exodus Rabbah 19:4; Leviticus Rabbah 6:5. For the minority point of view, disapproving of converts, see Yevamot 47b.

78. Avot de-Rabbi Natan 15:3, 24b.

79. Berakhot 60a. This tale points to Hillel's great trust. Evil can befall any man, even the righteous, but the faith of the righteous man precludes the expectation of evil.

80. Avot 1:15. The study of Torah must be regularly scheduled, not something occasional. If a man becomes too involved in worldly occupations, he will neglect the study of Torah altogether. One of the questions asked a person at the Final Judgment will be, "Have you set aside a definite time for study of the Torah?"

Abraham is an illustration of the righteous man who says little and does much. He promised only bread to the three visitors (Gen. 18:5) but gave them oxen and meal. But the wicked are like Ephron the Hittite who says much but does little (Gen. 23:15–16). If a man gives another the finest gifts but with an unpleasant countenance, it is as though he has given nothing. But if he receives another with cheerful countenance, even though he gives him nothing, it is as though he has given him the finest gifts (Avot de-Rabbi Natan 80:13).

81. Beiẓah 16a; Pesikta Rabbati, Piska 3, Aseret ha-Dibrot. Shammai feels that adequate preparation for the Sabbath must begin the previous Sunday, so important is the day. Hillel agrees on the Sabbath's sanctity, but his trust in God's goodness gives him the cer-

tainty that God will provide. Both revere the Sabbath, but they differ in their attitude to the weekday. The Sabbath engages Shammai's attention all week. Hillel feels that each day deserves his entire attention as it comes along, for each day has its opportunities for hallowing life.

82. Ḥagigah 9b. Hillel would explain the verse as making a distinction between one who has studied but who has ceased to do so, and he who constantly studies. It is the latter "that serves God." Learning must never end.

83. Leviticus Rabbah 34:3. This is an illustration of Judaism's refusal to denigrate the body, for the body has its own sanctity (cf. Epictetus, *Discourses* 4.11.2).

84. Leviticus 34:3. The midrash connects this tale with Prov. 11:17. The Stoics often compared the soul to a guest in the body (see Louis Ginzberg, "Kitvei Midrash ve-Haggadah," *Ginzei Schechter* [3 vols., New York, 1928–29], 1:87).

85. Tosefta Berakhot 2:21; cf. Derekh Ereẓ Zuta 5:5. A man should endeavor to be inconspicuous and considerate.

86. Sukkah 28a; Bava Batra 134a; Avot de-Rabbi Natan 14:1, 23b. The latter version describes the second thirty as being worthy enough that the intercalation of the years could be determined by them. Such calculations were made only by the leading members of the Sanhedrin. Jonathan ben Uzziel is named in Megillah 3a as the author of an Aramaic translation of the Prophets. The extant Targum is not his. The interpretation of the verse from Proverbs indicates that the "substance" and "treasures" promised by wisdom are not material but spiritual and intellectual. The mention of Abaye (ca. 273/280–338/339 C.E.) and Rava (ca. 280/299–352 C.E.) indicates the later inclusion of this phrase. The version in Avot de-Rabbi Natan does not contain the reference to the later scholars.

87. Yerushalmi Nedarim 5:7, 39b; Sukkah 28a; Sanhedrin 11a.

88. Soferim 16:8, 41b.

89. Sanhedrin 11a; Yerushalmi Nedarim 39b; Songs Rabbah 8:9; Sotah 48b; Yerushalmi Sotah, near end; Tosefta Sotah 13:3.

90. Bava Batra 133b–134a. The thrust of Jonathan's argument was that he had come into legal possession of the property and it was his to do with as he liked. Therefore, he was not violating the deceased's wishes, for it was not the latter's property Jonathan gave to the sons but his own. Another version of the story is found in Yerushalmi Nedarim 5:6 where it is Jonathan's father who disinherits his son and leaves his possessions to Shammai who sells one part, consecrates one part, and gives the remainder to Jonathan with the same kind of explanation for his action.

91. Yoma 77b and Sukkah 2:8 respectively. Washing is prohibited to adults on Yom Kippur, but here an exception is made for the sake of feeding a young child. Women, servants, and young children are not required to fulfill the commandment of dwelling in a sukkah on the Feast of Tabernacles. Women are generally absolved from those positive commandments dependent on a definite time for their observance. A higher priority, that of the care of young children, may preclude the observance of such a commandment at a certain fixed time. Here in the case of the sukkah, the definition of "young children" is that of children who, when awaking from sleep, call for their mother. Shammai did what he did for his grandchild because he felt that the

training of a child in religious observances should begin even before the child develops awareness (see also Beizah 16a). The early Karaites interpreted the pertinent biblical laws in similar fashion (see Eshkol Hakofer 135).

92. Shabbat 19a. The day is called "a hard one" for the Jewish people because Hillel was the nasi, the head of the Sanhedrin, and because of his great modesty (Rashi ad locum).

93. Sanhedrin 5a. The exilarch was the highest official of Babylonian Jewry (Reish Galuta, "Head of the Diaspora"). Those who occupied the post traced their ancestry to David. The Persian court considered the Reish Galuta as the representative of Jewry and responsible for the taxes to be collected from the Jews. The descendants of Hillel filled the office of nasi, "patriarch," in the land of Israel for sixteen generations, for nearly half a millennium, in unbroken succession until the Romans put an end to the Patriarchate in the fifth century. The greatest of Hillel's descendants was Rabbi Judah ha-Nasi, compiler of the Mishnah about the year 200 C.E.

11. Jonathan ben Uzziel

94. Megillah 3a. See the previous section on Hillel and Shammai for several other stories involving Jonathan ben Uzziel. Our current Targum or Aramaic translation of the books of the prophets is not that of Jonathan. Aramaic was the popular spoken language of the Jews in the land of Israel during the rabbinic period. The Writings or Hagiographa, the third division of the Scriptures, contains the Book of Daniel to which the tradition ascribed messianic allusions.

Part VIII

The First Generation of Tannaim

1

The School of Shammai
and the School of Hillel

The school of Shammai and the school of Hillel held differing views with regard to Creation. The school of Shammai maintained that the heaven was created first and the earth afterward, in accordance with the text, *When God began to create the heaven and the earth* (Gen. 1:1). The school of Hillel argued that the earth was created first, as it is written, *When the Lord God made earth and heaven* (Gen. 2:4). Both gave logical reasons for their opinions. The school of Shammai said that the matter may be compared to the case of a king who made himself a throne and then made a footstool for it. So speaks the verse, *Thus said the Lord: The heaven is My throne and the earth is My footstool* (Isa. 66:1). The school of Hillel said that it is like a king who builds a palace. First he sets the lower stories and then the upper ones.

The sages say that heaven and earth were created at the same time, as it is said, *My own hand founded the earth, My right hand spread out the skies. I call unto them, let them stand up* (Isa. 48:13).[1]

The schools of Shammai and Hillel differed about the creation of the embryo in the time to come. The school of Shammai said that in this world it begins with flesh and skin and ends with sinews and bones. But in the time to come it will begin with sinews and bones and end with skin; for so is it written of the dead in the vision of Ezekiel, *I looked and there were sinews on them and flesh had grown, and skin had formed over them* (Ezek. 37:8). The school of Hillel maintained that the formation of the embryo in this world will be like its formation in the time to come. In this world it begins with skin and flesh and ends with sinew and bones and in the time to come it will be the same, for thus said Job, *Consider that You fashioned me as clay . . . surely you will pour me out like milk* (Job 10:9–10). It does not say, "You have poured me out," but *You will pour me out*, and later, *and You will congeal me like cheese* (Job 10:10). It does not say, "You have congealed me," but *You will congeal me*, and *You will clothe me with skin and flesh* (Job 10:11). It does not say "You did clothe me," but *You will clothe me . . . and will weave me with bones and sinews* (Job 10:11). It says not, "You did weave me," but *You will weave me*.[2]

The schools of Shammai and Hillel debated the following question for two and a half years. One side argued that it would be better for a man not to be born than to be born. The opposing side argued contrariwise. Finally, the votes of the scholars were counted and the conclusion was that it would be better for a man not to be born, but once having been born, let him look to his deeds![3]

The school of Shammai said, "A master should teach only those who are wise, meek, of good family, and well-to-do." But the school of Hillel said, "He should teach everyone, for in this way many sinners in Israel have been brought to the study of the Torah, and from them have issued righteous, pious, and worthy men."[4]

For three years did the schools of Shammai and Hillel differ, each asserting that the law was to be decided in accordance with its views. Then a heavenly voice was heard to say, "The words of both schools are the words of the living God, but the law is in accordance with the school of Hillel." If the words of both are those of the living God, why did the school of Hillel deserve that the law should be decided according to its opinions? Because the scholars of that group were gentle and modest, studying also the opinions of their opponents, the school of Shammai. In addition, they would quote the words of the school of Shammai before mentioning their own. This teaches that he who humbles himself the Holy One, praised be He, will raise up, and he who exalts himself the Holy One, praised be He, will bring low. He who pursues greatness, greatness will flee from him but he who flees from greatness, greatness will pursue him. He who impatiently tries to force time, time pushes him aside, but he who bides his time, time submits to him.[5]

The school of Shammai taught that divine judgment distinguishes three categories of people: the completely righteous, the completely wicked, and those in between. Upon their death the completely righteous are at once inscribed and sealed for life in the world to come. The completely wicked are at once inscribed and sealed for Gehenna, as it is said, *Many of those that sleep in the dust of the earth will awake, some to eternal life, others to reproaches, to everlasting abhorrence* (Dan. 12:2). Those neither altogether righteous nor altogether wicked go down to Gehenna, pray, and come up again, as it said, *That third I will put into the fire, and I will smelt them as one smelts silver and test them as one tests gold. They will invoke Me by name, and I will respond to them* (Zech. 13:9). Concerning this category of people, Hannah said, *The Lord deals death and gives life, casts down into Sheol and raises up* (1 Sam. 2:6). But the school of Hillel taught that He who abounds in mercy inclines the scale of judgment toward the side of mercy. It is concerning this group of people that David said, *I love the Lord for He hears my voice, my pleas* (Ps. 116:1). In fact, the full chapter may be applied to them, especially, *I was brought low and He saved me* (Ps. 116:6), and *You have delivered me from death* (Ps. 116:8).[6]

What should be sung in praise of the bride when dancing before her? The school of Shammai said, "A bride as she actually is." The school of Hillel said that, whatever the reality of the bride's appearance, the words to be sung before her are, "O lovely and graceful bride." The school of Shammai said to the school of Hillel, "Suppose the bride is lame or blind, should one still sing, 'O lovely and graceful bride?' Does the Torah not say, *Keep far from a false charge* (Exod. 23:7)?" The school of Hillel replied, "According to your opinion, when one buys a bad bargain in the marketplace, should one commend it or point out all its faults to the purchaser? Surely, it is more considerate that praise be spoken at such a time."[7]

Yet, despite the differences between the schools of Shammai and Hillel and notwithstanding the fact that the one school prohibited what the other permitted, and one declared unfit what the other called fit, the men of both schools did not hesitate to marry a daughter of a scholar of the opposing school. Despite all the disputes about what is clean and unclean wherein one school declared ritually clean what the other declared unclean, neither refrained from using anything that pertained to the others in matters concerned with ritual cleanness. This teaches that they practiced affection and friendship toward each other, in keeping with the verse, *You must love honesty and integrity* (Zech. 8:19).[8]

2

Ben Bag Bag and Ben He He

Ben Bag Bag said, "Turn the Torah and turn it again for everything is in it. Contemplate it, wax gray, and become old in it. Do
not stir from it for you can have no better virtue than this."[9] He
also said, "Do not enter the courtyard of another without permission, even to take your own property, lest he think you a thief.
But if he is reluctant to return your property, give him a good
blow and say, 'I am taking what belongs to me!' "[10]

Ben He He said, "According to the labor is the reward."[11]
Another time, he was asked by Elijah, "What is the meaning of the
verse, *See, I refine you, but not as silver; I test you in the furnace
of affliction* (Isa. 48:10)?" The explanation he gave was that the
Holy One, blessed be He, carefully considered all possible good
qualities and found none more fitting for Israel than poverty.[12]

3

Akavyah ben Mahalalel

Akavyah ben Mahalalel said, "Think about three things and you
will not sin: know where you came from, where you are going,
and before whom you will some day have to give account and
reckoning. Where did you come from? From a putrid drop. Where
are you going? To a place of dust, worm, and maggot. And before whom will you some day have to give account and reckoning? Before the King of the kings of kings, the Holy One, blessed
be He."[13]

Akavyah ben Mahalalel testified in four different legal cases. The sages said to him, "Akavyah, retract these four opinions you have stated and we shall make you head of the court." He replied, "Better that I be called a fool all my days than be a wicked person before God for even one hour; for people will say of me, 'He retracted for the sake of an appointment to power.' "

What were the four opinions he proclaimed? He declared unclean the residuary hair and the yellow blood in a leprosy symptom; but the sages declare them clean. If the hair of a blemished firstling animal fell out and one put it in a niche of the wall, and afterward slaughtered the beast, he used to permit the hair to be used; the sages, however, forbid it. He said that "the water of bitterness" is not given to a proselyte or a freed bondwoman to drink; the sages say it is. They said to him, "It happened to Karkemit, a freed bondwoman who lived in Jerusalem, that Shemaiah and Avtalyon gave her 'the bitter water' to drink." He answered, "Being proselytes and, therefore, in a similar legal category with her, they made her drink." The sages excommunicated him for his remark, which was offensive to the memories of the great scholars, Shemaiah and Avtalyon. He died while he was still under the ban, and the court stoned his coffin. But Rabbi Judah said, "God forbid that it should be that Akavyah was excommunicated! For the Temple Court was never closed on any man in Israel as great in wisdom and the fear of sin as Akavyah ben Mahalalel." But whom did they excommunicate? Rabbi Eleazar ben Enoch, because he cast doubt on the teaching of the sages concerning the law about the cleansing of hands. And when he died the court placed a stone on his coffin, which teaches us that when a man dies still under the ban, his coffin is to be stoned in like manner.[14]

As he lay dying, Akavyah said to his son, "My son, retract the four differing opinions that I used to defend." The son asked, "Why did you not retract them?" He answered, "Because I heard these opinions from an earlier group of sages and my opponents also heard their opinions from an earlier group of sages. Therefore, I held fast to the traditions I had heard and they stood by the traditions they had heard. But you have heard my position from an individual, myself alone, and their point of view from a group of scholars. It is better to reject the opinion of an individual in favor of the opinion of a majority."

"Father," asked the son, "Commend me to your friends." He

replied, "I shall not do that." "Have you found some wrong in me?" inquired the son. "No," the father answered, "but your own deeds will bring you close to men or remove you from them."[15]

== 4 ==

Gamaliel I the Elder

Hillel, his son Simon, Rabban Gamaliel the Elder, and Simon II served as nasi during the one hundred years before the destruction of the Second Temple.[16]

Rabban Gamaliel said, "Provide yourself with a teacher, stay away from doubtful matters, and do not make too much use of guesswork in giving your tithes."[17]

It once happened that a king and queen ordered their servants to have the Passover offering slaughtered on their behalf. The servants went and had two paschal offerings slaughtered for them, a lamb and a kid. They came and asked the king what to do under the circumstances—which animal was the legitimate paschal offering, or was neither? He said, "Go and ask the queen." They went and asked her. She said, "Go and ask Rabban Gamaliel." They went and asked him. He replied, "With a king and queen, to whom it is immaterial whether it be a lamb or a kid, let them eat from the one first slaughtered. If it were one of us who was involved, we should be permitted to eat from neither."

Again, it happened that a lizard was found in the slaughtering area of the Temple where animals were being slaughtered for a feast. It was thought that because of the lizard, which was presumed to be dead at the time of the slaughtering, all the slaughtered animals, in keeping with the laws of ritual purity, would have to be pronounced unfit for eating. They came to ask the king. He said, "Go, ask the queen." They did so and she said, "Go ask Rabban Gamaliel." They went and asked him. He inquired, "Was the area where the lizard was found warm or cold?" They replied, "Warm." He said, "Go, pour a glass of cold water upon it." They went, poured a glass of cold water upon the lizard, and it suddenly moved. Thus Rabban Gamaliel rendered the entire feast fit for eating. It appears that the king depended upon the queen, the queen depended upon Rabban Gamaliel, and the entire feast depended upon Rabban Gamaliel.[18]

Rabban Gamaliel the Elder would separate students into four categories: the unclean fish, the clean fish, the Jordan fish, and the Mediterranean fish. What is meant by these descriptions? The unclean fish describes the son of poor parents who though he has learned Scripture, Mishnah, laws, and lore remains without understanding. The clean fish is the son of wealthy parents who when he has learned Scripture, Mishnah, laws, and lore has understanding. The Jordan fish is the student who has learned Scripture, Mishnah, Midrash, laws, and lore but lacks the ability to discuss it. The Mediterranean fish describes the student who has learned Scripture, Mishnah, Midrash, laws, and lore and has the ability to discuss it.[19]

There is a story told about Rabban Gamaliel that once, as he was walking about the Temple Mount, he saw an attractive gentile woman and he uttered a blessing. Not that it was his practice to look at women, but the path was narrow and he could not help himself. And it was not that he was stunned by her beauty that he uttered the blessing, for it was his practice when he saw a fine donkey, a fine camel, or a splendid horse to exclaim, "Blessed is He who has such handsome creatures in His world!"[20]

When the daughter of Rabban Gamaliel married Simon ben Netanel, a priest, he made a special agreement with the bridegroom that his family would observe all the pharisaic laws of purity.[21] It was the custom of the house of Rabban Gamaliel to give white clothing to the laundry three days before the Sabbath but colored garments even on a Friday.[22]

Rabban Gamaliel sat and taught: In the messianic era a woman is destined to bear every day, as it is written, *Those with child and those in labor* (Jer. 31:8). But a certain student of his scoffed at him, quoting, *There is nothing new beneath the sun* (Eccles. 1:9). He replied, "Come, and I shall show you an example of this in the present age." He went out and showed him a hen.

Again, Rabban Gamaliel sat and taught: Trees in the messianic era are destined to yield fruit every day, as it is written, *And it shall bring forth boughs and produce fruit* (Ezek. 17:23)—just as there are boughs every day so shall there be fruit every day. But that pupil laughed at him, saying, "It is written, *There is nothing new beneath the sun* (Eccles. 1:9)." Rabban Gamaliel answered, "Come, and I shall show you an example of this in the present age." He went out and showed him a caper bush.

Again, Rabban Gamaliel sat and taught: In the messianic era the land of Israel is destined to bring forth loaves of white delicious bread and cloaks of fine wool, as it is written, *Let abundant grain be in the land* (Ps. 72:16). But that disciple again scoffed, saying once more, *There is nothing new beneath the sun* (Eccles. 1:9). Rabban Gamaliel said to him, "Come, and I shall show you an example of this in the present age." He went out and showed him mushrooms and truffles (for the loaves) and for the cloaks of fine wool, the bark of a young palm shoot.[23]

It was accepted practice to bow at thirteen different locations in the Temple. Among the members of the house of Rabban Gamaliel and of Rabbi Ḥananiah, the deputy high priest, the practice was to bow at fourteen. And where was the additional place? Facing the woodshed, for they had received a tradition from their ancestors that in that place the Ark had been concealed. It once happened that a priest, going about his duties, saw that a certain part of the floor was different than the rest. He came to tell the other priests, but before he could finish the story he suddenly died. They knew that he had come upon the spot where the Ark was hidden.[24]

The story is told that Rabban Gamaliel and the elders were sitting on the steps of the entrance hall on the Temple Mount and Johanan, the scribe at the time, was sitting before them. They said to him, "Go and write: 'To our brothers of upper Galilee and lower Galilee, may your peace increase! We inform you that the time has come for the removal of all tithes. Take the tithe from the olive vats!' 'To our brothers of the upper southern region and the lower southern region! We inform you that the time has come for the removal of all tithes. Take the tithe from the sheaves of grain!' 'To our brothers of the diaspora in Babylonia, Media, Greece, and the other lands of exile, may your peace increase! We inform you that the lambs are still small and the doves lean, so that the days of spring have not yet come, and I and my colleagues deem it proper, therefore, to intercalate the calendar and add to this year another thirty days.' "[25]

Once Rabbi Ḥalafta went to visit Rabban Gamaliel II in Tiberias and found him sitting at the table with the Targum translation of Job in his hand, reading it. Rabbi Ḥalafta said to him, "I remember Rabban Gamaliel, your father's father, while he was sitting at the side of a building under construction on the Temple Mount, when a Targum translation of Job was brought to him. 'Remove a course of stones,' he ordered the builder, 'and bury this under it.' " Thereupon, Rabban Gamaliel II ordered that his copy also be concealed.[26]

When the wicked Turnus Rufus ploughed over the Temple site, a decree was issued that Rabban Gamaliel be executed. An officer came to the academy and cried out, "The best-known man is being sought!" Rabban Gamaliel heard and hid himself. The officer quietly came to him and asked, "If I save your life, would you assure me of a place in the world to come?" Rabban Gamaliel replied, "Yes." The officer demanded, "Swear it!" He swore. The officer then ascended to the roof, threw himself off, and was killed. It is known by tradition that if one of the signers of a death warrant dies, the warrant becomes void. A voice came forth from heaven and declared, "This officer is ready for life in the world to come!"[27]

It is told of Rabban Gamaliel that once he ordered, "Have seven scholars ready for me for the court chamber for tomorrow morning to decide on the intercalation of the year." The next day he arose to find eight. He directed, "Whoever has come up to the court chamber without permission, let him go down." Whereupon Samuel the Small got up and said, "It is I who came up without permission, but not for the purpose of being among those who intercalate the year, but only for the purpose of learning the application of the law to realities." Rabban Gamaliel said to him, "Be seated, my son, be seated. All the years to be intercalated can so be done by no one worthier than you." But the sages have taught us that the year is not to be intercalated except by scholars invited for that purpose on the evening before. In reality, it was not Samuel the Small who was the uninvited one, it was someone else. He said it was he to save the guilty person from public embarrassment.

There was a similar story about Rabbi Judah ha-Nasi who, as he was teaching, smelled the odor of garlic. He ordered, "Whoever has eaten garlic, let him leave!" Rabbi Ḥiyya stood up and walked out. Then all the rest arose and departed. The next morning Rabbi Simon, son of Rabbi Judah ha-Nasi, happened to meet Rabbi Ḥiyya and asked him, "Are you really the one who upset my father?" He replied, "Heaven forbid! I would never eat garlic before coming to the house of study. I walked out, taking the blame on myself, so that the guilty person should not be embarrassed publicly and to give the signal that all should leave."

From whom did Rabbi Ḥiyya learn this? From Rabbi Meir. For we have learned that once a woman came to Rabbi Meir's house of study and said to him, "My master, one of you here married me through intercourse." Rabbi Meir at once got up and wrote her a bill of divorcement and handed it to her. Whereupon each one there did the same.

And where did Rabbi Meir learn this? From Samuel the Small. And whence did he learn it? From Shecaniah ben Jehiel, as it is written, *Then Shecaniah son of Jehiel of the family of Elam spoke up and said to Ezra, "We have trespassed against our God by bringing into our homes foreign women from the peoples of the land; but there is still hope for Israel despite this"* (Ezra 10:2). And from whom did Shecaniah ben Jehiel learn it? From Joshua, as it is written, *But the Lord answered Joshua: "Arise! Why do you lie prostrate? Israel has sinned!"* (Josh. 7:10). But Joshua protested, "Master of the Universe, who has sinned?" God answered, "Am I then a tale-bearer? Cast lots and find out!" Others say that Shecaniah learned it from Moses, as it is written, *And the Lord said to Moses, "How long will you men refuse to follow My commandments and My teachings"* (Exod. 16:28).[28]

When Samuel the Small died, they suspended his key and writing tablet from his coffin, because he had no son. When Rabban Gamaliel the Elder and Rabbi Eleazar delivered their funeral orations over him, they exclaimed, "For such a person it is fitting to weep, for such a person it is fitting to mourn. When kings die they leave their crowns to their sons; when wealthy men die they leave their riches to their children; but Samuel the Small has taken away with him all the desirable things in the world and has departed."[29]

In earlier years burial expenses were so great that they added to the grief and concern of the relatives. So costly did burial become that relatives would abandon the body and flee. Rabban Gamaliel set an example by his instructions for an inexpensive burial for himself, and he was buried in a simple linen shroud.[30] When Rabban Gamaliel the Elder died, the honor of the Torah was dealt a severe blow, as were the causes of ritual purity and religious abstinence.[31] Each person should be honored with the respect due Rabban Gamaliel.[32]

From the time of Joshua until Rabban Gamaliel the Torah would be studied while standing. When Rabban Gamaliel the Elder died, sickness and weakness became more prevalent and the Torah would be studied while sitting. And this is the meaning of the Mishnah, "When Rabban Gamaliel the Elder died, the honor of the Torah was dealt a severe blow."[33]

When Rabban Gamaliel the Elder died, the proselyte Onkelos burned more than eighty Tyrian minas in his honor. They asked him, "What was your purpose in doing this?" He answered, "It is written, *You will die a peaceful death; and as incense was burned for your ancestors, the earlier kings who preceded you, so they will burn incense for you* (Jer. 34:5). And is not Rabban Gamaliel worth more than a hundred useless kings?"[34]

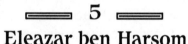

5
Eleazar ben Harsom

Of Rabbi Eleazar ben Harsom it was said that his father bequeathed to him a thousand villages and an equal number of ships. Yet each day he would place a jug of flour on his shoulder and journey from town to town and from region to region in order to study Torah. Once in one of his own villages his servants, who did not know him, thinking he was one of the villagers, seized him and pressed him into forced labor demanded by the owner of the village of all its inhabitants. He pleaded with them, "I beg you, let me go that I may study Torah." They said to him, "By the life of Rabbi Eleazar ben Harsom we swear that we shall not let you go!" He gave them much money to free him. All his days he was not in touch with his servants nor did he attend to his properties. He only sat and studied Torah day and night. So when a rich man is asked, "Why have you not studied Torah?" and he replies that he is rich and busily involved with financial matters, he is asked, "Are you then richer than Rabbi Eleazar ben Harsom?"[35]

He served as high priest for eleven years. It was told of him that his mother made a priestly garment for him worth twenty thousand manehs. His fellow priests did not let him wear it because, wearing it, he appeared naked.[36]

6

Abba Saul ben Batnit

It is told of Abba Saul ben Batnit that he used to fill up his measures on the eve of a festival day and give them to his customers on the festival day. Abba Saul says that he used also to do so during the intermediate days of the festival for the sake of clearness of measure. The sages say that he also did so on ordinary days for the sake of exactness of measure.[37] He collected three hundred kegs of wine that he felt were not his because of the inexactness of measuring in selling wine to customers, and he brought them to the managers of Temple property in Jerusalem as a gift to the Sanctuary. His fellow shopkeepers likewise collected three hundred barrels of oil and for the same reason brought them to the managers of Temple property. The latter said to them, "You do not have to do this, it is really yours." They replied, "We do not wish to keep it, for we do not consider it ours." Whereupon they were told, "Since you would be so strict with yourselves and not keep it, give it away to benefit the community at large."[38] Once Abba Saul ben Batnit fell ill and the rabbis came to visit him. He said to them, "You see this right hand of mine that has always given true and honest measure and yet it now pains me."[39]

He said in the name of Abba Joseph ben Ḥanin, "Woe is me because of the house of Boethus, woe is me because of their clubs! Woe is me because of the house of Ḥanin, woe is me because of their malicious gossip! Woe is me because of the house of Katros, woe is me because of their evil decrees! Woe is me because of the house of Ishmael ben Phiabi, woe is me because of their fists! For all of them were high priests, their sons were managers of Temple property, their sons-in-law were treasury trustees, and their servants would beat the people with rods."[40]

He told his sons, "Bury me at the feet of my father and remove the thread of blue from the fringes of my cloak."[41]

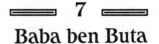

7

Baba ben Buta

Once Hillel the Elder brought an animal for a burnt offering to the Temple court on a festival. The disciples of Shammai the Elder gathered about him and asked, "What kind of an animal is this?" He answered, "It is a female and I have brought it for a peace offering." He moved its tail to and fro, making believe it was a female animal. They left. That day the school of Shammai rose in esteem above the school of Hillel and the attempt was made then to have the law decided in all cases in accordance with their opinions. But there was present an old man, a disciple of Shammai the Elder, and Baba ben Buta was his name. He knew that the law was to be decided in accordance with the school of Hillel. He arranged that all the Kedar sheep in Jerusalem be brought to the Temple court, and he proclaimed, "Whoever wishes to offer any of these for a burnt offering, let him do so!" That day the school of Hillel prevailed over the school of Shammai and the law was decided in accordance with their opinions with none opposed.[42]

Once there was a man who was anxious to divorce his wife but who wanted to avoid the payment of the large amount stipulated in his marriage certificate due his wife under such circumstances. What did he do? He invited his friends to his home, gave them food and much drink and, when they became intoxicated, put them into one bed and poured the white of an egg among them to create suspicion that they had made love with his wife. He brought witnesses to the scene and then took them to the court to testify against his wife—all so that he might be permitted to divorce her without any payment. There was present an old man, a disciple of Shammai the Elder, and Baba ben Buta was his name. He said to the court, "This is the tradition that I have received from Shammai the Elder—a stain on bedclothes made by the white of an egg contracts and hardens when heated, whereas male ejaculation becomes absorbed and does not solidify." The court investigated accordingly and discovered the truth. It ordered the husband flogged and made him pay the full amount designated in the marriage certificate.[43]

There was a certain Babylonian who came to the land of Israel and married a native of that country. One day he said to his wife, "Cook me a couple of lentils." She took him literally and cooked exactly two lentils." He was furious. The next day, thinking that if he said the same thing she would again understand him literally, he said to her, "Cook me a measure of lentils." She cooked a huge measure of them. He then said to her, "Go bring me two young pumpkins." She went and brought him two lamps—for the Aramaic word *butzini* may mean both young pumpkins and lamps. He became very angry and shouted, "Go break them on top of the gate!" (The word for gate in Aramaic is *baba*.) At that moment Baba ben Buta was sitting at the gate of the town presiding over the court. The wife thought that her husband meant for her to break the lamps on Baba's head. She went and broke them on his head! He asked her, in astonishment, "What is the meaning of this?" She answered, "This is what my husband has directed me to do." Recognizing her simple naiveté, he said to her: "You have indeed done your husband's will. May God reward you with two sons who will be scholars as great as Baba ben Buta."[44]

It was told of Baba ben Buta that each day he used to offer of his own free will a suspensive guilt offering except for the day after the Day of Atonement. Even then he swore, "By this Temple! If they permitted me, I would bring one on the day following Yom Kippur as well, but they tell me, 'Wait until you have some doubt whether you have sinned!'"[45]

═══ 8 ═══

Ḥanina the Deputy High Priest

While all others prostrated themselves at thirteen different places in the Temple, it was the practice of the members of the households of Rabban Gamaliel and of Rabbi Ḥanina, the deputy high priest, to do so at fourteen places. And which was the additional place? Facing the woodshed. For it was a tradition that they had inherited from their ancestors that it was in that place that the Ark had been hidden.[46]

Rabbi Ḥanina, the deputy high priest, said, "My father would inconspicuously nudge aside from the altar those priests who possessed any blemish.[47] He gave the reason for the office of deputy high priest—in case a blemish would befall the high priest rendering him unfit, his deputy could at once take his place.[48]

Rabbi Ḥanina, the deputy high priest, said, "I used to serve in the Temple and would witness miracles with the Menorah. It would be kindled at the beginning of the year and its flames would not go out until the beginning of the next year." One year the olive crop was poor and oil was not available. The priests began to weep. But Rabbi Ḥanina said, "I was in the Temple and I found that the Menorah burned more brilliantly than at other times."[49] To Rabbi Ḥanina the altar flame appeared to be in the shape of a crouching dog.[50]

He related that forty years before the destruction of the Temple the people of Jerusalem would lock their doors at night and would wake up to find them open, as it is said, *Throw open your gates, O Lebanon, and let fire consume your cedars* (Zech. 11:1).[51]

Rabbi Ḥanina, the deputy high priest, said, "He who lays the words of the Torah to his heart will be freed from the anxieties of the sword, hunger, madness, lust, the evil inclination, adultery, empty thoughts, and the yoke of human cares; for so is it written in the Book of Psalms by David, king of Israel, *The precepts of the Lord are just, rejoicing the heart; the instruction of the Lord is lucid, making the eyes light up* (Ps. 19:9). And he who does not lay the words of the Torah to his heart will be burdened with the anxieties of the sword, hunger, madness, lust, the evil inclination, adultery, empty thoughts, and the yoke of human cares; for so is it written in the book of Deuteronomy by Moses our teacher, *They shall serve as signs and proofs against you and your offspring for all time. Because you would not serve the Lord your God in joy and gladness over the abundance of everything, you shall have to serve—in hunger and thirst, naked and lacking everything—the enemies whom the Lord will let loose against you* (Deut. 28: 46–48)."

What does *in hunger* mean? When a man longs to eat barley

bread and does not have even that, his enemies demand of him white bread and rich meat. What does *in thirst* mean? When a man longs to drink a drop of sour wine or a drop of beer and does not have even that, his enemies demand of him the best wine that can be found in any land. What does *naked* mean? When a man wants to wear a woolen or linen shirt and does not have even that, his enemies demand of him the finest silks and satins that can be obtained in any land. And what does *lacking everything* mean? He will lack a candle, a knife, a table—or some say, vinegar and salt. For that is a popular curse—"May you have no vinegar and no salt in your home!"

He used to say, "It is written, *Don't stare at me because I am swarthy, because the sun has gazed upon me. My mother's sons quarreled with me, they made me guard the vineyards; my own vineyard I did not guard* (Songs 1:6). The reference is to the councilors of Judah who cast off the yoke of the Holy One, blessed be He, and set a human king over themselves."[52]

Rabbi Ḥanina, the deputy high priest, said, "Pray for the welfare of the government, for were it not for the fear of it, men would swallow each other alive."[53] And he interpreted the closing of the priestly benediction, *The Lord bestow His favor upon you and grant you peace* (Num. 6:26), to mean "peace in your house." He said, "Great is peace, for it is weighed in the balance against all of Creation, for so is it written, *I form light, and create darkness; I make peace, and create woe* (Isa. 45:7)."[54]

On the twenty-fifth of Sivan, Rabban Simon ben Gamaliel, Rabbi Ishmael ben Elisha, and Rabbi Ḥanina, the deputy high priest, were killed (by the Romans).[55]

9

Simon ben Gamaliel I

Simon, the son of Gamaliel the Elder, said, "All my days I have grown up among the sages and I have found nothing better for a person than silence." He also taught, "Not learning but doing is the principal thing." He said, "Whoever talks too much increases the likelihood of sin."[56]

Rabbi Joshua told Rabbi Neḥunia ben Ha-kanah of Emmaus, "I shall relate to you not just something heard by my ears, but what my own eyes have seen. Once I went up to the upper market at the Dung Gate in Jerusalem and I found there Rabban Simon ben Gamaliel and Rabban Johanan ben Zakkai. They were sitting with two open scrolls in their laps and Johanan of Haileh, the scribe, was standing before them, with pen and ink ready. They instructed him, 'Write the following: From Simon ben Gamaliel and Johanan ben Zakkai to our brethren in the upper and lower regions of the south, in Shaḥlil and in the seven districts of the south. Peace be unto you! Be it known to you that the fourth year has arrived and you have not as yet cleared from your possession the sacred offerings. Therefore, hasten to bring five sheaves of wheat, otherwise you will not be able to recite the declaration— "I have cleared the holy offerings from my home." And it is not we who have originated this procedure but our fathers, who wrote in like manner to your fathers.' They further instructed the scribe, 'Write a second letter: From Simon ben Gamaliel and Johanan ben Zakkai to our brethren in upper and lower Galilee, in Simonia, and in Oved Bet Hillel. Peace be unto you! Be it known to you that the fourth year has arrived and you have not as yet cleared from your possession the sacred offerings. Therefore, hasten to bring baskets of olives, otherwise you will not be able to recite the declaration—"I have cleared the holy offerings from my home." And it is not we who have originated this procedure but our fathers who wrote in like manner to your fathers.' "[57]

He was concerned, like his father, Rabban Gamaliel the Elder, about the legal disabilities of women. The law was that if a woman experienced five issues that were in doubt or five miscarriages that were in doubt, she need bring but one offering; she may then eat of the animal offerings, and she is not required to bring the other offerings. If she had five miscarriages that were not in doubt or five issues that were not in doubt, she need bring but one offering; she may then eat of the animal offerings, but she is required to bring the other offerings. Once in Jerusalem a pair of doves cost a golden dinar. Rabban Simon ben Gamaliel exclaimed, "I swear by this Temple! I will not let the night pass before a pair of doves cost but a silver dinar!" He went into the court and taught, "If a woman suffered five miscarriages that were not in doubt or five issues that were not in doubt, she need bring but one offering and she may then eat of the animal offerings; and she is not required to bring the other offerings." That very day the price of a pair of doves dropped to a quarter of a silver dinar.[58]

Rabban Gamaliel II, the son of Rabban Simon ben Gamaliel I, said, "Once a Sadducee lived with us in the same alley in Jerusalem and my father said to us, 'Hasten and put out all the needed vessels in the alley before he brings out his own vessels and so restricts you.'"[59] From barrels and goatskin bottles of non-Jews with wine of Jews in them, the wine may not be drunk by Jews but it is permitted to have benefit otherwise from it. Simon ben Guda testified before the son of Rabban Gamaliel that Rabban Gamaliel once drank such wine in Acre but his testimony was not accepted.[60]

They used to tell about Rabban Simon ben Gamaliel that at the ceremony of the Rejoicing at the Libation he would throw eight flaming torches into the air in succession, catching each in turn, and none would touch the other. And when he would prostrate himself in the Temple he would press his two thumbs on the floor, supporting himself on them, kiss the floor and then spring upright—a feat of which not every person is capable![61] There is a story about Rabban Simon ben Gamaliel that he was once standing on a high point of the Temple Mount and he beheld a very beautiful gentile woman. He exclaimed, *How many are the things You have made, O Lord* (Ps. 104:24).[62]

Rabban Simon ben Gamaliel says in the name of Rabbi Simon the deputy high priest, "The thickness of the curtain in the Temple was that of a handbreadth. It was woven of seventy-two cords, each cord of twenty-four strands. Its length was forty cubits, its width twenty. It was woven by eighty-two myriads of women and two such curtains were made each year. When it became unclean, it took three hundred priests to immerse it in water."[63]

Rabbi Judah said in the name of Samuel that Rabban Simon ben Gamaliel applied the verse, *My eyes have brought me grief over all the maidens of my city* (Lam. 3:51), as follows: "A thousand young children studied in father's house—five hundred studied Greek wisdom and none of them was left alive (by the Romans) but I and the son of my father's brother."[64]

Samuel the Small (under the influence of the Holy Spirit)

spoke thus at the time of his death, "Simon (ben Gamaliel) and Ishmael (ben Elisha the high priest) are destined for the sword and the rest of the people for spoliation; great distress will befall Israel after them." He uttered these words in Aramaic.[65]

When they seized Rabban Simon ben Gamaliel and Rabbi Ishmael ben Elisha the high priest and were leading them to execution, Rabban Simon was perplexed in his mind and said, "Woe to us that we are to be put to death like common desecrators of the Sabbath or idolaters or fornicators or murderers!" Rabbi Ishmael ben Elisha asked, "May I say a word to you?" He said, "Speak," and Rabbi Ishmael said, "It may be that when you were sitting down to a meal, poor persons came and stood at your door, and you did not allow them to enter and eat with you." Rabban Simon replied, "I swear by Heaven that I never did so. I set watchmen at the door and when poor persons came they brought them to me and they ate and drank with me and blessed the name of Heaven." Then Rabbi Ishmael said, "Perhaps when you were sitting and expounding the Torah on the Temple Mount and all the multitudes of Israel were sitting before you, your mind was puffed up. Or did no one ever come to you seeking justice and you asked him to wait until you had adjusted your sandal or put on your cloak? And does not the Torah say, *If you do mistreat them . . . My anger shall blaze forth and I will put you to the sword* (Exod. 22:22–23)?" Rabban Simon said, "You have consoled me, Master. A person must be ready to receive his due punishment."

They both pleaded with the executioner. One said, "I am a priest, son of a high priest, put me to death first so that I do not witness the death of my colleague." The other said, "I am a nasi, the son of a nasi, put me to death first so that I do not witness the death of my colleague." The executioner said, "Draw lots." They did and the lot fell upon Rabban Simon ben Gamaliel. The executioner took the sword and cut off his head. Rabbi Ishmael ben Elisha picked it up, held it to his bosom, wept, and exclaimed, "Holy mouth, faithful mouth! Holy mouth, faithful mouth! Mouth that gave forth beautiful gems, precious stones, and pearls! Who has buried you in the dust and filled your ear with dust and ashes? Concerning you was it stated, *O sword! Rouse yourself against My shepherd, the man in charge of My flock* (Zech. 13:7)." He had not finished the words when the sword was lifted up and cut off his head. Of them Scripture states, *My anger shall blaze forth and I will put you to the sword, and your own wives shall become widows and your children orphans* (Exod. 22:23).[66]

On the twenty-fifth day of Sivan there were executed Rabban Simon ben Gamaliel, Rabbi Ishmael ben Elisha, and Rabbi Ḥanina, the deputy high priest.[67]

= 10 =
Naḥum of Gimzo

Naḥum of Gimzo was blind in both eyes, crippled in both arms and both legs, and his entire body was covered with sores. He lay in a bed the legs of which stood in pails of water so that worms could not climb up. His house was tottering. It was told of him that when his disciples wanted to remove first him and his bed and then his furniture, he said to them, "My sons, first take out all the furniture and then my bed and me, for you can be assured that as long as I am in the house it will not collapse." They took out the furniture and then him and his bed and at once the house collapsed.

His disciples asked him, "Master, since you are so righteous why are you so afflicted?" He replied, "My sons, I myself am the cause. For once I was on my way to the house of my father-in-law and with me there were three donkeys, one laden with food, another with drink, and the third with various delicacies. A poor man stood on the road and asked me, 'Master, give me food.' I said, 'Wait until I can unload one of the donkeys.' Before I could do so, he died. I fell on his face and cried out, 'May my eyes that had no pity for your eyes go blind! May my arms that had no pity for your arms be cut off! May my legs that had no pity for your legs be crippled.' I was still not satisfied until I added, 'May my entire body be covered with sores.'" His disciples said, "Woe unto us that we look upon you in such a state!" He replied to them, "Woe would be unto me, if you did not!"[68]

And why was he called Naḥum of Gimzo? Because to whatever would befall him, he would say, "*Gam zo le-tovah*" ("This too is for good"). It once happened that the Jews wished to send a gift to the royal residence. They discussed the question of who should go and decided upon Naḥum of Gimzo for he could work miracles. They sent in his charge a casket full of precious stones and pearls. On his way he lodged at an inn for the night, and thieves stole the contents of the casket and filled it with earth. The next morning when he discovered it, he said, "This too is for good." When he arrived at his destination and presented the gift, it was seen that the casket was full of earth. The king, in his anger, wanted to kill all the Jews for he was certain the Jews had mocked him. Elijah appeared, in the guise of one of his counselors, and said, "Perhaps this earth is of the same soil that Abraham their father possessed. When he threw some of it upon his foes, their swords were turned into earth and their arrows became straw, as it is written, *has rendered their swords like dust, their bows like wind-blown straw* (Isa. 41:2)." There was one land the royal forces could not conquer. They tried using the special soil against the enemy and they were victorious. They then brought the earth to the royal treasury and filled the casket with precious stones and pearls and sent Naḥum on his way with much honor. When he stopped again at the same inn, the men there asked him, "What did you bring as a gift that such great honor should be paid you?" He answered, "That which I brought from here." Thinking that their soil must be very valuable, they tore down their houses, gathered up the soil, and brought it to the royal residence. They said, "That earth that he brought here was from our possessions." The soil they brought was examined and found to be unlike the first and all were killed.[69]

Rabbi Ishmael once asked Rabbi Akiba when they were on the road, "You served Naḥum of Gimzo twenty-two years. He expounded the meaning to be derived from all the particles *et* found in the Torah. How did he explain that particle as found twice in the first verse of the Bible?" Rabbi Akiba replied, "If the two particles were omitted, one might have thought that *heaven* and *earth* are names for the Holy One, blessed be He, but as the verse now reads one understands that the meaning is that God created them. The second time the particle *et* is used in the verse is to teach that the creation of heaven preceded the creation of earth."[70]

Rabbi Ishmael asked Rabbi Akiba, "Since you served Naḥum of Gimzo for twenty-two years and he interpreted every instance in the Scriptures where the particle *et* is found, tell me what of the *et* found in the verse, *God was with* [et] *the boy and he grew up* (Gen. 21:20)." He answered, "If the text stated, 'God was the boy' it would be unintelligible." Thereupon, he cited to him, "*This . . . is not too baffling for you* (Deut. 30:11)—meaning, if it is trifling, it is for you, on your account, because you are unable to interpret it rightly. However, *with* [et] *the boy* means 'with him, his mule drivers, his camel drivers, and his household.' "[71]

═══ **11** ═══
Eliezer ben Jacob

Ben Azzai said, "I found a family scroll in Jerusalem and in it was written that a certain man was a bastard and there was also written in it that the teaching of Rabbi Eliezer is small in quantity but excellent in quality. There was written in it also that Menasseh killed Isaiah.[72]

Rabbi Eliezer ben Jacob said, "They once found my mother's brother asleep (at his watch) and burned his garment.[73] Rabbi Eliezer ben Jacob said, "I have heard a tradition that a court may order lashes or even execution although it may not be called for by the law, the purpose being not to transgress the teachings of the Torah but to strengthen it at a critical time. So it happened during the time of the Greek rule that a man was riding a horse on the Sabbath and he was brought before the court, which ordered that he be stoned to death. Not that this was his legal punishment but the times demanded it. It also happened that a man was having intercourse with his wife under a fig tree and he was brought before the court (for indecent behavior) and he was lashed. Not because this was the fit punishment according to law but the times demanded it.[74]

Rabbi Eliezer ben Jacob said that the Gates of Nicanor in the Temple were of Corinthian bronze, which glittered like gold.[75]

Rabbi Eliezer had a disciple whose practice it was to study silently. After three years he forgot all he had studied.[76] He had another disciple who committed a wrong for which he merited execution by fire but they said, "Let him live for he served a great man."[77] At the school of Rabbi Eliezer ben Jacob it was taught that even at a time of danger let not a man remove from himself the mantle of authority, as it is written. *So these men, in their shirts, trousers, hats, and other garments, were bound and thrown into the burning fiery furnace* (Dan. 3:21).[78]

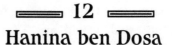

12
Ḥanina ben Dosa

Once Rabbi Ḥanina ben Dosa saw the inhabitants of his city bringing vowed offerings and freewill offerings to Jerusalem. He exclaimed, "All are taking vowed offerings and freewill offerings to Jerusalem and I take nothing!" What did he do? He went out to the waste land of his city and saw there a stone that he chipped, chiseled, and polished. He then vowed, "I take it upon myself to bring it up to Jerusalem." He sought to hire laborers, and five men happened to go by. He asked them, "Will you carry this stone for me up to Jerusalem?" They replied, "Pay us five selas and we will do it." He looked for the coins but at the moment he had no money with him. They left him and went on their way. The Holy One, blessed be He, arranged for five angels to appear to him in the likeness of men. He asked them, "Will you carry up this stone for me?" They answered, "Pay us five selas and we will do it, provided that you help us." He lent his hand and they found themselves standing in Jerusalem. He wanted to pay them the agreed sum but he could not find them. He entered the Hall of Hewn Stones (the locale of the Sanhedrin) and inquired for them. The men there said to him, "It seems that the ministering angels carried your stone up to Jerusalem," and they applied to him this verse, *See a man skilled at his work—he shall attend upon kings* (Prov. 22:29)—"read not *upon kings* (*melakhim*), but read 'upon angels' (*malakhim*) shall he attend."[79]

Once Rabbi Ḥanina ben Dosa was walking along the road

when it began to rain. He prayed, "Master of the Universe, every-one rejoices (because of the rain) but Ḥanina is upset." Whereupon it stopped raining. When he arrived home, he said, "Master of the Universe, Ḥanina is happy, but everyone else is sad." Whereupon the rains came. Rabbi Joseph commented upon this tale, "How could the prayer of even the high priest be compared to that of Rabbi Ḥanina ben Dosa?"[80]

Once in a certain place there was a poisonous lizard that would bite people and do them harm. They told Rabbi Ḥanina ben Dosa about it. He said to them, "Show me its hole." They went and showed him the hole and he placed his heel upon it. The lizard came up, bit him, and at once died. Rabbi Ḥanina carried it on his shoulder to the academy and said to the students, "See, my sons, it is not the lizard that causes death—it is sin that causes death." At that time people would say, "Woe to the man who meets a poison-ous lizard and woe to the lizard who meets Rabbi Ḥanina ben Dosa!"[81]

Every day a heavenly voice goes forth and says, "All the world is granted sustenance only through the merit of Ḥanina, My son, but Ḥanina, My son, is satisfied with one measure of carob to last him from Sabbath eve to Sabbath eve."[82]

Every Sabbath eve the wife of Rabbi Ḥanina would make a fire of twigs in her oven (even though there was no food) so that she would not be embarrassed by her neighbors (seeing no smoke). But she had one unkind neighbor who thought to herself, "Let me see, I know they have nothing. I shall go and look." She went and knocked on their door. Ḥanina's wife, embarrassed, went to her bedroom. A miracle occurred, for her oven suddenly became full of bread and her kneading basin full of dough. The neighbor cried out to her, "Woman, woman, bring your breadshovel or your bread will burn!" Rabbi Ḥanina's wife replied, "I have just gone to fetch it," because she was accustomed to having miracles occur to her.[83]

Rabbi Ḥanina's wife once said to him, "How long shall we suffer so for lack of our daily bread?" He answered, "What can we do?" She said, "Pray for His compassion that He give you something." He prayed and there appeared something like a hand that gave him a leg of a golden table. Later he saw in a dream that in the next world all the righteous were eating on golden tables with three legs and he on a golden table with two legs. He said to his wife, "Would you like it if all the righteous will eat on a golden table with three legs and we on a golden table with two legs?" She said to him, "Pray that the golden leg be taken back." He prayed and it was taken back. We have been taught that this latter miracle was even greater than the first for the tradition has it that Heaven bestows, it does not take back.[84]

One Friday at twilight Rabbi Ḥanina saw that his daughter looked sad. He asked her, "My daughter, why are you sad?" She replied, "Because I confused the oil and the vinegar and I poured the vinegar into the lamp." He said to her, "He who has ordained that oil should burn will decree that the vinegar shall burn." The lamp burned for twenty-four hours so that they could take fire from it to use for the havdalah ceremony the next evening.[85]

Rabbi Ḥanina ben Dosa had several goats and once was told that his goats were causing damage. He declared, "If my goats are indeed doing damage, may bears eat them! But if they are not doing damage, let them each return in the evening with a bear impaled on their horns!" In the evening each goat came with a bear on its horns. And where did the poor Rabbi Ḥanina get goats? The story is that once a man was passing by Rabbi Ḥanina's house and set down some chickens near the door. Rabbi Ḥanina's wife found them but her husband ordered her not to eat their eggs. Eggs and chickens multiplied so that they became a nuisance. She sold them all and with the money purchased goats. Some time later that same man came by again and inquired about the chickens he had left there. Rabbi Ḥanina heard and asked for some mark of identification. He gave identifying signs that satisfied Rabbi Ḥanina and he gave the man the goats. And they are the same goats that brought home bears on their horns.[86]

Rabbi Ḥanina had a neighbor who was building a house whose beams did not quite reach. She told him, "I am building a house and the beams are too short." He asked her, "What is your name?" She replied, "Aikhu." He said to her, "Aikhu, may your beams become longer." The beams became longer. Others say that they made the beams in links, that is, they joined pieces to them. Plimo said, "I saw that house whose beams were extended through the prayer of Rabbi Ḥanina and there was an additional cubit on each side. And people told me that this was the house whose beams were lengthened by Rabbi Ḥanina ben Dosa by means of his prayer."[87]

It once happened that the daughter of Neḥunia the welldigger fell into a deep well and people came and told Rabbi Ḥanina ben

Dosa. One hour went by and he told them, "No harm." After the second hour he told them, "No harm." After the third hour, he told them, "She has come out." Soon she appeared before them and he asked her, "My daughter, who took you out of the well?" She answered, "There went by a ram led by an old man and they rescued me." They asked Rabbi Ḥanina, "Are you then a prophet?" He replied, "Neither a prophet nor the son of a prophet, but I thought to myself, the very thing with which a righteous man is engaged cannot be a source of harm to his children."[88]

They used to say about Rabbi Ḥanina ben Dosa that when he would pray on behalf of the sick, he would say, "This one will live, that one will die." They asked him, "How do you know?" He told them, "If my prayer goes smoothly when I pray for a person, I know my prayer will be accepted. But if it does not, then I know that my prayer is rejected." Once it happened that the son of Rabban Gamaliel fell ill. He sent two scholars to Rabbi Ḥanina ben Dosa to pray for his son. When Rabbi Ḥanina saw the scholars, he went up to the upper story to pray. When he came down, he said to them, "You may go—his fever has left him." They asked him, "Are you then a prophet?" He replied, "Neither a prophet nor the son of a prophet, but I have this tradition, that when my prayer goes smoothly, I know it is accepted; if it does not, I know it has been rejected." They sat and wrote down the exact hour. When they returned to Rabban Gamaliel, he said to them, "By the Temple service! You fulfilled your mission to perfection! At that very hour (written down by you) his fever left him and he asked us for water to drink."[89]

In another story Rabbi Ḥanina ben Dosa went to study Torah under Rabban Johanan ben Zakkai and the master's son fell ill. Rabban Johanan said, "Ḥanina, my son, pray for him that he live." Ḥanina placed the son's head low between his knees and prayed for him and he lived. Whereupon Rabban Johanan ben Zakkai declared, "If my son had kept his head between his knees all the day long—that and nothing else—Heaven would not have responded." His wife asked, "Is then Ḥanina greater than you?" He replied, "No, but in the presence of God he is like a servant before the king, while I am like a prince before the king."[90]

Once Rabbi Ḥanina ben Dosa saw a lion. He said to the lion, "O weak king, have I not besworn you that you make no appearance in the land of Israel!" At once the lion ran away. Rabbi

Hanina ran after him, crying, "I beg your pardon for having called you a weak king when your Creator has called you 'mighty.' "[91]

Once the donkey of Rabbi Hanina ben Dosa was stolen by bandits. They tied it up in a courtyard and set before it hay, barley, and water, but it would neither eat nor drink. They said, "Why should we let it die here and befoul our courtyard with its stench?" So they proceeded to open the gate for it and let it out. The animal dragged itself all the way to the house of Rabbi Hanina ben Dosa. When it arrived, Rabbi Hanina's son heard its cry and exclaimed, "Father, father, the cry is like that of our animal!" Rabbi Hanina said, "My son, open the door for it is almost dead from hunger." He at once opened the door and set before it hay, barley, and water, which it ate and drank. Therefore, as the sages said, "Just as the righteous men of former times were pious, so too were their animals."[92] Rava ben Zemuna said, "If the sages of former times were like angels, then we are like men. And if they were like men, then we are like donkeys. And not like the donkey of Rabbi Hanina ben Dosa nor like the donkey of Phinehas ben Jair but like the ordinary run of donkeys."[93]

Rabbi Hanina ben Dosa said, "He in whom the fear of sin comes before wisdom, his wisdom shall endure. But he in whom wisdom comes before the fear of sin, his wisdom shall not endure." He used to say, "He in whom the spirit of his fellow creatures takes delight, in him the spirit of God takes delight. And he in whom the spirit of his fellow creatures finds no delight, in him the spirit of God finds no delight."[94] When Rabbi Hanina ben Dosa died, that was the end of the men who stressed action.[95] What does the term *magnate* (Isa. 3:3) mean? This refers to such whose merits are responsible for the divine forgiveness of the sins of his generation, like Rabbi Hanina ben Dosa.[96]

Rabbi Jonathan told this story: "Once I was aboard a ship and I saw in the sea a certain chest in which precious stones and pearls were set. Swimming around it was a shark. A diver went down to try to get the chest but it moved and almost broke his thigh. He threw a skin bottle containing vinegar at it and the chest sank. A heavenly voice was heard, saying, 'What have you to do with this chest that belongs to the wife of Rabbi Hanina ben Dosa into which she is destined to spin the purple-blue threads for the righteous in the world to come?' "[97]

══ 13 ══
Ḥananiah ben Hezekiah

The sages taught: Who wrote the Scroll of Taʻanit? Rabbi Ḥananiah and his colleagues who valued the recording of past calamities.[98]

Rabbi Judah said in the name of Rav, "We should remember for good that man, Ḥananiah ben Hezekiah by name. For had it not been for him the Book of Ezekiel would have been suppressed, for its words, in places, contradict the words of the Torah. What did he do? Three hundred kegs of oil (for light) were brought up to his upper chamber where he stayed until he had succeeded in reconciling all the contradictions."[99]

══ 14 ══
Neḥunia ben Ha-kanah

The students of Rabbi Neḥunia ben Ha-kanah asked him, "How have you managed to live so long?" He told them, "Never in my life have I sought honor through the degradation of a colleague, nor has my ill will against any fellowman lasted until bed time. And I was liberal with my money."[100] He taught: Whoever takes upon himself the yoke of the Torah will be delivered from the yoke of the government and the yoke of the search for sustenance. But whoever casts off the yoke of the Torah will have placed upon him the yoke of the government and the yoke of the search for sustenance.[101]

Rabbi Neḥunia ben Ha-kanah used to offer a short prayer

when he entered the house of study and a short prayer when he left. They asked him, "What is the nature of this prayer?" He answered, "When I enter I pray that no offense shall occur because of me and when I leave I offer thanks for my lot." The sages taught, "What did he say when he entered? 'May it be Thy will, O Lord, my God, that no offense shall occur because of me and that I not stumble in matters of law. May my colleagues rejoice in me. May I not pronounce the impure, pure nor the pure, impure. May my colleagues not stumble in matters of law, and may I rejoice in them.' What did he say when he left? 'I thank you, O Lord, my God, that you have placed my lot among those who come to the house of study and not among those who come to the street corners. For I arise and they arise. I arise to the study of words of Torah and they arise to things of vanity. I labor and they labor. I labor and receive reward and they labor and do not receive reward. I hasten and they hasten. I hasten to life eternal and they hasten but to the grave.' "[102]

═══ 15 ═══
Johanan ben Zakkai

Rabban Johanan ben Zakkai received the tradition from Hillel and Shammai. He used to say, "If you have studied much Torah, claim no special merit for yourself. It was for this that you were created."[103]

Hillel the Elder had eighty disciples. Thirty of them were worthy that the Divine Presence should rest upon them as upon Moses our teacher, but their generation was not worthy of it. Thirty of them were worthy that the intercalation of the years should be determined by them, and twenty were average. The greatest of them all was Jonathan ben Uzziel and the least of them all was Rabban Johanan ben Zakkai. Yet Hillel called him "the father of wisdom and the father of coming generations." It was said of Rabban Johanan ben Zakkai that he mastered Scripture,

Mishnah, Talmud, laws and lore, the minutiae of the Torah and the minutiae of the scribes, the hermeneutical rules of the sages, astronomy, arithmetic, the language of angels, the language of evil spirits, the language of palm trees, washers' fables and fox fables, little things as well as matters of great import. Not a word in the Torah did he not master, fulfilling the text, *I endow those who love me with substance; I will fill their treasuries* (Prov. 8:21). It was said of him that never did he speak profane language. He never walked four cubits without studying the Torah and without wearing phylacteries. He never slept in the house of study—neither a long sleep nor a short nap. No one arrived at the house of study earlier than he nor was anyone left there when he departed. He entertained no impure thoughts when passing through filthy alleys. No man ever found him sitting silently but he was always sitting and studying. No man ever opened the door for his students to enter but he. He always greeted the other person first, even a heathen in the market place. He never taught any tradition that he had not heard from his teacher. Never did he say in the house of study that it was time to stop learning except on the eve of Passover and the eve of Yom Kippur. His disciple, Rabbi Eliezer, emulated him in his conduct.[104]

But if the slave declares . . . "I do not wish to be freed," his master . . . shall pierce his ear with an awl; and he shall then remain his slave for life (Exod. 21:5–6). Rabban Johanan ben Zakkai interpreted this verse in a symbolic way, giving the passage an ethical significance: Why was the ear selected of all the parts of the body? For the Holy One, praised be He, said, "The ear that heard My voice on Mount Sinai declare, 'To Me are the children of Israel servants and not servants to other servants,' and yet this fellow went and willingly took a master unto himself, let his ear be pierced!"[105]

The disciples of Rabban Johanan ben Zakkai asked him, "Why was the Torah more severe with the thief than with the robber?" He answered, "The robber at least places the honor of his Creator on the same level as that of His servant, but the thief does not even do that, thinking that the eye of Heaven does not see and the ear of Heaven does not hear." So is it said, *Ha! Those who would hide their plans deep from the Lord! Who do their work in dark places and say, "Who sees us, who takes note of us?"* (Isa. 29:15). And (the evil-doers think), *"The Lord does not see it, the God of Jacob does not pay heed"* (Ps. 94:7). And it is written, *For they say, "The Lord has forsaken the land and the Lord does not see"* (Ezek. 9:9).[106]

The disciples of Rabban Johanan ben Zakkai once asked him a question about a certain matter and he gave them an answer. They said to him, "But on this same matter you taught us otherwise." He said to them, "You have well spoken, for should I forget that which my own hands have done and my own eyes have seen? And in a matter where my own ears have heard, how much more so!" It was not that he really had forgotten the correct answer, but his purpose was to stimulate the thinking of his disciples.[107]

Once Rabban Johanan ben Zakkai asked his disciples, "My sons, what is the meaning of the verse, *Righteousness exalts a nation; sin is a reproach to any people* (Prov. 14:34)?" Rabbi Eliezer replied, "When the verse says, *Righteousness exalts a nation*, it refers to Israel, as it is written, *And who is like Your people Israel, a unique nation on earth?* (2 Sam. 7:23); the second half of the verse, *sin is a reproach to any people*, means that any righteous or pious deed of a heathen people is accounted as a sin, for their purpose is only self-serving, as it is written, *So that they may offer pleasing sacrifices to the God of heaven and pray for the life of the king and his sons* (Ezra 6:10)." Rabbi Joshua answered as did Rabbi Eliezer except for this difference: ". . . any righteous or pious deed of a heathen people is accounted as a sin, for their purpose is only that the life of their kingdom be prolonged, as it is written, *Therefore, O king, may my advice be acceptable to you: Redeem your sins by beneficence and your iniquities by generosity to the poor; then your serenity may be extended* (Dan. 4:24)." Rabban Gamaliel answered as did his colleagues except for this difference: "The heathen do righteous or pious deeds only to boast of them and boasters go to hell, as it is written, *The proud, insolent man, scoffer is his name, acts in a wrath of insolence* (Prov. 21:24). The word *wrath* implies hell, as it is written, *That day shall be a day of wrath* (Zeph. 1:15)." But Rabban Gamaliel went on to say, "For the real interpretation of this verse we still need the Modaite; for Rabbi Eliezer the Modaite explained it as did the others but with this difference: 'The righteous and pious deeds of the heathen peoples are accounted as sins, for their purpose is only to insult Israel, as it is written, *And now the Lord has brought it about. He has acted as He threatened, because you sinned against the Lord and did not obey Him. That is why this has happened to you* (Jer. 40:3)." Then Rabbi Neḥunia ben Hakanah offered his interpretation: *Righteousness exalts a nation* (Prov. 14:34) refers to Israel, for whom it is deemed "piety" as well; however for the heathen peoples, it is accounted as a "sin offering." Whereupon Rabban Johanan ben Zakkai said to his disciples, "I prefer the interpretation of Rabbi Neḥunia ben Hakanah to both your interpretations and mine, for he offers to Israel righteousness and piety and to the heathen nations the opportunity of the sin offering." What had Rabban Johanan ben Zakkai said in this connection? He had said, "Just as a sin offering atones for Israel, so do righteousness and piety atone for the peoples of the world."[108]

Rabban Johanan ben Zakkai said, "Come and see how important is human dignity. When a thief steals, slaughters, and sells an ox that goes about on its feet, he must pay five times its value. But for a sheep, for which the thief had to demean himself by carrying it on his shoulders, he pays only four times its value."[109]

Rabban Johanan ben Zakkai said, "Come and see how concerned is God with the honor of human beings. For when the afraid and disheartened returns (from military service), people will say that it is because he has built a new house (and has had no opportunity to dedicate it) or because he has planted a vineyard (and has not yet eaten of its fruit) or because he has spoken for a woman (and not yet married her), and in all these cases witnesses are required except for the case of the afraid and disheartened who needs no further proof."[110]

Once it happened that Rabban Johanan ben Zakkai was riding out of Jerusalem on his donkey and his disciple, Rabbi Eleazar ben Arakh, was riding behind him. The latter asked, "My master, teach me a chapter concerning the mystical subject of the Divine Chariot." To which Rabban Johanan replied, "My son, have I not taught you and the others that this subject is not to be taught to a single individual alone unless he be a wise man who can understand through his own knowledge?" Rabbi Eleazar then said, "My master, permit me to say one thing that you have taught me." Rabban Johanan answered, "Speak!" and so saying he at once got down off his donkey, wrapped his garment around himself, and sat down on a stone beneath an olive tree. Rabbi Eleazar asked, "My master, why have you dismounted from the donkey?" He replied, "How can I remain riding on a donkey when you are about to discuss the mystical subject of the Divine Chariot and the Heavenly Presence will attend us and the ministering angels accompany us?" At once Rabbi Eleazar ben Arakh began to expound upon the subject of the Divine Chariot. Suddenly a fiery flame leaped down from the heavens lighting all the trees in the field and the trees broke out in song. What song did they sing? *Praise the Lord, O you who are on earth, all sea monsters and ocean depths, . . . all fruit trees and cedars, . . . Hallelujah* (Ps. 148:7, 9, 14). From out of the fire an angel responded and declared, "Surely this is truly spoken concerning the Divine Chariot." Rabban Johanan ben Zakkai stood up and kissed Rabbi Eleazar on his forehead and said, "Blessed be the Lord, God of Israel, who has given a descendant to Abraham our father like Eleazar ben Arakh, who is able to understand, to investigate deeply and to expound upon the subject of the Divine Chariot. There are those who teach well but do not do well or who do well but do not teach well, but you, Eleazar ben Arakh, you teach well and do well. Happy are you, Abraham our father, that Eleazar ben Arakh has sprung forth from your loins!"

This story was told to Rabbi Joshua when he and Rabbi Jose the priest were riding along the road. They said to each other, "We too shall expound upon the subject of the Divine Chariot." Rabbi Joshua began—that day was during the month of Tammuz, the dry season—when suddenly clouds covered the sky and something like a rainbow appeared in the clouds. And the ministering angels gathered to hear, like people who crowd around to hear the musical entertainment at a wedding. Rabbi Jose the priest recounted all this to Rabban Johanan ben Zakkai. He exclaimed, "Blessed are you both and blessed those who gave you birth! Blessed are my eyes that have beheld this! I too have had a dream in which you two and I were seated on Mount Sinai and we heard a heavenly voice—'Come you here! Come you here! Great banqueting couches are spread for you with beautiful cloths. You, your disciples, and your disciples' disciples are invited to the Third Order.' "[111]

Once it happened that Rabban Johanan ben Zakkai had a dream in which he saw that his sister's sons would lose seven hundred dinars. He asked them to give him this amount for charity. They secretly retained seventeen dinars. On the eve of Yom Kippur officials came and seized the seventeen dinars. Rabban Johanan said to them, "Do not be upset, you kept seventeen dinars and it was that sum that was taken from you." They asked, "How did you know?" He replied, "I saw it all in my dream." Whereupon they asked, "Why did you not tell us and we would have given you the entire amount for charity?" "Because," he answered, "I wanted you to give charity for its own sake."[112]

Concerning the details of measuring bulk merchandise, Rabban Johanan ben Zakkai said, "Woe is me if I explain it and woe is me if I do not. Woe is me if I do, for the swindlers will also learn how to cheat their customers. Woe is me if I do not, for then swindlers will say that the scholars are no experts in their trade." Did Rabban Johanan finally teach it or not? Rabbi Samuel son of Rabbi Isaac said that he did and he found support in this verse, *For the paths of the Lord are smooth; the righteous can walk on them, while sinners stumble on them* (Hos. 14:10).[113]

There was a certain family in Jerusalem whose members would die at the age of eighteen. They came to tell Rabban Johanan ben Zakkai. He said to them, "You may be, perhaps, descendants of Eli of whom it is written, *all the increase of your house shall die as [ordinary] men* (1 Sam. 2:33). Go, study the Torah and you will live." They went and studied the Torah and they did live. Their family was thereafter called by his name, the family of Johanan.[114]

It is related of Rabban Johanan that he once grew very faint because of hunger. He went to Emmaus and ate of its figs and was cured. He was asked, "How do you know that the fig is a remedy?" He replied, "From David, as it is written, *He was also given a piece of pressed fig cake. . . . He ate and regained his strength* (1 Sam. 30:12)." They applied to him the text, *The advantage of intelligence is that wisdom preserves the life of him who possesses it.* (Eccles. 7:12).[115]

Simon of Sikhnin was a clever man who used to dig wells, trenches, and caves in Jerusalem. Once he said to Rabban Johanan ben Zakkai, "I am as great a man as you." "How is that?" he was asked, to which he replied, "I work for the public as do you. If a man comes to you for a decision or for an inquiry, you tell him to drink from a certain well that I dug, whose waters are pure and cold. Or if a woman questions you concerning her ritual impurity, you tell her to immerse herself in a certain well that I dug, whose waters cleanse." The rabbi applied to him this verse, *More acceptable is obedience than the offering of fools, for they know nothing [but] to do wrong* (Eccles. 4:17).[116]

Rabban Johanan ben Zakkai had five outstanding disciples: Rabbi Eliezer ben Hyrcanus, Rabbi Joshua ben Ḥananiah, Rabbi Jose the priest, Rabbi Simon ben Netanel, and Rabbi Eleazar ben Arakh. He would praise their qualities in this fashion: Eliezer ben Hyrcanus, a cemented cistern that does not lose a drop of its water; Joshua ben Ḥananiah—happy is she who bore him; Jose the priest, a most pious man; Simon ben Netanel, a sin-fearing person; Eleazar ben Arakh, a spring flowing ever more strongly. He would say, "If all the sages of Israel were placed on one scale of the balance and Rabbi Eliezer ben Hyrcanus on the other, he would outweigh them all." But Abba Saul quoted Rabban Johanan as having said that if all the sages of Israel, including Eliezer ben Hyrcanus, were placed on one balance of the scale and Eleazar ben Arakh on the other, he would outweigh them all.[117]

When the son of Rabban Johanan ben Zakkai died, his disciples came to console him. Rabbi Eliezer came and sat before him and asked, "Master, is it your wish that I say a word in your presence?" He replied, "Speak." He said, "Adam, the first man, had a son who died and he permitted himself to be comforted in his loss. Whence do we know that? It is stated, *Adam knew his wife again* (Gen. 4:25). So should you also be comforted." He retorted, "Is it not enough that I have my own grief that you must also mention Adam's grief?" Then Rabbi Joshua entered and asked, "My master, is it your wish that I say a word in your presence?" He answered, "Speak." He said, "Job had sons and daughters who all died in one day and he permitted himself to be comforted; you too should find comfort. How do we know that Job found comfort? It is written, *The Lord has given, and the Lord has taken away; blessed be the name of the Lord* (Job 1:21)." He retorted, "Is it not enough that I have my own grief, that you must also mention Job's grief?" Next Rabbi Jose entered and asked, "My Master, is it your wish that I say a word in your presence?" He replied, "Speak." He said, "Aaron had two grown sons and both died in one day, yet he allowed himself to be comforted, as it is said, *And Aaron was silent* (Lev. 10:3), signifying that he was comforted. Therefore, you too be comforted." He retorted, "Is it not enough that I have my own grief that you must mention Aaron's grief?" Rabbi Simon then came in and asked, "My master, is it your wish that I say a word in your presence?" He replied, "Speak." He said, "King David had a son who died, yet he allowed himself to be comforted; you too be comforted." How do we know that David was comforted? It is stated, *David consoled his wife Bathsheba; he went to her and lay with her. She bore a son and she named him Solomon* (2 Sam. 12:24)." He retorted, "Is it not enough that I have to bear my own grief that you have to mention King David's grief?" Finally Rabbi Eleazar ben Arakh entered. When Rabban Johanan saw him coming, he said to his attendant, "Take my clothes and follow me to the bathhouse because this man is so distinguished and I cannot appear before him as I am." Then Rabbi Eleazar came in and said, "Let me tell you a parable. To what is the matter like? To the example of a man with whom a king had deposited an article of value. Every day the man wept and cried out, 'Woe is me! When shall I be free of the responsibility of this trust?' You, too, my master, had a son versed in the Torah, who had studied the Pentateuch, Prophets, and Hagiographa, Mishnah, laws, and legends—and he departed from this world sinless. Surely you should derive comfort from having returned your trust intact!" Rabban Johanan said to him, "Eleazar, my son, you have comforted me as much as man can comfort."[118]

Rabban Johanan said to his disciples, "Go and see which is the good way to which a man should cleave." Rabbi Eliezer said, "A good eye"; Rabbi Joshua, "a good friend"; Rabbi Jose, "a good neighbor"; Rabbi Simon, "foreseeing the consequences of an action"; Rabbi Eleazar, "a good heart." He said to them, "I prefer the answer of Eleazar ben Arakh, for your answers are all included in his."

He said to them, "Go forth and see which is the evil way from which a man should keep his distance." Rabbi Eliezer said, "An evil eye"; Rabbi Joshua, "A bad friend"; Rabbi Jose, "A bad neighbor"; Rabbi Simon, "A borrower who does not repay," whether from man or from God, as it is said, *The wicked man borrows and does not repay; the righteous is generous and keeps giving* (Ps. 37:21); Rabbi Eleazar, "An evil heart." He said to them, "I prefer the answer of Eleazar ben Arakh, for your answers are all included in his."[119]

Rabban Johanan ben Zakkai was asked, "How would you describe the man who is both learned and sin-fearing?" He answered, "He is a craftsman who has the tools of his craft in his hand." "And the man who is learned and not sin-fearing?" He replied, "He is a craftsman who does not have the tools of his craft in his hand." "And the man who is sin-fearing but not learned?" He replied, "He is no craftsman although he has the craftsman's tools in his hand."[120]

What were the beginnings of Rabbi Eliezer ben Hyrcanus? He was twenty-two years old and had not as yet studied Torah. One day he said to his father, "I shall go and study Torah with Rabban Johanan ben Zakkai." His father, Hyrcanus, replied, "You shall not taste a morsel of food until you shall have ploughed a complete furrow." He rose early in the morning and ploughed the entire furrow and left. It is told that that day was the eve of the Sabbath and he went for the Sabbath meal to the house of his father-in-law. Some say he tasted nothing from six hours before the Sabbath to six hours after the Sabbath. As he was walking on the way he saw a stone. He picked it up and put it in his mouth. Some say it was cattle dung. He kept on walking until he came to an inn where he spent the night. Then he finally came to Rabban Johanan Zakkai in Jerusalem and sat before him. A bad breath came from his mouth and Rabban Johanan ben Zakkai asked him, "Eliezer, my son, have you eaten anything today?" He did not reply. The same question was put to him again and he still remained silent. The innkeeper was sent for and was asked, "Did Eliezer eat with you?" He replied, "I thought that he would eat with you, my master." "And I thought that he had likely eaten at your table," said Rabban Johanan. "Between us we could have lost Rabbi Eliezer." Then Rabban Johanan said to Eliezer, "Just as a bad breath came forth from your mouth, so will your name go forth as a master of the Torah."

When his father, Hyrcanus, heard that he was studying Torah with Rabban Johanan ben Zakkai, he declared, "I shall go and ban my son, Eliezer, from deriving any benefit from my estate." It is told that on that day Rabban Johanan ben Zakkai was expounding the Torah in Jerusalem and the notables of Israel were sitting before him. When he heard that Hyrcanus was coming, he appointed guards and told them, "If Hyrcanus comes, do not let him sit down." When he arrived and wished to sit, they did not let him. He was compelled to move forward until he reached the place where Ben Zizit Ha-Kasat, Nakdimon ben Guryon, and Ben Kalba Savua were sitting. He sat down near them overawed. It is told that on that day Rabban Johanan ben Zakkai turned to Rabbi Eliezer and asked him to begin the exposition. "I am unable to speak," he said. The master and the other disciples urged him, whereupon he began the discourse and expounded matters that no ear had ever heard before. As the words came from his mouth, Rabban Johanan ben Zakkai stood up and kissed him on the head. But Rabbi Eliezer exclaimed, "It is you, my master, who have taught me the truth." Before the time of adjournment arrived, his father, Hyrcanus, stood up and said, "My masters, I came here for the purpose of banning my son, Eliezer, from my possessions. Now all my property shall be given to my son, Eliezer, and all his brothers are hereby dispossessed and deprived of everything."[121]

Rabban Johanan ben Zakkai had one opinion and Rabbi Akiba later on had another, said Rabbi Judah. One maintained that when the Lord made a covenant with Abram, He revealed this world to him—the future of the Jewish people in this world. The other held that He revealed to him both this world and the next.[122]

The verse in Ecclesiastes reads, *Let your clothes be always white and your head never lack oil* (Eccles. 9:8). Rabban Johanan ben Zakkai was of the opinion that this verse cannot be taken literally. He said, "If the text speaks of white garments, how many of these do the peoples of the world have? And if it speaks of good oil, how much of it do the peoples of the world possess? Therefore, it must refer to precepts, good deeds, and Torah."[123]

Once an idolater asked Rabban Johanan ben Zakkai, "These ceremonies that you perform look like a kind of witchcraft. You bring a heifer, burn it, pound it, and then take its ashes. If one of you is defiled by a dead body, you sprinkle upon him two or three drops of the ashes' mixture and say to him, 'You are clean!' " Rabban Johanan asked him, "Has the demon of madness ever possessed you?" "No," he replied. "Have you ever seen a man possessed by this demon of madness?" "Yes," said he. "And what do you do in such a case?" "We bring roots," he replied, "and make them smoke under him, then we sprinkle water upon the demon and it flees." Rabban Johanan said to him, "Do not your ears hear what your mouth is saying? Exactly so is this spirit of uncleanness—as it is written, *And I will also make the prophets and the unclean spirit vanish from the land* (Zech. 13:2). Water of purification is sprinkled upon the unclean and the spirit flees." When the idolater had gone, Rabban Johanan's disciples said to him, "Master! This man you have put off with a makeshift explanation, but how will you explain it to us?" He replied, "By your life! It is not the dead that defiles nor the mixture of ashes and water that purifies! The Holy One, blessed be He, simply says, 'I have laid down a statute, I have issued a decree. You are not permitted to transgress my decree.' So is it written, *This is the ritual law that the Lord has commanded* (Num. 19:2)."[124]

Once a heathen put a question to Rabban Johanan ben Zakkai, "We have festivals and you have festivals. We have the kalends, Saturnalia, and Kratesis. You have Passover, Pentecost, and Tabernacles. Which is the day when we rejoice alike?" Rabban Johanan ben Zakkai replied, "The day when rain falls. For it is said, *The meadows are clothed with flocks, the valleys mantled with grain; they raise a shout, they break into song* (Ps. 65:14). And what follows immediately afterward? *A song, a psalm. Raise a shout for God, all the earth* (Ps. 66:1).[125]

The Roman general, Agentus, put a question to Rabban Johanan ben Zakkai, "Moses, your teacher, was either a thief or else he did not know arithmetic." Said he to him, "Why?" "Because," answered Agentus, "there were twenty-two thousand firstborn plus an additional two hundred and seventy-three, and the Omnipresent commanded that the Levites should redeem the firstborn. Reckon twenty-two thousand Levites against the twenty-two thousand firstborn. Now there were still three hundred Levites over and above the twenty-two thousand, as is calculated in detail in the first numbering. Why did these three hundred Levites not redeem the two hundred and seventy-three firstborn who were over and above the twenty-two thousand firstborn? Instead, we find that those two hundred and seventy-three gave five shekels each! Moreover, why is it that when Moses sums up the number of Levites at the end, he deducts three hundred of them from the original number? Evidently he subtracted them from the correct number so that the two hundred and seventy-three firstborn might each give five shekels to his brother, Aaron. Or was he perhaps unable to do arithmetic?" Rabban Johanan ben Zakkai said to him, "He was no thief and he knew arithmetic. But there is one thing He whispered to me that I should tell you." He said to him, "Say it." Rabban Johanan said to him, "You are able to read the Scripture, but you cannot expound it. Moses thought those twenty-two thousand Levites will redeem the twenty-two thousand firstborn, but there will still remain of the Levites another three hundred, and of the firstborn another two hundred and seventy-three. Now those three hundred Levites were firstborn themselves and a firstborn cannot redeem another firstborn.

Therefore, when he added up their number, he omitted them because they were firstborn." Having heard the explanation Agentus took his leave of him.[126]

For forty years before the destruction of the Temple the lot never appeared in the right hand, the tongue of crimson wool did not turn white, the westernmost light in the candelabrum did not burn, and the Temple gates opened by themselves. Until Rabban Johanan ben Zakkai rebuked them, saying "O Temple, Temple, why play a role in your own destruction? I know that you are destined for destruction. Zechariah ben Iddo has prophesied about you, *Throw open your gates, O Lebanon, and let fire consume your cedars!* (Zech. 11:1)."[127] When adulterers became many, the rite of the bitter waters ceased. And it was Rabban Johanan ben Zakkai who put an end to it.[128]

For three and a half years Vespasian surrounded Jerusalem, and four generals were with him: the generals of Arabia, Africa, Alexandria, and Palestine. Two teachers differed as to the name of the general of Arabia, one saying it was Killus, the other, Pangar. In Jerusalem there were four councilors: Ben Zizit, Ben Guryon, Ben Nakdimon, and Ben Kalba Savua. Each of them was capable of supplying food for the city for ten years, so wealthy were they. The nephew of Rabban Johanan ben Zakkai, Ben Batiah, was appointed in charge of the stores. He arose and burned down the storehouses so that the people would go out to fight to obtain food. When Rabban Johanan ben Zakkai heard of this he exclaimed, "Woe!" It was reported to Ben Batiah, "Your uncle exclaimed, 'Woe!'" He had him brought before him and asked, "Why did you exclaim 'Woe'?" He replied, "I did not exclaim 'Woe' but "Wah.'" He asked, "Why did you make that exclamation?" He answered, "Because so long as the stores were intact the people would not expose themselves to the dangers of battle." Through the difference between *Woe* and *Wah* Rabban Johanan escaped death; and the verse was applied to him, *The advantage of intelligence is that wisdom preserves the life of him who possesses it* (Eccles. 7:12).[129]

Three days later Rabban Johanan ben Zakkai went out to walk in the marketplace and saw how people boiled straw and drank its water. He said to himself, "Can men who boil straw and drink its water resist the armies of Vespasian?" He concluded, "I must leave here."

When Vespasian came to destroy Jerusalem, he proclaimed

to its people, "Fools, why do you seek to destroy this city and burn the Temple? What do I ask of you? Merely that you deliver to me one bow or one arrow and then I shall leave." They answered him, "As we went forth against your two predecessors and slew them, so we will go out against you and slay you." When Rabban Johanan ben Zakkai heard this, he appealed to the men of Jerusalem, "My sons, why would you destroy this city and burn the Temple? What does he ask of you? Only one bow or one arrow and then he will leave." They answered, "As we went forth against his two predecessors and slew them, so we shall go out against him and slay him."

Some men loyal to Vespasian lived within the walls of Jerusalem and close to them and whatever they heard they wrote upon an arrow and shot it beyond the wall. So they reported that Rabban Johanan ben Zakkai was a friend of Caesar.

After he had pleaded with the men of Jerusalem for several days and they would not agree with him, he sent a message to Ben Batiah, also called Abba Sikra, his sister's son, "Come to me so that no one knows." When he came, Rabban Johanan said to him, "How long will you carry on this way, resulting in starvation for all the people?" He answered, "What can I do? If I say anything, the others will kill me." "Find some way for me to leave the city," said Rabban Johanan, "perhaps there will be some chance of rescuing something." He replied, "We have made an agreement among ourselves that none shall leave the city but the dead. Therefore, pretend to be sick and let people come to visit you. Get something with a bad odor and let the smell become overpowering, and people will then say you have died. Then let your disciples carry you out and no one else, so that they will not be able to sense that you are light in weight and so understand that you are alive"—for a live person is lighter than a dead one. He carried out this procedure. Then Rabbi Eliezer carried him by the head and Rabbi Joshua by the feet and Abba Sikra walked in front. When they reached the city gate, the guards asked, "What is this?" They replied, "A dead man. Do you not know that a corpse may not be kept overnight in Jerusalem?" They wanted to pierce him through to make certain he was a corpse. Abba Sikra said to them, "The Romans will say, 'They pierced through their own Master!'" They then wished to throw him down. Abba Sikra said, "They will say that you threw down the body of our teacher." They opened the gate and the group left. Rabban Johanan was carried to a cemetery outside the city; the others left him there and returned. He went to the camp of Vespasian and asked the soldiers, "Where is the king?" They went and told Vespasian, "A Jew is asking for you." He said to them, "Let him enter." When he came in he exclaimed, "Peace be to you, O king! Peace be to you, O king!" Vespasian said to him, "You deserve execution twice: first, because I am no king and should the king hear about it, he will put me to death. Secondly, if I am a king, why have you not come to me before this?" He answered, "If you are not now the king, you will be, because the Temple will only be destroyed by the hand of a king, as it is written, *And the Lebanon trees shall fall in their majesty* (Isa. 10:34), *majesty* means a king, and Lebanon refers to the Temple, as it is said, *That good hill country, and the Lebanon* (Deut. 3:25). As to your second question—if you are a king, why did I not come sooner—our rebels did not permit me." They took him and placed him in the innermost of seven chambers—into which no light could seep through —and asked him what hour of the night it was and he told them. How did he know it? From his studying.

Three days later Vespasian went to take a bath at Gofna. After he had bathed and put on one of his shoes, a courier arrived from Rome and exclaimed, "Rise, Nero has died and the nobles of Rome have chosen you as king." He wished to put on the other shoe but it would not go on his foot. He sent for Rabban Johanan and asked, "Explain to me why it is that these two shoes always fitted me and now one fits and the other does not." He replied, "Do not be concerned. It is because you have been told good news, as it is written, *Good news puts fat on the bones* (Prov. 15:30). "What is the cure for the condition?" Vespasian asked. He answered, "Is there someone you hate or who has done you wrong? Let him pass before you and your flesh will shrink, as it is written, *Despondency dries up the bones* (Prov. 17:22). He did as he was advised.

Then they began to speak to Rabban Johanan in riddles, in order to trap him. "If a snake rested in a cask, what is to be done?" He replied, "Bring a snake charmer to charm the snake out and leave the cask intact." Pangor, the general of Arabia, said, "Kill the snake and break the cask." Then they asked, "If a snake rested in a tower, what is to be done?" Rabban Johanan answered, "Bring a snake charmer to charm away the snake and leave the tower intact." Pangar said, "Kill the snake and burn the tower." Rabban

Johanan said to Pangar, "All neighbors who do harm, in the end do harm to their neighbors' neighbors. Instead of pleading in our defense, you argue against us!" He replied, "I seek your welfare. As long as the Temple exists, the heathen kingdoms will attack you. Once it is destroyed, they will not longer attack you." Rabban Johanan said to him, "The heart knows whether it is for *akel* or *akalkalot!*"

Vespasian said to Rabban Johanan ben Zakkai, "I am about to leave this area and another will be sent in my place. Ask of me something and I shall grant it." He answered, "I beg that you abandon this city of Jerusalem and depart." He said to him, "Did the Romans proclaim me king that I should abandon this city? Make some other request of me and I shall grant it." He replied, "I beg that you leave the Western Gate that leads to Lod and permit everyone who leaves up to the fourth hour to be spared." He then said to him, "Give me Jabneh with its sages and the descendants of Rabban Gamaliel."

When the city was about to fall, Vespasian asked Rabban Johanan, "Have you any friend or relative there? Send and bring him out before the troops enter." Rabban Johanan sent Rabbi Eliezer and Rabbi Joshua to bring out Rabbi Zadok. They went and found him in the city gate. When he arrived Rabban Johanan stood up before him. Vespasian asked, "You stand up before this emaciated old man?" He answered, "By your life, if there were in Jerusalem one more like him, you would not be able to conquer it." He asked, "What is his power?" He replied, "He eats one fig and on the strength of it teaches at one hundred sessions in the academy." "Why is he so lean?" he inquired. "Because of his many abstinences and fasts," was the answer. Vespasian sent and brought physicians who fed Rabbi Zadok on small doses of liquid until his strength returned to him. What was the nature of the remedy? On the first day they gave him bran water to drink, on the next day coarse flour water mixed with bran, on the following day flour water, until bit by bit his intestines were healed. His son Eleazar said to him, "Father, give them their reward in this world so that they should have no merit in the world to come because of their treatment of you." He gave them calculation by fingers and scales for weighing.

When Vespasian had subdued the city, he assigned the destruction of the four ramparts to the four generals. The Western Gate was allocated to Pangar. It had been decreed by Heaven that this should never be destroyed because the Shekhinah dwelt in the west. The others demolished their sections but he did not demolish his. Vespasian sent for him and asked, "Why did you not destroy your section?" He replied, "By your life, I acted so for the honor of the kingdom, for had I demolished it, nobody would know in the time to come what it was that you destroyed. When people will look at the Western Wall, they will exclaim, 'See how great was the might of Vespasian from what he destroyed!'" He said, "Enough! You have spoken well, but since you have disobeyed my command, you shall go up to the roof and throw yourself down. If you live, you shall live, if you die, you will die." Pangar went up, threw himself down, and died. Thus the curse of Rabban Johanan ben Zakkai was fulfilled for him.[130]

At the moment Jerusalem was captured Rabban Johanan was sitting and anxiously waiting for the news, as Eli had sat and waited for news, as it is stated, *Eli [was] sitting on a seat, waiting beside the road—his heart trembling for the Ark of God* (1 Sam. 4:13). As soon as Rabban Johanan ben Zakkai heard that Jerusalem was destroyed and the Temple in flames, he rent his clothes, his disciples did the same, and they wept, cried out, and lamented.[131] The words *her downfall*, in the verse *[enemies] gloated over her downfall* (Lam. 1:7), alludes to Rabban Johanan ben Zakkai who no longer lived in Jerusalem.[132]

Why does Scripture use the term *notable person* in the verse, *And all the houses of Jerusalem he burned down, and the house of every notable person* (2 Kings 25:9; Jer. 52:13)? Because it has in mind a particular house, the study house of Rabban Johanan ben Zakkai, where they used to acclaim the greatness of the Holy One, blessed be He.[133]

Justice, justice shall you pursue (Deut. 16:20) can be interpreted to mean: "Follow after an excellent court of scholars, for example, after Rabban Johanan ben Zakkai to Bror Ḥayil." It may also be interpreted as follows: "Follow after the wise to an academy of learning, for example, after Rabban Johanan ben Zakkai to Bror Ḥayil."[134]

It once happened that Rabban Johanan ben Zakkai was coming out of Jerusalem, followed by Rabbi Joshua, and he beheld the Temple in ruins. "Woe to us," cried Rabbi Joshua, "for this House that lies in ruins, the place where atonement was effected for the sins of Israel!" Rabban Johanan said to him, "My son, be not grieved, for we have another means of atonement which is as effective, and that is the practice of loving-kindness, as it is said, *For I desire goodness, not sacrifice* (Hos. 6:6)."[135]

On the first Rosh Hashanah after the destruction the question arose whether to sound the shofar in Jabneh. Until then it had been permitted only in the Temple. "Let us debate the matter in assembly," said some of the sages. Rabban Johanan ben Zakkai declared, "There is no time for debate; it is a time to act." The shofar was sounded. "Let us now debate," they said. "We have already set a precedent," he answered.[136]

Rabban Johanan taught, "If you have a seedling in your hand and they say to you, 'Look, here comes the Messiah!'—go and plant the seedling first and then come out to meet him."[137]

He used to say, "He who dies in a tranquil frame of mind, it is a good omen for him; if in a state of delirium, it is a bad omen for him. If while speaking, it is a good omen; if while silent it is a bad omen. If while conversing about the Torah, it is a good omen; about business matters, it is a bad omen. If while engaged in a religious act, it is a good omen; upon a worthless pursuit it is a bad omen. If in the midst of a joyous atmosphere, it is a good omen; amidst sadness, it is a bad omen. If he dies smiling, it is a good omen; if weeping it is a bad omen. If he dies on the eve of the Sabbath, it is a good omen; at the conclusion of the Sabbath, it is a bad omen. If he dies on the eve of the Day of Atonement, it is a bad omen; at the conclusion of the Day of Atonement, it is a good omen."[138]

When Rabban Johanan ben Zakkai was about to depart from this world, his disciples came to visit him. When he saw them he began to weep. They said to him, "Our Master! Light of Israel! Exalted pillar! Mighty hammer! Why do you weep?" He replied, "If I were now to be brought before a mortal king, who is here today and in the grave tomorrow, who, if he be angry with me, his anger does not last forever, if he imprison me, it is not an eternal imprisonment, if he kills me, my death is only for this world, and it might even be possible for me to appease him or to bribe him—and yet, were I now about to appear before such a mortal king, I would weep. But now, I am about to be brought before the King who is King of Kings, the Holy One, blessed be He, who lives and exists forever and for all time, who, if He be angry at me, His anger is forever, if He imprison me, His imprisonment is for all time, if He slay me, my death is forever and Him I cannot appease or bribe—more, before me there are two roads, one to Paradise and the other to Gehenna and I know not along which I am to be brought—with all this, should I not weep?"

They said to him, "Master, bless us!" He answered, "May it be His will that you should fear Heaven as you fear men." They said, "Master, no more than that?" He replied, "Would that it were so! Know, that when a man commits a transgression, he says, 'I hope no *person* sees me.'" As he was about to die, he said to them, "Remove all vessels from the house that they be not defiled and prepare a throne for Hezekiah, king of Judah, who will soon come!"[139]

The years of Rabban Johanan ben Zakkai were one hundred and twenty. Forty years he engaged in affairs of business, forty years he studied, forty years he taught.[140] When Rabban Johanan died, the glory of learning died with him.[141]

Rabbi Joshua said, "I have received as a tradition from Rabban Johanan ben Zakkai, who heard it from his teacher, and his teacher from his teacher, as a halakhah given to Moses from Sinai, that Elijah will come not to declare families unclean or clean or to remove them afar or to bring them closer but to remove afar those families who were brought close by violence and to bring closer those who were removed afar by violence."[142]

Rabbi Joshua exclaimed, "O Rabban Johanan ben Zakkai, who will remove the dust from your eyes? All your days you expounded that Job served God out of fear, as it is said of him, *that man was blameless and upright; he feared God and shunned evil* (Job 1:1). Now Joshua ben Hyrcanus, your disciple's disciple, has taught that Job served God out of love (Job 13:15, 27:5)."[143] As long as Rabban Johanan ben Zakkai lived, his five disciples sat before him. When he died, they went to Jabneh."[144]

Notes

VIII. THE FIRST GENERATION OF TANNAIM

1. The School of Shammai and the School of Hillel

1. Genesis Rabbah 1:15; Leviticus Rabbah 36:1; Ḥagigah 12a.

Hillel and Shammai are considered the last of the *zugot,* the pairs. Their students in the schools bearing their names are counted among the first generation of tannaim (see Strack, *Introduction to the Talmud,* p. 109).

2. Genesis Rabbah 14:5; Leviticus Rabbah 14:9. The new translation of *The Prophets* (Philadelphia, 1978) translates all these verbs in the past tense. The school of Hillel understood them to be in the future.

3. Eruvin 13b.

4. Avot de-Rabbi Natan 2:9.

5. Eruvin 13b; Yerushalmi Yevamot, end of chap. 1. Evidently the members of the school of Hillel practiced the ethical virtues of their founder. A. Hyman (*Toledot tannaim ve-amoraim,* 1:373) states that the total number of differences of opinions between the two schools was 316. He lists nine instances where the school of Hillel deferred to the opinions of the school of Shammai and cites Yerushalmi Beiẓah 1:3 and Sotah, end of chap. 4, as stating that in twenty-four cases the school of Shammai was more lenient in its decisions than the school of Hillel. In all the others the reverse was true. In a few instances the law was ultimately fixed as being in accordance with neither school (see Eduyyot 1:2–4).

6. Rosh Ha-Shanah 16b–17a.

7. Ketubbot 16b. The disciples of Shammai, being literalists, would describe the bride exactly as she is when dancing before her at a wedding. The followers of Hillel, true to their master, were more compassionate and did not mind stretching the truth, if need be, for the sake of kindness and consideration toward the bride at the moment of her great personal happiness.

8. Yevamot 1:4; Yevamot 13a–b; Eduyyot 4:8. The last-mentioned practice referred to the fact that the members of the two schools did not hesitate to borrow vessels and utensils from each other despite their differences in laws of ritual cleanliness. The uprising of the Zealots against Rome was not approved by the disciples of Hillel, not because of the latter's love of Rome but because they were so convinced of the great importance of the study of Torah that by comparison all political ambitions paled into insignificance (see J. Klausner, *The Messianic Idea in Israel* [New York, 1955], p. 393). The verse from Zechariah is better understood here in the Hebrew, the second object of "love" is *shalom,* "peace," rather than "integrity."

2. Ben Bag Bag and Ben He He

9. Avot 5:35; Avot de-Rabbi Natan 12:10, 23a–b (quoted in Hillel's name). Ben Bag Bag and Ben He He are reputed to have been students of Hillel. Ben Bag Bag's first name was Johanan (Kiddushin 10b; Yerushalmi Ketubbot 5:4). His patronymic, some authorities believe, indicates that either he, his father, or an earlier ancestor was a proselyte. The theory is that the patronymic is an acronym for *Ben Ger Bat Ger,* "son of a proselyte, daughter of a proselyte," or an acronym for *Ben Gerim,* "a son of proselytes." Tosafot, Ḥagigah 9b, quotes Rashbam to say both Ben Bag Bag and Ben He He were proselytes, Ben He He meaning a son of Abraham and Sarah, to whose respective names God added the letter, *he,* and who are the spiritual parents of all proselytes. *Bag* equals *he* in the numerical value of the

letters. One suggestion is that Ben Bag Bag was the heathen turned proselyte who asked Hillel to teach him the entire Torah while he stood on one foot. W. Bacher (*Aggadot ha-tannaim* [Tel Aviv, 1928]) suggests that Ben Bag Bag may have been the heathen later turned proselyte who desired to learn only the Written Torah but who rejected the Oral Torah and who was cured by Hillel of his contempt for the oral tradition by showing him that the very names of the letters of the alphabet depended on oral tradition. B[*et*] and g[*imel*], the second and third letters of the Hebrew alphabet, thus constituted his name or nickname. The same could hold for Ben He He, *he* being the fifth letter. Here Ben Bag Bag teaches the all-inclusive aspect of the Torah. All wisdom is to be found in it, provided the study of Torah is lifelong and its contents examined in depth and repeatedly.

10. Bava Kamma 27b.

11. Avot 5:26; Avot de-Rabbi Natan 12:10, 23b (quoted in Hillel's name). See previous note on Ben Bag Bag. Evidently a popular proverb is here applied to the study of Torah. This and the teaching of Ben Bag Bag above are in Aramaic. The suggestion has been made that both these names are, in reality, the names of the same person, since the numerical value of *b-g*, five, is indicated by the letter *he* (see Tosefta Ḥagigah 9b). Tosafot Yom Tov on Avot ad locum says the names of these two scholars are omitted and only their patronymics given, because they did not live long (cf. Ben Zoma and Ben Azzai, Avot 4:1–2). See the earlier section on Hillel for a dialogue between him and Ben He He.

12. Ḥagigah 9b. Another opinion in the Talmud states that the question was asked of Rabbi Eleazar. The Hebrew word for *affliction* has the same root as the word for *poverty*, hence the deduction that poverty and hardship refine a people.

3. Akavyah ben Mahalelel

13. Avot 3:1; Avot de-Rabbi Natan 19:1. (Cf. Ecclesiastes Rabbah on Eccles. 12:1 and Yerushalmi Sotah, chap. 2, where Rabbi Akiba deduces all three from one word in that verse.) Remembering one's origin should lead to humility. Remembering one's end should remind a man of the futility of earthly possessions. Remembering the Judgment should arouse a person to the study of Torah and the keeping of its commandments. Akavyah was a contemporary of Hillel and was invited to succeed Shammai as head of the court and deputy to the nasi (see Frankel, *Darkhei ha-Mishnah*, p. 58). Some say the invitation was extended after Menaḥem left and before Shammai took the post (see Hyman, *Toldot tannaim ve-amoraim*, p. 987). Other authorities place him later, as contemporary with Gamaliel I or even Gamaliel II (see Jacob Brüll, *Mavo ha-Mishnah*, p. 271). One indication of an earlier placement is the fact that he was not called "rabbi." Another lies in the fact that he evidently lived at a time when a scholar did not take a position in law opposed to the majority of his contemporaries. Hence his peers called upon him (see later in the text) to abandon his solitary position. In post-Temple times individual scholars did not hesitate to take lone stands.

The version given in Avot de-Rabbi Natan 19:1 mentions four, not three, things: "whence he came—from a place of darkness; whither he is going—to a place of thick darkness; what he is destined to become —dust, worms, and maggots; and who is his Judge—the King of kings, the Holy One, blessed be He" (see L. Finkelstein, *Akiba: Scholar, Saint and Martyr* [New York, 1936], p. 159 f., where this saying of Akavyah's is described as "this unequivocal denial of personal immortality"). Derekh Erez Rabbah 3:1 quotes the saying (as found in the variant version of Avot de-Rabbi Natan) in the name of Ben Azzai, and still another variant is given there.

14. Eduyyot 5:6; see also Numbers Rabbah 9:28 and Berakhot 19a. Precedent is most important in Jewish law and Akavyah here testifies to having heard earlier legal traditions on these four subjects that differed from the opinions of the scholars of his time. He preferred to be thought a fool because he turned down the offer of being appointed to the post of av bet din, second in power in the Sanhedrin to the nasi, rather than surrender his integrity. Concerning the offer and at what point in history it could have been made, see previous note. For the four subjects of the traditions testified to by Akavyah see Nega'im 5:3; Niddah 2:6; Bekhorot 3:4; and Num. 5:12 ff., respectively. Concerning Shemaiah and Avtalyon, see the earlier section and notes dealing with them. Akavyah's response to the sages' citation of the action by Shemaiah and Avtalyon is not clear. Commentators on the mishnaic text differ as to the intent and meaning of the two words in his answer. Rabbi Ovadiah of Bartinoro explains that Akavyah referred to the ancestry of the two great scholars who were said to be descendants of Sennacherib (see Rashi on this passage, Berakhot 19a). Reference to their non-Jewish ancestry was considered by the sages to be a slighting remark explains Maimonides in his Commentary on the Mishnah, and therefore, the sages excommunicated Akavyah. (Maimonides clarifies Akavyah's answer in this way. The two earlier scholars gave the freed bondwoman "the bitter water" to drink because as proselytes themselves they wished to make no differentiation between a native-born Jewess and a proselyte who was in the same legal category as a freed bondwoman.) Rabbi Ovadiah offers a second explanation: "they made her drink a substitute that resembled 'the bitter water' in order to overawe her, so that she should confess if she were really guilty." Tosafot Yom Tov ad locum explains the answer in this way: the reference to the Temple Court being closed is to the practice on the eve of Passover when the Jews would bring their paschal lambs to the Temple for slaughtering. When one large group would enter, the Temple Court was closed until they had finished, then opened again for the next group. So the phrase simply means, "there was no Jew . . ." (see Pesaḥim 64a–b). Eleazar ben Enoch (so explains Maimonides) made light of the practice of the cleansing of hands, which is not biblical in origin but rabbinic (see Yadayim 3:2). The coffin is not actually, but only symbolically, to be stoned, as the language of the Mishnah states here, by the placing of a stone on the coffin as a sign that his peers thus drew the line between him and them.

15. Eduyyot 5:7. The four opinions are those mentioned in the preceding story. Of course, Scripture teaches that one must follow the opinion of the majority as against an individual but the point here is

that even though an individual may have heard a legal tradition from *many* earlier teachers, if a contrary tradition, also heard from many earlier teachers, is now maintained by a *group*, the group's position now is preferred to that of the individual now (see the commentary of Rabbi Ovadiah of Bartinoro ad locum). The Talmud decides the final law against the opinion of Akavyah in the four cases in dispute and in favor of his opponents. Hyman (*Toledot tannaim ve-amoraim*, 3:987) says that the name of Akavyah's son may have been Ḥananiah. He rejects as worthless the opinion of the author of *Mavo ha-Mishnah* that the son's name was Issi ben Akavyah, a contemporary of Rabbi Judah ha-Nasi. That would have placed Akavyah himself more than a century later than when he actually lived.

4. Gamaliel I the Elder

16. Shabbat 15a. This is the only time that Simon, Hillel's son, is mentioned. Evidently, his term of office was of short duration. There are those who argue that there was no such person, that Gamaliel was the son of Hillel and that this text is faulty.

17. Avot 1:16; Avot de-Rabbi Natan 22:1. The latter version reads, "Provide yourself with a teacher and get a companion: a teacher for wisdom and a companion for study. . . ." Maimonides and others say the text is the advice to a rabbi that he should choose another scholar whom he respects as a greater authority than himself, whom he should consult in cases of difficulty and doubt before rendering a decision. The opening of this quotation in our text is the same as that ascribed to Joshua ben Peraḥyah in Avot 1:6.

Gamaliel I is called *ha-zaken*, the Elder, to distinguish him from his grandson, Gamaliel II. He himself was the grandson of Hillel (although some scholars identify him as Hillel's son) and president (nasi) of the Sanhedrin in the first century c.e. He was the first nasi without a deputy (av bet din). H. Graetz (*History of the Jews* 2:130, 192), says that Hillel's son, Simon, was nasi for twenty years, but, according to I. Halevy (*Dorot ha-rishonim*, 2:707), only for a very short time. He was succeeded as nasi by his son, Gamaliel I the Elder. He is the first teacher to be known as rabban, "our master" (see Shabbat 15a). It is possible that some of his statements have been erroneously attributed to his grandson and vice versa. David Hoffmann (*Die erste Mischna und die Controversen der Tannaim* [Berlin, 1882], p. 26) says the text here is that of Rabban Gamaliel II, as does E. Levi (*Pirke Aboth*, p. 19). Geiger insists it is Gamaliel I. Like Hillel he was lenient in legal matters, recognizing the needs of the times (see Orlah 2:12; Rosh Ha-Shanah 2:5). He is the author of the principle, "One must not impose upon the public a restriction that the majority cannot endure." Many of his rulings are based on the principle of *mi-pnei tikkun ha-'olam*, "for the general improvement," i.e., to promote the general good; also, *mi-pnei derkei shalom*, "to promote amity and concord in society," i.e., to avoid strife and conflict. He is especially concerned about the rights of women. Thus he permitted a woman to remarry even if there were only one witness (and not two, as usually required) to testify that her husband had died (Yevamot 16:7; Ketubbot 10b; Gittin 4:2–3). However, in matters of ritual purity and when there was no question of human rights involved, he was more inflexible (see Bekhorot 38a; Tosefta Avodah Zarah 3:10).

In Acts 22:3 Paul declares that he was brought up at the feet of Gamaliel and "taught according to the perfect manner of the law of the fathers. . . ." Herford (*Pirke Aboth*, p. 35) states that Rabban Gamaliel the Elder was the teacher of the apostle Paul; so too does Strack (*Introduction to the Talmud*, p. 109).

Acts 5:34–39 tells of how Gamaliel stood up in the council at the trial of Peter and the apostles—"a Pharisee, named Gamaliel, a doctor of the law, had a reputation among all the people"—to warn the council against harming the apostles. Because of this action, Christian legend regards him as a saint.

Hoenig (*Great Sanhedrin*, p. 41) says that this was no regular court and, hence, the story does not contradict the possibility that Gamaliel was then nasi in the Great Sanhedrin as recorded in the Talmud. Gamaliel was invited only after the council was "assembled," so it was not a regular court.

18. Pesaḥim 88b. Also see Pesaḥim 8:2 and Tosefta Pesaḥim, chap. 2, where there are a number of differences. The king here is assumed to be King Agrippa I, grandson of Herod and the Hasmonean princess, Mariamne. He was rightly regarded abroad as a friend of Greek culture, but at home he conformed to Jewish law and practice. Claudius reunited the whole of Palestine, as held by Herod the Great, in the hands of the latter's grandson. Agrippa's queen, Cypros, who was his cousin and a granddaughter of Mariamne, was evidently a wise and learned woman. Both favored Rabban Gamaliel the Elder and regarded him as their authority in matters of Jewish law. The point of the first story is that an ordinary person would care if the paschal offering were a lamb or a kid because of the difference in cost. Since instructions were not given to the servant as to which to slaughter and both were slaughtered, neither could be legally fit for eating as a paschal offering, for the master's mind could not have been known and two offerings for one person were not within the law. But royalty would not care which was offered. In the second story the lizard, *ḥalta'ah*, was one of eight kinds of creeping things the touch of whose corpse renders objects ritually unclean.

19. Avot de-Rabbi Natan 40:9. Instead of "the son of poor parents" the meaning may be "the student of poor intellect" (cf. Nedarim 41a: "No one is poor save him who lacks knowledge"). The student who is without understanding, even though he has studied, is like the unclean and, therefore, inedible fish, useless. The "son of wealthy parents" may be understood instead as "the student of rich intellect." The Jordan fish is small; the student compared to it is narrow and restricted, and his knowledge is limited because it cannot grow through discussion. The Mediterranean fish is large; the student compared to it is proficient and discerning, and through discussion and argumentation his knowledge develops.

20. Yerushalmi Avodah Zarah 1:9. A similar story is told about his son, Rabban Simon.

21. Tosefta Avodah Zarah 3:10. According to another version the bride was the granddaughter of Rabban Gamaliel. This story is an

illustration of the sage's strictness in matters of ritual purity even though he was liberal in matters affecting human rights.

22. Shabbat 19a. The Talmud explains that white garments are more difficult to clean than colored and, therefore, more time would be needed to launder white clothing for the Sabbath.

23. Shabbat 30b (see also Ketubbot 111b and Kallah Rabbati 2:3). The first century of the common era was marked by severe Roman oppression of the Jews and, consequently, by much messianic speculation and messianic claims among Jews. Here Rabban Gamaliel sets forth "signs of the messianic age." They are somewhat similar to the descriptions found in the Barukh Apocalypse (Syriac Barukh 29:5–8) and in Papias, one of the first Church Fathers. The words of Papias are quoted in Irenaeus, *Against Heresies* 5.33; see J. Klausner, *Jesus of Nazareth* (New York, 1925), p. 401.

In Kallah Rabbati 2:3 there is simply a short form, "Woman is destined to bear a child every day," and the analogy of the hen is given. It is quoted to refute the statement given earlier there that there is no procreation in the world to come.

The translation of *gluska'ot* as "loaves of white delicious bread" derives from the explanation of the Aramaic word, in the singular, as a contraction of *glusbika* (the guttural before the *l*) and referring to Lesbos, an island in the Aegean Sea noted for its fertility, delicacies, and luxuries. Therefore, in Syriac the word means a brand of white flour or a white bread. The word *milat* is translated as "cloaks of fine wool," like the famed robes of soft, very fine wool from the city of Miletus. In the verse from Psalms quoted by Rabban Gamaliel, he takes *pisat* to mean "robes of Milat" or "cloaks of fine wool" from the expression *ketonet pasim* (Gen. 37:3, 2 Sam. 13:18). See Rashi on Shabbat 30b. So too, *bar* is interpreted by Gamaliel as "cakes of Lesbos" or "loaves of white delicious bread."

In Ketubbot 111b the last sentence is given in the name of Ḥiyya bar Joseph, a much later scholar, an amora. But he must have been the transmitter of the baraita.

The question of who was that pupil of Gamaliel's who repeatedly scoffed at his master and quoted the verse from Ecclesiastes has engaged the attention of scholars. J. Klausner (*From Jesus to Paul*, pp. 310–11) says it is Paul. "I am almost certain, in spite of the ill-tempered attack on me on account of this on the part of Jewish apologists, that this is the Rabban Gamaliel I the Elder, and that 'that pupil' is Paul, who sat at the feet of Gamaliel (Acts 22:3). In like manner, Jesus is called 'that man.'"

On the story in our text, see Klausner, *The Messianic Idea*, pp. 506–7.

24. Shekalim 6:1. The Temple Mount was entered from the right and exited from the left. During the circuit there were thirteen places where a prostration took place. The Ark was concealed during the latter days of the First Temple (Bartinoro says ad locum) by King Josiah. Another belief had it that the Ark had been carried off to Babylonia by those who destroyed the First Temple. Hananiah, the deputy high priest, is so called regularly and, therefore, the conjecture is that he was probably the last to hold this office before the destruction of the Second Temple (see Strack, *Introduction to the Talmud*, p. 109).

25. Yerushalmi Ma'aser Sheni 5:4 (56c); see also Sanhedrin 11b.

He who delayed giving his tithes had to remove them from his possession at the end of the third year and the sixth year in the sabbatical year cycle: the priest's portion, *terumah*, went to the priest, the first tithe to the Levite, the tithe of the poor (every third year) to the poor (see Rashi, Sanhedrin 11b). Northern Galilee was rich in olives, the southern region in wheat. It was unnecessary to communicate by message concerning the intercalation of the year to those Jews living near the rabbinic court, but it was necessary for those living in foreign lands so that they would know the exact dates of the holidays and not eat leavened foods on Passover (see Rashi, ad locum). This baraita is quoted in Tosefta Sanhedrin, chap. 2, with important variations. Rabbenu Ḥananel, Rashi, and the scholars of the Tosafot ascribe this story as it occurs in the Babylonian version to Rabban Gamaliel II of Jabneh. But I. Halevy (*Dorot ha-rishonim*, 1:31), Z. Frankel (*Darkhei ha-Mishnah*, p. 59), D. Hoffman (*Die Erste Mischna*, p. 31), and others argue that it is Rabban Gamaliel I. They point out that the Temple had been destroyed before Rabban Gamaliel II became nasi, and what, therefore, could be the meaning of, "were sitting on the steps of the entrance hall on the Temple mount"? (It should be noted that the Babylonian version has a variant reading for these words: "The story is told that Rabban Gamaliel was sitting on the height of the Temple Mount.") On the other hand, A. Hyman (*Toldot tannaim ve-amoraim*, 1:306) supports Rashi's contention, pointing out also that the Gemara's statement, "after they had removed him," is a proof. And it is further argued that after the Temple had been destroyed, the site continued to be visited (see Berakhot 58a et al.). But if there be the possibility for debate concerning the text of the Babylonian baraita, the Yerushalmi text would seem to leave no room for doubt that the Rabban Gamaliel mentioned is the Elder. For the locale—the "steps of the entrance hall" on the Temple mount, *ma'alot ha-'ulam be-har ha-bayit*—indicates it took place before the destruction of the Temple. The reason Gamaliel's title, "the Elder," is not mentioned is because the passage reads "Rabban Gamaliel and the elders" and it would have been stylistically difficult for the reading to have been "Rabban Gamaliel the Elder and the elders."

26. Shabbat 115a; Soferim 5:15; Tosefta Shabbat 13:2. My translation is based on the first two sources. The earlier Rabban Gamaliel who is here remembered by Rabbi Ḥalafta is Rabban Gamaliel I the Elder. The one to whom he speaks is his own contemporary, Rabban Gamaliel II. The succession was Hillel, Simon (see Shabbat 15a), Rabban Gamaliel I, Rabban Simon son of Gamaliel I, Rabban Gamaliel II, Rabban Simon II son of Gamaliel II, Rabbi Judah ha-Nasi, Rabban Gamaliel III, Judah Nesiah, Gamaliel IV, Judah III, Hillel II, Gamaliel V, and Gamaliel VI. Targum is the Aramaic translation of biblical books. The Targum mentioned here must have been an earlier work than the one we now possess. The objection at the time to a written, as against an oral, Targum was the concern that the same sanctity might be attached to it as to the original Hebrew text.

27. Ta'anit 29a. Turnus Rufus (Tinneus Rufus) was governor of Judea in the first century (see *Jewish Encyclopedia*, 10:510).

28. Sanhedrin 11a; Semaḥot 8:7. Rabban Gamaliel as the nasi arranged for the invitation to be extended to the members of the Bet Din, the court, the evening before, in keeping with the law. The reason for

this was that each member of the court was to observe the moon on his own the night before the court was to assemble to determine whether or not there was to be intercalation. The ethical teaching embodied in these three stories and ascribed to Samuel the Small is that it is forbidden to embarrass another publicly. It is even better to leave off studying Torah, as in the story of Rabbi Hiyya, and to accept the statement of a strange woman, make her one's wife, and to issue a divorce to her, as in the story of Rabbi Meir. Shecaniah said, "*We* have broken faith . . . *we* have married foreign women. . . ." He had not, but he used the first person plural so as not publicly to embarrass those who had. Similarly in the story of Joshua and God, God refuses to point the finger; so too God uses the second-person plural in His accusation to Moses.

The text in Semaḥot is not in good order. It is omitted by the Gaon of Vilna and printed in the Romm-Vilna edition in brackets. Eldad and Medad mentioned in the Semaḥot version were worthy that the Divine Spirit should rest upon them (see Num. 11:26).

Samuel the Small explained that he had not intended to take part in the proceedings without invitation. The passage indicates the high esteem in which Samuel the Small was held by his teacher, Rabban Gamaliel. See Pirkei Avot 4:24 for a maxim quoted in the name of Samuel the Small (in reality, two biblical verses, Prov. 24:17–18), warning against rejoicing at the misfortune of one's enemy. Weiss (*Dor dor ve-doreshav*, vol. 1, takes it to refer to the period of Jewish rebellious actions against Rome. Herford (*Christianity in Talmud and Midrash*, pp. 132–34) deals with the chronology of Samuel the Small, arguing that he died not earlier than about 80 C.E. and was then a very old man. This is contrary to the opinion of many scholars that he died young; some explain his name this way, since *katan* may mean "young" as well as "small." He was called upon by Rabban Gamaliel II of Jabneh to draw up the formula against the sectarians (Berakhot 28b), and was not rebuked by Gamaliel II even though he had disobeyed his orders (Yerushalmi Sanhedrin 8c). The nasi instead addressed him with praise and reverence. Hyman (*Toldot*, p. 1148) says that Samuel the Small studied even with Hillel—that would make Samuel about ninety when he died (see also *Pirke Abot*, ed. Herford, p. 119). However, Strack (*Introduction to the Talmud*, p. 112) places Samuel the Small in the second generation of tannaim (90–130 C.E.).

29. Semaḥot 8:7. Perhaps the words, "the Elder," in our text were incorrectly inserted by a copyist, and our text really refers to Gamaliel II. Other texts say Samuel the Small was alive and active when Gamaliel II was nasi (Berakhot 28b; Yerushalmi Sanhedrin 8c).

30. Ketubbot 8b. See Josephus, *Wars* 2.1.1, describing the funeral banquet of Archelaus after Herod's burial. Rabban Gamaliel set the practice of democracy in death and simplicity in funeral practices, which are the tradition in Judaism. Many scholars, however, affirm that this passage speaks of Rabban Gamaliel II and not Gamaliel I the Elder. But S. Zeitlin (*The Rise and Fall of the Judaean State*, 2:300) states, "Gamaliel the Elder left a will in which he directed that his funeral be simple. Thereafter, many Judaeans followed his example." See Tosefta Niddah 9:17.

31. Sotah 9:15. Although liberal in his interpretation of laws affect-

ing human welfare, Gamaliel I was strict in laws concerning ritual purity.

32. Kallah Rabbati, chap. 9, opening baraita.

33. Megillah 21a. Perhaps scholars and students were weaker because of the Roman harassments and the instability of the times, which resulted in food scarcities.

34. Semaḥot 8:6. The preceding passage reads, "We may burn articles at the funerals of kings but not at the funerals of princes" (cf. Avodah Zarah 11a). The Jeremiah verse quoted by Onkelos is addressed to King Zedekiah of Judah. Onkelos, commonly called Onkelos the Proselyte, was a scholar who lived in the latter part of the first century c.e. and the early part of the second. Frequently he is confused with Aquila the proselyte, the author of the translation of the Bible. He is usually associated with Gamaliel II and there are scholars who identify the Gamaliel in our text with Gamaliel II, in which case, the words, "the Elder," would have to be ascribed to a copyist's error. The Tyrian mina was the standard unit of the Tyrian monetary system, equaling one sela or four zuzim (see Bekhorot 49b and Rashi ad locum).

5. Eleazar ben Harsom

35. Yoma 35b; Yerushalmi Ta'anit, chap. 4:5. Maimonides, in his introduction to Zera'im, places Eleazer in the time of Antigonus, but there is no evidence to support this early dating (see Hyman, *Toldot*, 1:176). Just as the example of Hillel is cited as a reproof to those who plead poverty as an excuse for not studying Torah, so Eleazar ben Harsom is cited to refute those who argue they cannot study Torah because their wealth and its care require all their time.

36. Yoma 9a, 35a; Yerushalmi Yoma, chap. 3:5–6. The tale illustrates the fact that his family was extremely wealthy. A maneh was a weight in gold or silver equal to one hundred common shekels. The expensive priestly garment was evidently loosely woven of fine thread and his body could be seen through it. The version in the Palestinian Talmud is fuller. It tells that Eleazar had ascended toward the altar and had offered a sacrifice. His fellow priests brought him down because of the immodesty of his attire. To remedy the situation, Eleazar soaked the garment in water, the loose weaving became thick, and the whiteness of the garment lost its sheen. He then walked around the altar seven times so that the heat of the burning wood could dry the garment.

6. Abba Saul ben Batnit

37. Beiẓah 3:8; Yerushalmi Beiẓah chap. 3:5–8; Tosefta Beiẓah chap. 3. See also Shabbat 24:5. Abba Saul ben Batnit was a shopkeeper in Jerusalem before the destruction of the Second Temple. He sold wine and oil, and his business practices were highly ethical. He would not benefit in the slightest way from that which was not his, and he was especially meticulous in giving his customers a full measure. He would fill his measures with wine and oil on the eve of a holiday to

give to his customers on the festival because the law forbade giving customers a measure of wine or oil on a festival day itself since it would appear to be a sale. (See the opening sentence of this same mishnah.) He also filled the measures the evening before an intermediate day of the festival because the froth on top of a measure of wine when it is poured makes it impossible to give a full measure—unless it be done the evening before. Then the wine can settle, the froth disappear, and the measure be filled to the brim. Besides, many would come to his shop to study with him on the intermediate days since they did not work on these days, and he would have to fill the measures for his customers hastily, thus preventing a full measure, unless he prepared the measures the evening before. (See *Ikkar Tosafot Yom Tov* and *Tiferet Yisrael* ad loc.) Even on ordinary days he would fill his customers' measures of oil the evening before. Oil sticks to the sides and bottom of the seller's measure as he pours it into the customer's measure. Therefore, Abba Saul would let the oil drip from his measures into those of his customers all night long so that they would get every drop coming to them. (See Ovadiah of Bartinoro ad loc.)

According to J. Derenbourg (*Mas'a Erez Yisra'el* [Jerusalem, 1969–70], p. 223), the mother of Abba Saul was a Batanian proselyte, which explains his name. But in Nedarim 23a Batnit is a masculine proper name. Abba Saul was engaged in commerce with Rabbi Eleazar ben Zadok, and together they issued a regulation concerning the Sabbath law (Shabbat 24:5).

38. Beizah 29a; Yerushalmi Beizah chap. 3:5–8; Tosefta Beizah chap. 3. Abba Saul knew that he had purchased so many measures of wine per barrel. In selling individual measures to his customers, despite his concern about giving full measures, the froth prevented the measure from being absolutely full. The result was that after he had sold the number of measures supposed to be in a barrel, there would still be some wine left at the bottom. It was this wine that he collected until he had three hundred kegs. Not wanting to keep it or sell it, since he did not believe it to be his, he sought to give it to the Temple. His ethical scrupulousness was shared by his fellow shopkeepers in Jerusalem as is evidenced by their collecting three hundred kegs of oil and their desire to give it to the Temple. Oil adheres to the seller's measure so that after he sells the total number of measures supposedly equaling the content of his barrels, he still has some left. Their ethical behavior was beyond what was required by law.

39. Yerushalmi Beizah chap. 3:5–8 (see *Korban ha-Edah* ad locum).

40. Pesahim 57a; Tosefta Menahot, end of chap. 13. This is a protest against the corrupt practices, the nepotism, and the violence practiced by the high priests.

41. Semahot 12:11. He speaks of the removal of the *tekhelet* from the *zizit* of the cloak.

7. Baba ben Buta

42. Beizah 20a–b; Yerushalmi Hagigah 2:3 (with some differences). Hillel and Shammai differed as to whether an animal could be brought on a festival for a burned offering, with Hillel in the affirmative and Shammai in the negative. A female animal could not be a burnt offer-

ing, hence the question of Shammai's disciples and Hillel's deceptive answer. For Hillel, the pursuer of peace, wanted no controversy. Kedar sheep were the very best. For the role played by Baba ben Buta in the reconstruction of the Temple by Herod, see the earlier section on the rebuilding of the Second Temple.

43. Gittin 57a.

44. Nedarim 66b. The fact that husband and wife were born in different countries where different dialects of Aramaic were spoken only added to the confusion of the poor wife who was, evidently, a very simple woman of little understanding. Courts commonly sat at the gate of a city or town. That too was the site for marketing and business transactions. The story is meant to illustrate the goodness of Baba in being so quick to understand and forgive the poor woman who had struck with two lamps so great a scholar as Baba, all because she was so anxious to please her husband and to obey his every order. The prayer of Baba for two sons for the woman was to balance the number of lamps with which she had struck him.

45. Keritot 6:3. A suspensive guilt offering, the sacrifice of *asham talui*, was brought when the person was in doubt whether or not he had committed a sin for which, if done intentionally, he would be liable to the punishment of *karet*, "extirpation," and if done unintentionally, to the bringing of a sin offering. Yom Kippur, of course, effaces sins committed in man's relationship to God provided that he follows the path of repentance, prayer, and righteous living. The tale illustrates the great piety of Baba ben Buta.

8. Ḥanina the Deputy High Priest

46. Shekalim 6:1. Ḥanina is sometimes called Ḥananiah, sometimes Neḥunia. Strack says he was probably the last deputy high priest to hold that office before the destruction of the Temple by the Romans in 70 C.E. (*Introduction to the Talmud*, p. 109). He lived some years after the destruction and is quoted in the Talmud as one who could give reliable testimony as to Temple practices (see Pesaḥim 14a; Zevaḥim 103b; Eduyyot 2:1–3).

All who entered the Temple Mount would do so on the right, proceed through the area, making thirteen prostrations, and exit on the left. The tradition was that during the last years of the First Temple, the Ark had been hidden by King Josiah (see *Tiferet Yisrael* ad locum).

47. Zevaḥim 84a; Tosefta Zevaḥim, chap. 9. Priests with blemishes were not to offer sacrifices. Rabbi Ḥanina's father did not wish to put any such to public embarrassment, so he nudged them aside inconspicuously.

48. Yoma 39a; Sotah 42a. In Nazir 47b the explanation is ascribed to Rabbi Ḥanina ben Antigonus.

49. Midrash Tanḥuma Teẓaveh.

50. Yoma 21b.

51. Avot de-Rabbi Natan (ed. Schechter), second recension, 11a–b.

52. Ibid., chap. 20. A more concise statement stressing a similar thought is found in Avot 3:6, quoted in the name of Rabbi Neḥunia

ben Ha-kanah. On the last part of the passage see A. Büchler, *Studies in Sin and Atonement* (Oxford, 1928), pp. 63 ff., and idem, *The Economic Conditions of Judaea* (Oxford, 1912), p. 28, n. 2. Rabbi Ḥanina here laments the low spiritual state to which his fellow Jews had fallen during the years before the war with Rome. He criticizes the political leaders, the powerful and the wealthy. He calls for the renewed study of Torah and the ordering of one's life in accordance with its teachings.

53. Avot 3:2; Avot de-Rabbi Natan (ed. Schechter), second recension, p. 34b. Perhaps Rabbi Ḥanina is here expressing his concern about a possible civil war among the Jews. During the years before the war with Rome there were those counseling accommodation, others violence. Internecine strife was common; factionalism was acute. Authorities understand this passage to mean, pray for the welfare of Rome (see Frankel, *Darkhei ha-Mishnah*, pp. 61–62; Weiss, *Dor dor ve-doreshav*, 1:191; Bacher, *Agada der Tannaiten*, 1:56). Weiss says that later Rabbi Ḥanina changed his mind and joined the party of the Zealots. This would explain his opposition, in the previous passage, to any earthly government. Compare this passage with Shakespeare, *Coriolanus*, act 1, scene 1, "You cry against the noble Senate, who . . . keep you in awe, which else would feed on one another." Compare also Jer. 29:7. The version found in the second recension of Avot de-Rabbi Natan gives the name as Rabbi Neḥunia, the deputy high priest, and inserts an additional clause, "Pray for the welfare of the government, *that rules over us all the days. . . .*"

54. Sifrei, Naso 42. As in the previous passage, Rabbi Ḥanina speaks out of his deep concern lest civil war break out. "Peace in one's house" could mean peace within the nation, among the Jewish people in their stand against Rome. The entire passage may also refer to his conservative position in opposition to the Zealots who urged war against Rome.

55. Megillat Ta'anit, last chapter. It is hardly likely that Rabbi Ḥanina, the deputy high priest, lived so long as to have been killed by the Romans during the Hadrianic persecution. On the other hand, the others mentioned here with him may have been executed long after Rabbi Ḥanina, but on the same day and month of the calendar. The theory of Weiss, *Dor dor ve-doreshav*, 1:191, that Rabbi Ḥanina in his later years changed his pacific views and joined the Zealots lends some plausibility to such a possibility. But some scholars believe that our text here is incorrect and in place of the name of Rabbi Ḥanina should be substituted the name of his son. The text then should read "and Rabbi Simon son of the deputy high priest" (see Halevy, *Dorot ha-rishonim*, 1:5, 174–81 and Maimonides, introduction to Zer'aim).

9. Simon ben Gamaliel I

56. Avot 1:17. Simon, son of Rabban Gamaliel I and great-grandson of Hillel, was the last nasi, president of the Sanhedrin, before the destruction of the Temple by the Romans (see Shabbat 15a). He belonged to the party advocating peace with the Romans in the closing years of the Jewish state, Josephus (*Wars* 4.3.9) describes him as

"one of the chief men just before the siege of Jerusalem." Again (*Life* 38.39) Josephus speaks of him as an official of the provisional government, a learned Pharisee active in political affairs. Josephus was concerned only with Simon's political activity and, therefore, did not state that he was head of the Sanhedrin, the nasi. It can be assumed that when the Sanhedrin was dissolved about 66 c.e. that Simon became one of the heads of the provisional government, a coalition of Pharisees and Sadducees. Josephus describes Simon as a native of Jerusalem, son of a lofty family, belonging to the party of the Pharisees whose influence was strongly exerted upon all that they keep the commandments of the Torah. He was a man of great wisdom and reason and capable of restoring public affairs by his prudence when they were in a bad state. All this by Josephus despite the fact that Simon must have suspected Josephus of potential treachery when Josephus served as commander of the Jewish forces in Galilee, and together with his colleagues in the provisional government, Ḥanan ben Ḥanan and Joshua ben Gamla, sent a military party to seize Josephus and return him to Jerusalem.

Comparatively few teachings are directely attributed to Simon but it may be assumed that his teachings are included in those of the school of Hillel since he was a direct descendant and third-generation successor to Hillel. The three teachings here quoted in Avot may also reflect, in part, the political conditions of the times. Under normal circumstances garrulousness can lead to incorrect or even foolish utterances. Biblical and rabbinic literature warn against loquacity (see Prov. 10:19, 17:28; Megillah 18a; Gittin 36b). But during the troubled years of the first century preceding the war with the Romans that led to the destruction of the Temple and Jerusalem, it was especially important to be cautious in one's speech so as not to divulge information that might be useful to the Roman enemy or to opposing parties among the Jews themselves, who advocated different policies as to the Jewish course of action vis-à-vis Rome.

Moreover, Simon here teaches the importance of the right deed. He does not derogate study but indicates that the good life is even more important. Study should lead to a life of righteousness (see Avot 3:12, 19, 22; Yevamot 63b; Kiddushin 40b; Yerushalmi Ḥagigah 1:7). The third teaching, reflecting Prov. 10:19, points to the possibility of the talkative person not only saying inaccurate or stupid things but also sinning through slander and tale-bearing.

Simon is not called Rabban here, perhaps because he taught these aphorisms before he became nasi.

57. Midrash Tannaim on Deut. 26:13. Rabbi Joshua ben Ḥananiah, referred to in the Mishnah as simply Rabbi Joshua, was a member of the second generation of tannaim (about 90–130 c.e.) and active at Peki'in. Nehunia ben Ha-kanah was of the first generation of tannaim. His town of Emmaus was renowned in talmudic days for its hot springs and high standard of living. The text here has the Hebrew *Haileh* as though it were a place name, perhaps the locale of the meeting place of the Sanhedrin. It may be a family name. The Tosefta has the word begin with *h* (*he*) rather than with *ḥ* (*ḥet*) as here. The Babylonian Talmud has the same reading for the first letter as the Tosefta but changes the last letter to *z* (*zayin*). The word would then mean "this

here" or "that there" (see Sanhedrin 11b; Yerushalmi Ma'aser Sheni 5:4, 56c, top).

The letters mention the fact that the fourth year had arrived. This was because the duty of "clearing out" or "removal" was to be fulfilled on the eve of the first day of Passover (some texts read "last"), in the fourth and seventh years of the sabbatical year cycle (see Ma'aser Sheni 5:6; Deut. 14:28; Shevi'it 9:2). Yerushalmi Ma'aser Sheni 5:4, 56c tells of similar letters sent by Rabban Gamaliel the Elder.

58. Keritot 1:7; Rashi ad locum; Lev. 15:25–30. By eliminating the need to bring the other offerings, Rabban Simon quickly brought down the price of doves. The doubt referred to about issues was whether the issues had occurred in the seven days of her menstrual separation or in the eleven days during which they must be reckoned fluxes (see Lev. 15:25–30). The doubt about miscarriages was whether the miscarriage was of the kind that required an offering (Keritot 1:4) or of the kind that did not (Keritot 1:5). The woman then would bring a turtledove or a pigeon for a sin offering required in cases of doubt. She is then allowed to eat of the offerings. A gold dinar was the equivalent of twenty-five silver dinars. Rabban Simon's innovation was in reality contrary to the law. He so taught, however, in accordance with the principle, "The time has come to do for the Lord's sake or else Your teachings will be set aside." Had he not acted to bring down the price of doves, by decreeing that only one pair not five was required where there was no doubt, poor women could not have afforded to pay the high price. Consequently they would not have brought the doves as a sacrifice and they would have eaten of the offerings in a state of ritual impurity. That would have been far worse, Rabban Simon reckoned, than his setting aside the requirement for the additional four pairs of doves (see Bartinoro ad locum). Maimonides decides that the law is according to Rabban Simon here.

59. Eruvin 6:2. The alley space is held in common by the abutting householders. Unless by means of an *eruv* they all combine to form a single "family," making all the houses, alley, and courtyard into a single domain, the householders are "restricted" in that they cannot move anything from the house into the alley or courtyard on the Sabbath, or vice versa. If one of the householders is a non-Jew, the others must, for the Sabbath, rent from him his rights in the alley or courtyard (see Eruvin 6:1). Here Rabban Simon ben Gamaliel, the father of the narrator, holds that the Sadducee is to be regarded legally not as a Gentile, but as a dissenting Jew. If he brings out his own vessels first, he thereby asserts his own rights in the alley. In the latter part of this Mishnah, Rabbi Judah interprets the words of Rabban Simon differently—"Hasten and do what is needed (i.e., pay the Sadducee rent for his rights in the alley during the Sabbath) before the eve of the Sabbath is over and he so restricts you." According to this interpretation Rabban Simon would regard the Sadducee legally as a non-Jew.

60. Avodah Zarah 32a. The same text is found in Tosefta Avodah Zarah 5 and there the words "the Elder" are used to identify Rabban Gamaliel.

61. Sukkah 53a. During the festival of Sukkot, as water was drawn from the well for libation on the holiday, there was a joyous procession to and from the well with music and dancing (see Sukkah 5:1).

The Talmud declares that he who has not witnessed the rejoicing at this ceremony has never seen rejoicing (Sukkah 51a).

62. Avodah Zarah 20a. A similar story is found in Yerushalmi Avodah Zarah 1:9 and Yerushalmi Berakhot 9:2 but there the subject is Rabban Gamaliel the Elder.

63. Ḥullin 90b. This text is cited in the Talmud on this page as an example of rabbinic hyperbole, together with other examples of such exaggeration in biblical, prophetic, and rabbinic literature.

64. Sotah 49b; Tosafot on Avodah Zarah 32a. There is some question as to whether the Simon ben Gamaliel here is Simon son of Gamaliel the Elder who is the subject of our discussion or his grandson of the same name who lived in the second century C.E.

A similar text is found in Gittin 58a referring to Lam. 3:51: "Rabbi Judah said in the name of Samuel that Rabban Simon son of Gamaliel applied the verse, *My eyes have brought me grief over [what occurred to] all the maidens of my city* as follows: There were four hundred synagogues in the city of Betar, in each there were four hundred teachers, each of whom taught four hundred little children. When the enemy entered, the soldiers smote them with their staffs and when complete victory was theirs, the enemy soldiers wrapped them in their scrolls and set them ablaze." In this text the Rabban Simon is clearly the scholar of the second century, Rabban Simon of Jabneh. Rabbi Judah bar Ezekiel (died 299) is usually called Rav Judah and was a pupil of Rav, founder of the academy at Pumbedita in Babylonia. He was of the second generation of amoraim. Samuel (died 254) was of the first generation of amoraim and served as director of the academy at Nehardea in Babylonia.

65. Semaḥot 8:7 (47a); Sotah 48b; Sanhedrin 11a. For Samuel the Small see supra, section 4, on Gamaliel the Elder. Simon and Ishmael ben Elisha met their death at the hands of the Romans after the capture of Jerusalem.

66. Avot de-Rabbi Natan 38:3 (33a). Parallel texts occur in Mekhilta, Mishpatim 18; Semaḥot 8:8; Midrash Aggadah Mishpatim 22:21; and version 2, Avot de-Rabbi Natan, p. 41. Since our text here follows the statement, "The sword comes upon the world for the delay of justice," it would seem logical that this is the explanation. Semaḥot 8:8 offers a similar explanation: "Perhaps you were having a meal or were sleeping when a woman came to ask a ruling concerning her ritual impurity (or a man about his vow) and they were kept waiting."

In our text Rabban Simon was upset by the coming execution. In Semaḥot the roles are reversed and it is Rabbi Ishmael who broke into tears and Rabban Simon says to him, "Avrekh (a title of honor), why do you weep? Two steps more and you will be in the bosom of the righteous, and yet you weep!" There Rabbi Ishmael explains that he is distressed not at the fact of the impending execution but its nature—the same kind that is used against murderers and desecrators of the Sabbath. In our text here Rabban Simon is disturbed for the same reason. However, the text in Semaḥot concludes, "Some say it was Rabban Simon ben Gamaliel who was weeping and Rabbi Ishmael who answered him in those words." This would reconcile that text with ours (see Büchler, *Studies in Sin and Atonement*, pp. 195 ff.).

These two rabbis were two of the "Ten Martyrs" executed by the government of Rome at various times because they insisted on teaching the Torah despite the Roman ban. But Bacher (*Agada der Tannaiten*, 1:234, n. 3) states that the Simon mentioned in this account was not Rabban Simon ben Gamaliel.

Rabban Simon in our text does not forcefully reject Ishmael's second question as he does the first. Evidently, the explanation that perhaps it was his pride at the sight of so many standing and listening to his teaching that accounted for his impending doom and the nature of his execution struck home. And Rabban Simon then acknowledged God's justice by stating that "a man must be prepared to accept his fate."

Weiss (*Dor dor ve-doreshav*, 1:191, n. 1) states his opinion that this tale does not describe the death of Rabban Simon ben Gamaliel the Elder but that of Rabbi Simon, of the second century, his grandson. Frankel rejects this notion (*Darkhei ha-Mishnah*, p. 63, n. 96).

67. Megillat Ta'anit, last chapter; Lamentations Rabbah, chap. 2; Midrash on Ps. 9:13; Hilkhot Rabbati (Jellinek, *Bet ha-midrash* 1:4). Frankel (*Darkhei ha-Mishnah*, p. 163), explains that although Rabbi Akiba is mentioned in several of these texts, this does not disprove the fact that it is Rabban Simon I who is the subject of the text, for Rabbi Akiba was already a prominent scholar before the destruction of the Temple.

10. Naḥum of Gimzo

68. Ta'anit 21a. Gimzo is in southwestern Judea (2 Chron. 28:18 and Lamentations Rabbah 1:64). Naḥum of Gimzo was the teacher of Rabbi Akiba (Ḥagigah 12a; Berakhot 22a), though little is known of his actual teachings.

69. Ibid. Abraham supposedly used the earth in his battle with the four kings (Gen. 14).

70. Ḥagigah 13a–b, Genesis Rabbah 1:14. The particle *et* is used to connote the direct object of the verb and precedes the object. Rabbi Ishmael and Rabbi Akiba were tannaim of the second generation (about 90–130 C.E.). Naḥum formulated the hermeneutical principle that *akh* (save that) and *rak* (except) are limitations, while *et* and *gam* (also) are extensions. In the first verse of the Bible if *et*, the sign of the accusative, were omitted, "Heaven" and "earth" might be regarded as nominatives and either additional subjects of the verb, "created," or in apposition to "God." The version in Genesis Rabbah has several variations. "Serving" a master means to study with him, since it was the practice for disciples to render personal service to their teacher.

71. Genesis Rabbah 53:15. See previous note for Naḥum's hermeneutical principle.

11. Eliezer ben Jacob

72. Yevamot 49b; Gittin 67a. Rabbi Eliezer, son of Jacob the Elder, taught much about the Temple and its furnishings. The traditional matter taught by him is pronounced *kav venaki*, small in quantity but trustworthy. A teacher of the same name lived in the second half of the second century C.E. Frequently, it is difficult to determine which of the two is meant in a particular text. Ben Azzai was of the second

generation of tannaim and was one of the four scholars who immersed themselves in theosophic speculation of whom only Rabbi Akiba emerged without harm (see Ḥagigah 14b, 15b; Yerushalmi Ḥagigah 2:77b).

73. Middot 1:2; Tamid 27a. The Levites kept watch at twenty-one places in the Temple. The officer of the Temple Mount made the rounds and if he found any of the Levites asleep at his post, he would beat him with his staff. He also had the right to burn his garment. Rabbi Eliezer's uncle was a Levite.

74. Yevamot 90b. The discussion in the Talmud here is about the source of authority for the court and the limit of its powers. Here it is stated that the court may be even harsher than the laws of the Torah require if the purpose be to enforce the observance of such laws at a critical time when there is a general breakdown in observance.

75. Yoma 38a. The Talmud reports that all the gates in the Temple were covered with gold except for the Gates of Nicanor. Since they were involved in miracles they were left as they were. Elsewhere the Talmud explains that it was because the bronze of which they were made had the color of gold. Rabbi Eliezer offers his own explanation. The miracles relate to the story in the Tosefta, Yoma 2:4, that when the gates were being brought by sea from Alexandria the ship was hit by a severe storm. To lighten the ship the crew threw one of the gates overboard. When the second gate was about to follow, Nicanor asked to be thrown after it. The storm at once ceased and when they landed at Acre, the first gate was found beneath the ship's keel (see also Yoma 3:10; Shekalim 6:3; Sotah 1:5; Middot 1:4, 2:3, 2:6; Negaʿim 14:8).

76. Eruvin 54a. The usual practice was to study the tradition aloud so as to fix it in one's memory.

77. Eruvin 54a. A disciple served his master in a literal sense.

78. Sanhedrin 91a. This comment may have been prompted by the fact that during the first century of the common era Roman oppression made leadership among Jews dangerous. The leader was an easily and quickly identifiable target. Indeed, rabbis were seized and executed. The teaching here urges the Jewish leaders to resist the temptation to surrender their role. The verse quoted from Daniel sets forth the example of Shadrach, Meshach, and Abednego. The verse's mentioning of their garments is interpreted as the symbolic mantle of leadership.

12. Ḥanina ben Dosa

79. Ecclesiastes Rabbah 1:1. A variant version is found in Songs Rabbah 1:1. The slight differences in this second version include his having painted the stone; the first group of five men demanded a hundred gold coins while the second group, the angels, asked for only five selas; and upon his not finding them to pay them, he gave the sum to the sages of the Sanhedrin. The difference between a vowed offering and a freewill offering lies in the following: a vowed offering is when one says, "I vow to dedicate a burnt offering"; a freewill offering when one says, "This animal is to be a burnt offering." In the latter case a specific animal is involved (see Kinnim 1:1). Ḥanina's objective was to make a gift of the stone to the Temple. The condition set by the angels that Ḥanina also help them to carry the stone—in

the Hebrew, "provided that you place your hand and finger with us"—is probably a suggestion that religion demands personal service. The Hall of Hewn Stones was the chamber in the Temple where the Sanhedrin held its sessions. The proof-text quoted (Prov. 22:29) involves a play on words. The verse reads *melakhim*, "kings," which is replaced by the word, *malakhim*, "angels."

Rabbi Ḥanina ben Dosa was among the last group of tannaim of the first generation who lived during the latter part of the first century c.e. The literature portrays him as a legendary performer of miracles.

80. Yoma 53b; Ta'anit 24b; Ecclesiastes Rabbah 1. Rabbi Joseph ben Ḥiyya, of the third generation of Babylonian amoraim, died in 333. He was honored by being called "Sinai" because of his comprehensive knowledge of traditional lore. The version in Ecclesiastes Rabbah differs somewhat in that it has Rabbi Ḥanina walking with a basket of salt on his head, which rain could spoil.

81. Berakhot 33a. The *arod* is a species of lizard, as also in Ḥullin 127a, although usually the word means a wild ass.

82. Ta'anit 24b. The measure referred to in the text is a kab, which equals four logs, and one log is the equivalent of the contents of six eggs. The carob or Johnnybread (or St. John's bread) grows plentifully in Israel.

83. Ta'anit 24b–25a. The second version is contained in a baraita following the original passage in the Talmud.

84. Ta'anit 25a.

85. Ta'anit 25a. The last sentence in the story is contained in a separate baraita following the tale in the Talmud.

86. Ta'anit 25a. The reason for the question about the goats belonging to Rabbi Ḥanina was that it was known that he was a desperately poor man.

87. Ibid. *Aikhu* may be extended to *ya'arikhu*, "may they be long."

88. Yevamot 121a; Bava Kamma 50a, with a variation in one word. The mention of the ram rescuing the young woman may be an allusion to the sacrifice of Isaac and perhaps the old man is Abraham. Neḥunia dug wells so that the pilgrims coming up to Jerusalem would have water.

89. Genesis Rabbah 34.

90. Ibid.

91. Midrash Tanḥuma Hakadum on Vayiggash. The lion was always described as the king of the beasts.

92. Avot de-Rabbi Natan, chap. 8, end. For the Hebrew original, here translated as "dragged itself," there is a variant reading, translated as "being merry," which makes no sense. Schechter in his edition of the text reads still another variant, translated as "braying." Here, "dragged itself" makes sense because the donkey was weak from lack of food and water.

93. Shabbat 112b; Shekalim, chap. 5, beginning; Yerushalmi Demai 1:3. Phinehas ben Jair was of the fourth generation of tannaim. He lived during the second century c.e., was an ascetic, the son-in-law of Rabbi Simon bar Yoḥai. His name is associated with Midrash Tadshe. His donkey, like that of Rabbi Ḥanina ben Dosa, was supposed to have been gifted with cleverness. Concerning Rava ben Zemuna, this passage is the only teaching ascribed to him. In Shekalim his name is given as Abba ben Zemina, in the Yerushalmi as Abba ben Zevina.

94. Avot 3:11–13. Wisdom is not the summum bonum. The good life is to be prized even above wisdom. Wisdom is a means to an end—righteous deeds, and the kind of actions that endear a man to his fellows. Such a person is the one whom God also loves (see 1 Sam. 2:26; Prov. 3:4; cf. Avot de-Rabbi Natan 22:3; Ps. 111:10; Prov. 1:7).

Rabbi Ḥanina ben Dosa was a ḥasid whose life was marked by great piety and much prayer, with his heart directed toward Heaven. His friend Rabbi Jose the priest, was a ḥasid as well. Both were students of Rabbi Johanan ben Zakkai.

95. Sotah 49a. A hyperbole but perhaps the sense here is that Rabbi Ḥanina personified the type, no longer seen, who prayed much, studied much, but who placed his greatest emphasis on actions pleasing to man and God. He was renowned for his piety, for his character, for his saintliness, and for God's readiness to hearken to his prayers.

96. Ḥagigah 14a.

97. Bava Batra 74a–b. Rabbi Jonathan was a pupil of Ishmael and belonged to the third generation of tannaim (ca. 130–160 C.E.). The kind of fish Rabbi Jonathan called kresha is here translated as "shark." The tekhelet that the wife of Rabbi Ḥanina is destined to spin refers to the purple-blue or cerulean-dyed threads used for the show-fringes (see Num. 16:37–41). The dye was made from the shell—or the shell's contents—of a sea creature. The formula for the making of the dye was lost long ago.

13. Ḥananiah ben Hezekiah

98. Shabbat 13b. Ḥananiah ben Hezekiah ben Garon was of the first generation of tannaim and a follower of the school of Shammai. See Bacher, Tannaiten, 1:22. In his chamber the teachers met and decided eighteen questions to suit the Shammaites for he was the head of the school of Shammai in the generation before the destruction of Jerusalem (see Shabbat 1:4; Zavim 5:12). The Scroll of Ta'anit (Fasts) lists those days when it is not permissible to fast, for the reason that some joyous event had occurred on such days at one time or another. The Aramaic text was probably composed in part before the destruction of Jerusalem; its present text dates from the reign of Hadrian. Near the end of the Scroll of Ta'anit there is mention of Eleazar ben Hananiah as the author. It may be that father and son wrote the work, or the father started it and the son finished it or revised it (see Ta'anit 2:8; Eruvin 62b; S. Zeitlin, Megillat Ta'anit [Philadelphia, 1922], pp. 3–4).

99. Shabbat 13b; Ḥagigah 13a; Menaḥot 45a. Thus Ḥananiah ben Hezekiah is credited with having restored the Book of Ezekiel to its place in the canon. See G. F. Moore, Judaism in the First Centuries of the Christian Era, 1:246.

14. Neḥunia ben Ha-kanah

100. Megillah 28a. His secret for longevity involved constant consideration of others, the daily removal of his own feelings of hostility, anger, and bitterness and the practice of generosity to others, especially

scholars. Neḥunia ben Ha-kanah, of the first generation of tannaim, was the teacher of Ishmael (Shevu'ot 26a) and student of Rabbi Johanan ben Zakkai (Bava Batra 10b). The name, Ha-kaneh or Ha-kanah, is of uncertain etymology. Neḥunia is probably a form of Ḥonia (Onias) or of Johanan. Kanah occurs in Josh. 16:8 and 17:8 as the name of a brook or wadi and in 19:28 as a place-name. Geiger, relying on a reading that renders the last letter as an *aleph*, conjectures "the Zealot" (see Bacher, *Tannaiten*, 1:58, n. 1). Neḥunia was looked upon by later generations as a mystic. The prayer recited after the counting of the omer is attributed to him, as is the prayer, *onna be koaḥ* and the book, *Sefer Ha-bahir* or *Sefer Ha-pli'ah*.

101. Avot 3:5. The multitude of commandments in the Torah is likened to a yoke, not in the sense of burden or oppression, but of obedience. Maimonides explains "yoke of the Torah" as "diligent study." The yoke of the kingdom refers to the Roman taxation and general oppression. The yoke of search for sustenance refers to the anxieties and hardships attendant upon the earning of a livelihood. Absorption in study of Torah frees a man from all cares.

102. Berakhot 4:3, 28b. Compare also Megillah 28a; Bava Batra 10b; Bacher, *Tannaiten*, 1:58–61. The prayer he recited when departing from the house of study is a part of the prayer recited today by one concluding the study of a tractate of the Talmud.

15. Johanan ben Zakkai

103. Avot 2:9. Although the study of Torah was deemed most praiseworthy, the scholar should not regard it as reason for boasting or self-righteousness. To the contrary, study of Torah should result in humility. Maimonides points out that because Rabban Johanan had neglected nothing that was to be studied he could properly tell others not to take credit for whatever they had studied (cf. Deut. 10:12–13 and Micah 6:8). Rabban Johanan ben Zakkai was of the first generation of tannaim but his life and works served as an effective bridge to the second generation and, indeed, with all the generations of scholars to follow. His foresight in founding the Academy at Jabneh just prior to the destruction of the Temple resulted in the preservation of Judaism. He raised up brilliant disciples and was responsible for many regulations important because of the radically changing conditions of his times. The tradition has it that he lived 120 years like Moses and Ezra. In any case, he lived a long life. He probably survived the fall of Jerusalem in 70 c.e. by several years, and he must have been born near the beginning of the common era. Hoenig (*Great Sanhedrin*, p. 189) calls him a coleader with Rabban Simon ben Gamaliel I, who was occupied with the immediate problem of the hostilities with the Romans. Rabban Johanan, Hoenig says, may have served as head of the religious court and the position of coleader was reestablished as in the days of the *zugot*. This opinion is based on the reliability of the passage in Midrash ha-Gadol to Deut. 26:13 (cf. Midrash Tannaim, ed. Buber [Berlin, 1909], p. 175 and G. Alon, *Toldot ha-Yehudim be-Erez Yisrael bi-tekufat ha-Mishnah ve-ha-Talmud* [2 vols., Tel Aviv, 1952–55], 1:56), which speaks of the letter sent jointly by the nasi, Rabban Simon ben Gamaliel I, and Rabban Johanan ben Zakkai to the Jews of the Diaspora

concerning the tithe. Alon suspects the authenticity of the passage. S. Zeitlin, "The Hebrew Scrolls and the Status of Biblical Scholarship," *Jewish Quarterly Review*, n.s. 42 (1951–52):153, calls the letter inauthentic. For the text of the letter see earlier in this part, section 9, second paragraph. Louis Finkelstein says that Rabban Johanan was the av bet din, the head of the religious court, and, as such, second in command to the nasi, during the last decades of the Second Temple.

104. Avot de-Rabbi Natan 14:1; Sukkah 28a; Ta'anit 20b; Berakhot 26a; Yerushalmi Berakhot 2:10b. There are slight variations between the passages in the first two sources; e.g., in Sukkah the second group of Hillel's students are described as being worthy that the sun halt in its course for their sake as it did for Joshua. The passage in the former source ends with "the hermeneutical rules of the sages." Hillel's description of Rabban Johanan is found in Yerushalmi Nedarim 5:7. The intercalation of the years was made only by the leading members of the Sanhedrin. His disciple mentioned here was Rabbi Eliezer ben Hyrcanus.

105. Kiddushin 22b; Pesikta Rabbati 21:22. Here the teacher underscores Judaism's emphasis upon human freedom and its thrust from early biblical times toward the abolition of slavery. No human being is to accept another as his master. God alone is to be recognized as master.

106. Bava Kamma 79b. The thief (*ganav*) is one who steals surreptitiously, the robber (*gazlan*) takes openly, by force. The former fears to face his victim, the latter confronts him. The law punishes the thief more severely than the robber. For the thief fears man but not God; the robber fears neither man nor God.

107. Tosefta Oholot.

108. Bava Batra 10b. This entire passage constitutes one baraita, except for the explanation of Rabban Johanan at the end, which constitutes another baraita. The disciples are all tannaim of the second generation (about 90–130 C.E.). Rabban Gamaliel II was the son of Rabban Simon ben Gamaliel I and to set him apart from his grandfather of the same name is frequently called Gamaliel of Jabneh. He was the successor to his master, Rabban Johanan ben Zakkai, and served as nasi and head of the academy. Rabbi Eliezer ben Hyrcanus, usually in the Mishnah just Rabbi Eliezer, was the brother-in-law of Rabban Gamaliel II. Rabbi Joshua ben Hananiah, usually just Rabbi Joshua in the Mishnah, is frequently found in controversy with Rabbi Eliezer. He was active at Peki'in. Rabbi Eliezer the Modaite was from the town of Modi'im. For Nehunia ben Ha-kanah, see above legend.

109. Bava Kamma 79b; see Exod. 21:37.

110. Sifrei, Deuteronomy 192 on Deut. 20:1–8; Sotah 44b; Yerushalmi Sotah 5:9; Midrash Tannaim (Hoffman edition), p. 120. Compare with the Scroll of the War of the Sons of Light in which the same admonition is given, plate 10, lines 1 through 10, translation by M. Burrows, *The Dead Sea Scrolls* (New York, 1955), p. 397. See also J. Neusner, *A Life of Yohanan ben Zakkai* (2d ed., Leiden, 1970). The frightened soldier would return from battle with the newlywed and the new owner of a house or vineyard and no one at home would know the reason for his return. So he would be spared embarrassment and humiliation.

111. Hagigah 14b; Yerushalmi Hagigah 2:77a–b. Eleazar ben Arakh

was of the second generation of tannaim (ca. 90–130 C.E.) and a disciple of Johanan ben Zakkai. The rabbis were concerned about probing too much into the great mysteries of the Creation and of Ezekiel's vision of the Divine Chariot (see Ezek. 1), for such probing, they feared, could lead to insanity or apostasy. So Ben Azzai, Ben Zoma, Elisha ben Avuyah, and Rabbi Akiba immersed themselves in such theosophic speculation; but only Rabbi Akiba emerged without detriment to faith and intellectual faculty (see Ḥagigah 15b). For Rabbi Joshua, see n. 108. Jose the priest was a disciple of Rabban Johanan ben Zakkai and of the second generation of tannaim (ca. 90–130 C.E.; see Avot 2:10). The month of Tammuz falls in about the middle of the hot dry summer in Israel when the skies are cloudless. The *bat kol* or heavenly voice assured them that their reward in the hereafter was already prepared. Concerning the "Third Order," see Midrash Tehillim on Ps. 11:7: "there are seven classes (or orders) of people who will (after death) be admitted into the presence of the Ever-Living" and again, "these are the seven classes (or orders) of righteous persons." The Third Order or Class is that of the righteous of the world who are seated in a choice place in Paradise.

112. Bava Batra 10a. This story is quoted in connection with the statement that just as the income of a person is determined in heaven on Rosh Hashanah, so too his losses. If he merits it, then he will be able to share his good fortune with others; if not, then ill fortune will strike his household.

113. Bava Batra 80b. The talmudic passage deals with ways by means of which a seller of merchandise is likely to cheat his customer and the regulations prescribed by the sages to prevent it. If Rabban Johanan expounded upon the subject, would-be cheaters might learn from the prohibitions new ideas on cheating. If he did not deal with the subject, would-be cheaters would assume that the sages are ignorant of the practices of the trade, and would, therefore, be encouraged to cheat.

114. Rosh Ha-Shanah 18a; Yevamot 105a.

115. Ecclesiastes Rabbah 7:12. Evidently he suffered no simple faintness because he was hungry but because he was ill.

116. Ecclesiastes Rabbah 4:17. The welldigger meant that since he provided the wells necessary for the carrying out of the rabbi's instructions, he was cooperating with him as an equal. The rabbi's quotation of the verse implied that the welldigger, ignorant of the law, did not know what was ritually clean or unclean and he was presumptuous in considering himself the rabbi's equal.

117. Avot 2:10–12, Avot de-Rabbi Natan 14:3–4 (see also Bava Batra 10b for another group of disciples; and Pesikta de-Rav Kahana 12b; Bacher, *Tannaiten*, 1:38–39). The master here singles out the special characteristic that distinguishes each of the five. "Cemented cistern" is a figure of speech for a retentive memory. Eliezer was known for his exact recollection of traditional teachings and was a teacher of Rabbi Akiba. "A spring always flowing with fresh water," in contrast to "a cemented cistern," denotes an original mind with new and fresh ideas. The praise of Eliezer as one who outweighs all the other scholars is because Johanan places greater value on accurate retention of tradition than on sharpness of dialectical ability. But Abba Saul, who was of the third generation of tannaim and lived during the second century,

had an opposite tradition, that Johanan valued Eleazar ben Arakh and his original mind the most. The passage in Avot de-Rabbi Natan differs in certain aspects. Eliezer is described as "a glazed pitcher that preserves its wine"; Joshua, as "a threefold cord not easily severed"—alluding to three unspecified virtues; Jose, as "the saint of the generation"; and Ishmael (*sic*) ben Ḥananiah, as "an oasis in the desert which retains its waters."

118. Avot de-Rabbi Natan 14:6. Each disciple evidently was unaware that a colleague had preceded him in the mission of trying to console their master and his irritation must have gathered momentum with each vain attempt. When Rabbi Eleazar approached his home, Rabban Johanan changed his clothing from the mourner's garments he had been wearing. He complimented his disciple for having comforted him as far as it is within human ability to do so. This story would seem to support Abba Saul in the previous passage. See previous note. The words that finally did comfort him are reminiscent of those of Beruriah, wife of Rabbi Meir of the second century C.E., after the death of their two sons (Berakhot 10a).

119. Avot 2:13–14; Avot de-Rabbi Natan 14:5. The teacher here asks his students to state that quality the ethical person should strive to develop within himself above all others. The "good eye" implies seeing good in others, defects within oneself; it is the eye that is also free of jealousy and animosity. The "good heart" is one that is unselfish, generous, and loving. In the Hebrew the heart is the seat of all emotion as well as understanding. Avot de-Rabbi Natan adds to Rabbi Jose's answer: ". . . a good impulse and a good wife." The second dialogue is the converse of the previous one, except for the answer of Rabbi Simon. A version in Avot de-Rabbi Natan gives a different answer for Rabbi Jose: "An evil eye, an evil neighbor, and an evil wife." The same source adds explanatory words to Rabbi Eleazar's answer: "a heart that is evil towards Heaven and is evil towards all creatures."

120. Avot de-Rabbi Natan 22:1. Learning is exalted as the means to the virtuous life, but it is worthless unless it is so used.

121. Ibid., 6:3; see also Genesis Rabbah on Gen. 14:1 where several details are different. Eliezer's brothers were ploughing in the plain, while he was ploughing on the side of the mountain. As a consequence, his cow fell and was maimed. Therefore, he fled to Rabban Johanan to study in his academy. There he ate clods of earth because of his poverty. The verses upon which he was expounding, at the climax of the story, are given as Ps. 37:14–15. The story there concludes with Eliezer replying to his father that he refuses to profit from his learning and he will take only an equal share with his brothers in his father's estate. Because the guards prevented Hyrcanus from sitting down in the rear as he would have preferred, he had to push forward until he found himself close to the front, among the distinguished and famous, where he could witness his son's distinction. The three notables named are mentioned in Gittin 56a as being extremely wealthy. The text here continues by explaining that Ẓizit Ha-Kasat was so named "because he used to recline on a silver couch at the head of all the notables of Israel." The correct form of the name would then be Ẓizit Ha-Keset, i.e., "Ẓizit of the silver (couch)." See L. Finkelstein, "Introductory Study to Pirke Abot," *Journal of Biblical Literature* 57 (1938): 13–50). In the Talmud (Gittin 56a) the name is explained as follows:

because the fringes (*zizit*) of his garments would trail on cushions (*keset*) or because his seat (*kisei*) was among those of the Roman nobility (see also Nedarim 49b).

122. Genesis Rabbah on Gen. 15:18. Rabbi Akiba was of the younger group of the second generation of tannaim and one of the greatest scholars of the talmudic period. He was thus separated by a full generation from Rabban Johanan. His leadership was exercised especially between 110 C.E. and 135 C.E. Rabbi Judah bar Ilai was his pupil, a member of the third generation of tannaim (ca. 130–160 C.E.).

123. Ecclesiastes Rabbah 10:8.

124. Numbers Rabbah 19:8; Peskita Rabbati 14:14. For the purification ceremony of the red heifer, see Num. 19. The answer is given to the idolater in terms familiar to him, but the disciples cannot accept it, it smacks too much of demonology. Their teacher tells them that there is no rational explanation for the rite of the red heifer. It is a divine commandment that must be carried out because it is God's will.

125. Deuteronomy Rabbah 7:7. See also Genesis Rabbah 13:6, where the same story is told about Rabbi Joshua ben Korha. The Roman festivals here mentioned are the kalends, the first day of the month in the Roman calendar; Saturnalia, observed in December, beginning on the seventeenth and Kratesis, a Roman festival marking the conquest of the countries of the East (see also Avodah Zarah 8a).

126. Numbers Rabbah 4:9. Agentus may be a corruption of Quintus or Quietus, the name of a Roman general at the time of Rabban Johanan. The expression, "he whispered to me," may mean that it can be deduced from Scripture. Another reading of it is "Whisper to me," that is, "Permit me" to tell it to you. The point made here is that a mere surface reading of the Scripture does not suffice to get at its meaning.

127. Yoma 39b. The "lot" refers to the casting of lots on Yom Kippur for the selection of the scapegoat and the goat to be offered on the altar (see Yoma 6:1). Here the reference is to the lot reading, "For the Lord," designating the goat to be offered on the altar. The "tongue" refers to the crimson tongue-shaped strip that would turn white after the high priest would conclude the atonement ceremonies (see Yoma 6:8). In the verse quoted (Zech. 11:1), "Lebanon" is taken to refer to the Temple. The root of Lebanon means "whiten" and the Talmud here cites Rabbi Isaac ben Tablai who explains that the Temple is called Lebanon because it whitens the dark sins of the Jewish people. Iddo was the grandfather of Zechariah but the Scriptures will occasionally attach an individual to a distinguished grandfather rather than to the father. Hoenig (*Great Sanhedrin*, p. 112 and p. 273, n. 25) suggests a reading of four years instead of forty. Josephus records a similar episode for the year 66 C.E. and his testimony is parallel to that of the Talmud (see *Wars* 6.5.3).

128. Sotah 9:9; see Num. 5:19. The Mishnah here quotes Hos. 4:14 as a proof-text and Sotah 47b explains that the rite of the bitter waters administered to a wife suspected of adultery is effective only when the husband is above reproach. But during the chaotic years under the Romans before the war with Rome (66–70 C.E.), law and order broke down. The wife suspected of immorality could not be put to the test of bitter waters if the husband was himself immoral.

129. Lamentations Rabbah 1:5, Ecclesiastes Rabbah 7:12; see also

Gittin 56a. In Gittin 56a the number of councilors is three, two names being combined: Nakdimon ben Guryon. Ben Batiah was a leader of the Zealot party, the Sicarii. *Wah* was an exclamation indicating approval. Ben Batiah would not have hesitated to kill his venerable uncle had he thought that the scholarly leader had expressed disapproval. Rabban Johanan opposed the Zealots who had revolted against Rome (66 c.e.) and he counseled surrender to Vespasian, the Roman general who commanded the siege of Jerusalem. In Avot de-Rabbi Natan 6:3 it is told that the Zealots burned down all the storehouses.

130. Lamentations Rabbah 1:5; Gittin 56a–b, Avot de-Rabbi Natan 4:5. The narrative in our text is derived from a blending of elements in all three sources. The importance of the story lies in the action of Rabban Johanan that assured the survival of Judaism and the Jewish people after the destruction of Jerusalem and the Temple by the Romans in 70 c.e. Heretofore, the Temple had served as the central force uniting the people. In the future it would be the study of Torah. This was made possible by the creation of an academy of learning at Jabneh by Rabban Johanan with the permission of the Roman authorities. His counsel of peace to his fellow Jews was not a desire for appeasement at all costs or because he was opposed to nationalism. He showed his wisdom—Hillel had praised him as "the father of wisdom" and "the father of coming generations"—and his political acumen by his grasp of the hopelessness of the Jewish revolt against Rome. He opposed the Zealots, even though his nephew was one of their chief leaders, and counseled peace and submission to Rome. When he realized that his efforts were futile and that Jerusalem was doomed, he escaped from the besieged city not to save himself but to rescue the cause of Judaism. He was received graciously by Vespasian, the Roman general, and was granted his request—what must have seemed to Vespasian a trifle—immunity for the small group of Torah scholars at Jabneh, a rural town, until then insignificant. But Jabneh replaced Jerusalem and the Temple as the focal point of Jewish peoplehood. The Jewish future was thus assured and from the jaws of disaster Rabban Johanan had snatched Jewish eternity.

So bad was the famine in Jerusalem during the siege that the people were reduced to boiling straw and drinking its water. The conversation between Rabban Johanan and the men of Jerusalem is found in Avot de-Rabbi Natan 4:5. The use of the name Caesar here has the meaning of the Roman emperor or the Roman government. The one bow or arrow demanded by Vespasian was to serve as a token of submission. His "two predecessors" are, according to Zeitlin (*Megillat Ta'anit*, p. 104), the generals Florus and Cestius, whose armies were defeated in 66 c.e., but the generals were not slain by the Jews. In some sources Rabban Johanan's nephew is called Ben Batiah, in others, Abba Sikra, literally, Father of the Sicarii, the extremists in violence against the Romans.

The passage in Gittin 56a calls him the chief of the Biryoni in Jerusalem. They refused to make peace with the Romans despite the urging of the rabbis and declared they would fight the Romans. They burned the stores of wheat and barley so that the Jews would join them in fighting against the Romans for their survival. What the relationship was between the Sicarii and the Biryoni is difficult to determine. Professor Klausner sees the Biryoni as a corrupt faction of the more extreme group of Jewish resistance against Rome, ". . . part of the Zealot and Sicarii riffraff . . ." (Klausner, *Historiyah shel ha-bayit ha-sheni* [5 vols. in 3, Jerusalem, 1949–51], 5:233). He says the Zealots organized into a faction in 6 c.e. and the Sicarii during Felix's procuratorship (52–66 c.e.), the Sicarii evolving from the Zealots into a more extreme position. Zeitlin differs with Klausner in evaluating the nature and purposes of the Sicarii (see S. Zeitlin, "Massada and the Sicarii," *Jewish Quarterly Review*, n.s. 55 [1964–65]:302). Elsewhere Zeitlin writes that the Sicarii of Masada are called robbers by Josephus and in the Talmud, Biryoni, although in still another article he states that the Hebrew name of the Sicarii is not mentioned in the sources (*Bitzaron* 58 [May–June, 1968], No. 6, 272, pp. 71–78 and "Ha-essenim," *Sefer Ha-doar* [New York, 1957]), pp. 48–53. Joseph Nedava states that the term Biryoni may refer to "a political party, affiliated in some way with the Zealots and dedicated in particular to the defense of the vital fortress of Jerusalem" ("Who Were the 'Biryoni'?" *Jewish Quarterly Review*, n.s. 63 (1973):317–22), and he says that they may have been the precursors of the Sicarii. For a comprehensive summary of the authorities see Morton Smith, "Zealots and Sicarii: Their Origins and Relations," *Harvard Theological Review* 64 (1971):1–19.

Avot de-Rabbi Natan 35:2 states, "No dead bodies were kept overnight" in Jerusalem, and for Rabban Johanan's disciples, see earlier in this section.

Vespasian had served with distinction in Germany and Britain, and the emperor Nero gave him the chief command to quell the Jewish revolt. He began his campaign in the spring of 67 c.e., advancing from the north and had under his command three complete legions, twenty-three cohorts, six wings of cavalry, and the auxiliary troops of King Agrippa, altogether some sixty thousand men. By the spring of 68 c.e. he had taken the whole north of the country, all of Transjordan, and the lowlands of Judea and Idumea. By June of 69 he was proclaimed emperor by the legions stationed in the East. On his way to Rome, in Alexandria, the news reached him that Vitellius, who had been proclaimed emperor by the army of the Rhine, had been murdered (December 20, 69). He remained in Alexandria until the beginning of the following summer, and the command of the war against the Jews was left to his son Titus.

Lamentations Rabbah 1:5 has Rabban Johanan hail the king in Latin: "*Vive domine Imperator!*" ("Live, O lord Emperor!"). In the innermost chamber where Rabban Johanan was placed there was only pitch blackness. He could tell his questioners the hour from his practice of reviewing his studies in his mind and knowing how long they took. When placed in the chamber, he spent his time this way and thus was able to fix the hour. Gofna is located about fifteen miles northeast of Jerusalem, the modern Jifna. In the riddles the "snake" is Israel, the "cask" is Jerusalem, and the "tower" is the Temple. Pangar was a general of the Arabs, the neighbors of the Jews, and he advised that a harsh course be used against them by Vespasian. Rabban Johanan tells him he will regret it for in the end he and his people will be treated the same way by the Romans. At the end of the story Pangar is killed by Vespasian—presumably, Titus, because it was Titus who succeeded Vespasian and destroyed the Temple. Pangar gave

Rabban Johanan a deceptive answer, to which the sage retorted with a proverbial expression (see Sanhedrin 26a). The root of both words, *akel and akalkalot* means "to bend" or "to twist," i.e., either woven or crooked. The meaning is—your heart knows what your real intention is. Only Lamentations Rabbah has Rabban Johanan ask Vespasian for Jerusalem and then the Western Gate (or Western Wall) and, later, the rescue of Rabbi Zadok. Avot de-Rabbi Natan mentions only one request—for Jabneh—where he can establish an academy for his disciples. The Talmud mentions Jabneh with its sages and the family of Rabban Gamaliel and the healing of Rabbi Zadok. Ancient Lod was near modern Lod, a town southeast of modern Tel Aviv, and the site of Israel's largest airport. Rabban Gamaliel I lived earlier than the first century of the common era. At the time of the revolt against Rome his son, Rabban Simon ben Gamaliel I, was active. Rabbi Zadok had a grandson by the same name who was an associate of Gamaliel II, Eliezer, and Joshua, Johanan's disciples at Jabneh. The Zadok mentioned here was famous for his great piety and ascetic life. It was said of him that he carried on a fast for forty years to avert the destruction of Jerusalem. "Calculation by fingers" is a kind of game, says one scholar or it could have been some mathematical device. See part 9 for more on the Western Wall and the dwelling of the Shekhinah, the Heavenly Presence, in the west.

Josephus (*Wars*, 3.8.9) tells that he too predicted to Vespasian that he would become emperor, as would his son, Titus.

131. Avot de-Rabbi Natan 4:5.

132. Lamentations Rabbah 1:7. The departure of the great sage left the city desolate. The enemy gloats or, preferably, "rejoices"—the Hebrew verb may also mean "laughed with joy"—when the great scholars and teachers of Israel are forced to leave her.

133. Pesikta Rabbati 14:15. Because of their probing into the esoteric doctrines of Creation and of *ma'asei merkavah* in Ezek. 1. So says *Yefei Anaf* on Lamentations Rabbah, end of *petihah* 12 (see *Pesikta Rabbati*, trans. William G. Braude [2 vols., New Haven, 1968], 1:294, n. 107).

134. Sanhedrin 32b. Bror Hayil was the actual location of Rabban Johanan's academy near Jabneh (perhaps pronounced Bror Heil). The other illustrations given in the Talmud are to follow the court of Rabbi Eliezer to Lod, to follow his academy of learning similarly, and to follow after the sages to the Chamber of Hewn Stones, the seat of the Sanhedrin in Temple times.

135. Avot de-Rabbi Natan 4:5. This tale reflects Rabban Johanan's insight into religion's essence, his love for his fellow human beings, and the value he placed upon acts of benevolence.

136. See Rosh Ha-Shanah 4:1. In similar fashion did Rabban Johanan ben Zakkai transfer the celebration of the seven days of Sukkot with *lulav* and *etrog* from the Temple (as distinct from one day elsewhere) to the synagogue and even the home. He also transferred the practice of the *kohanim* ascending without shoes for the priestly blessing to the synagogue congregation.

137. Avot de-Rabbi Natan (ed. Schechter), second rescension, chap. 31, p. 34. The Messiah may be arriving but finish the practical things you are doing first.

138. Ibid., 25:2. The dying man with a tranquil mind can put his affairs in order properly. The man who dies on Sabbath eve will enter into rest at once. But he who dies on the eve of Yom Kippur dies with his sins unexpiated.

139. Genesis Rabbah 28; Avot de-Rabbi Natan 25:1 (cf. Berakhot 28b). They called him "exalted pillar" for upon him rested the Jewish world. The last words of Rabban Johanan testify to his strong belief that the King-Messiah would soon make his appearance. But while waiting, he built for eternity. In the time of later tannaim, Hezekiah was still considered almost identical with the Messiah (see Klausner, *The Messianic Idea*, p. 396). In Avot de-Rabbi Natan the words, "who will soon come" are lacking (see also Yerushalmi Sotah 9:16 and Yerushalmi Avodah Zarah 3:1, where the reading is, "and prepare (or place) a throne for Hezekiah, king of Judah." While there are no messianic sayings from the time before the destruction of the Temple, there is a whole series of such sayings from the first years after the destruction.

140. Rosh Ha-Shanah 31b. The number of his years was like that of Moses, Hillel, and Akiba. He died ca. 80 C.E.

141. Sotah 49a. A hyperbole intended as a tribute to the greatness of Rabban Johanan's learning.

142. Eduyyot 8:7. This mishnah is the principal passage concerning the mission of Elijah in the messianic age. Elijah in the tradition is to be the forerunner of the Messiah. Other tannaim in the same mishnah express differing opinions as to Elijah's role: Rabbi Judah, "to bring closer but not to remove afar"; Rabbi Simon, "to bring agreement where there is a matter for controversy"; the sages, i.e., the majority opinion, "to bring peace," as found in Mal. 3:23–24. Joshua ben Hananiah, one of Rabban Johanan's five principal disciples, was of the second generation of tannaim (ca. 90–130 C.E.). He is quoted usually as Rabbi Joshua, without the patronymic, and his name is found about eighty times in the mishnah. The teacher of Rabban Johanan was Hillel. The point of the passage is that Elijah will make no change in the law; he will come only to put an end to injustice (see Klausner, *The Messianic Idea*, p. 453, and n. 9 on same page).

143. Sotah 5:5. Rabbi Joshua, see previous note. To "remove the dust from the eyes" is an expression for "to come to life again."

144. Ecclesiastes Rabbah 7:7; Avot de-Rabbi Natan 14:6. The five disciples were Rabbi Eliezer ben Hyrcanus, Rabbi Joshua ben Hananiah, Rabbi Jose the Priest, Rabbi Simon ben Netanel, and Rabbi Eleazar ben Arakh (Avot 2:10). The text here goes on to say that the last named did not go to Jabneh, where Rabban Johanan had established the academy, but to join his wife at Dimsit (a watering place identical with Emmaus, so Jastrow [*Dictionary*, p. 300]). In Shabbat 147b the place is called Diomsit. It is a town in the plain of Judah and in talmudic times it was renowned for its warm springs and luxurious life. The result, says the text, was that Rabbi Eleazar forgot his learning; indeed, he is mentioned in the Mishnah only in Avot, chap. 2.

Part IX

The Last Years
of the Second
Commonwealth

1

Rome

On the day that Solomon married Pharaoh-Necho's daughter, Michael, the great prince among angels, came down from heaven and stuck a reed in the sea. Mud arose on each side so that the place became like a thicket of reeds, and that was the site on which the great city of Rome was built. On the day on which Jeroboam made the calf of gold the first two huts were built in Rome. They kept falling in until an old man named Abba Kolon said to the builders, "Unless you bring water from the river Euphrates and mix it with the clay, the buildings will not stand." They asked him, "Who will do this for us?" He answered, "I will." He dressed up like a wine carrier and went from one town to another and from one country to another until he came to his destination. When he arrived there, he went to the Euphrates, took water from the river, returned to Rome, and mixed it with the mortar and the buildings stood. From that time on they used to say: Any country that does not have an Abba Kolon is no country. They called the place "Rome-Babylon." On the day on which Elijah of blessed memory died, a king was established in Edom (Rome); for it says, *There was no king in Edom; a viceroy acted as king* (1 Kings 22:48).[1]

When God desired to judge the world, He entrusted the mission to two men, Romulus and Remus, so that if one wished to do something that was unjust, the other could veto it.[2] It is written, *You do look! You take note of mischief and vexation! To requite is in Your power. To You the hapless can entrust himself; You have ever been the orphan's help* (Ps. 10:14). The community of Israel said to the Holy One, blessed be He, "Master of the Universe, *You do look* [and see] that the wicked Esau will come and destroy the Temple and carry Israel away from their land and fasten their necks with chains. *You take note.... To requite is in Your power*—and yet, You caused Your divine presence to rest on

Isaac so that he said to Esau, *See, your abode shall enjoy the fat of the earth . . . yet by your sword you shall live* (Gen. 27:39–40). *To You the hapless can entrust himself*—tomorrow he will come and seize orphans and widows and lock them in prison and say to them, 'Let Him of whom it is written that He is *the father of orphans, the champion of widows* (Ps. 68:6) come and deliver you from my hands.' But in truth *You have ever been the orphan's help*—two orphans were left by Esau, namely Remus and Romulus, and You gave permission to a she-wolf to suckle them and afterward they arose and built two great tents in Rome."[3]

Ten measures of wealth descended upon the world. Nine were taken by Rome and one by all the rest of the world.[4] All the silver and gold in the world were collected by Joseph and brought to Egypt, as it is said, *Joseph gathered in all the money that was to be found in the land of Egypt* (Gen. 47:14). But this tells only about Egypt. Whence do we know what happened to this treasure later, in Canaan and the rest of the lands? The verse says, *So all the world came to Joseph in Egypt to procure rations* (Gen. 41:57). When Israel went up out of Egypt, they carried that wealth with them, as it is said, *Thus they stripped the Egyptians* (Exod. 12:36). It stayed with them until the time of Rehoboam, son of Solomon. Then Shishak, king of Egypt, came up against Jerusalem and took it away from Rehoboam, as it is said, *In the fifth year of King Rehoboam, King Shishak of Egypt marched against Jerusalem and carried off the treasures of the House of the Lord and the treasures of the royal palace. He carried off everything; he even carried off all the golden shields that Solomon had made* (1 Kings 14:25–26). Then Zerah, king of Cush, came and took it away from King Shishak of Egypt. Then Asa, King of Israel, took it from Zerah and sent it to Hadrimon son of Tabrimon. Jehoshaphat came and took it from the Ammonites and it remained until the time of Ahaz. Sennacherib came and took it from Ahaz. Hezekiah came and took it back from Sennacherib and it stayed until the days of Zedekiah. Then the Chaldeans came and took it from Zedekiah. The Persians took it from the Chaldeans, the Greeks from them, and the Romans from the Greeks. In Rome it still remains.[5]

The blessing of Isaac to Esau, *See, your abode shall enjoy the fat of the earth* (Gen. 27:39), refers to Italy.[6] The verse, *All streams flow into the sea, yet the sea is never full* (Eccles. 1:7), can be interpreted as meaning that all wealth goes only to the empire of

Rome, and the Roman empire is never sated. For Rabbi Levi said, "It is written, *Nor can the eyes of man be satisfied* (Prov. 27:20), that is, the eyes of Rome are never satiated." Does this mean that when wealth enters Rome it never again will return to its owners? Therefore, the verse states, *To the place [from] which they flow the streams flow back again* (Eccles. 1:7). From the place where wealth accumulates, that is, the kingdom of Rome in premessianic times, thence it will be dispersed in the days of the Messiah, as it is written, *But her profits and "hire" shall be consecrated to the Lord* (Isa. 23:18).[7]

There is no successful war in which the descendants of Esau, i.e., the Romans, have no part.[8] Were it not for the sound of the sun's revolution, the tumult of the troops of Rome could be heard everywhere. And were it not for the tumult of the troops of Rome, the sound of the sun's revolution could be heard. The rabbis taught that three sounds go from one end of the earth to the other: the sound of the sun's revolution, the sound of Rome's troops, and the sound of the soul as it leaves the body. Others add the sound of birth, while still others include the sound of Ridya, the angel of rain. The heathen troops swing their shields, blow their trumpets, and they shout and tread down with their galloping horses.[9]

Moses said to Israel, "If you see that Esau [Rome] seeks to make war on you, then do not stand up to him but hide yourselves from him until his world of might will have passed." Israel complained before God, "Master of the universe, Esau's father blessed him with the words, *Yet by your sword you shall live* (Gen. 27: 40), and You did approve of the blessing, now You say to us, 'Hide yourselves before him?' Where shall we flee?" God replied, "When you see that he would attack you, then flee to the Torah." Another explanation is that the Holy One, blessed be He, said to Israel, "Wait, the King Messiah has yet to come to fulfill the words of the Scriptures, *How abundant is the good that You have in store for those who fear You* (Ps. 31:20)."[10]

Yet by your sword you shall live—another interpretation of *your sword*: Esau (Rome) is Your sword, for with him You chastise the world.[11]

When the emperor is counted with the Decumani, the legion is complete. When he is counted with the Augustiani, the legion is complete.[12]

In the time to come the Holy One, blessed be He, will bring a scroll of the Torah, place it in His lap, and declare, "Let any who have been engaged in the Torah come and receive their reward!" The peoples of the world will come forward and gather in disarray. The Holy One, blessed be He, will tell them, "Do not enter before Me in disarray but let each people, together with its scribes, enter in order." At once the kingdom of Rome will enter first because of its importance. Whence do we know that it is important? For it is written, *The fourth beast [means]—there will be a fourth kingdom upon the earth which will be different from all the kingdoms; it will devour the whole earth, tread it down, and crush it* (Dan. 7:23). And Rabbi Johanan explained, "This means Rome whose sway extends over all the world." The Holy One, blessed be He, will ask them, "With what have you engaged yourselves in this world?" They will answer, "Master of the Universe, we have established many markets, we have built many bathhouses, we have multiplied much silver and gold—and all of this we have done only for the sake of the Jewish people so that they could busy themselves in the study of Torah." "Fools!" the Holy One, blessed be He, will reply. "Whatever you did, you did for your own benefit—markets, so that you could establish your prostitutes in them; bathhouses, so that you could get physical satisfaction from them. As for the silver and gold, they really belong to Me, as it is said, *Silver is Mine and gold is Mine—says the Lord of Hosts* (Hag. 2:8). Have you then anyone who has engaged in Torah?" At once they will depart, disconsolate.[13]

Rebecca was told by the Lord: There are two proud rulers of nations in thy womb, each taking pride in his world and in his kingdom. Two peoples hated by the nations are in your womb: all nations hate Esau (Rome) and all heathens hate Israel. The rejected of your Creator is in your womb, as it is written, *And [I] have rejected Esau* (Mal. 1:3).[14] The verse reads, *Now Esau harbored a grudge against Jacob* (Gen. 27:41). He was filled with hatred, hostility, and vindictiveness toward him, so that to this very day one speaks of the *senatores* (hateful ones) of Rome.[15]

Another exposition of *The Lord bless you*—with wealth—*and keep you* (Num. 6:24)—that you not be compelled to take office in the province of Paneas and that no fine be imposed upon the district as a result of which the Romans should say to you, "Give gold!"[16]

The wicked state (Rome) casts an envious eye upon a man's wealth, saying, "So-and-so is wealthy; let us make him a councilor."[17] A man may be rich and put out his money on interest and so accumulate much wealth. But he may die without having children and his entire wealth will go to swell the state treasury. What does the king do with that money? He builds pedestals for idols, public baths, terraces, and lavatories to answer the needs of the poor.[18] Three things did the wicked state (Rome) receive from Greece: laws (justice), literature, and language.[19]

There are four languages of special value to human society: Greek for song, Persian for lamentation, Hebrew for conversation, and Latin for military purposes. A certain border villager fashioned the Latin language out of the Greek.[20] How confounded, how senseless, is the laughter in which the heathen peoples indulge in their circuses and theaters! What cause can a disciple of the sages have to enter such places?[21]

Ruth told Naomi, "I am fully resolved to become converted under any circumstances, but it is better that it be at your hands than at those of another." When Naomi heard this, she began to explain to her the laws of conversion, saying, "My daughter, it is not the custom of daughters of Israel to frequent gentile theaters and circuses." To this Ruth replied, *For wherever you go, I will go* (Ruth 1:16).[22]

It is written, *Those who sit in the gate talk about me* (Ps. 69:13). This refers to the peoples of the world who sit in theaters and circuses. *I am the taunt of drunkards* (Ps. 69:13)—after they sit eating and drinking and become intoxicated they sit and talk about me, scoffing at me, and saying, "We have no need to eat carobs like the Jews!" They ask one another, "How long do you wish to live?" To which they reply, "As long as the shirt of a Jew worn on the Sabbath!" They take a camel into their theaters, put shirts upon it, and ask, "Why is it in mourning?" To which they reply, "The Jews observe the law of the sabbatical year and they have no vegetables, so they eat this camel's thorns, and that is why it is in mourning!" Next they bring a clown into the theater, his head shaven, and ask one another, "Why is his head shaven?" To which the reply is given, "The Jews observe the Sabbath and whatever they earn during the week they eat on the Sabbath. Since they have no wood to cook with, they break up their beds and use them as fuel; consequently they sleep on the ground and get covered with dust, so they anoint themselves with oil, which therefore, becomes very expensive."[23]

Behemoth and Leviathan will engage in a contest before the righteous in the time to come, and whoever has not been a spectator at the wild beast contests of the heathen nations in this world will be given the opportunity of seeing this one in the world to come. How will they be slaughtered? With its horns Behemoth will pull Leviathan down and tear it asunder and Leviathan, with its fins, will pull Behemoth down and pierce it through.[24]

The verse, *Do not be vexed by the prospering man* (Ps. 37:7), refers to Esau (Rome) of whom it says, *Why does the way of the wicked prosper?* (Jer. 12:1). Because of the man *who carries out his schemes* (Ps. 37:7). This refers to Esau (Rome) who conducts trials with guile. How? A judge of the (Roman) government tries a man for murder and asks him, "Why did you murder?" The accused denies the charge. He is then asked, "With what did you murder the man—with a sword, a spear, or a knife?"[25]

The verse, *The way of man may be tortuous and strange* (Prov. 21:8), refers to Esau (Rome) who is constantly planning evil decrees with which to harass Israel. Thus the Romans accuse them, "You have stolen!" and they answer, "We have not stolen." "You have been guilty of murder!" and they answer, "We have not been guilty of murder." "You have not stolen? Who then stole with you?" "You have not been guilty of murder? Who then murdered with you?" The Roman judge thereupon fines them on false charges, saying, "Bring the records of your *annonae,* your poll tax, your state tax."[26]

David wrote the seventh psalm with reference to the seat of judgment of wicked Rome. Like Nimrod, a mighty hunter before the Lord, Rome snared people with words, saying with cunning, "Yes, you have not stolen, but tell us, who was your partner in the theft; you have not killed, but who was your accomplice in the murder?"[27]

If you see Esau (Romans) in the great city of Rome oppressing the lowly and robbing the poor, and the Holy One, blessed be He, granting them prosperity, you will see applied to them the divine attribute of justice in the future.[28]

The verse, *The life you face shall be precarious* (Deut. 28: 66), applies to one who lies in the prison at Caesarea.[29] To what can the word, *mazor,* "bastion" be applied, in the verse in Psalms, *Would that I were brought to the bastion* (Ps. 60:11)? It can be applied to Rome. And why does David call it *mazor?* Because it is a city that oppresses (*mezirah*) and diminishes (*mevazerah*) Israel.[30]

The swine is symbolic of Edom (Rome). It does not accord

the stranger the treatment due him. It does not exalt righteous men—even worse, it kills them. This is alluded to in what is written, *I was angry at My people, I defiled My heritage; I put them into your hands, but you showed them no mercy. Even upon the aged you made your yoke exceedingly heavy* (Isa. 47:6).[31] The swine symbolizes Edom (Rome) in that it does not extol the Holy One, blessed be He. But not only does it not extol, it reviles and blasphemes, saying, *Whom else have I in heaven?* (Ps. 73:25).[32]

Of all the prophets only two, Moses and Asaph, exposed Rome's perfidy. Asaph said, *Wild boars gnaw at it* (Ps. 80:14), and Moses said, *Also the swine . . . although it has true hoofs* (Deut. 14:8). Why is Rome compared to a swine? When the swine is lying down it puts out its hoofs, as if to say, "See! I am clean." In like fashion this wicked state robs and oppresses, yet pretends to be executing justice.[33]

The boar symbolizes Rome in the verse, *Wild boars gnaw at it* (Ps. 80:14)—that kingdom that consumes the wealth of other peoples and that derives status from Abraham, saying, "I descend from him since Esau was the son of Isaac who was the son of Abraham." Everyone appears before Rome with pieces of silver; for even when one has sinned against her and she is angry with him, yet she opens her palm to accept the bribe that is offered and she becomes reconciled. She disperses Israel when assembled for the study of Torah, and gathers them in such places where the Evil Inclination takes delight.[34]

The river Perat (Euphrates) refers to Edom (Rome) for it was fruitful (*parat*) and multiplied because of the prayer of the old man—Isaac. Another explanation is: Perat is a name applicable to Edom (Rome), because it was fruitful and multiplied and oppressed His children; or, because it was fruitful and multiplied and besieged His Temple; or, Perat, because of Edom's end, as it is said, *I trod out a vintage* [purah] *alone* (Isa. 63:3).[35]

The verse reads, *Awesome as bannered hosts* (Songs 6:10). Rabbi Joshua said, "It is like the fear inspired by earthly powers, such as generals and commanders and field marshals." How do we know that these inspire fear? Because it says, *A fourth beast* [applied to Rome]—*fearsome, dreadful, and very powerful* (Dan. 7:7).[36]

Rabbi Judah said, "*The little foxes* (Songs 2:15) are Esau (Rome) and his generals, as it is said, *I will make you least among nations* (Obad. 1:2). *That ruin the vineyards* (Songs 2:15)—vine-

yards signifies Israel, as it is written, *For the vineyard of the Lord of Hosts is the House of Israel* (Isa. 5:7)."[37] *When all the flocks were gathered there* (Gen. 29:3)—this symbolizes the wicked state (Rome) that levies troops from all the nations of the world.[38]

The verse, *Hark! My beloved! There he comes* (Songs 2:8), refers to the Messiah. When he will say to Israel, "In this month you will be redeemed," they will say to him, "How can we be delivered since the Holy One, blessed be He, has sworn that He will subject us to the seventy nations?" He will answer, "This state of Rome levies troops from all over the world, from every nation. Therefore, if one Cuthean or one Barbarian comes and rules over you, it is as if his entire nation had ruled over you and as if you had served all the seventy nations. Hence in this month you are to be delivered after all, as the verse says, *This month shall mark for you the beginning of the months* (Exod. 12:2)."[39]

The following verse may also be applied to Rome. *He who increases his wealth by loans at discount or interest amasses it for one who is generous to the poor* (Prov. 28:8). But is Rome gracious to the poor? Does not Rome rather oppress the poor? The explanation lies in the examples of generals, commanders, and governors who go out to cities to plunder and despoil them and upon their return say, "Bring us the poor that we may feed them." The popular proverb says it, "She prostitutes for apples and distributes them among the sick."[40]

Rabban Simon ben Gamaliel said, "Although the earlier generations experienced only part of what is inflicted upon us by the foreign kingdoms, they gave voice to their suffering. In connection with our forefathers, it is written, *But the people grew restive on the journey* (Num. 21:4). Daniel said, *As for me, Daniel, my spirit was disturbed* (Dan. 7:15). Isaiah said, *Therefore, my loins are seized with trembling* (Isa. 21:3). Jeremiah said, *We get our bread at the peril of our lives* (Lam. 5:9). But we, who are set in the midst of the four kingdoms, how much more should we complain!"[41]

The people of Israel cried out before God, "Master of the Universe! Is it not enough that we have been subject to the seventy nations but must we also be subject even to this one as well—Rome—whose men practice immoral abuses, using each other as women?" The Holy One, blessed be He, answered them, "Therefore will I punish them with those very words, as it is said, *And the heart of Edom's warriors in that day shall be like the heart of a woman in travail* (Jer. 49:22)."[42]

In Roman practice one must not call himself by the name of a king, Caesar or Augustus, even though the king is but a mortal, for if one assumed the king's name, he would be executed for treason. Yet God called Moses by His own name, as it says in Scriptures, *See, I place you in the role of God to Pharaoh* (Exod. 7:1).[43] When the Roman legions throw the purple cloak of royalty before a general, what does he do? He remits the tax arrears, burns the roll, and leads the legions out on parade, and this is counted as the beginning of his reign.[44]

He who cuts his hair in Roman fashion violates the biblical prohibition against imitating the ways of the Amorites. An exception was made in the case of Abtolumus ben Reuben because he had to associate with members of the Roman regime.[45]

These things are concealed from man: the day of death, the day of comfort, and the absolute truth of judgment. No man knows through what he will profit. No person knows what kind of child a woman is bearing, nor when the wicked state of Rome will fall.[46]

A time will come when Rome, the destroyer of the Second Temple, will fall into the hands of the Parthians. But another opinion has the contrary, Parthia will fall into the hands of Rome. For it has been taught that the Messiah, descendant of David, will not come until Rome will have spread its dominion over all the world for nine months, as it is said, *Truly, he will leave them [helpless] until she who is to bear has borne; then the rest of his countrymen shall return to the children of Israel* (Mic. 5:2).[47]

The prayer of the psalmist, *O Lord, do not grant the desires of the wicked; do not let their plan succeed* (Ps. 140:9), may be interpreted: Sovereign of the Universe, do not grant that the wicked Esau (Rome) fulfill the schemes of his heart that he has schemed against Jacob. And what is the interpretation of the second part of the verse, *Do not let their plan succeed*? It is as follows: Sovereign of the Universe! Make a muzzle for the wicked Esau (Rome), so that he may not enjoy complete tranquillity. And what was the muzzle that the Holy One, blessed be He, made for Esau (Rome)? Rabbi Ḥama bar Rabbi Ḥanina said that it was the Barbarians and the Germans of whom the Edomites (Romans) are afraid.[48]

The patriarch Abraham saw the ram (at the time of the sacrifice of Isaac) extricate itself from one thicket only to become entangled in another. The Holy One, blessed be He, said to him, "So will your descendants be entangled among the peoples, from Babylon to Media, from Media to Greece, and from Greece to Edom (Rome). But eventually they will be redeemed by the ram's horn, as it is written, *My Lord God shall sound the ram's horn. . . . The Lord of Hosts will protect them* (Zech. 9:14–15)."[49]

The King Messiah who will one day punish Edom (Rome) lives with them in that land.[50] In the millennium to come all the nations will bring gifts to the King Messiah. Egypt will be the first. The Messiah will hesitate to accept their gifts and God will say to him, "My children found hospitality in Egypt," for it says, *Tribute-bearers shall come from Egypt* (Ps. 68:32). Whereupon the Messiah will immediately accept their gifts. Ethiopia will then draw an inference for itself: "If the Messiah receives gifts from Egypt which enslaved them, how much more will he receive gifts from us who have never subjected them to slavery?" Therefore, the verse says, *Cush* [Ethiopia] *shall hasten its gifts to God* (Ps. 68:32). When the other kingdoms will hear this, they too will bring gifts, as it says, *O kingdoms of the earth, sing to God* (Ps. 68:33). The kingdom of Edom (Rome) will then draw an inference for itself: "If gifts were received from those who are not their brothers, then how much more will they be received from us—who are their brothers?" But when Rome will be about to offer its gift to the King Messiah, God will say to him, *"Blast the beast of the marsh* (Ps. 68:31), for that entire nation is like a wild beast of the marsh."[51]

When Edom (Rome) falls, it will not bring in its train another empire to follow it. And why is it called *ḥazir*, "swine"? Because it will restore (*ḥazor*) the crown to its proper owner. This is indicated by what is written, *For liberators shall march up on Mount Zion to wreak judgment on Mount Esau; and dominion shall be the Lord's* (Obad. 1:21).[52]

Just as God has used Michael and Gabriel as His instruments in this world, so will He execute His will through them in the future, for it says, *For liberators shall march up on Mount Zion to wreak judgment on Mount Esau* and this refers to Michael and Gabriel. Our holy teacher (Rabbi Judah ha-Nasi) is of the opinion that this refers only to Michael, for it says, *At that time, the great prince, Michael, who stands beside the sons of your people* (Dan.

12:1), because it is he who presents Israel's requirements and pleads for them, as it says, *Thereupon the angel of the Lord exclaimed, "O Lord of Hosts! How long will You withhold pardon from Jerusalem"* (Zech. 1:12), and again, *No one is helping me against them except your prince, Michael* (Dan. 10:21).[53]

This is an interpretation of the verse in Psalms, *On Edom I would cast my shoe* (60:10). God asks what will I do? I will draw off My shoes and tread upon them and trample them down with My heel. Similarly does another verse read, *I trod out a vintage alone* (Isa. 63:3). This is illustrated by a parable. To what may it be compared? It may be compared to a king of flesh and blood who built four palaces in four cities. He went to the first and ate and drank without removing his shoes. He did the same in the second and the third. When he came to the fourth he ate and drank and took off his shoes, saying to his attendants, "Go and bring all the prominent men in this city and have them set food before me." They asked him, "How is it that when you entered the other palaces you ate and drank without taking off your shoes, while here you removed your shoes when you ate and drank?" He replied, "When I entered the first palace my mind was not at ease. The same was true with the second and third. I was constantly thinking, When shall I see the hour when I can enter the fourth palace? Now that I have entered it, my mind has at once been put at ease." It was the same with the Holy One, blessed be He. He made war against Pharaoh, Amalek, Sisera, Sennacherib, Nebuchadnezzar, Haman, and the kings of the Greeks. But His mind will not be calmed until He will have executed vengeance upon Edom (Rome). This explains the verse, *On Edom I would cast my shoe; acclaim me, O Philistia!* (Ps. 60:10). This means, I will cast down the foundations of Edom (Rome) and will achieve your redemption.[54]

The link between the downfall of Rome and the coming of the Messiah may be compared to the case of a woman eagerly awaiting the return of her husband who had gone abroad. He had said to her before his departure, "Such and such will be a sign for you. Whenever you see such a sign, know that I shall soon be back." In like manner Israel has eagerly awaited salvation since the rise of Edom (Rome). God said, "Let this be a sign to you. The night that will witness the overthrow of Rome will be followed by the morning of salvation for you, but if the night does not occur, then do not believe that salvation is at hand, for the time has not yet come." So do the Scriptures say, *I the Lord will speed it in due time* (Isa. 60:22), and *In just a little while longer I will shake the heavens and the earth* (Hag. 2:6), and *I will over-turn the thrones of kingdoms* (Hag. 2:22). Moreover, God said, "Just as I have overthrown the Egyptians, so will I overthrow all idol worshipers." For it says, *Such nations shall be destroyed* (Isa. 60:12), and also *So that it seizes the corners of the earth and shakes the wicked out of it* (Job 38:13).[55]

God's actions may be compared to those of a person who found a serpent, crushed its head with a stone, and cut off its tail. Of what value was it then? In like manner did the Egyptians and Edom (Rome) subject Israel to unendurable slavery. What did God do? In Egypt He punished them, for it says, *[He] hurled Pharaoh and his army into the Sea of Reeds* (Ps. 136:15). Concerning Edom, it is written *I trod out a vintage alone* (Isa. 63:3). The Holy Spirit said, *Egypt shall be a desolation and Edom a desolate waste* (Joel 4:19). God will one day deliver Israel from Edom. *Jerusalem and Your people have become a mockery among all who are around us* (Dan. 9:16), and will you not redeem us? God replied, "Yes." They then asked Him, "Swear!" And He swore that just as He had delivered us from Egypt so would He deliver us from Edom. More than that, when nobles of the peoples will see even the most ordinary Israelite, they will desire to kneel before him because of God's Name inscribed on each Israelite, as it is said, *Thus said the Lord, the Redeemer of Israel, his Holy One, to the despised being, to the abhorred nation, to the slave of rulers: Kings shall see and stand up* (Isa. 49:7). It is as if a beautiful tree were set in the bathhouse, and when the chief of the army with his suite came to bathe, they trampled upon the tree, and all the villagers and everyone else were eager to tread upon it. Some time later, the king sent his bust to that province so that they might put up a statue of him, but they could find no wood except that from the tree in that bathhouse. The workmen said to the local ruler, "If you wish to set up the statue, you must bring the tree that is in the bathhouse, for it is the best wood there is." They brought it, prepared it thoroughly, and placed it in the hands of a carver, who fashioned of it a pedestal for the statue and placed it within the palace. Then came the ruler and bowed before it; and afterward the general, the prefect, the imperial officers, the legionaries, the people, and everyone else. Then the workmen said to them, "Yesterday you were trampling on this tree in the bathhouse, and now you are bowing to it." They answered, "It is not to the tree that we are bowing, but to the bust of the king set upon it." So will the men of Gog say, "Until now we did atrocious things to Israel—as it is said, *To the despised being, to the abhorred nation*—but now we bow down to them!" God said to them, "Yes, it is because of My Name that is proclaimed over them," for it says, *To the honor of the Lord, who is faithful* (Isa. 49:7). Moses also said, *And all the peoples of the earth shall see that the Lord's name is proclaimed over you, and they shall stand in fear of you* (Deut. 28:10). When God took Israel out of Egypt, He took the lantern—to illumine their path—and went before them, as it says, *The Lord went before them . . . in a pillar of fire by night, to give them light* (Exod. 13:21). So will He do when He takes them out of Edom, as Isaiah said, *For the Lord is marching before you, the God of Israel is your rear guard* (Isa. 52:12), and it is written, *See, the things once predicted have come* (Isa. 42:9). All this in order that the prophecy be fulfilled, *Egypt shall be a desolation and Edom a desolate waste* (Joel 4:19).[56]

The chaos and void, which prevailed before Creation, have not yet gained the upper hand in this world. When will they prevail? In the great city of Rome, as it is said, *He shall measure it with a line of chaos and with weights of emptiness* (Isa. 34:11).[57]

The wicked state (Rome), because it blasphemes and reviles, saying, *Whom else have I in heaven?* (Ps. 73:25), is to be punished with fire, as it is said, *The beast was killed as I looked on; its body was destroyed and it was consigned to the flames* (Dan. 7:11). Israel, however, who is despised and lowly in this world will be comforted with fire, as it is said, *And I Myself—declares the Lord —will be a wall of fire all around it, and I will be a glory inside it* (Zech. 2:9). The fire that will consume Rome shall never be quenched. It will burn night and day forever because the Romans burned the Temple of God, of which it is written, *And the House kept filling with smoke* (Isa. 6:4). Therefore it is written about Edom (Rome), *Its smoke shall rise for all time* (Isa. 34:10). Because they disturbed Israel's study of the Torah, God will avenge Himself on the wicked city with fire.[58]

With the threefold priestly benediction are the children of Israel to be blessed. This may be linked to what is written in Scripture, *Do not envy a lawless man or choose any of his ways* (Prov. 3:31). *A lawless man* refers to the wicked Esau (Rome) and the reason for the verse saying *Do not envy* is because the Holy One, blessed be He, knew that Israel is destined to be enslaved to the power of Edom (Rome) and will be oppressed and crushed in their midst. At that time Israel will raise angry protest against this. Therefore, the Holy Spirit, speaking through Solomon, said, *Do not envy the lawless man*—do not envy the well-being enjoyed by the wicked Esau; *or choose any of his ways*—you must not do according to their ways. Why not? Look how it will all end some day! For behold, a day will come when God will abhor all who sneer at the commandments. On the other hand, he who directs his course properly in His presence shall be among the men of His counsel.

The curse of the Lord is on the house of the wicked (Prov. 3:33) applies to the wicked Esau; as can be read in Scripture, *They may build, but I will tear down. And so they shall be known as the region of wickedness, the people damned forever of the Lord* (Mal. 1:4). *But He blesses the abode of the righteous* (Prov. 3:33) applies to Israel, about whom it is written, *And your people, all of them righteous, shall possess the land for all time* (Isa. 60:21).

Every day they scoff at Israel because of the sufferings that have come upon them. In the future the Holy One, blessed be He, will mete out to them according to their own measure; as Scripture says, *As you did, so shall it be done to you; your conduct shall be requited* (Obad. 1:15). *But to the lowly He shows grace* (Prov. 3:34), refers to the people of Israel who are poor and go about in humility and suffer the burdens imposed upon them in order to sanctify the name of the Holy One, blessed be He. In the future He will show grace to them and execute justice upon their traducers. So is it written, *Truly the Lord is waiting to show you grace* (Isa. 30:18), and as it says, *Then the humble shall have increasing joy through the Lord* (Isa. 29:19); and it also says, *O people in Zion, dwellers of Jerusalem, you shall not have cause to weep* (Isa. 30:19). *The wise shall obtain honor* (Prov. 3:35) applies to the people of Israel who are called wise when they fulfill the Torah and the commandments. Because the people of Israel observe the Torah while among the nations, the Holy One, blessed be He, will in the future cause them to inherit a throne of glory and restore to Israel its sovereignty. But as for the fools, they *get disgrace as their portion* (Prov. 3:35). This applies to the Edomites (Rome). What is the meaning of *get disgrace as their portion?* That they will raise a conflagration in their territory; that is, they will ultimately go up in flames.[59]

God commands those who study Torah, "Never say 'I understand' to something you do not understand, nor prohibit to another that which you permit to yourself, but let all the utterances that proceed from your mouth be reliable, as were those that proceeded from Moses, and I will make you behold My beauty face to face," as it says, *When your eyes behold a king in his beauty* (Isa. 33:17). Israel then asked, "How can we behold You for You have delivered us into the hands of Edom (Rome)?" But God replied, "Do not be afraid of them, for one day you will ask Me where they are, as it is written, *No more shall you see the barbarian folk* (Isa. 33:19), but instead you shall see the joy of Zion, for it says, *When you gaze upon Zion, our city of assembly, your eyes shall behold Jerusalem as a secure homestead* (Isa. 33:20)."[60]

Israel said to God, "Lord of the universe! How long will You delay judging the heathen?" The reply was, "Until the time of vintage comes; as it says, *In that day, they shall sing of it: 'Vineyard of Delight'* (Isa. 27:2)." Is it done, to glean one's vineyard before the grapes ripen? No, only after they are ripe does a man pluck them, place them in the vat, and tread them, while his fellow workers sing with him. So did God say to Israel, "Wait until Edom's (Rome's) time is ripe and then I will tread upon her, as it says, *On Edom I would cast my shoe* (Ps. 60:10). I will begin [singing] and you will respond after Me. Therefore, does it say, *In that day, they shall sing of it: 'Vineyard of Delight.' I the Lord keep watch over it, I water it every moment* (Isa. 27:2–3). I am biding My time with her to make her drink many cups. [If I willed it] I would only have to glance at them to destroy them completely from this world, but *there is no anger in Me* (Isa. 27:4) as it is in them against My children. What will I do to them? [When their measure of sin is full], *I will ... set all of them on fire* (Isa. 27:4)."

God said to the heathen, "Israel is Mine, as it says, *For it is to Me that the Israelites are servants* (Lev. 25:55), and fury is Mine, as it says, *The Lord is vengeful and fierce in wrath* (Nah. 1:2), yet you are filled with the fury that is Mine against Israel that is Mine!"

God gave another answer to Israel: "If I were to alter My procedure in judgment [which is patient and long-suffering], I would destroy them in a flash. But what do I do? *My hand lays hold on judgment* (Deut. 32:41) [adhering to the usual divine procedure]."[61]

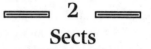

2

Sects

Antigonus of Sokho had two disciples who taught his doctrine to their students and they to their disciples: "Be not like servants who serve the master for the sake of reward, but be like servants who serve the master without expectation of reward." They rose up and considered the matter and said, "Why did our predecessors say this? Is it right for a laborer to work all day and not be paid in the evening? Had our predecessors known that there was another world and that there would be resurrection of the dead they certainly would not have taught as they did!" So they arose and turned away from the Torah. Two sects sprang from them, the Sadducees and the Boethusians—the Sadducees named after Zadok and the Boethusians after Boethus. They always used vessels of silver and gold, but not because they were arrogant of spirit. The Sadducees said that it was the Pharisees' tradition to subject themselves to austerity in this world, and yet in the world to come they possess nothing.[62]

Twenty-four groups of sectarians existed in Jerusalem at the time of the destruction of the Second Temple. Indeed, Israel was not rejected until it had given rise to twenty-four sects of heretics.[63] Heretics who reject the Torah, who do not believe in the resurrection of the dead, who separate themselves from the practices of the community, rulers who make themselves hated in the land of the living, who sin and cause others to sin—as did Jeroboam ben Nebat and his associates—go straightway down to Gehenna and are there judged and sentenced for countless generations, as it is said, *They shall go out and gaze on the corpses of the men who rebelled against Me: their worms shall not die, nor their fire be quenched* (Isa. 66:24). Even after Gehenna will be ended, their fate will not come to an end.[64]

The following have no share in the world to come: he who says the Torah offers no warrant for the resurrection of the dead;

he who denies the divine authorship of the Torah; and the irreverent skeptic.[65]

Rabbi Mattnah and Rabbi Simon ben Zoma both said that according to law the Ten Commandments should be recited each day. Why was this not prescribed? Because of the error of the sectarians who would say that only the Ten Commandments were given to Moses on Mount Sinai.[66]

A certain Sadducee once asked Gebiha ben Pesisa, "Woe to you, you sinners, who say that the dead will live again; if the living die, how can the dead live?" He replied, "Woe to you, you sinners, who say the dead will not live again; if those who never existed come to life, how much more so those who have existed!" The Sadducee retorted, "You call me sinner! If I get up, I shall give you such a kick as to knock your hump off your back!" Gebiha responded, "If you do so, you will be known as a skillful physician and you will be highly paid!"[67]

Only one man was created in the beginning so that the sectarians might not say there is more than one heavenly power. The first man was created on the eve of the Sabbath—as the six days of Creation were ending—so that the sectarians might not say that he was a partner to the Holy One, blessed be He, in the work of Creation.[68]

If a person be pursued by a would-be murderer or a poisonous snake, let him better take refuge in a temple of idol worship than in the house of a sectarian.[69] A person may not go to be cured by the sectarians even if it be doubtful whether otherwise he will live more than a short time.[70]

On the eve of Yom Kippur senior members of the Court would read the ordained practices of Yom Kippur to the high priest. They then delivered him to the elders of the priesthood who made him swear: "My lord high priest, we are the agents of the Bet Din and you are our agent and the agent of the Bet Din, we ask you to swear by the One who caused His Name to dwell in this House that you will change nothing of what we have said to you." He turned aside and wept and they did the same. Why did they weep? Because the oath implied that he might be a Sadducee. Why did they then feel obliged to take so stringent a measure? To make certain that when alone on Yom Kippur in the Holy of Holies, he would not follow the Sadducean practice of preparing the incense outside and then bringing it inside the Holy of Holies. Once it happened with a high priest who turned out to be a Sadducee that he prepared the incense before entering the Holy of Holies and then brought it within. When he came out he rejoiced greatly. His father met him and told him, "My son, it is true that we are Sadducees, but we must be careful not to let the Pharisees know." His son replied, "All my life I have been anxious to see the fulfillment of the verse, *For I appear in the cloud over the cover* (Lev. 16:2). I have said to myself, 'When shall I have the opportunity to realize it?' Now when the opportunity is present, shall I not seize it?" It is said that not too many days passed before he died and his body was flung upon an ash heap and worms were coming out of his nostrils. Others say that he was stricken just as he left the Temple.[71]

The verse, *Your sons and daughters shall be delivered to another people* (Deut. 28:32), refers to the Sadducees. So does the verse, *The benighted man thinks, "God does not care"* (Ps. 14:1).[72]

Ḥanina, the son of Rabbi Joshua's brother, came to Capernaum and the sectarians worked a spell on him so that he rode upon a donkey on the Sabbath. He went to his uncle, Joshua, who anointed him with oil and he recovered from the spell. Rabbi Joshua said to him, "Since the donkey of that wicked person has roused itself against you, you can no longer live in the land of Israel." He consequently moved to Babylonia where he died in peace.[73]

━━ 3 ━━

Jerusalem and Its Inhabitants

There are ten measures of beauty in the world—nine in Jerusalem and one in the rest of the world. There are ten measures of suffering in the world—nine in Jerusalem and one in the rest of the world. There are ten measures of wisdom in the world—nine in Jerusalem and one in the rest of the world. There are ten measures of smooth talk in the world—nine in Jerusalem and one in the rest of the world. There are ten measures of Torah in the world—nine in Jerusalem and one in the rest of the world. Rabbi Natan said, "There is no beauty like the beauty of Jerusalem."[74]

David said of Jerusalem, *fair-crested, joy of all the earth, Mount Zion, summit of Zaphon, city of the great king* (Ps. 48:3). This verse was explained in this way. A merchant once went to Jerusalem to sell his merchandise, but after sitting there a whole day, he had sold nothing. He then bitterly exclaimed, "Is this the city of which people say that it is the *joy of all the earth?*" An hour later he had sold all his goods and then he burst forth, "Verily she is *Fair-crested, joy of all the earth.*" There was a counting-house just outside Jerusalem where all accounts were totaled and anyone who wished to make up his accounts would go in order that he might not make his reckoning in Jerusalem and perhaps become distressed; one must not be grieved there, because it is the *joy of all the earth.* Why did Jerusalem possess all this honor? Because it was the *city of the great king.* With its destruction *the sun has set on all joy, the gladness of the earth is banished* (Isa. 24:11). In this world the *joy of all the earth* has ceased, but when God will rebuild Jerusalem He will restore all the joy in it, as it says, *Truly the Lord has comforted Zion, comforted all her ruins; He has made her wilderness like Eden, her desert like the Garden of the Lord. Gladness and joy shall abide there, thanksgiving and the sound of music* (Isa. 51:3).

He who has not seen Jerusalem in her splendor has not seen a desirable city in his life. There is no wisdom like the wisdom of the land of Israel. There is no beauty like the beauty of Jerusalem. Jerusalem is the light of the world . . . and who is the light of Jerusalem? God. There are six things that were chosen: the priestly family, the levitical family, Israel, the royal house of David, Jerusalem, and the Sanctuary. Jerusalem is destined to expand until it reaches the throne of Glory.[75]

Once King Agrippa wished to know how many people there were in Jerusalem. He said to the priests, "Set aside for me one kidney from each paschal offering." They set aside for him twice 600,000 kidneys, double the number of those who went out of Egypt, and there was not a single paschal offering in which less than ten persons participated. Rabbi Ḥiyya taught, "The number might have been forty or fifty persons, apart from those who were unclean and those away on a distant journey." On one occasion there were so many people on the Temple Mount that there was no space and an old man was crushed to death. They consequently called that Passover "the Passover of the Crushers."

How did the population get so large? A man married his son at the age of twelve to a wife capable of bearing children. Then he married his grandson at the age of twelve, so that before he was himself twenty-six years old he saw grandchildren. This is to fulfill what was said, *And live to see your children's children. May all be well with Israel!* (Ps. 128:6).[76]

There were four hundred and eighty synagogues in Jerusalem. In each there was an elementary school and an advanced school: an elementary school for the study of Scripture and an advanced school for the study of Mishnah. Vespasian went up and destroyed them all.

There were twenty-four thoroughfares in Jerusalem, each thoroughfare had twenty-four side-turnings; each side-turning had twenty-four roads; each road had twenty-four streets; each street had twenty-four courtyards; each courtyard had twenty-four houses; and each courtyard, residents double the number of those who came out of Egypt. Know that it was really so, because Rabbi Eleazar told this story. It once happened that a merchant was traveling to Jerusalem with two hundred camels loaded with pepper. He passed by the city of Tyre and met a tailor sitting at the city gate. The tailor asked, "What are you carrying?" He replied, "Pepper." He asked, "Will you not let me have a small quantity?" He answered, "No"—the whole stock would be sold only to one buyer. The tailor then said, "Then you can sell it only in another town." When he arrived in Jerusalem, he met a tailor sitting at the entrance of the gate who asked, "What are you carrying?" He answered, "Go on with your cutting!" Another tailor met him and asked what he was carrying. He replied, "Go on with your sewing!" The tailor said to him, "Tell me; if I am able to buy it, well and good, and if not, I shall bring you someone who will buy your entire stock. So what is it you are carrying?" He replied, "Pepper." The tailor took him to a dwelling place, showed him a pile of dinars, and said to him, "Look at this coin. If it has currency in your country, take of the coins for your pepper." The next day the merchant went to walk in the street and met a friend who asked him what wares he was carrying. He answered, "Pepper." The friend said, "Will you sell me a hundred dinars worth as I am giving a party today?" He replied, "I have already disposed of it to a certain person." He went to this man and inquired, "Have you the pepper that you bought? Let me have a little because I am giving a party." He replied, "What can I say to you? I have already sold it to a certain tailor, but I shall speak to him and he will let you have some." He went and found the house full of buyers, so that those who were in the first room got an ounce each, those in the second room got only half an ounce each, while those in the third room got none. This is to fulfill what was said, . . . *the city once great with people!* (Lam. 1:1).[77]

There were three very wealthy men in Jerusalem: Ben Ẓiẓit Ha-Kasat, Nakdimon ben Guryon, and Ben Kalba Savua. Why was Ẓiẓit Ha-Kasat so named? Because he used to recline upon a silver couch at the head of all the notables of Israel. About the daughter of Nakdimon ben Guryon it is told that her bed had been outfitted at the cost of twelve thousand gold dinars and that she would spend a Tyrian gold dinar each week on confections. At the time she was a childless widow awaiting the decision of her late husband's brother to marry her or not. Why was Nakdimon ben Guryon so named? Because the sun broke through again for his sake. Once when all Israel had come up to Jerusalem for the festival, there was no water for them to drink. Nakdimon went to a certain official and said to him, "Lend me twelve wells of water until such and such a day and if I do not repay you with twelve wells of water I will give you twelve talents of silver." He fixed a time limit for repayment. When the agreed upon day arrived and the morning came without rain, the official sent him a message: "Deliver either the twelve wells of water or the twelve talents of silver." He replied, "The day has not yet ended." The official sneeringly retorted, "There has been no rain the entire year, will it rain now?" In a happy mood the official went off to the bathhouse while Nakdimon ben Guryon went to the Temple, wrapped himself in his cloak, and stood up to pray. "Lord of the universe!" he said. "Before You it is revealed and known that it was not for my glory that I acted nor for the glory of my father's house, but for Your glory, that the pilgrims should have water to drink." Immediately, the sky became overcast and rain began to fall until the twelve wells were filled to overflowing. He left the Temple and ran into the official who had just left the bathhouse. Nakdimon said to him, "Pay me money for the additional water you have because of me." He replied, "You still owe me the money because the sun has already set; the day is over and the rain has fallen in my possession." Nakdimon returned to the Temple, wrapped himself in his cloak and again stood up in prayer, saying, "Lord of the Universe! Perform a miracle for me now as You did before." Immediately, the wind blew, the clouds dispersed, and the sun shone through. When they met the official said, "I know that it was only for your sake that the Holy One, blessed he He, disrupted the natural processes of His world and caused the sun to break through again so that I should not be able to demand the money of you." Nakdimon's real name was Buni. He was called Nakdimon because the sun broke through for his sake.

Why was Ben Kalba Savua so named? Because whoever entered his house hungry as a dog came out fed to the full.[78]

The rabbis taught that there were three men for whose sake the sun broke through again after it had set: Moses, Joshua, and Nakdimon ben Guryon.[79]

When Nakdimon ben Guryon would leave his house to go to the house of study, fine woolen cloth would be spread out for him to walk upon. Then the poor would come and roll up the wool for themselves.[80]

The people of Jerusalem would eat white bread and drink aged wine. Rabbi Ḥanina bar Papa so interpreted the verse, *Those who feasted on dainties lie famished in the streets* (Lam. 4:5). They used to drink snow, making their complexion clear. They would drink milk for a bright complexion.

What is meant by *The precious children of Zion; once valued as gold* (Lam. 4:2)? It cannot mean that they were covered with gold since in the school of Rabbi Shela it was said that two measures of gold coins came down into the world, of which one went to Rome and the other to the rest of the world. What it means is that their beauty outshone fine gold. In earlier times the important people of Rome used to keep handsome figures set in a signet ring in front of them when they engaged in sexual intercourse. But now they brought Israelites and tied them to the foot of the bed.[81]

The responsible people of Jerusalem did not sign a note without first ascertaining who was signing with them; did not sit as judges on a case without first ascertaining who was sitting with them; and did not join in a meal without first ascertaining who their companions would be.[82]

The verse reads, *The precious children of Zion* (Lam. 4:2). Wherein were the inhabitants of Jerusalem precious? One interpretation is that they were like a golden ornament, their bodies like precious stones and pearls. Another interpretation is that when a man of one of the other towns in the land married a woman of Jerusalem he gave her her weight in gold. When a Jerusalemite married a woman of superior status to his own, he would spend more for the wedding feast than for the home furnishings. When she was of inferior status he spent more to furnish their home than for the wedding feast. Another explanation is that no Jerusalemite would attend a banquet unless he was invited twice; another that no Jerusalemite had a child who was defective in limb or blemished in body, and another that no Jerusalemite would attend a dinner without changing his buckle from the right to the left shoulder. For what reason? So that another person should not extend to him an invitation that would be wasted.[83]

No Jerusalemite ever made a claim that he could not support. Rabban Simon ben Gamaliel said that there was a fine custom in Jerusalem whereby, at the beginning of a meal, a cloth was spread over the door and as long as it was there guests could enter. But after three introductory courses had been served and the cloth was removed a guest was not to enter. Another explanation for *the precious children of Zion* is that they would entrust the dinner to a caterer. If he spoiled anything, he would be fined in proportion to the status of the host and his guests. Still another explanation is that whenever one of them gave a dinner, he indicated all the courses on a menu. This was to inform those who were fastidious with their food so that no one should have to eat that which was distasteful to him.[84]

Once a Jerusalemite went to a distant place and while there took ill and soon lay on his deathbed. He called the owner of the house where he was staying and entrusted him with his possessions, saying, "If one comes from Jerusalem who says he is my son and if he performs three clever things, give him my possessions; otherwise do not." The man then died and went to his eternal rest. The inhabitants of the place had arranged that none should disclose the address of his neighbor to a stranger. After a while the son arrived and when he reached the entrance to the town he saw a man carrying a load of twigs. He asked, "Will you sell that load of twigs?" The man replied that he would. "Then take the money for it and carry it to so-and-so (naming the man at whose house his father had stayed)." He took the money and carried the twigs to that person. As he walked the son followed until he arrived at the person's house. The bearer of the twigs called out to the owner of the house, "Hello, there! Come and take this load of twigs!" He exclaimed, "Did I ask you to bring me a load of twigs?" The man answered, "True, you did not tell me to do so, but it belongs to the man who is following me." He opened his house at once to the son who entered and they greeted each other. This was the first clever act.

The owner of the house asked him, "Who are you?" He replied, "I am the son of the man who died in your house." He took him in and arranged that a meal be prepared. This man had two sons and two daughters. When the hour of the meal came, the host set before the visitor five chickens as a course. When they were ready to eat, the host said to him, "Take it and serve." He replied, "This is not mine that I should do the serving." The man said, "I wish you to take it and serve." He then apportioned one chicken between the man and his wife, a second between the two sons, a third between the two daughters and set two before himself. They ate without comment. That was the second clever act.

In the evening the host brought a fat capon to the table and asked him to serve it. He declared, "This is not mine." He said to him, "Serve it at my request." He then apportioned the head to the host, the entrails to the wife, the two thighs to the two sons, the two wings to the two daughters, and set the carcass before himself. That was the third clever act.

The host asked, "Is this how they serve where you come from? The first time you served I said nothing. But now you again act in this manner!" He answered, "Did I not tell you that it was not mine? Nevertheless, what I have served I did apportion properly. On the first occasion you brought five chickens at the meal. You, your wife, and one chicken total three; your two sons and one chicken total three; your two daughters and one chicken total three; and I and two chickens total three. So have I taken any of your portion? At the present occasion you brought a capon. I took the head and gave it to you because you are the head of the house. I took the entrails and set them before your wife because children issue from the womb. I took the two wings and gave them to your daughters because in the future they will fly away from your house and go to their husbands. I took the carcass that is shaped like a boat because I came in a boat and will leave in a boat. Now come and give me the possessions that my father entrusted to you and I shall leave at once." He gave him his property and he departed in peace. This is to fulfill what is said, *She that was great among nations* (Lam. 1:1), that is, great in intellect.[85]

Once an Athenian came to Jerusalem where he met a child to whom he gave some money and said, "Go bring us figs and grapes." The child replied, "Thank you—you with your money and I with my legs." When he returned, the man said to him, "Take and share it." The child placed the poorer fruit before himself and set the better before the man. The man exclaimed, "Rightly do they say that the people of Jerusalem are very clever. Since this child knew that he had laid out no money of his own, he took the inferior fruit for himself and gave me the good." The child then said, "Come now and let us cast lots. If I throw and win, then I take your share. If you win, you take my share." They both agreed, and the child won and took the man's portion.[86]

Once an Athenian came to Jerusalem where he met a child to whom he gave money and said, "Go and bring me something of which I can eat my fill and have something left over to take on my journey." He went and brought him salt. The man said to him, "Did I tell you to bring me salt?" He replied, "But did you not tell me to go and bring you something of which you can eat your fill and still have some left over to take on your journey? By your life, here you have something of which you can eat all you want and have a good portion of it left over to take on your journey!"[87]

Once an Athenian came to Jerusalem where he met a child to whom he gave some money and said, "Bring me eggs and cheese." When he returned the man said to him, "Show me which cheese is from a white goat and which from a black goat." The boy retorted, "You are a grown man. You show me which egg is from a white hen and which from a black!"[88]

Once an Athenian came to Jerusalem and entered a school where he found the children sitting, but their teacher was not in the room. He put questions to them, which they answered. Then they said to him, "Come, let us make up that if one of us asks a question which the other cannot answer, the latter's clothing shall be taken from him." He agreed and said, "Since you live here, you answer first." They replied, "You answer first since you are so much older." They then asked him, "What are the following— nine go in but eight come out, two pour out but only one drinks, and twenty-four serve?" He could not answer and they took his clothing. He went to Rabbi Johanan, their teacher, and said to him, "O rabbi, what great mischief there is among you! When a stranger comes among you, you deprive him of his clothing!" He answered, "I suppose they put a question to you which you could not answer and they took your clothing?" "Yes," he said. "What was the question they asked you?" He told him and the teacher explained, "The nine that go in are the nine months of pregnancy and the eight that come out are the eight days of circumcision. The two that pour out are the two breasts that supply milk and the one who drinks is the child who has been born; and the twenty-four that serve are the twenty-four months of nursing." The man went to the children, gave them the answer, and regained his clothing. They quoted against him, *Had you not plowed with my heifer, you would not have guessed my riddle* (Judg. 14:18).[89]

Once an Athenian came to Jerusalem where he met a priest and said to him, "How much of that load of wood there will become smoke?" He answered, "When moist it all becomes smoke. When dry, a third becomes smoke, a third ash, and a third fire." Where had he learned this? From observing the wood on the altar.[90]

Once an Athenian came to Jerusalem. He found a mortar that had been thrown away because it was cracked. He picked it up and took it to a tailor and said, "Sew this broken mortar for me." The tailor picked up a handful of sand and said, "Twist this into threads for me and I will sew it."[91]

Once an Athenian came to Jerusalem where he studied for three and a half years to learn wisdom but he could not master it. After the three and a half years had passed he bought a slave who, it turned out, was blind in one eye. In disgust at his folly he exclaimed, "After three and a half years of study I have bought a slave who turns out to be half-blind!" The seller said to him, "By your life, he is very wise and can see great distances." When they came out of the gate, the slave said to him, "Hurry so that we shall overtake the caravan!" "Is there then a caravan ahead of us?" he asked. "Yes," replied the slave, "and there is a she-camel in front of us blind in one eye. It carries twins in its womb and on its back two skin-bottles, one containing wine, the other vinegar. It is four miles ahead and the camel driver is a gentile." He said to the slave, "O you who belong to a stiff-necked people! With one eye how do you know the camel is blind in one eye?" He answered, "I notice that one side of the road has been grazed but not the other." "And how do you know that there are twins in its womb?" He answered, "It lay down, and I noticed the trace of the two of them." "And how do you know that it is carrying two skin-bottles, one containing wine and the other vinegar?" He replied, "From the drippings; those of wine are absorbed in the ground but those of vinegar ferment." "And how do you know that the camel driver is a gentile?" He explained, "Because he urinated in the middle of the road. A Jew would not do that but would withdraw to the side." "And how do you know that it is four miles ahead?" He said to him, "Up to four miles the mark of the camel's hoof can be observed but not beyond that distance."[92]

Once an Athenian visited Jerusalem and made great fun of the inhabitants of that city and then returned home. They said, "Who will go and bring him back to us?" One said, "I will not only go but bring him back with his head shaven." The Jerusalemite went to Athens and was given hospitality by that man. In the morning the two of them went out to walk in the marketplace. One of the sandals of the Jerusalemite broke and he said to a workman, "Take this tremis and mend this sandal." He did it for him. The next day the two of them went out again to walk in the marketplace, and the other sandal broke. He said to the Athenian, "Take this tremis and get the workman to repair my sandal." Noticing the high price voluntarily paid for the repair of the two sandals, the Athenian asked, "Are then sandals so expensive in Jerusalem?" "Yes," the Jerusalemite replied. "How many dinars?" he inquired. "Nine or ten," he answered, "and when they are cheap, seven or eight dinars." He said to him, "If I were to come to you with a stock of sandals, could you sell them for me?" "Certainly," he replied, "only you must not enter Jerusalem without first informing me."

When the Athenian finished the work on which he was engaged, he bought a stock of sandals, set forth for Jerusalem, and sat outside the gate of the city. He sent for the Jerusalemite, who came to him. He told the Athenian, "We have agreed among ourselves that no one may enter the city to sell his wares unless his head is shaven and his face blackened." He replied, "What do I care if my head is shaven so long as I sell my goods?" After shaving his head, he took him and seated him in the middle of the marketplace. When a person came to buy sandals of him and asked how much a pair cost, he answered, "There are some at ten dinars and some at nine; but I will not take less than eight." Upon hearing this the prospective purchaser hit him on the head with one of the sandals and left without buying. Understanding now that a trick had been played on him, the Athenian said to the Jerusalemite, "Did I treat you so badly when you were in my city?" He replied, "From now on do not make fun of the people of Jerusalem."[93]

Four Jerusalemites came to Athens, and a certain man gave them hospitality. In the evening he made them a meal and after they had eaten and drunk he prepared four beds for them, one of them damaged and held up by the next. When they got up to retire he said to himself, "I have heard that the men of Jerusalem are very clever. I shall listen to their conversation." He went to spend the night in the room adjacent to theirs. During the night the man sleeping in the damaged bed got up and said to his friends, "Do you think I am sleeping in a bed? I am sleeping on nothing else than the floor and I am suspended in midair!" Another remarked, "And the meat we ate in the evening had a flavor about it like dog's flesh." Still another said, "And the wine we drank had the flavor of the grave." The fourth man exclaimed, "Why should you be surprised at all this? Our host is not even his father's son!" When the man heard what they said, he declared, "The one who said he slept on the floor spoke the truth, the other three uttered lies."

The next morning he went to the butcher and said, "Give me some of the same meat you supplied me last night." The butcher answered, "I have no more." He asked, "What was so special about it?" He replied, "I had one lamb sucking but its mother died. I had a she-dog and the lamb sucked from her. In the evening I was short of meat and you came to buy some. I had no other and gave you some of it." He said to himself, "Two spoke the truth and two uttered lies." He went to the wine merchant and said to him, "Give me some of the wine you supplied me last night." He replied, "I have no more." He asked, "What was special about it?" He answered, "I had one vine planted over my father's grave. I pressed its grapes and poured the wine into casks. I was short of wine when you came to buy some; I had no other so I gave you some of it." He said to himself, "Three spoke the truth and one uttered a lie." Then he went to his mother and asked her, "Whose child am I?" She answered, "My son, you are your father's child." He said to her, "Tell me the truth, whose child am I? Otherwise, I will cut off your head." She then said to him, "My son, your father was incapable of having a child. I was afraid that if he died childless, his relatives would deprive me of my property. Did I do wrong by my misconduct when by it I secured for you all this wealth and property?" He said to her, "You see what is happening! The Jerusalemites will come and make us all illegitimate. No more hospitality for them!"[94]

A Jerusalemite went to see a merchant in Athens. When he arrived he put up at an inn where he found several persons sitting and drinking wine. After he had eaten and drunk he wished to sleep there. They said to him, "We have agreed among ourselves not to accept a guest until he has made three jumps." He said, "I do not know how you jump. You do it first and then I shall do the same." One of them stood up and jumped to the middle of the room. The second jumped from that point to the door at the entrance of the inn. The third jumped from there and found himself outside, with the first two watching and following. The Jerusalemite got up and bolted the door in their face and said to them, "By your lives, what you intended to do to me I did to you!"[95]

Wherever one of the men of Jerusalem would go the people of the place would set up an armchair for him to sit on in order to hear the wisdom he would speak.[96]

It once happened that a red heifer was needed for the ritual purification ceremony and none could be found. At long last one was found at a heathen's. Some Jews went to him and said, "Sell us the heifer you have for we need one." He replied, "Give me my price for her and take her." (And what was the going price for a heifer? Three gold coins or four at the most.) They replied, "We shall give it." As they went to fetch the money the heathen guessed the purpose for which they needed the heifer. And so when they came back and brought the money for her, he said to them, "I shall not sell her to you." They asked, "Perhaps you wish to increase the price? If so, we shall give you all you ask."

Now that the wicked man saw that they were pressing for the heifer, he decided to put the price up as high as possible. When they said, "Take five gold coins," he refused. "Take ten, take twenty," they went on until they reached one hundred and still he refused. In fact—so some of our masters say—they went up to a thousand gold coins. Then he agreed to give them the heifer for a thousand gold coins. What did the wicked man do?

He said to another heathen, a close friend of his, "Come and see how I fool those Jews. The only reason they are trying to get the heifer from me and are willing to give me all the money is that a yoke has never been upon her. Watch me take the yoke and put it upon the heifer. I'll have some fun at their expense and get my money just the same." This is what he did. He took the yoke and put it on the heifer for the entire night.

Now you can tell a heifer that has never borne a yoke by the fact that on her neck, in the place where the yoke is set, are two particular hairs that stand upright as long as she has never borne a yoke. But as soon as a yoke is placed upon her, the two hairs are bent down. And there is still another sign. As long as no yoke has been put upon her, both eyes look straight ahead. After a yoke has been upon her, her eyes have an anxious look, as she turns her head and rolls her eyes, trying to see the yoke.

When they came with all the gold to take the heifer from the heathen and showed him the gold, he went in and, first removing the yoke from the heifer, led her out to them. When he led her out, they proceeded to examine her for the two signs of her never having borne a yoke, but the two particular hairs that should have been straight were bent down, and in addition her eyes were rolling back because of the yoke. They said to him, "Take your heifer. We can do without her. Fool around with your own mother!" When the wicked heathen saw that they were returning the heifer to him and that he had come out with hands empty of all the gold coins, his mouth, which had said, "I will have some fun at their expense," proceeded to say, "Blessed is He who chose His people." Then he went into his house, strung up a rope and hanged himself—*So may all Your enemies perish, O Lord!* (Judg. 5:31).[97]

4

The Destruction of Jerusalem
and the Temple

Rabbi Johanan said, "What may illustrate the verse, *Happy is the man who is anxious always, but he who hardens his heart falls into misfortune* (Prov. 28:14)? The following—the destruction of Jerusalem came about because of Kamza and Bar Kamza; that of Tur Malka because of a cock and a hen; that of Betar because of a pig."

The destruction of Jerusalem brought about by Kamza and Bar Kamza occurred as follows. A certain man had a friend named Kamza and an enemy named Bar Kamza. Once when he was making a party he said to his servant, "Go and bring Kamza." The servant went and brought Bar Kamza. The host found Bar Kamza seated among the invited guests and said to him, "You are my enemy! What are you doing here? Get up and leave!" The humiliated man pleaded, "Since I am already here, let me stay and I will pay you for whatever I eat and drink at your party." "No!" was the answer. "I will pay for half the cost of the party," Bar Kamza continued. The reply again was "No." "I will pay all the costs of the party," said Bar Kamza. "No," replied the host, and taking Bar Kamza by the hand he pulled him up and put him out.

Bar Kamza thought to himself: "The rabbis were sitting there and did not stop me; evidently my conduct did not bother them; therefore I shall go and inform against them to the Roman emperor." He went and told the emperor, "The Jews are rebelling against you." The ruler said, "Prove it!" He answered, "Send them a sacrifice and see if they will offer it." He sent a calf of a fine quality. While it was on the way, Bar Kamza made a blemish on its upper lip or, some say, on the white of its eye, which to Jews counts as a blemish but to the heathen does not. The rabbis were inclined to offer it so as not to offend the government, but Rabbi

Zechariah ben Avkulus said to them, "People will say that animals with blemishes may be offered on the altar." They then thought they should kill Bar Kamẓa so that he should not again inform the authorities. But Rabbi Zechariah ben Avkulus said to them, "Is the one who blemishes an animal for the altar to be executed for it?" It was about this that Rabbi Johanan remarked, "The great concern of Rabbi Zechariah ben Avkulus led to the destruction of our House, the burning of our Temple, and our exile from our land." Rabbi Eleazar said, "See how serious a thing it is to embarrass a person. For the Holy One, praised be He, took up the cause of Bar Kamẓa and destroyed His House and burned down His Temple."

The emperor sent against them Nero Caesar. As he was approaching he shot an arrow toward the east and it fell in Jerusalem. He then shot one toward the west and it fell in Jerusalem. He shot arrows in all four directions and each fell in Jerusalem. He said to a boy he saw, "Tell me the biblical verses you have learned most recently." The child replied, "*I will wreak my vengeance on Edom through My people Israel* (Ezek. 25:14)." He said, "The Holy One, blessed be He, wishes to destroy His House and to place the blame upon me." So he fled and became a convert to Judaism and Rabbi Meir was his descendant.

The emperor then sent against them Vespasian Caesar who came and besieged Jerusalem for three years. There were in the city these three wealthy men: Nakdimon ben Guryon, Ben Kalba Savua, and Ben Ẓiẓit Ha-Kasat. Ben Ẓiẓit Ha-Kasat was so called because the fringes of his garment would trail on cushions. Others say it was because his seat was placed among those of the Roman noblemen. One of these rich men said to the people of Jerusalem, "I will supply you with wheat and barley." Another pledged wine, salt, and oil and the third, wood. The rabbis praised the offer of wood as most generous, for Rabbi Ḥisda would hand all his keys to his servant except the key for the wood, saying that a storehouse of wheat needs sixty storehouses of wood for fuel. These three men had enough so that they could have kept the city supplied for twenty-one years.

The rebels belonging to the war party were in the city. The rabbis said to them, "Let us go make peace with the Romans." They would not let them. Instead they said, "Let us go make war against them!" The rabbis said, "You will not succeed." The rebels rose up and burned the stores of wheat and barley and a famine resulted. Martha, daughter of Boethus, was one of the wealthiest women in Jerusalem. She sent out her manservant for fine flour. By the time he arrived it was sold out. He returned and told her, "There is no more fine flour, but there is the ordinary white flour." She told him to buy it but by the time he got there that too was sold. He came back and reported, "There is no more white flour, but there is dark flour." By the time he went it was sold. He returned and said, "There is no more dark flour, but there is barley flour." By the time he got back this too was sold. She had already taken off her shoes but she said, "I shall go out and see if anything to eat can be found." Some dung stuck to her foot and she died of shock. Rabban Johanan ben Zakkai applied to her the verse, *And she who is most tender and dainty among you, so tender and dainty that she would never venture to set a foot on the ground* (Deut. 28:56). Others say she ate a fig left by Rabbi Zadok and fell ill and died. For Rabbi Zadok observed fasts for forty years so that Jerusalem might not be destroyed. In between fasts when he would eat anything the food could be seen as it passed through his throat, so thin had he become. In order that he might gain strength they would bring him a fig. He would suck its juice and then throw it away. It was one of these that Martha ate. When Martha was on the verge of death, she brought out all her gold and silver and threw it into the street, saying, "What good is it to me?" So is it written, *They shall throw their silver into the streets, and their gold shall be treated as something unclean* (Ezek. 7:19).[98]

"Through a cock and a hen Tur Malka was destroyed." How? The custom was that when a bridegroom and a bride were led in a procession, a cock and a hen were carried before them as though to say, "Be fruitful and multiply like fowl." One day a troop of Roman soldiers passed by such a procession and seized the fowl. The Jews fell upon them and beat them. They went and reported to the emperor that the Jews had rebelled against him, and he marched against them. There was among them a certain Bar Deroma who could jump a mile and he slaughtered the Romans. The emperor took his crown, put it on the ground, and said, "Master of all the universe, may it please You not to deliver me and my kingdom into the hands of one man!" Bar Deroma was tripped up by the words of his own mouth. He said, *"But You have rejected us, O God; God, You do not march with our armies"* (Ps. 60:12). But did not David say the same? The difference is that David was wondering if it were so. Bar Deroma entered a privy, a snake came, and from fright he dropped his large intestine and died. The emperor said, "Since a miracle occurred on my behalf, this time I shall let them off," and he left. They danced, ate, drank, and kindled so many lights that the stamp made by a seal could be detected by the light a mile away. The emperor said, "Are the Jews then rejoicing because of me?" He marched against them again. Rabbi Assi said, "Three hundred thousand men, their swords drawn, went up against Tur Malka and slaughtered for three days and three nights, while on the other side carousing and feasting were going on, and one group did not know about the other."[99]

When the Emperor Vespasian came to destroy Jerusalem the Zealots sought to burn all the food supplies. Ben Kalba Savua said to them, "Why do you destroy this city and seek to burn all the supplies? Wait until I go in and see what I have in the house." He went in and found that he had enough to supply food for every citizen in Jerusalem for twenty-two years. He gave orders at once and the wheat was stacked and cleaned, ground and sifted, kneaded and baked into bread, thus providing a food supply for every citizen in Jerusalem for twenty-two years. The Zealots, however, paid no heed to him. They took the loaves of bread, cut them through, and dirtied them with mud. As a result the people of Jerusalem had to cook straw and eat it. Every man of Israel who was encamped near the walls of Jerusalem would call out, "For five dates I will go down and bring back five heads of the enemy." One man was given five dates and he went down and brought back five heads of the men of Vespasian. When Vespasian examined the excrement of the besieged men and saw that it was without a trace of wheat, he remarked to his soldiers, "If these men who subsist on straw alone can kill so many of you, how many more of you could they kill if they were to eat and drink like you!"[100]

During the siege the people of Jerusalem would lower a basket of gold over the city wall for which enemy soldiers gave them a basket filled with wheat. Later when they lowered a basket of gold the enemy gave them a basket filled with barley. Still later when they lowered a basket of gold they were given a basket filled with straw. What did they do? They cooked it and drank its water. Finally, when they lowered a basket of gold they received nothing in return.[101]

During the siege of Jerusalem by the Babylonians people died from the smell of the thistles they had to eat. But during the siege by the Romans there were not even thistles to eat. What did the enemy do to make it even worse? They brought kids which they roasted to the west of the city and the smell carried by the wind so aroused the appetite of the starving people that they died.[102]

The story is told about a child by the name of Doeg ben Joseph whom his father left to his mother when he was very young. Every day his mother would measure him by her hand-breadths and she would then give in gold the additional weight he had grown to the Temple. When, however, the besieging enemy army surrounded Jerusalem, she slaughtered him and ate him. It is concerning her that the lament of Jeremiah is to be applied, *See, O Lord, and behold, to whom You have done this! Alas, women eat their own fruit, their new-born babes!* Whereupon the Holy Spirit replied, *Alas, priest and prophet are slain in the Sanctuary of the Lord!* (Lam. 2:20).[103]

The Holy One, blessed be He, declared, "The women were responsible for My not stretching forth My hand against My world to punish the Jewish people fully for their sins." For if one of them had a loaf of bread enough only for herself and her husband for one day and her neighbor's son died, she would take it to her neighbor and comfort her. Scripture counts it to their merit as though they had cooked their own children. That is what is meant by the verse, *With their own hands tender-hearted women have cooked their children.* For what purpose? So that, *Such became their fare* (Lam. 4:10).[104]

A woman said to her husband during the siege, "Take my bracelet or an earring and go to the marketplace and see if you can find anything there for us to eat." He went and looked around, but could find nothing. He writhed in agony and died. She then said to her son, "Go and see what has happened to your father." He went to the marketplace and saw his father dead; so he writhed in agony and died at his side. That is the sense of the verse, *As they languish like battle-wounded in the squares of the town*, which alludes to her husband and grown son. *As their life runs out in their mothers' bosoms* (Lam. 2:12), refers to her young son who wished to suck but found no milk, and he writhed in agony and died.[105]

It happened that one of the eminent men of Jerusalem said to his servant, "Go and bring me some water," and he watched him from the top of the roof. The servant returned and said, "I did not find any water." The master then told him, "Throw down your pitcher in front of me," and he did so. He then threw himself from the top of the roof and died, and his limbs were mingled with the pieces of earthenware. It is about him that the verse declares, *Alas, they are accounted as earthen pots* (Lam. 4:2).[106]

Those starving Jews who had concealed themselves would eat the flesh of their slain brethren. Every day one of them would venture out and would bring the corpses, which they then ate. One day one of them went out and found the slain body of his own father, which he took and buried, marking the spot. He turned and reported that he had found nothing. They said, "Let another go and if he find anything, let him bring it and we shall have something to eat." When the second man went out he found a scent and followed it. Making a search, he discovered the body. He brought it to them and they ate it. After they had consumed it, they asked him, "Where did you find this corpse?" He replied, "In such and such a spot." They then asked, "What distinguishing mark was over it?" He told them what it was. The son exclaimed, "Woe is me! I have eaten the flesh of my father!" This is to fulfill what was said, *Assuredly, parents shall eat their children in your midst, and children shall eat their parents* (Ezek. 5:10).[107]

A water channel ran from Etam but the besiegers destroyed it and turned its water away. When a man would take his child to the water channel and found no water, his tongue would stick *to its palate for thirst* (Lam. 4:4).[108]

Rabban Johanan ben Zakkai was once walking in the marketplace when he noticed a young woman picking up grains of barley from under the feet of the cattle of Arabians. He said to her, "My daughter, who are you?" She at first remained silent and then said to him, "Wait a moment." She wrapped her hair around her, sat down before him, and said, "I am the daughter of Nakdimon ben Guryon." He asked, "My daughter, what has become of your father's wealth?" She answered, "Master, is there not a popular proverb in Jerusalem, 'The salt that preserves wealth is its decrease by gifts to charity,' or, according to another version, 'The salt that preserves wealth is kindness.'" "And what became of the wealth of your father-in-law?" he asked. She answered, "The one destroyed the other." Then Rabban Johanan ben Zakkai turned to his disciples and said, "All my life I have read the verse, *If you do not know, O fairest of women, go follow the tracks of the sheep* (Songs 1:8), but I did not grasp its meaning until today —that Israel will come under the domination of the most inferior of the nations, and more than that, they will be among the dung of their cattle." The young woman then asked him, "Master, do you remember when you signed my marriage contract?" "I do," he replied. Turning to his disciples he exclaimed, "By the Temple service! I signed this young woman's marriage contract and it mentioned a sum of one million gold dinars as a dowry from her father apart from the sum given by her father-in-law." He wept and said, "How fortunate are you, O Israel, that when you do God's will, no people can rule over you. But when you do not, He delivers you into the hands of an inferior people. And not only are you beneath them, but their cattle too!" It is told that so rich were the members of the family to which the young woman belonged that they never set out from their house to go to the Temple until the finest woolen rugs were spread before them.[109]

At the time of the invasion by Vespasian the rabbis decreed against the wearing of garlands by bridegrooms and the beating of drums at weddings.[110] The Decumanian and Augustan legions suggested to Vespasian that he should go up and destroy the Temple and God exterminated them and raised up others in their place. These were the Joviani and Herculanei.[111]

The emperor Vespasian placed guards eighteen miles from Emmaus who would question the pilgrims and ask them, "To whom do you belong?" They would reply, "We are the men of Vespasian or Trajan or Hadrian."[112]

It is told that Martha, the daughter of Boethus, was married to Joshua ben Gamla, whom the king appointed high priest. Once she went to see him, saying to herself, "I shall go and see him reading on the Day of Atonement in the Temple." They laid carpets for her from the door of her home to the entrance of the Temple so that her feet might not feel the dampness. So delicate was she that they did feel it. When her husband died the rabbis allowed her two measures of wine a day. Rabbi Eleazar, son of Rabbi Zadok, said, "May I not live to see the consolation of Zion if I did not see the Romans bind her hair to the tails of Arabian horses and make her run from Jerusalem to Lydda. And I quoted this verse as being apropos, *And she who is most tender and dainty among you, so tender and dainty that she would never venture to set a foot on the ground* (Deut. 28:56)."[113]

It is related of Miriam, the daughter of Nakdimon, that the rabbis gave her an allowance of five hundred gold dinars each day for perfumes. Nevertheless, she stood up and cursed them, "Make such a niggardly allowance for your own daughters!" Rabbi Aḥa said, "We answered with 'Amen!' " Rabbi Eleazar said, "May I not live to see the consolation of Zion if I did not see her gathering barley from beneath the horses' hoofs in Acco. I quoted this verse of her, *If you do not know, O fairest of women, go follow the tracks of the sheep, and graze your kids* (Songs 1:8). Read not *gediyotayikh* ('your kids') but *geviyotayikh* ('your bodies')." A similar occurrence befell the daughter-in-law of Nakdimon. The sages awarded her an allowance of two measures of wine weekly for the making of mincemeat pudding. She said to them, "Make such a stingy allowance for your own daughters!" They did not reply "Amen" this time because she was awaiting the decision of her late husband's brother as to whether or not he would take her in levirate marriage.[114]

It is told of Miriam, the daughter of Tanḥum, that she and her seven sons were taken captive. The emperor placed them in the innermost of seven rooms. He had the eldest brought and said to him, "Prostrate yourself before the idol." He replied, "God forbid! I will not prostrate myself before an idol." "Why not?" asked the king. "Because it is written in our Torah, *I the Lord am your God* (Exod. 20:2)." He had him taken out at once and killed. He had the second brought and said to him, "Prostrate yourself before the idol." He replied, "God forbid! My brother did not prostrate himself and I will not." "Why not?" the king asked. "Because it is written in our Torah, *You shall have no other gods beside Me* (Exod. 20:3)." He immediately commanded that he be killed. He had the third brought and said to him, "Prostrate yourself before the idol." He answered, "I will not prostrate myself." "Why not?" asked the king. "Because it is written in the Torah, *For you must not worship any other god* (Exod. 34:14)." He immediately ordered him to be slain. He had the fourth brought, who quoted, *Whoever sacrifices to a god other than the Lord alone shall be proscribed* (Exod. 22:19), and he was ordered to be slain. He had the fifth brought, who quoted, *Hear, O Israel! The Lord is our God, the Lord alone* (Deut. 6:4), and he was ordered to be slain at once. He had the sixth brought who quoted similarly, *For the Lord your God is in your midst, a great and awesome God* (Deut. 7:21), and he was ordered to be slain. He had the seventh brought, who was the youngest of them all, and the king said, "My son, prostrate yourself before the idol." He answered, "God forbid!" "Why not?" asked the king. "Because it is written in our Torah, *Know therefore this day and keep in mind that the Lord alone is God in heaven above and on earth below; there is no other* (Deut. 4:39). Not only that, but we have sworn to our God that we will not exchange Him for any other god; as it is said, *You have affirmed this day that the Lord is your God* (Deut. 26:17). And as we swore to Him, so He swore to us not to exchange us for another people; as it is said, *And the Lord has affirmed this day that you are, as He promised you, His treasured people* (Deut. 26:18)." The emperor said to him, "Your brothers have had their fill of years and life, and experienced happiness. Prostrate yourself before the idol and I will bestow favors upon you." He answered, "It is written in our Torah, *The Lord will reign for ever and ever!* (Exod. 15:18), and it is said, *The Lord is king for ever and ever; the nations will perish from His land* (Ps. 10:16). You are of no account and so are His enemies. A human being lives today and is dead tomorrow; but the Holy One, blessed be He, lives and endures for all eternity." The emperor said to him, "See, your brothers are all dead before you. Look, I shall throw my ring to the ground in front of the idol. Pick it up in order that all may be sure that you have obeyed my command." He replied, "Woe unto you, O emperor! If you are afraid of the opinion of human beings who are the same as yourself, shall I not fear the supreme King of Kings, the Holy One, blessed be He, the God of the universe!" He asked him, "Does the universe, then, have a God?" He answered, "For shame, O emperor! Do you, then, behold a world without a Master?" He asked, "Has your God a mouth?" He replied, "About your gods it is written, *They have mouths, but cannot speak* (Ps. 115:5). About our God it is written, *By the word of the Lord the heavens were made* (Ps. 33:6)." The king asked, "Has your God eyes?" He replied, "About your gods it is written, *They have eyes, but cannot see* (Ps. 115:5). About our God it is written, *The eyes of the Lord, ranging over the whole earth* (Zech. 4:10)." "Has your God ears?" He replied, "About your gods it is written, *They have ears, but cannot hear* (Ps. 115:6). About our God it is written, *The Lord has heard and noted it* (Mal. 3:16)." "Has your God a nose?" He replied, "About your gods it is written, *Noses, but cannot smell* (Ps. 115:6). About our God it is written, *And the Lord smelled the pleasing odor* (Gen.

8:21)." "Has your God hands?" He replied, "About your gods it is written, *They have hands, but cannot touch* (Ps. 115:7). About our God it is written, *My own hand founded the earth* (Isa. 48:13)." "Has your God feet?" He replied, "About your gods it is written, *Feet, but cannot walk* (Ps. 115:7). About our God it is written, *On that day He will set His feet on the Mount of Olives* (Zech. 14:4)." "Has your God a throat?" He replied, "About your gods it is written, *They can make no sound in their throats* (Ps. 115:7). About our God it is written, *The sound that comes out of His mouth* (Job 37:2)." The king asked, "If your God possesses all these attributes, why does He not rescue you out of my hand as he delivered Hananiah, Mishael, and Azariah from the hands of Nebuchadnezzar?" He answered, "Hananiah, Mishael, and Azariah were worthy men and King Nebuchadnezzar was deserving that a miracle be performed through him. You, however, are undeserving. And as far as we are concerned, our lives are forfeit to Heaven. If you do not kill us, the Omnipresent has many executioners. There are numerous bears, wolves, serpents, leopards, and scorpions to attack us and kill us. But in the end the Holy One, blessed be He, will avenge our blood on you." The king at once ordered that he be put to death.

The child's mother said to the king, "By the life of your head, O emperor, let me embrace my son and kiss him." They gave him to her and she bared her breasts and suckled him. She said to the king, "By the life of your head, O emperor, put me to death first and then slay him." He answered her, "I cannot because it is written in your Torah, *However, no animal from the herd or from the flock shall be slaughtered on the same day with its young* (Lev. 22:28)." She retorted, "You unspeakable fool! Have you already fulfilled all the commandments except for this one!" He immediately ordered him to be killed. The mother threw herself upon her child and embraced him and kissed him. She said to him, "My son, go to our father Abraham and tell him, 'My mother said, Be not boastful, saying I built an altar and offered up my son, Isaac. Our mother built seven altars and offered up seven sons in one day. Yours was only a test, but mine was a reality.'" While she was embracing him and kissing him, the king gave an order and they killed him in her arms. When he had been slain, the sages calculated his age and learned that he was two years, six months, and six and a half hours old. When it happened, all the peoples of the earth cried out, "What does their God do for them that they are all the time slain for His sake!" Concerning them it is written, *It is for Your sake that we are slain all day long* (Ps. 44:23). After several days, disturbed by her grief, the woman fell from a roof and died, to fulfill what was written, *She who bore seven is forlorn* (Jer. 15:9). A voice came forth from heaven saying, *A happy mother of children* (Ps. 113:9), and the Holy Spirit cried out, *For these things do I weep* (Lam. 1:16).[115]

It is told of Miriam, the daughter of Tanḥum, that she was taken captive and was ransomed at Acco. The people bought her a dress and when she went to wash it in the sea, a wave came and carried it away. They bought her another and when she went to wash it in the sea, a wave came and carried it away. They wished to buy her still another, but she said to them, "Let the Collector of debts collect His debt." As soon as she thus justified the heavenly decree against herself, the Holy One, blessed be He, gave a hint to the sea and it restored her garments to her.[116]

In the verse, *All around me He has built misery and hardship* (Lam. 3:5), the word *hardship* refers to Vespasian.[117] And in the verse, *He is a lurking bear to me* (Lam. 3:10), the word *bear* refers to Vespasian.[118]

The verse reads, *I will not reject them or spurn them so as to destroy them, annulling My covenant with them: for I the Lord am their God* (Lev. 26:44). Rabbi Ḥiyya explains it: *I will not reject them*—in the days of Vespasian; *or spurn them*—in the days of Trajan; *so as to destroy them*—in the days of Haman; *annulling My covenant with them*—in the days of the Romans; *for I the Lord am their God*—in the days of Gog and Magog.[119]

Samuel explained the same verse in this manner: *I will not reject them*, refers to the days of Antiochus; *or spurn them*, to the days of Vespasian Caesar; *so as to destroy them*, to the days of Haman; *annulling My covenant with them*, to the days of the Romans; *for I the Lord am their God*, to the days of Gog and Magog.

Still another explanation is: *I will not reject them*, refers to the days of the Persians, when I sent them Daniel, Hananiah, Mishael, and Azariah; *or spurn them*, to the days of Haman, when I sent them Mordecai and Esther; *so as to destroy them*, to the days of Antiochus, when I sent them Simon the Just and Mattathias, son of Johanan the Hasmonean, the high priest, and his sons; *annulling My covenant with them*, to the days of the Romans when I sent them Rabbi Judah the Patriarch and his descendants and the sages of the various generations; *for I the Lord am their God*, to the messianic future when no heathen people or tongue shall have dominion over them.[120]

To whom may the verse be applied, *The voice is the voice of Jacob but the hands are the hands of Esau* (Gen. 27:22)? The *voice of Jacob* is the cry caused by the emperor Vespasian who killed in the city of Betar four hundred myriads or, as some say, four thousand myriads. *The hands are the hands of Esau*, this is the wicked government of Rome that destroyed our Temple, burned down our Sanctuary, and exiled us from our land.[121]

The punishment of Nebuchadnezzar will last for three and a half years and that of Vespasian for the same because that is the length of time each of them besieged Jerusalem.[122]

Vespasian sent Titus who mocked, *Where are their gods, the rock in whom they sought refuge?* (Deut. 32:37). This was the wicked Titus who blasphemed and insulted Heaven. What did he do? He entered the Holy of Holies and with his sword slashed the curtain. Through a miracle blood spurted forth and he thought that he had killed God Himself. He brought two harlots and, spreading out a scroll of the Torah beneath them, transgressed with them on top of the altar. He began to speak blasphemies and insults against Heaven, boasting, "One who wars against a king in a desert and defeats him cannot be compared to one who wars against a king in his own palace and conquers him." He gathered together all the vessels of the Temple and placed them in the curtain that he had shaped like a basket; others say that he collected them in a net. He then set sail on a ship to take them to his city for his triumphal procession. A violent gale struck the sea and threatened to drown him. He said, "Evidently their God has power only on the water. He punished the generation of the Flood by water. He did the same to Pharaoh and his army. When Sisera came He drowned him in water. And in my case too, when I was in His own house and within His own domain He could not withstand me, but now here on the water He attacks me. If He is really mighty let Him come up on the dry land and fight with me!" A voice came forth from Heaven and said, "Villain, son of a villain, descendant of Esau! By your life, I shall inflict punishment upon you by one of My smallest creatures, a mosquito. Go up on the dry land and make war with it!" Then the Holy One, blessed be He, signaled to the sea and it became calm. When Titus reached Rome all the citizens of Rome came out and sang his praise, "O conqueror of the barbarians!" They immediately kindled the fire of the bathhouse for him and he bathed. When he came out they mixed for him a cup of wine with a vial of poterion. The Holy One, blessed be He, caused a mosquito to be in the goblet, which entered into his nose and made its way to his brain. It gnawed at his brain for seven years, devouring it, until it became as large as a dove weighing two pounds. One day as he was passing a blacksmith's place it heard the noise of the hammer and stopped its activity. He said, "I see there is a remedy." So every day a blacksmith was brought to hammer before him. If he was a non-Jew he was given four zuzim. If he was a Jew he was told, "It is enough that you see the suffering of your enemy." This went on for thirty days but then the creature got used to the hammering. Titus ordered, "Call the physicians to come to open my skull to find out what it is that the God of this people uses to inflict punishment upon me." The doctors opened his brain and found in it something resembling a young dove weighing two pounds. Rabbi Eleazar, son of Rabbi Jose, said, "I was in Rome at the time. They placed the young dove on one side of the scales and two pounds on the other and they balanced." They set the creature in a bowl and as it gradually shrank, so did Titus. When the mosquito flew away, the soul of Titus flew away to destruction and eternal abhorrence. As he died, he said, "Burn me and scatter my ashes over the seven seas so that the God of the Jews should not find me and bring me to judgment."[123]

Onkelus, son of Kolonikus, was the son of Titus's sister. He was interested in converting to Judaism. He went to a necromancer and raised Titus from the dead. He asked him, "Who are the foremost people in the next world?" He replied, "Israel." "What then of my joining them?" He answered, "Their teachings are burdensome and you will not be able to carry them out. Instead, go and attack them in your world and you will be a leader, as it is written, *Her enemies are now the masters* (Lam. 1:5), that is, whoever torments Israel becomes a master." He asked him, "What is your sentence in the next world?" He answered, "What I decreed for myself. Each day my ashes are collected and reconstituted; and sentence is passed on me again and I am burned and my ashes are scattered over the seven seas."[124] *Her enemies are now the masters,* refers to Vespasian. *Her foes are at ease* (Lam. 1:5), refers to Titus.[125]

How was Jerusalem captured? They brought to the Roman

commander a catapult, which he directed against the wall of Jerusalem. Then they brought him logs of cedar, which he inserted in the catapult and hurled them at the wall until he breached it. Then they brought to him the head of a pig, which he inserted in the catapult and shot so that it landed among the sacrificial parts that were on the altar. At that moment Jerusalem was captured.[126]

It is written, *He readies deadly weapons, and makes his arrows sharp* (Ps. 7:14)—*le-dolkim*. What does this word mean? Rabbi Judah ha-Nasi said, "It refers to the wicked Romans who, during the siege of Jerusalem, hurled fire upon the Jews." Rabbi Jacob of Kefar Ḥanan said, "It refers to the Romans who set fire to the structure in their destruction of the Temple."[127]

When the Temple was set afire the chief priests who were in the Temple took their keys in their hands and hurled them skyward, exclaiming to the Holy One, blessed be He, "Lord of the Universe! Here are Your keys that You entrusted to us, since we have not been faithful custodians to carry out the duties set by the King and we are no longer worthy to eat from the King's table." It is to this that the verse refers: *Throw open your gates, O Lebanon, and let fire consume your cedars!* (Zech. 11:1). The patriarchs, Abraham, Isaac, and Jacob, and the twelve tribes wept and cried out, saying, *Howl, cypresses, for cedars have fallen! How the mighty are ravaged! Howl, you oaks of Bashan, for the stately forest is laid low* (Zech. 11:2). *Howl, cypresses, for cedars have fallen*, refers to the Temple; *How the mighty are ravaged*, refers to Abraham, Isaac, and Jacob and the twelve tribes; *Howl, you oaks of Bashan*, refers to Moses, Aaron, and Miriam; *for the stately forest is laid low*, refers to the Holy of Holies. *Hark, the wailing of the shepherds, for their rich pastures are ravaged* (Zech. 11:3), refers to David and his son Solomon. *Hark, the roaring of the great beasts, for the jungle of the Jordan is ravaged* (Zech. 11:3), refers to Elijah and Elisha.[128]

During the war with Titus the sages decreed that no longer would brides wear wreaths around their heads and no more would a man teach his son Greek wisdom.[129]

Five things happened to our ancestors on the seventeenth day of Tammuz and five on the ninth day of Av. On the seventeenth day of Tammuz the tablets of the Ten Commandments were broken and the daily offering ceased and the city of Jerusalem was breached and Apostomos burned the scrolls of the Torah and set up an idol in the Sanctuary. On the ninth of Av it was decreed that our ancestors not enter the land of Israel and the Temple was destroyed the first and second time and Betar was captured and the city of Jerusalem was ploughed over. When Av begins, gladness must be limited.[130]

As long as the Temple service continued, the world was a source of blessing to all its inhabitants and the rains fell in their seasons. But when the Temple service ceased, the world was no longer a source of blessing to its inhabitants and the rains did not fall in their seasons.[131]

When the pagans entered the Temple, they placed their hands behind their necks—to support their heads—and turned their faces upward. They blasphemed and reviled and the nails of their boots made scratches upon the floor. This is what is written, *He has handed over to the foe the walls of its citadels; they raised a shout in the House of the Lord as on a festival day* (Lam. 2:7).[132]

Rabbi Joshua ben Levi said that when the Roman enemies came to destroy Jerusalem, there were sixty thousand myriads of evil spirits standing at the gate of Jerusalem ready to engage them in battle. But when they saw the Heavenly Presence looking on in silence, as it is written, *He has withdrawn His right hand in the presence of the foe* (Lam. 2:3), they too gave way.[133]

Rabbi Judah ben Simon said that Moses foretold that at a much later date Rome, descendant of Esau, would be triumphant over Israel. Moses said to Israel, "God sees the enemy destroying His house and He is silent and yet you wish to attack him; the reward for the honor he showed his parents is still owing him."[134]

And your descendants shall seize the gates of their foes (Gen. 22:17). Rabbi Judah ha-Nasi said that this refers to Tadmor (Palmyra). Happy is he who will see the downfall of Tadmor which took part in the destruction of both Temples. At the destruction of the First Temple Tadmor supplied eighty thousand archers and at the destruction of the Second, eight thousand archers.[135]

Many were the tragedies that resulted from the destruction of the Second Temple and Jerusalem. It is related that the son and daughter of Rabbi Ishmael ben Elisha were carried off and sold to two different masters. Some time afterward the two masters met. One said, "I have a male slave so handsome that none in the world can compare to him." The other said, "I have a female slave who is the most beautiful in the world." They said, "Let us marry them to each other and divide the children between us." They put them in the same room. The young man sat in one corner of the room and the young woman in another. He said to himself, "I am a priest descended from high priests and shall I marry a slave?" She said to herself, "I am a priest's daughter descended from high priests and shall I marry a slave?" They wept the entire night. When day dawned they recognized each other. They fell upon each other and burst forth into such weeping that their souls left them. It is of such as these that Jeremiah laments, *For these things do I weep, my eyes flow with tears* (Lam. 1:16).

Rabbi Joshua ben Ḥananiah once went to the great city of Rome. He was told that there was in the prison a child with beautiful eyes and face and said, "*Who was it gave Jacob over to despoilment and Israel to plunderers?* (Isa. 42:24)." The child answered, "*Surely, the Lord against whom they sinned, in whose ways they would not walk, and whose Teaching they would not obey* (Isa. 42:24)." He said, "I am certain that this child will be a teacher in Israel. I swear by the Temple service that I shall not leave here until I shall have ransomed him no matter what the price may be!" It was told that he redeemed him at a high figure. It did not take long before he became a teacher in Israel. And who was he? Rabbi Ishmael ben Elisha.[136]

The story is told of a young woman who was taken captive together with her ten maids. A pagan acquired her and she grew up in his house. One day he handed her a jug and said, "Go bring me some water!" One of her former maids arose and took the jug from her. "What is the meaning of this?" the master asked. The woman replied, "By your life, master! I was one of five hundred maids of this young woman's mother." When he heard these words he at once set her free together with her ten maids.[137]

Another story is told of a young woman who was taken captive. A pagan acquired her and she grew up in his house. The Master of Dreams appeared to him and said, "Send the young woman away from your house." His wife said to him, "Do not send her away." Again the Master of Dreams appeared to him and said, "If you do not send her away, I will kill you," and he let her go. He followed her, saying to himself, "I must go and see what will happen to this young woman." As she proceeded along her way she grew thirsty and went down to a spring to drink. She placed her hand on the wall and a snake came out and bit her so that she died instantly, her body floating on the water. He went down, retrieved her body, and buried her. Upon his return home he told his wife, "This people whom you see must bear the anger of none other than their Father in heaven."[138]

Four hundred boys and girls were taken captive by the Romans and set aboard ship for Rome for immoral purposes. They guessed their fate and said, "If we drown in the sea we shall attain life in the world to come." The eldest among them expounded the verse, *The Lord said, "I will retrieve from Bashan, I will retrieve from the depths of the sea"* (Ps. 68:23). *I will retrieve from Bashan*, means from between a lion's teeth; *I will retrieve from the depths of the sea*, means those who drown in the sea. As soon as the girls heard this, they all leaped into the sea. The boys deduced a moral for themselves, saying, "If these for whom the contemplated shameful act was at least a natural one behaved so, how much more so should we follow their example, for whom the contemplated shameful act is an unnatural one!" They too all leaped into the sea. Concerning them the verse says, *It is for Your sake that we are slain all day long, that we are regarded as sheep to be slaughtered* (Ps. 44:23).[139]

It is told about a certain woman named Zafnat, daughter of Peniel—Zafnat, because she was so beautiful all gazed at her; daughter of Peniel, because she was the daughter of the high priest who served in the inner shrine—that she was abused by a Roman brigand a whole night. The next day he put seven wraps around her and took her out to sell her. A certain man, unusually ugly, came and said, "Show me how beautiful she is." The first man replied, "Fool! If you want to buy her, buy her, for her beauty has no comparison in all the world." The man retorted, "Nevertheless!" The first man took six wraps off her and she herself tore off the seventh and rolled in the dust, crying out, "Master of the Universe, if you have no pity on us, why do You not have pity on the sanctity of Your great Name?" It is about one like her that Jeremiah laments, *My poor people, put on sackcloth and strew dust on yourselves! Mourn, as for an only child; wail bitterly, for suddenly the destroyer is coming upon us* (Jer. 6:26). It does not say "upon you" but *upon us*: the spoiler has come, if it may be said, upon Me and upon you.[140]

Rabbi Eleazar, son of Rabbi Zadok, said, "May I not behold consolation, if this be not true—although my father lived many years after the destruction of the Temple, his body never became normal again. So the verse was fulfilled, *Their skin has shriveled on their bones, it has become dry as wood* (Lam. 4:8)."

He said again, "A beggar once came and stood at the door of my father's house and my father told me, 'Go and see whether he is a Jerusalemite.' I went and found there a woman whose hair had fallen out through hunger so that no one could tell whether she was a woman or a man. She begged only for a dried fig; to fulfill the verse, *They are not recognized in the streets; their skin has shriveled on their bones* (Lam. 4:8)."[141]

▬ 5 ▬
After the Destruction

The Holy One, blessed be He, weeps with Jerusalem. The ministering angels weep with her. Heaven and earth weep as well, as do the mountains and the valleys.[142]

The Holy One, blessed be He, summoned the ministering angels and asked them, "When a king of flesh and blood loses a son, what does he do?" They replied, "He drapes his palace gate with sackcloth." He said, "So shall I do," as it is written, *I clothe the skies in blackness and make their raiment sackcloth* (Isa. 50:3). He again asked them, "What more does a human king do when mourning?" They replied, "He extinguishes the lamps." He said to them, "I shall do likewise," as it is said, *Sun and moon are darkened, and stars withdraw their brightness* (Joel 4:15). "What more," He asked, "does a mortal king do?" They answered, "He overturns his couch." He said to them, "I shall do the same," as it is stated, *Thrones were set in place, and the Ancient of Days took His seat* (Dan. 7:9). "What more does a human king do in mourning?" They replied, "He goes about barefoot." He said to them, "I will do likewise," as it is said, *He travels in whirlwind and storm, and clouds are the dust on His feet* (Nah. 1:3). "What more does a mortal king do?" They answered, "He rends his purple robes." He said to them, "So shall I do," as it is written, *The Lord has done what He purposed, has carried out the decree* (Lam. 2:17). And Rabbi Jacob of Kefar Ḥanan explained that the Hebrew words translated as "*has done what He purposed*," should be understood to mean "He tore His purple." Further He asked, "What more does a human king do in mourning?" They replied, "He sits in silence." He said to them, "I will do likewise," as it is stated, *Let him sit alone and be patient* (Lam. 3:28). "What more does a mortal king do when mourning?" They answered, "He sits and weeps." He said to them, "I will do likewise," as it is written, *My Lord God of hosts summoned on that day to weeping and lamenting, to tonsuring* (Isa. 22:12).[143]

The rabbis asked, "What is the meaning of the word *be-mistarim* in the verse, *My soul shall weep in secret (be-mistarim) because of your pride* (Jer. 13:17)." Rav was quoted as explaining, "There is a place where the Holy One, blessed be He, weeps and its name is *mistarim.*" And what is the meaning of *your pride?* God weeps because the Jewish people has lost its source of pride, taken from them and given to other peoples. Another explanation is that God weeps because the Kingdom of Heaven has lost its source of pride—the Temple and Jerusalem. The verse continues, *My eye must stream and flow with copious tears, because the flock of the Lord is taken captive.* Why the three "weepings" implied here? One for the First Temple, one for the Second Temple, and one for the exile of the Jewish people from their home.[144]

Rabbi Jose said, "Once I was walking along the way and I entered one of the ruins of Jerusalem to pray. Elijah of blessed memory appeared and guarded the entrance until I ended my prayers. When I finished, he said to me, 'Peace be to you, my Master.' I replied, 'Peace be to you, my Master, my Teacher.' He then said to me, 'My son, why did you enter this ruin?' I answered, 'To pray.' He said, 'You should have prayed outside on the road.' I replied, 'I was concerned lest passersby interrupt my praying.' He said, 'Then you should have prayed more briefly.' At that moment he taught me three things: not to enter a ruin, that one may pray on the road, and that such prayer should be abbreviated. He asked me further, 'What kind of sound did you hear in this ruin?' I told him, 'I heard a divine voice mourning like a dove and lamenting, "Woe to My children that because of their iniquities I have had to destroy My House and burn My Temple and exile My children among the nations."' Elijah then said to me, 'My son, I swear by your life and by the life of your head, this lament was uttered not only at this time but it is voiced every day, three times a day. More, each time Jews enter their synagogues and their houses of study and, in their prayers, respond, "Let His great name be praised forever and for all eternity," the Holy One, blessed be He, nods His head and declares, "Happy is the king who is so praised in his house but of what good is it to a father who has exiled his children among the nations, and woe to children who have been exiled from their father's table!" ' "[145]

The night is divided into three watches and at the beginning of each watch the Holy One, blessed be He, roars like a lion, crying out, "Woe to My children because of whose iniquities I have had to destroy My House and burn My Temple and exile My children among the nations."[146]

Balza asked Rabbi Akiba, "Where does thunder come from?" He replied, "When the Holy One, blessed be He, beholds the heathen temples and their worshipers enjoying peace and prosperity in this world and He sees His Temple destroyed and in the hands of idolaters, He becomes furious and begins to roar. Immediately heaven and earth tremble and break into thunder, as it says, *And the Lord will roar from Zion, and shout aloud from Jerusalem, so that heaven and earth tremble* (Joel: 4:16)."[147]

The Heavenly Presence has never departed from the Western Wall of the Temple, as it is said, *There he stands behind our wall* (Songs 2:9).[148]

Since the day the Temple was destroyed there has been no day without its curse; and the dew has not fallen in blessing and the fruits have lost their taste; some add, they have also lost their fullness. From the day the Temple was destroyed the *haverim* and the freemen were put to shame and walked with covered head, and the men of good works became enfeebled; men of violence and men of loud tongue prevailed. And now, there are none to expound to Israel and none to seek compassion for them and none to seek their welfare. On whom can we depend? Only on our Father in heaven.

From the day the Temple was destroyed the sages became like schoolteachers, schoolteachers like sextons, and sextons like run of the mill people; and the people became feeble, and there was no one to seek compassion for them. On whom can we depend? Only on our Father in heaven.[149]

From the day the Temple was destroyed wine formed into a jelly, and white glass was no longer used at a dinner.[150] When the Second Temple was destroyed the number of people increased who would not eat meat nor drink wine. Rabbi Joshua approached them and asked, "My children, why do you not eat meat and drink wine?" They replied, "Shall we eat meat of which offerings were brought on the altar, which is no more, and shall we drink wine of which libations were poured at the altar, which is no more?" He said to them, "If so, let us not eat bread since the meal offering is no more." They said, "We can eat fruit." He said, "We should not eat fruit since the offering of the firstfruits is no more." They said, "We can eat other fruits that were not brought as an offering." He said, "We should not drink water for the ceremony of libation of water is no more." They fell silent. He then told them, "My children, not to mourn at all is impossible for the decree has gone forth. But to mourn overly much is wrong for a decree is not issued unless a majority of the public can endure it." Therefore, the sages said that when a person paints his house he should leave a small area unpainted—approximately a cubit square—and it should be opposite the entrance. A person may prepare an entire meal but leave out one item, such as a pie of fish-hash and flour. A woman may put on all her adornments but omit one small thing, such as a forehead adornment. For it is said, *If I forget you, O Jerusalem, let my right hand wither; let my tongue stick to my palate if I cease to think of you, if I do not keep Jerusalem in memory even at my happiest hour* (Ps. 137:5–6). Rabbi Isaac said, "This refers to the ashes placed on the forehead of bridegrooms." And whoever mourns for Jerusalem will merit to witness her joy, as it is said, *Rejoice with Jerusalem, and be glad for her, all you who love her! Join in her jubilation, all you who mourned over her* (Isa. 66:10).

Rabbi Ishmael ben Elisha said, "From the day the Temple was destroyed it would have been right to decree upon ourselves not to eat meat nor to drink wine but a decree must not be issued unless the majority of the public can endure it. And from the day the Roman government extended its sovereignty and decreed harsh edicts against us, suspending the study of Torah and the practice of the commandments, it would have been right that we decree against ourselves not to marry nor to have children and the result would have been that Abraham's descendants would have ended their history. Therefore, leave it to the Israelites—better that they be unintentional rather than intentional transgressors."[151]

Both Rabbi Johanan and Rabbi Eleazar said, "As long as the Temple was in existence, its altar was the means of atonement for Israel, but now each person's table is the means of atonement."[152]

Esau (Rome) put a stop to the sacrifices but of Jethro it is said, *And Jethro, Moses' father-in-law, brought a burnt offering and sacrifices for God* (Exod. 18:12).[153]

The House of Israel says, "I am asleep with regard to the sacrifices, but my heart is awake for the recital of the Shema and prayer. I am asleep with regard to the Temple, but my heart is awake for synagogues and houses of study."[154]

Rabbi Eleazar son of Rabbi Jose said, "I actually saw the Temple curtain in Rome and it had upon it many drops of blood. When I asked the source of this blood, the reply I received was, 'This is from the blood which the high priest used to sprinkle in the Holy of Holies on the Day of Atonement.' "[155]

An explanation for the verse, *. . . behind your veil. Your hair is like a flock of goats streaming down Mount Gilead* (Songs 4:1): the mountain from which you streamed away I made into a heap and a witness for the nations of the world. What was this? The Temple, as it says, *You are awesome, O God, in your holy places* (Ps. 68:36). Whence issues awe? Is it not from the Temple? For so we read, *You shall keep My sabbaths and venerate My sanctuary* (Lev. 26:2), which indicates that it is hallowed in its ruin as it was hallowed when it still stood.[156]

The biblical words, *Your neck is like the Tower of David* (Songs 4:4), refer to the Temple. Why is it compared to a neck? Because as long as the Temple was standing Israel's neck was stretched high among the nations of the world, but when the Temple was destroyed, then Israel's neck was bowed; and so is it written, *And I will break your proud glory* (Lev. 26:19), namely, the Temple. Another explanation: Just as a man's neck is at the highest part of him, so the Temple was at the highest part of the world. And just as ornaments are hung around the neck, so the priests and the Levites were attached to the Temple. And just as if the neck be removed a man cannot live, so since the Temple was destroyed there has been no life for Israel.

The biblical words, *built to hold weapons (talpiot)* (Songs 4:4), mean that what was once beauty has been turned into a ruin. The Holy One, blessed be He, said, "It is I who made it into a ruin in this world; it is I who will make it a thing of beauty in the world to come."[157] Another explanation: *talpiot* means the ruin *(tel)* for which all mouths *(piyot)* pray. Hence it was prescribed that those who stand up to pray outside the land of Israel turn their faces to the land of Israel, as it says, *and they pray to You in the direction of their land* (1 Kings 8:48). Those who pray in the land of Israel turn toward Jerusalem, as it says, *and they pray to You in the direction of the city* (2 Chron. 6:34). Those who pray in Jerusalem turn toward the Temple, as it says, *when he comes to pray toward this House* (1 Kings 8:42). Those who stand on the Temple mount turn toward the Holy of Holies, as it says, *then they pray toward this place* (1 Kings 8:35). All this can be proof for the time when the Temple was still standing. Whence do we know it for the time when it is in ruins? Rabbi Avin said, "From the text, *built to hold weapons* (*talpiot*), that is, the Temple for which all mouths pray."[158]

Rabbi Simon ben Lakish interpreted the biblical words, *Ah, those who add house to house* (Isa. 5:8), as follows: you have joined the destruction of the First Temple to that of the Second Temple. As with the First Temple, *Zion shall be ploughed as a field* (Jer. 26:18), so with the Second Temple, *Zion shall be ploughed as a field.*[159]

Abandon our dwellings! (Jer. 9:18). The plural form, *dwellings*, alludes to the destruction of the First Temple and the Second Temple.[160] *With that he embraced his brother Benjamin around the neck and wept* (Gen. 45:14). Joseph wept for the two destructions, the destruction of the First Temple and the destruction of the Second Temple.[161]

Rabbi Judah said in the name of Rav, "What is meant by the verse, *By the rivers of Babylon, there we sat, sat and wept, as we thought of Zion* (Ps. 137:1)?" This indicates that the Holy One, blessed be He, showed David the destruction of both the First Temple and the Second Temple. Of the First Temple, as it is written, *By the rivers of Babylon, there we sat, sat and wept*; of the Second Temple, as it is written, *Remember, O Lord, against the Edomites the day of Jerusalem's fall; how they cried, "Strip her strip her to her very foundations!"* (Ps. 137:7).[162]

Rabbi Abbahu in the name of Rabbi Jose ben Ḥanina opened his discourse with the text, *And her gates shall lament and mourn* (Isa. 3:26): lamenting is internal—grief in the heart—and mourning is external—the outward manifestations of grieving. *Her gates* —plural—refers to the destruction of the First and Second Temples.[163]

The prophet Jeremiah prophesied, *My eye must stream and flow with copious tears, because the flock of the Lord is taken captive* (Jer. 13:17). Rabbi Eleazar asked, "Why (in the Hebrew original) does the verse speak of tears three times? Once for the

First Temple, once for the Second Temple, and once because Israel has been exiled from its land." Others say that the third time was because of the interruption of the study of Torah.[164] *Bitterly she weeps in the night* (Lam. 1:2), says the book of Lamentations. Why (in the Hebrew original) is weeping mentioned twice? Rabbah said in the name of Rabbi Johanan, "Once for the First Temple and once for the Second Temple."[165]

Of the leper the Bible says, *And he shall cover over his upper lip* (Lev. 13:45). Rabbi Alexandri applied those words to Israel. When the people were exiled among the nations of the world, not one of them was able to bring a word of Torah out of his mouth. *And he shall call out, "Unclean! Unclean!"* (Lev. 13:45)—that is, the destruction of the First and Second Temples.[166]

The destruction of the Second Temple was worse than that of the First. The destruction of the First Temple was like the splintering of a house that causes a leak. It is said, *Through lazy hands*— that is, because of Israel's reluctance to repent in the days of Jeremiah—*the house caves in* (Eccles. 10:18). And it is said, *For the Lord will command, and the great house shall be smashed to bits, and the little house to splinters* (Amos 6:11). From a smashing to bits, escape is possible. But the destruction of the Second Temple was like a smashing into splinters. And from such a splintering no escape is possible. They are not like one another.[167]

In the construction of the Temple and of the tabernacle that preceded it no mention is made of iron. Why? Because Rome, who destroyed the Temple, was likened to iron and the verse teaches that God will accept gifts from all the kingdoms in the time to come but not from Edom (Rome). But did not Babylonia also destroy the Temple? Yes, but it did not raze it to the ground, while of Edom it is written, *How they cried, "Strip her, strip her, to her very foundations!"* (Ps. 137:7). They said to each other in amazement while destroying the Temple, "What! It still has a foundation? Then let us destroy it!" It is on this account, because Edom (Rome) is compared to iron that no mention of iron is made in the construction of the tabernacle or the Temple.[168]

As long as the Temple was standing not one Israelite was in distress, for when a man entered it laden with sin and offered a sacrifice, he was forgiven. Could he have a greater joy than the feeling that he had when he left the Temple forgiven and righteous once again? Therefore, it is said of the Temple, *Fair-crested, joy of all the earth* (Ps. 48:3).[169] Just as oil gives forth light so did the Temple give light to the whole world, as it says, *And nations shall walk by your light* (Isa. 60:3).[170]

Before Jerusalem was destroyed no province was held in any esteem. But after it was destroyed, Caesarea became a metropolis.[171] If anyone should tell you that both Caesarea and Jerusalem are destroyed, do not believe him; if he says both are inhabited, do not believe him. If he says Caesarea is destroyed and Jerusalem inhabited or Jerusalem is destroyed and Caesarea is inhabited, believe him. When one flourishes, the other must be waste; both cannot flourish or be desolate at the same time.[172]

In response to *My Lord God of hosts summoned on that day to weeping and lamenting* (Isa. 22:12), the ministering angels said to Him, "Sovereign of the Universe, it is written, *Glory and majesty are before Him* (1 Chron. 16:27), and You tell us to weep! We do not know how to lament since our daily task is to sing of Your majesty." He replied to them, "I will teach you. It is said, *Strip yourselves naked, put the cloth about your loins! Lament upon the breasts* (Isa. 32:11–12); so will you lament." *Lament upon the breasts*, because of the destruction of the First and Second Temples.[173]

There is a seeming contradiction between two verses in the Bible. One verse reads, *Can His troops be numbered?* (Job 25:3). This implies that there is no number. Another verse reads, *Thousands upon thousands served Him* (Dan. 7:10), implying there is a number. The only explanation is that before the Temple was destroyed the praise of the Holy One, blessed be He, used to ascend in complete, unlimited form, but since the Temple was destroyed, the Holy One, blessed be He, if it may be said, reduced the size of His household.[174]

After Jerusalem was destroyed there was added to the grace said after meals, "Who will rebuild Jerusalem." When the Israelites entered the land in the beginning, they added, "For the land and for the food." Before they entered the land they used to recite only one blessing, "Who feeds all."[175]

The Heavenly Presence did not go into exile when the Sanhedrin was banished nor when the priestly watches were exiled. When, however, the children were exiled, the Heavenly Presence went into exile with them, so beloved are children by the Holy One, blessed be He. As it is written, *Her infants have gone into captivity before the enemy.* This is followed immediately by *Gone from fair Zion are all that were her glory* (Lam. 1:5–6)— the glory of Jerusalem being the Heavenly Presence.[176]

From the day the Temple was destroyed the gift of prophecy was taken away from the prophets but not from the wise. This is the opinion of Rabbi Avdimi of Haifa. But Rabbi Johanan said that from the day the Temple was destroyed the gift of prophecy was taken from the prophets and given to fools and children.[177]

From the day the Temple was destroyed rain has not come with the south wind, as it is written, *They snatched on the right, but remained hungry, and consumed on the left without being sated* (Isa. 9:19), and it is also written, *North and south—You created them* (Ps. 89:13). Moreover, from the day the Temple was destroyed, the rains do not come from the heavenly treasure, as it is said, *The Lord will open for you His bounteous store, the heavens, to provide rain for your land in season* (Deut. 28:12). When Israel did God's will and lived in its own land, the rains came from the *bounteous store,* but now that Israel is no longer in its own land this is not so any more. From the time the Temple was destroyed there has been no day without its curse. Moreover, the dew that brings blessing has not fallen. Fruit has lost its taste and even its richness.[178]

Since the Temple was destroyed the world has not witnessed the true radiance of the sun nor the true brightness of the sky. And ever since the Temple was destroyed God does not laugh anymore, as it is written, *I have kept silent far too long, kept still, and restrained Myself* (Isa. 42:14).[179] From the day the Temple was destroyed the gates of prayer were closed, as it is said, *And when I cry and plead, He shuts out my prayer* (Lam. 3:8). But although the gates of prayer were closed, the gates of tears were not closed, as it is said, *Hear my prayer, O Lord; give ear to my cry; do not disregard my tears* (Ps. 39:13). And from the day the Temple was destroyed the iron wall separating Israel from their Father in heaven has been broken, as it is said, *Then take an iron plate and place it as an iron wall between yourself and the city* (Ezek. 4:3).[180]

From the day the Temple was destroyed the Holy One, blessed be He, has in His world for His satisfaction only the four cubits where the Halakhah is studied. This is the meaning of the passage, *The Lord loves the gates of Zion . . . more than all the dwellings of Jacob* (Ps. 87:2), that is, the Lord loves the gates marked for study of the Halakhah more than the synagogues and the houses of study.[181]

From the day the Temple was destroyed a decree was issued against the houses of the righteous that they be destroyed, as it is said, *Surely, great houses shall lie forlorn, spacious and splendid ones, without occupants* (Isa. 5:9). For a servant should not be better off than his master. And in the future the Holy One, blessed be He, will again cause them to be inhabited, as it is said, *Those who trust in the Lord are like Mount Zion that cannot be moved, enduring forever* (Ps. 125:1). Just as the Holy One, blessed be He, will cause Mount Zion again to be peopled, so will He cause the houses of the righteous to be inhabited again.[182]

Why was Jerusalem destroyed? Abaye said because its people profaned the Sabbath. Rabbi Abbahu said it was because they neglected their prayers, to recite the Shema mornings and evenings. Rabbi Hamnuna said because they stopped teaching Torah to their children. Ulla said it was because they lost their sense of shame. Rabbi Isaac said because they paid no respect to people who deserved it. Rabbi Amram, quoting his father, Rabbi Simon ben Abba, who had quoted Rabbi Ḥanina, said it was because they did not admonish each other when it was called for; they turned their faces away and saw no evil. Rabbi Judah said Jerusalem was destroyed because they held scholars in contempt. Rava said it was because there were no more trustworthy people in the city, although Rabbi Ketina said that even at its worst Jerusalem always had some trustworthy people.[183]

Jerusalem was destroyed only because justice was perverted, as it is said, *Your rulers are rogues and cronies of thieves, every one avid for presents and greedy for gifts* (Isa. 1:23).[184] Rabbi Johanan said, "Jerusalem was destroyed because people insisted on taking everything to court instead of seeking to settle disputes and litigations by compromise. They insisted upon the fulfillment of the exact law and never sought equity."[185]

What was the cause of the destruction of the First Temple? Idolatry. And of the Second Temple? Causeless hatred. And causeless hatred is worse than idolatry. Whence do we know this? For it is written, *Ephraim is addicted to images—let him be* (Hos. 4:17). As long as they are joined together—even to worship their idols, let them alone. And it is also written, *Their hearts divided; now shall they bear their guilt* (Hos. 10:2).[186]

The First Temple was destroyed because the people practiced

idolatry, immorality, and murder. But during the period of the Second Temple they were engaged in the study of Torah, the fulfillment of the commandments, and the practice of charity. Why then was the Second Temple destroyed? Because there was causeless hatred among them, which teaches you that causeless hatred is equal to the transgressions of idolatry, immorality, and murder together.[187]

At the very beginning of the creation of the universe the Holy One, blessed be He, made for Himself a booth in Jerusalem and, as it were, used to pray in it, "May it so be that My children will do My will so that I shall not have to destroy My House and My Sanctuary."[188]

The doom of Jerusalem was sealed as is explained by this story told by Rabbi Judah in the name of Rav to illustrate the meaning of the verse, *They defraud men of their homes, and people of their land* (Mic. 2:2). Once a certain man, a carpenter's apprentice, cast his eyes upon his master's wife. It happened that his master had to borrow some money from him. The apprentice said, "Send your wife to me and I will lend the money to her." He sent his wife to him and she stayed three days with him. The master went to him and demanded, "Where is my wife whom I sent to you?" The apprentice replied, "I sent her away at once but I heard that the young fellows had sport with her on the way." "What shall I do?" he asked. "If you listen to my advice, divorce her." "But she has a large marriage settlement provided for her in our marriage certificate," said the master. "I will lend you the money," said the apprentice, "you pay her." The master then divorced her and the apprentice married her. When the time came for the payment of the debt and he was not able to pay, his former apprentice said to him, "Come and work off your debt with me." So the new couple would sit and eat and drink and he would serve them, his tears falling into their cups. From that hour the doom of Jerusalem was sealed. Others say the real reason was for two wicks in one candle.[189]

Why was the Temple destroyed? Because it was taken as a pledge for our sins. Therefore the verse says, *These are the records of the Tabernacle* (mishkan), *the Tabernacle of the Pact* (Exod. 38:21). Do not read *mishkan*, "Tabernacle," but *mashkon*, "a pledge."[190] When the two Temples were standing they were called "tents," but when they were destroyed, they were called "pledges." That is what Balaam said, *How fair are your tents, O Jacob, your dwellings, O Israel!* (Num. 24:5). Two dwellings are referred to. God says, "It is not because I am in debt to the heathen nations that I have pledged My tabernacle to them, but it is your iniquities that have caused Me to hand over to them My Sanctuary. Were this not the case, why was I then obliged to do this? Does it not say, *Thus said the Lord: Where is the bill of divorce of your mother whom I dismissed?* (Isa. 50:1)? With Moses too did I make this condition concerning them." Moses asked, "Shall they remain in pledge forever?" God replied, "No, only until the sun appears, that is, until the coming of the Messiah"; for it says, *But for you who revere My name a sun of victory shall rise to bring healing* (Mal. 3:20).[191]

There is a difference of opinion as to whether the Divine Presence came to dwell in the Second Temple. Some say it did not for the Holy One, blessed be He, had said, "If Israel—all of them—come up to the land, the Presence will dwell in it; but if they do not, they will have only the echo of the Divine Voice to depend upon." So when the Second Temple was built half the people were weeping and half were shouting with joy. The old men who had seen the glory of the House in which the Heavenly Presence itself had dwelt and now saw the second House in which the Presence was not dwelling were those who wept; but their children who had not seen the glory of the first House and now saw the second House being built shouted for joy. Rabbi Isaac said, "Why did not the Presence dwell in the second House which the exiled Children of Israel built?" Not, as has been said, because all the exiles failed to return to the land, but because Cyrus king of Persia was responsible for their building it. Since he was a descendant of Japheth, the Presence would not rest on the handiwork of Japheth's seed. But in the first House, which the children of Israel—Shem's descendants —had built, there the Presence had dwelt. As Scripture says, *May God enlarge Japheth, and let him dwell in the tents of Shem* (Gen. 9:27).

But others say that He dwelt there during the days of the First Temple when the Ark was there and even during the days of the Second Temple, when the Ark was not there and only the rock was there. God's glory still reposed, *Dwelling in the rock, lodging upon the fastness of a jutting rock* (Job 39:28).

Before the Temple was destroyed the Divine Presence dwelt within it, for it says, *The Lord is in His holy palace* (Ps. 11:4). But when the Temple was destroyed the Divine Presence removed itself to heaven, as it is said, *The Lord has established His throne in heaven* (Ps. 103:19). This was said by Rabbi Samuel ben Naḥman. But Rabbi Eleazar said, "The Divine Presence did not depart from the Temple, for it is said, *My eyes and My heart shall always be there* (2 Chron. 7:16)." So it also says, *I cry aloud to the Lord, and He answers me from His holy mountain* (Ps. 3:5). For although it was laid waste, it still retained its holiness. See what Cyrus said, *The God that is in Jerusalem* (Ezra 1:3), implying that though Jerusalem is laid waste, God had not departed from there. Rabbi Aḥa said, "The Divine Presence will never depart from the Western Wall, as it is said, *There he stands behind our wall* (Songs 2:9)." *Wall* alludes to the Western Wall of the Temple, which will never be destroyed. Why? Because the Divine Presence is in the West. And because God has sworn to Himself that it will never be destroyed; nor will the Gate of the Priests nor the Gate of Ḥuldah ever be destroyed until God shall renew them.[192]

Why did God swear that the Western Wall would never be destroyed? Because when lots were drawn at the time the Temple was constructed it fell to the poor to build the Western Wall. The wealthy men of Israel took the golden earrings from the ears of their wives and their daughters, as well as all their jewels, which were very precious. They brought cedar wood for the floors and the walls, cypress wood for the doors, and olive wood for the lintels. They hired day laborers from the Sidonians and the Tyrians and others of the heathen who lived in the land; and over them they appointed foremen to press them on, saying, "You slackers, finish your work!" Thus the work was speedily ended and the responsibilities of the wealthy were fulfilled. Only the work of the poor was delayed for they could not bring materials from afar and they did the work themselves, the men, women, and children hewing stone. When the holy work was ended the Divine Presence descended and rested upon it and the Lord chose the Western Wall, for He said, "The toil of the needy and the poor is precious in My eyes, and My blessing shall be upon it." And a heavenly voice went forth and proclaimed, "Never shall the Western Wall be destroyed."[193]

The verse reads, *There he comes, leaping over mountains, bounding over hills* (Songs 2:8). The Divine Presence leaped from mountain to hill, but found no repose in all the places that it visited —neither in all the burning bush, nor on Sinai, nor in the Tent of the Congregation, until it came to rest in the Holy Temple at the

Western Wall. *There he stands behind our wall* (Songs 2:9). From there He observes the actions of men. The Holy One, blessed be He, stands, as it were, behind the wall and peeps through the crevices. He sees but is not seen.[194]

Once Rabbi Natan entered the site of the destroyed Holy Temple and found only one wall standing—the Western Wall. He wondered what were the properties of this wall that it was not destroyed. Someone said, "I shall show you." He took a ring and inserted it into a crevice in the wall and the ring moved to and fro, showing that the wall was actually trembling in awe of the Divine Presence that never departs from it. And Rabbi Natan saw the Holy One, blessed be He, prostrating Himself with grief and bewailing the destruction of the Temple and the exile of His people, Israel.[195]

The Holy One, blessed be He, said to His people, "My children, now accept from Me a measure of comfort." Whereupon Israel replied, "Master of the Universe, You became angry at us and exiled us among the peoples of the world and now You come to comfort us?" The Holy One, blessed be He, answered, "I shall tell you a parable to which it may be likened. A man married his niece and later became angry at her and divorced her. Some time later he came to comfort her. She said to him, 'You were angry at me and drove me from your home and now you come to comfort me?' He replied, 'You are my sister's daughter. Do you think that from the day you left my home there has been another woman in it? I swear by your life, not even I have entered my house.'" So said the Holy One, blessed be He, to Israel, "My children, from the day that I destroyed My house below, I have not gone up to sit in My house above. I have instead been weeping, sitting amidst the dew and the rain. And if you do not believe Me, touch My head and you will feel the dew upon it."[196]

On the day the Temple was destroyed, the Messiah was born. It happened once that a man was ploughing when suddenly his cow began to low. A man of Arav was passing by and heard its voice and asked, "Who are you?" He replied, "I am a Jew." The man of Arav said, "Jew, Jew, unharness your cow and unhitch the plough." "Why?" asked the Jew. "Because the Temple of the Jews has been destroyed." "How do you know this?" the Jew asked. He answered, "From the lowing of your cow." While they were talking, the cow lowed again. The man of Arav said, "Jew, Jew, harness your cow and hitch up the plough for the Messiah has been born, the Redeemer of Israel." The Jew asked, "What is his name?" "Menaḥem," was the answer. "And what is his father's name?" "Hezekiah," he replied. The Jew asked, "Where does he live?" The man of Arav answered, "In Birat Araba near Bethlehem in Judah." The Jew went and sold his cow and his plough and became a seller of linen garments for children. He set out, going from one area to another and from town to town until he reached the place. Women from all the nearby villages came to buy the linen garments, but that woman, the mother of Menaḥem, did not buy anything from him. He heard the women calling, "Mother of Menaḥem! Mother of Menaḥem! Come and buy linen garments for your son." She said, "May the enemies of Israel choke!" They asked, "Why do you say this?" She replied, "On the day my son was born the Temple was destroyed." He said to her, "I am certain that as the Temple's destruction was associated with him, so too will be its rebuilding." She said to him, "I cannot buy for I have no money." He replied, "What difference does that make? Come, take linen garments for your son and after several days I shall come to your house and you will pay me." Some days later he came to her village and he thought to himself, "I shall go and see that child and what he does." He came to her and said, "Tell me about your son's actions." She replied, "Soon after you saw me stormy winds came, snatched him out of my hands, lifted him up, and carried him away." He said to her, "Did I not tell you that both the destruction and the rebuilding of the Temple are associated with him?"

Rabbi Abun said, "Why should I learn this from an Aravite when there is an explicit scriptural text in which it is stated, *And the Lebanon trees*—that is, the Temple—*shall fall in their majesty*, which is followed by, *But a shoot*—that is, the Messiah—*shall grow out of the stump of Jesse, a twig shall sprout from his stock* (Isa. 10:34–11:1).[197]

Rabbi Isaac interpreted the verse, *On the third day Abraham looked up and saw the place from afar* (Gen. 22:4), and said, *The place*—that is, the place of the sacrifice of Isaac and the future Temple—*shall one day be alienated*—*afar*—from its owner. Forever? No, for it is stated, *This is My resting-place for all time; here I will dwell, for I desire it* (Ps. 132:14)—when the one comes of whom it is written, *Humble, riding on an ass* (Zech. 9:9).[198]

God, if it may be said, is called *first*, as it says, *I am the first, and I am the last* (Isa. 44:6). Zion is called *first*, as it says, *O Throne of Glory exalted from of old, our Sacred Shrine!* (Jer. 17:12). Esau was called *first*, for it says, *The first one emerged red* (Gen. 25:25). And the Messiah is called *first*, for it says, *The first I will give to Zion—Behold, here they are! And again I send a herald to Jerusalem* (Isa. 41:27). God who is called *the first* will come and rebuild the Temple, which is also called *first*, and will exact retribution from Esau, also called *first*. Then will the Messiah who is called *first* come in the first month, as it is said, *This month shall mark for you the beginning of the months* (Exod. 12:2).[199]

It is written, *But confirm the word of My servant and fulfill the prediction of My messengers* (Isa. 44:26). God appeared to Jacob, His servant, to fulfill the decree of that angel who had said to him, *"You shall be called Jacob no more,"* and God too spoke to him thus, as it says, *God said to him, "You whose name is Jacob, you shall be called Jacob no more"* (Gen. 35:10). Then how much more will God fulfill the words of His prophets concerning Jerusalem, for all the prophets prophesied about it—that it would be rebuilt and returned to its former glory.[200]

All the talk of human beings generally has to do with matters of the earth. Will the earth produce? Will it not? And all their prayers are on the same subject. "Master of the Universe, cause the earth to produce! Master of the Universe, cause the earth to prosper!" But all the prayers of Israel have only to do with the Temple. "Master of the Universe, may the Temple be rebuilt! Master of the Universe, when will the Temple be rebuilt?"[201] The one who mourns for Jerusalem will merit seeing it rejoice once more, and he who does not mourn for Jerusalem will not see the city rejoice again, as it is said, *Rejoice with Jerusalem and be glad for her, all you who love her! Join in her jubilation, all you who mourned over her* (Isa. 66:10).[202]

At the time the Temple was being destroyed the Holy One, blessed be He, found Abraham standing within it. He asked him, *Why should My beloved be in My house?* (Jer. 11:15). Abraham replied, "I have come because of my children's concerns." He told him, "Your children have sinned and are to be exiled." Whereupon Abraham pleaded, "Perhaps they sinned unintentionally." God replied, *Who—Israel—executes so many vile designs* (Jer. 11:15). Again Abraham pleaded, "Perhaps only a few sinned." God answered, "Many." Abraham argued, "You should have remembered for their merit the covenant of circumcision." God replied, *The sacral flesh will pass away from you* (Jer. 11:15). Abraham pleaded, "Perhaps had You waited they would have repented." God said, *For you exult while performing your evil deeds* (Jer. 11:15). At once Abraham put his hand on his head, cried out and wept, "Is there then, Heaven forfend, no remedy for them?" A voice came forth from heaven and said, *The Lord named you verdant olive tree, fair, with choice fruit* (Jer. 11:16); just as the olive tree brings forth its best at the end, so Israel will be at its best in the end.[203]

The Torah states, *He who started the fire must make restitution* (Exod. 22:5). The Holy One, blessed be He, said, "I must make restitution for the fire that I kindled. I kindled the fire on Zion, as it is said, *He kindled a fire in Zion which consumed its foundations* (Lam. 4:11), and I shall in the future rebuild it through fire, as it is said, *And I, Myself—declares the Lord—will be a wall of fire all around it, and I will be a glory inside it* (Zech. 2:9)."[204]

Rabban Gamaliel, Rabbi Eleazar ben Azariah, Rabbi Joshua, and Rabbi Akiba were walking along the road when they heard the noise of the Roman crowds in their wide avenues a great distance away. All of them wept except Rabbi Akiba. He laughed. They asked, "Why are you laughing?" He asked them, "And you, why are you weeping?" They replied, "These heathen who bow down to idols and offer incense to them live in security and quiet and we—our God's Temple burned down by fire—shall we not cry?" He said to them, "For the same reason I laugh. If it is so for those who transgress His will, how much more will it be for those who do His will!"

On another occasion they were going up to Jerusalem. When they reached Mount Scopus they rent their garments. When they reached the Temple Mount they saw a fox coming out from the ruins where the Holy of Holies once stood. They broke into weeping but Rabbi Akiba laughed. They asked, "Why are you laughing?" He asked them, "Why are you weeping?" They replied, "Of this place it has been written, *And any outsider who encroached was to be put to death* (Num. 3:38). Now foxes are going through it, and shall we not cry?" He said to them, "For the very same reason, I am laughing, for it is said, *And call reliable witnesses, the priest Uriah and Zechariah son of Jeberechiah, to witness for Me* (Isa. 8:2). What does Uriah have in common with Zechariah? Uriah lived during the time of the First Temple and Zechariah during the days of the Second Temple. But the explanation must be that Scripture makes Zechariah's prophecy depend upon Uriah's. The prophecy of Uriah was, *Assuredly, because of you Zion shall be plowed as a field, and Jerusalem shall become heaps of ruins, and the Temple Mount a shrine in the woods* (Mic. 3:12). Zechariah's prophecy was, *There shall yet be old men and women in the squares of Jerusalem* (Zech. 8:4). Had Uriah's prophecy not been fulfilled I would have been concerned that Zechariah's would not have been. Now that the prophecy of Uriah has been fulfilled, certainly the prophecy of Zechariah will be fulfilled." They then spoke these words to him, "Akiba, you have comforted us, Akiba, you have comforted us!"[205]

Notes

IX. THE LAST YEARS OF THE SECOND COMMONWEALTH

1. Rome

A number of passages pertaining to Rome and the Romans in rabbinic literature are not included in this section because they can be definitely dated after the destruction of the Second Temple, the terminus ad quem of this book. However a number of passages of later origin are included when they describe the rabbinic attitude to Rome.

1. Songs Rabbah 1:6; Shabbat 56b; Sanhedrin 21b. This entire passage seeks to link the weakening of the religious character of the Jewish people with the disasters that befell it. So, the intermarriage of King Solomon and the idolatry of King Jeroboam are connected with the beginning of Roman power. Similarly, the passing of a strong moral leader like Elijah weakens the people. Edom is frequently used in rabbinic literature as an appellation for Rome, see n. 7. Abba Kolon (Colonus) is a legendary character associated with the founding of Rome. This aspect of the passage might possibly speak of the importance for Roman growth of the conquest of the East. For Solomon's marriage to the daughter of Pharaoh, see 1 Kings 3:1.

2. Genesis Rabbah 49:9. Rome was seen by the rabbis as part of God's plan, as a rod in His hand to punish the sinning nations. The prophets, earlier, had the same view of history. Assyria, Babylonia, and Persia were, to them, God's instruments for executing judgment against the sinning Jewish people. The word *judge* in the midrashic passage is to be understood in the sense of visiting judgment upon, or punishing. The reference to the veto power that Romulus and Remus had against each other is used in contrast to God's power. He is One, with none to veto Him; therefore, He must do justly. The reference here may be to the early Roman system of dyarchy under which a duum-

virate ruled; appeal could be made from the decision of one to the other. The passage is quoted in the name of Rabbi Judah, most likely the rabbi by that name who was of the fourth generation of amoraim.

3. Esther Rabbah 3:5. Rome is frequently referred to in rabbinic literature as Esau or Edom (see n. 7). The "two great tents" may possibly be a reference to the early Roman system of dyarchy under which a duumvirate ruled and appeal could be made from the decision of one to the other. See the passage immediately before this one.

4. Kiddushin 49b; Esther Rabbah 1:17. A statement about Roman opulence.

5. Pesaḥim 119a, still another passage testifying to Roman wealth. Shishak, king of Egypt, ruled 947–925 B.C.E. Rehoboam, king of Judah, 933–917; Asa, 915–875; Jehoshaphat, 875–851; Aḥaz, 735–720; Hezekiah, 720–692; Zedekiah, 597–587. Sennacherib, king of Assyria, 705–681 B.C.E. Chaldeans in the text are to be understood as Babylonians. See 2 Chron. 14:8 ff. for Asa's defeat of Zeraḥ, the Ethiopian or Cushite, and 1 Kings 15:18 for Asa's shipment of gold to Damascus.

6. Genesis Rabbah 67:6. Here Isaac's blessing for Esau involving materialistic wealth is seen as fulfilled in the fertility of the land of which Rome was the capital.

7. Ecclesiastes Rabbah 1:7, Isa. 23:18. Throughout this passage the word *Rome* is actually not used; instead, as is frequently the case in rabbinic literature, *Edom* is used. Rabbi Levi made use of a play on words. The verse in Proverbs (27:20) quoted by him reads, *Nor can the eyes of man* (adam) *be satisfied*. He reads *adam* as though it were vocalized *edom*. Edom is used as a substitute for Rome, frequently as *malkhut Edom*, "the kingdom of Edom," i.e., the Roman Empire. The word *edom* in Hebrew means "red" and the ancient rabbis saw Rome as bloody in its conquests. Moreover, Esau, regarded by the rabbis as the prototype for Rome (see Gen. 27:40, *Yet by your sword you shall live*), took up his residence in Edom (see Gen. 32:4, 36:8). Esau is himself called Edom (see Gen. 36:1, 8) and is regarded as the progenitor of the Edomites or Idumeans (see Gen. 36:9). In addition Herod the Idumean was dependent on Rome. Hence, in rabbinic literature, as is seen here, Esau and Edom are used interchangeably for Rome. In subsequent ages, after Christianity became the official religion of the Roman Empire, Edom was used for Christianity or the Church. This passage states that the wealth of Rome will not always remain hers. Through divine intervention, with the coming of the Messiah, her unjustly gotten gains will be taken from her.

8. Gittin 57b. By "the descendants of Esau" the rabbis here mean Rome (see n. 7). The statement constitutes a reluctant tribute to the fighting ability of the Roman legions.

9. Yoma 20b–21a and Sotah 42b. For Ridya, the angel of rain, see also Ta‘anit 25b; associated with it is Ps. 42:8. This is a hyperbolic statement testifying to the size and sound of Roman military forces, in themselves psychological weapons against the enemy.

10. Deuteronomy Rabbah 1:19. The rabbis interpret the words in Deut. 2:3, *now turn north* (ẓafonah). This Hebrew word is similar to ẓafon, "to hide," hence the play on words. The Scriptures here deal with the instructions to Moses and the children of Israel to detour around the land of Edom, called by the verse, *the descendants of Esau*, and not to make war upon them. This rabbinic passage then expresses

support for a pacific policy toward Rome, although it must be pointed out that the rabbis who are the interpreters of the biblical verses in this passage are all late, the earliest being of the fifth generation of tannaim, who lived at the close of the second century of the common era.

11. Genesis Rabbah 75:1. Rome is regarded as the whip of God, not because of its own merit but because it is used in God's plan for mankind (see supra, n. 2).

12. Genesis Rabbah 94:9. The Decumani and the Augustiani were two famous royal Roman legions. The point being made here is that without the emperor, the legions may be described as incomplete. This farfetched deduction is drawn by the rabbis from Gen. 46:8. Although the purpose of the verse is to state the names of the children of Jacob—it begins by mentioning Jacob himself—without him the numbering of his sons, his "legion," as it were, would be incomplete.

13. Avodah Zarah 2a–b (Dan. 7:23 is interpreted as a prophecy concerning Rome). Rabbi Johanan, referred to here, is of the second generation of amoraim. He was born in the latter part of the second century and died in the latter part of the third. The question and his answer to it may, however, be a later addition to the text. It is clear that the rabbis were not impressed with the physical aspects of Roman civilization.

14. Genesis Rabbah 63:7 on Gen. 25:23. The *ketiv* of the word, usually translated in this verse as "nations," is *ge'im*, which can mean "proud ones." Israel takes pride in its world of Torah; Esau, standing here for Rome, as is frequent in rabbinic literature (see n. 7), takes pride in its world of war and violence. Israel takes pride in its world of the hereafter; Esau (Rome) in its world of the present. All peoples fear and hate Rome, the conqueror of the world. All pagan nations hate Israel, for Israel is the medium of God's message. Since Esau is regarded as the prototype for Rome the midrash here goes so far as to associate Rome's beginnings with Rebecca and Isaac! Of course, the rabbis recognized that this was but a fanciful play on words, on the *ketiv, ge'im.*

15. Genesis Rabbah 67:8. The Hebrew, *vayistom* (hated) is read as an abbreviation of *son'ei* (hate), *nokem* (take revenge), and *noter* (be vindictive) and is, therefore, so interpreted in the midrash here. Through a play on words, using both languages, Hebrew and Latin, *senator* is connected with *son'ei.*

16. Numbers Rabbah 11:5 on the priestly benediction. Paneas, the modern Banias, the province of Caesarea Philippi, is notorious for the extreme oppression to which its inhabitants were subjected by the Romans. In ancient times Pan was worshiped at the site. Getting an office under the Romans was costly, as was keeping it. Appointment to office by the Romans was frequently only a means of extortion. The officeholder was the instrument for extortion from the people.

17. Genesis Rabbah 76:6 on Dan. 7:8. See above, n. 16.

18. Exodus Rabbah 31:11 on Exod. 22:24, interpreting Prov. 28:8. The word here translated as terraces is translated by others as balconies or basilicas. A rabbinic reference to the mixed value of Roman contributions to civilization.

19. Genesis Rabbah 16. The rabbis here evidently credit Greece with the admirable aspects of Roman culture. Greek was used by the

Romans as a language of culture, in addition to Latin. When the rabbis said "the wicked state," as they frequently did, there was no misunderstanding their meaning—Rome.

20. Esther Rabbah 4:12. The effect of the last sentence is a denigration of Latin, that it is a mere dialect or offspring of Greek.

21. Ecclesiastes Rabbah 2:1 on Eccles. 2:2. A rabbinic derogation of two aspects of Roman culture.

22. Ruth Rabbah 2:22. A fanciful interpretation of the dialogue between Ruth and Naomi, used by the rabbis to voice their opposition to Roman circuses and theaters, which had among them a reputation for lewdness.

23. Lamentations Rabbah 3:14. This postdestruction passage reflects the scoffing by Romans at Jewish religious practices, eating, and dress. But it also reflects the poor economic conditions prevailing among Jews under Roman rule. The clown's shaven head is a sign of his mourning, as it turns out, because the price of oil is so high.

24. Leviticus Rabbah 13:3. Behemoth is a mythological beast; see, for example, Job 40:15. It is sometimes translated as water ox. Leviathan is a legendary sea animal. Both are reserved for the righteous in the world to come (see Leviticus Rabbah 22:13; Avodah Zarah 3b; Mo'ed Katan 25b). In this postdestruction passage the rabbis show their antipathy to the wild beast contests staged by the Romans and their disapproval of attendance at them by Jews.

25. Deuteronomy Rabbah 1:17. Again, as in earlier passages, Esau refers to Rome. Here the examining judge is trying to entrap the accused. In the eyes of the rabbis this is not justice. For the rabbinic point of view about criminal confessions in general, see Aaron Kirschenbaum, *Self-Incrimination in Jewish Law* (New York, 1970).

26. Ruth Rabbah, Proem 3. As in the previous passage the rabbis here point to the unfairness of Roman courts. The Roman accusers seek to entrap the accused. They ignore the denials of the accused and proceed with the questioning. Different kinds of Roman taxes are meant: in addition to the poll tax, taxes on cattle, crops, and land.

27. Genesis Rabbah 37.2. The logical link with Ps. 7:1 is tenuous at best. Perhaps the explanation lies in the fact that the land of Benjamin was southward and, similarly, that of Edom was in the south, and Edom is for the rabbis a code word for Rome. Gen. 10:9 reads, *Like Nimrod a mighty hunter by the grace of the Lord,* implying that there was another one like him who "hunted" men, understanding the verb metaphorically. In this midrash the rabbinic thrust is against the Roman legal practice of entrapment, as in the two previous passages.

28. Ecclesiastes Rabbah 5:7 on Eccles. 5:7. The biblical verse states that one should not wonder that the poor are oppressed and that justice and righteousness are perverted by the state, for One who is higher watches—the inference being that in due course divine retribution will follow. The author of the midrashic statement, Rabbi Jose ben Ḥanina, a second-generation amora, applies the verse in Ecclesiastes to Rome.

29. Esther Rabbah, Proem 1. Caesarea was the seat of the Roman government in the land of Israel. Many of the rabbis quoted in Esther Rabbah are Palestinian amoraim of the fourth century who read conditions of their own time into the biblical text.

30. Deuteronomy Rabbah 1:16. In the second half of Ps. 60:11

Edom is mentioned, frequently applied by the rabbis to Rome. The first verse in this psalm ascribes it to David.

31. Leviticus Rabbah 13:5, referring to Lev. 11:7. The prophecy is directed at Babylonia but the rabbis here take the *Mistress of King-doms* (Isa. 47:5) to refer to Rome.

32. Leviticus Rabbah 13:5, see previous note. The quoted verse is here twisted out of its original meaning, which is the direct opposite of blasphemy. Verse 11 in the same psalm would have been far more appropriate.

33. Genesis Rabbah 65:1; Leviticus Rabbah 13:5. A number of the psalms are ascribed to Asaph whom the rabbis depict as a prophet. The word in Psalms for swine is the usual one, *ḥazir*, but it is there translated as boar because of the context, *creatures of the field*, a wild swine being a boar. The *ḥazir* is ritually unclean and may not be eaten because, while it has cloven hooves, it does not chew its cud. The swine puts out its cloven hooves while lying down as though to deceive those looking upon it into thinking it is a permitted animal. Its cunning and perfidy, says this midrashic passage, make it an appropriate symbol for Rome. The text, at the end, reads literally, "setting up a dais," which is understood to mean, setting up a dais in a court of law, hence, executing justice. The text in Leviticus Rabbah indicates that Rome is guilty of the very crimes it charges against the accused. Its perfidy lies in the fact that while pretending to carry out justice, it commits crimes.

34. Exodus Rabbah 35:5. Support for the interpretation is drawn from Ps. 68:31 with a play on words: *adat abirim* is read as though it were *adat Abraham*. The places referred to at the end of the passage are most likely such places as circuses and theaters. See earlier passages in this section for rabbinic opposition to Jews attending such attractions.

35. Leviticus Rabbah 13:5; Gen. 2:14. Isaac blessed Esau (Gen. 27:39 ff.) and Esau was regarded by the rabbis as the progenitor of Rome. The last-quoted verse is from a prophecy against Edom, the name used by the rabbis for Rome. By the familiar technique of play on words the rabbis hang on a framework of biblical verses their own attitudes toward Rome.

36. Songs Rabbah 6:10. Rabbi Joshua is probably Rabbi Joshua ben Hananiah who, in the Mishnah, is usually cited without the patronymic. He was of the second generation of tannaim, about 90–130 C.E. and a disciple of Rabban Johanan ben Zakkai.

37. Songs Rabbah 2:15. The verse in Obadiah is the prophecy against Edom. Here Rabbi Judah contemptuously refers to Rome as *the little foxes* despite its great power. He is Rabbi Judah bar Ilai, of the third generation of tannaim, about 130–160 C.E. In the Mishnah he is always referred to without the patronymic over six hundred times and because of his eloquence called *rosh ha-medabrim*.

38. Genesis Rabbah 70:8. See also Genesis Rabbah 76:6 on Dan. 7:8. A reference to the unjust levy of soldiers from the peoples conquered by Rome.

39. Songs Rabbah 2:8. The month of future redemption, according to the rabbis, is the month of Nisan, the month when the children of Israel were redeemed from Egyptian slavery. The Cutheans were the sect also called Samaritans. In medieval editions of the Talmud and Midrash printed under the watchful eyes of censors the word is fre-

quently a substitute for *goy*, *akum*, *min*, and for "gentile" generally. Cuth or Cuthah was a Babylonian town from which Assyrian colonists were introduced into Samaria (see Bava Batra 91a; Pirkei de-Rabbi Eliezer, chap. 26). A variant reading gives the word not as *Kuti*, "Cuthean," but as *Kushi*, "Ethiopian" or "black man." The Aramaic word *barbaron*, barbarian, is, of course, from the Greek. It has several meanings in Aramaic: a foreigner, an inhabitant of Germania Barbara, Britannia, or the east African coast, Azania. The point made here is that Rome levies its troops from all the known world. The "seventy nations" to the rabbis denoted all the peoples of the world. Therefore, if any Roman soldier from whatever people has power over any Jew or group of Jews, it is as if that soldier's people had ruled over all the Jews. This was for the sake of fulfilling the prediction that all the peoples of the world would rule over the Jews before the Messiah would come to deliver them.

40. Exodus Rabbah 31:16. The midrashic passage here is a satiric comment upon Roman welfare policy—aiding the poor from booty stolen from others. Evil modalities cannot achieve good.

41. Lamentations Rabbah 5:9. Simon ben Gamaliel I lived during the time of the war with Rome. Simon II ben Gamaliel II was of the third generation of tannaim (ca. 130–160 B.C.E.). Although Rome held sway over most of the ancient world during the rabbinic period and most Jews were subject to its rule, there were Jews in the Parthian Empire and in the Hellenized and eastern regions of the Roman Empire.

42. Genesis Rabbah 63:10. The rabbis express their abhorrence here at such Roman sex practices as homosexuality and sodomy. The verse, in which Edom is taken to stand for Rome, as is commonly found in rabbinic literature, is interpreted here to mean that since the Romans use men like women, their men will become as women and will cry out in pain on the day of divine punishment, similar to the fierce pain felt by a woman in labor.

43. Exodus Rabbah 8:1. The words "for treason" are not found in the original text and are here added to explain the reason for the execution. The midrash contrasts Roman imperial pride with God's lack of it. The Jewish Publication Society's new translation renders the word *elohim*, translated here as God, as "oracle" (cf. Exod. 4:16). Other translations give "prophet" and "spokesman."

44. Exodus Rabbah 15:13, quoting Prov. 8:15. The purple cloak is a sign of royalty and throwing it before a general would mean that the legions declare him to be the new emperor. Burning the roll probably refers to the roll containing the records of the tax arrears. The burning of such records would show a complete break with the previous reign, as the new emperor comes to power.

45. Bava Kamma 83a. The prohibition against imitating "the ways of the Amorites"—the expression means the ways of the heathen generally—is based on Lev. 18:3. The style of haircutting referred to here as Roman included trimming the front of the hair like a fringe on the forehead and letting the curls hang down on the temples (see Sifra, Aharei, Par. 9, chap. 13, referring to Lev. 18:3). Abtolumus could have been Eutolomos. Reference to him as son of Reuben is found also in Sotah 49b.

46. Genesis Rabbah 65:12. The absolute truth of judgment, literally "depth of judgment," refers to the fact that however hard a judge may

try to give a fair judgment, there will always be facts that will remain hidden from him. No person knows what child a woman will bear— i.e., the nature of the child to be born. Finally, the power and might of the Roman Empire are so great that no one can predict its downfall.

47. Yoma 10a. The talmudic statements quoted here are in the names of scholars who lived in the latter part of the second and during the third centuries of the common era. The fifth chapter of Micah is a prophecy concerning the messianic king and the destiny of the Jewish people among the nations comparable to the better known prophecy in the eleventh chapter of Isaiah. The verse from Micah here speaks of God surrendering Israel into the power of its enemies. But their oppression and suffering are temporary and will end with the appearance of the Messiah. The nine months dominion of Rome is deduced from the clause in the verse, "Until she who is to bear has borne"— a reference to Zion again inhabited by her children. The original text here calls Rome's adversary Persia, but the land called Persia was ruled by the Parthian monarchs from 250 B.C.E. to 226 C.E.

48. Genesis Rabbah 75:9. Of course, the ancient rabbis were well aware of the fact that the psalmist was not literally referring to Rome. But here, as frequently elsewhere, they attached their own attitudes, ideas, or emotions to biblical verses to give them traditional rooting. The interpretation of the second part of the verse is based on "device" —in the Hebrew, zemamo, which sounds like zemam, which in Hebrew means "muzzle" or "bit," preventing the animal from grazing, from eating and enjoying its food. Rabbi Ḥama bar Ḥanina was of the second generation of amoraim in Roman Palestine living during the second half of the third century of the common era. He directed a school at Sepphoris and was renowned as an aggadist. He was aware of the Roman fear of the Goths and the Huns.

49. Genesis Rabbah 56:9 on Gen. 22:13. A rabbinic expression of hope for redemption from Roman rule by the coming of the Messiah.

50. Exodus Rabbah 1:26. Just as Moses who was to liberate the Jews from Egyptian bondage lived in Egypt, so does the Messiah who is to liberate the Jews from Roman oppression live in Rome (see also Sanhedrin 98a). The proof-text cited in Exodus Rabbah 1:26 is Isa. 27:10, the rabbis applying the fortified cities in the verse to Rome and the calves to the Messiah.

51. Exodus Rabbah 35:5 and Pesaḥim 118b. Rome deems itself a brother to Israel since, according to the rabbis, Esau is also a code word for Rome (see n. 7), and Esau and Jacob or Israel were brothers, the sons of Isaac and Rebecca. The description of Rome as "the beast of the marsh" may have various interpretations. In Pesaḥim 118b, it is interpreted to mean a nation, all of whose deeds may be written with one quill, i.e., they are uniformly wicked. The word kaneh may be translated as "reed" or "quill." Another interpretation explains it as a nation whose existence is based on the quill, and with it she writes down her demands and the tributes she wants from other nations. There may also be an allusion here to the legend that when Solomon married Pharaoh's daughter, the angel Michael descended and planted a reed into the sea, upon which Rome was eventually built (see the beginning of this section). The idea here is that Rome will never be forgiven for her oppression of the Jews. For although the Jews experienced sub-

jection under a number of nations, that of Rome was the worst of all.

52. Leviticus Rabbah 13:5. Rome's might is so great and universal and its oppression of the Jews so fearful that the rabbis could only envisage the coming of the Messiah as the means for its destruction and as the consequence of the worst in Jewish suffering. The verse is interpreted here to mean that the final judgment will be meted out from Mount Zion against the mount of Esau (Rome) with the result being that the kingdom and dominion shall be the Lord's. See the next passage. The play on words, *hazir*, "swine," and *hazor*, "to return," is a common rabbinic device.

53. Exodus Rabbah 18:5. Rabbi Judah ha-Nasi or Prince or Patriarch, frequently just Rabbi, Rabbenu, or Rabbenu ha-kadosh, as here, meaning holy, not in the sense of a saint in the Church's meaning, but as a man of the highest morals, piety, scholarship, and character. He was born about 135 C.E., the son of Rabban Simon ben Gamaliel, whom he succeeded as patriarch, president of the Sanhedrin. After the death of his father, he moved his home and the Academy from Usha to Bet Shearim, also in Galilee. During the last years of his life he lived in Sepphoris. His great achievement was the redaction of the Mishnah. The date of his death is uncertain; most scholars place it some time after the start of the third century C.E. (see Frankel, *Darkhei ha-Mishnah*, pp. 191–97; Bacher, *Tannaiten*, 2:454–86). The sense of the passage is that with the ending of historical times judgment will be meted out from Mount Zion in Jerusalem upon Esau (Rome) by the two angels, the instruments of God, Michael and Gabriel. According to Rabbi Judah the Patriarch, it will be done by Michael alone.

54. Numbers Rabbah 14:1. The reference to the kings of the Greeks is probably to Antiochus Epiphanes, king of Hellenistic Syria, one of the successor states to the empire of Alexander the Great. The deduction of "I will cast down the foundations," from the word Philistia in the verse is through a play on words: "Philistia" in Hebrew, *peleshet*, and *apil shashot*, "cast down the foundations," in Hebrew. "I will achieve your redemption," is probably connected with the Hebrew verb *ra'o'a*, "to be inclined favorably," while the last word in Ps. 60:10 is *hitro'a'i*. As has been seen in previous passages the rabbis saw Rome as the worst of the oppressors of the Jews, and the last. The divine overthrow of Rome would begin the posthistorical era.

55. Exodus Rabbah 18:12, based on Isa. 21:12, where, by a play on words, *ata*, "come," is read as *ot*, "a sign." The verse then is understood as, "A sign that there will be morning, is the night [of the Egyptians, i.e., their overthrow]." The sense here is, Do not believe any self-pronounced redeemer or messiah who appears before the final overthrow of Rome. That event must precede redemption.

56. Exodus Rabbah 15:17. The thrust of this passage is to compare Egypt's fate in the past to that which awaits Rome. The principal proof-text is Joel 4:19, where the same word is used for both Egypt and Edom, *shemamah*, "desolation." The verse in Joel indicates that the same desolation that overcame Egypt will befall Rome. Isa. 49:7 is seen by the rabbis as referring to Israel and to the individual Israelite. The phrase, "chief of the army" is with Jastrow's reading of *praepositus*, a title of several imperial officers, especially, *magister militum*, "chief of the army." "The legionaries, the people . . ." may be "the legionaries, the city council." Gog and Magog are the legendary

nations whose defeat will precede the redemption of Israel (see Ezek. 38; Eduyyot 2:10; Berakhot 13a; Sanhedrin 95b).

57. Leviticus Rabbah 6:6. This midrashic passage comments upon the plague of thick darkness and heavy gloom that befell Egypt. In this connection the comment is made that such chaos or confusion (*tohu*) and void or emptiness (*bohu*), as existed before Creation (Gen. 1:2) had not occurred in Egypt and would not be seen again until Rome would be overthrown. In Isa. 34:11 the prophecy is directed against Edom, which the rabbis use for Rome.

58. Leviticus Rabbah 7:6. The proof-verse from Psalms raises a question because the original words constitute praise of God and loyalty to Him, not blasphemy as here suggested. The latter meaning can only come from a disregard of the meaning in situ or a distortion. Perhaps the proof-text meant here was Ps. 73:11, *How could God know? Is there knowledge with the Most High?* The verse from Daniel refers to the fourth beast in his vision, which is generally taken in rabbinic exegesis to refer to Rome. This midrashic passage actually does not mention Rome but refers to it as "the wicked state." The second statement, from Exodus Rabbah 9:13, compares Rome's future fate with that that befell Egypt. The verses quoted from Isaiah refer to Tyre and Edom. When Tyre is written in Hebrew without the intermediate *vav*, it is interpreted by the rabbis as a reference to Rome, for so written, the Hebrew letters may also mean "adversary," and Rome was their adversary par excellence.

59. Numbers Rabbah 11:1 on the priestly benediction, Num. 6:23. The thrust of this lengthy midrash is to comfort the Jews suffering under Roman oppression, to warn them against envy of the seemingly superior status of the Romans, and to assure them of Israel's ultimate survival and Rome's ultimate destruction by fire. Our English translation of this passage omits a number of the proof-texts chosen by the rabbis from Scripture in support of their statements. The interpretation of the last verse depends upon a play of words: *merim*, "carry away," is read *yarimu*, "they will raise"; and *kalon*, "shame," is understood as though it were derived from the verb, *kaloh*, "to burn, roast, parch."

60. Exodus Rabbah 25:9. Despite the oppression of Rome it is for Jews to study Torah and to refine the qualities that emanate from it. For Roman power will pass away and the special relationship between God and the Jewish people will remain.

61. Exodus Rabbah 30:1. This midrashic section begins with an explanation of Ps. 99:4. To answer Jews questioning God's justice, with Roman tyranny supreme and Israel abjectly cast down, the explanation is that the time of Rome will surely come. But God's ways in meting out justice are not to be set aside even for so despicable an enemy as Rome. God is patient and long-suffering even with the wicked. Only when Rome will have filled its full measure of sin, will God execute justice against her. But then she will be made to drink many cups of divine wrath.

2. Sects

62. Avot de-Rabbi Natan 5:2. The two disciples, Zadok and Boethus, are mentioned later. For a more historical discussion of these two

sects see the articles on them in the *Jewish Encyclopedia*. See also Louis Finkelstein, *The Pharisees*, p. 80 and p. 663, n. 20. The word, *not*, in "but not because they were arrogant of spirit" is doubtful; for the text here is uncertain. Josephus, *Antiquities*, 18.1.3, says of the Pharisees, "The Pharisees live simply and despise delicacies." For an interpretation of the text see L. Finkelstein, "Introductory Study to *Pirke Abot*," pp. 35–37.

63. Yerushalmi Sanhedrin 15, quoted in the name of Rabbi Johanan, who was one of the second generation of amoraim during the third century C.E. The second statement is from Yerushalmi Sanhedrin 10:5. See also Maimonides, Hilkhot Teshuvah 3:6 ff.

64. Rosh Ha-Shanah 17a. Some hold that this talmudic passage is directed at specific enemies of the pharisaic tradition. "Heretics who reject the Torah," for example, refers to the new Christians who denied the Torah and said that it was replaced by the New Covenant. Those "who do not believe in resurrection" refers to the Sadducees. "Rulers who make themselves hated" refers to the Roman rulers. One conjecture would explain those "who separate themselves from the practices of the community" as referring to Jews who would inform against their fellow Jews to the Roman authorities.

65. Mishnah Sanhedrin 10:1. Aimed at the Sadducees and other sectarians. "The irreverent skeptic" in the Hebrew original is *apikoros*, which is an epithet often applied both to Jews and others who oppose rabbinic teaching. It is not to be understood as applying to the followers of the philosopher Epicurus. To the ancient rabbis it sounded like the Hebrew word *pakar*, "to be free of restraint," therefore, irreverent skeptic.

66. Yerushalmi Berakhot, chap. 1; Yefei Mareh, 7b, 17. Rashi ad locum comments, "that the sectarians might tell the ignorant the rest of the Torah is not true. . . ." Rabbi Simon ben Zoma, usually called Ben Zoma, was of the second generation of tannaim, ca. 90–130 C.E. The word for sectarian in this passage is *min;* see n. 68.

67. Sanhedrin 61a. Gebiha ben Pesisa, according to Megillat Ta'anit, chap. 3, was a priest who lived during the time of Alexander the Great and served as a gatekeeper at the Temple (see also Genesis Rabbah, chap. 61, end, where the name is Gebiha ben Kosem). To "knock your hump off" is used idiomatically with the meaning "to drive out your arrogance," but Gebiha was a hunchback.

68. Sanhedrin 33b. The Hebrew word *min*, translated here as "sectarian," especially refers to a Jewish apostate and is often applied in rabbinic literature to the Jews who joined the new Christians (see Horoyot 11a; Gittin 45b; Yerushalmi Berakhot 9:12; Tosefta Bava Meẓia 2:33; Avodah Zarah 26b; Berakhot 28b).

69. Shabbat 116a; see also 139a.

70. Avodah Zarah 27b; Tosefta Ḥullin 2:20–21, Ecclesiastes Rabbah 1:8, 10:5. Again in this passage "sectarian" is the translation of *min* (see n. 68). The early tannaim, according to Klausner, *Jesus of Nazareth*, p. 47, knew that Jesus' disciples used to heal the sick in his name. They prohibited this method of healing even when there was danger of the illness proving fatal. M. Friedländer (*Die religiösen Bewegungen innerhalb des Judentums in Zeitalter Jesu* [Berlin, 1905], pp. 172–78) tries to show that this has nothing to do with the new Christians but with the antinomians among the Jews and pagans. See T. Herford,

Christianity in Talmud and Midrash (London, 1903), pp. 177–89. Klausner says that the rabbis in the earlier period were more averse to the *minim* than to Jesus himself since in them they saw a danger to national existence. It is this that accounts for the benediction concerning the *minim* (Berakhot 28b–29a). See Herford, pp. 392–93 and 125–37. This benediction was instituted at Jabneh toward the end of the first century; so too the law about breaking off all relations with the *minim* (see Tosefta Ḥullin 2:20–21).

71. Yoma 1:3, 1:5, 19b.

72. Yevamot 63b. The statement is quoted in the name of Rabbi Eliezer of the second generation of tannaim, ca. 90–130 C.E. He was the brother-in-law of Rabban Gamaliel II, and his school was at Lydda. He was the son of Hyrcanus but in the Mishnah is usually (more than 320 times) referred to simply as Rabbi Eliezer.

73. Ecclesiastes Rabbah 1:8. "Sectarians" here is the translation of *minim*; see nn. 68 and 70. Rabbi Joshua ben Ḥananiah was of the second generation of tannaim, ca. 90–130 C.E. Capernaum, a town in Galilee, is known in the New Testament, see Matt. 4:13. Some assume that "that wicked person" is an allusion to Jesus, although most believe that any references to Jesus in talmudic literature are late additions. See M. Friedländer, *Die religiösen Bewegungen innerhalb des Judentums in Zeitalter Jesu*. Other works on the subject, apart from the books by Klausner and Herford already mentioned, include the following: Gustaf Dalman, *Jesus Christ in the Talmud, Midrash, Zohar, and the Liturgy of the Synagogue* (Cambridge, 1893); M. Friedländer, *Der Antichrist in der vorchristlichen Quellen* (Göttingen, 1901); J. Z. Lauterbach, "Jesus in the Talmud" (in *Rabbinic Essays*, pp. 473–570 [Cincinnati, 1951]); Origen, *Contra Celsum* (trans. H. C. Chadwick, Cambridge, 1965); E. B. Nicholson, *The Gospel according to the Hebrews* (London, 1879). From the time of Abraham Geiger, there have been Jewish scholars who have seen references to Jesus in certain talmudic passages where Balaam is mentioned. See A. Geiger, "Bileam und Jesus," *Jüdische Zeitschrift* 6 (1868):31–37. Friedländer denies that Jesus is ever referred to under the pseudonym of Balaam in any early rabbinic passage. H. P. Chajes also disagrees; see his *Markus-Studien* (Berlin, 1899), p. 25, n. 2. For a discussion of this aspect of the problem, see Klausner, *Jesus of Nazareth*, pp. 32–35. Klausner states that Jesus is mentioned openly by name in an early baraita in which Rabbi Eliezer ben Hyrcanus (of the second generation of tannaim, ca. 90–130 C.E.) is the central figure (see Klausner, op. cit., pp. 37–38, and Avodah Zarah 16b–17a; Tosefta Ḥullin 2:24). Again Friedländer argues that "every Talmudist worthy of the name knows that the few talmudic passages which speak of Jesus are a late addition." See *Der vorchristliche judische Gnosticismus* (Göttingen, 1898), pp. 71–74, and his *Der Antichrist*, introd., pp. xix–xx, and his *Die religiösen Bewegungen*, pp. 191–92, 206–7, 215–21.

Klausner's conclusions as to the early statements in the Talmud about Jesus are that they date back to the first generation of the tannaim who lived after the destruction of the Temple in 70 C.E. Their attitudes to Jesus, he says, do not reflect the bitter hatred and hostility found later among Jewish scholars, when Christians had begun to oppress and persecute the Jews. The earliest talmudic references to Jesus came from Rabbi Eliezer ben Hyrcanus and his contemporaries. In their eyes, Klausner says, Jesus may have been "an Israelite who had sinned" or "a transgressor in Israel," but he remained a Jew. His attitude to the Law, which at one time he emphatically says he has come to support and at another he sets aside and mocks the words of the wise, aroused the anger and condemnation of the talmudic rabbis. They agreed that Jesus worked miracles but they asserted that they were performed through sorcery (see Mark 3:22, Matt. 4:34, 12:24). His birth, they stated, was an illegitimate one. It is only later, Klausner argues, at the end of the tannaitic period, about 200 C.E., that we find a rabbi, Eliezer ha-Kappar, accusing Jesus of "making himself God." The earlier tannaim knew nothing of this. They knew only that his disciples used to heal the sick in his name and they prohibited this method of healing. In the earlier period they were more opposed to the *minim* (see nn. 68 and 70) than to Jesus himself since they saw in them a danger to the national existence (see Klausner, op. cit., pp. 46–47).

3. Jerusalem and Its Inhabitants

74. Avot de-Rabbi Natan, version 2, 48, and 28:1. Rabbi Natan was a fourth-generation tanna who came from Babylonia to Palestine.

75. Exodus Rabbah 52:5; see also Lamentations Rabbah 2:15. Not only is Jerusalem beautiful but the city so affected those within it as to dispel sadness and anxiety and to increase joy. The countinghouse just outside Jerusalem may have been a kind of exchange. The explanations are offered in the names of Rabbi Jonathan ben Eleazar and Rabbi Johanan, amoraim of the first and second generations, respectively. The second group of statements about Jerusalem come from Sukkah 51b; Avot de-Rabbi Natan, chap. 28; Genesis Rabbah 59:5; Numbers Rabbah 3:2; Songs Rabbah 7:5.

76. Lamentations Rabbah 1:1; Pesahim 64b. Agrippa was of Edomite descent and is mentioned in the Mishnah in Bikkurim 3:4 and Sotah 7:8. The largest crowds came to Jerusalem for Passover and a lamb was offered on Passover eve as a paschal sacrifice on behalf of each family, then roasted whole and eaten by the family at night. By ordering the counting of the kidneys the king achieved his purpose of a census of the number of people crowded into Jerusalem for the festival: 1,200,000 kidneys representing the same number of families with an average of 10 per family or 12,000,000. That would seem to be an exaggerated figure and Rabbi Ḥiyya of the fifth generation of tannaim, looking back at past glories, inflates the figures even more. The explanation for the large population comes from Lamentations Rabbah 1:2.

77. Lamentations Rabbah, Proems 12, 1:2, 4:1; Songs Rabbah 5:12. The number must be less than scientifically accurate. Rabbi Phinehas is the author of the statement, quoting it in the name of Rabbi Hoshaiah. The former was of the fifth generation of amoraim, the latter, of the first. The calculation of the number is based upon the numerical value of the Hebrew letters of the word *filled* in Isa. 1:21, *that was filled with justice.* The actual total is 481, the discrepancy explained in one of two ways: the Temple is included in the total number or the Hebrew word for *filled* is spelled without the letter *aleph*, whose numerical value is one. Vespasian commanded the Roman army that laid siege to Jerusalem. The story about the pepper is another hyperbolic state-

ment to describe the size and the metropolitan character of Jerusalem before its destruction. Its author is Rabbi Samuel, an amora who died in 254 c.e., sometimes called "the astronomer." Rabbi Eleazar was of the second generation of tannaim, about 90–130 c.e.

78. Gittin 55b, 56a; Avot de-Rabbi Natan 6:3; Ta'anit 19b-20a. The story given here combines elements from all three sources. The source in Ta'anit implies that the "official" is a Roman. The argument has been offered that the name of the first of the three extremely wealthy men should be properly Zizit Ha-Kasat, that is, Zizit "of the silver (couch)," since it is the latter that is given as the explanation of his name. See Finkelstein, *The Pharisees*, p. 135, for some manuscript support. See also part 8, n. 121. The daughter of Nakdimon, a childless widow, was awaiting the decision of her late husband's brother to marry her or not in accordance with the law of levirate marriage as given in Deut. 25:5 ff. The name, Nakdimon, is connected in this story with the Hebrew root, *nakad*, "break through" or "pierce." Adolf Büchler in *Studies in Jewish History* [London and New York, 1956], pp. 99 ff., states that "though many legendary features are interwoven in this story, there is no ground for doubting the actual occurrence related." *Kalba* in Aramaic means "a dog" and *savu'a*, "satiated." The Hebrew word here translated as "talents" (of silver) is the plural of *kikar*, a weight of gold or silver or a talent equal to the weight of three thousand shekels. A shekel weighed about seven grams (see Danby, *The Mishnah*, p. 798). The name, Nakdimon, can be Nicodemus; in one edition the name is given as Nikodimon. Kalba Savua was the father-in-law of Rabbi Akiba (see Ketubbot 62b, 63a).

79. Ta'anit 20a. The explanation for Nakdimon is the story just given before in our text. The source quoted in the Talmud for Joshua is, of course, the story of the sun standing still at Gibeon (Josh. 10:13). As for Moses, the rabbis offer two deductions from word analogies to prove that Moses too worked the same miracle. Another rabbi says it is to be inferred from the words of Deut. 2:25 (see Ta'anit 20a for these rabbinic explanations).

80. Ketubbot 66b–67a; Avot de-Rabbi Natan 17:4. This story about Nakdimon tells not only about his wealth and high standard of living but also about his generosity to the poor. This would seem to conflict with the story in section 4 below, where his daughter explains to Rabban Johanan that the reason for the disappearance of her father's fortune was because he was not charitable. The rabbis in the Talmud (Ketubbot 67a) resolve the conflict by explaining that either he performed such charitable acts as described in the first story for the sake of his own honor and prestige or else he did not give according to his means.

81. Lamentations Rabbah 4:5. Rabbi Hanina bar Papa (or Pappai, the Aramaic form of the Greek, *Pappos*) was of the third generation of amoraim (early part of fourth century c.e.). The statement about drinking snow and milk are from Lamentations Rabbah 4:7. One emendation changes "drink snow" to "wash in snow." As for drinking milk, see Ketubbot 59b, "He who wishes his daughter to have a bright complexion, as she approaches maturity, let him feed her with young fowls and give her milk to drink." The interpretation of Lam. 4:2 is from Gittin 58a. Rabbi Shela was of the first generation of Babylonian amoraim, early third century. The reason for the Roman practice was in order that beautiful children be born.

82. Sanhedrin 23a.

83. Lamentations Rabbah 4:1–2. This midrashic passage contains a series of interpretations on the opening words of Lam. 4:2 that in their general thrust have some relation to reality in the sense that Jerusalemites had the reputation of being a notch or two above the general population. When a woman enjoyed higher status and was married by a Jerusalemite, he spent more on the wedding feast as an indication that it was upon him that the honor was bestowed. The reverse situation brought the opposite result. A Jerusalemite had to be invited twice to a dinner to be certain that the first invitation was not sent him in error. The tragic result of an invitation sent by mistake can be seen in the story of Kamẓa and Bar Kamẓa to be found later in this part. At a dinner when the guest changed his buckle from the right to the left shoulder, it was a sign that he intended to stay (see Yerushalmi Avodah Zarah 39c).

84. Lamentations Rabbah 4:2 on the opening words of the verse in Lamentations of the same chapter and number, continuing the series of interpretations immediately before. The wording of Rabban Simon is given here in accordance with Tosefta Bava Batra 4:8. The original text here is that when the cloth was removed, guests were permitted to take only three paces into the house. In Bava Batra 93b the reading is "no wayfarers entered." It would seem that the Tosefta has the preferable reading. Rabban Simon ben Gamaliel I was active at the time of the war with Rome. His grandson, Rabban Simon II ben Gamaliel II, lived during the second century of the common era and transferred the seat of the Sanhedrin from Jabneh to Usha. He was the father of Rabbi Judah ha-Nasi, the redactor of the Mishnah.

85. Lamentations Rabbah 1:1. This tale, illustrating the cleverness for which the residents of Jerusalem were famous, is attached to the words descriptive of Jerusalem in Lam. 1:1. Jerusalem's greatness among the nations is attributed not to the power nor the wealth of its citizens but to their wisdom.

86. Lamentations Rabbah 1:1. The child's proposal on the casting of lots was similar to "heads I win, tails you lose." In talmudic literature Athens is frequently cited for its wisdom. If a Jerusalemite child can get the better of an Athenian man, it is tribute indeed to Jerusalemite cleverness.

87. Lamentations Rabbah 1:1.

88. Lamentations Rabbah 1:1.

89. Lamentations Rabbah 1:1. The story indicates inter alia that children were not usually weaned until the age of two. When the name of Rabbi Johanan is mentioned without patronymic it is usually Rabbi Johanan bar Nappaḥa. He was of the second generation of amoraim (third century c.e.). Halevy, Dorot ha-rishonim, 2:306, attempts to show that he was born between 175 and 180 c.e. and died about 279 c.e. The reputation of the people of Jerusalem—and their children—for wisdom and cleverness continued through the centuries.

90. Lamentations Rabbah 1:1. The Warsaw edition reverses the answer as between moist and dry, but the fact is that it is moist wood that smokes more.

91. Lamentations Rabbah 1:1.

92. Lamentations Rabbah 1:1; Sanhedrin 104a–b. Here the wisdom of the people of Jerusalem is shown by contrasting an Athenian student

in pursuit of wisdom and a half-blind Jewish slave of Jerusalem. The story given in Sanhedrin has several minor variations.

93. Lamentations Rabbah 1:1. A tremis was a Roman coin, a third of an aureus, a gold piece. It was a ridiculously high price to offer for the repair of a sandal. Two dinars equaled one shekel, so the price mentioned by the Jerusalemite as the going price of sandals in Jerusalem was also exorbitant, enticing the Athenian to come to Jerusalem to earn a quick large profit.

94. Lamentations Rabbah 1:1. A similar story, with several variations, is found in Yalkut Shimoni.

95. Lamentations Rabbah 1:1.

96. Lamentations Rabbah 1:1.

97. Pesikta Rabbati 14:1; another story illustrating the wisdom of the people of Jerusalem and of how their cleverness made it impossible for others to fool them. Num. 19:1–22 is the section in the Scriptures concerning the red heifer and the use of its ashes, after its sacrifice, for rendering ritually pure those who had become unclean. The red heifer had to be without blemish and one which had never been under a yoke. In Mishnah Parah 2:1 there is a difference of opinion between Rabbi Eliezer and the sages as to whether the red heifer may be bought from a heathen. Rabbi Eliezer said that it may not; the sages declared that it may. The text of Pesikta Rabbati here asks for Rabbi Eliezer's reason, and he answers that idolaters are under suspicion of wishing to bring Israel to sin. Then follows the story presented here, as an illustration. This story is found also in Tanḥuma Hakadum.

4. The Destruction of Jerusalem and the Temple

98. Gittin 55b, 56a, 57a; see also Lamentations Rabbah 1:5, 4:2; Ecclesiastes Rabbah 7:12; Avot de-Rabbi Natan, 4:5, and supra, n. 77. For a story involving Rabban Johanan ben Zakkai, Vespasian, and the destruction of Jerusalem see part 8, section 15, and n. 130. The illustrations of this verse show the results of hardness of heart. A triviality, the outcome of stubbornness, set in motion a chain of events leading to the destruction of the Temple and Jerusalem. So too with the fall of Betar, the mountain fortress southwest of Jerusalem, which was finally captured by the Romans in 135 C.E., the last battle in the revolt against Rome led by Bar Kokhba (132–135 C.E.). Tur Malka, the Aramaic for "The Mountain of the King," is variously identified. One opinion makes it Mount Ephraim, as in Pseudo-Jonathan, Judg. 4:5, rendering Mount Ephraim as Tur Malka. Israel Wolf Horowitz, *Erez Yisrael u-shekheinoteha* (Vienna, 1923), p. 240, identifies it as the entire mountainous region running from the Valley of Jezreel to the south of Judah, including the mountains of Samaria, and is called also by the Hebrew name, *Har Hamelekh*, "The Mountain of the King" (see A. Büchler, "Die Schauplätze des Bar-Kochbakrieges und die auf dieser bezogenen jüdischen Nachrichten," *Jewish Quarterly Review*, o.s. 16 [1904]:143–205, and esp. 180 ff.). Maurice Simon, in his notes to the English translation of Gittin, ad locum, conjectures that perhaps the name was given to the region because it lay within the area of conquest of King John Hyrcanus. Büchler, op. cit., pp. 186 ff. places the destruction of Tur Malka during the war, 66–70 C.E. Rabbi Johanan

bar Nappaḥa (the "smith"), usually in talmudic literature simply
Rabbi Johanan, was of the second generation of amoraim, about the
middle of the third century C.E. He was born in Sepphoris where he
was a teacher, and he taught later in Tiberias. He lived a long life;
Halevy, *Dorot*, 2:149, calculates that he was born between 175 and 180
C.E. and died about 290. The word *kamẓa* in Aramaic means "locust."
For "a calf of fine quality" the text has "a third calf," which could
mean a calf in its third year, one that has reached a third of its full
growth, or the third born. Non-Jews could offer animals for sacrifice
on the altar in the Temple (see Ḥullin 13b). Of course, animals with
a blemish were not acceptable from anyone. Josephus, *Wars*, 2.17.2,
ascribes the start of the war with Rome to the refusal of the Jews to
accept the offering of the emperor for a Temple sacrifice in 66 C.E.
Since the days of Augustus sacrifices had been offered in the Temple
on behalf of the emperor and Rome. In 65 C.E. the extremists proposed
the ending of this practice, an act tantamount to revolt. The Pharisees
opposed this but lost (see Zeitlin, *The Rise and Fall of the Judaean
State*, 2:238–39). The reference in the legend to Nero is not historical
for Nero never came to Palestine. In rabbinic literature *Edom* is a code
word for Rome; see supra, n. 7. There was a legend that Nero, who
had committed suicide, was still alive and would come back to the
throne (see *Jewish Encyclopedia* 9:225). Nero was emperor from 54
to 68 C.E. and to quell the Jewish rebellion sent in 67 C.E. his general
Vespasian who had served with distinction in Germany and Britain.

For the three wealthy men in Jerusalem see the previous section
in this part. The text uses the word *biryoni*, here translated as "the
rebels belonging to the war party." See Joseph Nedava, "Who Were
the 'Biryoni?,'" pp. 317–22, where he suggests they were a political
party affiliated in some way with the Zealots, perhaps the predecessors
of the Sicarii. The word is derived perhaps from *birah*, "palace," so
that the meaning originally would be palace guard or soldier, hence
rebel, outlaw, highwayman. The word is found in these various senses
in rabbinic literature. Here the reference is to the Zealots, the "hawks."
Their leader was Johanan of Gush Ḥalav, and they gained the upper
hand in Jerusalem in 68 C.E. Most of the rabbis were in the peace party,
including Simon ben Gamaliel, descendant of Hillel, and the leader of
the Pharisees. A still more extreme and belligerent faction was led
by Simon bar Giora (see Margolis and Marx, *A History of the Jewish
People*, pp. 199–203).

The death of Martha is here ascribed to shock. A similar cause
is ascribed to the eating of a fig thrown away by Rabbi Ẓadok. Rashi,
ad locum, explains that she was shocked either by the odor of the fig
caused by Rabbi Ẓadok's illness or by his long and frequent fasting.

See part 8, section 15, for the well-known story about Vespasian
and Rabban Johanan ben Zakkai and the permission granted to the sage
by Vespasian to save Jabneh and its scholars; see also part 8, nn. 129
and 130.

99. Gittin 57a. For Tur Malka see the previous note. *Bar Deroma*
in Aramaic means "son of the south." He uttered the verse as an affirmative statement and was, therefore, punished, while David, according to
the rabbinic explanation, voiced it as a question.

100. Avot de-Rabbi Natan 6:3. The Zealots or members of the
war party in Jerusalem were concerned that ample food supplies in the

besieged city would give time and opportunity to their opponents who advocated suing for peace with the Romans. For the Zealots and the peace party, see supra, n. 98; for Kalba Savua, one of the three wealthiest men in Jerusalem at the time, see the previous section in this part. After the Zealots had destroyed the food supplies, famine followed; see above, part 8, section 15, for Rabban Johanan ben Zakkai and the story about his nephew burning the food supplies.

101. Lamentations Rabbah 1:2 on the verse, *All her inhabitants sigh as they search for bread* (Lam. 1:11).

102. Lamentations Rabbah 4:9 on the verse, *Better off were the slain of the sword than those slain by famine* (Lam. 4:9).

103. Yoma 38b; Lamentations Rabbah 1:16: The story as given here is a blending of both sources. In the latter source, however. Doeg ben Joseph is the name of the father who dies young. The text of the discussion in the Talmud would confirm its reading of the name as that of the unfortunate child rather than of the father as the midrash has it. The midrash also states that the child's additional weight each year would be given to the Temple. The first half of Lam. 2:20 is interpreted as the complaint of the prophet to God, the second half, God's answer, viz., the Jews had behaved despicably in putting to death the prophet, Zechariah ben Johoiada (2 Chron. 24:20–22). It is cause and effect, sin and punishment. The generous practice of the mother in giving her child's additional weight in gold to the Temple shows both her intense love for her child and her wealth. Yet the effects of the Roman siege were so horrible as to nullify both.

104. Lamentations Rabbah 4:10. The author of this midrash thus indicates that the verse is not to be taken literally and would reject the previous story about Doeg ben Joseph. It is an important *mizvah* for neighbors to provide the food for the mourners' meal following the funeral. The fulfillment of Jewish law in this regard by the women, this act of compassion, caused God to withhold the full punishment due the Jewish people for their sins.

105. Lamentations Rabbah 2:12.

106. Lamentations Rabbah 4:3. Lam. 4:2 refers to *the precious children of Zion; once valued as gold*. The principal sources of water for the inhabitants of Jerusalem were beyond the walls of the city so the Roman siege resulted in cutting off both water and food supplies. The flat roofs of the Jerusalem homes were favorite places for relaxation in the cool of a summer's evening.

107. Lamentations Rabbah 1:16. This story may refer to the siege of Jerusalem by the Romans or to Hadrianic times some sixty-three years later when the revolt of the Jews under Bar Kokhba was finally suppressed by the Romans. Indeed, a number of the stories in this section may refer to the siege of Jerusalem, to the years following its destruction, or to Hadrianic times.

108. Lamentations Rabbah 4:7. The place-name, Etam, must be corrupt in the text. Zevaḥim 54b mentions the well of Etam in the land of the tribe of Benjamin. This passage is attributed to Rabbi Abba ben Kahana who was of the third generation of amoraim.

109. Avot de-Rabbi Natan 17:3; Ketubbot 66b; Sifrei to Deuteronomy, par. 305. As for the proverb, salt was the most widely used preservative. The two versions of the proverb hinge on the reading of one Hebrew letter. The first version has the word, *ḥaser*, meaning "decrease,

diminution"; the second, *ḥesed*, meaning "kindness, benevolence." The difference lies in the last Hebrew letter, whether it be *dalet* or *resh*, and in the printed form both letters are similar. The young woman's answer about one fortune destroying the other explains that the fortunes of her father and her father-in-law were interlocked.

110. Gittin 7a; Sotah 9:14. Joyous practices were to be suppressed at a time of national sorrow. See also Lamentations Rabbah 5:16 where Rabbi Jeremiah, an amora of the fourth generation, is rebuked for his practice of dancing before wedding-couples with a crown of olive branches on his head.

111. Esther Rabbah 1:19. The reference may be to the Praetorian Guards, who often deposed emperors and chose their successors until Constantine the Great disbanded them. The text in this midrashic passage says Nebuchadnezzar instead of Vespasian, but frequently the Midrash will confuse Roman and Persian personalities, practices and institutions. A bodyguard created by Diocletian was called the Joviani.

112. Lamentations Rabbah 1:17. The text has as the place-name Pumeus, and commentators take this to be another reading for Parmeas (Caesarea Philippi) in the far northeast of Palestine. But the logic of the text, speaking as it does of pilgrims supposedly on their way to Jerusalem, leads one to follow the emendation of Pumeus to Emmaus as suggested by the translator of Lamentations Rabbah in the Soncino edition. Emmaus was about twenty-two miles from Jerusalem. The pilgrims gave the answer they did, acknowledging their allegiance to the emperor, for fear of their lives.

113. Lamentations Rabbah 1:16; Ketubbot 66b–67a. Boethus was the name of a family that, with a few others, was favored by the Roman procurator or members of the Herodian dynasty for the appointment of high priests. During these years of the first century the Temple worship was an object of imperial concern and protection. One of the wives of Herod was a daughter of Boethus. The name following "daughter of" or "son of" in ancient texts was not always the father. It could have been the grandfather, the founder of the family or clan, or its most prominent member. Joshua ben Gamla was famous as the creator of the elementary universal educational system. The high priest would read the Scriptures on Yom Kippur, a procedure detailed in Yoma 7:1. Rabbi Eleazar, son of Rabbi Zadok, was of the second generation of tannaim, about 90 to 130 C.E.; he had a grandson of the same name (see Frankel, *Darkhei ha-Mishnah*, pp. 97–99; Hyman, *Toldot tannaim ve-amoraim*, 1:201–5). Jerusalem to Lydda, called Diapolis by the Romans, was about a day's journey; see Ma'aser Sheni 5:2, though the statement in the passage may be hyperbole.

114. Lamentations Rabbah 1:16; Ketubbot 66b–67a; Avot de-Rabbi Natan 17:4. The rabbinic tribunals were generous in their awards to the daughter and daughter-in-law of Nakdimon from the legacies of their husbands because the sages were aware of the costly style of living to which the women had been accustomed. There were two scholars by the name of Rabbi Eleazar during the second generation of tannaim, ca. 90–130 C.E.: Rabbi Eleazar of Modi'im and Rabbi Eleazar Ḥisma, who was younger. The quoted verse is interpreted: If you know not how to observe the Torah, then the time will come when you will have to go out among the footsteps of the flocks to look for grain to feed your bodies. The rabbinic judges did not reply "Amen" to

the daughter-in-law because her late husband's brother was very young and she had to wait until he came of legal age and would be able to decide whether he would take her in levirate marriage or not (for levirate marriage, see Deut. 25:5 ff.). Such a fate was not one the rabbis would wish for their own daughters. The two measures of wine awarded to the daughter-in-law were for the purpose of preparing a pudding of mincemeat mixed with wine and spices. The word for measure here is sa'ah, a liquid measure equal to 1,144 eggs (see Danby, *The Mishnah*, p. 798).

115. Lamentations Rabbah 1:50 and Gittin 57b. The midrashic text has "daughter of Naḥtum"; in the talmudic story the name of the woman is not stated. In general the story as related in the Midrash is much more expansive. This story is similar to the popular story related in the second book of Maccabees about Hannah and her seven sons, where the emperor is Antiochus IV Epiphanes. See Dan. 1–3, for the story about Hananiah, Mishael, and Azariah. The youngest son refused to pick up the king's ring not only because it would appear that he was stooping before the idol but also, explains Rashi ad locum in the Talmud, because the seal on the ring had engraved on it the image of the king and by bending down to pick it up he would make it appear that he was worshiping the image. Buber's reading for the age of the youngest son is six and a half years and two hours.

116. Lamentations Rabbah 1:49. The text has "daughter of Naḥtum." By her words she admitted that God was justified in punishing her for the wrongs she must have committed.

117. Lamentations Rabbah 3:5. The first application of the word is to Nebuchadnezzar, the destroyer of the First Temple.

118. Lamentations Rabbah 3:10. The midrash applies the word first to Nebuchadnezzar.

119. Esther Rabbah, Proem 4. Rabbi Ḥiyya was of the fifth and last generation of tannaim, about the end of the second century. He was born in Babylonia and came to Palestine advanced in years, settling in Tiberias. Trajan was emperor of Rome from 98 to 117. During the latter part of his reign the Jews of Egypt, Cyrene, and Cyprus revolted against Rome, and so too did the Jews of Babylonia. The Romans put down the insurrections, at times with barbaric cruelty. To what extent the Jews of Palestine participated in these struggles is not definite (see Margolis and Marx, *A History of the Jewish People*, pp. 211–12). One would conjecture that logically the third section of the verse should have been applied to Hadrian who was emperor of Rome from 117 to 138, for he followed Vespasian and Trajan. But of course Esther Rabbah is a midrashic commentary on the story of Esther. "The days of Gog and Magog" refers to the battle at the end of human history, which will precede the Day of Judgment and the redemption of the Jewish people (see Ezek. 38–39; Sanhedrin 95b; Eduyyot 2:10).

120. Megillah 11a. Samuel (died 254) was of the first generation of amoraim. He headed the academy at Nehardea in Babylonia. The third interpretation is anonymous and is from a baraita, the generic name for all tannaitic teachings and utterances not included in the Mishnah. For Persians the text actually reads Chaldeans who with the Medes formed the Persian empire. For Simon the Just, see part 7, section 1. Mattathias was not a high priest but a rural priest residing in Modi'in, northwest of Jerusalem on the road to the present-day city of Tel Aviv.

Antiochus IV, the villain of the Hanukkah story, was king of the Seleucid empire of Syria from 175 to 164 B.C.E. Rabbi Judah ha-Nasi, head of
the Sanhedrin, was called simply Rabbi, the master par excellence. He
was the final redactor of the Mishnah. He became nasi in 170 C.E. and
his activity covered half a century.

121. Gittin 57b. The fall of Betar to the Romans was the last event
in the revolt led by Bar Kokhba against the Romans. This rebellion
began in 132 C.E. and the fortress of Betar fell, after a long and stubborn
defense, in 135. The Roman emperor at the time was not Vespasian but
Hadrian (117–138). A myriad is ten thousand, but the statistics here
are evidently exaggerated.

122. Lamentations Rabbah 1:12. Nebuchadnezzar, king of Babylonia, besieged and destroyed Jerusalem and burned the First Temple
in 586 B.C.E. Vespasian was dispatched to Palestine in 67 C.E. by the
emperor Nero to put down the rebellion of the Jews. By June 69 all
of Palestine except for Jerusalem and the three fortresses of Herodium,
Machaerus, and Masada were in Roman hands. Before the end of July
69 Vespasian had been proclaimed emperor by his legions. The conduct
of the war against the Jews was left to his son Titus. With the main
part of his army he reached the immediate vicinity of Jerusalem a few
days before Passover in the year 70. About four months later the
Temple was destroyed and Jerusalem fell. The war continued until
the capture of Masada in April 73. The term of three and a half years
of siege is, therefore, a round number, or the length of time between
Vespasian's taking command of the Roman army in Palestine to the
destruction of the Second Temple and Jerusalem by the Roman legions
led by Vespasian's son Titus. The midrashic passage here notes that
the punishment of the wicked in Gehenna lasts twelve months. The
destroyers of the two Temples were punished for a much longer period
because of the great and unusual suffering they inflicted upon the
Jewish people.

123. Gittin 56b; Leviticus Rabbah 22:3, 20:5; Ecclesiastes Rabbah
5:8; also Genesis Rabbah. Elements of these several sources are interwoven to create the story as given here. The story as given in these
sources varies in detail; it is fullest in Leviticus Rabbah 22:3. See the
previous note for Vespasian's return to Rome in 69 C.E. to be crowned
emperor and his delegation of the military command to his son Titus
who captured Jerusalem and destroyed the Second Temple the following year. The Temple is called by Titus the palace of God. The triumphal procession of Titus after his sea voyage from Alexandria to
Rome included hundreds of Jewish captives. He led the procession
together with his father, the emperor Vespasian, and his brother Domitian, followed by the vanquished Jewish leader Simon bar Giora who
was executed afterward in the prison next to the Forum. Among the
booty carried in the triumphal procession were two valuable golden
pieces of the Temple furnishings: the table of the bread of display and
the seven-branched candelabrum. The arch of triumph, upon which
these objects and other sacred Jewish symbols are depicted, was constructed after the death of Titus and is a favorite of tourists today.
As for water being used as an instrument of God against Sisera, see
Judg. 5:21, *the torrent Kishon swept them away*. Mixed with Titus's
wine was poterion, the extract of a shrub taken medicinally after a
bath. Rabbi Eleazar, son of Rabbi Jose, was of the fourth generation of

tannaim (160–200 C.E.). In the story as related in Gittin the name of the rabbi is given as Rabbi Phinehas ben Aruvah. At the end of the tale the two-pound creature resembling a dove, a pigeon, or a swallow—the sources differ—shrank to its original size and shape as a mosquito. At the same time Titus shrank, as it were; his strength left him.

124. Gittin 56b–57a. Onkelus—perhaps originally Ocellus—is the supposed translator of the Pentateuch into Aramaic. In rabbinic literature his name is frequently followed by the appellation, "the proselyte." He is identified often with Aquila, the alleged author of a Greek translation of the Bible (see Avodah Zarah 11a; Megillah 3a; Tanḥuma Mishpatim 5; Songs Rabbah 1:11). According to H. Graetz, *History of the Jews* (6 vols., Philadelphia, 1891–98), 2:387 (see also J. Derenbourg, *Mas‘a Erez Yisra'el* [Jerusalem, 1969–70], 2:178), the son of the sister of Titus was Flavius Clemens, corrupted to Kalonymus or Kalonikus. The nephew of Domitian, the brother of Titus, and nephew, therefore, also of Titus, was put to death as an atheist about the year 96 C.E. The Romans, and pagans generally, regarded belief in one invisible God as atheism. Klausner, *Jesus of Nazareth*, pp. 33–34, thinks this story is earlier.

125. Lamentations Rabbah 1:5.

126. Avot de-Rabbi Natan 4:5. The text does not say who was in command of the Roman troops when Jerusalem was captured. In the preceding sentence Vespasian is the subject. But he was proclaimed emperor before the end of July 69 C.E. by his legions and was in Alexandria on the way to Rome when the news reached him of the murder on December 20, 69, of Vitellius, who had been proclaimed emperor by his legions in Germany. Vespasian stayed in Alexandria until the summer of 70 and the leadership of the war against the Jews was given to his son Titus. It was Titus who began the siege of Jerusalem in the spring of 70 and who captured it during the summer.

127. Ecclesiastes Rabbah 5:2. The word *dolkim* is from the root meaning to kindle or to burn, hence, "those who kindle or burn." Rabbi Judah ha-Nasi was the final redactor of the Mishnah ca. 200 C.E. Jacob of Kefar Ḥanan or Ḥanin in Yerushalmi Berakhot 5:2 is mentioned as quoting Resh Lakish, an amora of the third century.

128. Avot de-Rabbi Natan 4:5, end. The story of the priests illustrates the rabbinical explanation of the catastrophe that befell the Jewish people in the destruction of the Temple and Jerusalem, the end of the Second Commonwealth, and the consequent Diaspora. It was all due not to the mortal enemies of the Jews but to their own wrongdoing. The theme is repeated in Jewish legend and liturgy. See infra, on the cause of the destruction of the Second Temple. The fault lay with the Jews themselves in failing to live up to their lofty responsibilities. The tragedy was none the less great and all the leading figures of the Jewish past wept and mourned.

129. Sotah 9:14. See earlier in this section and n. 110 for the prohibition against bridegrooms wearing wreaths during the war with Vespasian. For "Titus" the Cambridge manuscript of the Mishnah reads "Quietus," who was governor of Judea in 117 C.E. At a time of national sorrow it was natural also to strike out against the culture of the alien, for after the introduction of Greek culture a series of catastrophes occurred, reducing national dominion and diminishing national independence. However, this prohibition against Greek philos-

ophy and learning was neither enforced nor obeyed, for leading medieval Jewish philosophers were exponents and interpreters of Greek philosophy, reconciling it with the Bible and Jewish tradition.

130. Ta'anit 4:6. The daily offerings on the Temple altar came to an end during the siege of Jerusalem by the Romans because of lack of animals for sacrifice and lack of priests to perform the sacred rite. For a description of the breaching of the several walls of Jerusalem and of the Temple itself by the Romans, see Margolis and Marx, *A History of the Jewish People*, pp. 201–2. Apostomos or Posthumus is said to have been a Syrian general, but about whom nothing is known. Syrian soldiers fought in the Roman army against the Jews during the war and the siege of Jerusalem. The decree against the Jews entering the land of Israel is stated in Num. 14:29 ff. The two destructions of the Temple were by Nebuchadnezzar in 586 B.C.E. and by Titus in 70 C.E. Betar, south of Jerusalem, was the scene of Bar Kokhba's final defeat in 135 C.E.

131. Avot de-Rabbi Natan 4:4, quoting Deut. 11:13–16.

132. Lamentations Rabbah 2:11. This statement is quoted in the name of Rabbi Samuel ben Naḥman, who was of the third generation of Palestine amoraim and a noted aggadist, by his pupil, Rabbi Ḥelbo, and by rabbis Berekhiah and Aibo, the latter of the fourth generation of amoraim, like Rabbi Ḥelbo. Rabbi Berekhiah was a disciple of Rabbi Ḥelbo and of the fifth generation of Palestinian amoraim. He is often mentioned as a transmitter of traditions.

133. Deuteronomy Rabbah 1:17. Rabbi Joshua ben Levi was a Palestinian amora of the first generation in the first half of the third century. He lived at Lydda and was noted for his involvement with the Aggadah.

134. Ibid. Of course this is an anachronism. Esau and Rome are identified with each other; see n. 7 in this chapter. Because Esau was reverential toward his parents, especially his father, Rome was not hindered by God in the destruction of the Temple and Israel's military efforts against Rome were doomed to failure. Rabbi Judah ben Simon was a Palestinian amora of the fourth generation who lived in Lydda.

135. Genesis Rabbah 56:11 on Gen. 22:17, a part of the divine blessing given to Abraham. Rabbi Judah ha-Nasi was the final redactor of the Mishnah, ca. 200 C.E. Palmyra or Tadmor was an oasis town in the Syrian desert. See also Lamentations Rabbah 2:4, where the number of archers supplied at the destruction of the Second Temple is given as forty thousand and a second opinion gives it as eighty thousand. See also Yerushalmi Ta'anit 4:69b and Yalkut Genesis 102.

136. Gittin 58a. Ishmael ben Elisha was a high priest. A similar story is found in Lamentations Rabbah 1:16, where the father is called Zadok the priest. More details are given in the midrashic version. Rabbi Joshua ben Ḥananiah was of the second generation of tannaim (90–130 C.E.). The second tale, wherein the name of the child in the Roman prison is given as Ishmael ben Elisha, makes it hard to accept the name of the father in the first story as the same and therefore it may be better to accept the father's name as Zadok the priest as in Lamentations Rabbah 1:16.

137. Avot de-Rabbi Natan 17:5. One of several anecdotes of the miserable plight of even the richest families in Israel during and after the Roman war against the Jews.

138. Ibid., 17:6. The expression "Master of Dreams," literally, "Dream," may mean an angel or the One who is the ultimate cause of all dreams, God; cf. Berakhot 10b where the same expression is found.

139. Gittin 57b. The Talmud quotes the story in the name of Rabbi Judah who quoted Samuel or Rabbi Ammi, while some say it was taught in a baraita. Samuel was a Babylonian amora of the first generation; he died in 254 C.E. But if the source for the story is a baraita, it would be earlier, for a baraita contains tannaitic teachings not included in the Mishnah. *Bashan* was read by the expounder of the verse as a contraction of the Hebrew words, *bein shein*, "between the teeth."

140. Gittin 58a. Zafnat is taken to be derived from the Aramaic, *zofin*, meaning "they look at"; Peniel from *lifnei el*, "before God." This story is quoted in the name of Resh Lakish, Rabbi Simon ben Lakish, who was of the second generation of amoraim active during the middle part of the third century.

141. Lamentations Rabbah on Lam. 4:8. Rabbi Eleazar, son of Rabbi Zadok, was of the second generation of tannaim, about 90–130 C.E. He had a grandson of the same name. His father had suffered hunger, the story tells, during the siege of Jerusalem by the Romans before the destruction of the Temple.

5. After the Destruction

142. Lamentations Rabbah on Lam. 1:2. The statement is quoted in the name of Rabbi Joshua ben Levi who was of the first generation of amoraim in the early part of the third century. He was known for his preoccupation with the Aggadah.

143. Lamentations Rabbah 1:1, quoted in the name of Rabbi Joshua ben Levi, as with the passage before. Overturning the couch was an ancient custom in observance of mourning; see Mo'ed Katan 15a. The rending of the divine purple raiment refers to the curtain before the Holy of Holies, which God allowed Titus to rend.

144. Ḥagigah 5a. In Jer. 13:17 the Hebrew word *dim'ah*, "tear," is used three times in the verb and noun forms. Hence the interpretation of three "weepings." God participates in the sorrow of His people and weeps with them.

145. Berakhot 3a. Rabbi Jose the Galilean was of the younger group of the second generation of tannaim, about 90–130 C.E. He is the author of a number of statements concerning the Temple service.

146. Berakhot 3a. The statement is quoted in the name of Rav, a third-century amora.

147. Exodus Rabbah 29:9; Yerushalmi Berakhot 9:13; Midrash Tehillim 18:12, 104:25. Rabbi Akiba, one of the greatest of the rabbis, was active ca. 110–135. The Palestinian Talmud and the Midrash Tehillim make the asker of the question Elijah rather than Balza, and the person asked, Rabbi Nehorai instead of Rabbi Akiba. Rabbi Nehorai was a third-generation tanna (ca. 130–160 C.E.).

148. Tanḥuma Hakadum, Exodus. The author of the statement is Rabbi Aha of the fourth generation of amoraim in Palestine. The Western Wall, the sole remaining wall of the Temple area, has been

revered by Jews through the centuries as a holy place. Many aggadic statements are associated with the Wall.

149. Sotah 9:12, 9:15; and also in Genesis Rabbah 32:49. The first statement is quoted in the name of Rabban Simon ben Gamaliel, who quotes Rabbi Joshua. The latter was of the second generation of tannaim, ca. 90–130 C.E.; the former was of the third generation of tannaim, ca. 130–160 C.E. The second statement is that of Rabbi Phinehas ben Jair, of the fourth generation of tannaim, about 160–200 C.E. The Cambridge text reads Rabbi Eliezer. The last statement is ascribed to Rabbi Eliezer the Great, son of Hyrcanus, who was of the second generation of tannaim; the Cambridge reading ascribes the text to Rabbi Joshua. The midrash inserts an additional comparison in the last statement: ". . . the sages became like scribes, the scribes like schoolteachers. . . ." Moreover, the midrash has "students" for "sextons." The ḥaverim were those who were scrupulous in observing the law to the full, in particular the laws of tithing and of ritual cleanness (see Moore, *Judaism*, 3:26).

150. Lamentations Rabbah 4:2. The utterance is quoted in the name of Rabbi Samuel ben Naḥman of the third generation of amoraim and an eminent aggadist. White glass was of very fine quality and was used for festive dinners. Bad luck caused the wine to jell and so to be unusable.

151. Bava Batra 61b. See also Ta'anit 30b. Rabbi Joshua was of the second generation of tannaim, about 90–130 C.E. Rabbi Isaac, frequently cited in the Mekhilta and Sifrei, was of the fourth generation of tannaim active during the latter part of the second century. Rabbi Ishmael ben Elisha, usually called just Rabbi Ishmael, was of the younger group of the second generation of tannaim active during the early third of the second century. Leaving one small area of a house unpainted was, through the centuries to modern times, one of the practices observed by Jews to commemorate the destruction of Jerusalem. One cubit equals 22.08 inches or 56.1 cm. The placing of ashes upon the forehead of a bridegroom did not persist.

152. Berakhot 55a. The point here is that the home should be a miniature temple and the table an altar. The home becomes a temple *in parvo* when within its walls there are found love and kindness, piety, and sanctity, and exemplary relations between husband and wife, parents and children. The table becomes an altar when its food is prepared according to the dietary laws and when words of Torah are spoken by those seated at it. Rabbi Johanan and Rabbi Eleazar, both originally of Alexandria, were of the third generation of tannaim, ca. 130–160 C.E., and were students of Rabbi Akiba.

153. Exodus Rabbah 27:1, a contrast between two non-Jewish figures.

154. Songs Rabbah 5:2 interpreting the verse in the biblical book of the same chapter and verse. The Shema is the declaration of Jewish belief in God's unity, Deut. 6:4, recited during the daily morning and evening prayers and before retiring each night. It is proclaimed at the end of the services on Yom Kippur and uttered by the Jew upon his or her deathbed. The sacrifices upon the Temple altar are replaced by prayer and the Temple itself by the synagogue and the school.

155. Exodus Rabbah 50:4. Rabbi Eleazar, son of Rabbi Jose Ha-Gelili was of the third generation of tannaim, ca. 130–160 C.E. Evidently

the Temple curtain was part of the booty carried to Rome by the conquerors.

156. Songs Rabbah 4:4. The Temple ruins retain the sanctity that was the Temple's. And it is God who was ultimately responsible for its destruction, the Romans being His instrument, because of the sins of the Jewish people. It is a point the rabbis make time and again, and they include it in the Sabbath and holiday liturgy.

157. Songs Rabbah 4:4. *Built to hold weapons* (*talpiot*) is the continuation of the verse, *Your neck is like the Tower of David* (Songs 4:4). It is Ḥiyya, son of Rabbi Bun, who divided the word *talpiot* into two, as the basis for his interpretation: *yofi*, "beauty," and *tel*, "a ruin."

158. Songs Rabbah 4:4. See also Berakhot 30a for the passage on the direction one faces in prayer, referred to here. Rabbi Avin or, in abbreviation, Rabin, was a member of the fourth generation of amoraim, first half of the fourth century C.E. He read *talpiot* as *piyot mitpalelot* (literally, "mouths praying"). Archaeological excavations in Israel in recent years have revealed that synagogues in the land of Israel followed, without exception, the directions stated here—that is, all faced Jerusalem.

159. Lamentations Rabbah, Proems 22. Rabbi Simon ben Lakish, called Resh Lakish, was an amora of the second generation, the middle of the third century C.E. Under the Roman governor, Tinneus Rufus, after Jerusalem had been retaken by the Romans from the Jewish rebels led by Bar Kokhba in 134 C.E., the ruins were cleared and the earth was freshly ploughed up as a sign of the foundation of a new city (see Lamentations Rabbah 1:13; Yerushalmi Ta'anit 4:5, 69b).

160. Lamentations Rabbah, Proems 8.

161. Genesis Rabbah 93:12; Megillah 16b. Joseph is credited with such prescience because the Hebrew word for *neck* is in the plural form, literally *necks*. The neck is symbolic of pride, as in an earlier midrash. Both Temples were in the territory of the tribe of Benjamin. The First and Second Temples, the pride of Benjamin's tribe in the future, Joseph foresaw, were both to be destroyed. Rabbi Eleazar said that Joseph foresaw through the Holy Spirit.

162. Gittin 57b. Since the rabbis held David to be the author of Psalms, the interpretation here of two verses from Ps. 137 would have David aware of the future destruction of both Temples. Rav was a Babylonian amora of the first generation, early part of the third century.

163. Lamentations Rabbah, Proems 7. Rabbi Abbahu was a Palestinian amora of the third generation and Rabbi Jose ben Ḥanina, of the second generation, latter part of the third century. Rabbi Jose taught Rabbi Abbahu and served as principal of the school in Caesarea.

164. Ḥagigah 5b. The root *damo'a*, "to shed tears," is found in the verse in three forms (Jer. 13:17), twice as verb forms and translated as *flow with copious tears* and once as a noun. Rabbi Eliezer ben Hyrcanus was of the second generation of tannaim, ca. 90–130 C.E. He had his school at Lydda.

165. Sanhedrin 140b. The Hebrew text has the verb form of "to weep" doubled to indicate intensity and it is translated, *bitterly she weeps*. Rabbah was an amora of the third generation, early fourth century. He was for some time in Palestine and later in Babylonia at the academy at Sura. Rabbi Johanan was an amora of the second generation and was active during the third century at Tiberias.

166. Lamentations Rabbah, Proem 21. Rabbi Alexandri (or Alexandrai or Alexander) was a Palestinian amora of the second generation, early third century. The repetition of the word *unclean* is interpreted as referring to the destruction of the two Temples.

167. Leviticus Rabbah 19:4. The First Temple is called the *great house* and the Second Temple, the *little house* (Amos 6:11) because the sanctity attaching to the latter was less than to the former. An escape, a way out, was possible after the destruction of the First Temple in the return from Babylonia and the rebuilding of the Temple. But such was not possible after the destruction of the Second Temple. Hence the destruction of the First Temple may be compared to nothing worse than the piercing of a roof, which caused leaking, while the destruction of the Second Temple was like a complete smashing into splinters.

168. Exodus Rabbah 35:5 on Exod. 25:3 where gold, silver, and copper are mentioned as offerings from the people for the building of the tabernacle. Gold is compared to Babylonia, silver to Persia, and brass to Greece (see Dan. 2:32, 38). Rome is compared to iron in Daniel's vision of the four kingdoms (see Dan. 2:40). Edom is the speaker in Ps. 137, who is depicted by the psalmist as urging that it be utterly destroyed down to its foundations.

169. Exodus Rabbah 36:1. Elsewhere in this chapter the rabbis point out that with the destruction of the Temple prayer took the place of the sacrifice (see supra, n. 154). Rabban Johanan ben Zakkai said that acts of benevolence were a substitute for the sacrificial cult. In a supposed conversation between Abraham and God, Abraham is assured by God that his descendants will survive the destruction of the Temple because their reading about the sacrifices in their daily prayers will serve as a substitute for the sacrifices (Ta'anit 27b).

170. Exodus Rabbah 36:1.

171. Lamentations Rabbah 1:5 on Lam. 1:5, *Her enemies are now the masters*. Caesarea was a Roman city, originally built by Herod, on the site of Straton's Tower. The Roman governors or procurators had their residence at Caesarea, where the temple of Augustus was erected. Nero denied Jews citizenship in the city but the city continued to have a large, prosperous Jewish community. After the destruction of the Temple the country was administered from Caesarea by the Roman governors, as alluded to in this midrashic passage. In addition to being the Roman capital of the land of Israel and the seat of the Roman administration, it was also the headquarters of the Roman army. Buber's text of this passage reads "Caesarea became a metropolis, Antipatris a province, and Neapolis a Roman colony." Antipatris was built by Herod in memory of his father, Antipater, in the place of the ancient Kefar Saba, near Rosh ha-Ayin of modern Israel, ten miles northeast of Jaffa. The ruins of Caesarea and Antipatris can be seen in Israel today.

172. Lamentations Rabbah 1; Megillah 6a. Jerusalem was the center of Judaism and the capital of the Jewish people while Caesarea was its antithesis, the center of Roman influence and the capital of Roman administration in the land of Israel. See the previous note.

173. Lamentations Rabbah, Proems 24. The Temple is compared to a breast as a source of spiritual nourishment, and the plural refers to the two Temples.

174. Leviticus Rabbah 31:6. God shares the grief of His people by diminishing the volume of the songs of praise sung before Him by the ministering angels and by reducing their number.

175. Numbers Rabbah 23:7. A midrashic explanation of the development of the prayers included in the grace recited after a meal.

176. Lamentations Rabbah 1:6. Rabbi Judah ben Ilai, a tanna of the third generation, about 130–160 C.E., is the author of this statement about God's love for children.

177. Bava Batra 12a–b. Rabbi Avdimi was a Palestinian amora of the fourth generation, first half of the fourth century C.E. Rabbi Johanan bar Nappaḥa was an amora of the second generation, middle of the third century C.E.

178. The first group of statements, containing the scriptural explications, are from Bava Batra 25b, and are attributed to Rafram I, son of Papa, who quotes them in the name of his teacher, Rabbi Ḥisda. The former was a Babylonian amora of the fifth generation, second half of the fourth century; the latter, a Babylonian amora of the third generation, known for his preeminence in Aggadah and for his ten years as head of the academy at Sura. His student Rabbi Rafram was head of the academy at Pumbedita. The second group of statements is to be found in Sotah 48a, attributed to Rabban Simon ben Gamaliel, quoting Rabbi Simon, son of the deputy high priest. The former was a tanna of the third generation, ca. 130–160 C.E.

179. Berakhot 32a and Avodah Zarah 3b. Not only does God share the grief of Israel—as has been asserted in earlier passages—but nature as well.

180. Bava Batra 59a and Berakhot 32b. This text is in conflict with an earlier passage, which states that after the destruction of the Temple prayer became the substitute for the animal sacrifices. Rabbi Eliezer ben Hyrcanus, a tanna of the second generation who was active after the Temple's destruction (ca. 90–130 C.E.), is the author of this statement. He had his school at Lydda.

181. Berakhot 8a, a statement attributed to Rabbi Rafram quoting his teacher Rabbi Ḥisda (see n. 178 above). The argument here is that the place where Halakhah ("law") is studied has the highest priority. Zion and ziyun ("mark") are spelled alike in Hebrew hence the homiletical interpretation of the verse.

182. Berakhot 58b. This passage is quoted in the name of Rabbi Johanan, an amora of the second generation, about the middle of the third century C.E. God's house was destroyed; the righteous, His servants, should not wish to enjoy a superior fortune.

183. Shabbat 119b; Ḥagigah 14a. Each rabbi quotes a biblical verse to support his contention. In order they are: Abaye, Ezek. 22:26; Abbahu, Isa. 5:11; Hamnuna, Jer. 6:11; Ulla, Jer. 6:15; Isaac, Isa. 24:2–3; Amram, Lam. 1:6; Judah, 2 Chron. 36:16; Rava, Jer. 5:1; Ketina, Isa. 3:6. Abaye lived from approximately 280 to 338/339 C.E. Abbahu was a Palestinian amora of the third generation; Hamnuna, a Babylonian amora of the same generation, early part of the fourth century C.E. Ulla too was a Babylonian amora of the same generation. Rabbi Isaac was most likely of the third generation of amoraim. Rabbi Amram was a fourth-generation Palestinian amora and Rabbi Judah, a second-generation amora, died in 299 C.E. Rava, a fourth-generation Babylonian amora, a contemporary of Abaye with whom he entered into frequent

talmudic debate, lived from 299 to 352 C.E. Ketina was a second-generation Babylonian amora.

184. Midrash Aggadah 21:1; Midrash Tehillim 82:1.

185. Bava Batra 30b. Rabbi Johanan was an amora of the second generation. He was born between 175 and 180 C.E. and died during the last quarter of the following century after a long scholarly career in Sepphoris and Tiberias.

186. Kallah Rabbati 54b. Unity among the people even for a base purpose such as idolatry excused them to a degree. But worse was when the people were divided through enmity without cause. The story of Kamza and Bar Kamza, told earlier, is an illustration. The late Rabbi Abraham Isaac Kook, chief rabbi of Palestine, would say that the Third Temple—or the Third Commonwealth—would be built when Jews would be marked by causeless love, that is, love for each other without ulterior motive. The translation of the verse from Hosea is from the Jewish Publication Society's 1917 translation, *The Holy Scriptures*. It shows more clearly the rabbinic deduction from the verse.

187. Yoma 9b. The three transgressions mentioned are deemed by the rabbis to be the very worst. For they teach that a person, for the sake of saving his life, may transgress any of the commandments in the Torah except these three. But even worse than the three transgressions together is causeless hatred.

188. Midrash Shoher Tov 76, quoted in the name of Rabbi Bere-khiah who was of the fifth generation of Palestinian amoraim, latter part of the fourth century C.E. He was known as an expert in the traditions.

189. Gittin 58a. Rav was a Babylonian amora of the first generation, early third century C.E. The story is an illustration of the immorality and injustice considered by this rabbi to be responsible for the destruction of Jerusalem. "Two wicks in one candle" is a euphemism for one woman marrying two men under such circumstances.

190. Exodus Rabbah 51:5. By a play on words, changing only the vocalization, the rabbis equate the Tabernacle with a pledge by God that will be forfeited to the heathen nations if Israel sins. It is a meaningful insight into rabbinic character and theology that they blamed not their enemies but the sins of their own people for the national disaster. Moreover, their faith in God was not shaken. It was not His lack of power but their own moral and ethical weakness that was responsible for their people's tragedy.

191. Exodus Rabbah 31:10. The plural forms—*tents* and *dwellings* (Num. 24:5)—are interpreted to refer to the two Temples. There is also a play on words here, whereby *mishkenotekha* (*your dwellings*) is read as *mashenotekha* (*your pledges*) with only a slight change in the vocalization. The midrash supports the statement that God made the same bargain with Moses—that the two Temples would be a pledge against the conduct of the Jews—by the use of a biblical verse, Exod. 22:25, where *your neighbor's garment* is taken as a symbol for the Temple. *If you take your neighbor's garment in pledge, you must return it to him before the sun sets* (Exod. 23:25) is here made to read ". . . until the sun appears."

192. Pesikta Rabbati 35:1, 15:10, 47:3; Exodus Rabbah 2:2; Tanhuma Hakadum Exodus; Numbers Rabbah 11:2. Rabbi Isaac was a fourth-generation tanna, frequently mentioned in Mekhilta and Sifrei.

Rabbi Samuel ben Naḥman was a Palestinian amora of the third generation, early fourth century C.E., an eminent aggadist who was active in Tiberias. Rabbi Aḥa belonged to the next generation of Palestinian amoraim and lived at Lydda. The "echo of the Divine Voice," *bat kol*, is frequently translated "heavenly voice." The "rock" is the foundation stone of the Temple, the rock upon which the near-sacrifice of Isaac took place. Not only was the Temple holy but its site is also holy and the Divine Presence, the Shekhinah, an aspect of the Godhead, remains there, especially at the Western Wall, the only wall that has remained standing through the years. The Divine Presence is said to be in the west because the principal entrance to the Temple was at the east and the Holy of Holies at the west. The translation, "Gate of Ḥuldah," follows Rashi on 2 Kings 22:14. Some translate it as "Carts Gate," a back entrance used for loading and unloading. One of Vespasian's four generals to whom he had assigned the task of destroying the four ramparts of Jerusalem failed to carry out his assignment, so the story goes. The general, Pangar by name, was ordered to destroy the Western Wall but did not, and was, therefore, executed. See the story (part 8, section 15) about Rabban Johanan ben Zakkai and part 8, n. 130. Vespasian in the story is presumably Titus. According to Josephus, *Wars*, 7:1:1, Titus left Phasael, now known as the Tower of David, standing "in order to demonstrate to posterity what kind of a city it was and how well fortified, which the Roman valor had subdued."

193. Source unknown. See Zev Vilnay, *Legends of Jerusalem* (Philadelphia, 1973), pp. 177–78 and n. 197.

194. Commentary of Naḥmanides on Songs 2:9. See also Songs Rabbah 2:24. The Holy of Holies was placed toward the west in the Temple.

195. Lamentations Rabbah, Proems 2; Midrash on Ps. 105:1; Eliyahu Rabbah 38, p. 149. Rabbi Natan was of the fourth generation of tannaim and a contemporary of Rabbi Judah ha-Nasi, ca. 200 C.E.

196. Genesis Rabbah 100:17. Still another legend to portray God's grief at the destruction of the Temple and Jerusalem, forced upon Him by the wrongdoings of Israel, a grief He shares with His people.

197. Lamentations Rabbah 1:16; Yerushalmi Berakhot 2:4. The details vary in the two versions, and I have blended elements from both. Where I have translated "a man of Arav" the usual translation is "an Arab." The town of Arav was near Sepphoris in Upper Galilee (see Shabbat 16:7). Arav was the town where Rabban Johanan ben Zakkai lived for eighteen years; see Yerushalmi Shabbat 16, end 15d; Yerushalmi Ta'anit 4:67c; Tosefta Bava Kamma 6:22; Yerushalmi Bava Kamma 6:5c. For Birat Araba the Yerushalmi version has Birat Malka. Y. Yadin, "Expedition D," *Israel Exploration Journal* (1961): 36–52, quotes a suggestion of S. Klein that these two place-names may refer to two ruins near Solomon's Pools south of Jerusalem, Khirbet el-Bireh and Khirbet Arib. There are places in the story where the text is uncertain. The fact that the stormy winds carried off the child was proof to the Jew that the child was destined for a supernatural purpose. The Jewish proverb has it that the healing comes before the blow, so here the Messiah is born on the day the Temple is destroyed. A later interpretation understands this to mean that on the same calendar date on which the Temple was destroyed—the ninth day of Av— the Messiah will be born. In later versions of the story the peddler of

children's clothes is told that the child was taken away for safekeeping and meanwhile waits in Paradise until the appointed time for the Messiah to appear (see Midrash Eikhah Zuta [ed. Buber, 1894], p. 133; cf. L. Ginzberg, *Peirushim ve-ḥiddushim bi-yerushalim* [4 vols., New York, 1941–61], 1:339 ff.; also Abraham Berger, "Captive at the Gate of Rome: The Story of a Messianic Motif," *Proceedings of the American Academy for Jewish Research* 44 [1977]:1–17).

Rabbi Abun or Abin was a fourth-generation amora, born in Babylonia, but active chiefly in Palestine during the early part of the fourth century C.E.

198. Genesis Rabbah 56:2. The tradition was that Mount Moriah, where the testing of Abraham took place with the binding of Isaac, was the location of the future Temple. Its "owner" could be God or Israel. All this is deduced from *the place from afar* (Gen. 22:4). Ps. 132:14 supports the argument that the alienation would not be for all time. Zech. 9:9 is compared to *You stay here with the ass* (Gen. 22:5), where the Hebrew for "stay" may also be translated as "return"; hence, you will return when he (the Messiah) comes riding on an ass.

199. Exodus Rabbah 15:1. The words in Jeremiah, *exalted from of old,* may be translated *exalted from the beginning,* the Hebrew being amenable to either. The rabbis said, "In Nisan were they redeemed, in Nisan will they be redeemed," hence here the Messiah will come in the first month of the year—all an exposition of Exod. 12:2.

200. Genesis Rabbah 78:3. Since the first half of the verse from Isaiah was fulfilled with Jacob, the second half dealing with the prophets, God's messengers, and their prophecies about Jerusalem's future will also be fulfilled.

201. Genesis Rabbah 13:2.

202. Ta'anit 30a.

203. Menaḥot 53b. The replies of God and the "heavenly voice" (*bat kol*) are sections of scriptural verses, where Jeremiah's exhortation is addressed to Judah. The plea of Abraham on behalf of his descendants as portrayed here by Rabbi Isaac is reminiscent of the biblical story of Abraham's plea on behalf of Sodom and Gomorrah, Gen. 18:23–32. Abraham's principle is that the Judge of all the earth must judge justly (Gen. 18:25). Rabbi Isaac was a fourth-generation tanna; he is frequently mentioned in the Mekhilta and Sifrei.

204. Bava Kamma 60b. The God of justice is subject to His own law.

205. Makkot 24a–b. Rabban Gamaliel II, Rabbi Eleazar ben Azariah, and Rabbi Joshua belonged to the older group of the second generation of tannaim, ca. 90–130 C.E., Rabbi Akiba, to the younger group, and he was trained in the schools of Rabbi Eleazar and Rabbi Joshua. The four sages mentioned in the two stories are said to have undertaken a sea voyage to Rome in the year 95 C.E. (see Derenbourg, *Mas'a Erez Yisra'el*, pp. 334–40, and Bacher, *Agada der Tannaiten* 1:84 ff.). Gamaliel II succeeded Johanan ben Zakkai as head of the academy at Jabneh; for a brief period he was replaced by Eleazar ben Azariah and was restored to the dignity of nasi after a reconciliation with the offended Joshua ben Ḥananiah. Rabbi Joshua ben Ḥananiah was active at Peki'in. Rabbi Eleazar ben Azariah was a wealthy priest and, after the reconciliation between Gamaliel II and Joshua, delivered discourses at the Jabneh academy on one Sabbath to Gamaliel's every three. Rabbi

Akiba's school was at Bnei Brak but he was also at Lydda and Jabneh. The period of his greatest activity was between 110 and 135 C.E. He supported Bar Kokhba in the rebellion against Rome, 133–135 C.E., and was executed by the Romans. One of the greatest of the rabbis of the Talmud, he is mentioned more than 270 times in the Mishnah. Sifra on Leviticus is a midrashic work following his system. The distance from which the four sages heard the noise coming from the Roman crowds is stated in the text to be 120 mil, a mil equaling 2,000 cubits; a cubit is 22.08 inches or 56.1 cm. Upon entering Jerusalem at Mount Scopus the four sages rent their garments as a sign of mourning, but soon Rabbi Akiba was to comfort them with the assurance of the future fulfillment of divine prophecy.

Bibliography

Name and Place Index

Subject Index

Passages Cited

Bibliography

Postbiblical Sources

Apocrypha and Pseudepigrapha of the Old Testament. Edited by R. H. Charles. 2 vols. Oxford, 1913.
Bickerman, Elias. *The First Book of Maccabees.* New York, 1948.
―――. *From Ezra to the Last of the Maccabees.* New York, 1962.
―――. *The Maccabees.* New York, 1947.
Divrei ketuvim aḥronim. Edited by J. L. Barukh. Jerusalem, 1937.
Josephus, Flavius. *Works.* Translated by William Whiston. New York, 1872; New York, 1974.
Ketuvim Aḥronim. Translated by Seckel Isaac Frankel. Berlin, 1927.

Rabbinic Sources

Aboth: Sayings of the Fathers. Edited and translated by Joseph H. Hertz. London, 1943; New York, 1945.
Aggadat Bereishit. Edited by Salomon Buber. Vilna, 1925.
Aggadat Esther. Edited by Salomon Buber. Cracow, 1897.
Aggadat Shir ha-Shirim. Edited by Solomon Schechter. Cambridge, 1896.
Avot de-Rabbi Natan. Edited by Solomon Schecter. Vienna, 1887; reprint, New York, 1967.
The Babylonian Talmud. Translated into English. Edited by Isidor Epstein. 34 vols. London, 1935–48. 16 vols. London, 1961.
Bereishit Rabbati. Edited by Chanoch Albeck. Jerusalem, 1940.
The Fathers According to Rabbi Nathan. Translated by Judah Goldin. Yale Judaica Series 10. New Haven, 1955.
Masekhet Avot im Talmud Bavli ve-Yerushalmi. Edited by Noah Chaim. New York, n.d.
Masekhet Derekh Ereẓ Zuta. Edited by Jacob Landau. Tel Aviv, 1970–71. With commentary by Daniel Sperber. Jerusalem, 1979.
Masekhtot Ketanot [The minor tractates of the Talmud]. Translated under the editorship of Abraham Cohen. London, 1965.
Masekhtot Ze'irot. Edited and translated by Michael Higger. New York, 1929.
Megillat Ta'anit. Edited and translated by Solomon Zeitlin. Philadelphia, 1922.
Mekilta de-Rabbi Ishmael. Edited and translated by Jacob Z. Lauterbach. 3 vols. Philadelphia, 1933–35.

Mekilta de-Rabbi Shimon ben Johai. Edited by J. N. Epstein and Ezra Zion Melamed. Jerusalem, 1955.

Midrash Aggadah. Edited by Salomon Buber. Vienna, 1894.

Midrash Aggadat Bereishit. Edited by Hanoch Zundel ben Joseph. Warsaw, 1876; Jerusalem, 1962.

"Midrash Aseret Melakhim." Edited by Chaim Meir Horowitz. In *Bibliotheca Haggidica*, vol. 1, pp. 16–33, 38–55. Frankfurt-am-Main, 1881.

"Midrash Aseret Melakhim." In *Ozar midrashim*, edited by Judah David Eisenstein, vol. 2, pp. 461–66. New York, 1915.

Midrash Eikhah Rabbah. Edited by Salomon Buber. Vilna, 1899.

Midrash ha-Gadol. Genesis. Edited by Mordecai Margoliot. Jerusalem, 1947.

———. Exodus. Edited by Mordecai Margoliot. Jerusalem, 1956.

———. Leviticus. Edited by Adin Steinsalz. Jerusalem, 1975.

———. Numbers. Edited by Zvi Meir Rabinowitz. Jerusalem, 1967.

———. Deuteronomy. Edited by Shlomo Fish. Jerusalem, 1972.

Midrashim ketanim. Edited by Salomon Buber. Vilna. 1925.

Midrash Iyyob. Edited by Solomon Aaron Wertheimer. Jerusalem, 1920.

Midrash Lekah Tov. Edited by Salomon Buber. 2 vols. Vilna, 1884.

Midrash Mishlei. Edited by Salomon Buber. Vilna, 1893.

Midrash on Psalms. Translated by William G. Braude. 2 vols. New Haven, 1959.

Midrash Otiyot de-Rabbi Akiva ha-shalem. Edited by Solomon Aaron Wertheimer. Jerusalem, 1914.

Midrash Rabbah. 3 vols. Vilna, 1878, translated by H. Freedman and Maurice Simon. London, 1939.

Midrash Shemuel. Edited by Salomon Buber. Cracow, 1893.

Midrash Tanhuma. Edited by Salomon Buber. Vilna, 1885.

Midrash Tannaim. Edited by Salomon Buber. Berlin, 1909.

Midrash Tannaim. Edited by David Hoffmann. Berlin, 1908–9; reprint, Tel Aviv, 1962.

Midrash Tehillim. Edited by Salomon Buber. Vilna, 1891.

Midrash tish'ah aggadot. Edited by Salomon Buber. 2 vols. Vilna, 1925.

The Mishnah. Horeb edition. Berlin, 1924.

The Mishnah. Edited by Chanoch Albeck. 6 vols. Jerusalem, 1952–58.

The Mishnah. Edited and translated by Herbert Danby. Oxford, 1933.

Mishnat Rabbi Eliezer. Edited by Hyman G. Enelow. New York, 1933.

Pesikta de-Rab Kahana. Edited by Salomon Buber. Vilna, 1925; New York, 1962.

Pesikta de-Rab Kahana. Edited by Bernard Mandelbaum. 2 vols. New York, 1962.

Pesikta de-Rab Kahana. Translated by William G. Braude and Israel J. Kapstein. Philadelphia, 1975.

Pesikta Rabbati. Edited by Meir Friedmann. Vienna, 1880.

Pesikta Rabbati. Translated by William G. Braude. 2 vols. New Haven, 1968.

Pirke Abot: With Commentary. Edited by Eliezer Levi. Tel Aviv, 1951–52.

Pirke Aboth. Edited and translated by R. Travers Herford. London, 1930.

Pirke Aboth: Sayings of the Fathers. Edited and translated by Isaac Unterman. New York, 1964.

Pirke de-Rabbi Eliezer. Edited by Samuel Luria. Warsaw, 1852; New York, 1946.

Pirke de-Rabbi Eliezer. Translated by Gerald Friedlander. London, 1916; New York, 1965.

Seder Eliyahu Rabbah. Edited by Meir Friedmann. Vienna, 1900.

Seder Eliyahu Rabbah ve-Seder Eliyahu Zuta. Edited by Meir Ish Shalom (Friedmann). Vienna, 1907; Jerusalem, 1960.

Seder Olam Rabbah. Edited by Jeruchim Leiner. Warsaw, 1904; New York, 1952.

Sheva Masekhtot Ketanot. Edited and translated by Michael Higger. New York, 1930.

Sifrei de-aggadeta al Megillat Esther. Edited by Salomon Buber. Vilna, 1886.

Sifrei de-ve-Rav. Edited by Meir Ish Shalom (Friedmann). Vienna, 1864; New York, 1948.

Talmud Bavli [The Babylonian Talmud]. Zhitomir, 1863.

Talmud Yerushalmi [The Palestinian Talmud]. Krotoschin, 1866. New York, 1948–49, based on Krotoschin, Venice, and Cracow editions.

Talmud Yerushalmi [The Palestinian Talmud]. Leiden manuscript. With introduction by Saul Lieberman. Jerusalem, 1970.

Tanna de-be Eliyyahu. Translated by William G. Braude and Israel J. Kapstein. Philadelphia, 1981.

Tanna de-ve-Eliyahu. Warsaw, 1881–1908. Jerusalem, 1965–66.

Targum Sheni. Translated into Hebrew by J. A. Handelsalz. Tel Aviv, 193?.

The Tosefta. Edited by Moses Samuel Zuckermandel. Pasewalk, 1880; Jerusalem, 1937.

The Tosefta. Translated by Jacob Neusner. 5 vols. New York, 1981.

Yalkut Shimoni. Vilna, 1908–9; New York and Berlin, 1926.

Postrabbinic Sources

Bonfils, Immanuel ben Jacob. *The Book of the Gests of Alexander of Macedon.* Edited and translated by Israel J. Kazis. Mediaeval Academy of America Publications 75. Cambridge, Mass., 1962.

Callisthenes, Pseudo-. *The Life of Alexander of Macedon.* Edited and translated by Elizabeth H. Haight. New York, 1955.

Ibn Ḥabib, Jacob. *Ein Ya'akov.* 4 vols. Vilna, 1922. Translated by S. H. Glick. 5 vols. New York, 1916–22.

Ibn Yahya, Gedaliah. *Shalshelet ha-kabbalah.* Jerusalem, 1961–62.

Ma'aseh Book. Translated by Moses Gaster. 2 vols. Philadelphia, 1934; reprint (1 vol.), Philadelphia, 1981.

Origen. *Contra Celsum*. Translated by Henry Chadwick. Cambridge, 1965.

General Sources

Abramski, Samuel. *Jerusalem in the Time of the Second Temple*. Jerusalem, 1968.
Aggadot Talmud Yerushalmi. With commentaries of Moses Margalit and Elijah ben Solomon Abraham ha-Kohen. Jerusalem, 1964–65.
Albeck, Chanoch. *Mavo la-Mishnah*. Jerusalem–Tel Aviv, 1959.
———. *Mishnah Mo'ed*. Jerusalem, 1952.
———. *Ha-Sanhedrin u-nesi'ah*. Tel Aviv. 1942–43.
Alon, Gedaliah. *Meḥkarim be-toldot Yisrael*. 2 vols. Tel Aviv, 1957–58.
———. *Toldot ha-Yehudim be-Erez Yisrael bi-tekufat ha-Mishnah ve-ha-Talmud*. 2 vols. Tel Aviv, 1952–55.
Ashkenazi, Shmuel Yafeh. *Yefei Mar'eh*. Warsaw, 1898.
Bacher, Wilhelm. *Die Agada der Tannaiten und Amoräer*. 2 vols. Strassburg, 1902. Hebrew translation by A. Z. Rabinowitz. *Aggadot ha-tannaim*. Tel Aviv, 1928.
Baeck, Leo. *The Pharisees and Other Essays*. New York, 1947.
Bahat, Dan. *Carta's Historical Atlas of Jerusalem*. Jerusalem, 1973.
Belkin, Samuel. "Ha-midrash ha-simli ezel Philon be-hashva'ah le-midrashei hazal." In *Harry Austryn Wolfson Jubilee Volume on the Occasion of His 75th Birthday*, edited by Saul Lieberman, pp. 33–68. Jerusalem, 1965.
Ben-Israel, Asher. *Aggadot ha-arez*. 2 vols. Tel Aviv, 1936.
Bentwich, Norman. *Josephus*. Philadelphia, 1914.
———. *Philo-Judaeus of Alexandria*. Philadelphia, 1910.
Berger, Abraham. "Captive at the Gate of Rome: The Story of a Messianic Motif." *Proceedings of the American Academy for Jewish Research* 44 (1977): 1–17.
Bergman, Judah. *Ha-folklor ha-yehudi*. Jerusalem, 1953.
Bialostotzky, Benjamin Jacob. *Fun unzer oytser*. New York, 1939.
Bin Gorion [Berdyczewski], Micha Joseph. *Me-ozar ha-hashva'ah*. 2 vols. Berlin, 1913; Tel Aviv, 1938.
———. *Mimekor Yisrael*. Edited by Emanuel Bin Gorion, translated by I. M. Lask. 3 vols. Bloomington, Ind., and London, 1976.
Büchler, Adolf. *Das Synhedrion in Jerusalem*. Vienna, 1902.
Cary, George. *The Medieval Alexander*. Edited by J. A. Ross. Cambridge, 1956.
Chajes, Hirsch Perez. "Ben Stada." *Hagoren* 4 (1903): 33–37.
Churgin, Pinkhos. *Meḥkarim bi-tekufat bayit sheini*. New York, 1949.
Cohen, Abraham. *Everyman's Talmud*. New York, 1949.
Cohen, Gerson D. "Ma'aseh Ḥannah ve-shiv'at baneha be-safrut ha-ivrit." In *Mordecai M. Kaplan Jubilee Volume*, edited by Moshe Davis, pp. 119–22. New York, 1953.
Dalman, Gustaf. *Jesus Christ in the Talmud, Midrash, Zohar, and the Liturgy of the Synagogue*. Cambridge, 1893.
Damesek, Gershon Zeeb. *Le-or ha-aggadah*. New York, 1955.

Daube, David. *The New Testament and Rabbinic Judaism*. London, 1956.

Derenbourg, Joseph. *Mas'a Erez Yisra'el* [History of the land of Israel from Cyrus to Hadrian according to the scholars of the Mishnah and Talmud]. Translated by Menaḥem M. Mibashan. 2 vols. in 1. Jerusalem, 1969–70.

Donath, Leopold. *Die Alexandersage in Talmud und Midrasch*. Fulda, 1873.

Dubnow, Simon. *Divrei am olam*. 11 vols. Tel Aviv, 1923–40.

Eisenstein, Judah David. *Ozar ma'amarei ḥazal*. 2 vols. New York, 1922.

———. *Ozar midrashim*. New York, 1915.

Encyclopedia Judaica. 16 vols. Jerusalem, 1971–72.

Enziklopediyah Talmudit. 16 vols. Jerusalem, 1969–80.

Epstein-Halevi, Elimelech. *Ha-aggadah ha-historit-biografit*. Tel Aviv, 1975.

Finkelstein, Louis. *Akiba: Scholar, Saint and Martyr*. New York, 1936.

———. "Introductory Study to Pirke Abot." *Journal of Biblical Literature* 57 (1938): 13–50.

———. *Mavo le-masekhtot Avot ve-Avot de-rabbi Natan*. Texts and Studies of Jewish Theological Seminary 16. New York, 1950.

———. "The Maxim of the Anshe Keneset ha-Gedolah." *Journal of Biblical Literature* 59 (1940): 455–69.

———. *Ha-Perushim ve-Anshei Keneset ha-Gedolah*. Texts and Studies of Jewish Theological Seminary 15. New York, 1950.

———. *The Pharisees: The Sociological Background of Their Faith*. 2 vols. Philadelphia, 1938.

———. "The Pharisees: Their Origin and Their Philosophy." *Harvard Theological Review* 22 (1929): 185–261.

Fishman, Zekhariah. *Aggadot erez ha-kedoshah*. Tel Aviv, 1927.

Frankel, Zacharias. *Darkhei ha-Mishnah*. Warsaw, 1923.

Gans, David. *Zemaḥ David ha-shalem*. Edited by Chaim Hominer. Jerusalem, 1966.

Gaster, Theodor H. *The Dead Sea Scriptures*. Garden City, N. Y., 1956.

Ginzberg, Louis. *Al halakhah va-aggadah*. Edited by Judah Nadich. Tel Aviv, 1960.

———. *Legends of the Bible*. Philadelphia, 1956.

———. *Legends of the Jews*. 7 vols. Philadelphia, 1909–46.

———. *On Jewish Law and Lore*. Philadelphia, 1955.

———. *Peirushim ve-ḥiddushim bi-yerushalmi*. 4 vols. New York, 1941–61.

———. "The Religion of the Jews at the Time of Jesus." *Hebrew Union College Annual* 1 (1924): 307–321.

Glatzer, Nahum N. *Hillel the Elder: The Emergence of Classical Judaism*. New York, 1956.

Goldin, Judah. *The Living Talmud—The Wisdom of the Fathers*. New York, 1957.

———. "Mashehu al bet midrasho shel Rabban Johanan ben Zakkai." In *Harry Austryn Wolfson Jubilee Volume on the Occasion of His 75th Birthday*, edited by Saul Lieberman, pp. 58–92. Jerusalem, 1965.

Goodspeed, Edgar J. *The Story of the Apocrypha*. Chicago, 1939.

Graetz, Heinrich H. *History of the Jews*, 6 vols. Philadelphia, 1891–98.

Grayzel, Solomon. *A History of the Jews*. Philadelphia, 1948.

Gross, Moses David. *Ozar ha-aggadah*. 3 vols. Jerusalem, 1953–54.

Gutman, Mattathias Ezekiel. *Aggadot Talmud Yerushalmi*. Jaffa, 1953–54.

Halevy, Isaac. *Dorot ha-rishonim*. 6 vols. Pressburg and Jerusalem, 1897–1939; reprint, Jerusalem, 1966–67.

Halperin, Jehiel. *Seder ha-dorot*. Warsaw, 1897.

Herford, R. Travers. *Christianity in Talmud and Midrash*. London, 1903; reprint, Clifton, N.J., 1966.

———. *Pharisaism: Its Aims and Its Method*. London, 1912.

———. *The Pharisees*. New York, 1924.

Hershberg, A. S. "Tenu'at ha-hitga'irut ha-gedolah bi-tekufat ha-bayit ha-sheni." *Ha-Tekufah* 12 (Warsaw, 1921):129–48; 13 (Warsaw, 1922):189–210.

Hesronot ha-Shas. Cracow, 1895.

Higger, Michael. *Aggadot ha-Mishnah*. New York, 1937.

———. *Aggadot ha-tannaim*. New York, 1929.

———. "Al mivneh ha-Sanhedrin." *Hadoar* 1945:712–14.

———. *Halakhot ve-aggadot*. New York, 1933.

———. *Ozar ha-braitot*. New York, 1938.

Hoenig, Sidney B. *The Great Sanhedrin*. New York, 1953.

Horowitz, Israel Wolf. *Erez Yisrael u-shekheinoteha*. Vienna, 1923.

Hurwitz, Chaim Meir. *Aggadat aggadot*. Frankfurt-am-Main, 1888.

———. *Bet aked ha-aggadot*. Frankfurt-am-Main, 1881.

Hyman, Aaron. *Toldot tannaim ve-amoraim*. 3 vols. London, 1910.

Jackson, F. J. Foakes. *Josephus and the Jews*. London, 1930.

Jastrow, Marcus. *A Dictionary of the Targumim, the Talmud Babli and Yerushalmi, and the Midrashic Literature*. New York, 1926.

Jellinek, Adolf. *Bet ha-midrash*. 6 vols. Jerusalem, 1938.

Jewish Encyclopedia. 12 vols. New York, 1901–6.

Juster, Jean. *Les Juifs dans l'Empire Romain*. Paris, 1914.

Kadushin, Max. *Organic Thinking: A Study in Rabbinic Thought*. New York, 1938.

———. *The Rabbinic Mind*. New York, 1952.

———. *The Theology of Seder Eliahu*. New York, 1932.

Kahn, Israel Meir. *Hafez Haim al aggadot ha-Shas*. Edited by Samuel Charlap. Jerusalem, 1964.

Kaminka, Aaron. *Kitvei bikoret historit*. New York, 1944.

Kasher, Aryeh. "The Isopoliteia Question in Caesarea Maritima." *Jewish Quarterly Review*, n.s. 68 (1977): 16–27.

Kasowski, Chaim Joshua. *Ozar leshon ha-Talmud*. Jerusalem, 1953–54.

Katz, Ben-Zion. *Perushim, Zedukim, Kanaim, Nozrim*. Tel Aviv, 1947.

Kaufmann, Yehezkel. *Toledot ha-emunah ha-yisra'elit*. 8 vols. in 4. Tel Aviv and Jerusalem, 1955–60.

Klausner, Joseph. *Bi-yemei bayit sheini*. Berlin, 1923; Jerusalem, 1954.

———. *Ha-bayit ha-sheini be-gadluto*. Tel Aviv, 1930.

———. *Historiyah shel ha-bayit ha-sheini*. 5 vols. in 3. Jerusalem, 1949–51.

————. *Historiyah yisra'elit.* 4 vols. Vol. 1, Odessa, 1909; vols. 2–4, Tel Aviv, 1924–25.

————. *Mi-Yeshu ad Paulus (From Jesus to Paul).* 2 vols. Tel Aviv, 1939–40. Translated by William F. Stinespring. Boston, 1961.

————. *Ha-ra'ayon ha-meshiḥi be-Yisrael (The Messianic Idea in Israel).* Tel Aviv, 1949–50; reprinted 1956. Translated by William F. Stinespring. New York, 1955.

————. *Yehudah ve-Romi.* Tel Aviv, 1946.

————. *Yeshu ha-Noẓri (Jesus of Nazareth).* 2 vols. Jerusalem, 1922. Translated by Herbert Danby. New York, 1925.

Landau, Abraham. *Sefer rav pe'alim.* With notes by Moses Simon Hunes. Warsaw, 1894; reprint, Tel Aviv, 1967. With notes by Salomon Buber. New York, 1959.

Lauterbach, Jacob Z. "Jesus in the Talmud." In *Rabbinic Essays*, pp. 473–570. Cincinnati, 1951.

Lévi, Israel. "La légende d'Alexandre dans le Talmud." *Revue des Études Juives* 2 (1881): 293–300.

————. "La légende d'Alexandre dans le Talmud et le Midrasch." *Revue des Études Juives* 7 (1883): 78–93.

Levine, Israel Lee. "The Jewish-Greek Conflict in First-Century Caesarea." *Journal of Jewish Studies* 25 (1975): 381–97.

Levner, J. B. *Kol aggadot Yisrael.* Jerusalem, 1943–44.

Lichtenstein, Hans. "Die Fastenrolle." *Hebrew Union College Annual* 8–9 (1931–32): 257–351.

Lieberman, Saul. *The Greek in Jewish Palestine.* New York, 1942.

————. *Hellenism in Jewish Palestine.* New York, 1950.

————. *The Martyrs of Caesarea.* New York, 1944.

————. *Midrashei Teiman.* Jerusalem, 1970.

————. *Tosefta ki-peshuta.* 8 vols. New York, 1955–73.

————. *Ha-Yerushalmi ki-peshuto.* Jerusalem, 1934.

Lilienblum, Moses L. *Kol kitvei.* Cracow, 1910.

Lurie, Benzion. *The Western Wall.* Jerusalem, 1969.

Magoun, Francis P. *The Gests of King Alexander of Macedon.* Cambridge, Mass., 1929.

Mantel, Hugo. "The Nature of the Great Synagogue." *Harvard Theological Review* 60 (1967): 69–91.

————. *Studies in the History of the Sanhedrin.* Cambridge, Mass., 1961.

Marcus, A. Z. *Le-toldot dat Naẓeret.* Jerusalem, 1937.

Marcus, Ralph. "A Selected Bibliography of the Jews in the Hellenistic-Roman Period." *Proceedings of the American Academy for Jewish Research* 16 (1946–47): 97–183.

Markus, Mordecai Zvi. *Mafteaḥ ha-aggadot mi-kol ha-Shas.* Vilna, 1870.

Margolis, Max, and Marx, Alexander. *A History of the Jewish People.* Philadelphia, 1945.

Melamed, Ezra Zion. *Midrashei halakhah shel ha-tannaim be-Talmud Bavli.* Jerusalem, 1943.

————. *Parashiyot mei-aggadot ha-tannaim.* Jerusalem, 1962.

Mishkin, Mordecai. *Agodes fun Talmud un Midrash.* New York, 1932.

Moore, George Foot. *Judaism in the First Centuries of the Christian Era: The Age of the Tannaim.* 3 vols. Cambridge, Mass., 1950–54.

———. "Simon the Righteous." In *Jewish Studies in Memory of Israel Abrams*, pp. 348–64. New York, 1927.

Nahmad, H. M. *A Portion in Paradise*. New York, 1970.

Nedava, Joseph. "Who Were the 'Biryoni'?" *Jewish Quarterly Review*, n.s. 63 (1973): 317–22.

Neusner, Jacob. *Early Rabbinic Judaism*. Leiden, 1975.

———. *Eliezer ben Hyrcanus*. 2 vols. Leiden, 1973.

———. *From Politics to Piety: The Emergence of Pharisaic Judaism*. Englewood Cliffs, N.J., 1973.

———. *A History of the Jews in Babylonia*. 5 vols. Leiden, 1965–70.

———. *A Life of Yohanan ben Zakkai*. 2d ed., Leiden, 1970.

Patai, Raphael. *Ha-mayim*. Tel Aviv, 1935–36.

Petuchowski, Jakob J. *Heirs of the Pharisees*. New York, 1970.

Pin, Benjamin. *Jerusalem contre Rome*. Paris, 1938.

Piron, Mordecai. *Bi-netivei aggadot Ḥazal*. Tel Aviv, 1970.

Plutarch. *Lives of Noble Grecians and Romans*. Translated by John Dryden; revised by Arthur Hugh Clough. New York, n.d.

Rabinowitz, Chaim Dov. *Yemei ha-bayit ha-sheini*. Jerusalem and New York, 1963.

Rabinowitz, Raphael Nathan. *Dikdukei soferim*. 15 vols. Munich, 1867–97.

Radin, Max. *The Jews among the Greeks and Romans*. Philadelphia, 1915.

Raphael, Chaim. *The Walls of Jerusalem*. New York, 1968.

Rapoport, Solomon Judah. *Sefer erekh millin*. Warsaw, 1914; Jerusalem, 1969–70.

Rappoport, Angelo. *The Folklore of the Jews*. London, 1937.

Ravnitzki, Joshua H., and Bialik, Hayyim Nahman. *Sefer ha-aggadah*. 6 vols. in 3. Vol. 1, Cracow, 1905; vols. 2–3, Odessa, 1910; reprint (1 vol.), Tel Aviv, 1952.

Raz, Simhah. *Yerushalayim shel aggadah*. Tel Aviv, 1976.

Rosenstein, Abraham Moses, and Karlin, Arye. *Ha-tannaim u-mishnatam*. Tel Aviv, 1952–53.

Roth, Cecil. *History of the Jews*. New York, 1964.

———. "The Jewish Revolt against Rome." *Commentary* 27 (June 1959): 513–22.

———. "Simon bar Giora: Ancient Jewish Hero." *Commentary* 29 (Jan. 1960): 52–58.

Ryle, Herbert E. *The Canon of the Old Testament*. London, 1914.

Sachar, Abram Leon. *A History of the Jews*. New York, 1965.

Sandmel, Samuel. *The First Christian Century in Judaism and Christianity*. New York, 1969.

———. *Herod: Profile of a Tyrant*. Philadelphia, 1967.

———. *A Jewish Understanding of the New Testament*. Cincinnati, 1957.

———. "Myths, Genealogies and Jewish Myths and the Writing of the Gospels." *Hebrew Union College Annual* 27 (1956): 201–11.

Schürer, Emil. *Geshichte des judischen Volkes in Zeitalter Jesu Christi*. 3 vols. Leipzig, 1898–1901.

Smith, Morton. "Zealots and Sicarii: Their Origins and Relations." *Harvard Theological Review* 64 (1971): 1–19.

Solomon, Nissim N. *Enziklopediah le-aggadot ha-Talmud.* New York, 1951.

Strack, Herman L. *Introduction to the Talmud and Midrash.* Philadelphia, 1931.

Taubes, Z. *Ha-nasi be-Sanhedrin ha-Gedolah.* Vienna, 1925.

Taxin, Menahem Zvi. *Orah yesharim.* Pietrokov, 1909; Vilna, 1910; Tel Aviv, 1968–69.

———. *Or yekarot.* New York, 1947.

Tcherikover, Victor. *Hellenistic Civilization and the Jews.* Translated by S. Applebaum. Philadelphia, 1959.

Tchernowitz, Chaim. *Toldot ha-halakhah.* 4 vols. New York, 1934–40.

Urbach, Ephraim E. *The Sages—Their Concepts and Beliefs.* 2 vols. Jerusalem, 1975.

Vilnay, Zev. *Legends of Jerusalem.* Philadelphia, 1973.

———. *Legends of Judea and Samaria.* Philadelphia, 1975.

———. *Legends of Palestine.* Philadelphia, 1932.

Wallach, L. "Alexander the Great and the Indian Gymnosophists in Hebrew Tradition." *Proceedings of the American Academy for Jewish Research* 11 (1941): 47–83.

Waxman, Meyer. *History of Jewish Literature.* 6 vols. New York, 1960.

Waxman, Samuel. *Yalkut Shemuel al masekhet Avot.* Jerusalem, 1937–38.

Weiss, Isaac Hirsh. *Dor dor ve-doreshav.* 5 vols. New York, 1924.

Wertheimer, Solomon Aaron. *Batei midrashot.* 2 vols. Jerusalem, 1952–53.

———. *Midrashim kitvei yad.* Jerusalem, 1923.

———. *Ozar midrashim.* Jerusalem, 1913–14.

Wohlman, M. *Misterei ha-aggadah.* Tel Aviv, 1929–30.

Wolfson, Harry Austryn. *Philo: Foundations of Religious Philosophy in Judaism, Christianity and Islam.* Cambridge, Mass., 1947.

———. *The Philosophy of the Church Fathers.* Cambridge, Mass., 1956; 2d rev. ed., 1964.

Wünsche, A. "Die Alexandersage nach judischen Quellen." *Die Grenzenboten* 33 (1879): 272–74.

Yadin, Yigal, ed. *Jerusalem Revealed: Archaeology in the Holy City, 1968–74.* Jerusalem, 1975.

Zahavi (Goldenbloom), Yosef. *Eretz Israel in Rabbinic Lore.* Jerusalem, 1962.

———. *Midrashei Erez Yisrael.* Jerusalem, 1959.

———. *Midrashei Zion ve-Yerushalayim.* Jerusalem, 1963.

Zeitlin, Solomon. "The Crucifixion of Jesus Re-examined." *Jewish Quarterly Review,* n.s. 31 (1940–41): 327–69; 32 (1941–42): 175–89, 279–301.

———. "The Hebrew Scrolls: Once More and Finally." *Jewish Quarterly Review,* n.s. 41 (1950): 1–58.

———. "Historical Books on Judea, The Second Commonwealth, the Pharisees and Josephus." *Jewish Quarterly Review,* n.s. 29 (1938–39): 287–300.

————. *Megillat Ta'anit As a Source for Jewish Chronology and History in the Hellenistic and Roman Periods*. Philadelphia, 1922.

————. "The Origins of the Synagogue." *Proceedings of the American Academy for Jewish Research* 2 (1930–31): 69–81.

————. *Ha-Perushim*. New York, 1939.

————. *The Rise and Fall of the Judaean State*. 3 vols. Philadelphia, 1962–78.

————. "Simeon the Just and the Kenesset ha-Gedolah." *Ner Ma'aravi* 2 (1925) 137–42.

————. Takkanot Ezra. *Jewish Quarterly Review*, n.s. 8 (1917–18): 107–38.

————. *Ha-Zedukim ve-ha-Perushim*. Jerusalem, 1936.

Zisling, Judah. *Yalkut Erez Yisrael*. Vilna, 1890; Jerusalem, 1979.

Zunz, Leopold. *Ha-derashot be-Yisrael*. Edited and translated by Chanoch Albeck. Jerusalem, 1946–47.

Name and Place Index

Darius, 4, 10, 24–25, 27n, 32n, 49n,
   103–4, 144n
David, 18, 30n, 104, 119, 147n,
   155n, 164, 166, 190, 203, 207,
   230n, 235, 266–68, 314, 317,
   327, 341–42, 352, 361, 377n,
   388n, 397n
   house of, 119, 149, 327
Dead Sea, 158n
Deborah (nurse of Rebecca), 47
Decumani, 311, 345, 375n
Demetrius, 82n
Derenbourg, J., 288n, 393n, 402n
Diaspora, xxi, 240, 298n, 393n
Dimsit (Diomsit), 306n
Dio Cassius, 84n
Diocletian, 390n
Dios, 49n
Dirdimus (king of the Brahmans),
   55n
Dobiel, 8, 9, 28n
Doeg, 164
Doeg ben Joseph, 343, 389n
Domitian, 392n–93n
Donath, L., 50–53n
Dragon, 27n, 98n

Ecbatana, 88, 90, 95n–96n
Eden, 13
Edom (Rome), 29n, 309, 314–15,
   318–23, 362, 373n–74n, 376n–
   78n, 381n, 388n, 398n
Edomites (Romans), xvi, 317, 322,
   374n
Egypt, xviii, 9, 13–15, 27n, 43–47,
   56n, 73, 79n, 89, 94n–95n, 97n,
   99n, 117, 128, 189, 195, 217n,
   219n, 310, 318, 327–28, 374n,
   379n–81n, 391n
Egyptian(s), xix, 10, 27n, 38–39,
   43, 50n–51n, 54n, 96n, 320,
   380n
Ein Sokher, 129
Eisenstein, J. D., xv, 96n
Elam, 10, 14
Eldad, 286n
Eleazar (Maccabee), 71
Eleazar (rabbi), 83n, 157n, 242,
   328, 340, 346, 359, 368, 385n,
   390n, 396n–97n
Eleazar (victim of the Syrians), 64
Eleazar ben Arakh, 264–65, 267–
   68, 280n, 299n, 301n, 306n

Eleazar ben Azariah, 173, 181n,
   372, 402n
Eleazar ben Enoch, 221n, 237,
   281n
Eleazar ben Hananiah, 297n
Eleazar ben Harsom, 110, 243,
   287n
Eleazar ben Jose Ha-Gelili, 351,
   360, 392n, 396n
Eleazar ben Poirah, 74
Eleazar ben Simon, xxvi
Eleazar ben Zadok, 182n, 275,
   288n, 345, 355, 390n, 395n
Eleazar Hisma, 390n
Eleazar of Modi'im, 390n
Eli, 276
   descendants of, 266
   sons of, 116
Eliehoenai ben Hakof, 185
Eliezer (ben Hyrcanus), 262–63,
   267–70, 273, 275, 299n–301n,
   305n–6n, 361, 383n, 387n,
   396n–97n, 399n
Eliezer ben Jacob, 126, 254–55,
   294n–95n
Eliezer ha-Kappar, 384n
Eliezer the Modaite, 263, 299n
Elijah, 21, 25–26, 31n, 166, 196,
   236, 253, 278, 306n, 309, 352,
   357, 373n, 395n
Elisha, 189, 352
Elisha ben Avuyah, 300n
Ellasar, 10, 14
Emmaus, 249, 266, 291n, 306n, 345,
   390n
Englander, Henry, 175n
Ephraim, 83n, 214n
Ephron the Hittite, 228n
Epictetus, 229n
Epicurus, 382n
Esarhaddon, 87
Esau, 310, 370–71
Esau (Rome), 309–12, 314–15, 317,
   321–22, 359, 374n–77n, 379n–
   80n, 394n
Essene(s), 215, 224n–25n
Esther, 66, 178n, 185, 349, 391n
Etam, 344, 389n
Ethan, 23
Ethiopia, 318
Euphrates (Perat; river), 6, 7, 13,
   227n, 309, 315
Eutolomos, 378n

Evil-merodach, 7, 10
Ezekiel, 209, 300n
Ezra, xvii, 17–23, 31n, 103, 161,
    176n, 185, 202–3, 223n, 298n

Felix, 306n
Finkelstein, Louis, 50n, 80n, 176n,
    181n, 214n–15n, 217n, 223n,
    281n, 299n, 301n, 382n, 385n
Flavius Clemens, 393n
Florus, xxv, 303n
Foundation Stone, 108, 119
Frankel, Z., 212n, 214n–17n, 223n,
    280n, 285n, 290n, 294n, 380n,
    390n
Friedländer, M., 382n–83n

Gabinius, 182n
Gabriel (angel), 8, 9, 25, 28n, 74,
    95n, 213n, 220n, 318, 380n
Gadil, 188
Gagot-Zerifin, 129
Galba, xxvi
Galilee, xx, xxii–xxiv, 87, 194,
    220n, 240, 249, 285n, 291n,
    380n, 383n, 401n
Gamaliel (son of the proselyte),
    208
Gamaliel I (the Elder), 172, 181n,
    223n, 227n, 238–43, 247, 249–
    50, 258, 280n, 282n–87n, 292n–
    93n, 299n, 305n
  descendants of, 275
Gamaliel II (of Jabneh), 57n, 223n,
    240–41, 250, 263, 280n, 282n,
    285n–87n, 299n, 305n, 372,
    383n, 402n
  family of, 305n
Gamaliel III, 285n
Gamaliel IV, 285n
Gamaliel V, 285n
Gamaliel, VI, 285n
Gaon of Vilna, 286n
Garmu, house of, 117, 148n–49n
Gaskalgas, 72, 185, 213n
Gaster, M., 49n
Gaul, xxiv, 11, 16
Gebiha ben Kosem, 38–39, 50n–
    51n, 382n
Gebiha ben Pesisa, 50n, 325, 382n
Gebini, 120, 144, 150n, 158n
Gehazi, 164, 189

Gehenna (Hell), 10, 80n, 171, 235,
    261, 278, 324, 392n
Geiger, Abraham, 80n, 282n, 298n,
    383n
Germania Barbara, 378n
Germans, 317
Germany, 304n, 388n, 393n
Gershon, 146n
Gibeon, 385n
Gibeonites, 20, 146n
Gihon (river), 13
Gilead, 69
Gimzo, 294n
Ginzberg, Louis, xii, xiii, xv, xvii,
    27n–31n, 144n–45n, 153n,
    177n–78n, 215n, 220n–21n,
    223n–24n, 229n, 402n
Glatzer, Nahum, 224n, 226n–28n
Gofna, 274, 304n
Gog, 30n, 81n, 321, 349, 380n, 391n
Goiim, 10, 14
Goldin, Judah, 177n
Gomorrah, 402n
Goodspeed, Edgar, 95n, 97n–99n
Goths, 379n
Graetz, H., 212n, 220n, 282n, 393n
Greece, xvi, xvii, 9–15, 28n–30n,
    44, 55n–56n, 79n, 81n–82n,
    240, 313, 318, 375n, 398n
Greek(s), 43–45, 54n, 57n, 61, 63,
    66–67, 69–70, 78n, 96n–98n,
    173, 213n, 227n, 310, 319, 380n
Gurya, 210
Gutman, Joshua, 178n

Haazati, Nathan, 96n
Habakkuk, 5, 27n, 195, 221n
Hadrian, 54n, 297n, 345, 391n–92n
Hadrimon (son of Tabrimon), 310
Haggai, xvi, 8, 16–17, 30n, 104, 107,
    177n
Hai Gaon, 31n
Hakufa, 103
Halafta, 240, 285n
Halevy, Isaac, 182n, 212n, 214n,
    217n, 282n, 285n, 290n, 386n,
    388n
Hama bar Hanina, 317, 379n
Haman, 10, 14, 30n, 66, 81n, 103,
    185, 319, 349
Hamnuna, 365, 399n
Hamor, 47
Hanamel the Egyptian, 185

Nittai the Arbelite, 189–90, 215n–16n
Noah, 5, 8, 44–45, 97n

Ocellus, 393n
Olshefsky, Samuel, xxvii
Onias, 61, 62, 69–70, 78n–79n, 212n, 298n
Onias III (son of Simon the Just), 78n–79n, 187
Onkelos, 243, 287n, 351, 393n
Origen, 98n, 383n
Ovadiah of Bartinoro, 281n–82n, 284n, 288n, 292n
Oved Bet Hillel, 249
Ovid, 213n

Palestine, xvii, 6, 28n, 151n, 163, 178n, 222n, 272, 283n, 379n, 384n, 388n, 390n–92n, 395n, 397n, 400n, 402n
Palmyra (Tadmor, Thedmor), 227n, 353, 394n
Palmyrans, 206, 227n
Pangar, 272, 274–75, 304n, 401n
Papias, 284n
Paradise (Garden of Eden), 40, 41, 53n, 55n, 63n, 278n, 300n, 402n
Parthia, 28n, 317, 378n
Parthians, xxii–xxiii, 317
Paul, 283n–84n
Peki'in, 291n, 299n, 402n
Peniel, 355, 395n
Perea, 158n
Persia, xvi, 3, 7–15, 23, 28n–30n, 49n, 56n, 75, 82n, 97n, 169, 175n, 367, 373n, 379n, 398n
Persian(s), xvii, 8, 9, 14–16, 23, 27n–28n, 53n, 82n, 95n, 97n, 104, 154n, 158n, 310, 349, 390n–91n
Pfister, F., 50n
Pharisee(s), xix–xxi, xxv, xxvi, 74–76, 83n, 99n, 137, 156n, 169, 176n, 180n, 187, 215n–20n, 283n, 291n, 324, 326, 382n, 388n
Pharaoh, 170, 203, 319, 350, 373n, 379n
Pharaoh-Necho, 309
Phasael, 220n, 401n
Philip (son of Herod), xxiii

Philistines, 166
Philo, xiii, 51n, 57n, 96n
Phinehas (Num.), 76, 84n, 116
Phinehas (rabbi), 384n
Phinehas (stone cutter), 110
Phinehas ben Aruvah, 393n
Phinehas ben Jair, 259, 296n, 396n
Phoenicia, 79n, 227n
Pinkai, 116
Pishon (river), 13
Plimo, 257
Plutarch, 51n–52n, 55n
Poleyeff, Moshe Aaron, xxvii
Pollion, 220n–21n
Pompey, xxi, xxii
Pontius Pilate, xxiv
Potiphar, xiii
Praetorian Guards, 390n
Ptolemy(ies), xviii, 28, 45–46, 79n, 95n
Ptolemy II Philadelphus, xviii
Ptolemy XIV, 220n
Ptolemy Philopater, 50n, 78n
Pumbedita, 293n, 399n
Pumeus (Caesarea Philippi, Parmeas), 390n

Quietus (Quintus), 302n, 393n

Rabbah, 362, 397n
Rachel, 12
Rafram I ben Papa, 399n
Ragae (Rhages), 87–89, 95n
Raguel, 88–89
Raphael, 88–89, 95n
Rapoport, S., 51n, 52n
Rashbam, 279n
Rashi, 26n, 28n–29n, 51n, 52n, 81n, 84n, 148n–49n, 157n, 216n, 218n, 227n, 230n, 281n, 284n–85n, 287n, 292n, 382n, 388n, 391n, 401n
Rav, xiii, 228n, 260, 293n, 357, 361, 366, 395n, 397n, 400n
Rava (Raba, Abba), 83n, 197, 209, 221n, 229n, 365, 399n
Rava ben Zemuna (Abba ben Zemina, Abba ben Zevina), 259, 296n
Ravin, 83n
Ravnitzky, Y. H., xv
Rawidowicz, Simon, 176n
Rebecca, 47, 103, 312, 375n, 379n

Subject Index

calendar:
  announcing intercalation of, 240, 285n
  Babylonian names in, 3
cannibalism, 343, 344
captives, ransoming of, 111
charity:
  anonymous, 121
  clothing the naked as, 87
  feeding the poor as, 21, 87, 199, 251, 252
  for its own sake, 265–66
  loans as, 87
  peace engendered by, 204
  providing employment as, 48
  to those formerly wealthy, 205, 227n
  unharvested corner as, 172
children:
  fasting by, 113
  naming of, 39–40
  prophecy by, 364
  schools established for, 218n, 219n, 390n
  Shekhinah in exile with, 363–64
circumcision:
  as covenant, 111
  time of, 111
citron (etrog), 156n
coffins of excommunicated, 237
commercial documents, God's name prohibited in, 70
complexion, beauty hints for, 330, 385n
confession, for share in world to come, 173
conformity, virtue of, 209
congregations, prayer in, 225n
corpses:
  respect accorded to, 87, 88, 95n, 242
  uncleanliness of, 188
courts:
  days for sessions of, 21
  God's ratification of decrees by, 19
  precedent underlying decisions of, 165, 277, 281n
covenant with God:
  Abraham's sealing of, 10
  messianic era and, 15
Creation:
  chaos before, 321

God as sole author of, 325
  order of, 40, 51n, 233, 253

dead:
  resurrection of, 324, 325
  treatment of, 87, 88, 95n, 242
death:
  of high priest, 110–11
  moment of, 277
  on Sabbath, 277
  sins as cause of, 256
  on Yom Kippur, 277
death penalty:
  for adultery, 93
  after dissolution of Sanhedrin, 174
  four methods of, 63, 174
  mourning victims of, 173
  rare imposition of, 173
  for witchcraft, 192
  witnesses required before imposition of, 191
death warrants, voiding of, 241
deeds:
  of gentiles, 263–64
  learning vs., 249
  man measured by, 234
  see also Torah observance
descendants, providing for, 196–97
divine justice, 14–15, 16, 68, 74, 350–51
  inevitability of, 173
  in messianic era, 16, 322
divine plan, invincibility of, 4
Divine Presence, camp of, 121

eating, in honor of Sabbath, 208
elementary school system, introduction of, 218n, 219n, 390n
embarrassment, shielding others from, 137, 241–42, 286n, 289n, 339–40
embryo, formation of, 233–34
employers:
  charity of, 48
  duty owed to, 198–99
envy, 21, 193–94
eruv, law of, 292n
Esther, Book of, Torah study during reading of, 142
etrog (citron), 156n

Greek language (*continued*)
  special use of, 45, 313
  translation of Torah into, 45–46
  for understanding Torah, 47
guilt offerings, suspensive, 246,
  289n

hair:
  ritual bath and combing of, 21
  women's covering of, 115
Halakhah:
  Great Assembly's development
    of, 162
  place for study of, 399n
Hallel:
  composition of, 152n
  sacrifice of paschal lamb and
    recitation of, 127
Hanukkah, 67–68
hatred:
  Jerusalem destroyed by, 365
  Second Temple destroyed by,
    365–66
havdalah, Great Assembly's
  establishment of, 162
Hebrew language:
  characters in, 17, 20
  special uses of, 45, 313
hell, in messianic era, 25
heroism, *see* bravery
high priests:
  clothing of, 110–11
  death of, 110–11
  in First vs. Second Temple, 109
  kings vs., 111
  sages vs., 111
  selling office of, 186
  sins of, 116–17
  Yom Kippur and cleanliness of,
    115, 143
  Yom Kippur and preparation of,
    131–32
  see also priests, priesthood
Holy of Holies:
  on earth vs. in heaven, 119
  entrance to, 38
  gold not worn in, 111
  high priests in, 111–12, 137
  spring from, 119
  on Yom Kippur, 112, 115
Holy Scriptures:
  canonization of, 161–62
  consistency of, 260

Great Assembly's interpretation
    of, 161
  transcription of, 23
hospitality:
  to all, 189, 330
  to poor, 189
  to wise, 187–88
house painting, 359
human dignity, value of, 264
humility:
  exaltation in, 205
  placing others first as, 234
  reward of, 322
  in service of God, 187, 211–12
  in Torah study, 298n

idolatry:
  atonement for, 110
  First Temple destroyed by, 365–
    66
  foolishness of, 4–5, 347–48
  prohibition against, 64–65, 346–
    47
impudence, atonement for, 110
incense:
  honoring dead by burning of,
    243
  making of, 117–18
  potency of, 143–44
incest, evil inclination and, 164
intermarriage:
  Jewish people weakened by,
    373n
  with *natin*, 146n–47n
Israel, land of:
  as center of earth, 119
  holiness of, 6
  Jewish right to, 38–39, 50n–51n
Israelites:
  camp of, 121
  relative position of, 111

jealousy, 21
Jerusalem, 325–28
  adding on to, 172
  beauty of, 326–27
  as center of Israel, 119
  measures of Torah in, 327
  in messianic era, 371
  reasons for destruction of, 365
  room for pilgrims in, 143
  sanctity of, 78
  schools in, 328

serpents and scorpions in, 143
wisdom in, 326, 327
Jewish people:
  infighting among, 77
  prophecy among, 17
  purity of, 20
  sins of, 9, 21
  uniqueness of, 138, 263
judges:
  awesome responsibility of, 191
  empathy necessary for, 204,
    226*n*
  qualifications for, 165–66
judgments:
  before God, 277–78
  impartiality of, 190–91
  leniency in, 189
  unnecessary delay in, 251
justice:
  Jerusalem destroyed for perver-
    sion of, 365
  see also death penalty; divine
    justice; judges; judgments;
    punishment; witnesses

kiddush, Great Assembly's estab-
    lishment of, 162
kindness, world sustained by, 185
kings:
  counting years on throne of, 6
  high priests vs., 111
  as judges, 84*n*
  reading from Torah on Sukkot
    by, 141
  relationship with, 40
  sages vs., 111

labor pains, Israel's sufferings
    likened to, 15
language, priests' use of, 114
Latin:
  origin of, 45, 313
  special use of, 45
laundry work, day for, 21
levirate marriages, 72–73, 346,
    390*n*–91*n*
Levites:
  camp of, 121
  relative position of, 111
  tithing and, 18–19
life, saving of, 111
lineage, 18, 20

lizards, impurity associated with
    corpse of, 238–39
loans:
  charity in form of, 87
  sabbatical year and repayment
    of, 222*n*
locusts, eating of, 188
longevity:
  of Sanhedrin members, 166
  secret to, 260
lulavim, 137–38

magreifah, 120
majority, decisions made by, 237
mankind, love of, 203
manslaughter, atonement for,
    110–11
marriage:
  consummation of, 96*n*
  levirate, 72–73, 346, 390*n*–91*n*
  peace within, 203
marriage contracts, alimony
    stipulated in, 245–46
martyrdom, 62, 64–66
materialism, anxiety produced by,
    204
meal offerings:
  priests' share of, 123
  value of, 124
Menorah:
  miracle of, 247
  Shekhinah's presence signaled
    by, 114–15
mercy, mercy rewarded by,
    234–35
Messiah:
  birth of, 369–70, 401*n*
  Edom (Rome) as home of, 318
  greeting of, 277
  tribe of, 103
  Writings' revelations of, 212
messianic era:
  abundance in, 239–40
  childbearing in, 239
  covenant fulfilled in, 15
  divine justice in, 16
  hell in, 25
  Jerusalem in, 371
  Temple rebuilt in, 103
  Torah in, 25
  trees in, 239–40
mezuzahs, Hebrew used in, 45

Midrash, Great Assembly's
development of, 162
might, sign of, 40
milk, complexion improved by,
330, 385n
miracles:
of Menorah, 247
natural means vs., 9
in Temple, 142–44
of wind on Sukkot, 143
miscarriages:
fasting and prevention of,
113–14
from odor of holy flesh, 143
Mishnah, 228n
modesty:
low public profile as, 200
women's hair covered for, 147n
monotheism, 9
months, Hebrew, origin of, 3
mourners:
comforting of, 268–69
food provided for, 343, 389n
mourning:
customs of, 356–57
of death penalty victims, 173
of sages, 242
musical instruments in Temple,
120–21

natin:
intermarriage with, 146n–47n
relative position of, 111
nations:
God's judgment of, 16, 311–12,
323
Torah study by, 16, 311–12
Nazirite's vow, 185–86
Nissan, Messiah's coming in month
of, 370–71, 402n
nursing mothers, fasting by, 113–14

oaths:
gravity of, 73
by high priest on Yom Kippur,
131
see also vows
obesity, good news as cause of,
274
omer:
defects never found in, 143
offering of, 128–29
prayer for counting of, 298n

priests sated by, 115, 186
Oral Law:
codification of, 228n
components of, 162
messianic era's clarification of,
25
Written Law vs., 206–7, 228n
orphans, treatment of, 61

palm branches (lulavim), 137–38
paschal lamb:
non-Jews' eating of, 128
sacrifice of, 127–28
Passover:
crowds at Temple during, 127–
28
offering of omer on, 128–29
peace:
charity leading to, 204
God's love of, 71
government as securer of, 248
love and pursuit of, 203
in marriage, 203
penalties, see punishment
Pentateuch, see Torah; Written
Law
perjury, punishment for, 94,
98n–99n
perpetual fire, 19–20, 26
Persian language, special use of,
45, 313
phylacteries, Hebrew used in, 45
pilgrims, divine protection of,
124–25
polygamy, witchcraft engendered
by, 226
poor:
anonymous care of, 121
avoiding embarrassment of, 137
clothing for, 87
employment of, 48
feeding of, 21, 87, 199, 251, 252
hospitality to, 189
loans to, 87
sacrifices of, 123–24
Torah study by, 200–201
unharvested food left for, 172
Western Wall and merit of, 368
poverty, as virtue, 236
power, love of, 190
prayer:
answers found in, 19, 77–78
in congregations, 225n

direction faced in, 360–61
Great Assembly's contributions
    to, 162–63
Jerusalem destroyed for neglect
    of, 365
to relieve sickness, 258
on road, 357
as substitute for sacrifices, 399*n*
precedent in Jewish law, 165, 277,
    281*n*
pregnant women, fasting by, 113–
    14
pride, 68, 294*n*
priestly blessing:
    comfort provided by, 321–22
    God's name chanted during,
        112, 115
    staring at priests during, 124
priests, priesthood:
    Aaron's descendants as, 207
    blemishes on, 247, 289*n*
    blessing of, *see* priestly blessing
    bribery for attainment of, 109–
        10
    clothing worn by, 110
    disqualification of, 172
    duties delegated among, 126–27
    fighting among, 126–27
    gluttony among, 115, 186
    language used by, 114
    qualifications for, 74, 76, 114
    sins of, 116–17
    sleeping on watch by, 126
    special skills retained by, 117–19
    witchcraft used by, 109
    see also high priests
procrastination in studying, 204
procreation in messianic era, 239
property:
    disposition of, 210
    retrieval of, 236
prophecy:
    children and gift of, 364
    fools and gift of, 364
    among Jewish people, 17
proselytes, relative position of, 111
prozbul, 222*n*
punishment:
    for adultery, 93
    of angels, 8
    for arrogance, 70, 116
    for blasphemy, 63–64, 71–72, 321
    for boasting, 263

for bribery, 116
exile as, 24
for greed, 253
for hindering construction of
    Temple, 103
of Israel's enemies, 14–15, 68
legal vs. necessary, 254
for perjury, 94, 98*n*–99*n*
for sleep during Temple watch,
    295*n*
of wicked, 392*n*
see also death penalty
purchases, treasure found in, 193
Purim, Great Assembly's introduc-
    tion of, 163
purity, ritual, *see* ritual purity

rainbows:
    as sign of God's covenant, 161
    staring at, 124
ram's horn (shofar):
    redemption signaled by, 10
    Rosh Ha-Shanah and sounding
        of, 277
redemption:
    signal of, 10
    Torah observance leading to, 15
red heifer:
    purchase from gentiles of, 387*n*
    rationality lacking in rite of,
        271, 302*n*
repentance:
    after chastisement, 204
    divine decrees reversed through,
        24
    life through, 17
    martyrdom as, 62
    after seeing God's powers, 168
    suicide as, 62–63
resurrection of dead, 324, 325
ritual bath, hair combed before, 21
ritual purity:
    immersion for, 21, 266
    lizard corpses and, 238–39
    miscarrying women and, 249–50,
        292*n*
    spring from Holy of Holies and,
        119
    strictness of laws of, 239
    see also uncleanliness, laws of
robbery, theft vs., 262–63, 299*n*
Rome, 309–23
    descent from Esau, 310

Rome (*continued*)
destruction of, in messianic era, 317–23
founding of, 309–19
swine as the symbol of, 314–15, 318
warriors of, 311
wealth of, 310–11
Rosh Hashanah:
income preordained on, 300*n*
shofar sounded on, 277
rudeness, 204
rulers, relationship with, 40

Sabbath:
adherence to, 26
animal labor prohibited on, 215*n*
baking loaves for, 21
carrying knives for sacrifices on, 202
death on, 277
eating in honor of, 208
Jerusalem's destruction and profaning of, 365
kiddush for, 162
laws of sacrifices on, 201–2
permissible distance to go on, 158*n*
permissible violation of, 200–201
preparation for, 208, 228*n*–29*n*
sexual relations on, 31*n*–32*n*
use of alley space on, 292*n*
utensils and vessels handled on, 26
sabbatical year cycle:
fourth year of, 249, 292*n*
repayment of loans and, 222*n*
seventh year of, 292*n*
sacrifices:
animals subject to, 122
on behalf of all vs. individuals, 142
blemished animals for, 339–40
before completion of Temple, 104
of miscarrying women, 249–50, 292*n*
of night vs. day, 121
of paschal lamb, 127–28
of poor, 123–24
prayer substituted for, 399*n*
priest with blemishes ineligible for, 247, 289*n*

replacement of, 113
Sabbath superseded by, 201–2
of Sukkot, 138, 142
Torah study vs., 142
sages:
high priests vs., 111
Jerusalem destroyed for treatment of, 365
kings vs., 111
sailors, fasting by, 113
saliva, uncleanliness of, 115
Sanhedrin, 165–75
as center of Temple, 166
death penalty imposed by, 173–74
exile of, 174
heavenly counterpart to, 166
language interpreters unnecessary for, 171
legislative role of, 171–72
longevity of members of, 166
number of members in, 47
origins of, 166
as protector of Torah, 171, 173
qualifications for membership in, 169, 170–71
wisdom of members of, 170
schools:
establishment of, 218*n*, 219*n*, 390*n*
in Jerusalem, 328
scribes:
transcription of Holy Scriptures by, 23
transcription of Torah by, 21
Second Temple:
beauty of, 106, 107
building materials of, 6, 12, 106, 108
courts of judgment in, 121
design of, 119–21
dimensions of, 104
disunity's destruction of, 6
First Temple vs., 107, 108, 109
hatred's destruction of, 365–66
items missing from, 107
number of priests in, 109–10
priests barefooted in, 113
sacrifices before completion of, 104
see also Temple
Seder, four cups of wine at, 15
self-interest, 203

semen, distinguishing between egg
white and, 245–46
sex stimulant, garlic as, 21, 31n–
32n
sexual offenses, atonement for, 110
shame, Jerusalem destroyed for
lack of, 365
Shekhinah (Heavenly Presence):
bare feet and, 113
dwelling place of, 275–76
exile of, 174, 363–64
menorah light as omen of, 114–
15
Western Wall and, 368–69
Shema:
God's name in, 163
hour for reading of, 108
interruption of, 190
Jerusalem destroyed for neglect
of, 365
recitation of, 396n
Shetiyah (Foundation Stone), 119,
134
shewbread, see bread of display
shofar (ram's horn):
redemption signaled by, 10
Rosh Hashanah and sounding
of, 277
shyness, learning hindered by, 204
sickness, prayer for relief of, 258
silence:
Torah study and, 254, 295n
virtues of, 248–49
sinar, wearing of, 21
sins:
bounty withheld because of, 191
death caused by, 256
idle talk leading to, 248–49
of Jewish people, 9, 21
of leading others to sin, 190
thoughts for avoidance of, 236
wisdom and fear of, 259
see also specific sins
slander, 21
idle talk leading to, 291n
prohibition against, 105
slaves, relative position of, 111
sleep, heavy eating as cause of, 131
snow, complexion improved by,
330, 385n
songs:
after dissolution of Sanhedrin,
174–75

Greek used for, 45, 313
soul:
body as host of, 209
sound made by, 311
speech:
care in, 193
of priests, 114
spitting, on Temple Mount, 109
strangers, treatment of, 153n
suicide, 66, 104–5
in bereavement, 66
after repentance, 63
sukkah, women and children
absolved from mizvah of,
210–11
Sukkot, 137–42
eighth day of, 141–42
king's reading from Torah on,
141
miracle of wind on, 143
sacrifices of, 138, 142
water libation of, 138–41
suspensive guilt offerings, 246,
289n
swearing, see oaths; vows
synagogue, development of, xxii,
20, 305n

tabernacle, building materials of, 12
Talmud, 228n
Tammuz, seventeenth day of, 352
Targum, composition of, 17
teachers:
association with, 189, 238
temperament of, 204
tekhelet, dye for, 297n
Temple:
additions to, 172
altar fire unaffected by rain in,
143
bowing in, 240, 246–47
as center of Jerusalem, 119
column of smoke in, 143
cries heard within court of, 116
flies in slaughterhouse of, 143
Foundation Stone of, 119, 134
images prohibited in, 39
in messianic era, 103
miracles of, 142–43
musical instruments in, 120–21
room for prostration in, 142–43
Sanctuary of, 119
Torah study vs. building of, 103

va-yehi (*bimei*), unhappy events
in Bible preceded by, 3, 162
vengeance, enduring power of, 167
violence, violence produced by,
204, 226n
vows:
of Nazirites, 185–86
see also oaths

water:
for altar use, 139
for ritual laver, 108
wealth:
distribution in world of, 310–11
love of, 43
sign of, 40
spiritual merit vs., 201
Torah study vs., 243
of wicked, 312–13
weaning, age of, 334, 386n
wedding feasts, 89, 331
at time of national sorrow, 345,
352, 390n
Western Wall:
permanence of, 368
Shekhinah in, 358, 368–69
survival of, 275–76
wicked:
association with, 189
fools vs., 237
God's curse upon, 322
punishment of, 392n
wealth of, 312–13
treatment of, 61
willow branches, gathering of, 139
wine:
for altar use, 139
gentiles' handling of, 26
power of, 24, 32n, 92
wisdom:
distribution in world of, 326
fear of sin and endurance of, 259
in Jerusalem, 326, 327
life preserved by, 266, 272
of Sanhedrin, 170
schooling as source of, 204
sign of, 40
surrounding oneself with, 187–88

witchcraft:
death penalty for, 192
polygamy and, 226
priests' use of, 109
witnesses:
for capital offense, 191
examination of, 93–94, 99n, 191
required number of, 93
wives, obedience to husbands by,
246
women:
charity by, 199
commandments not applicable
to, 229n
hair covered by, 115
as heroines, 91–92
idle talk with, 189
in messianic era, 239
power of men vs., 24, 41
work, love of, 193
Writings, secrets of Messiah's
coming revealed in, 212
Written Law:
messianic era's clarification of,
25
Oral Law vs., 206–7, 228n
wrongdoing, appearance of, 149n,
192–93, 236

year, intercalation of, 240, 241,
285n
Yom Kippur (Day of Atone-
ment):
cleanliness of high priest on, 115,
143
confession of high priest on,
154n–55n
as day of joy, 137
death on, 277
entering Holy of Holies on, 112,
115, 133–34
high priest's preparation for, 131
ritual of two goats on, 114, 132–
33, 134–35
Temple service on, 131–37
washing hands to feed child on,
210
washing on, 229n

PSALMS (*continued*)

16:11	150
18:7	14
19:6	44
20:8	70
22:25	123
30:2	130
31:20	150, 311
33:6	347
36:7	43
37:7	314
37:14–15	301
37:21	268
39:13	364
42:8	374
44:23	80–81, 349, 355
45:14	116
46:8	375
48:3	327, 362–63
57:3	31
60:10	319, 323, 380
60:11	314, 376
60:12	341
65:14	271
66:1	271
68:6	310
68:20	208
68:23	355
68:31	318, 377
68:32	318
68:33	318
68:36	360
69:13	313
72:16	240
73:11	381
73:25	314, 321
75:7f.	26
77:6	44
78:38	162
80:14	162, 314
87:2	364
89:13	364
93:4	42, 54
94:7	262
96:1	15
98:4	150
99:4	381
103:19	368
104:24	250
105:15	164
109:4	141
111:10	297
112:1	214

112:7	208
113–18	152
113:9	66, 349
115:5	347
115:6	347
115:7	348
116:1	235
116:6	235
116:8	235
118:20	42
118:25	69, 138
120–34	157
122:1	153
122:2	153
125:1	365
126:1	196
128:5–6	140
128:6	328
132:14	368, 402
136:15	320
137	398
137:1	361
137:5–6	359
137:7	29, 361, 362
138	30
140:9	317
145:9	168
146–49	30
148:7,9,14	265
150:1	153
150:6	153

PROVERBS

1:7	297
3:1–2	226
3:4	149, 297
3:15	146, 147
3:31	321
3:33	322
3:34	322
3:35	322
4:8	75, 76, 84
6:23	106
8:15	378
8:21	209, 210, 262
8:35	226
9:11	226
10:7	126
10:19	291
10:22	193

MARK (*continued*)

15:43–46	95
21:31	228

LUKE

8:3	98
10:27	228
22:52	153
23:50–52	95

JOHN

8:1–11	98
19:38	95

ACTS

5:34–39	283
22:3	283, 284

REVELATION

12:15	95
21	96

HELLENISTIC LITERATURE

PHILO

Life of Moses

1.25.140–42	51

De Monarchia

1.7	228

De Poenitentia

1	228

JOSEPHUS

Antiquities

2.2.14	84
7.12.3	150
11.3.1	33
11.3.3–9	33
11.5.5	32
11.8.3–5	49
12.2.5	212
12.4.1	212
12.4.10	212
12.9.1	82
12.9.7	80, 82
12.10.5	82
13.5.5	219
13.8.4	82
13.9.1	82
13.10.3	82, 213
13.10.5	83–84
13.13.5	83, 157
13.15.5	84
14.1.10	79
14.2.1	84, 221
14.9.3	84
14.9.4	220
14.16.4	84
15.1.1	220
15.10.4	220–21
18.1.3	214, 382
18.1.4	218
20.4.1	146
20.9.4	146

Wars of the Jews

1.4.6	84
2.1.1	286
2.8.9	32
2.8.14	152
2.14.3	158
2.17.2	388
2.18.7–8	56
3.8.9	305
4.3.9	290
6.5.3	302
7.1.1	401

Life

38.39	291

BABYLONIAN TALMUD

BERAKHOT

Mishnah

4:3   298

Gemara

3a	395
7a	158
8a	399
10a	301
10b	395
13a	381
19a	219, 221, 226, 281
22a	294
26a	299
28b	286, 306, 382
28b–29a	383
29a	53, 82, 216, 226
30a	397
32a	399
32b	399
33a	178, 296
33b	178
44a	183
48a	84, 217–18
55a	396
58a	285
58b	399
60a	228
63a	226
67b	32

PE'AH

Mishnah

1:1	95
1:2	181
2:6	181, 214
2:7	79

KILAYIM

Mishnah

1:9	53
9	224

SHEVI'IT

Mishnah

6:1	53
9:2	292

TERUMOT

Mishnah

8:4   157

MA'ASEROT

Mishnah

2:5   215

MA'ASER SHENI

Mishnah

5:2	390
5:6	292

ORLAH

Mishnah

2:12   282

BIKKURIM

SHABBAT

ERUVIN

PESAḤIM

SHEKALIM

YOMA

SUKKAH

BEIZAH

4:24	286
5:8	158
5:25–26	225
5:26	280
5:35	279

HORAYOT

Mishnah

3	146

Gemara

11a	382
13a	146

ZEVAHIM

Mishnah

9:7	146, 157

Gemara

54b	389
62a	30, 144
84a	289
103b	289

MENAHOT

Mishnah

6	152
6:6–7	152
7:4	146, 157
8	150
13:8	215

Gemara

28b	82

45a	297
53b	402
64b	84, 153
65a	180
73b	181
86b	147
100a	155
104a	151
109b	147, 213, 217

HULLIN

Gemara

5a	180
13b	388
90b	149, 293
127a	296

BEKHOROT

Mishnah

3:4	281
5:5	176

Gemara

38a	283
49b	287

ARAKHIN

Mishnah

2:3	150
2:5	158
9:4	222

Gemara

10b	150
11a	150
13b	150

LAMENTATIONS RABBAH
(*continued*)

1:1	384, 386–87, 395
1:2	384, 389, 395
1:5	302–4, 387, 393, 398
1:6	78, 182, 399
1:7	305
1:12	392
1:13	397
1:16	80, 389–90, 394, 401
1:17	153, 390
1:19	56
1:42	28
1:49	391
1:50	391
1:64	294
2	294
2:4	179, 394
2:11	394
2:12	389
2:15	384
3:4	179
3:5	391
3:10	391
3:14	376
4:1	384
4:1–2	386, 396
4:2	386–87
4:3	389
4:5	385
4:7	385, 389
4:8	395
4:9	389
4:10	389
4:15	182
5:8	28
5:16	390

3:6	150
4:1	179
6:5	228
6:6	30, 381
7:6	381
10:9	158
11:5	177
11:7	26
11:8	180
12:5	56
13:3	376
13:5	27–29, 49, 80, 377, 380
14:9	279
15:9	29
16:1	57
19	180
19:4	398
20:4	155
20:5	145, 392
20:11	147
21:6	147
21:9	146, 213
21:10	146
21:12	213
22:3	392
22:13	376
27:1	53–54
28:2	152
28:5	153
29:2	29
29:10	28
30:11	179–80
31:6	399
31:7	150
32:8	180
33:2	180
34:3	229
35:10	145, 218
36:1	278

LEVITICUS RABBAH

1:2	228
1:5	227
1:8	178
2:2	179
2:9	180
2:10	146
2:11	31, 224
3:5	150

NUMBERS RABBAH

1:4	179
2:26	147
3:2	384
3:13	31
4:9	302
5:9	179
6:1	146
6:3	179

ANCIENT LITERATURE

EPICTETUS

Discourses
4.11.2   229

PLUTARCH

Lives
p. 847   52

Morals
1:382   55

MEDIEVAL BIBLE COMMENTATORS

ABARBANEL

Isa. 45   32

IBN EZRA

Zech. 9:9   81
Zech. 9:13–14   81

KIMḤI

Zech. 2:1   29
Zech. 3:9   31

NAḤMANIDES

Songs 2:9   401

RASHI

Isa. 1:18   147
Hag. 2:22   28

Zech. 6:1   29
Zech. 9:9   81
Zech. 9:13–14   81
Mal. 1:10   148

OTHER MEDIEVAL WRITINGS

ESHKOL HAKOFER

135   230

HALAKHOT GEDOLOT

32

HILKHOT RABBATI

Bet ha-Midrash
1:4   294

JOSIPPON

3   31
3:5b   32
3:10a–11a   32
3:11d–12a   33
17d   51
9   82
19   81
21   82
22   82
24   82

MAIMONIDES

Commentary
on the
Mishnah   281